Political

Oppositions

in Western

Democracies

POLITICAL

OPPOSITIONS

IN WESTERN

DEMOCRACIES

edited by

ROBERT A. DAHL

༒

New Haven and London

Yale University Press

1966

To the memory of Otto Kirchheimer

ACKNOWLEDGMENTS

This book was made possible through the generous support of the Rockefeller Foundation. The authors are also indebted, singly and jointly, to Mr. and Mrs. John Marshall for their many gracious kindnesses at the Villa Serbelloni, Bellagio, Italy, where much of this book was formulated and discussed in a setting that could not have been more attractive or more hospitable; and to our rapporteurs at the two conferences there, Ian Budge and Mary Dahl.

We are obligated to Marian Ash for her skillful editing at the Yale University Press.

I should like to express my own thanks to Yale University and the Henry L. Stimson Fund for their generous assistance, and to my wife Mary for her help from the beginning of this undertaking to the end.

R.A.D.

April 1965
New Haven, Conn.

CONTENTS

PREFACE

Somewhere in the world, at this moment, a political group is probably engaged in the antique art of imprisoning, maiming, torturing, and killing its opponents. Somewhere, as you read these words, a government and its opponents are no doubt trying to coerce one another by violent means. For without much question the most commonplace way for a government to deal with its opponents is to employ violence.

Of the three great milestones in the development of democratic institutions—the right to participate in governmental decisions by casting a vote, the right to be represented, and the right of an organized opposition to appeal for votes against the government in elections and in parliament—the last is, in a highly developed form, so wholly modern that there are people now living who were born before it had appeared in most of Western Europe.

Throughout recorded history, it seems, stable institutions providing legal, orderly, peaceful modes of political opposition have been rare. If peaceful antagonism between factions is uncommon, peaceful opposition among organized, permanent political parties is an even more exotic historical phenomenon. Legal party opposition, in fact, is a recent unplanned invention that has been confined for the most part to a handful of countries in Western Europe and the English-speaking world. Even more recent are organized political parties that compete peacefully in elections for the votes of the great bulk of the adult population who can exercise the franchise under nearly universal suffrage. Universal suffrage and enduring mass parties are, with few exceptions, products of the past century. It should not be altogether surprising, then, that of the 113 members of the United Nations in 1964, only about 30 had political systems in which full legal opposition among organized political parties had existed throughout the preceding decade.

If political systems with legal opposition parties are a minority as we move into the last third of the twentieth century, what can we expect for the twenty-first century? Are the 30 systems that now exist merely the exotic flowers of a unique and passing historical climate? Or are they vigorous products of a long evolution, a political species now rugged enough to thrive in other, perhaps harsher, climes? In short, if systems with legal party opposition do not fully reflect the present world, do they merely reflect the past—or do they provide patterns for the future?

A Few Preliminary Assumptions

The fact that a system of peaceful and legal opposition by political parties is a comparative rarity means that it must be exceedingly difficult to *introduce* such a system, or to *maintain* it, or both. To explain how and why these systems start is difficult; historical explanations tend to dissolve into minutiae that do not altogether "explain," while ahistorical explanations remain on the surface or recede into shadowy uncertainties because the data needed for a satisfactory explanation do not exist.

The novelty of peaceful opposition does suggest, however, that governments have usually tried to prevent the development of opposition. One could convert this historical observation into a simple axiom about the behavior of any political group that controls the central government of any political association: A governing group will use the coercive powers of the government to deny opponents the opportunity to oppose it, in every instance where the governing group expects that coercion has a fair chance of succeeding *and* the gains of a successful denial will exceed the costs. The plausibility of this axiom, you will notice, gains from the fact that it does not say very much. But let us now turn the axiom around: Opposition is likely to be permitted in a political system if (1) the government believes that an attempt to coerce the opposition is likely to fail, or (2) even if the attempt were to succeed, the costs of coercion would exceed the gains.

This excessively simple axiom suggests two interrelated questions: What factors increase the chances that a government will fail if it tries to coerce its opponents? And what factors increase the relative costs of successful coercion?

Consider the first question. Ordinarily a government has access to much greater resources for coercing opponents than opponents have for coercing government. (Otherwise, the chances are that the opposition would soon control the government.) Our initial conjecture is, however, that peaceful opposition is more likely to be introduced and maintained in a system where there is a kind of limited preponderance, so to speak, in the government's access to resources of coercion: that is, where a governing group stands a significant chance of failure if it tries to coerce its opponents, and hence permits or even encourages the development of institutions for peaceful negotiation. Would systems of legal opposition ever have developed if governing groups had known that they could, unquestionably, coerce their opponents and get away with it?

Specifically, then, the nature of the military and police forces has a bearing on the prospects of opposition. The potential effectiveness of military or police forces as instruments for coercing opposition may be limited because the standing army is small and police forces are under local control as in eighteenth-century Britain where an insular position and a navy eliminated the need for a large standing army while the country gentry and the justices of the peace maintained law and order;[1] or because the military forces consist of a citizen militia, as in Switzerland; or because the loyalty and obedience of the military or the police would be doubtful if they were employed to put down the opposition. This last constraint on the coercive power of the government may develop because bonds exist between military elements and the opposition. Or tradition and even law may deny legitimacy to a government that uses military forces for settling internal political wrangles; norms of this kind seem to have developed in the Netherlands during the fifteenth and sixteenth centuries, in Britain following the Revolution of 1688, and in Sweden during the course of the eighteenth century.

The prospects of successful coercion also decline when opposition groups improve their own opportunities to resort to defensive violence if they are threatened with coercion. Defenses against coercion by the central government may be relatively strong because of equality or superiority in numbers; because efficient weapons and military skills are widely diffused, as in the United States during the eighteenth and early nineteenth centuries; or because an opposition receives the loyalty of a population in a region with good natural defenses, economic supremacy, or other advantages.

Thus it is plausible to think that the existence of a limited preponderance of coercive forces, as these are perceived by government[2] and opposition, plays a key part in the transition to a system in which government and opposition are both prepared to renounce the use of violence. I say "limited preponderance" to cover an inescapable vagueness in the formula. An opposition might renounce violence because it sees that in an outright conflict, given the enormous potential power of the government, it would have no chance at all; one thinks here of the strategy of nonviolent resistance in British India and in the American South in recent years. For its part a government may renounce violence because, though it *might* succeed, the strategy of coercion is heavily fraught with risks of failure.

1. Ernest Barker, *The Development of Public Services in Western Europe, 1660–1930* (London, Oxford University Press, 1944), pp. 28–34, 50–52.

2. For convenience, I use "government" here, as later, as a shorthand for the more cumbersome "groups that control the government." The context will indicate sufficiently whenever the term is used this way.

The element of coercion, the requirement for a limited preponderance of coercive potential, is worth stressing because it is not uncommon to understate the importance of violence and coercion in the evolution of democratic institutions. Nonetheless, even if some rough balance may help to initiate a phase of growing tolerance of opposition by government and of government by its opponents, it seems unlikely that the growth of full-fledged systems of legal opposition could have rested entirely, or even mainly, on such precarious foundations. Limited preponderance is, conceivably, a necessary condition, but it is hardly sufficient. What weight should we give, then, to the factors posed a moment ago in our second question: factors that increase the relative costs of successful coercion? For a governing group might believe that it could coerce its opponents, and yet not do so because the costs would be too great.

What turns "successful" coercion into costly failure? Among other things, one surmises, are matters of belief, ideology, values. Costs of coercion rise, one may assume, whenever elites and the general population of a country develop a sense of nationhood that includes the opposition; a distaste for violence; a commitment to a liberal ideology; or economic and social goals that require internal stability. Finally, once a system that permits peaceful party opposition is highly institutionalized and surrounded with legal protections, the costs of destroying it are likely to be extremely high. For a government can destroy the opposition only by wrecking the constitutional system. At this stage of evolution, to destroy the opposition requires a revolution. And the costs of revolution often run high.

These speculations as to the introduction and maintenance of a system of peaceful opposition suggest two further observations. First, the conjunction of the necessary factors depends heavily on historical developments over which it is difficult to exercise precise control. Second, the rise and conjunction of the appropriate factors take *time*; until now, stable systems with legal oppositions have evolved rather slowly. It is by no means clear whether or how the process can be deliberately contrived or greatly speeded up. Yet it would be hard to find other questions on which knowledge is more urgent.

A New Form: Opposition Parties

Political systems with organized political parties protected by law are, as I have already said, a modern development. Historical analogies can generally be found for any innovation; nonethless, the opposition political party as we know it today represents a radical break with older forms of opposition.

Because some conflict of views seems to be unavoidable in human affairs, political societies have always had to deal somehow with the fact

of opposition. Nevertheless, that there might legitimately exist an organized group within the political system to oppose, criticize, and if possible oust the leading officials of government was until recently an unfamiliar and generally unacceptable notion. When the men at the American Constitutional Convention of 1787 expressed their fear of "factions"
as the bane of republics, they spoke the traditional view. The most long-
lived republic in history, the aristocratic republic of Venice, deliberately
inhibited the formation of enduring political organizations. Venice, like
Rome before it, sought to provide in its constitutional arrangements sufficient checks and balances among officials to prevent arbitrary decisions
and to insure a large measure of consensus for the laws; thus organized
opposition was seen as unnecessary and a danger to the stability of the
Republic.[3] Not all the premodern democracies and republics went quite
as far as Venice. Factions, coalitions, and alliances of one kind or another
existed in and outside the popular assemblies of Athens,[4] and in the late
Roman Republic political alliances sought votes both for candidates and
for laws in the various popular assemblies. But evidently these groups
were never highly organized, had no permanent structure, and even
lacked definite names.[5] Moreover, like the Guelphs and Ghibellines of
medieval Italy or the Piagnoni and the Arrabiati of Savonarola's Florence,
factions typically settled their differences sooner or later, as they came to
do during the last century of the Roman Republic, by bloodshed.

The system of managing the major political conflicts of a society by
allowing one or more opposition parties to compete with the governing
parties for votes in elections and in parliament is, then, not only modern;
surely it is also one of the greatest and most unexpected social discoveries

3. All the more so because the aristocracy was acutely aware of the danger,
particularly after the strife of the thirteenth century, that a split within the aristocracy would endanger its exclusive control over the constitutional machinery
of the Republic. For a thoroughgoing description of this constitution and the pre-
occupation of the aristocracy with the prevention of internal conflict see Giuseppe
Maranini, *La Costituzione di Venezia* (Venice, La Nuova Italia Editrice), Vol. 1,
Dalle Origini alla Serrata del Maggior Consiglio (1927), and Vol. 2, *Dopo La
Serrata del Maggior Consiglio* (1931), particularly Vol. 1, pp. 168–71; the description
of the highly complex method for electing the doge at pp. 187–90; and 324–50;
also Vol. 2, pp. 99, 115, 122.

4. "There were no parties in anything like the modern sense, either among
the politicians or the general public. At the one end of the scale there were groups
or cliques among the politicians. But such alliances were probably based on personalities rather than principles, and seem to have been temporary." A. H. M. Jones,
Athenian Democracy (Oxford, Blackwell, 1957), pp. 130–31. Jones concludes, however, "that Athenian policy was really determined by mass meetings of the citizens
on the advice of anyone who could win the people's ear." (p. 132). See also Fustel
de Coulanges, *The Ancient City* (Garden City, N.Y., Doubleday Anchor Books,
n.d.), pp. 340 ff.

5. Lily Ross Taylor, *Party Politics in the Age of Caesar* (University of California,
Berkeley and Los Angeles, 1961). Also F. E. Adcock, *Roman Political Ideas and
Practice* (Ann Arbor, University of Michigan Press, 1959), pp. 60–62.

that man has ever stumbled onto. Up until two centuries ago, no one had accurately foreseen it. Today one is inclined to regard the existence of an opposition party as very nearly the most distinctive characteristic of democracy itself; and we take the absence of an opposition party as evidence, if not always conclusive proof, for the absence of democracy.

Yet there are signs, as the essays in this volume show, that this new form, which was unknown before the nineteenth century and had spread to some 30 countries in the twentieth, is, nearly everywhere, undergoing profound changes. One task of these essays is to discover what these changes are.

The Meaning of Opposition

The term "opposition" is rather difficult to define precisely. This is not unusual with key terms in social theory, though it is often annoying. A preliminary definition will, I think, prove satisfactory enough for our purposes. Suppose that A determines the conduct of some aspect of the government of a particular political system during some interval. We need not specify the interval exactly; it may be a period in the past, the coming year, etc. Suppose that during this interval B cannot determine the conduct of the government; and that B is opposed to the conduct of government by A. Then B is what we mean by "an opposition." Note that during some different interval, B might determine the conduct of the government, and A might be "in opposition." Thus it is the *role* of opposition that we are interested in; we are concerned with A and B only insofar as they perform that role in different ways.

This preliminary definition can be clarified a little, at the price of adding logical embellishments of doubtful beauty. To begin with, the "conduct" of the government is deliberately broad and vague, and I propose to leave it undefined; it remains therefore what logicians sometimes call a primitive term. But it is intended to be comprehensive enough to include, for example, the mere fact that A comes from an ethnic, racial, or religious group that B is opposed to having in high government offices. What it means to "oppose" might also be left undefined, but a few comments may help to specify the meaning. As the term is used here, A is opposed to B's action or strategy S_b if A believes that S_b will prevent A from successfully pursuing his own preferred action or strategy S_a. In this sense one cannot speak of an "objective" opposition of "interests" that is independent of the perceptions or beliefs held by the parties themselves.[6] Nonetheless, it is useful to distinguish between *active* op-

6. To say that A and B are "objectively" opposed, even though they are not aware of it, presumably means, in our terms, either: (1) An observer can demonstrate, or believes he can demonstrate, that A's strategy makes it "objectively" impossible for B to pursue his preferred strategy S_b; or (2) given certain "objective" characteristics of A and B, such as occupation or class, an observer holds that he

position, which occurs when *B* undertakes a deliberate course of action intended to modify the conduct of government, and *passive* opposition, which exists when *B* recognizes the conflict but does not deliberately undertake any action directed toward a change in the conduct of government. In this volume we are almost entirely concerned with active opposition.

Second, in some political systems the role of opposition might be difficult to distinguish, either because one is uncertain whether it is *A* or *B* that determines the conduct of the government, or because both do. In systems like this, opposition is not distinctive; it dissolves into the system, so to speak. As we shall see later, something like this seems to happen so often in the United States that it is difficult or even impossible to locate "the opposition."

Third, you will notice that our preliminary definition is highly abstract. It refers to the government of *any* political system. In this volume, however, we are concerned with the national government of a territorial state. A study of patterns of opposition in other kinds of political systems —local governments or trade unions, for example—would be highly instructive; but we have nonetheless restricted our attention to national systems because the national patterns are of crucial importance, we have more information about them than about other patterns, and they provide some basis for comparison.

Finally, the definition does not explicitly restrict itself to "democratic" political systems. Admittedly, it would be important to know more about the ways in which opposition operates in nondemocratic systems, but in this volume we deliberately confine ourselves to the operation of oppositions in democracies.

Our preliminary definition need not be taken too seriously. It is not intended to serve as a rigorous definition in a deductive system; it will serve, rather, as a pointer. In the essays, the meaning of the term is usually clear enough from the context.

Questions and Problems

I had originally intended to provide an introduction to this volume that according to currently fashionable and sufficiently ambiguous jargon would probably be called an analytical framework—something, that is, rather more than a classification scheme and less than a tightly knit theory. But as the discussions among the contributors proceeded, our analytical framework kept changing—for the better, one hopes. A candid portrayal of the relation between the essays in this volume and the

---

can predict from certain theoretical or hypothetical conditions that *A* and *B* will come to believe that they pursue conflicting strategies; or possibly (3) both of these.

analytical scheme that eventually emerged would have to show the final scheme less as a format for the essays than as their product. I have therefore placed the whole comparative analysis in the final chapters.

Discussions of drafts and revised papers that ultimately led to these essays took place at the Villa Serbelloni, in Bellagio, Italy, first through a week in August 1962 and again during a week in July 1963. Between these meetings and after the second one, all the authors exchanged their revised essays for additional comments. Thus, more than is usually the case, the result is, I think, a joint product.

Our discussions and written exchanges continued to demonstrate that it was easier to dismantle our various "frameworks" than to build an enduring one. For one thing, the range of countries examined provided such a diversity of experience that generalization was all too easily torpedoed by its natural enemy, some stubborn fact that would not consent either to fit the generalization or to be ignored. Moreover, our attempt to understand modern democratic politics by examining oppositions provided a perspective that constantly produced new questions, hypotheses, tentative explanations, and reevaluations.

In these circumstances, the most profitable course, it began to appear, was to leave each author considerable leeway in describing and explaining the pattern of political oppositions in the country for which he was responsible. Some of the authors have placed a relatively heavy emphasis on the historical and developmental factors that seem to account for present patterns; others have given greater weight to more recent factors. The differences in treatment stem, I think, partly from differences in intellectual temperament, partly from differences in the character of the problem and the amount of knowledge the author can assume his readers possess about the country, and partly from unsettled differences, which mirror the current state of the social sciences, over the place of historical explanation in social analysis. Since these essays enter upon a domain that had not been well charted before we began, a tight, authoritative analytical scheme would have compelled our essayists to chop off a good deal of information and explanation that would not have fitted a Procrustean framework. I cannot help feeling that in the end both the reader and future progress on this subject would have been a good deal poorer.

Moreover, much of the experience described in these essays lies almost completely outside the main body of knowledge about the political systems of advanced countries. Knowledge of the political systems of Norway, Belgium, Holland, and Austria, for example, rarely enters into comparative political analysis: there are the major developed countries —Britain, France, Germany, the United States—and there are the developing countries, but we generally ignore the experiences of the smaller

European nations in an advanced state of social, economic, and political development. Because of our relatively greater ignorance about these countries, it seemed wise to permit more descriptive material, and perhaps more variation in treatment, than would otherwise be required. The result is that the number and variety of democratic systems examined in this volume are large in comparison with most comparative efforts.

Even so, there are important omissions. Some of these are accidental. The lengthy illness of a distinguished Swiss colleague prevented him from writing what would surely have been a highly important contribution to our understanding of oppositions in the unique and venerable democracy of Switzerland. Simple considerations of space and the availability of contributors eliminated many other potential chapters; thus only two of the five Nordic democracies are included, and only two of the English-speaking democracies; Israel, an outpost of democracy in the Middle East, has been excluded, along with all the non-Western democracies, even such important ones as Japan and India.

It would be grossly misleading, however, to leave the implication that each of the essays that follow takes off, without guide or map, into an unknown territory. For one thing, to examine the problem of oppositions is sometimes a matter of employing a new perspective to look at fairly familiar things—political parties, elections, legislatures, for example. For another, and this is the more important point, our discussions and the resulting essays do reflect our concern for a common set of questions that have confronted us from the outset.

These questions fall into two sets. As to the *patterns within countries*, what are the principal characteristics of political oppositions, particularly their goals and strategies? How has the prevailing pattern developed in each country? Has the pattern of opposition goals and strategies undergone important changes in recent years? How can this pattern, its development, and its changes be explained? As to *comparisons among countries*, is there a single more or less standard pattern of political oppositions in all countries examined here? If not, what are the main patterns? What factors seeem to account for variations? To what extent have there been general changes in the patterns of oppositions associated with the kind of economy and society emerging since the Second World War? In particular, to what extent have patterns of opposition been changing in Western Europe and the United States as a result of declining structural opposition, social cleavages, polarization, or political alienation?

The authors of the chapters on the individual countries were naturally concerned primarily with the first set of questions. The second set, which asks for comparisons among countries, I have tried to deal with in the concluding chapters.

R.A.D.

Political

Oppositions

in Western

Democracies

1

GREAT BRITAIN:
OPPOSITION WITH A CAPITAL "O"

Allen Potter

Peaceful political opposition has had a long history in Great Britain. It antedates the Industrial Revolution of the late eighteenth century and the series of Reform Acts, starting with those of 1832, which turned the parliamentary electoral system of an oligarchy into that of a representative democracy. Perhaps one in twelve adult males could vote before 1832, one in seven thereafter, one in three after 1868, and three in five after 1884. The Second Reform Acts, of 1867 and 1868, whose general effect was to enfranchise the male working-class householders of the towns, constituted the decisive step in the "transition to democracy." They increased the electorate proportionately more than any of the other nineteenth-century Acts. The Ballot Act of 1872 made voting secret.

The situation since the late nineteenth century has had the following features:

a mass electorate, including rural workers on the same basis as urban workers from 1884, almost all adult males and almost all females aged 30 and above from 1918, and women on the same basis as men from 1928;

a constitutional system in which there is, owing to the principle of parliamentary sovereignty, no formal limit to the power of a Government with a parliamentary majority and, when the two-party system is fully operative, no possibility between elections of a Government losing its majority;

a consensus, especially among political leaders, about the general nature of the rights, privileges, and duties of the Opposition, which makes the propriety of opposition as integral a part of the constitutional structure of conventions and understandings as the authority of government; and

a social cleavage along class lines, which is more or less institutionalized in the contest between the two major political parties for governmental power, and whose political effects are thereby contained within the

3

conventional structure restraining the governing of the Government and the opposing of the Opposition.

The British constitution, with its implicit recognition of the legitimacy of opposition, is an inheritance from aristocratic times. There were forebodings in 1867 that it would not be preserved by a democratic age. It would fall victim to the war between "the masses" and "the classes." That war seemed to begin in earnest in the politics of the early years of this century, but it was the crisis over Irish Home Rule that then seemed most likely to destroy the constitution. After the First World War the prospect of an uncomplicated and full confrontation between the proletariat and privilege opened, as the incubus of Ireland was lifted from internal British politics and the Labor Party with its socialist program replaced the Liberal Party with its measures of social reform. The conditions preserving the British constitution in an age of a mass electorate may be discerned in the failure of that straight class struggle for power to materialize.

The Situation

THE HISTORICAL BACKGROUND   In 1937 the Ministers of the Crown Act provided for the payment of a salary from public funds to the Leader of the Opposition in the British Parliament. In debate on the provision Kenneth Pickthorn, M.P., remarked that the position of Leader of the Opposition, in anything like the modern sense, was hardly older than the oldest member:

> it was not until the late sixties, when Mr. Gladstone threw his hat into the ring in competition with Lord Stanley, that there was a Leader of the Opposition in the sense not of a man who most criticised the Government on the way they were doing their business and hoped that, in the long run, his criticism would get the Government out; but in the sense of a man who put up a different programme, with different subjects on which to base his programme and upon which he fought, who looks round to see what is likely to interest the public—the Irish Church or the means test.[1]

As befitted a member for Cambridge University, Pickthorn thought it premature to give formal recognition to this constitutional innovation. The Home Secretary, Sir John Simon, agreed with Pickthorn's account, but added that "the conception that you were discharging a public duty when you were opposing is one of the oldest conceptions in the history of British politics."[2]

1. 323 H.C. Deb. 5s. 621.
2. Ibid., 642.

The constitutional settlement within which the institutions of cabinet government and official opposition eventually developed followed upon the civil war of the seventeenth century. The tendency thereafter to avoid pushing political differences to extremes reflected a similar tendency in religious controversy, which was more central in the politics of the seventeenth century than later; and the growth of religious toleration was in the first instance much less a matter of positive conviction or religious indifference than of a reluctant realization that the cost of imposing uniformity was too great. Charles II's Declaration of Breda in 1660, the acceptance of which by the Convention Parliament put Charles on the throne, stated:

> because the passion and uncharitableness of the times have produced several opinions in religion, by which men are engaged in parties and animosities against each other (which, when they shall hereafter unite in a freedom of conversation, will be composed or better understood), we do declare a liberty to tender consciences, and that no man shall be disquieted or called in question for differences of opinion in matter of religion, which do not disturb the peace of the kingdom.[3]

Although the ensuing Cavalier Parliament disquieted those who refused to take the sacrament according to the rites of the Church of England, in doing so it recognized dissent as lawful for the first time. The acceptance of the constitutional settlement was also for some time less than complete, with plots or rumors of plots disturbing the political conversation before and after the Revolution of 1688; as usual, Scotland was the last to lay the old aside, but the 'Forty-five was a political anachronism even there.

In the late seventeenth century the country was decidedly becoming a business nation, and intolerance was thought bad for trade. After the Glorious Revolution Britain engaged in long wars with France. By way of contrast with French intolerance and absolutism the British ruling class pointed with pride to British liberties. That class, the landed aristocracy, dominated society and politics in the century after the Glorious Revolution. Divergences of opinions and interests could be tolerated within and to some extent outside that class, which was in any case never defined with legal precision, because its position seemed unassailable.

The events of the French Revolution frightened the upper classes. In 1792 the Government embarked on a policy of outright repression of unrest in "the mob," though not of opposition to its measures among gentlemen in Parliament. The worst social tension was during the period of unsettled economic conditions caused by the end of the Napoleonic wars. But it was followed by adjustments to changes in society brought about

3. S. R. Gardiner, *The Constitutional Documents of the Puritan Revolution 1628–1660* (Oxford, Clarendon Press, 1889), p 352.

by the Industrial Revolution which ensured, in the language of the day, that the "age of improvement" would not be suddenly transformed into an age of "disruption." [4] The outcome was the Victorian compromise in which social and political leadership remained largely in the hands of the hereditary but absorbent ruling class, though government policy was now more directly responsive to the interests and opinions of the middle classes; and, since social, political, and economic power was less concentrated in a single class than in the previous century, the working classes were also not without influence as long as they did not, as in the case of the Chartists, frighten all the classes above them.

"It has been said," Walter Bagehot wrote in the mid-1860s in *The English Constitution*, "that England invented the phrase, 'Her Majesty's Opposition'; that it was the first Government which made a criticism of administration as much a part of the polity as administration itself. This critical opposition is the consequence of Cabinet Government." [5] It might equally well be put that cabinet government is the consequence of critical opposition. Once the supremacy of Parliament was established in the constitutional settlement of the late seventeenth century, the problem arose of relating the conduct of administration to opinion in Parliament in some regular way. The ultimate solution was a cabinet controlling administration and commanding the confidence of a majority in the House of Commons against its opponents in the chamber. The solution was long in emerging, though rudiments of it were discernible almost from the start. It was not fully realized until the support of the electorate completely displaced the favor of the monarch as the determinant of who should govern.

The development of opposition in Parliament was essentially from an opposition to particular men or measures to an opposition offering an alternative government. From the Restoration the fact that the monarch needed at least to consider the ability of ministers to manage Parliament was an element in politicians' calculations. This made it worthwhile to attempt to marshal opposition in Parliament against particular ministers or their policies. Throughout most of the eighteenth century the king's ministers maintained themselves in Parliament as the "Court Party," against the active and hostile politicians of the "Country Party," the majority of whose members, however, were not playing for office and, though independent of the Court, were not generally unfriendly to ministerial policy. The Court and Country parties were kaleidoscopic combinations of family and other personal connections, "Whigs" and "Tories" alike, active politicians supporting or opposing the Court in accordance with the immediate political interests of the groups to which they be-

4. Asa Briggs, *The Age of Improvement* (London, Longmans, 1959), p. 259.
5. Fontana Library ed. London, Collins, 1963, p. 72.

longed. The originally opprobrious nicknames "Whigs" and "Tories" date from the time of Lord Shaftesbury's Country Party, in the 1670s and '80s, and, though they persisted as the main political denominators for a century and a half, soon lost most of whatever value they had had as differentiating indicators of political behavior.

The theory of parliamentary supremacy was combined with the practical leadership of the king and his ministers. They had the support of placemen in the House. They attached groups to themselves by patronage and contracts, and corruption also ensured that they gained more support from elections than did their opponents. But for their majority ministers had to obtain the approval of enough independent members. Opposition politicians sought to harass ministers sufficiently to be bought off or to induce the king to replace one or more of his ministers; or, looking to the future, they attached themselves to the Prince of Wales. There was neither a formed general majority nor a formed general opposition.

Both started to emerge in the 1780s. Difference of opinion about public policy grew more important. An increasing number of social and political interests articulated issues. Reforms reduced the influence of patronage and contracts. Ministerial policy began to be based on public political attitudes. This meant that the question of parliamentary reform was bound to be raised, for a ministerial policy more directly related to "opinion" than in the past would not necessarily be a policy that the monarch could be induced personally to accept: ultimate support must come from "the people." The First Reform Acts completed the transition to responsible government, which had in essence been demanded by the Long Parliament in the Grand Remonstrance of 1641; "in 1841, for the first time, the opposition won a general election and the Crown accepted the decision at the polls." [6]

A straightforward connection between elections and cabinets was not established, however, until after the electorate was almost doubled and the constituencies made more uniform by the Second Reform Acts. The parliamentary political parties thereafter took the lead in mass political organization; the party labels became increasingly important in elections, and the independence of M.P.'s was considerably reduced. In the period between the first two sets of Reform Acts, glittering as the golden age of parliamentary government in Bagehot's classic account of *The English Constitution*, it came to be accepted that neither Her Majesty's Government nor Her Majesty's Opposition was, in theory at least, any more or less the Queen's Friends than the other. But the absence of a simple two-party system meant that Her Majesty's Opposition was not the alternative government that it is now. When the Government fell, the Opposition might not be prepared to take its place, though the four successive Parlia-

6. John P. Mackintosh, *The British Cabinet* (London, Stevens, 1962), p. 17.

ments elected from 1841 began under one sort of cabinet and ended under another, indicating the degree to which the connection between elections and cabinets was broken by the interposition of the House of Commons.

With the development of a strong and disciplined two-party system after the Second Reform Acts, Her Majesty's Opposition became the alternative government, but now normally unable to displace the Government during the life of a Parliament. Its appeal must be to the electorate; and from the late 1860s the party leaders tended to base their campaign appeals on one or two issues. A generation later these were becoming "programs." The party contest of British representative democracy took form, an essential element of which is official opposition—opposition with a capital "O."

THE CONSTITUTION   The constitutional principles of contemporary British government are conceived in terms of the other classic account of the nineteenth-century English constitution, A. V. Dicey's *Introduction to the Study of the Law of the Constitution*. The basic principle of the British, or at least the English, legal order is simple: Parliament, by which in this context is meant the Queen, Lords, and Commons or, under the provisions of the Parliament Acts of 1911 and 1949, the Queen and Commons alone, is sovereign. That means, in Dicey's words, "that Parliament thus defined has . . . the right to make or unmake any law whatever; and, further, that no person or body is recognized . . . as having a right to override or set aside the legislation of Parliament." [7] The principle of parliamentary sovereignty describes legal competence, the conditions of whose exercise are determined, according to Dicey, by the conventions of the constitution. The queen acts on the advice of her ministers. Her ministers command the confidence of the House of Commons. The House of Commons is chosen in free elections, in which the Government and Opposition parties in effect contend for the control of the state. It is as the arbiters of this contest that the electors were described by Dicey as "the true political sovereign of the State." [8]

The last phrase is vacuous: the aggregation of the individual decisions of voters in a general election determines which team of party leaders becomes the Government, and this makes the leaders responsive to opinion in its various manifestations, in the parties, pressure groups, the press, and public opinion polls; but the electorate, *qua* electorate, is in no significant sense the ultimate source of the content of the laws. In the British political system with its two highly disciplined parties, the victory of one of them in a general election gives to its leaders governmental authority without formal limit. Its exercise is tempered by thoughts of the next free election.

7. 10th ed. London, Macmillan, 1959, pp. 39–40.
8. P. 429.

But the prior question is why in their relations with each other the Government and the Opposition behave so that the Government allows the next election to be free, or rather why that question does not overtly arise in British politics.

Under a constitution that permits the Government always to get its own way, the Opposition is not protected by any institutional arrangements of the state. But the legitimacy of opposition is incorporated in the structure of constitutional conventions and understandings, so that the conditions preserving legitimate opposition are in Great Britain the conditions preserving its constitution.

> We may say [Dicey wrote] that the constitution is pervaded by the rule of law on the ground that the general principles of the constitution (as for example the right to personal liberty, or the right of public meeting) are with us the result of judicial decisions determining the rights of private persons in particular cases brought before the courts; whereas under many foreign constitutions the security (such as it is) given to the rights of individuals results, or appears to result, from the general principles of the constitution.[9]

As Dicey's examples indicate, the rights of private persons under the "rule of law" are essential to legitimate opposition. Dicey has been correctly criticized for attempting to derive the constitution from ordinary law, but he was fundamentally right in perceiving that no constitution is less a creator and more a creation of the arrangements it regulates than the British.

THE PARTY SYSTEM   That description of the constitutional position discounts the capacity of the House of Commons to check the actions of the Government, except insofar as the House is one of the media and sources of opinion to which the political leaders, in a system of free elections and competitive parties, respond. When its members belong to two disciplined parties, with too few M.P.'s outside them to hold the balance and with such dissident members of the main parties as there are usually on the extreme wings, and therefore more in disagreement with the other party than with their own, the House is not an independent factor in determining who governs and how. For that—for it to be the case that in bestowing its confidence in a Government the House "assumes the initiative, and acts upon its discretion or its caprice"—there must be a center element of independent and independent-minded members—as there was when Bagehot wrote the quoted words.[10]

It has been said that the Church of England is rightly named because it

9. Pp. 195–96.
10. *The English Constitution*, p. 151.

is the church that most Englishmen stay away from; likewise, even since the 1860s, the British two-party system has been the system from which the British have more often than not departed. The Liberal Unionists for two decades after 1885, the Irish Nationalists from 1874 to 1918, the independent Labor Party from 1906 to after the First World War, and the Liberals from then to near the end of the interwar period, provided elements of confusion in a parliamentary system whose conventions were increasingly institutionalizing the contest between the two front benches of the Government and the official opposition. But the Liberal Unionists soon were a few political leaders without independent voting support; and, like the Liberal Nationals (later National Liberals) who allied themselves to the Conservatives from 1931, became part of the Conservative side with little more than the pretence of independence. The Irish Nationalists provided the only parliamentary opposition of any significance that was unwilling to operate the British parliamentary system and, except for a couple of members among the representatives of Northern Ireland, were eliminated from the British Parliament by the establishment of the Irish Free State. The split in the Liberal Party in 1916 enabled the Labor Party to become the second party of the country by 1922, though it took another decade, during which there were two minority Labor governments, to settle that the only alternative governing party to the Conservatives was Labor. Once that was settled, any real resemblance to a three-party system came to an end.

The two-party system is the system to which the British return, and with which they have abided, in general elections, since the Second World War—as the table indicating the results of the elections from 1945 to 1964 shows. The increase in the Liberal percentage of the total vote in each of the last two general elections was largely accounted for by the increase in the number of Liberal candidates, of whom there were 110 in 1955, 216 in 1959, and 365 in 1964. However, the average Liberal vote as a percentage of the vote cast in the constituencies in which Liberal candidates stood rose from 15.1 per cent in 1955, to 16.9 per cent in 1959, and to 18.5 per cent in 1964 (just short of the 18.6 per cent of 1945).

The electoral system of single-member constituencies electing by simple majority favors a two-party system. The Representation of the People Act of 1918 introduced the requirement of a £150 electoral deposit, forfeited by all candidates failing to receive one-eighth of the votes cast in a constituency, in order to discourage "freak" candidacies. The average cost of contesting a constituency is a good deal higher than the amount of the deposit. The greatest financial problem of smaller parties is to raise funds for matching the services of the central party organizations of the major parties, especially the Conservative Party, which now include expensive advertising campaigns between elections that, unlike electioneering activities in the constituencies, are not subject to any legal limit as to the amount of money spent on them.

	General Election 1945		General Election 1950		General Election 1951	
	% of M.P.'s elected (640)	% of total vote (25.1 million)	% of M.P.'s elected (625)	% of total vote (28.8 million)	% of M.P.'s elected (625)	% of total vote (28.6 million)
Labor	61.4	47.8	50.4	46.1	47.2	48.8
Conservative	33.3	39.8	47.7	43.5	51.4	48.0
Two-party total	94.7	87.6	98.1	89.6	98.6	96.8
Liberal	1.9	9.0	1.4	9.1	1.0	2.5
Communist	0.3	0.4		0.3		0.1
Other	3.1	3.0	0.5	1.0	0.5	0.6

	General Election 1955		General Election 1959		General Election 1964	
	% of M.P.'s elected (630)	% of total vote (26.8 million)	% of M.P.'s elected (630)	% of total vote (27.9 million)	% of M.P.'s elected (630)	% of total vote (27.7 million)
Labor	43.9	46.4	40.9	43.8	50.3	44.1
Conservative	54.6	49.7	57.9	49.4	48.3	43.4
Two-party total	98.5	96.1	98.9	93.2	98.6	87.6
Liberal	1.0	2.7	1.0	5.9	1.4	11.2
Communist		0.1		0.1		0.2
Other	0.5	1.1	0.2	0.8		1.1

Besides the conservatism of party loyalties, the emphasis on choosing a Government in a general election buttresses the position of the existing major parties. The evidence for this lies not only in the way election campaigns are conducted, but also in the differences in voting behavior between general elections and by-elections, when non-major-party candidates often do comparatively well, and in the results of public opinion polls that compare how electors intend to vote in the next general election with how they would vote if "the Liberals had a chance." It is reasonable, therefore, to surmise that if the Liberals were thought to have gained a chance, the electoral system would aid and accelerate a shift of support to that party, but it has in the existing circumstances acted as a brake on the "Liberal revival."

Television is now the chief medium of mass communication and, unlike the press, subject to stringent regulation in party political matters. Both the British Broadcasting Corporation and the commercial Independent Television service are charged with maintaining political impartiality in their programming, and the latter cannot accept political advertisements of any kind. The services provide free facilities for a limited number of party political broadcasts, which are entirely under the control of the parties giving them. For 1965 the television allocation is five programs totaling 60 minutes to each of the two major parties, two programs totaling 20 minutes to the Liberal Party, and one five-minute program apiece to the Scottish National Party and the Welsh Nationalists. This is the first time that others than the three main parties have shared in the annual allocation. During the 1964 general election period the Conservative and Labor parties each had five programs of 15 minutes apiece and the Liberal Party three. There are similar arrangements for sound programs on the B.B.C. Since 1949 it has been agreed by the party managers of the three leading parties, who work out the arrangements with the broadcasting authorities, that any other party running 50 candidates qualifies for an election broadcast. In 1950 the Communist Party ran 100 candidates and was allotted one ten-minute sound program, at a time when there was no television electioneering. No party has qualified in that way since.

Until the advent of commercial television as provided for in the Television Act of 1954 led to a competition for audiences, a blackout had been imposed on news and comment about election campaign activities, apart from the party political broadcasts. It was ended by a commercial company during a by-election in 1958. There is now a good deal of coverage, though the broadcasting services must do nothing to promote the election of particular candidates. Between general elections the chief political beneficiaries of the change have so far undoubtedly been the Liberals, whose by-election candidates are treated on a par with those of the two major parties, and whose by-election gains have been well publicized. In general elections they and to some extent the small parties have been represented, along with the two main parties, on discussion programs put out by the broadcasting bodies. But the inevitable consequence of unbiased reporting of general election campaigns is on balance to call more attention to and thereby reinforce the tendency to reduce a general election to the contest for office between the leaders of the two main political parties.

The inertia of the present two-party system is large. But its continuance is conditional on the absence of strong and diverse political passions, which would burst out of a system that treats the political attitudes of electors as constituting a single linear distribution with the two parties competing for the "floating voters" at the mean point of the distribution: "offering bait to the same fish." [11] There seems little likelihood of a change in this respect. The system also assumes the occasional alternation of the

11. W. Ivor Jennings, *The British Constitution* (Cambridge, Cambridge University Press, 1946), p. 50. Cf. D. E. Butler and Anthony King, *The British General Election of 1964* (London, Macmillan, 1965), p. 54.

parties in office. After the third successive Conservative victory in 1959, it was fashionable to ask whether in the existing two-party alignment the Labor Party could ever win power again. But the Labor victory in 1964 and its narrowness ensure the continuance and probably the intensification in the immediate future of the present two-party contest.

The variations in the two-party system during the last hundred years ought not to obscure the fundamental and permanent change that took place in the latter part of the nineteenth century with respect to the influence of party on parliamentary voting. After 1832 the Government sought increasingly to guide the House: in 1836, the first year in which division lists were printed, Government whips acted as tellers on less than half the divisions, from 1851 to 1860 on seven-tenths, and in 1894 on nearly nine-tenths. But the percentage of divisions on which nine-tenths of the Conservative members who voted went into the same lobby was 56 per cent in 1836 and only 31 per cent in 1860; for members of the Whig-Radical or Liberal Party the comparable figures were 40 in 1836 and 25 in 1860; and the percentage of divisions in which nine-tenths of the members of each of the parties who voted went into opposite lobbies was 23 per cent in 1836 and only 6 per cent in 1860. In 1871 the figures under all three headings were greater than in 1836; and in 1894 the percentage of divisions on which nine-tenths of the Conservative and Liberal Unionist members who voted went into the same lobby was 91 per cent, that for Liberals and the two groups of Irish Nationalists taken together was 81 per cent, and that for nine-tenths of the members of each of the parties who voted going into opposite lobbies was 76 per cent.[12] Divisions in the House of Commons had become occasions on which the Government and the Opposition deployed their parliamentary forces against each other, and the only development since has been to perfect and institutionalize the change.

When the two-party system is fully functioning (as it was not in the two world wars as well as the periods of minority Government), it is politically impossible to bring the Government down by adverse votes or abstentions in the House of Commons. Backbench pressure in the majority party may more or less successfully be brought to bear on the Government off the floor of the House, though less successfully if the Government is determined to resist it. This pressure may mount if the Government seems unpopular among its supporters or the voters in the country. But it is not a force for preserving the rights of the Opposition.

OPPOSITION WITH A CAPITAL "O"   Like cabinet government, the official opposition is part of the conventional British constitution. The Leader of the Opposition, like the Prime Minister, holds an office that arose out

12. A. Lawrence Lowell, "The Influence of Party upon Legislation in England and America," in *Annual Report of the American Historical Association for the Year 1901, I* (Washington, 1902), 321–29.

of practice. His position has no official functions according to legislation or the rules of the House of Commons. The rights, privileges, and duties of Her Majesty's Opposition are subjects in which the ambiguities of constitutional interpretation, with its mixture of descriptive and prescriptive elements, cannot be resolved by recourse to courts of law.

That the official opposition has privileges is evident in the practice of the House of Commons. Thus a convention of more than 60 years' standing permits the Opposition to select the topics of debate on days allotted to the consideration of the Estimates and the bills by which they are finally authorized. In general the two front benches of Her Majesty's Government and Her Majesty's Opposition between them set the great majority of topics of parliamentary debate. The Government's legislative program perforce determines most of the broad subjects, but the leaders of the Opposition have the greatest influence in deciding what specifically to discuss. This is mainly at the expense of backbench members on the two sides. In relation to their small numbers in the House of Commons the members of any minor parties and "rebels" are given at least proportionate opportunities to express their points of view.

More and more, the Leader of the Opposition is treated in effect as Her Majesty's alternative prime minister, in public ceremonies and in private conversations with the Prime Minister on confidential matters, though it is constitutionally improper to describe him thus, since the choice of a new Prime Minister is the personal prerogative of the monarch. There is disagreement about how far the possible future position of the Leader of the Opposition casts its shadow before. Leaders of the Opposition are cautious about receiving the confidences of the Government, of which their backbenchers are naturally suspicious. It is argued that the leaders of the Opposition have responsibilities, not to damage the security of the state and other public interests in their criticism and to keep themselves informed as potential advisers of the queen, which require them to receive confidential information; but once they have received it, they are not in a position to dispute with the Government about the value of imparting it in the particular case. They sometimes refuse it, when it seems likely to be incompatible with the constitutional function of criticism and without compensating advantages for themselves or the public interest as they conceive it.

Generally, while recognizing that the Opposition has duties as well as rights and privileges, Leaders of the Opposition resist attempts to impose restraints on their conduct. Near the end of 1937, a Conservative M.P. put down a motion inviting the House to pass a vote of censure on the Labor Leader of the Opposition for speeches Attlee had made during a visit to the Spanish Republican government. Attlee made a personal statement in the House of Commons, in which he said in part:

In his Motion, the Hon. Member . . . has specifically referred to me as 'the Leader of His Majesty's Official Opposition,' and seems to imply that this places me in a special category. The Leader of the Opposition is a private Member. He owes no allegiance to the Government. No action of his can in any way implicate the Government. He is responsible only to his constituents and to the Members from whom he derives his position. He is, I think, under a special obligation to defend the rights and privileges of private Members, particularly the right of every Member to express his opinion freely on all matters of public policy.[13]

That was the end of the matter.

Her Majesty's Opposition is not a "licensed" opposition: the status of being the official opposition is not in the gift of the Government. The payment of a salary to its Leader necessitated a legal definition of his position, which appears in the Ministers of the Crown Act of 1937: " 'Leader of the Opposition' means that member of the House of Commons who is for the time being the Leader in that House of the party in opposition to His Majesty's Government having the greatest numerical strength in that House." [14] But on the formation in 1940 of Churchill's Coalition Government embracing the Conservative, Labor, and Liberal parties, leaving only the four Independent Labor Party members and one Communist M.P. outside the government supporters, the Speaker ruled that "it cannot be said that there is now an Opposition in Parliament in the hitherto accepted meaning of the words; namely, a party in Opposition to the Government from which an alternative Government could be formed." [15] The Prime Minister announced that the provision of the Ministers of the Crown Act relating to the payment of a salary to the Leader of the Opposition was in abeyance for the time being. The practice of the House of Commons required that someone act as Leader of the Opposition. Some of the older Labor leaders had been left out of the Government and were, in Attlee's words,

> available to lead the Party in the House. By tacit consent, first Lees Smith and, after his death, Pethick-Lawrence . . .—although both were wholehearted supporters of the Government—performed the duties of a Leader of the Opposition, asking questions as to the business of the House and so on. The Labor Party continued to sit on the Opposition benches. The Front Bench was filled by leading members of both Parties who were sometimes found in temporary alliance.[16]

Opposition with a capital "O" is provided by a party—or parties,

13. 330 H.C. Deb. 5s. 824.
14. 1 Edw. 8 & 1 Geo. 6c. 38, s. 10 (1).
15. 361 H.C. Deb. 5s. 27
16. *As It Happened* (London, Heinemann, 1954), p. 116.

though the conception fits more naturally in a two-party than a multi-party system—prepared to become the Government; and that entails a willingness to govern as well as to oppose which is, however, not a willingness to govern, or to oppose, too much. Her Majesty's Opposition as well as Her Majesty's Government behaves so as not to call into question the structure of constitutional conventions and understandings regulating their relationship. "What we mean by the 'Opposition,' " wrote Lord Campion, formerly Clerk to the House of Commons, "is the party for the time being in the minority, organized as a unit and officially recognized, which has had experience of office and is prepared to form a Government when the existing Ministry has lost the confidence of the country. It must have a positive policy of its own and not merely oppose destructively. . . . Our system, alone," he added with insular pride, "can produce a responsible Opposition, one with a consistent policy known to the country in broad outline, one which is not anxious to win at the expense of ruining the game." [17]

THE SOCIAL SETTING   Great Britain is a populous, highly urbanized, and mature industrial country, whose class structure relates to disparities of income and wealth and also, both reinforcing and modifying the influence of money, differences in education, occupation, ancestry, and behavior. Class differences are politically the most significant social cleavages in a society whose people have perhaps an even stronger sense of their homogeneity than the facts warrant. This unity is partly accounted for by the greater homogeneity among the leaders of opinion than among the population as a whole.

The population of Great Britain in 1961 was 51.3 million, of whom 43.4 million lived in England, 2.6 million in Wales and Monmouthshire, and 5.2 million in Scotland. Eighteen and seven-tenths million lived in Greater London and six other conurbations. That was a smaller proportion of the population than lived in them in 1901, but the urbanization of the countryside continues: the percentage of the total occupied population engaged in agriculture or fishing was 9 per cent in 1901 and 4 per cent in 1961.

Estimating the distribution of income and wealth is an undertaking of great difficulty; and the data on personal wealth, derived mainly from estate duty statistics, undoubtedly underestimate the concentration at the top, owing to the ease with which the tax may be avoided. Even so, "the concentration of ownership of capital is much greater than the concentration of income. Out of total real disposable income the top one per cent of income units received in 1954 only about 7 per cent; out of total

17. "Developments in the Parliamentary System Since 1918," in *British Government Since 1918* (London, Allen and Unwin, 1950), p. 19.

personal net capital (excluding pension and trust funds) the top one per cent of persons aged 20 and over in 1954 owned 43 per cent. Wealth is much more unequally distributed in Britain than in the United States." [18]

To give a very rough idea of the educational situation in England and Wales in the late 1950s: of every 20 boys aged twelve, 19 were in state-supported schools, of whom 4 were in grammar schools providing the most academic education and the rest in schools from which the great majority left at fifteen. One of the 20 was in a "public" or other independent school. Not one in a hundred was in the 20 best-known public schools. One in 20 boys went on to a university. Oxford and Cambridge had more than a fifth of the university population, a quarter of the male and a tenth of the female full-time students. At least two-fifths of their intake were from the public schools.

Less than one per cent of the population have gone to one of the leading public schools or to Oxford or Cambridge. But social analysis of the top people in the City, in the Foreign Service, in the armed services, on the Bench, or in the Church shows that a majority of them have been educated at the leading public schools; and if they have attended an English university, it has almost invariably been Oxford or Cambridge.[19] Studies of managers and directors of larger public companies indicate that a third to a half have been to a public school, and "the advantages of being an old Etonian become more marked the higher up you go." [20] A large proportion of top managers have not attended a university, but recruitment by industry from the public schools and Oxford and Cambridge is increasing. A study of senior civil servants in 1958 showed that one-fifth had been educated at six leading public schools and two-thirds at Oxford or Cambridge.

Of 304 Conservative M.P.'s elected in 1964, 68 had been to Eton, 17 to Harrow, 12 to Winchester, and 132 to other public schools. Of 317 Labor M.P.'s, 2 had been to Eton, 2 to Winchester, and 52 to other public schools. Of the 192 Conservative members who had been to a university, 159 had been to Oxford or Cambridge. Of the 134 Labor members who had been to a university, 60 had been to Oxford or Cambridge.[21] In 1961 more than one-third of the incumbent Conservative ministers had been to Eton and Harrow, and two-fifths to other public schools. Of 34 Labor

18. H. F. Lydall and D. G. Tipping, "The Distribution of Personal Wealth in Britain," *Bulletin of the Oxford University Institute of Statistics, 13* (1961), 97. Cf. Richard M. Titmuss, *Income Distribution and Social Change* (London, Allen and Unwin, 1962).

19. There is a summary table with bibliographic references in W. L. Guttsman, *The British Political Elite* (London, Macgibbon and Kee, 1963), pp. 336–37.

20. Roy Lewis and Rosemary Stewart, *The Boss* (London, Phoenix House, 1958), p. 96.

21. Butler and King, *The British General Election of 1964,* p 237.

ministers who served in cabinets between 1916 and 1931, 6 had been to public schools; of 34 who served between 1940 and 1951, 11 had been; and of 23 entering the cabinet formed in October 1964, 8 had been. Of Conservative ministers who have been university graduates, the overwhelming majority have always gone to Oxford or Cambridge. Of Labor ministers who served in cabinets between 1916 and 1931, 7 had been to Oxford or Cambridge, 7 to other universities, and 20 to none; of those who served between 1940 and 1951, 11 had been to Oxford or Cambridge, 6 to other universities, and 17 to none; [22] and of those entering the cabinet formed in October 1964, 11 had been to Oxford, 1 to Durham, 1 to Glasgow, and 10 to no university. By far the larger number of editors of the quality national newspapers and periodicals, "the governors of culture and the arts," [23] the leading satirists of "the Establishment" as well as the leading members of it, if they have been to a university (and most of them have), have been to Oxford or Cambridge.

Education, it seems, largely determines occupation and the chances of success in it; but the occupation of parents tends to determine the education of their children even in the state system of free schools and free places. In the generation educated in English schools after the Second World War, fewer than one-sixteenth of the children admitted to grammar schools were children of unskilled manual workers, though one-eighth of men aged 20–64 were such workers; and, while seven-tenths of men aged 20–64 were manual workers of all kinds, their sons constituted only half that fraction of the male entry to British universities from grammar schools and only about a quarter of the total male entry. Among university entrants from grammar schools there were 62 children from white-collar (professional, managerial, and clerical) homes for every child of an unskilled manual worker. The state system, however, provides for much greater social mobility than the independent system, which is most closed at the top. Three-fifths of Etonians are sons of Old Etonians, and the remainder are practically indistinguishable from them. Fewer than an eighth of the male entrants to Oxford and Cambridge universities are sons of manual workers.

Thus continues the process by which social mobility at the top of British society is more or less contained within the established social hierarchy. In the nineteenth century the landed aristocracy lost its economic dominance. There was a formal transfer of ultimate political power to first the middle-class and then the working-class electorate. But the landed aristocracy retained a large measure of its social leadership; and it joined with the plutocracy in an alliance of old families and new wealth to form a "governing class," set apart from "the masses" by ancestry,

22. Guttsman, *The British Political Elite*, pp. 313, 244, 103, 106.
23. Ibid., p. 346.

education, and affluence, and knit together by family and marriage connections, the leading public schools, Oxford and Cambridge, and continual
contacts among its members. In this century the governing class has become looser and its social influence less pervasive: "the hereditary Establishment of interlocking families, which still has an infectious social and
political influence on the Conservative party, banking and many industries, has lost touch with the new worlds of science, industrial management
and technology." [24] It has never been a "power elite" organized to overcome the opposition of the rest of the population, but its members have
on the whole had the greatest access to and command of what the British
by their strivings define as the good things of life. When the process of
absorbing new elements has worked smoothly, the standards of behavior
of the established gentlemen have predominated; when it has not, the
standards have succumbed to the pursuit of money and pleasure.

Throughout the period of mass party politics the bulk of the governing class have been in the Conservative Party and most working-class
electors have usually voted against Conservative candidates. The middle
classes were divided more evenly and less certainly between the Conservatives and Liberals, but have always been predominantly anti-Labor. Concerning recent years "all the published studies of British voting behavior
support the same general conclusion: that the way a British elector votes
is closely related to his social and occupational status and, more particularly, to the way in which he sees his own status." [25] In the 1950s the
two-party vote of the manual working classes divided between 2 to 1
and 3 to 2 in favor of the Labor party; the two-party vote of the classes
above them taken as a whole divided about 4 to 1, and that of the upper
class overwhelmingly, in favor of the Conservative Party, with a shift
in general toward the latter. This meant that about half the Conservative
vote and about four-fifths of the Labor vote came from the manual
working classes.

The social cleavage between the two parties can be traced from top
to bottom, with manual workers disappearing from the Conservative
Party before the top and being present in varying proportions at different
levels of the Labor Party, though most preponderantly at the bottom.
There are few manual workers among Conservative constituency party
leaders and only two among the 304 Conservative M.P.'s elected in 1964,
assessing the latter by their first or formative occupations. Manual workers are a smaller proportion of Labor constituency party leaders than of
Labor voters. In 1918 they were over nine-tenths of 61 Labor and Co-

24. Anthony Sampson, *Anatomy of Britain* (London, Hodder and Stoughton,
1962), p. 632.
25. Graeme C. Moodie, *The Government of Great Britain* (New York, Crowell,
1961), p. 61.

operative M.P.'s elected, in 1935 nearly two-thirds of 154, and in 1964 a little under one-third of 317. The great majority of them have always been the "sponsored" candidates of trade unions affiliated to the Labor Party. Officials of the working-class movement—trade unions, consumer cooperatives, and the Labor Party organization—made up about half the membership of every Labor cabinet before 1964, the rest of whose members, with a single exception in each of two cabinets, had come into politics from non-working-class occupations and in the great majority of cases non-working-class backgrounds.[26] Of the 23 members of the cabinet formed in 1964, 9 were from the trade union movement.

Other social differences are much less determinant of variations in voting behavior. There is, however, an intrusion into a few localities of Great Britain of the division—still exacerbating the politics of Northern Ireland—between Irish Catholics and Orangemen among working-class voters, the first being more Labor, the second less so, than the working classes as a whole. In some places, too, Anglican working-class voters are more Conservative than are non-conformists; and in the House of Commons after the 1964 election there were 30 known Jews and 47 known nonconformists among 317 Labor M.P.'s as compared with 2 and 6 respectively among 304 Conservatives.

Only about a tenth of the adult population are Roman Catholics. Present estimates put the number of colored people in Britain at between 750,000 and 1,000,000 (less than 2 per cent of the population). The Commonwealth Immigrants Act of 1962 was passed to check their influx. The great majority of the British are of white Protestant stock. They set the tone of British politics and life. The differences among them, of religious belief and indifference, of regional or national sentiment associated with the North or South of England, with Scotland, or with Wales, are not only less important politically than what unites them but also less important than what otherwise divides them—class.

OPPOSITION WITH A LITTLE "o"   Mass political organization in Great Britain first developed outside the parliamentary system. That was necessarily so at a time when the great majority of the masses were without the vote. The Catholic Association founded by Daniel O'Connell in Ireland as part of a campaign for Catholic Emancipation (which was conceded in 1829) and Home Rule was the model for Thomas Attwood's Political Union agitating for parliamentary reform. In the 1830s and '40s the working-class Chartist movement failed to secure universal manhood suffrage, annual parliaments, and the secret ballot. But the middle-class Anti-Corn Law League led by Manchester men organized opinion so successfully that its structure and methods were later adopted by the political parties.

26. Guttsman, *The British Political Elite*, p. 242.

The Birmingham Liberal "caucus" proved the most effective device for organizing the enlarged electorate created by the Second Reform Acts; and in 1877 Joseph Chamberlain's supporters formed the National Liberal Federation of local associations to bring advanced Radical opinion in the country to bear on the parliamentary Liberal Party. Birmingham, with its small workshops making for less of a division between masters and operatives than the large factories of the cotton district around Manchester, was the natural center of the new Radicalism seeking to bring together the middle- and working-class electors of the industrial towns for—in Chamberlain's words—"the politics of the future . . . social politics." [27] Although the Federation was incorporated in the official party machinery after Chamberlain left the Liberals over Home Rule, it continued to reflect the opinions of militant Liberals in the constituencies. From 1867 the Conservative Party provided its constituency organizations with a National Union, which apart from a brief period in the 1880s, when Lord Randolph Churchill used it to further his own ambitions, has never played an important part in the counsels of the party.

At the turn of the century, trade unions were persuaded to join a simple organization for putting independent Labor representatives in Parliament. In 1918 the Labor Party outside Parliament was transformed into a national party of affiliated trade unions and individual members. The trade unions have always had a great majority of the votes at the extraparliamentary Labor Party conference, at which the individual members are represented through the constituency parties. But the notion, derived in part from the former necessity to organize working-class opinion outside the parliamentary system, that the party conference should guide the parliamentary Labor Party succumbed to the tradition, also coming from the time when the masses were beyond the pale of the constitution, that extraparliamentary efforts to instruct or coerce M.P.'s are unconstitutional. It is persuasively argued that in representing the electorate members of Parliament and the Government must not submit to the orders of any outside body, which however representative of its party cannot be so representative of the country as Parliament itself. On both the Conservative and Labor sides "the mass parties are primarily the servants of their respective parliamentary parties." [28]

During the last hundred years there has been an enormous increase in the number of bodies in the country organizing sectional interests and promoting causes. But the trend has been to separate the activities of these bodies as political pressure groups from party politics. Most of them maintain strict impartiality.

---

27. Donald Read, *The English Provinces c. 1760–1960* (London, Arnold, 1964), p. 181.
28. R. T. McKenzie, *British Political Parties* (2nd ed. London, Heinemann, 1964), p. 647.

The business community is closely identified with the Conservatives, but trade associations consult and bargain with any Government on behalf of their industries. They oppose any Labor proposals to nationalize their industries, but they insist that the opposition, which may take the form of extensive and expensive advertising campaigns asking electors to reject nationalization at the next election, is aimed only at the proposals. The connections between the trade unions and the Labor Party are more formal than those between business and the Conservative Party, but the trade unions likewise (and increasingly) insist that their prime function is to protect their members' interests under any Government. "It is our long standing practice," stated the General Council of the Trades Union Congress when the Conservatives were returned to office in 1951, "to seek to work amicably with whatever Government is in power. . . . On our part we shall continue to examine every question solely in the light of its industrial and economic implications."[29]

The system of disciplined political parties occasionally alternating in power deters groups whose concerns are mainly "defensive" from committing themselves wholly to one party, because if they do they are bound at some time to lose. Because the constitutional authority of a Government with a parliamentary majority is unlimited, groups behave so as not to invoke its full exercise against them; and this tends to remove much of the activity shaping public policy from electoral politics. It may be argued in any case, as it was by the Webbs about the time of the First World War and as it has been by many political commentators in recent years, that governmental policy is the resultant of a continuous political process only marginally affected by "who loses and who wins; who's in, who's out." This is a valuable corrective to the "mandate" theory of British politics which describes governmental policy as the direct result of the electorate's choice between alternatives.

But the argument should not be pushed too far. The ways in which groups press and persuade take into account that the Government wants to be popular and successful at the next general election. That the great majority of them forbear from intervening openly in the choice of a Government is to make a virtue of necessity. At close hand who's in, who's out often seems to matter, especially on questions of major importance, about which ministers may be reluctant, for various political, administrative, or diplomatic reasons, to consult outside bodies in advance of announcing their policies. "The result of all this," Sir Raymond Streat, a leading spokesman of the cotton textile industry for over a quarter of a century, pointed out, "is that new departures of a major kind are often made with little consultation whereas new departures of a minor and non-

29. *Report of the 84th Annual Congress* (London, Trades Union Congress, 1952), p. 300.

controversial type can be the subject of extremely detailed and adequate inquiry and consultation. This is a rather ironical consequence of government by politicians but it is hard to see how to avoid it." [30]

There is virtually no opposition in Britain with a little "o," in the sense of organized activity outside the parliamentary party system aimed at displacing the holders of governmental power. The last agitation by and on behalf of those without the vote was the woman suffrage movement. The only mass agitations against parliamentary authority to achieve any success among the enfranchised were those in Ireland, South and North, prior to the granting of Home Rule. There was a syndicalist strain in the trade union movement in the second decade of this century, and in 1920 the labor movement's threat of strike action to stop British intervention against the Russian Soviet government was effectual in a nation weary for peace. But the General Strike of 1926 was considered by the General Council of the T.U.C. to be for an industrial end: to resist the proposed worsening of miners' wages or hours. Neither the trade union leaders nor the Labor Party ever contemplated using the General Strike to displace the Government. There is not the slightest chance that direct-action nuclear disarmers, Trotskyists, or those few Scottish and Welsh nationalists prepared to use direct action will overturn the central government or achieve regional independence by either civil disobedience or force. Opposition in Great Britain, as well as government, is by politicians, offering an alternative government in accordance with the conventions of the parliamentary system—opposition with a capital "O."

The Conditions

THE CONSTITUTION IN PERIL   The one time in the last hundred years when the constitutional structure of conventions and understandings seemed in peril was just before the First World War. There was a series of constitutional crises, over the budget of 1909, the Parliament Bill, and Irish Home Rule. There was recourse to direct action by suffragettes in the woman suffrage movement, syndicalists in the trade union movement, and, above all, in Ireland where the crisis over Home Rule appeared to be leading to a civil war in Ulster.

By the beginning of this century the landed interest was breaking up and the national landed aristocracy merging with the capitalist plutocracy. "The apparently stable Edwardian society had in fact resolved upon a social revolution, the liquidation of the landed interest, whose full accomplishment was but deferred by the First World War." [31] Among "the

---

30. "Government Consultation with Industry," *Public Administration*, 37 (1959), 5–6.

31. F. M. L. Thompson, *English Landed Society in the Nineteenth Century* (London, Routledge, 1963), p. 326.

classes" accepted social distinctions were sapped by the influence of money. The result was class bitterness among all strata of society, but also an assimilation of the interests of the old and newer sources of great wealth. Among "the masses" the notion of the "laboring classes" or "working classes" in the plural tended in the last quarter of the nineteenth century to yield to the concept of a single "working class." "The Education Act of 1870 tended to separate the population more clearly into those who were educated at their parents' expense and those who went to the 'Board' schools or the church schools; nearly all the manual workers fell into the latter category." [32] Changes in industry and the new unionism of the 1880s among the unskilled also made for a more homogeneous industrial class.

In politics, the Whig landed families had been leaving the Liberal Party in reaction against concessions to Radicalism before 1885, when Gladstone's adoption of the policy of Home Rule for Ireland made their secession almost complete. The Liberal Government of 1886 was turned out of office on that issue; the Liberal Governments of 1892–95 were too weak and divided to fight the House of Lords, which rejected a Home Rule Bill in 1893 by a majority of 419 to 41; but the Liberal Government that won the general election of 1906 was strong. It was essentially a Government composed of the "educated and professional classes." For the first time the landed aristocracy might be effectually challenged by a Government in which it was not substantially represented. The Liberal politicians were, moreover, increasingly responsive to working-class claims, though they fought the 1906 election on other issues. Fifty-three Labor candidates were elected in 1906, 29 of them candidates of the Labor Representation Committee and the rest, 13 of whom were sponsored by the Miners Federation, more or less associated with the Liberal Party. A secret agreement between L.R.C. and Liberal leaders had also freed the great majority of the independent 29 from direct Liberal opposition.

In the eighteenth century "governmental power was never used to challenge the natural social order, in which family, property, rank and intelligence were the attributes which counted." In the absence of any apparatus of centralized administration the country was governed "not by 'politicians' or by a civil service, but by a miscellaneous collection of unpaid local authorities, all of which, efficient or inefficient, gave a paramount place to rank and property. Indeed it was rank and property which conferred authority and not the other way round." [33] In the course of the nineteenth century the apparatus of professional government was formed. By the turn of the century the administrators recruited from the reformed

32. Henry Pelling, *A Short History of the Labour Party* (London, Macmillan, 1961), p. 2.
33. Briggs, *The Age of Improvement*, p. 100.

universities as the result of Gladstone's reorganization of the civil service in 1870 were reaching the top, and the importance of the central departments in the governmental process began to be recognized. In the country the County Councils Act of 1888 brought to an end the rule of the justices of the peace. It was now conceivable that a Government not representative of the governing class might govern in opposition to the natural social order. This was, however, a conception that the representatives of the governing class were reluctant to accept. In an election speech in 1906, A. J. Balfour, the Leader of the Unionist (Conservative) Party, declared that it was the duty of everyone to see that "the great Unionist party should still control, whether in power or whether in Opposition, the destinies of this great Empire." [34]

The Lloyd George budget of 1909, a revolutionary departure from Gladstonian public finance, epitomized the use of the ordinary operations of government to attack the natural social order. For faced with the need to raise more money, the Chancellor of the Exchequer proposed, among other things, increases in death duties, more graduation of the income tax, and the introduction of land taxes, of which the most spectacular was a duty of 20 per cent on the unearned increment of value when land changed hands. The Lords, many of whom were substantial landowners, rejected the budget in a constitutionally questionable exercise of their legally equal legislative power with the Commons, thereby putting themselves clearly in opposition not only to the Irish but also to "the people." After a general election in January 1910 the Government introduced a Parliament Bill to remove the veto power of the Lords over money bills and to reduce it over other legislation to a power to delay for two years. After a second general election in December it was made known that the King had promised Asquith, the Prime Minister, that he would create enough peers to ensure the enactment of the Parliament Bill. Under that threat the Lords accepted the Bill in August 1911 by a majority of 131 to 114. "The division lists show most strikingly how complete had been the desertion of the Whigs": "for the first time in the advance to political democracy . . . there was hardly a patrician who would aid the process." [35]

From 1910 the Liberal Government was dependent on the Irish Nationalists in the House of Commons for its parliamentary majority. In the December election the Liberals and Conservatives each won 272 seats. The Labor Party (which the miners had joined in 1909) won 42 and the Irish Nationalists 84. The Nationalists were resolved upon securing Home Rule for a united Ireland. But the Protestants of Ulster were at least equally determined that Home Rule would not mean "Rome rule" from Dublin for them. This conflict between the Catholic and Protestant peoples of

34. Roy Jenkins, *Mr. Balfour's Poodle* (London, Heinemann, 1954), pp. 18–19.
35. Ibid., pp. 183–84.

Ireland was too intense to be contained within the conventions of the British constitution. It also had ominous repercussions in British society as a whole.

"I can imagine no length of resistance to which Ulster will go," Bonar Law, who had succeeded Balfour as Leader of the Conservative Party in the House of Commons and who was himself the son of an Ulsterman, declared publicly in July 1912, "which I shall not be ready to support and in which they will not be supported by an overwhelming majority of the British people." [36] In November he wrote to the King's Private Secretary that the results of the Government's policy would be the coercion of Ulster, civil war, and a situation in which the position of the Crown would be made impossible. "Well, if it is in our power to prevent it," he explained, "we shall not permit this; and sooner or later, if the tension does not come to an end in some other way, we shall have to decide between breaking the Parliamentary machine and allowing these terrible results to happen. When faced with the choice of such evils as these, we shall not, I think, hesitate in considering that the injury to the House of Commons is not so great an evil as the other." [37]

In 1914 the Conservative leaders considered amending in the House of Lords the annual Mutiny Act, the palladium of the subordination of military power to parliamentary authority, so as to prevent the use of the army against Ulster. Bonar Law had decided against that, when the Curragh incident in March made it unnecessary. General Sir Arthur Paget, the Commander-in-Chief in Ireland, upon being ordered to concentrate his troops in Ulster, extracted from the War Office permission to tell his officers who were Ulstermen that they would be allowed to "disappear" from Ireland and his other officers that they could elect to be dismissed from the service. Fifty-seven of 70 officers of the 3rd Cavalry Brigade, stationed at the Curragh, chose dismissal rather than accept orders that might involve the initiation of military operations against Ulster. This, to say the least, cast doubt on the readiness of the army to coerce Ulster, while Orangemen prepared to fight. What the consequences of provoking them would have been for British politics, had not the First World War led to the postponement of Irish self-government to a time when the Ulster claim was met, can only remain a matter of conjecture.

The Irish question was *sui generis* in modern British politics, but it is important to remember that it was not alone in giving rise to a constitutional crisis in the years just before the First World War, nor the only question to introduce an unaccustomed note of violence. The class cleavage both amplified and dampened the Irish crisis. Home Rule had always had class implications, with Irish landowners part of the United Kingdom

36. Harold Nicolson, *King George the Fifth* (London, Constable, 1952), p 199.
37. Ibid., p. 202.

landed interest. In the army "the class from which most officers came tended by 1914 to be overwhelmingly Conservative, whereas fifty or sixty years before it would probably have divided fairly evenly between Tory and Whig." [38] But if officers had little regard for, in a phrase reportedly used by General Paget in March 1914, "those dirty swine of politicians" in Asquith's Government, they were concerned for the natural social order. According to the major-general commanding the 5th Division in Ireland, Paget said that "it was reported by the Secret Service that great internal trouble was brewing in London, Liverpool, and other large towns, and that there was great anxiety on this score. I understood him to say that the Labour party was determined to make a big effort to advance their policy by taking advantage of the crisis." For the major-general, as for many other officers, the "king's order" was enough. But in succeeding in keeping most of his own officers from choosing dismissal he told them

> Logically, we Officers could not refuse to obey the present orders, and yet expect our men to obey orders when they, on strike duty for instance, were placed in difficulties similar to those now confronting us.
> I spoke of the far reaching consequences of a disruption of the Army. That the country without a disciplined and united Army would be at the mercy of the mob. I alluded to the probability of even bigger questions arising if the Army broke up, that the Monarchy, Society and Empire itself might be shattered. [39]

One of the considerations deterring Conservative leaders from amending the Mutiny Act was the dangerous precedent it might give in the event of labor unrest.

THE CONSTITUTION SECURE   In 1918 the Labor Party adopted a socialist program. In 1922 it replaced the Liberals as the second largest political party. In 1924, in a Parliament with 258 Conservative, 191 Labor, 159 Liberal, and 7 other M.P.'s, the Labor Party formed a minority Government with Liberal support. The King and the outgoing Conservative Prime Minister, Stanley Baldwin, who was not, however, consulted by the monarch as to who his successor should be, thought it desirable to give Labor a fair chance to learn the British way of governing. As Asquith, the Liberal Leader, pointed out, the Labor Government would be too weak without a majority in the House of Commons to introduce a socialist regime even if it wanted to. It lasted less than a year. The upper and middle classes were much more alarmed by the General Strike of 1926. On

38. Robert Blake, "Great Britain. The Crimean War to the First World War," in Michael Howard, ed., *Soldiers and Governments* (London, Eyre and Spottiswoode, 1957), p. 36.
39. A. P. Ryan, *Mutiny at the Curragh* (London, Macmillan, 1956), pp. 142, 137, 145–46.

May 3rd Prime Minister Baldwin told the House of Commons that the Government "found itself challenged with an alternative Government" and that the trade union leaders were "threatening the basis of ordered government, and going nearer to proclaiming civil war than we have been for centuries past." [40] On May 12th the King wrote in his diary that "the Government have remained firm & backed up by the people have won a great victory for law & order." [41]

The General Strike was a mistake, not a crime against constitutional government. The Labor movement focused its political efforts on increasing its parliamentary representation, and in 1929 the second minority Labor Government took office. In August 1931 it split under pressure from the City and American bankers to introduce drastic economies as a condition for receiving help to stop a run on sterling. The Prime Minister, Ramsay MacDonald, and a few of his colleagues joined Conservative and Liberal leaders in a "National" Government led by MacDonald and supported by the Conservative and Liberal parties. In October the new Government, in an unprincipled campaign for a "doctor's mandate," won an overwhelming victory at the polls which gave the Conservatives more than three-fourths of the seats in the House of Commons and disrupted the Labor parliamentary leadership still further.

After the events of 1931, it was not altogether implausible to argue, as Harold Laski did in his *Parliamentary Government in England* in 1938, that the propertied classes might use unconstitutional means to prevent a socialist Government with a majority from implementing its program. "What was possible over a relatively minor controversy like Ulster," he wrote, "is certainly not impossible over a major controversy like the foundations of the economic system." [42] The Labor Government of 1945, the first with a parliamentary majority, set about changing the economic system about as much as Laski seemed to have had in mind in 1938. But the constitutional conventions and understandings that he thought might be destroyed remained secure.

From the time when Labor leaders joined the Coalition Government of the First World War, the leaders of the party have sought to demonstrate their "fitness to govern" in the traditional manner. A second generation served in the Coalition Government of the Second World War. That was useful to a party whose continuity of leadership had been broken in 1931; and the experience gained enabled the Labor Government of 1945 to take over very much more smoothly than would otherwise have been the case. It also confirmed Labor's acceptance of the established ways of governing. Since these derive from an era when governing was the preserve of a small class, they tend to sustain elitist attitudes of which the governing class, as

40. 195 H.C. Deb. 5s. 70–71.
41. Nicolson, *King George the Fifth*, p. 420.
42. London, Allen and Unwin, 1938, p. 37.

the social elite, is inevitably a beneficiary, even though Labor Governments bring some people with other backgrounds into the governing circles. The traditional ways, for example, keep a great deal of information about the working of the decision-making processes from the wider public.

It is too simple to say that the Labor leaders have thus succumbed to the "aristocratic embrace." The Fabian strain of socialism has always been elitist: the "meritocracy" bestows social justice on the masses instead of teaching them to seek it for themselves. In this respect Fabianism has had an affinity with "Tory Democracy," in which the "aristocracy" is the counterpart of the "meritocracy." The convergence of the "political formulas" of the two parties is the ideological reflection of the fact that both the "meritocracy" and "aristocracy" are, increasingly, educated at Oxford and Cambridge.

Incorporating by far the greater part of the governing class, the Conservative Party tends to lay claim to rule as of right, and regards its periods in Opposition as contrary to the natural order of things. It tends, therefore, to be a more fractious Opposition than Labor, which accepts a decision of the mass electorate as conclusive on the question of who should govern. But the Conservatives opposed the Labor Government after the Second World War in a much milder fashion than they had opposed the Liberal Government before the First. During the Second War something like a socialist regime had come into being. There was a planned and controlled economy. Tax, rationing, labor, and other policies, together with full employment and inflation, produced a much greater measure of social equality. The parties were not far apart in principle about the need for social security, both major parties generally associating themselves with the plan of an eminent Liberal, Sir William Beveridge. The parties were not very far apart in practice about the need for the Government to reorganize the coal, rail, and utility industries; and the only nationalization measure of the Labor Government to which the Conservatives offered uncompromising opposition was that for the iron and steel industry.

Although attitudes toward economic planning and organization have shifted back and forth in the postwar years, the parties have generally moved in tandem. It was Harold Wilson who, as Labor President of the Board of Trade in 1948, lit the first "bonfire of controls." It was the Conservative Government of Harold Macmillan which set up the National Economic Development Council late in 1961. The nationalization issue now affects only a few industries. In the 1964 election Labor, Conservatives, and Liberals alike promised an expansion in public services based on greater economic growth to be achieved by "modernizing" Britain.

THE PLURALISTIC SOCIETY   In Great Britain a considerable concentration of economic and social privilege coexists with a mass electorate. Of the two major political parties, one is closely associated with the most privileged sections of the community and the other with the organized working-class movement. The party that wins a general election obtains constitutional power without limit. Those points have been emphasized in this account because a class struggle for state power would end—in Laski's words—"the long habituation to peace which the party system has secured" the British people.[43]

The danger is now wholly illusory. The habituation to peaceful procedures has been strengthened by further experience. The Irish settlement of 1921–22 left only class cleavages as a significant politically divisive force. Class distinctions, though still in many respects strongly felt, are much less raw than at the turn of the century. The condition of the people has been greatly improved since then and since Laski wrote *Parliamentary Government in England*. The British people are becoming more "middle class." The percentage of the occupied population engaged in manual work is falling at something like a rate of one-quarter of one per cent a year. Changes in consumption habits and self-images are assimilating large numbers of manual workers to people in middle-class occupations. Because of its association with the organized working-class movement, the Labor Party has had difficulty in shifting its appeal from the "working-class" to the "classless" masses, though the Conservative Party lost the 1964 election through failing to continue to meet the rising expectations of the people. In the more fluid class structure neither party can afford to talk the political language of the 'thirties. There is also a growing awareness that the problem of political leadership is not simply to capture the "commanding heights" of government but to make effective the social influence of political institutions.

A description of the British situation in terms of a class struggle for state power has always required qualifications. It is convenient in conclusion to indicate the general nature of the qualifications mainly by referring to present details. Together with the long habituation to peace, the qualifications are the conditions preserving the British constitution: viz., there is not a sharply defined and unified class at the top of British society entrenched against the mass electorate; the British political parties are not the agents of coherent bodies of interests and opinions; and the social power of British government is confined within the structure of a pluralistic society.

1. The landed aristocracy was not a class apart from others so much as the apex of a social order of extended families and connections cutting through the layers of society. It was always permeable to the heirs and heiresses and the opinions and interests of rising groups. Indefiniteness and flexibility are even more the characteristics of the broader governing class formed in the latter part of the last century. This is what makes

43. *ibid.*, p. 110.

serious discussion of "the Establishment" in Britain so difficult. If it is not equated with the hereditary but absorbent governing class, it is impossible to specify the attributes that distinguish its members from others except that they are at the top; but if it is equated with the governing class, there are many important people outside it. The widespread feeling in Great Britain that there is a single "Establishment" in positions of power is probably accounted for by the stable hierarchy of social prestige. The men of power are varied; but the "gentleman" is, for almost all of them, the exemplar—to be deferred to, imitated, or joined.

To say that there is a considerable concentration of economic and social privilege at the top of British society is not to say that the privileged groups are united. There are many diverse interests and real conflicts among them. A study of the "revolt" under a Conservative administration by the leaders of productive industry against the City's influence on national economic policy, which led eventually to the creation of the National Economic Development Council, would illuminate more of the inner workings of British capitalism than all the statistics of interlocking directorships in British finance and industry compiled by political sociologists and "New Left" polemicists.

2. The diversity of interests in the circles from which the Conservative Party draws its money, and with which its leaders have close personal connections, gives the leaders considerable freedom of action. So does the existence of the mass electorate. To win a general election the Conservative Party must be supported by the great majority of middle-class electors, and about half its vote must come from the working class. Rational policy requires concessions, and habit has taught the privileged classes reason. Dishing the Whigs and their successors is the oldest surviving Conservative principle.

The diversity of interests at the top is more than matched by the crosscurrents of opinions below. Members of both parties agree as to which occupational groups support each of the major parties, though the stereotypes regarding political allegiances are not always correct. The main conclusion to be drawn from studies of political attitudes "appears to be this: to the great mass of the British electorate, at all social levels, the party contest is seen primarily in terms of competition between two great classes of the population for material satisfactions." [44] But there are many working-class Conservatives. Studies of their attitudes indicate that they have tended to regard members of the governing class as the natural leaders of society, though this "deferential" support may be declining compared with support based on an assessment of Conservative performance in the national and for particular interests. Conservative values are indeed widely spread among working-class electors: many who vote

44. John Bonham, *The Middle Class Vote* (London, Faber, 1954), p. 94.

Labor are on many points more in agreement with Conservative than Labor Party positions.[45]

Studies of political opinions have indicated on the one hand that the ordinary members of each party disagree a great deal among themselves on political questions: "the Labour members, in particular, disagree with one another to such an extent that a common outlook on political issues can hardly be said to exist among them." [46] The studies have indicated on the other hand that "there is a broad measure of agreement on political matters among supporters of both parties" and that at least two-fifths of the supporters of both regard the other party as equally likely to deal satisfactorily with some important matters as the one they support.[47] A lot depends, however, on the questions in the sample surveys. When asked which party would do the best job for a particular class, the voters again refer to the stereotypes of party alignments, with a sizable fraction of Conservative working-class voters agreeing with Labor working-class voters that in terms of purely class interests the Labor Party would do best for the working class.

The attitudes of the electorate to the parties and the behavior of the parties toward the electorate reinforce each other in making partisanship in Britain more significant than in the United States, but about as moderate. A larger proportion of the supporters of each of the two main parties are harsh in their appraisals of voters for the other, as compared with Americans, but the majority of British party supporters who are indifferent to the marriage of a son or daughter across party lines is almost as overwhelming.[48] British party discipline makes differences in party programs usually seem more meaningful than in the United States. But in a two-party system in which there is habitually a large turnout in general elections, the parties are even more likely than those in the American two-party system, with its greater variations in turnout, to bid for floating voters between the parties with moderate appeals, instead of attempting to mobilize occasional voters on their extreme wings. There is some evidence to suggest that the parties' stereotypes of floating and occasional voters may be at least as incorrect as the voters' stereotypes of the parties' supporters. But erroneous beliefs of that kind can alter a situation so as to make them more correct.

3. In the past England lacked a centrally controlled police force and had a very small army. The eighteenth-century constitution was—in G. M.

45. Robert McKenzie and Allan Silver, "The Working-Class Tories," *The Observer* (September 6, 1964), p. 11.

46. A. H. Birch, *Small-Town Politics* (Oxford, Oxford University Press, 1959), p. 94.

47. Mark Abrams et al., *Must Labour Lose?* (London, Penguin, 1960), p. 19.

48. Gabriel A. Almond and Sidney Verba, *The Civic Culture* (Princeton, Princeton University Press, 1963), pp. 124–26, 135–36.

Trevelyan's phrase—"aristocracy tempered by rioting." [49] The police (and education) are still far from fully centralized, though the organized forces of the state are now adequate for imposing the Government's will as long as the forces remain loyal. But as a method of dealing with constitutional opposition that course is unthinkable among political leaders, who are not only imbued with British traditions but also well aware of the consequences of calling an army into politics.

In governing a modern industrial society, moreover, the administrative structure of the British state is hardly more than a shell, which would break if not supported by thousands of organizations—public bodies of all sorts, voluntary services, and affected interests. There are again "rules of the game," well understood by those who work them, which while recognizing that the Government always has the last word dispose it not to utter it as long as "there is not yet sufficient agreement among those concerned." [50] The formal authority to govern is unlimited. The effective power to manage is vitiated by the inadequacy of public administration for the task. The apparatus of professional government was developed in Britain without destroying the tradition that "public" arrangements are part of the natural social order rather than the function of "the state." The result is professional government without professionals: there is a distinct organization of full-time officials, and politics is also increasingly a profession, but administrative class civil servants as well as ministers are largely uneducated in fields directly related to the needs of running a modern industrial society. This "cult of the amateur" is currently a subject of controversy among those interested in public affairs. One of the arguments in defense of the present civil service is that its incompetence as an industrial management puts a limit on the potential tyranny of officials.

Any social and political system that is reasonably successful in meeting expectations tends to be self-sustaining. This means that the degree to which political power has been used consciously to mold society tends to define the limits of its exercise. In that sense the formal power of British government cannot be used instantly to make or prevent changes in the natural social order outside the broad limits set by the structure of that order and its development, in which the longer-term effect of governmental action is only one of the factors. Great Britain is, socially and politically, a pluralistic society, in which the government no more than any other group or institution is outside the interaction of social forces that constitute the society. British politics is by nature the politics of compromise.

49. *History of England* (London, Longmans, 1926), p. 533.
50. Words often used by ministers in Parliament. Allen Potter, *Organized Groups in British National Politics* (London, Faber, 1961), p. 233.

2

THE AMERICAN OPPOSITIONS:
AFFIRMATION AND DENIAL

Robert A. Dahl

The normal pattern of oppositions in the United States is roughly this:

Oppositions seek limited *goals* that do not directly challenge the major institutions or the prevailing American system of beliefs.

Oppositions employ a wide variety of *strategies:* they combine a heavy emphasis on winning presidential and congressional elections with an equally heavy emphasis on bargaining, logrolling, and pressure-group activities in policy-making.

Oppositions are not usually very *distinctive;* they are not even clearly identifiable as oppositions; they melt into the system.

Oppositions are not combined into a single organization of high *cohesion;* they usually work through one or both major parties, each of which has rather low internal unity.

These two parties are highly *competitive* in national elections but in Congress members of different parties are both *competitive* and *cooperative.*

Oppositions try to gain their objectives by seeking out encounters with policy-makers at a great variety of official *sites*—bureaucratic, congressional, presidential, judicial, local, etc.

A distinctive, persistent, unified structural opposition scarcely exists in the United States. Overt and organized oppositions ordinarily affirm their support for the prevailing ideology and the basic social, economic, and political institutions; these oppositions concentrate on limited changes within the established framework of ideas and institutions. Oppositions, then, are typically opposed only to specific policies or the personnel of government. Thus it is nearly always impossible to refer precisely to "the" opposition, for the coalition that opposes the government on one matter may fall apart, or even govern, on another. To say where "the government" leaves off and "the opposition" begins is an exercise in metaphysics.

So far I have been speaking of "normal" oppositions. There are, however, other chapters in the story of oppositions in the United States. For example, groups opposed to existing policies and frustrated by their inability to achieve changes sometimes go beyond the conventional strategies of American politics: they defy national law, call the legitimacy of one or more major institutions into question, and even resort to individual or collective violence.

These oppositional groups shade off into an indeterminate collection of alienated Americans whose opposition is even more out of line with the pattern of normal opposition described a moment ago. Even if we put to one side the small radical or revolutionary parties and political movements that have existed from time to time on the fringes of American political life, commitment to the prevailing ideology and institutions among the general population is highly uneven. There are, and probably always have been, Americans who reject some or most of the key elements in the dominant ideology and some or most of the major institutions. The size and social content of this group probably varies from one generation to another. Since it is extremely difficult for these individuals and groups to express their opposition through the usual processes of American politics, they may either resort to other means or lapse into apathy and withdraw from politics. These Americans are the neglected side of the American political system.

To explain the normal pattern of opposition, and its dark underside, I propose to rely mainly on three sets of factors:

1. The characteristic pattern of consensus.
2. The characteristic pattern of cleavage.
3. The structure of government and politics.

Consensus

That American opinions tend to converge has been emphatically stressed by foreign observers ever since Tocqueville and Harriet Martineau visited the United States in the 1830s. If caution and even skepticism are justified in evaluating their assertions as to what Americans believe or once believed, it is nonetheless difficult to explain American politics without invoking the familiar proposition that a predominant number of Americans arrived fairly early in their national history at a rough concordance on attitudes on some important political questions—questions of a kind that have led to profound and enduring cleavages in other countries.

What usually strikes foreign observers is the extent to which Americans profess the virtues of a government ruled by the elected representatives of the people, that is, popular government or "democracy." Americans publicly disagree about liberty; they do not, in this strict sense, publicly disagree over "democracy." The question whether there might be alternatives open to Americans other than popular government was settled very early. When Hamilton stressed the virtues of monarchy at the Constitutional Convention of 1787 his views and proposals were looked on as irrelevant: not necessarily intrinsically wrong but simply irrelevant because so obviously unacceptable to the overwhelming majority of Americans. Federalists sometimes tried to accent the virtues of an aristocratic republic—but after 1800 they did so less and less frequently in public; and the demise of the Federalists as a party was a lesson to others. Consider the fate of John Adams, whose early works, "Defence of the Constitutions" and "Discourses on Davila," were widely interpreted (incorrectly, Adams later insisted) as defenses of monarchy and aristocracy. A dozen years after he had left the White House, Adams wrote to Jefferson, his old political enemy, now his personal friend: "In truth, my 'Defence of the Constitutions' and 'Discourses on Davila' were the cause of that immense unpopularity which fell like the tower of Siloam upon me. Your steady defence of democratical principles, and your invariable favorable opinion of the French Revolution, laid the foundations of your unbounded popularity."[1] Doubtless Adams exaggerated the effect of his writings, but there can be no doubt that his political opponents, the Republicans, hung his words about his neck like a millstone. Given his instructive example, no one seriously interested in a political career was likely thereafter to utter words—in public—that might be interpreted as favorable to any system other than popular government. Later, when the Whigs challenged Jackson's notions of presidential leadership, they did so in the name of popular government itself, and chose the very title of their party to emphasize the point.

If one excludes the Federalists (simply in order to ignore a controversial case that could not be analyzed properly in a few sentences), it is correct to say that no political party openly in favor of an alternative to popular government has ever elected a single representative to Congress or captured one electoral vote in a presidential election. Thus a question on which, in other countries, political elites and party followings have often generated opposition has been excluded in the United States.

Support for popular government was interwoven with support for specifically American forms of government. The tendency to identify republican government or, later, democracy with the particular American political system evidently developed quite early. Most of the men who attended the Constitutional Convention lived to see their patchwork of compromises, the American Constitution, become an object of veneration. Within a few years it had already become dangerous to attack the Constitution, perhaps even before it had become politically dangerous—and

---

1. Adams to Jefferson, July 13, 1813, quoted in Joseph Charles, *The Origins of the American Party System* (New York, Harper Torchbooks, 1956), p. 56.

futile—to attack popular government. An understanding quickly developed that all controversies, particularly constitutional controversies, must
take for granted the overriding legitimacy of the Constitution and the
superiority of American political institutions. Opposition groups were
therefore restricted to changes that (so supporters would argue) were
consistent with the Constitution. The view of the Massachusetts Anti-
slavery Society and William Lloyd Garrison that the U.S. Constitution
was "a covenant with death and an agreement with hell" was, even in the
heat of the controversy over slavery, eccentric. Most opponents in this
controversy assumed the legitimacy of the Constitution: the quarrel was
over what the Constitution meant. Thus just as avowedly antidemocratic
parties were effectively excluded from politics, so anticonstitutional
parties also had little prospect of success.

Given the flexibility of the document and the political institutions it
chartered, the worship of the Constitution was less restrictive than for-
eigners who encountered that fetish might suppose. Indeed one could even
advocate changes in the Constitution itself provided these were shown to
be in harmony with the principal institutions it established. The main outlines of the constitutional system and the principle that changes, including
of course, changes in the Constitution, must take place within the limits of
that framework, thus set imprecise but nonetheless important boundaries
to the goals and strategies of the opposition groups.

The proposition that support for popular government, for the constitutional system, and for constitutional rather than revolutionary change
has been widespread among Americans since the 1830s is about as reliable
as any we are likely to get from historical evidence about attitudes. Two
things seem reasonably certain: First, political leaders came to believe that
they could not win elections without giving at least lip service to popular
government, the Constitution, and constitutional change; second, opposition to these principles did not in fact flourish.

In the third place, there is the complex matter of American beliefs about
"equality." Although the evidence for a wide commitment to "equality" is
impressive, the nature and bounds of that commitment cannot be precisely
described, for there were (and are) too many variations on the theme. The
notes from Tocqueville's journey to America contain a record of his conversation with John Quincy Adams in which the former President
remarked:

> Slavery has altered the whole state of society in the South. There the
> whites form a class to themselves which has all the ideas, all the passions,
> all the prejudices of an aristocracy, but do not be mistaken, nowhere is
> equality between the whites so complete as in the South. Here we have
> great equality before the law, but it simply does not affect our ways of
> life. There are upper classes and working classes. Every white man in

the South is an equally privileged being whose destiny is to make the
Negroes work without working himself . . . I remember a Southern
congressman who was dining with me in Washington, and who could
not conceal his surprise at seeing white servants serving us at table.
He said to Mrs. Adams: "I feel that it is degrading the human race to
have white men for servants. When one of them comes to change my
plate, I am always tempted to offer him my place at table." [2]

Complex and contradictory as they were, commitments to equality
encouraged a rapid expansion of the suffrage, facilitated the incorporation
of new groups (except Negroes) into the political system, and reduced
the influence of class and status as sources of political cleavages. As compared with some of the countries in our study, the development of oppositions was not significantly shaped by resentments, hostilities, memories,
and struggles of excluded groups to gain entry into political life.

A fourth convergence of views is more difficult to assess; yet it is worth
stressing because it has probably been important in limiting the bounds of
successful opposition. This was a belief, evidently popular in the early
years of the Republic, in the virtues of private property. It is true that in
drafting the Declaration of Independence Jefferson and his colleagues
wrote "life, liberty, and the pursuit of happiness." Yet it was "life, liberty,
and property" that the men at the Constitutional Convention more obviously had in mind. And though small property owners quarreled with
large property owners, though landed property contested with commercial and banking interests, it is a fact that Americans were, from the
beginnings of national independence, a nation of small property owners.
They were, after all, a nation of small farmers; in 1820, 70 per cent of the
working population were farmers, and land was plentiful. Thus side by
side with the common ideology of popular government and constitutionalism there also developed an ideology favorable to private property. Even
after a great share of economic life came to be conducted by large corporations that had only a remote resemblance to the private property of the
small farmer, the ideology of private property proved to be extremely
durable.

Emphasis on the virtues of private property may be one example of a
fifth and more general constellation of values that foreign visitors have
encountered in Americans: a relatively weak sense of social solidarity,
particularly among social "classes," and a strong emphasis on individual

2. Alexis de Tocqueville, *Journey to America*, trans. George Lawrence, ed. J. P.
Mayer (New Haven, Yale University Press, 1959), p. 61. For another contemporary
observation on the nature of American beliefs in equality, see Francis J. Grund,
Aristocracy in America, from the Sketch-book of a German Nobleman (1839; New
York, Harper Torchbooks, 1959). S. M. Lipset has summarized and analyzed a wide
variety of nineteenth-century observations on the American character in *The First
New Nation* (New York, Basic Books, 1963), Ch. 3.

achievement, on personal success, on the desirability and the possibility of getting on in the world.[3] Tocqueville held that among Americans "the doctrine of self-interest rightly understood . . . finds universal acceptance," that is, intelligent, reasonable self-interest bounded by vaguely Christian or humanistic standards. Indeed, according to Tocqueville, even religious commitments were seen as "self-interest rightly understood." [4]

This emphasis on individual achievement was not an emphasis on individual distinction, on individuality; quite the contrary, as Tocqueville, Harriet Martineau, and many others complained.[5] Americans were often so afraid of being different that they lived in terror of their neighbors' opinions. Nor—to avoid another common error—did Americans rely solely on individual action to get ahead. They were not at all averse to pursuing individual self-interest by means of voluntary associations; indeed, according to Tocqueville, "the English often perform great things singly, whereas the Americans form associations for the smallest undertakings." [6] What is more, they quite freely used instruments of government; Tocqueville found that legislators were kept busy turning out laws to regulate the behavior of Americans.[7]

Nonetheless the constellation of values we are discussing undoubtedly did have some consequences highly relevant to our concern here with opposition. For the weak sense of social solidarity, the lack of class consciousness, and the concern for individual success made it difficult to

3. In 1889 Henry Adams wrote of America in 1800: "Reversing the old-world system, the American stimulant increased in energy as it reached the lowest and most ignorant class, dragging and whirling them upward as in the blast of a furnace. The penniless and homeless Scotch or Irish immigrant was caught and consumed by it; for every stroke of the axe and the hoe made him a capitalist, and made gentlemen of his children. Wealth was the strongest agent for moving the mass of mankind; but political power was hardly less tempting to the more intelligent and better-educated swarms of American-born citizens." *The United States in 1800* (Ithaca, N.Y., Great Seal Books, Cornell University Press, 1955), p. 115. This book consists of the first six chapters of Vol. 1 of Adams' *History of the United States of America During the First Administration of Thomas Jefferson, 1889*. This set of values has been reemphasized by sociologists, who find it a rich source of explanations for many different aspects of American behavior. For example, Robert K. Merton, *Social Theory and Social Structure* (rev. ed. Glencoe, Ill., Free Press, 1957), S. M. Lipset, *The First New Nation.*
4. Alexis de Tocqueville, *Democracy in America* (New York, Vintage Books, 1955), *1*, 130–35.
5. Ibid., *1*, 273 ff. Harriet Martineau, *Society in America* (New York, Anchor Books, 1961), pp. 251 ff.
6. Tocqueville, *Democracy in America, 2*, 115.
7. The common view that early Americans were implacably hostile to government regulation of the economy is without historical foundation and is largely (it would appear) an invention of later ideologues. As F. W. Coker observed, "In both our practice and our theory we have had, throughout our national history, a tradition of governmental intervention as well as of nonintervention." "Income Stabilization and the American Political Tradition" in Max Millikan, ed., *Income Stabilization for a Developing Economy* (New Haven, Yale University Press, 1953), p. 87.

appeal to Americans with political ideologies or programs based upon
class gains. (Americans, it appears, did not typically think of progress as
the progress of a class or social stratum to which they belonged but of
individuals or like-minded groups; they did not see conflict as the conflict
of classes but of individuals, groups, or perhaps regions) Government
therefore was not the central mechanism for social and economic progress
but a regulatory instrument—not the moving force, the motor, but the
regulator, the governor, or fly wheel. Government could be used to
eliminate barriers and to even up the chances of personal success, but
"success" was then a matter of action by individuals or voluntary groups.
Even the conflict over slavery was in this sense a question of regulation,
of laying down the terms under which free farmers and slaveholders could
carry their institutions into the Western territories.

Sample surveys over the last several decades show that these attitudes so
frequently ascribed to Americans in the nineteenth century remain widespread today.[8] The evidence from surveys indicates that:

1. It is very nearly impossible to find an American who says that he is
opposed to democracy or favors some alternative—at least for the United
States. On the contrary, nearly everyone professes to believe that democracy is the best form of government.[9]

2. Although substantial minorities see specific defects in the constitutional system, the broad elements of the system are widely endorsed.[10]

3. There is substantial agreement that if defects exist in the laws and
the Constitution they should be cured by legal processes of change.[11]

4. Most Americans also display complacency about their economic
institutions. Proposals for extensive reconstruction do not enjoy much

8. For analyses of greater breadth or depth than space permits here, the reader
should consult: Clyde Kluckhohn, "The Evolution of Contemporary American
Values," *Daedalus*, 87 (Spring 1958), 78–109; Robert Lane, *Political Ideology, Why
the American Common Man Believes What He Does* (New York, The Free Press,
1962); Gabriel A. Almond and Sidney Verba, *The Civic Culture, Political Attitudes
and Democracy in Five Nations* (Princeton, Princeton University Press, 1963); V. O.
Key, Jr., *Public Opinion and American Democracy* (New York, Knopf, 1961);
Herbert McCloskey, "Consensus and Ideology in American Politics," *American
Political Science Review*, 58 (June 1964), 361–82.

9. James W. Prothro and C. W. Grigg, "Fundamental Principles of Democracy:
Bases of Agreement and Disagreement," *Journal of Politics*, 22 (Spring 1960), 276–94.

10. The evidence is indirect. For example, "Should the Constitution be made easier
to amend?" No, 69%, AIPO, March 1, 1937, in Hadley Cantril, *Public Opinion 1935–
1946* (Princeton, Princeton University Press, 1951), p. 939. "Do you think the Constitution of the United States should ever be changed in any way?" No, 54%; Yes,
34%; Don't know, 12% (NORC, Nov. 1945, in ibid.)

11. One study provides as evidence the percentages of "political influentials"
($N = 3020$) and "general electorate" ($N = 1484$) *agreeing* to the following statement:
"There are times when it almost seems better for the people to take the law into their
own hands than wait for the machinery of government to act." Political influentials,
13%; general electorate, 27%. McCloskey, "Consensus and Ideology in American
Politics," *American Political Science Review*, p. 365.

support. The great corporations, it appears, have regained rather wide acceptance. A minority holds that corporations should be more severely regulated; a smaller minority holds that they should be nationalized. The trade unions are somewhat more unpopular than the corporations; many would like to see them more severely regulated by the government; but few say that they would like to see trade unions done away with altogether.[12]

5. Although a majority of Americans seem willing to place themselves in the "working class," their sense of class is obviously weak. The key word seems to be "working," not "class." Few believe that class lines divide Americans into hostile camps.[13]

6. Most Americans continue to profess a strong confidence in the possibilities of personal achievement in the American milieu. A great many continue to believe that personal success is attainable by hard work and skill.[14]

7. Thus Americans tend to express satisfaction rather than discontent with their lot. Most Americans claim that life in the United States is the best they could attain anywhere in the world; almost no one wants to emigrate. They expect that their own material conditions will improve, and that for their children life will be much better, provided there is no war.[15]

These propositions concerning American attitudes suggest two questions:

How deeply are these attitudes sustained?
How did such an astonishing unity of views ever come about?

DEPTH AND DISTRIBUTION   How deeply these attitudes run, how firmly they are held, and how they are shared among Americans are questions on which historical data shed almost no direct light, and modern survey data

12. The Survey Research Center, Institute for Social Research, University of Michigan, *Big Business from the Viewpoint of the Public* (Ann Arbor, 1951), pp. 18, 20, 26, 44, 56. In the midst of the Great Depression, responses to the question, "Should the government attempt to break up large business organizations?" were: No, 69%; Yes, 31% (= 100%), No opinion, 10%. (AIPO, July 19, 1937, in Cantril, *Public Opinion 1935-1946*, p. 345). On government ownership, see polls #14 and 16, p. 345; #53, #54, #59, p. 349; and #73, p. 351.

13. See V. O. Key's analysis, "Occupation and Class," Ch. 6 in *Public Opinion and American Democracy*. See also Robert R. Alford, *Party and Society* (Chicago, Rand-McNally, 1963), Ch. 8.

14. The hypothesis that there has been a decline in the motivations for personal achievement is highly dubious. See: Lipset's discussion of "A Changing American Character?" Ch. 3 in *The First New Nation;* the data cited in Key, *Public Opinion and American Democracy*, p. 47 n. 2 and 4 and p. 48 n. 5; and Fred I. Greenstein, "New Light on Changing American Values: A Forgotten Body of Survey Data," *Social Forces, 42* (1964), 441-50.

15. William Buchanan and Hadley Cantril, *How Nations See Each Other* (Urbana, University of Illinois Press, 1953), p. 53.

only a little more. Survey data do, however, lend some support for the following hypotheses:

1. Though Americans are agreed on abstract, general propositions about popular government, majority rule, the Constitution, the virtues of individual liberty, and so on, an attempt to apply these generalities to concrete problems is likely to produce extensive disagreements.[16]

2. Statistically speaking, the more formal education an American has, the more likely he is to express support for the general views we have been describing. The greater his income, the more likely his support, though we cannot be sure about the very rich, who are too small a group to show up in surveys. Support also increases with the status or social prestige of one's occupation; it is higher among professional people, for example, than among skilled workers. Again, we cannot be sure about small categories—corporate executives or Wall Street brokers, for example. Finally, the more active and involved one is in political affairs, the more likely he is to support these views.[17]

3. The connection between the word and the deed is rather uncertain. In particular, to express disagreement with widely prevailing views does not at all mean that one will actually do anything more to act out his dissent. Many—perhaps most—Americans who express disagreement do not, it seems, try to change the attitudes of others by discussion or bring about changes by joining dissident political movements or trying to secure the nomination and election of candidates favorable to their views. The reasons for inaction include political apathy and indifference, lack of strong feeling, pessimism over the prospects of success, ignorance, etc.[18]

Thus the patterns of support, disagreement, and apathy help to sustain the prevailing views and weaken the effectiveness of opposition to them. Since support tends to increase with education, income, occupational status, and political activity, and since political influence is also to a considerable extent a function of these same factors, the influence of

16. The best evidence is found in Prothro and Grigg, "Fundamental Principles of Democracy: Bases of Agreement and Disagreement," *Journal of Politics;* McCloskey, "Consensus and Ideology in American Politics," *American Political Science Review;* and Samuel A. Stouffer, *Communism, Conformity and Civil Liberties* (Garden City, N.Y., Doubleday, 1955).

17. See the survey data reported and analyzed in Fred I. Greenstein, *The American Party System and the American People* (Englewood Cliffs, N.J., Prentice-Hall, 1963), Ch. 3, pp. 18–36. See also S. M. Lipset, *Political Man* (Garden City, N.Y., Doubleday, 1960), Ch. 4, "Working Class Authoritarianism," pp. 97–130, and Stouffer, *Communism, Conformity and Civil Liberties,* passim.

18. The evidence is indirect but strong. See Herbert McCloskey, "Conservatism and Personality," *American Political Science Review,* 52 (March 1958), 27–45; Robert Lane, *Political Life* (Glencoe, Ill., The Free Press, 1959), Ch. 5, pp. 63–79, and Ch. 12, pp. 163–81; A. Campbell, P. E. Converse, W. E. Miller, D. E. Stokes, *The American Voter* (New York, Wiley, 1960), Ch. 5, pp. 89–115.

supportive attitudes tends to be disproportionately increased while opposition tends to be politically ineffectual.

SOURCES   How one explains the development of such a high degree of unity in political attitudes depends on the point in time at which one starts his explanation and on the relations one assumes to exist between "ideal" and "material" factors, between cognitive activity and everyday life. I can do no more here than to suggest a few of the more evident factors.

In 1776 Americans were, in the main, Englishmen; during a century and a half of colonial experience they had adapted English political ideas, attitudes, and institutions to the conditions of life in America. Among the Englishmen living in English colonies, American colonial experience, it seems fair to conclude, strengthened attitudes favorable to constitutionalism, the virtues of written constitutions, the supremacy of law, the values of representative government. In the colonial legislatures the English-Americans learned the arts and skills of self-government, made and enforced many of their own laws, and developed political elites with a high degree of expertness in managing political institutions. Unlike many countries that have recently acquired independence, by 1776 the United States was, in a sense, already an "old" country; though it would be easy to exaggerate the point, the fact is that by the time of the American Revolution, Americans had had a long and varied experience in operating some of the institutions of representative government. And they shared a common political tradition.

Their colonial experience and their common political tradition would not account, by themselves, for the speed with which the United States was transformed into a democratic republic. For in the United States the length of about one generation was needed in order to arrive at political conditions that in Britain were to require still another century. In fact, by 1800 or thereabouts a high proportion of white males could vote in local, state, and national elections.[19] The Democratic-Republicans were rapidly becoming a mass-based political party highly organized at all levels of government from towns and villages to the United States Congress and the presidency.[20] By 1832, there existed two such parties. When Tocqueville visited the United States—from May 1831 to February 1832—the

19. Although the question is still somewhat unsettled, the older view which held that property qualifications greatly limited the suffrage in most states until a decade or two after 1800 apparently has to be revised in the light of more recent evidence. See especially Robert E. Brown, *Middle-Class Democracy and the Revolution in Massachusetts, 1691–1780* (Princeton, Princeton University Press, 1960).

20. Charles, *The Origins of the Party System;* Noble E. Cunningham, Jr., *The Jeffersonian Republicans, The Formation of Party Organization 1789–1801* (Chapel Hill, The University of North Carolina Press, 1957); and Noble E. Cunningham, Jr., *The Jeffersonian Republicans in Power Party Operations 1801–1809* (Chapel Hill, University of North Carolina Press, 1963).

credo and institutions of democracy had, it seemed to him, already gained well-nigh universal acceptance among Americans.

Why this amazing speed? Given the background of traditions and experience, one reason for the rapid transition is undoubtedly to be found exactly where Tocqueville found it, in the "equality of condition" that prevailed among Americans. "America," he wrote, "exhibits in her social state an extraordinary phenomenon. Men are there seen on a greater equality in point of fortune and intellect, or in other words, more equal in strength, than in any other country of the world, or in any age of which history has preserved the remembrance." [21]

If one prefers to go yet further back in order to account for this equality of condition, that explanation too is surely to be found mainly where Tocqueville and later F. J. Turner found it: in the vast supply of cheap land. If the United States, like some recently independent countries, was launched by revolution it became a stable republic only as a result of a second silent revolution that accomplished what many new nations struggle painfully and even violently to achieve: a wide distribution of landholdings. For the land was there to be had. In 1803 the Louisiana Purchase alone provided the equivalent of 90 acres of land for every man, woman, and child then living in the United States. In 1850, the area of the public domain was still equal to 50 acres for every person in the country.[22] The problem of expropriation did not exist. The land did not have to be taken from a preexisting set of feudal barons. At most the land had to be obtained from foreign governments or seized from the Indians with the aid of the new federal government; it could then be bought from speculators or sometimes from the government itself. Everyone stood to profit by the diffusion of landholdings (except the Indian, who had no representatives in Congress): the would-be independent farmer, the speculator who sold him the land, the banker who lent him money on his mortgage note, the merchant and real estate dealer who thrived in the new towns.

The attitudes that developed out of the already existing traditions of English and American political thought were perfectly harmonious with the emerging structure of the American society, a nation of small independent farmers. Democratic ideas and institutions offered the farmers substantial control over government and laws; given the distribution of people, landed property, and muskets, and the state of civil and military technology, no elite could have ruled the Americans without their assent. Thus democratic ideas and institutions gave legitimacy to what was unavoidable, namely some kind of popular government. Once the constitutional equilibrium was established in their favor, the body of citizen

21. *Democracy in America, 1*, 55.
22. *Historical Statistics of the United States, Colonial Times to 1957* (Washington, U.S. Government Printing Office, 1960), Series A 1–3 and Series J 3–9.

farmers naturally supported the Constitution and constitutional change, for these insured that elites could not easily change the rules of the game. To a nation of landholders, moreover, the virtues of private property were obvious; where so many people were of roughly the same socioeconomic condition—small farmers—and had no landlord class as an enemy, feelings of class solidarity were bound to be weak. With land to be bought, land to be sold, towns of be built, roads, bridges, canals, and railroads to connect the towns, opportunities for personal success were everywhere.[23] Government was needed only to make sure that the framework for individual competition seemed fair to the preponderant majorities.

Yet it is one thing to explain how the unity of views among Americans happened to arise and quite another to explain how it continued to exist when the United States ceased to be a nation of small independent farmers. By 1880 workers in nonfarm occupations exceeded those in farming. Thereafter the farmers were an ever smaller minority; by 1957 less than one out of ten persons in the labor force was in agriculture, and of these only about half owned their own farms.[24]

Probably the sheer inertia of an already venerable tradition helped the United States through periods of crisis. But the crises themselves may have helped even more. The inertial force of the traditional attitudes must have increased as each great challenge to the liberal democratic, privatistic, success-oriented ideology was turned back. Each challenge offered the possibility of a rival ideology—aristocracy, slavocracy, socialism, plutocracy. Yet in each case these potential rivals for the minds of Americans were defeated, and the older, victorious ideology then became thoroughly intertwined with traditionalism. To attack the conventional ideas meant more and more to attack the whole course of American national history, to imply that Americans had failed, long ago, to take the right path.

These challenges might not have been successfully overcome, however, if the "equality of condition" that Tocqueville had observed had vanished: if, in short, blatant contradictions had developed between the lives led by ordinary Americans and the aspirations offered in the dominant ideology. Despite increasing economic inequalities that accompanied industrialization, particularly in its early stages after the Civil War, enough of the old

23. "The possession of land," Harriet Martineau reported with some exaggeration, "is the aim of all action, generally speaking, and the cure for all social evils, among men in the United States. If a man is disappointed in politics or love, he goes and buys land. If he disgraces himself, he betakes himself to a lot in the west. If the demand for any article of manufacture slackens, the operatives drop into the unsettled lands. If a citizen's neighbors rise above him in the towns, he betakes himself where he can be monarch of all he surveys. An artisan works, that he may die on land of his own. He is frugal, that he may enable his son to be a land-owner. Farmers' daughters go into factories that they may clear off the mortgage from their fathers' farms; that they may be independent land-owners again." *Society in America*, p. 168.
24. *Historical Statistics*, Series D 1–12 and K 8–52.

"equality of condition" evidently survived—if not in reality, at least in expectations—so that the old ideas won converts even among the very people who were worst off under industrial capitalism.[25]

Two additional elements have helped to sustain the dominant traditional ideology in the twentieth century. One of these is the educational system, which from the primary grades through high school and even on in the universities, emphasizes the values and institutions expressed in the dominant liberal-democratic ideology. While the relationship between formal education and ideas is complex, most of all with any specific person, one simple and imposing statistical fact is that, in survey after survey of political attitudes and ideas among Americans, the amount of formal education appears as a highly significant variable; indeed, more often than any other, education shows up as *the* most significant variable, even when the effects of socioeconomic status and occupation are canceled out.[26] As we have already observed (and this is the important point), the greater one's formal education, the more likely one is to endorse the key propositions in the prevailing ideology.

The other influence, that of the mass media—radio, television, newspapers, and mass circulation magazines—is harder to assess. Concrete data are few. Critics on the Left argue that the great bulk of Americans are lulled by the mass media into a complacent acceptance of the values in the prevailing ideology, chiefly the emphasis on private property and personal success, and that these beliefs in turn protect the position of certain important elite groups, business leaders, men of wealth, and so on. Critics among the ranks of the radical Right tend to view the mass media in much the same way; they see them as major instruments (along with the educational system) by which the Liberal Establishment acquires and retains its dominance over American institutions and attitudes.[27]

25. Comparative studies of rates of social mobility are still too few for confident conclusions. The view of S. M. Lipset and Reinhard Bendix that "the overall pattern of social mobility appears to be much the same in industrial societies of various Western countries" (*Social Mobility in Industrial Society* [Berkeley and Los Angeles, University of California Press, 1960], p. 13) appears, in the light of later studies, to be doubtful. Perhaps the most that one can say at this point is that social mobility is or has been relatively high in the United States, as compared with such European countries as Britain and the Netherlands, in some but not in all respects. See S. M. Miller, "Comparative Social Mobility: A Trend Report, "*Current Sociology, 9,* No. 1 (1960), 1–5; and also Thomas Fox and S. M. Miller, "Intra-Country Variations: Occupational Stratification and Mobility," in Richard L. Merritt and Stein Rokkan, eds., *Comparing Nations: The Use of Quantitative Data in Cross-National Research* (New Haven, Yale University Press, 1966), pp. 217–38.

26. Key, *Public Opinion and American Democracy*, Ch. 13, "The Educational System," pp. 315–43.

27. The following quotation could as easily have come from a source on the Left as on the Right: "the mass circulation media in this country have virtually closed their columns to opposition articles. For this they can hardly be blamed; their business is to sell paper at so much a pound and advertising space at so much a line. They must give the masses what they believe the masses want, if they are to maintain their mass

Both views, I think, exaggerate the direct, manipulative influence of the mass media on American attitudes. The opposition of three-quarters of the daily newspapers of the United States may have reduced the amount of support for Franklin D. Roosevelt, but it did not prevent him from being reelected three times. Or, to take a more recent example, differences in attitudes toward a highly controversial issue like medical care were in 1956 related in a very weak way to the amount of exposure to the mass media. Moreover, some of the differences were the opposite of what one might expect from simple theories of the influence of the media on "mass man." Thus among persons with only a grade school education, both support for (76 per cent) and opposition to (15 per cent) a government program of medical care was higher among those *most* exposed to the mass media.[28]

The explanation is not mysterious. There is a good deal of evidence that the individuals and groups who might be most susceptible to positive influences from the media because of weak social, psychological, and political ties—"mass man"—also pay much less attention to the media; whereas the individuals who are most exposed to the mass media are in general those with the strongest social, psychological, and political barriers between them and manipulative efforts.[29] The views of Left and Right also underestimate, I think, the extent to which the mass media themselves reflect stable values in the American culture; for better or worse, culture and media reinforce one another.

What is essentially correct, however, is that the amount of time and space devoted by the mass media to views openly hostile to the prevailing ideology is negligible.[30] An American who wishes to find criticisms of the

---

circulation business; and there is no doubt that the promises . . . reiterated by the propaganda machine of the government, have made it popular and dulled the public mind to the verities of freedom." The source is, in fact, an editorial note in a right-wing publication, *The Freeman* (June 1955), cited in Daniel Bell, "Interpretations of American Politics," in Daniel Bell, ed., *The New American Right* (New York, Anchor Books, 1964), p. 68 n. 23. The editorial was attacking the mass media for lulling the public into socialism. The best-known criticism from the Left, sounding many of the same themes, is in the late C. Wright Mills, *The Power Elite* (New York, Oxford University Press, 1956) Ch. 13, "The Mass Society," pp. 298–324.

28. V. O. Key, *Public Opinion and American Democracy*, p. 398.

29. A sophisticated and skeptical attempt to assess the influence of the mass media is V. O. Key, *Public Opinion and American Democracy*, Chs. 14 and 15, "Media: Specter and Reality" and "Media: Structure and Impact," pp. 344–410. On the general problem of manipulating attitudes, see also R. E. Lane and D. O. Sears, *Public Opinion* (Englewood Cliffs, N.J., Prentice-Hall, 1964), Ch. 5, "Leaders' Influence on Public Opinion." See also Elihu Katz and Paul F. Lazarsfeld, *Personal Influence* (Glencoe, Ill., Free Press, 1955).

30. "Extraordinarily few [American] journals, either daily newspapers or magazines, act as agencies of political criticism. They may dig to find the facts about individual acts of corruption, but the grand problems of the political system by and large escape their critical attention." Key, *Public Opinion and American Democracy*, p. 381.

basic social, economic, and political structures can indeed find them; but he will have to search outside the mass media. And, naturally, the number who are strongly motivated enough to do so is relatively small. Hence the general effect of the mass media is to reinforce the existing institutions and ideology.[31]

Cleavage

The ambience of unity that has just been described is impressive. It is, nonetheless, something of an illusion. The traditional ideology, which appears so monolithic, is a patchwork of ambiguities and potential contradictions that not only permit but even encourage a wide variety of conflicts.

European (and American) observers have often underestimated the pervasiveness of conflict in American politics because political conflict in the United States does not follow the expected patterns of class and ideological politics. The American "working class" is obviously not arrayed against "the bourgeoisie." The sound of conflict is muffled by the outward consensus on ideology: everyone seems to be employing the same ideology, the same phrases, even the same words.

Nevertheless, an examination of cleavage patterns in American politics suggests three conclusions:

1. Certain types of questions or issues have been the subject of political conflict for relatively long periods of time.

2. These questions have led to extremely severe conflict about once every generation.

3. Ordinarily, however, the severity of political conflicts is greatly reduced by, among other things, the pattern of cleavage, which encourages conciliation rather than conflict.

THE PERSISTENT SUBJECTS OF CONFLICT   Dispute over specific, concrete policy questions tends to be of a rather short-run nature. The particular issues that provoke controversy in one decade are likely to be superseded in the next by other specific questions. Nevertheless, certain types of issues have been recurrent subjects of conflict in American politics.

One of these is the nature and extent of democratic processes. This question has persistently reappeared in American politics in a multitude of forms. It was one of the basic cleavages of the Constitutional Convention itself, where a question at issue was whether the republic to be established under the new constitution was to be democratic or aristocratic in character. The Convention and the Constitution left the issue unsettled. A major difference between the Federalists and the Republicans during the first several decades under the new Constitution was the way they

31. For a similar conclusion, see Key, *Public Opinion and American Democracy*, p. 396.

answered this question.[32] After the demise of the Federalists, aristocratic themes were muted—at least in public. But even if the outward form of the dispute changed, differences have persisted to the present day over the extent, distribution, and kinds of civil and political rights and liberties that should be guaranteed. On matters of this kind, the seemingly massive consensus about "democracy" quickly breaks down; as we saw above, although certain general propositions in the American ideology are given well-nigh universal lip service, any attempt to apply these general principles to concrete cases reveals sharp differences. Thus a problem on which there has never been much deep agreement is the proper balance between the rights and duties of majorities and minorities. Spokesmen for regional minorities (the South, for example) frequently challenge the constitutional or moral authority of the Congress, the President, or the Supreme Court (or all three) to impose a national policy on the whole country. The rights of dissident, radical, or revolutionary opposition groups are invariably in dispute. Although conflicts over liberties and rights almost always wind up in the courts, and often produce epochal Supreme Court decisions, these conflicts are inescapably political as well. A recent example was supplied by Senator Joseph McCarthy, who formed the nucleus of an opposition movement on the Right that challenged existing government policies and procedures for dealing with Communists, alleged Communists, and other individuals and groups who, it was charged, endangered the national security.

Another highly visible kind of issue that generates conflict is the specific or general role of the government in the regulation and control of the economy. The absence of a sizable socialist movement in the United States and any large-scale challenge to the basic economic institutions can easily be misleading. For consensus breaks down here too. Ever since Alexander Hamilton, the first Secretary of the Treasury, presented his economic programs to the First Congress, government economic policies have stimulated sharp controversy. Indeed, probably conflict in national politics has occurred more frequently in this domain than in any other.

The single most concrete, persistent, and explosive issue in American politics from the Constitutional Convention to the present has, however, been the place of the Negro in American life, whether as slave or as freeman. Although the question has sometimes been removed from national debate by tacit understandings among white leaders, it seems safe to say that no other issue has exerted such a steady force on the patterns of coalition and opposition in American politics. To protect its peculiar institution, whether slavery before the Civil War or white supremacy

32. Some historians would probably disagree with the preceding three sentences, which telescope a complex development into a few words. The relevant literature is too vast to cite here. I am developing each of these points at length in a forthcoming book on American politics.

afterward, the South has always had to maneuver so as to prevent the triumph of a majority hostile to the racial practices of the White South. The South has steadily and skillfully used its political strength in Congress and in presidential elections to bargain with the North and West for protection of—or at least acquiescence in—its treatment of the Negro. On only two occasions has this strategy failed. It failed (at least in the eyes of some Southern leaders) just before and after the election of 1860; as a result these leaders induced the South to choose the path of secession and finally war. The second failure occurred during the period beginning with the Supreme Court decision outlawing segregation in the schools in 1954 and culminating in the passage of the Civil Rights Act in 1964. The eventual results of this second failure may prove to have important consequences for American politics.[33]

Finally, foreign policy, though a dormant question for long periods, sometimes generates fairly sharp conflicts. During the early years from 1789 to 1815 foreign policy was an important source of conflict between Federalists and Republicans. During the century that followed, widespread acceptance of neutrality, isolationism, and the Monroe Doctrine tended to inhibit sharp and persistent controversy over foreign affairs. But from the First World War onward, American foreign policies have frequently been the subject of political conflict: neutrality, the arming of merchant ships, and entry into the First World War; the Treaty of Versailles and the League of Nations; neutrality and aid to the Allies prior to our entry in World War II; since then the dimensions of foreign aid, how to deal with Communist nations, the wars in Korea and Viet Nam—all have provoked controversy.

THE RECURRENCE OF INTENSE CONFLICT   One of the commonest beliefs about American politics (rather widely shared by Americans themselves) is that although conflict does occur over these issues, it is rarely if ever very intense. Because there are no precise ways of measuring the severity or intensity of a conflict, and it is therefore difficult to compare the severity or intensity of one conflict with that of another, the validity of this belief is not easy to challenge. Yet if one is prepared to accept as indices threats or moves to disrupt the constitutional system, threatened or actual violence against or on behalf of national policies, or expressions by sober and informed observers or participants that a given conflict will lead to disruption, revolution, or civil war, then the weight of historical evidence seems to offer solid support to a contrary proposition:

> From the very first years under the new Constitution American political life has undergone, about once every generation, a conflict over national politics of extreme severity.

33. See pp. 68–69.

To suggest the evidence for this proposition, let me review some familiar historical episodes.

1. Before the Constitution had completed its first decade, the Alien and Sedition Acts (1798), which threatened the very existence of any organized political opposition, were challenged by the legislatures of Kentucky (1798) and Virginia (1799) in resolutions that hinted for the first time (but definitely not the last) that a state government might deliberately refuse to enforce a federal law which its legislators held to be unconstitutional. The specters raised by the Alien and Sedition Acts on the one side, and by the Kentucky and Virginia resolutions on the other, were temporarily banished by what Jefferson called "the Revolution of 1800."

2. Within hardly more than another decade (December 1814), New England Federalists, driven to desperation by the embargo policies enforced by the Republicans, assembled at Hartford in a convention that not only adopted a set of resolutions calling for extensive constitutional changes but issued a report asserting among other things that "in cases of deliberate, dangerous and palpable infraction of the Constitution, affecting the sovereignty of a State and liberties of the people; it is not only the right but the duty of such a State to interpose its authority for their protection, in the manner best calculated to secure that end." [34]

3. Less than another score of years went by before the United States approached civil war over the tariff.[35]

4. Thereafter, the middle years of the century were occupied with various aspects of the controversy over slavery, particularly whether slavery should be permitted in the great unsettled areas of the West, a question that touched the most sensitive interests of Northerners and Southerners. Finally, as everyone knows, the issue no longer could be contained; and for four terrible years men died of wounds and disease to settle the question—or so it was supposed.

34. Richard B. Morris, ed., *Encyclopedia of American History* (New York, Harper, 1953), p. 153.

35. In 1828 the legislature of South Carolina adopted a set of eight resolutions holding unconstitutional, oppressive, and unjust the newly passed "Tariff of Abominations," which ultimately hit cotton exporters with what seemed to them undue severity; in an accompanying document written by John C. Calhoun the legislature espoused the view that a single state might, in such cases, "nullify" an unconstitutional law. Four years later, when the South Carolinians were still chafing under the protective tariff, a convention called by the state legislature adopted an ordinance that "nullified" the tariff acts of 1828 and 1832, prohibited the collection of duties within the state, and asserted that the use of force by the federal government could be cause for secession. The state legislature passed laws to enforce the ordinance, to raise a military force, and to appropriate funds for arms. President Jackson thereupon sought and gained from Congress the legal authority to enforce the tariff laws by military means if necessary. A compromise tariff was worked out in Congress, South Carolina rescinded its Ordinance of Nullification, and civil war was avoided—or rather postponed for thirty years. Morris, *Encyclopedia*, pp. 166–72.

5. In fact, the issue was only partly settled: slavery was abolished, to be sure, but the freed Negroes were not permitted for long to enjoy equal political rights, to say nothing of economic, educational, or social privileges. Ten years after Appomattox, the election of 1876 brought the country to the verge of civil war, but as so often before and after the outcome was compromise rather than war; yet a compromise that tacitly allowed the restoration of white supremacy throughout the South and thus adjourned the whole problem of effective citizenship for Negroes until the middle of the present century.

6. This adjournment allowed economic questions to take over. During the last third of the century, discontented farmers and urban workers formed a pool of recurring opposition to the policies of a national government that responded less and less to their demands and more and more to those of the new men of business, industry, and finance. Out of economic dissatisfaction radical and reformist movements developed: Socialist Labor, the Greenbacks, the Farmers' Alliance, Populism, the Socialist Party, the IWW. The trade union movement also had a turbulent growing period: the Knights of Labor, the AFL, the railway unions. Strikes, lockouts, and protest meetings frequently led to severe violence.[36]

7. In the presidential elections of 1896, William Jennings Bryan, a man of primitive intellect and beguiling eloquence, whom Democrats and Populists had jointly nominated as their candidate, and who in his simple and confused protests evidently evoked support among farmers and urban workers who were opposed to the "domination of Eastern capital," was defeated by McKinley after a campaign period of unusually high tension.[37]

8. Sixteen years later a new Democratic President, the second since the Civil War, was elected, and under Wilson's leadership many of the specific reforms that had been demanded earlier by Populists and Socialists were carried out. Although these reforms were sharply opposed, the conflicts seem to have lacked some of the earlier intensity; the country was not viewed as approaching another civil war.

9. The next generation witnessed the Great Depression, mass unemployment, extensive discontent, the election of the third Democratic

36. In 1886 during a demonstration near the McCormick Reaper Works in Chicago, six strikers were killed by the police and many more were wounded. The next day two thousand persons attended a protest meeting in Haymarket Square; policemen ordered the meeting to disperse; a bomb was thrown, killing a policeman; in the ensuing battle, seven more policemen and four workers were killed, sixty policemen and fifty workers were wounded. Six men who had addressed the meeting were sentenced to death; four were hanged the following year. In 1894, Grover Cleveland, the first Democrat elected to the presidency since 1856, now in his second term as President, called out federal troops in order to break a great nationwide strike of railway workers against the Pullman Company.

37. Bryan won 47 per cent of the two-party vote and carried 21 states—all of them, however, agricultural states of the South, Midwest, and West.

President since the Civil War, new outbreaks of violence, the rise of quasi-democratic or antidemocratic political movements on both Right and Left, and extensive changes in national policies, changes that from 1935 onward were fought with increasing bitterness. Driven to extreme measures by a Supreme Court dominated by conservatives who steadily rejected the major items of the New Deal as unconstitutional, President Roosevelt even tried to "pack" the court in 1937. It was his first important unpopular move, and he was defeated.

10. Less than thirty years later the unsolved problem of equal rights and opportunities for Negroes has produced a new eruption of demonstrations, discontent, and violence not only in the South but also in the Negro ghettos of the large Northern cities. And in 1964 the long-frustrated opposition of the Radical Right, capitalizing on white reactions to Negro discontent, temporarily captured the Republican Party and at last found national spokesmen in the Republican nominees for President and Vice President, Senator Goldwater and Representative Miller.

Whoever supposes, then, that American politics has been nothing more than a moving consensus, a sort of national Rotary Club luncheon, has not sufficiently reflected on the recurrence of intense conflict, crisis, and violence in American history.

THE PATTERN OF CLEAVAGE   If cleavages have been persistent, and if at times they have led to intense conflicts, why, one might inquire, has the system not been disrupted more often? Why have American oppositions been, on the whole, so moderate? Why don't oppositions "debate the great issues" and "present clear-cut alternatives," as critics so often demand? Why is it that "opposition" and "government" are often so hard to distinguish from one another?

One reason was discussed in the preceding section: the ambience of concensus in which government and oppositions operate. As long as oppositions employ substantially the same ideology and accept much the same set of values as the administration, it is difficult for them to force debate on the great issues (for there are no great issues) or to present clear-cut alternatives (for alternatives clearly outside the common ideology are excluded).

A second reason, which will be discussed briefly in the next section, is the structure of government and politics in the United States.

But a third reason is to be found in the very patterns of cleavage that lead to conflict. Even though, as we have seen, Americans divide quite often on questions of democratic rights and privileges, on the place of Negroes in American life, and on the economic role of the government, and divide somewhat less often on foreign policy, these and other issues do not ordinarily divide them into exclusive camps. For two reasons, it seems, American politics is almost never highly polarized.

1. Differences in political attitudes and actions are not highly related to

differences in socioeconomic characteristics—region, status, occupation, etc. Even though there is some relationship, it is usually weak: people in the same regions, or the same status groups, or the same broad occupational categories do not form distinct, homogeneous clusters of attitudes. Consequently, polarization of politics along socioeconomic lines is inhibited.

2. Differences in political attitudes and loyalties are not highly interrelated among themselves. That is, persons who hold the same attitudes on one question frequently hold different attitudes on other questions. (To overstate the point, every ally is sometimes an enemy and every enemy is sometimes an ally.) Thus polarization of politics along ideological lines is inhibited.

As to the first explanation, it is difficult to find any distinctive and persistent clusters of attitudes in different regions of the United States, except on the question of the Negro. Regional differences in political attitudes do, of course, exist; but the differences are, on the whole, weak. Southerners are not, for example, more conservative about the economic role of the government than people in other regions. In fact, on the basis of 1956 survey evidence, V. O. Key suggested that "on some questions the South turns out to be a shade more 'liberal' than other regions." Key also pointed out, incidentally, that "even with respect to the Negro the unity of the South varies from aspect to aspect of race policy. Southerners take a far stronger position on school segregation than on such questions as the protection of the economic rights of Negroes." [38] Nor, despite its reputation, has the Midwest remained (assuming that it once was) notably more isolationist or less internationalist than the rest of the country.[39] The reputation of the Midwest was created in part by its representatives in Congress, of whom a larger percentage opposed foreign aid in the period before and after World War II than among the representatives from other regions. Yet much of this congressional isolationism was more closely related to party than to region: Democratic congressmen from the Midwest have been, unlike their Republican colleagues, predominantly internationalist.[40]

Relationships are often found between political attitudes and various indices of occupation, socioeconomic status, and class. But strong relationships are rare, and often they are surprisingly weak. Thus in 1956

38. Key, *Public Opinion and American Democracy*, pp. 102–03.

39. On a scale of "internationalism," the percentages in each region which ranked high in 1956 were 53 per cent in the Midwest, compared with 59 per cent in the Northeast, 58 per cent in the Far West, and 56 per cent in the South. Key, *Public Opinion and American Democracy*, p. 107.

40. Leroy N. Rieselbach, "The Demography of the Congressional Vote on Foreign Aid, 1939–1958," *American Political Science Review*, 58 (September 1964) 577–88, esp. 582–83.

percentages of persons who ranked high on a scale of internationalism did not seem to vary a great deal according to whether the occupations were white-collar, blue-collar, or farming.[41] As in other countries, however, manual workers tend to diverge from nonmanual workers in their views on the proper economic policies of the government. The effects of class identification seem to be even greater than the effects of occupation; in 1956 a white-collar worker who identified himself as a member of the working classes was somewhat more likely to be in favor of government intervention in the economy on a variety of fronts than a blue-collar worker who identified himself as middle class. (See Table 2.1). Yet be-

Table 2.1. Socioeconomic Status and Support for Stronger Economic Role of Government*

Occupation of head of family	Class with which respondent identified himself	
	Working	Middle
White-collar	40%	22%
Blue-collar	50%	35%
Farm operator	41%	32%

* Entries are percentages ranking high in support for government aid to cities and towns for building more schools; to Negroes for fair treatment in jobs and housing; in guaranteeing everyone a job; for medical care; and in providing electric power and housing.

Source: Key, *Public Opinion and American Democracy*, p. 143.

cause class identity is weak, manual workers do not differ as sharply from nonmanual workers in their voting for candidates and parties as they do in a number of countries. Among the major English-speaking democracies, class voting seems to be lower in the United States than in Britain and Australia (though higher than in Canada).[42]

Ethnic and religious loyalties and identifications introduce heterogeneity into regions and status groups. The common belief that distinctive ethnic and religious identifications are weakening in the United States as the descendants of the various immigrants become assimilated into American life has been recently challenged in a study of ethnic groups in New York; the authors conclude:

Religion and race seem to define the major groups into which American

---

41. White-collar workers who identified themselves as middle class ranked a little higher in internationalism; otherwise, differences were negligible. See Key, *Public Opinion and American Democracy*, Table 6.11, p. 144.

42. "A number of public opinion surveys taken between 1952 and 1962 indicate that class voting is consistently higher in Australia and Great Britain than in Canada and the United States. The countries may be ranked in the following order: Great Britain, Australia, the United States, and Canada." Robert R. Alford, *Party and Society*, pp. 101–02.

society is evolving as the specifically national aspect of ethnicity [i.e., the specific nation from which one's ancestors came] declines. In our large American cities, four major groups emerge: Catholics, Jews, white Protestants, and Negroes.[43]

Yet, like region, status, occupation, and economic position, ethnic and religious loyalties do not as such produce sharp political cleavages. Voting patterns are very much more distinctive than political attitudes. Jews and Catholics vote more heavily Democratic than Protestants; Negroes vote more heavily Democratic than whites; and voters of Irish, Italian, Polish, German, and Scandinavian descent often seem to have somewhat distinctive voting patterns. The differences may be more apparent in local elections than in national elections, and most distinctive when a representative of their own ethnic group—or an enemy of their ethnic group—has a leading place on one ticket.[44]

The extent to which religious differences cut across class differences is revealed in a very general way by the data in Tables 2.2 and 2.3. In national elections over the past generation, among both manual workers and nonmanual workers, Catholics have voted Democratic in considerably higher proportions than Protestants. (Table 2.2) The discrepancy was

Table 2.2. Religious Voting by Occupational Categories, 1936–1960 (non-Southern whites only): 7 Presidential, 2 Congressional Elections

Religious voting: % Catholics voting Democratic minus % Protestants voting Democratic

	Manual workers	*Nonmanual*	*Farmers*
High	41% (1960)	59% (1960)	39% (1956)
Median	20% ('52, '54)	28% (1956)	14% (1958)
Low	16% (1956)	17% (1952)	— 5% (1954)

Source: Data taken from Table II, pp. 92–94, in Seymour M. Lipset, "Religion and Politics in the American Past and Present," in Robert Lee and Martin Marty, eds., *Religion and Social Conflict* (New York, Oxford University Press, 1964).

greatest between middle-class (nonmanual) Catholics and Protestants; many Catholics who had moved into nonmanual occupations maintained their traditional loyalties as Democratic voters. The differences between

43. Nathan Glazer and Daniel Patrick Moynihan, *Beyond the Melting Pot* (Cambridge, Mass., the MIT Press and Harvard University Press, 1963), p. 314.
44. See the evidence in Louis Harris, *Is There a Republican Majority, Political Trends, 1952–1956* (New York, Harper, 1954), Ch. 6; Angus Campbell and Homer C. Cooper, *Group Differences in Attitudes and Votes, A Study of the 1954 Congressional Election* (Ann Arbor, Survey Research Center, 1956), Ch. 3; Alford, *Party and Society*, pp. 241 ff.; Campbell et al., *The American Voter*, pp. 319 ff. In the 1964 presidential election the fears aroused among Negroes by the candidacy of Senator Goldwater amplified to near unanimity their predisposition to vote Democratic.

Catholics and Protestants were smallest in the elections of 1952 and 1956, when General Eisenhower was the Republican candidate, and, as might be expected, greatest in 1960 when John F. Kennedy, a Catholic, was the Democratic candidate.

To look at the same data in another way (Table 2.3), Protestants split

Table 2.3. Class Voting by Catholics and Protestants, 1936–1960 (non-Southern whites only): 7 Presidential, 2 Congressional Elections

Class voting: % *manual workers voting Democratic minus* % *nonmanual voting Democratic*

	Catholics	Protestants
High	28% (1952)	29% (1936)
Median	16% (1948)	23% (1956)
Low	6% (1960)	18% (1954)

Source: See Table 2.2.

most sharply along class lines in 1936 in the midst of the Great Depression, when Franklin Roosevelt was running for a second term. Catholics split most sharply in 1952 when many middle-class Catholics succumbed to the appeal of Eisenhower; in 1960, on the other hand, Kennedy all but obliterated the appeal of class among Catholics by his appeal as a fellow Catholic.

Thus religion or ethnic identity may either amplify the effects of class and status on voting, as in the case of Negroes or working-class Catholics; or, conversely, religion or ethnic identity may depress the significance of class and status by providing a crosscutting cleavage, as in the case of middle-class Catholics and Jews or white working-class Protestants. Moreover, just as the impact of occupation and economic position on voting may vary depending on the state of the economy, so the impact of religion and ethnic identity is not a constant but a varying factor depending on current issues and on the candidates themselves.

More important, differences in voting and partisan loyalties among ethnic and religious groups do not seem to reflect significant differences in ideology or attitudes about policy. This is not to say that there are *no* discernible differences in political predispositions and beliefs among the different groups. It has been conjectured that "the sympathy which Catholic doctrine has had for trade union objectives, as contrasted with the greater emphasis on individualism inherent in Protestantism may in some part explain why even non-union middle-class Catholics are more supportive of union rights in this country."[45] In New York City, it has been

45. Lipset, "Religion and Politics," *The First New Nation*, p. 113. Lipset cites the following finding: "Ohio's counties were segregated (for analytic purposes) into twenty different levels of urbanism, income, and rural farm, and in all twenty of

said, "what attracts Jews is liberalism, using the term to refer to the entire range of leftist positions, from the mildest to the most extreme." [46] The kind of Christian pacifism exemplified by Martin Luther King's strategy of nonviolence quite possibly could not have succeeded with any other group of Americans as well as it did with Negroes.

Nonetheless, differences in attitudes and beliefs often reflect other factors like education and economic position; or else the differences are highly specific and depend on some particular issue that impinges directly on the group, as in the case of Catholic views on governmental aid to parochial schools or the views of Negroes on civil rights. On the whole, when these factors are removed it is difficult to find much distinctiveness in the political attitudes of the various ethnic and religious groups.[47]

In short, then, differences in political attitudes and actions are related to a number of different social and economic characteristics, but they are not highly related to any, and the variety of social and economic characteristics of any broad category of the population makes for a high degree of political heterogeneity. Hence polarization along social and economic lines is inhibited.

The second factor mentioned a moment ago—that differences in political attitudes and loyalties are not highly interrelated—contributes further to this process. Despite the relatively low level of differences in political attitudes and actions among people in different regions, occupations, classes, religions, and ethnic groups, it is conceivable that Americans might divide into two distinctive ideological blocs, each of which was internally a rather heterogeneous (though not random) mixture of socioeconomic groups. In a very rough way this might serve as a description of the Democratic and Republican parties. The difficulty is, however, that until the present the ideological distinctiveness of these blocs has been blurred because even on major issues persons who hold the same attitudes on one question diverge on others. Two issues of great recent salience—integration and medical care—furnish illustrations. One might speculate that at least in the North economic liberals who would favor medical care would also be civil libertarians who would favor racial integration in the public schools; conversely, the prosegregationists might also be economic conservatives. Doubtless there is some tendency of this kind. The relations are, however, very shaky. In a 1956 sample, among Northerners who favored medical care about half also favored racial integration

---

these groups the more Catholic counties exceeded the least Catholic in their opposition to right-to-work" (i.e. anti-union) legislation in a 1958 referendum. See also John H. Fenton, *The Catholic Vote* (New Orleans, Hauser Press, 1960), pp. 37–38.

46. Glazer and Moynihan, *Beyond the Melting Pot*, p. 167.

47. See, for example, the generalizations based on data from a survey made during the 1954 congressional elections, in Campbell and Cooper, *Group Differences*, pp. 79–80.

in the schools; but more than a third opposed it. Hence a Northern medical care coalition would, in the extreme case, lose a third of its support when it endorsed racial integration. Conversely, Northerners who opposed a federal medical care program were almost evenly divided on the question of racial integration; hence their coalition would (in principle) split wide open if it took any definite stand on the issue of segregation.[48]

Unless attitudes are highly polarized, it is impossible to divide a population into two like-minded collections of people. No matter what criterion is used for dividing people, as long as there are only two categories or collections, then within each category there will be many conflicting views. Given the existence of a two-party system, it follows inevitably that, unless attitudes are highly polarized, each of the two parties can hope to win only by constructing an electoral coalition made up of people whose views coincide on some questions but diverge on others. This is exactly what happens most of the time in the United States. And as long as (1) political attitudes are not polarized and (2) only two major parties exist, there can be no escape from two parties each with heterogeneous followings.[49]

Is the pattern I have been describing a recent one? It is difficult to say, for we have surveys and election studies only for the past quarter-century. Yet there is substantial reason for thinking that low polarization has been the usual condition of American politics, and that the reasons for low polarization have been about the same in the past as they are now: large socioeconomic groups have generally been heterogeneous in political attitudes, and persons who agree on one question disagree on others.[50]

Presumably there have been historical fluctuations; the tide of polarization ebbs and flows. Polarization has probably risen to high points during each of the major crises described earlier, and then receded. But polarization is rarely high in American politics and, it would appear, never persistent.

Structure of Government and Politics

After the patterns of consensus and cleavage, the third major factor that helps to account for the characteristics of oppositions in the United States

48. V. O. Key, *Public Opinion and American Democracy*, p. 170. In the 1964 election the voters in California supported President Johnson against Senator Goldwater by six to four and at the same time supported by two to one an amendment to the state constitution permanently nullifying all state legislation to eliminate racial discrimination in the sale of housing.

49. For some speculation as to the likelihood of a change, see pp. 68–69.

50. Although it covers only a limited period, a recent study of Jacksonian Democracy lends support to this interpretation. See Lee Benson, *The Concept of Jacksonian Democracy: New York as a Test Case* (Princeton, Princeton University Press, 1961), particularly Ch. 13, "Outline for a Theory of American Voting Behavior."

is the structure of government and politics: structure in large part prescribed by the Constitution but in some measure amplified by practice and tradition.

One critical element in this structure is of course the two major parties. Parties other than the two largest have less impact on politics in the United States than in any other country examined in this volume. The two parties are, however, decentralized; they do not command as high a degree of voting support from their members in Congress as most European parties seem to do; they tend to be pragmatic, even opportunistic, in approach; they seek and retain highly heterogeneous followings. Some of these characteristics, as we shall see, result from—or at any rate are strengthened by—the kinds of factors discussed up to this point. But the reasons an almost exclusive two-party system exists and persists in the United States are too complex and debatable to enter into here. I propose therefore to consider the two-party system as a given, and not try to account for it. Its existence helps us explain the characteristics of oppositions.

The other aspect of the structure of government and politics that bears most heavily on the characteristics of oppositions is the fragmentation of power that it facilitates. As everyone knows, the structure provides a great many checkpoints at which one set of officials can block, slow up, or significantly modify the actions of other officials—the White House, the executive agencies, the independent commissions, the House, the Senate, the rules of procedure in each house, the standing committees, conference committees of the two houses, the federal courts—and not least the federal system itself, in which all these features are in greater or lesser degree duplicated in 50 different states with a rather extensive amount of authority and power.

These features reinforce the heterogeneous character of the parties, primarily by providing to leaders who hold these offices, or can influence officeholders, an extensive opportunity to bargain for advantages by threatening to block, slow up, or modify the policies of other leaders who need their support, constitutionally or from long-standing tradition, practice, or law.

Illustrations abound. Ever since 1938 Democratic Presidents have suffered defeats at the hands of conservatives in Congress. In President Kennedy's first two years in office, a conservative coalition of Northern Republicans and Southern Democrats voted together on about one-fourth of the roll-call votes in the Senate and about one-sixth of the roll-call votes in the House. Considering only these votes, the coalition defeated the President by winning in the Senate more than half the time and in the House nearly two times out of three. The victories of the conservative coalition included measures dealing with foreign aid, farm laborers from

Mexico, mass transportation, and aid to depressed areas.[51] Or to take the example of civil rights: until 1964 opponents of laws designed to strengthen Negro rights regularly defeated these measures even when they had majority backing; the instruments were usually the House Rules Committee (controlled by a coalition of Southern Democrats and conservative Republicans) and the filibuster in the Senate. It was the Supreme Court, not the Congress, that ordered the principal changes in Southern patterns of segregation. Yet the Southern states, aided by the institutions of federalism, generally refused to comply; with relatively weak presidential leadership and enforcement under President Eisenhower, their opposition was on the whole successful. Southerners who defied the Court argued, moreover, that they were only obeying the law: the law of their own state.

Consequences for the Strategy and Tactics of Opposition

The strategy and tactics of opposition in the United States have been largely determined, I have suggested, by

1. The characteristic pattern of consensus
2. The characteristic pattern of cleavage
3. The structure of government and politics

Let me now describe some of the consequences in more detail.

First, a group opposed to existing American institutions is unlikely to gain much support if it mounts a comprehensive attack on the prevailing American ideology, or if it is widely perceived as doing so. To the extent that such a group is pragmatic and realistic in orientation, it will try to reduce its apparent divergence from the prevailing ideology by stressing aspects more consistent with its own ideology and objectives. Since the prevailing ideology is not all of one piece, it lends itself fairly readily to such treatment. However, the result within a radical opposition group is to create an esoteric ideology and an exoteric one; and this produces difficulties when naïve followers attracted by the exoteric ideology are repelled by the esoteric one. To some extent this has been a problem with the Communist Party.[52] Alternatively, an opposition that does not accommodate itself to the prevailing ideology is likely to be so unrealistic in its general behavior that its following is minuscule and made up of a disproportionate number of individuals low in political skills, realism, and effectiveness. The result is that few Americans are ever exposed to a

51. *Congressional Quarterly, Weekly Report, 21* (Week Ending April 17, 1964), "On Conservative Coalition," pp. 737–40. It should be pointed out that the victories of the conservative coalition were sometimes only marginal changes in the President's proposals, not outright defeats of the whole measure.

52. Irving Howe and Lewis Coser, *The American Communist Party, A Critical History* (New York, Praeger, 1962), pp. 538 ff

presentation of an alternative ideology that involves extensive criticism of the prevailing institutions or the belief-system that legitimizes these institutions.

Second, opposition is likely to be successful in bringing about the changes it seeks only if it affirms its support for the prevailing ideology and the basic institutions of American life, and concentrates its fire on some specific aspect of existing institutions, practices, or beliefs, e.g., free land for homesteaders, slavery, national regulation of banks, child labor, the sale of alcoholic beverages, and so on.

Third, given the dominance of two parties, low polarization, and the particular structure of government and politics, opposition is likely to be successful only if it enters directly into one of the two parties or bargains with both parties.

Although the option of forming a new party is theoretically open, there is not a single case in American history where an opposition has formed a third party, pushed one of the major parties aside, and subsequently won a national election. The electoral record of third parties in the United States is one of nearly total failure.[53] Of all the party systems in the world, the American two-party system has the longest continuous history of rivalry between the same two major parties. To anyone contemplating the formation of a third party, this historical fact should be (though evidently it not always is) a melancholy prospect to contemplate.

The upshot is, then, that to be effective in a concrete way an opposition will usually have to operate in league with, and make concessions to, leaders of groups whose attitudes on some questions will be in conflict with attitudes among its own followings.

Fourth, it is difficult or impossible to make a sharp distinction between "loyal opposition" and "government." Both merge imperceptibly into a system of coalitions, bargaining, and compromise in which no one coalition can be said to "govern" and none is definitely and persistently in opposition. Significantly, in Congress, in the state legislatures, and with rare exceptions in the press, Americans do not speak of "the loyal opposition" or even "the opposition." The closest terms are "the majority party" and "the minority party"; and even these terms cannot refer to both President and Congress during those periods when President, Senate, and House are not of the same party, which has been the case one-fourth of the time since 1789.

53. One might object that the Republicans began in 1854–56 as a third party, but the point is only technically true and of little relevance. For the Republican Party did not destroy the Whigs and take their place. The Whigs were destroyed by the slavery controversy, and the Republicans built their party, like Phoenix, on the ruins of the Whigs. This could perhaps happen again. The leaders of some third parties have impatiently awaited their Phoenix for a very long time. But after a full century the phenomenon has not yet been repeated.

Some Consequences for the System

Thus, just as the pervasive ideology provides support for the political system, so too the operation of the political system, in the ways I have just examined, provides support for the prevailing ideology.

To overstate the point somewhat: opposition cannot change the institutions because of the ideology; yet opposition cannot change the ideology because of the political institutions. Since most of the electorate accepts roughly the same ideology, it is possible (with the assistance of institutional factors such as presidential elections and single-member districts) for a two-party system—of a kind—to exist. Yet given the existence of only two major parties competing for votes, and given the initial acceptance of a single ideology among the electorate, competition between the two parties in turn undoubtedly reinforces the ideology.

This familiar process of reinforcement might be illustrated in the following way. Suppose we were to classify American adults according to the number of major propositions in the prevailing ideology with which each person disagrees: for example, support for popular government, for the constitutional system, for change by constitutional means, for private property, and for the desirability and possibility of personal success. Although we do not have the exact data we need, the evidence presented earlier suggests that most voters would not disagree with any of the major propositions; some, however, would disagree with one; a few with two or three; almost none with all five. A distribution would look something like Figure 2.1.

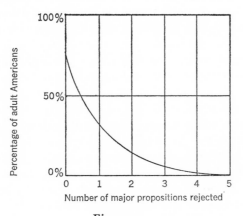

Figure 2.1

In conditions like these both parties direct their appeals to the great body of voters piled up on the left of the distribution. For either party to make any other appeal is to run the risk of losing a vast number of votes in order to gain a much smaller number among the political deviants.[54] When a party or a presidential candidate misreads the distribution, as Senator Goldwater did in 1964, the election confirms the risk of "extremism" by producing a resounding defeat. Further, the very fact that both parties are driven by the logic of numbers to adhere to roughly the same ideology means that the ideology is constantly reinforced, or, at the very least, that alternative ideologies are severely handicapped. Thus a typical election, far from generating long-lasting ideological tensions and conflicts as in many other countries, instead tends in the long run to strengthen the traditional ideology. For both major parties emphasize the virtues of that ideology and their faithful adherence to it.

The result is, then, that Americans have solved over long periods the problem of national unity that has weakened and even destroyed many other attempts to operate representative government. If the price for this success is high, the costs of failure could be even higher. Americans have their Civil War to remind them what failure can cost: one out of every dozen males of military age dead, an entire section of the country devastated, and the major question at issue, the place of Negroes in American life, given no more than a superficial, unstable, and morally intolerable solution. The twentieth century has revealed once more what enormous costs may be imposed on the people of a country, and on the world, when representative institutions fail from internal conflicts: Italy, Spain, and Germany, to mention only the three major European examples. The American achievement is all the more significant because of the differences in race, ethnic group, religion, and national origin of the American people, their sheer numbers, the vast size of the country, and the degree of economic specialization that has much of the time existed in the different regions.

Yet the costs of success (in this sense) are high—higher than most Americans are aware of, I think, and quite possibly higher than they need to be. For there are several additional consequences that must, I think, be weighed in the balance.

First, the system makes it easy for political leaders to ignore groups of people whose problems lie outside the attention, loyalties, values, and identifications of the great mass of voters, particularly if these groups lack bargaining power because of poor organization, low status, isolation, ignorance, lack of political incentives, and so on. In practical political terms, the political leader who seeks to find solutions for the problems of marginal groups runs the risk of gaining less support than he loses. It seems highly unlikely, for example, that the deprivation of Negro rights could have gone on so long, with so little national attention, if the United

54. This point was strongly stressed by E. E. Schattschneider in *Party Government* (New York, Rinehart, 1942).

States had had cabinet government, proportional representation, three or four major political parties, and more sources of ideological dissent. To say that this alternative would also have generated costs (costs that many of us would regard as excessive) does not gainsay the costs of the present system.

Second, criticism of the major structures and institutions of the United States tends to be rather limited, and examination of structural alternatives is ordinarily rather slight. The point is, no doubt, a familiar one; yet to weigh the balance of advantage and disadvantage flowing out of this consequence is not as easy as it is sometimes made to appear. Extensive, severe, and persistent criticism of the major social, economic, and political structures would put a serious strain on any democratic polity. Moreover, comprehensive and persistent criticism is almost inevitably grounded in ideologies; yet ideological controversy, like religious controversy, is rarely conducive to rational presentation, consideration, and appraisal of alternatives. Although nationwide shouting matches put a heavy burden on a democracy, they do not even compensate for that disadvantage by improving the grasp of the alternatives among citizens and leaders. Is it, as a practical matter, possible to have a rational, orderly examination in national politics of great structural alternatives? The question poses, I think, an unsolved problem. But to say that it is unsolved does not mean that the American solution is desirable. At one extreme, Italy, France, and Germany have in the past all incurred very high costs from implacable ideological controversy. At the opposite extreme, the immunity from comprehensive criticism that the major structures of American social, economic, and political life seem to possess may also impose heavy costs.

Third, if severe ideological cleavages often stimulate irrational controversy, it seems more than likely that the overwhelming ideological consensus of the kind I have described in this essay also encourages irrationalities. It may do so by compelling political dissenters to choose between futility and the two-party politics of compromise, thereby increasing their sense of frustration and political alienation. One enters here a doubtful terrain, and what follows is speculative. It is usually assumed that pragmatic, two-party politics American-style encourages reasonable compromises that mitigate frustration by yielding something to all the parties to a conflict. Yet this is surely not the whole story. Consider the lot of the political dissenter in the light of all that has been said up to this point. If he enters into a third party, he is condemned to political impotence. If he enters into one of the two major parties, he constantly sees his principles compromised or even forfeited. He has no satisfactory choice among candidates in elections. From his point of view, the relevant policy alternatives are rarely posed; national leaders, it seems, are unwilling to take his alternatives seriously. Differences among national leaders that are im-

portant to voters closer to the center of the political spectrum are, to our
political dissenter, too small to be noticeable. It is natural for him to interpret political conflict among national leaders as sham battles within a
unified power elite—or, as the American Right often calls it, taking a leaf
from the British Left, the Establishment (Eastern, Liberal).

For the political dissenter, continued political impotence and rejection
breed frustration. Frustration may produce apathy and withdrawal from
politics, but frustration may also turn to hostility, resentment, vengeful-
ness, and even hatred for national leaders in both parties. The political
dissenter, then, is likely to become alienated from the political system—
from its prevailing practices, its institutions, its personnel, and their assumptions. "Betrayed" by the leaders who dominate the system of politics,
the politically alienated dissenters look to some new leader for deliverance
—a leader who, like them, will shake off the shackles of two-party, pragmatic, compromising politics and offer a radical and uncompromising
alternative. In 1948 Henry Wallace may have briefly tapped a reservoir of
politically alienated voters on the Left; an alienated Right evidently responded to a Joe McCarthy in 1952, to a Barry Goldwater in 1964.

It is reasonable to surmise (if one continues this line of speculation)
that from the defeat of Populism in 1896 until the New Deal, the largest
alienated group in the United States was on the Left. Populism was in
many ways the American equivalent of European social democracy.[55] And
when it went down to defeat in 1896, the Left was confronted with the
familiar alternatives of supporting a separate socialist party that could not
win elections or entering one of the two major parties and compromising
with all the heterogeneous elements that made up these parties.

Since the advent of the New Deal, however, it is evidently the Right
that has been alienated, perhaps increasingly. Except for the fact that this
new Right is almost exclusively white, its composition seems to be socially
and economically heterogeneous. Attempts to locate the new Right in
particular social, economic, or educational strata have on the whole proved
unsuccessful. What distinguishes the new Right most sharply is not its
social-economic position but simply its dissenting ideology; and its alienation stems from a total inability to win national elections or, until 1964,
even to secure presidential candidates who would espouse its obviously
deviant minority views.[56]

55. Norman Pollack argues: "Had Populism succeeded, it could have fundamentally
altered American society in a socialist direction." *The Populist Response to Industrial
America* (Cambridge, Harvard University Press, 1962), p. 12.

56. This interpretation deliberately stresses the political sources of the radical Right.
Attempts to locate the socioeconomic sources of the new Right have been unsuccessful. In the first edition of *The Radical Right*, ed. by Daniel Bell (New York, Criterion
Books, 1955), the authors suggested such sources as anxieties over status and the new
rich. But the evidence for these hypotheses was slight; in the second edition (New

In national elections, the Right has had to look, in the North, to the Republican Party; in the South, to the Republicans or to a Southern third-party "Dixiecrat" movement. The Dixiecrats, like other third parties, have proved to be a political failure. As for the Republican Party, until 1964 it refused to nominate a presidential candidate wholly satisfactory to its right wing. The defeat of Senator Taft at the Republican convention in 1952, and the nomination and election of General Eisenhower, were dramatic and unmistakable victories for the moderates—the "Eastern, Liberal Establishment." Because Eisenhower was a Republican President, his attitudes and policies were perhaps all the more displeasing to the Right, since they demonstrated the ineffectiveness of the Right within its own party. In 1964, the Right at last had its way in the nomination of Barry Goldwater. The consequence was—as most responsible observers outside the Right predicted from the outset—overwhelming defeat.

In the conventional liberal-democratic theory of politics, political dissenters are a valuable source of enlightenment; by posing currently unpopular alternatives they force citizens and leaders to examine possibilities they could otherwise ignore. In the United States, however, it is doubtful whether the process has worked quite this way. Frustration and alienation seem to encourage paranoid interpretations of political life,[57] emotionalism and styles of thought that do not produce debate and discussion but

---

York, Anchor Books, 1964) the authors themselves are inclined to doubt them. As Lipset remarks, efforts to test their hypotheses about the effects of status incongruities "with the data now available proved unfruitful." (*The Radical Right*, p. 402). Oddly, in the first edition the authors all but ignored the most obvious possibility: the frustration of conservative Republicans unable to win elections. In 1960 Nelson Polsby called attention to the fact that the most significant distinction between those who supported and opposed McCarthy in various surveys was party identification: his supporters were mainly regular Republicans, while most Democrats opposed him. ("Towards an explanation of McCarthyism," *Political Studies*, 8 [1960]). Lipset, after acknowledging Polsby's finding, says that two surveys "suggest that the most important single attribute associated with opinion of McCarthy was education, while a 1954 national study . . . indicated that religious affiliation was of greater significance than party." (*The Radical Right*, p. 398. The findings were: the more educated the respondents, the more anti-McCarthy they were, and Protestants were more anti-McCarthy than Catholics.) In a more recent study of persons who attended a "San Francisco Bay Region School of Anti-Communism" (an extreme right-wing group) in 1962, the authors found that this particular group of right-wingers were Republicans of relatively high socioeconomic status and education. Their most salient characteristic was their support for Republican candidates. Ninety-two per cent of those who voted in the 1960 presidential election supported the Republican candidate, Richard Nixon, and two-thirds identified themselves as Republicans, 19 per cent as independents, and only 8 per cent as Democrats. Raymond E. Wolfinger, Barbara Kaye Wolfinger, Kenneth Prewitt, and Sheila Rosenhack, "America's Radical Right: Politics and Ideology" in David E. Apter, ed., *Ideology and Discontent* (New York, The Free Press, 1964), pp. 262–93.

57. Richard Hofstadter, "The Paranoid Style in American Politics," *Harper's Magazine* (November 1964), pp. 77–86.

hostility and rejection. The moderates close ranks against the threat. In the end, the attack of the political dissenters, far from clarifying alternatives by debate and discussion, may actually reinforce the prevailing ideology.

Changes

In emphasizing the recurring patterns of the American system, I have inevitably portrayed that system as more static over the long run than in fact it is. The system does change. Opinions change as to what the government should be doing in the issue-areas mentioned earlier—democratic rights and privileges, the Negro, the role of the government in the economy, foreign policy. And the policies enforced by the government also change.

An attempt to explain changes in political opinions and policies would take us into a vast area, important but not well charted. However, it might be useful to conjecture whether there are likely to be any important changes in the three main sets of explanatory factors discussed earlier. Of these three kinds of factors, the pattern of cleavages seems to offer the greatest likelihood of significant changes.

The pattern described earlier seems likely to change in two ways. First, it is reasonable to project a trend of gradually declining salience of objective differences within the American population as a result of affluence, widespread education, mass communications, the expansion of white-collar employment and declining proportions of farmers and manual workers. If this trend continues, then objective differences will become even less related than they are at present to differences in voting patterns and, more important, to political attitudes. Subjective factors only related in a loose way to these objective characteristics—values, ideology, psychological predispositions—may then become relatively more important. To the extent that this occurs, the appropriate strategy for the political parties will be to pay less attention to the presumed desires of particular socioeconomic categories in the population and more and more to general attitudes, aspirations, and policy-oriented views that cut across socioeconomic categories to like-minded voters in each of these categories. In this sense, American politics may become more, not less, "ideological." As a result of this change the parties may be even more heterogeneous than at present in the socioeconomic characteristics of their support, and at the same time less heterogeneous and more unified in the policies for which they can secure the support of their voters. To put it another way, one's political allies and opponents today would remain one's allies and opponents tomorrow.

This change might well be the result of two other changes that are very likely to occur in American politics: the removal of the ancient issue of Negro rights from its central (if not always public) place in politics by defeating the South on this question and providing such powerful juridical guarantees for the Negro that the process cannot be reversed, as it was after 1876; and the development of a two-party system in the South.

For one condition above all created the pattern of cleavage that has dominated American politics in which today's allies are tomorrow's opponents. This was the power of the one-party South in elections and in Congress and its virtually unbreakable unity on the institutions of white supremacy in the South. A party that would not do business with the South on its own terms, i.e., yield to white supremacy in the South, has for nearly a hundred years stood in perpetual danger of being defeated in elections or in Congress, or both, by a party that would. Both parties yielded to this imperative. As a result, the South was at once a permanent opposition (on all questions involving racial segregation) and a permanent partner in government.

If, however, the issue that has made this inevitable is removed from politics, and if the Republican Party gains an increasingly strong foothold in the South (not merely in presidential elections but also in elections to Congress and the state legislatures), there will be little left to distinguish Northern liberals and progressives from Southern liberals and progressives, Northern moderates from Southern moderates, or Northern conservatives from Southern conservatives. The parties may then regroup along lines of greater ideological and programmatic consistency.

Should this take place, however, it is not likely to produce two sharply differentiated parties with distinct ideologies. The kind of consensus, even pseudo-consensus, discussed earlier, makes this unlikely. The content of the beliefs at the center may—indeed, undoubtedly will—change. But the tendency for opinions and beliefs to converge will probably continue. The center will then continue to dominate political life, and dissenters will continue to be frustrated and alienated.

3

NORWAY:
NUMERICAL DEMOCRACY
AND CORPORATE PLURALISM

Stein Rokkan

28 Years In, 28 Days Out:
The Labor Government Is Ousted but
Returns to Power After a Brief Interlude

An extraordinary crisis was triggered off in Norwegian politics by the resignation of the Minister of Industrial Affairs on June 20, 1963. A disaster had occurred in a state-owned coal mine in Spitzbergen some months earlier and the Commission of Inquiry appointed by the government to look into the mining operations had concluded that the disaster was likely to have been caused by gross negligence on the part of the management and the government inspectors. The report of the Commission had not yet been published but the members of the Cabinet knew its conclusions. The mining company was administered by a board under the Department of Industrial Affairs, and the minister responsible for the Department decided to resign, apparently without consulting his colleagues in the Cabinet. His letter of resignation set off the first serious crisis in domestic politics since the early 1930s. The letter was made public the day before the Storting was to be prorogued; this was the first time anyone in the opposition had been given any information about the conclusions of the Commission of Inquiry. The rumor spread that the Cabinet had deliberately withheld the report from the Storting in order to gain time during the summer recess. The five opposition parties—the 2 Left Socialists (formally, the Socialist People's Party) as well as the 74 Liberals, Christians, Agrarians, and Conservatives to the right of the government—united in defense of their right to full information and decided to keep Parliament in session through the summer to allow detailed consideration

This chapter was written while I held a Simon Visiting Professorship at the University of Manchester. I am much indebted to William Mackenzie for support, encouragement, and advice and to Richard Rose for stimulating discussions. I also wish to record my indebtedness to Robert Dahl, Harry Eckstein, Egil Fivelsdal, Val Lorwin, Jens Arup Seip, Nils Stjernquist, Ulf Torgersen, Henry Valen, and Jörgen Westerståhl for comments on and criticisms of an early version of the chapter.

of the action to be taken on the report. This was a direct threat to the Labor government: if the Left Socialists sided with the four nonsocialist parties, there would be 76 votes for a motion of no confidence, the 74 Labor representatives would be outvoted, and the government would have to go. All hinged on the 2 Left Socialists: they could repudiate the Labor government, but they might make life equally impossible for a new government formed by the 74 nonsocialists.

Few political leaders had any holiday that summer. The Liberals, Christians, Agrarians, and Conservatives developed a united front and agreed to do their utmost to carry out the threat and, if they were successful, form a coalition government. The Labor Party rallied massive support behind the government and encouraged the trade unions to put heavy pressure on the Left Socialists to keep them from any act of disloyalty toward the working class. The young Socialist People's Party was indeed caught on the horns of an acute dilemma: the party might lose its raison d'être if it kept giving in to the Labor Party, but it might lose a lot of its electoral support among dissident trade unionists and other workers if it helped the "bourgeois" parties to power after 28 years of Labor rule.

The party leadership decided to follow a novel strategy: the 2 Left Socialists in the Storting would vote for the motion of no confidence but would not support a new government of what the Norwegians call the "bourgeois" parties. The implication was that they were prepared to support a new Labor government after appropriate changes in personnel and in policy: they wanted a more socialist and perhaps also more neutralist government, and they wanted to use their two strategic votes to force such a change.

When it was first announced, this strategy met with derision and scorn in the Labor Party. But when the Labor government was ousted from power after a memorable debate on August 23, this was in fact the strategy its leaders adopted in their counteroffensive. They forced the new Cabinet of the four opposition parties to present its policies in a broad program statement on September 16, and then immediately counterattacked with a far more radical and far more socialist program of their own: they proposed a comprehensive scheme of service pensions of the type the Swedish Social Democrats had introduced, and they also suggested a series of moves to strengthen the role of the state in the economy. The Storting was faced with two alternative programs of action: one moderate and emphasizing balanced welfare state policies very similar to those followed by Labor in the years after World War II; the other distinctly more radical, more socialist. The result was a foregone conclusion: the Left Socialists thought they had had their way and voted with Labor. The four-party coalition government was out, and Labor was again in power.

The opposition still had hopes, however. The debates in the Storting had taken place during local election campaigns and had been televised to a national audience of unprecedented size. The local elections were held only two days after Labor's return to power and in fact took the form of a national contest between the opposing political groups. The result came as a shock to all those who had hoped that the crisis had weakened the Labor Party. It gained more votes than any other party and kept the Left Socialists in check: Labor had mobilized its working-class electorate to a maximum in moving leftward and at the same time had held the dissidents to a minimum.[1]

1. Local elections since World War II have given these results:

Per cent of total
votes cast for

	1945	1947	1951	1955	1959	1963
Communist Party	11.4	10.0	6.1	5.3	3.9	1.9
Socialist People's Party	—	—	—	—	—	2.8
Labor	39.8	38.2	42.4	43.4	43.7	45.8
Middle parties (Liberal, Christian, Agrarian)	19.8	22.2	22.7	22.8	24.2	25.4
Conservatives	9.7	13.9	15.3	16.7	18.6	19.8
Joint "burgher" lists	6.2	8.2	6.2	4.3	2.3	1.2
Local, nonpartisan lists	13.2	7.6	7.4	7.5	7.3	5.1
Per cent voting	*65.5*	*71.6*	*72.7*	*71.5*	*72.9*	*81.0*

The 1959–63 gains registered for the Socialists in general (+2.9 per cent) and for Labor in particular (+1.9 per cent) seem to have resulted from two movements within the electorate: first, the increased turnout (+8.1 per cent), and second, the reduction in the number of votes for local nonpartisan lists (−2.2 per cent). Direct comparison with the results for national elections is difficult for three reasons: (1) differences in turnout levels between the two types of elections, (2) the presence of nonpartisan and joint "burgher" lists in local elections, and (3) variations in the number of constituencies and communes in which the new Socialist People's Party presented its own lists. To get around the first difficulty one can calculate party votes in per cent of the electorate rather than of the total valid vote. A comparison for two national and two local elections give these results:

	1957 national	1959 local	1961 national	1963 local
Total electorate in '000s = 100%	*2,298*	*2,314*	*2,340*	*2,363*
Turnout (incl. rejected votes)	77.9	72.9	79.1	81.0
Per cent for:				
Communist Party	2.6	2.8	2.3	1.5
Socialist People's Party	—	—	1.9	2.3
Labor	37.7	31.5	36.8	36.8
Middle	22.8	17.4	21.9	18.9
Conservative	14.7	13.4	15.7	15.9
Joint "burgher" and nonpartisan lists	—	6.9	—	5.1

The Socialist gains from 1959 to 1963 were indeed considerable: they advanced from 34.3 to 40.6 per cent of the electorate. But this was essentially due to the "nationalization" of the local elections of 1963: by comparison with the preceding national elections in 1961 there was very little change indeed. For details on traditional differences between local and national elections in Norway, see S. Rokkan and H. Valen, "The Mobilization of the Periphery," in S. Rokkan, ed., *Approaches to the Study of Political Participation* (Bergen, Chr. Michelsen Institute, 1962).

The four-party opposition to the right had again been reminded of a stubborn fact of Norwegian political life: the numerical majority of the mobilized citizens has been to the left in all elections since the war and a crisis such as the one of the summer of 1963 could only have been brought about through dissidence and splinter movements within this majority.

The Norwegian Party System:
Four Minor Parties Face One Major Party

The Norwegian party system hovers at some point halfway between the Anglo-American and the Continental. There are one "in" party but four "out" parties: the Labor Party has been close to the majority point for three decades; throughout this period the opposition has been divided into several organizationally distinct parties, each with its particular clientele. There is no possibility of regular alternation between major parties as in Britain or in the United States, yet there is no discernible trend toward an "all-party" or "most-party" coalition as in Austria, Switzerland, the Netherlands, and several German Länder. There is no great enthusiasm for this halfway system, and there have been assiduous advocates of change in one direction or the other: toward an Anglo-American system of alternation between major parties or toward a Continental system of proportional sharing of responsibilities among all national parties.

The pleas for an Anglo-Saxon solution have no doubt been loudest and most persistent: calls for unity among all antisocialists have been heard ever since the introduction of manhood suffrage in 1900, and the need for a broad alliance in opposition to Labor has been a central theme in all election debates since the early 'twenties. The idea of a merger into one great antisocialist opposition party has survived an endless series of setbacks. The brief period of coalition in the summer of 1963 gave fresh impetus to efforts in this direction, but subsequent debates over the rights and wrongs of the joint program of action made it clear that there was no basis yet for an organizational merger across the historically given lines of cleavage.

Pleas for a Continental solution have been fewer and more academic. The idea of shared government gained momentum during the years of war, occupation and resistance from 1940 to 1945 and was argued fervently by several leading publicists and one or two active politicians in the years that followed. The notion of a *Proporz* solution was never a central issue of public debate, however, and the bitter experiences of the summer of 1963 made the possibility of agreement on an all-party national government more remote than ever.

The advocates of change in the established halfway system, whether toward the Anglo-American or toward the Continental model, have tended to ignore the hard structural facts of Norwegian politics; they have underestimated the difficulties of introducing workable alternatives to a system of gradually formed alignments along inherited lines of cleavage in the national community. A realistic analysis of the problems and prospects of effective opposition in such a system must start with an account of the succession of conflicts, divisions, and realignments which led to the current constellation of parties, and seek to pinpoint the conditions for the continued functioning of this system.

A leading academic historian recently reviewed the history of Norway from 1814 to 1964 and divided this time span into three distinct periods: first, the *regime of the officials*, the 70 years of centralized bureaucratic rule from 1814 to 1884; second, the *multiparty regime*, the 60 years that followed of rapidly changing governments and frequent shifts in parliamentary constellations and alignments; and finally, from 1945 onward, the *one-party regime*, the rule of the Labor leaders and their allies in the central bureaucracy and in the giant interest organizations.[2] Paradoxically, this dialectical interpretation of the cyclical movement of Norwegian history appeared only a month after the greatest upheaval in national politics since the early 'thirties: the theory of the one-party state was propounded in the immediate wake of a severe, if unsuccessful, challenge to the continued dominance of the Labor movement in the affairs of the nation. In a sense the theory functioned as a self-falsifying prophecy: it was one item in a broad movement of Left Socialist opposition to the rigidities of the regime, and it was this very movement of Socialist dissent which had put the Labor leaders to their severest test since the victory in 1945.

The historian had joined the ranks of the *terribles simplificateurs* but in doing so had pointed to three crucial sets of factors in the development of the Norwegian polity; firstly the deep-rooted tradition of *centralized bureaucratic rule*, originally inherited from the absolutist regime under the Danish kings but later developed and reinforced as the farmers, the fishermen, and the workers rose to state their claims and pressed forward the twentieth-century service state; second, the heritage of *territorial and cultural opposition* to the governing officials and the allied urban elites of academics, merchants, and industrialists; and third, the intensification of *class contrasts* with the spread of the money and market economy throughout the national territory and with the development of industrial centers both in the traditional urban settings and in the peripheral countryside.

Norway was granted internal independence in the wake of the Napoleonic wars: it had to accept personal union with Sweden and the dominance of Stockholm in all external affairs, but it was granted full autonomy in the organization of its domestic administration and its internal political life. The Constitution of 1814 gave the new nation the most democratic

2. Jens Arup Seip, *Fra embedsmannsstat til ettpartistat og andre essays* (Oslo, Universitetsforlaget, 1963).

system of representation in Europe: all freehold peasants and most lease-holders were given the right to vote.[3] In practice, however, the government of the country continued to be in the hands of a small elite of officials and patricians; for decades after the grant of the franchise the great majority of peasants deferred to their "betters" and were content to leave the affairs of the nation in the hands of the educated administrators and the privileged burghers of the cities.

The peasantry was not to remain in this state of obedient apathy, however. A slow process of social, cultural, and religious mobilization got under way in the wake of independence and gradually prepared the ground for a political breakthrough. The decisive marshaling of forces against the regime of the officials took place from the 1860s onward. The peasants finally organized themselves for political action and established their allies among reformers and radicals in the cities—artisans, teachers, lawyers, and other groups—in opposition to the central administrative elite. This alliance soon gained the upper hand in the Storting and launched a long series of skillfully organized attacks against the supremacy and independence of the Cabinet and the administration.[4] The struggle was long and protracted but the opposition stuck to the rules of the game and was at every point careful to establish its rights through due process of law. Before every major decision it insisted on consulting the people in duly organized elections. The result was an unprecedented mobilization of new voters on each side in the struggle. The *Left*, as the alliance of rural populists and urban radicals came to be called, won overwhelming victories at the polls in 1879 and 1882, but its very success forced the official establishment to mobilize all the electoral counterforces it could command and to organize clubs and societies for the defense of the Constitution: this was the origin of the *Right*, the Conservative Party.

The final struggle between the forces of the Left and the forces of the Right was ugly and bitter. The country was on one or two occasions on the verge of civil war: there were rumors that the Swedish king was preparing to mobilize the army for a coup d'etat against Parliament, and the Left on its side organized a network of riflemen's associations to serve as a popular militia against the forces of the officials.[5] In the end, however,

3. For detailed estimates of the size and composition of the electorate under the original franchise criteria see S. Rokkan, "Geography, Religion and Social Class," in S. M. Lipset and S. Rokkan, eds., *Party Systems and Voter Alignments* (New York, Free Press, forthcoming 1966). The fullest discussion of early electoral arrangements is found in Alf Kaartvedt's volume of *Det norske Storting gjennom 150 år* (Oslo, Gyldendal, 1964), *1*, 51–138.
4. The best analyses of these struggles are found in J. A. Seip, *Et régime foran undergangen* (Oslo, Tanum, 1945); Alf Kaartvedt, *Kampen mot parlamentarisme 1880–1884* (Oslo, Universitetsforlaget, 1956); and in Rolf Danielsen's volume of *Det norske Storting gjennom 150 år* (Oslo, Gyldendal, 1964), *2*.
5. Kaartvedt, *Kampen mot parlamentarisme*, pp. 131–37, and 304–13.

both sides agreed to proceed within the law. The struggle ended in 1884 in a series of dramatic impeachment proceedings against the King's Council. The Left used its overwhelming majority in the Storting to pack the Court of Impeachment and the verdict itself was never in doubt: the members of the Cabinet had acted contrary to the Constitution and were to be divested of their offices. But what would the King do? This was the real issue: would he appoint another Cabinet of the Right from among his own officials or would he give in and accept the supremacy of the Storting? After much soul-searching, the King and his advisers took the safer course: they asked the leader of the Left majority to form the Cabinet and thereby took a decisive step toward the establishment of the principle of parliamentary rule in Norway.[6]

The critical contest for power between the Left and the Right generated a process of mass mobilization into politics, and this process soon acquired its own dynamics. It changed the conditions for political activity and set the stage for new alignments and new cleavage lines in the system. The system had lost its equilibrium, and each party was continuously pressed to bring in new allies on its side to achieve some balance. The result was an unprecedented expansion of the political arena: first through increased turnout among those already registered and through increased registration of those qualifying under the old franchise rules, later through a series of extensions of the suffrage.[7]

In 1876, at the last of the "prepolitical" elections, the total number of citizens on the electoral rolls was only 84,000 out of an adult male population of close to 400,000. In 1900, at the first election after the introduction of manhood suffrage, the total number on the rolls had risen to five times the 1876 figure even though the adult population had only increased by some 20 per cent. These masses of new entrants into the political system could not easily be absorbed by the original contestants; new lines of cleavage came to the fore in the body politic, new alliances were tried out, and an increasingly complex system of party constellations emerged.

In oversimplified structural terms we may say that the Norwegian multiparty system was generated by regional differences in the timing of the two decisive waves of mobilization: the mobilization of the peasants and the mobilization of the workers.

The original struggle between the Left and the Right was triggered off by the mobilization of the peasantry. The decisive lines of cleavage tended to be territorial and cultural. The provinces resented the dominance of the capital. The awakening rural communities resisted the influence of an alien and foreign-oriented urban culture. The peasantry found it more and

6. Ibid., Chs. 8, 10–12.
7. For statistical details of this process of mobilization see S. Rokkan, "Geography, Religion, and Social Class."

more difficult to accept the standards set by the officials and the patrician establishment: the urban language, the *riksmål*, so remote from the inherited dialects of the countryside, the rationalist Lutheranism of the State Church, the foreign manners, the tolerant morals, and the convivial drinking prevalent in the open urban society. The Left gained strength through the convergence of these resentments against the urban establishment: the Left did more than open up channels to influence political power—it met a widespread demand for cultural self-assertion and identification. In the early decades after independence, the peasantry had generally accepted the language and the cultural traditions of the king's officials and the educated bourgeoisie as superior to their own, but increasing contacts with urban manners and urban realities led to widespread frustration and alienation. The peasants felt awkward and uncertain when communicating with officials and others in authority; they felt inferior and exploited in their dealings with city folk; and they found little comfort in the teachings of the established Church. Mobilization did not lead to cultural integration; instead it produced a widespread breakdown in human communication and generated a number of "countercultures" essentially hostile to the established standards and models of the original elite.

The movement for a new national language, the *landsmål*, was the most direct and most forceful of these expressions of resistance against urban influence. The new language gave the peasants a concrete symbol of their historical identity and inspired pride and confidence in their national mission. The movement accentuated the regional contrasts in the nation; it entrenched itself firmly in the inner valleys of the East and in the fjords and on the coast of the South and the West but remained in a minority in the central rural areas and the cities of the East, in the Trøndelag and in the North.[8] The conflict over the language forms deepened the cleavage between city and countryside throughout the national territory but it was only one among a number of polarizing issues. Religious divisions often reinforced, sometimes cut across linguistic cleavage lines. Pietistic and fundamentalist doctrines and practices entrenched themselves in many rural districts early in the nineteenth century and prepared the ground for a broad movement of religious protest against the established Lutheran Church.

A number of educational endeavors helped to give the young peasantry

8. *Riksmål* was the name given to the language of the educated urban strata. This was, at least until 1907, essentially Danish in orthography and structure but East Norwegian in pronunciation and vocabulary. The contrast between the written and spoken form was reduced through a series of linguistic reforms in the twentieth century. The *landsmål*, later *nynorsk*, was originally the creation of a linguist of peasant origin, Ivar Aasen. It represented an attempt to reconstruct a common Norwegian standard language on the basis of the rural dialects least affected by the 400 years of Danish rule. For an attempt at a sociological interpretation of these cultural contrasts see S. Rokkan, "Geography, Religion, and Social Class."

a deeper consciousness of their historical mission and trained them for active citizenship: the Folk High Schools established from the 1860s onward became important recruiting stations for militants and leaders within the rural Left.[9] Even such essentially philanthropic and practical movements as the teetotal organizations fitted into this alignment of countercultures: the total rejection of alcohol was part of a general movement of protest against the moral disintegration brought about by urbanization. All these movements reflected deep divisions in the national community. There was no single acceptable medium of communication; there was only fragmentary consensus on national standards and national values and there were many built-in barriers against informal social contacts across the many cultural enclaves. Foreign observers have often found it difficult to understand the importance of alcohol as an issue in Nordic politics. It is tempting to interpret the strength of the teetotal movement within the Left as another expression of a basic refusal to accept communications from the established elite: the refusal to take part in convivial drinking was tantamount to a refusal to mix freely within the community and helped to maintain a multitude of local cultural enclaves from erosion through informal social contact with other milieux.

The Left offered a common platform for these varieties of cultural enclaves, whether linguistic, religious, or moral. The party did not stand for one integrated counterculture but was a temporary alliance of several, some in close communication with each other, others far apart. The unity of the heroic years of struggle did not last long. The first split came only four years after the victory in 1884: the fundamentalist wing of the party could no longer cooperate with the nationalist radicals. The two wings came together again after the settlement with Sweden in 1905, but the unity of the party was always precarious. The failure of the policy of alcohol prohibition in the 'twenties increased the strains between the fundamentalist and the nationalist factions of the party, and in 1933 led to the next split in the ranks of the defenders of rural cultural traditions: a Christian People's Party was formed by a dissident wing of the old Left and established itself as a serious competitor for votes, first in the West only, later, from 1945 onward, throughout the country.

However fragile the unity of the old Left, the territorial-cultural cleavages have persisted in Norwegian policies throughout the 80 years since the downfall of the old regime. The mobilization of the working class in the years after the introduction of manhood suffrage produced new lines of conflict within the system, but there was no polarization along any single dimension: the old center-periphery axis cut across the new upper-

9. For a lively description and comparison of the Danish, Swedish, and Norwegian Folk High School movements see Erica Simon, *Réveil national et culture populaire en Scandinavie* (Paris, Presses Universitaires, 1960).

lower axis and produced an increasingly complex system of alignments. The conflicts between the capital and the provinces, between the urban culture and the rural, were far from resolved at the time the workers entered the political arena, and the old issues of cultural policy proved distinctly more divisive than the new issues of class conflict throughout the period up to 1918. The core of the old Left continued its fight for the rural countercultures: it championed the recognition of *landsmål* as a standard national language, it fought for a reorganization of the established Church, it advocated stringent legislation against the sale of alcohol. There was no basis for an understanding with the Right: even the threatening specter of a giant working-class party could not bring the two cultures into close communication with each other.

This conflict between rural claims and urban dominance goes far to explain the difference between the Scandinavian multiparty system and the English two-party system. In Scandinavia there were few and only tenuous ties between the rural and the urban elites; in Norway this chasm was even deeper than in Denmark or Sweden as a result of centuries of foreign dominance channeled through the cities. In England the original conflict between Tories and Liberals pitted landed interests against commercial and industrial, but the great estate owners soon found allies in the boroughs and from 1885 onward there was a distinct trend toward a merger between rural, suburban, and urban elites.[10] This realignment brought about a polarization of English politics and paved the way for the rise of a distinct lower-class party, first under the wings of the embattled Liberals, later on its own. In England the decisive struggles between rural and urban interests came long before the mobilization of the lower classes for political action. In Scandinavia the two waves of mobilization came close on each other's heels and one set of issues had not come anywhere near settlement before the next set forced itself on the body politic. The result was a very different system of party constellations: there was the same tendency toward class polarization as in England, but it did not come through with equal force in all regions and the poles of the class conflict were not the same in the rural as in the urban areas.

In the Norwegian case the crosscutting of the two axes produced a complex system of regionally differentiated party oppositions along the lines indicated in the table on page 80.

The new wave of mobilization triggered off by the extension of the suffrage to the landless, the propertyless, and the wage earners accentuated the territorial differences in the system, not only between the central and the peripheral areas but also between the regions.

The equalitarian communities of the South and the West had long been

10. See especially James Cornford, "The Transformation of Conservatism in the Late 19th Century," *Victorian Studies*, 7 (1963), 35–66.

Territorial axis		Functional-economic axis	
		Least polarized: South, West	Most polarized: East, Middle, North
	Center: cities, suburbs, industrialized, rural	Labor vs. Left, Right	Labor vs. Right
	Intermediate rural: market farming, forestry	Labor weak, Agrarians, Liberals, Christians dominant	Labor vs. Agrarians
	Periphery: marginal farming, fisheries	Labor weak, Liberals, Christians dominant	Labor vs. Right

the strongholds of the movements of cultural defense against the influences from the cities and from the economic and administrative center of the nation. In these communities the old Left and its offshoots remained in dominance and offered stubborn resistance against the trend toward a class polarization of local politics. This was the case not only in the isolated periphery but even in areas of incipient urbanization and industrialization: the territorial opposition to the influences from the cities was stronger than the contrast between the old established electorate and the lower-class entrants, and the Labor Party found it very difficult to enlist support outside the few core groups of unionized industrial workers.[11]

In the other regions the spread of the money and market economy undermined the earlier traditions of cultural defense and created new alignments on functional lines. The result was another split within the ranks of the old Left—this time not on issues of religious orthodoxy but over questions of economic policy. The farmers and the forest owners felt increasingly unable to support the diffuse politics of cultural defense so central in the program of the Left, and insisted on action to protect their prices and to ensure regular government support for their efforts to expand and modernize. They were also worried about the rise of the rural lower classes and the entrenchment of the Labor Party among the agricultural wage earners and the forestry workers. They could not ally themselves with the Right: the age-old traditions of suspicion and distrust against the urban elite were too strong, and there were also direct clashes of interest between the producers of primary commodities and the managers of free enterprise commerce and industry. The market farmers and the forest owners were among the first to establish vigorous interest organizations, and the leaders of these organizations soon exerted heavy pressures both on nominations of candidates for the Storting and on the decisions of the representatives once they had been elected. It did not take

11. For details see S. Rokkan and H. Valen, "Regional Contrasts in Norwegian Politics," a chapter in E. Allardt and Y. Littunen, eds., *Cleavages, Ideologies and Party Systems* (Helsinki, Westermarck Society, 1964).

long, however, before they felt the need to go further and to establish their own party: steps in this direction were first taken in a few constituencies in 1915 and a full-blown nationwide Agrarian Party emerged in 1921. The crosscutting of the two axes had produced four parties: the old Left still remained culturally opposed to the Right, but the rise of the Labor Party had added another dimension to the system and pitted the lower classes against the Right in the cities and the industrialized countryside, but against the Agrarians in the majority of the farming and forestry communities.

The enfranchisement of the lower classes had brought about a profound change in Norwegian politics. The cities and the industrial centers were the first to be polarized between the middle and the lower strata, but the movement gradually spread to the traditional rural communities and to the coastal peripheries: very slowly, as we have seen, in the South and the West, surprisingly rapidly in the poorest of all the provinces, the North. The Labor Party, originally an offshoot of the burgeoning trade union movement in the cities, cut across the earlier territorial lines; it established alliances between rural and urban, peripheral and central forces and stimulated a series of moves toward the development of "nationalized" politics. It is deeply significant that the party had its decisive breakthrough not in the capital or in any of the larger cities but in the Northern periphery: it had built up its initial organizational strength in the central areas of the East, but the Socialist message spread much more quickly and with much more effect among the crofters, the fishermen, and the "navvies" of the far North. The first five Socialists to be elected to the Storting all came from the North: four from the fisheries districts of Troms and Finnmark, one from the new industrial center at Narvik. Class resentments in the traditional primary economy in fact proved as important for the growth of the Labor Party as the new cleavages within the industrializing centers. The waves of rapid industrialization after 1910 radicalized the party, and the experiences of inflation and unfettered speculation during the First World War strengthened its revolutionary wing. But the party remained an alliance between rural and urban interests, and the broad popular appeal of the movement in fact acted to restrain its ideologists and its leaders.

The Norwegian Labor Party went further to the revolutionary left than any of the other Scandinavian working-class movements. The radical wing gained the upper hand in the wake of the Russian Revolution and mobilized a majority for the Third International: the result was a split-off on the right. The Norwegians proved highly insubordinate in their relations with the Comintern, however, and the alliance was broken in 1923.[12] The result was another split-off, this time on the left. This anarchic state of

12. For details see K. Langfeldt, *Moskvatesene i norsk politikk* (Oslo, Universitetsforlaget, 1961).

affairs lasted for four years. By 1927 the majority party and the right-wing Social Democrats had finally decided to unite again and to build up a broad national organization for effective electoral action. The election that year proved decisive: the united Labor Party advanced from 32 to 59 seats in the Storting and constituted the largest group of representatives in the legislature. The divisions between the old, established parties, the Left and the Right, were still deep and bitter and in the Cabinet crisis that followed the election the King decided to ask the leader of the Labor Party to form an administration.[13]

This decision marked a turning point in the history of democratic politics in Norway. A revolutionary party representing hitherto under-privileged strata of the national community was admitted to power in accordance with the established rules of the parliamentary game. The party was not immediately domesticated as a result of this gesture of acceptance: there was widespread distrust of all varieties of "Ministerial Socialism" and a great deal of reluctance to take power without a clear parliamentary majority.[14] Nevertheless, the party decided to accept the challenge: its leaders presented a straight socialist program of action to the Storting and were voted out of power nine hectic days later.

Labor had had its first brief taste of power. Did the experience prove that the revolutionaries were right, that the fight for a socialist society could not be won through electoral and parliamentary procedures? Or did it only show how little could be achieved before a numerical majority had been won in people and Parliament? The Labor Party was rocked by debates over this question for the next three years: should it build itself up as a strong class party ready to fight the capitalist forces directly or should it broaden its appeal to the people at large and seek power through the regular channels of elections and majority voting? The revolutionaries again won out, and the party went into the 1930 election with a program even further to the left than the 1928 declaration. The result was a massive mobilization of the available counterforces in the community. The turnout rose to the highest level reached since the introduction of universal suffrage, and large numbers of women voting for the first time in their lives threw their weight against Labor. The party maintained most of its strength in absolute numbers but it lost grievously in the competition for new votes. To the revolutionary wing of the party this was not neces-sarily a loss; it wanted an organization of convinced Socialists, not a mass of mobilized sympathizers. But to the majority of the party leaders the defeat was a call for action: they wanted to win mandates, and they wanted to broaden the appeal of the party. The economic crisis of 1930–31 forced

13. An illuminating analysis of the background of these developments is given in Ivar Roset, *Det norske Arbeiderparti og Hornruds regjeringsdannelse i 1928* (Oslo, Universitetsforlaget, 1964).

14. Ibid., Ch. 3

them into concrete political action in their localities, and they became increasingly convinced that the revolutionary strategy of the party could only lead to despair and disillusionment. The world crisis, the disenchantment with the Soviet system, the threatening specters of Fascism and National Socialism made more and more of them rally to the defense of parliamentary democracy and made them willing to cooperate with other parties in the solution of concrete problems of policy. A fundamental change of orientation took place in the leadership during 1930–33: the party was about to enter the national political community and was preparing itself for its ascent to power.

This process of domestication was accelerated by the strains between the urban and rural wings of the party. Two young party ideologists, Dag Bryn and Halvard Lange, analyzed this contrast in great detail in a path-breaking article in 1930.[15] They pointed to the marked imbalance between the cities and the countryside in the member–voter ratios of the party and saw in this an expression of the strain between the two models of organization, the class party and the people's party. Their figures, in the accompanying table, are indeed striking.

	Members 1927 (in '000s)	*Voters 1927 (in '000s)*	*Ratio of members to voters*
Oslo	26.1	63.5	1:2.4
Other cities	15.4	79.1	1:5.1
Rural communes	26.5	225.6	1:8.5

In the capital the party came close to having direct organizational ties with at least one voter in every household on its side. In the rural districts the party had gathered votes from a great number of households without any such membership ties to the organization. In the capital and some of the larger cities the party could count on an organized body of committed members ready to support the Socialist cause not only in elections but also in demonstrations, in strikes, and in other forms of direct action. This core of convinced Socialists offered the best basis for the development of a centralized elite party on Leninist lines. In the provinces and in the rural areas the party was weak in organization but strong in votes. The steady worsening of conditions in the primary economy had rallied more and more fishermen, smallholders, and casual laborers behind the party, but only a few of these were swayed by considerations of ideology and long-term strategy. They wanted immediate relief from their economic difficulties, and they cast their votes for Labor because they trusted the party to defend their interests. This set the dilemma for the party leaders after

15. **Dag Bryn and Halvard M. Lange, "Klasse eller folk,"** *Det 20de århundrede, 31* (3) (March 1930), 67–75.

1927: should they give priority to ideology and organization and keep away from involvement in practical decision-making, or should they broaden the electoral appeal of the party and enter into cooperation with other parties in the solution of day-to-day problems of immediate urgency?

The events after 1930 in fact made the decision for the party: the revolutionary wing lost out and the parliamentary democrats took over. The party went all out for electoral victory in 1933 and came very close indeed: it won 69 out of the 150 seats in the Storting. The leaders immediately declared themselves willing to take over the government of the country. The old, established parties, the Right and the Left, resisted to the end, but the Agrarians finally agreed to back a Labor government under a guarantee of support for the primary economy. Again it is significant that a decisive change in the political system came about through an alliance in defense of the rural interests: the Agrarians represented a higher socioeconomic stratum than the rural Labor leaders, but this class cleavage proved less important in the concrete situation of economic crisis than the traditional conflict between the primary economy and the commercial and industrial interests centered in the cities.

The Labor Party acceded to power in 1935 and has dominated Norwegian politics ever since. The new government presented a cautious program of concrete action to relieve the current crisis—it did not want to risk a repetition of the brief intermezzo of 1928. The party wanted to establish its parliamentary trustworthiness and was concerned to discourage as far as possible any trend toward a merger of the opposition on its right. It still needed allies and was most likely to find these among the representatives of what were now called the Middle parties: the old Left and the emerging Christian People's Party no less than its current partner, the Agrarian Party. These parties helped to keep the system in balance under the strains of the transfer of power: the polity was not torn between two poles but was kept within bounds through the crosscutting of a number of cleavage lines.

Figures 3.1 and 3.2 give the strength of the parties on each side of the principal conflict line from the decisive election of 1882 to the latest contest in 1961. The most striking characteristic of this long sequence of electoral decisions is the continuity of alignments. From 1882 to 1924 the principal cleavage line in the system was between the Left on the one side and the Right on the other. The character of the opposition between the two changed fundamentally after 1900: the Left remained essentially a party of cultural and territorial defense but the Right was gradually transformed from a party of the official "establishment" to a party defending the broadening community of commercial and industrial interests. The extension of the suffrage to all adults accentuated class divisions: the rise of the Labor Party, the transformation of the farmers' interest groups into

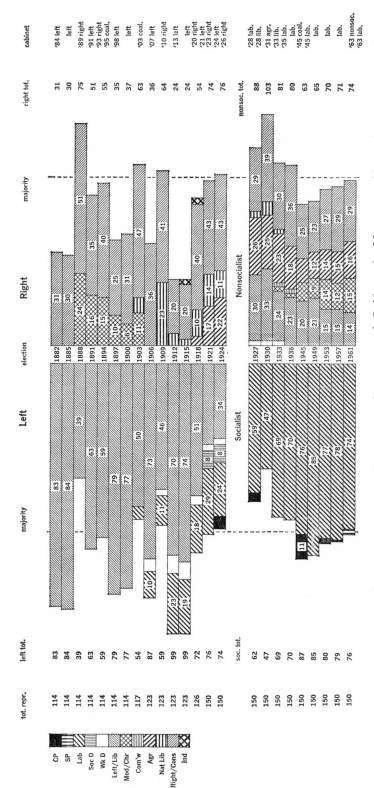

Figure 3.1 *The Political Composition of Parliaments and Cabinets in Norway, 1882–1963*

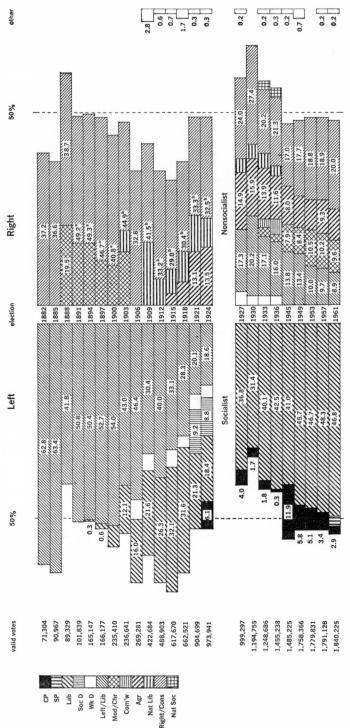

Figure 3.2. *The Voting Strengths of the Parties, 1882–1961*

a. *For these elections the statistics do not distinguish Moderate and Right votes: The percentages given therefore refer to the Moderate plus Right total.*

b. *For these elections the statistics do not distinguish National Liberal and Right votes.*

This ordering of the parties from a working-class left to a nationalist-elitist extreme right is not based on any detailed analysis of the dimensions of policy disagreements and the likelihood of coalitions. In its basic structure this ordering has been confirmed through analyses of differences in attitudes toward Labor policies (cf. Table 3.4), but the placement of some of the minor parties in the middle range of the spectrum is questionable and should not be interpreted to reflect detailed research on the "dimensionalities" of Norwegian politics.

Separate figures for the votes cast for the Moderates and Right have only been established for 1888, see *Indstilling S.XX* (1890). For subsequent elections through 1903 the combined percentage strength of the two groups has been entered under "Right" in Figure 3.2 and only approximate distributions have been indicated on the basis of the known ratios of seats.

Separate figures for the National Liberals and the Right are not given in the statistics from 1909 to 1924. In Figure 3.2 the percentages given for the Right therefore refer to the totals for these two parties.

Norwegian name	*Elections*	*English translation*	*Abbreviation*
Norges Kommunistiske Parti	1924–	Communist Party	CP
Sosialistisk Folkeparti	1961	Socialist People's Party	SP
Det Norske Arbeiderparti	1894–	Labor Party	Lab.
Norges Socialdemokratiske Arbeiderparti	1921–24	Social Democrats	Soc.D.
Arbeiderdemokratene	1906–18	Worker Democrats	Wk.D.
Radikale Folkeparti	1921–36		
Venstre	1882–	Left 1882–1924 / Liberals 1924–	Left. / Lib.
Moderate	1888–03	Moderates	Mod.
Kristelig Folkeparti	1933–	Christian People's Party	Chr.
Samfunnspartiet	1933–49	Commonwealth Party	Com'w.
Landmandsforbundet	1915–18	Agrarians	Agr.
Bondepartiet	1921–53		
Senterpartiet	1957–		
Frisinnede Venstre	1909–30	National Liberals	Nat.Lib.
Frisinnede Folkeparti	1933–36		
Høire (Høyre)	1882–	Right 1882–1924 / Conservatives 1927–	Right / Cons.
Nasjonal Samling	1933–36	National Socialists	Nat.Soc.

an Agrarian Party, the change in the ideology of the Right—all these developments cut across the earlier territorial-cultural cleavage line and produced new constellations of opposition and alliance. From 1927 the principal cleavage line was no longer between Left and Right, but between the Socialists and all the offshoots of the parties established before the extension of the suffrage: the Left, now better rendered into English as the Liberals, the Agrarians and the Right, now better translated as the Conservatives (for details on the party names and their translation, see the notes to Figures 3.1 and 3.2). The rise of the Labor Party to its position of dominance in the 'thirties did not decisively change this structure of party alignments. Nor did the five years of war, occupation, and resistance from 1940 to 1945. There was much talk of a broad coalition based on the experiences of cooperation in the exile government and in the resistance movement, but when it came to brass tacks in the summer of 1945 the old parties proved their vitality.[16] The election of 1945 did not produce any major changes in the system. The war had strengthened the working-class parties: the Communists made a spectacular comeback after their near disappearance in the 'thirties, and Labor won its first clear majority of seats, if not of votes. On the opposition side there was very little change: the Christian People's Party was transformed from a regional to a national movement but otherwise the alignment remained roughly as before. The subsequent elections of 1949, 1953, and 1957 produced little in the way of structural change: the Communist Party lost out after the coup in Czechoslovakia, and Labor consolidated its position. It is true that the party lost seats in 1953 and 1957; this did not reflect a loss in votes, however, but a change in the electoral law—the switch from the d'Hondt to the Sainte-Laguë allocation procedure lowered the threshold for the small parties and increased the number of votes required for additional seats for the largest party.[17] The first sign of potential change came in 1961: a dissident group of Left Socialists decided to move into competition with the mother party and won two seats in the Storting, one in the capital and one in the North. The Labor Party found itself in a minority position for the first time since 1945. The situation in the Storting became highly unstable: the two representatives of the Socialist People's Party held the balance between the 74 Laborites and the 74 members of the traditional

16. See T. Chr. Wyller, *Frigjøringspolitikk* (Olso, Universitetsforlaget, 1963).

17. Under the d'Hondt system the total number of votes cast for each party list is divided successively by 1, 2, 3, 4, and so on. This means that each new seat costs a party the same number of votes as the first seat gained. The Sainte-Laguë procedure is to divide successively by the odd numbers 1, 3, 5, 7, etc. This makes further seats progressively more expensive and gives the advantage to the one-seat parties. To increase the threshold of representation without favoring the large parties, the Scandinavian electoral systems have since 1952 set the first divisor at 1.4 instead of 1, but kept the subsequent Sainte-Laguë divisors. For details on the mathematics of these procedures see C.-G. Janson, *Mandattilldelning och regional röstfördeling* (Stockholm, Idun, 1961).

opposition. There was much soul-searching but the final outcome was clear: the Gerhardsen Cabinet stayed in power under a tacit agreement that it could rely on support from the opposition in carrying out major policies. The nonsocialist opposition had very little choice in the matter: it could not muster a majority for an alternative government and it was seriously split over a central issue of foreign policy—the stormy issue of Norwegian entry into the European Economic Community, which broke out shortly after the election. In this fight, the antagonists on the functional-economic axis of the political system, Labor and the Conservatives, were united in their advocacy of entry while the offshoots of the old party of territorial-cultural defense were either deeply split or entirely against any application for full membership in the EEC. Our reanalysis of Gallup data for the peak period of the campaign for and against entry [18] suggests a resurgence of the old alliance of the 'seventies and 'eighties: alienated urban radicals, primarily on the left wing of Labor and among the Eastern Liberals joined with the peasantry of the provinces in an attack on the "establishment." But the central authorities they attacked were very different: the radical-peripheral alliance was no longer directed against the King's administration and its ties with Swedish interests but against a complex of trade unions, business organizations, and public bodies, and their ties with the organs of European integration. The stakes of the game had indeed changed, but the conflict had retained something of its old structure.

The fight over the EEC issue kept Labor in power. Entry would require a change in the Constitution, and to bring this about the pro-EEC Liberals and the Conservatives had to cooperate actively with the majority faction within Labor. These unusual cross-party agreements lost their objective after January 14, 1963: General de Gaulle called off the campaign, and in fact changed the structure of Norwegian politics. The result was the Cabinet crisis of the summer of 1963—the point where we started our story.

The Sociology of Norwegian Politics:
The Struggle for the Majority Narrows the Range of Alternatives

Two blocs of voters have been pitted against each other in Norwegian politics at least since 1927: an "established" bloc essentially recruited from the strata already enfranchised under the *régime censitaire* and an "underprivileged" bloc recruited from the urban and industrial working class and the landless rural proletariat after the introduction of manhood suffrage in 1898. The registered electorate more than doubled from 1897 to 1900. If the Labor Party had been able to mobilize all these new voters it would have risen to a majority position right away. But the process of mobilization was slow and irregular, and the subsequent extension of the suffrage to adult women on the same terms as men in fact delayed the process of

18. See S. Rokkan and H. Valen, "Regional Contrasts," pp. 199-201.

polarization between the two blocs. The Labor Party came very close to one-third of all votes cast at the first election under universal suffrage for both sexes in 1915. Only half the women had voted, however, and in the subsequent struggle to mobilize this potential, the working-class parties clearly lost out, at least in the first round. The "underprivileged" bloc stayed at the 30 per cent level until 1924. The first breakthrough toward a majority position came in 1927 in the wake of the widespread economic crisis in the countryside: the Socialist parties for the first time polled beyond the 40 per cent mark. The "underprivileged" again lost out in the scramble for further electoral reserves in 1930 but continued the march toward the majority point in 1933 and 1936. The movement culminated in 1945, at the first election after the war: the two working-class parties reached 52.9 per cent of all votes cast and won a decisive majority of the seats in the Storting. The voting majority was only slightly reduced in the elections that followed: it never moved below 51.5 per cent in the period 1945 to 1961.

These majorities said a great deal about the balance of orientations in the electorate, but they were essentially socioeconomic, not political majorities. The working-class parties were deeply split over core issues of foreign policy and could not cooperate with each other at any level of political action. The dominant Labor Party could only hope to govern as long as it was in a position to marshal parliamentary majorities of its own. Any move toward a coalition with the left splinters would bring the entire system out of equilibrium. In terms of *Koalitionsfähigkeit* the Norwegian system was split in three, not two blocs of parties: the alienated Socialists to the left, the domesticated Labor Party in the center, the four parties of the "established" bloc to the right.

In this situation the strategies of the governing Labor Party were largely determined by two sets of concerns: it must hold the left splinter movements to a minimum, and it must keep its appeal broad enough to attract the votes of the less committed masses halfway between the poles of the political system. The programs and campaign messages of the party reflected the difficulties of reconciling these two strategic objectives: the old strains between class and nation, between ideology and policy, were still there. The Communists posed a real problem for the party until the Czechoslovak coup d'état in 1948 and the subsequent Stalinist-Titoist quarrels. The decline of the Communist Party from 1949 onward secured the left flank of the governing party for 12 years. Power and responsibility brought Labor closer to the established institutions of the nation, and agreement with the nonsocialist opposition on entry into the Western alliance system gradually brought about an ideological détente between the two blocs.[19] The four parties of the "established" bloc found themselves in

19. For a review of these tendencies toward "deideologization" in the 'fifties, see

agreement with the government over a wide range of issues of domestic policy, and the steadily expanding system of functional representation on decision-making boards within the central government tended to "de-politicize" much of the debate and to blunt the edges of the ideological conflict.[20]

Not everybody, of course, was equally happy with this drift toward the political center: there were highly articulate, and sometimes very influential dissidents both on the right and on the left.

The remarkably dynamic *Libertas* movement[21] mobilized widespread support in the business community for a radically antisocialist program and sought to infiltrate both the Conservative and the Agrarian party organizations in an effort to create a strong front against the Labor government. The nonsocialist parties fought off these attempts, however, and retained their welfare-state platforms: ironically, when in 1963 the broad opposition front did what Libertas had fought for, and defeated the government, it did not present a strong antisocialist counterprogram but a remarkably balanced plan for a continuation of agreed-upon policies at the center of the political spectrum.

The dissidents on the left flank of the Labor Party had much more success. A vigorous neutralist movement had been active within and on the fringes of the party ever since the decision to join NATO in 1949. For a number of years the Labor leaders nevertheless felt sure that these dissidents would continue to vote for the party or at worst simply abstain; the system did not give them any real alternative. This was true as long as the movement remained small. Even though the change-over in 1953 from the d'Hondt to the Sainte-Laguë procedure had lowered the threshold for the first seat in all the multimember constituencies, it still required a sizable number of core members and an extensive organization to launch a new party. The neutralist movement grew during the late 'fifties, however, and in 1961 a group of dissidents in Oslo took the decisive step of launching a party of their own, the Socialist People's Party. The party was able to present lists in only 6 of the 20 constituencies; against the predictions of all experts it succeeded in crossing the threshold in two of them. What was even more astounding was that these two members were to become the arbiters in an unprecedented deadlock between the government and the "established opposition": the additional crack in the old

Ulf Torgersen, "The Trend Towards Political Consensus: the Case of Norway," in S. Rokkan, ed., *Approaches to the Study of Political Participation* (Bergen, Michelsen Institute, 1962), pp. 159–72.

20. For accounts of these developments see J. Moren, *Organisasjonene og forvaltningen* (Bergen, Norges Handelshøyskole, 1958), and Per Stavang, *Parlamentarisme og maktbalanse* (Olso, Universitetsforlaget, 1964), Ch. 10.

21. The tactics of this movement have been analyzed in a comparative perspective by Arnold Heidenheimer, whose book on patterns of political finance in Germany, Japan, and Norway will be published in 1965–66.

bloc of the "underprivileged" had made rule by the routine procedures of parliamentary decision-making an impossibility, and the system was faced with its first serious crisis since the early 'thirties. The leaders of the Labor Party, after a long period of complacency, were face to face with a basic dilemma of electoral strategy: they could not continue to broaden the appeals of the party without risking losses on the left and they could not satisfy their clients on the left without risking defeat in the battle for the middle ranges of the electorate.

The government–opposition game in Norway might up to a point be analyzed in terms of the Downs model of two-party competition: [22] the votes at the center of the political spectrum decide the struggle for power, and each of the contestant blocs tends to focus its appeals on the uncommitted citizens halfway between the poles of the system. But this holds only up to a point: the low-threshold proportional representation system opens up possibilities of splinters at the extremes, and the leaders of the dominant parties have to temper their eagerness for indiscriminate, catch-all electioneering with concern for dissidence and defection among the militants and idéologues in each bloc. The Downs model assumes that the voters at the tails of the frequency distribution of policy positions have no real alternatives: however centrist the party strategy, the cost of dissidence would be greater than any conceivable payoff. In a PR system this may not hold: the lower the threshold of representation, the greater the likelihood of splinter movements.

The crucial electoral battles since 1945 have not been fought at the extremes, however, but over the middle ranges of the system. The Downs model would not take us far in the analysis of the strategies and counter-strategies of these battles. We have seen how the Norwegian party system was generated by a succession of crosscutting cleavages and how the earlier divisions persisted through lags in the processes of change from locality to locality. To fit all these dimensions of conflict into one model would be very difficult and probably not very illuminating. At the level of functional-economic conflict the simplest model would have to posit three poles of electoral attraction: the unions, the farmer organizations, and the business community. Figure 3.3 spells this out in further detail. The decisive electoral struggles have taken place at the halfway ranges between these three poles:

at the *L-F* front the fight has been for the votes of the declining population of subsistence farmers, smallholders, and fishermen in the peripheries of the nation;

at the *L-B* front it has been for the votes of the rising new middle class of salaried employees in the private and public bureaucracies;

22. Anthony Downs, *An Economic Theory of Democracy* (New York, Harper, 1957).

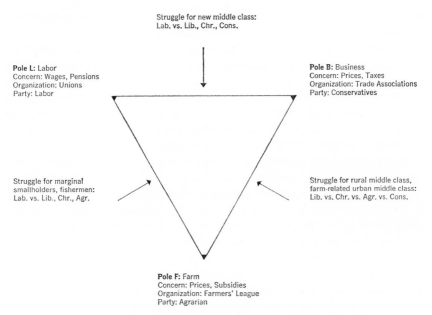

Struggle for new middle class:
Lab. vs. Lib., Chr., Cons.

Pole L: Labor
Concern: Wages, Pensions
Organization: Unions
Party: Labor

Pole B: Business
Concern: Prices, Taxes
Organization: Trade Associations
Party: Conservatives

Struggle for marginal
smallholders, fishermen:
Lab. vs. Lib., Chr., Agr.

Struggle for rural middle class,
farm-related urban middle class:
Lib. vs. Chr. vs. Agr. vs. Cons.

Pole F: Farm
Concern: Prices, Subsidies
Organization: Farmers' League
Party: Agrarian

*Figure 3.3. A Model of the Electoral "Fronts" in Norway:
The Functional-Economic Dimension*

and at the *F-B* front it has been for the votes of the owners, the managers, the organizers, and the professionals at the intersections between the primary and the secondary-tertiary economies.

The fights at the *L-F* and the *L-B* fronts have decided the balance between the government and the "established" opposition. The fight at the *F-B* front has essentially concerned the balance among the four opposition parties: it has been of minor importance both numerically and strategically. To the governing Labor Party the fights on the *L-F* and the *L-B* fronts have been of equal importance strategically but the numerical stakes have been rapidly changing.

The party rose to power through an alliance between the rural proletariat and the industrial working class. The continuing exodus from the rural peripheries and the primary economy has reduced the numerical weight of the smallholder-fisherman wing of the party but in a tight majority-minority situation the votes from this wing will still remain of strategic importance for years to come. Survey data for 1957 indicate that the Labor Party derives some 20 per cent of its votes from the primary economy: 12 per cent from farmers, smallholders, and fishermen and 8 per cent from agricultural and forestry workers.[23] Any move likely to alienate this clientele could have disastrous consequences for the balance

23. Calculated from Table 2.7 in S. Rokkan and H. Valen, "Regional Contrasts."

of power in the Storting. The result has been a series of complex compromises in the primary sector of the economy. The unions have been concerned to keep the prices of primary products down to protect the standard of living of the industrial and urban working class and have favored measures to increase the efficiency of farming and fishing through the establishment of larger units of production and the adoption of capital-intensive techniques. Electoral pressures have made it very difficult for the Labor leaders to go far in this direction, however; the farmers and the fishermen have strong and articulate lobbies, and the representatives from the peripheral provinces have again and again proved their power against the urban and industrial leadership.

With continuing economic growth, however, this wing of the party is bound to decline in electoral weight; about 26 per cent of all households were still in the primary economy in 1950 but by the 'seventies this proportion, it is estimated, will be down to only half that figure.[24] The crucial battles for parliamentary control will increasingly be fought over the votes of the new middle class of salaried employees, technicians, and administrative personnel. This broad stratum between the industrial working class and the old middle class has been gaining steadily in numerical weight since the beginning of the century and will soon number one-third of all the households in the nation.[25] No single political party has been

24. A classification of the active population in three sectors shows these trends since 1875:

	Total active (in '000s)	Per cent in		
		Primary sector (agric., forestry, fish.)	Secondary sector (mining, industry, construction)	Tertiary sector (services)
1875	736	52	18	30
1900	887	42	26	32
1930	1163	36	26	38
1950	1388	26	36	38
1960	1409	20	36	44

Sources: *Population Census 1950*, Vol. 4 (Oslo, N.O.S. XI 323, 1959), Table 12, p. 31, and *Statistisk ukehefte* 3(40) October 1962.
The remaining population in the primary sector is much older than the national average. This suggests a rapid decline in its share of the total during the 'seventies.

25. A classification of the active population by occupational status from 1875 to 1950 gives these trends (figures are percentages):

	Independents		Salaried	Workers	No information
	Primary	Other			
1875	28	10	5	52	5
1900	23.5	10	8	55.5	3
1920	19	8.5	13.5	48.5	0.5
1950	15.5	9.5	19.5	54.5	0.5
1960	19.4		24.9	55.7	—

Source: *Bidrag til en sosiologisk beskrivelse av norsk næringsliv* (Oslo, Institute of

able to stake any exclusive claim to this stratum. The new middle class
emerged as a political force after the parties had organized themselves
around their core groups of supporters and was too split, both in terms
of its socioeconomic origins and its political loyalties, to produce a distinctive nucleus of electoral action all its own. An expanding middle
ground was left open in the system and offered great opportunities for
mass electioneering. The new stratum became a major target of party
propaganda, and the efforts to attract scarce additional votes brought
about a convergence of policy lines and a softening of ideological oppositions.[26]

The new middle class divided its votes among Labor, the Liberals, the
Christians, and the Conservatives (see the detailed distributions in Table
3.1) but at the same time exerted a unifying influence on the system. Two
claims tended to unite the new middle class: the demand for explicit
recognition of training and experience in a system of differentiated
economic rewards, and the concern for long-term security through the
provision of collective and compulsory pension schemes. The one claim
went counter of the egalitarian ideology of the labor movement and the
policy of severely progressive taxation pursued by the government. The
other claim implied opposition to the ideology of individual self-reliance
and the belief in a beneficent free enterprise economy so strongly entrenched among the Conservatives. To meet these claims the Socialists
had to move closer to the recognition of a hierarchical structure of rewards and the Conservatives closer to the acceptance of the principles of
collective solidarity underlying the welfare society.

The result was a softening of class appeals and a greater emphasis on
the role of the state as an arbiter between economic interests: in fact a
convergence toward the position of the old Left. In the nineteenth century
the opposition to the regime had recruited a high proportion of its local
leaders in the salaried middle class: sheriffs, teachers, newspapermen.
Once in power the Left had placed increasing numbers of its loyal supporters in public employment, and through a natural process of entrenchment it became a defender of the apparatus of national government

---

Sociology, 1961), Tab. A 2.100.5, and, for 1960, E. Fivelsdal, *Funksjonærenes syn på
faglige og politiske spørsmål* (Olso, Universitetsforlaget, 1964), Tab. 1.1.

Exactly comparable figures for the 1960 census are not yet available. Interestingly
enough, the great number of intermediary positions between "workers" and "salaried"
forced the Central Bureau of Statistics to abandon this overall distinction in its 1960
census tabulations; see *Population Census 1960*, Vol. 3 (Oslo, N.O.S. XII 129, 1964),
p. 9. An extrapolation from social security data gives roughly these proportions by
1970: under 20 per cent independents, over 30 per cent salaried, and 50 per cent wage
earners (calculations by K. G. Åbyholm, Norwegian School of Economics and Business Administration, 1959).

26. For a detailed development of this point see S. Rokkan, "Geography, Religion,
and Social Class," sect. V.

Table 3.1. Party Choices Within Major Occupational Groups (survey data for 1957)

		Intended vote (percentage of N)				
	N	Socialist (CP/ Lab.)	"Left" (Lib./ Chr.)	Agr.	Cons. (incl. joint lists)	Unclear, nonvoter
Primary economy						
All	407	21	15	22	7	25
farmers	171	14	19	38	9	20
smallholders, fishermen	138	35	15	12	7	31
workers	98	57	9	6	3	25
Secondary and tertiary economy						
Wage earners	644	61	7	1	7	23
manufacturing	285	65	7	1	4	23
others	359	58	8	1	10	23
Self-employed	53	21	13	2	24	40
Salaried	319	28	19	2	28	23
public	130	30	27	2	22	19
private	189	26	13	2	33	26
Employers	92	10	12	0	46	32

Note: Dependent respondents have been classified by the occupation of the head of the household (current or, if retired, past occupation).

against the private interests of the unions no less than of the capitalists. The rise of the Labor Party did not change this overnight. The offshoots of the old Left, the Liberals and the Christians, still retain much of their hold on the salaried employees and officials of the public sector, most markedly so in the South and the West but also in the more polarized regions of the country. Table 3.1 shows a remarkably even division of allegiances within the public sector: the Conservatives, the heirs of the old defenders of the regime of the officials, can count on some 22 per cent of these votes, the offshoots of the old Left on 29 per cent, and the Labor Party on 30 per cent. A breakdown by region tells us a great deal about the conditions for the politicization of public bureaucracies: in the South and the West, the strongholds of the Middle parties, the Labor Party still gets as little as 5 per cent of the votes in this sector while in the rest of the country it reaches 40 per cent. The dominance of the old Left in public employment is especially marked in the least industrialized communes of the South and the West; in these areas the strong traditions of territorial and cultural defense have given particularly important leadership positions to such public employees and officials as teachers and clergymen and have served to contain the spread of polarized class politics from the cities and the centers of industry. Table 3.2 shows this clearly: in the cities and towns the South and West differ very little from the other regions in the level of class polarization, while in the typical

Table 3.2. The Distinctiveness of the South and West: Differences in the Politics of Major Occupational Groups in Communes at Different Levels of Industrialization Within Two Contrasting Divisions of the Country (1957)

Occupation	Community	Region	N	Intended vote (percentage of N)			Un-clear, non-voter
				Soc.	Middle	Cons.	
Worker	City, town	South, West	77	61	8	9	22
		Rest	230	63	7	9	21
	Industri-alized	SW	31	45	30	3	22
		Rest	161	65	6	5	24
	Other rural	SW	70	35	24	4	39
		Rest	173	64	10	4	22
Farmer, small-holder, fisherman	Industri-alized	SW	25	4	68	8	20
		Rest	40	32.5	30	2.5	35
	Other rural	SW	86	10	58	6	26
		Rest	228	32	35	11	22
Middle class	City, town, industri-alized	SW	84	13	25	29	33
		Rest	228	26	11	39	24
	Other rural	SW	77	16	72	18	25
		Rest	108	29	18	25	28

primary-economy communes the contrast is most marked indeed. The Labor Party has throughout its history remained an almost exclusively industrial movement in the South and the West: it found only minimal support in the primary economy (the *L-F* front in Figure 3.3) and it has been much weaker than elsewhere on the expanding front of the salaried middle class (the *L-B* front).

In the rest of the country, however, the Labor Party was not only successful on the rural front but also—and this has become increasingly important—in the battle for the votes of the new middle class. Several factors were at work in this process of "bourgeoisification." First of all,

there was the increasingly frequent upward mobility from the rural proletariat and the industrial and urban working class: many of the sons and
daughters who moved into the new stratum from below had been
brought up in the politics of Labor, and at least half remained loyal to the
family party even after the change from the parental milieu.[27] In many
cases there was indeed very little cross-pressure between the old working-
class and the new middle-class environment. This was especially the case
when the son or daughter had entered a salaried position in the public
sector or was a member of the Labor-oriented trade union movement,
the Norwegian Federation of Labor (Landsorganisasjon, LO). To a large
extent the growth of the middle-class wing of the party was in fact a
direct consequence of Labor's rise to power; not only had the party placed
an increasing number of workers' sons and daughters in municipal and
central government employment at the salaried and professional levels
but the very growth of the public sector since the 1930s had created a
number of new openings for such upward mobility. The LO kept a close
watch on this process of change and succeeded in unionizing remarkably
large proportions of the public employees and the civil servants.[28] The
LO was in fact able to cut across traditional class lines, and this opened
up important possibilities for a broadening of the appeal of the Labor
Party. In Sweden the new middle class had achieved a much higher level
of organizational unity and built up strong, distinctive unions for the
defense of its interests. In Norway the new middle class is much more
split—perhaps one-third is affiliated with the working-class movement
within the LO, around one-third has joined independent bargaining organizations without any overall federative ties, and the rest, mainly employees in the smaller units of family businesses, remain unorganized.[29]

27. For further details see S. Rokkan, "Geography, Religion, and Social Class,"
Tables 5.3 and 5.4, and H. Valen and D. Katz, *Political Parties in Norway* (Oslo,
Universitetsforlaget, 1964), Table 6.23.

28. Egil Fivelsdal, *Funksjonærenes syn*, Tab. 3.2, reports these results of a nationwide survey carried out in 1961–62:

Percentage of salaried employees (excl. professions) in service of

	National government		Municipalities		Cooperatives		Private firms	
	Men	Women	Men	Women	Men	Women	Men	Women
Member of								
LO union	70	31	71	27	75	(76)	21	17
Member of								
other union	15	28	9	29	9		17	8
Not unionized	15	41	20	44	16	(24)	62	75
Total	100	100	100	100	100	100	100	100
N =	344	85	196	48	44	17	469	208

Parentheses indicate too few cases for safe computation.

29. The membership figures published by the unions and the professional associations do not allow uniform breakdowns in conformity with the distinctions between

The result has been a steady strengthening of the middle-class wing of the Labor Party. Table 3.3 represents an attempt to gauge the generational changes in the party's clientele since the introduction of manhood suffrage.[30] In the early phase of growth the party was essentially a coalition of workers, smallholders, and fishermen without any appeal to the middle-class voters, whether of the new or the old stratum. The decisive change came in the 'thirties with the rise of the party to a position of political dominance; in this generation the party not only retained its important smallholder-fisherman wing but also developed a strong middle-class wing in the cities and the urbanized countryside. In the 'fifties the continuing processes of urbanization, industrialization, and bureaucratization brought about further changes in the structure of the party clientele: there is now very little recruitment in the primary economy but a steady influx of voters from the new middle class.

---

wage earners and salaried in the official occupational statistics. Rough estimates for 1959 give 30 per cent LO, 30 per cent other unions and professional associations, 40 per cent unorganized. Nationwide surveys have not produced exactly comparable results either:

Percentage of salaried employees

	LO	Other	Not organized
(a) NGI survey, 1954	29	20	51
(b) Election survey, 1957	24	27	49
(c) Fivelsdal survey, 1961	42	16	42
(excludes higher civil servants, teachers, academically trained employees but includes fixed-contract manual workers in the public services)			

Sources: (a) Norsk Gallup Institutt, *Funksjonærenes og tjenestemennenes organisasjonsforhold* (Oslo, Funksjonærsambandet, 1954); (b) unpublished data from the nationwide election survey carried out in 1957; (c) Fivelsdal, *Funksjonærenes syn.*

Fivelsdal's Table 3.4 shows a very clear relationship between the size of work organization (firm, department) and unionization:

Percentage of employees organized

	In units of less than 5	In units of more than 150
Men		
Governmental	75	88
Municipal	56	100
Private	14	59
Women		
Public	41	65
Private	14	33

30. This analysis has been developed in further detail in S. Rokkan, "Geography, Religion, and Social Class," sect. V.

Table 3.3. Changes in the Occupational Composition of the Socialist Vote,
1890s–1950s (estimates based on survey data for 1957)

	N	Manual workers	Farmers, small-holders	Salaried em-ployees	Inde-pendent, self-employed
			(percentage of N)		
1890s–1920s					
Resp. born before 1907: occupational distribution for fathers voting Socialist	*119*	76	13	3	8
1910s–1930s					
Resp. born 1907–27: occupational distribution for fathers voting Socialist	*267*	74	15	6	5
1930s–1940s					
Resp. born 1907–27: occupational distribution for respondents voting Socialist at their first election	*372*	65	13	15	5
1950s					
Resp. born after 1927: occupational distribution for those who said they had voted or would vote Socialist	*128*	72	5	20	3

This change in the structure of the clientele might have had very little influence on the policies pursued by the party if it had been in a clear majority position. In a tight situation at the 50 per cent mark, however, every vote counts and the party was forced to pay more for the uncertain votes at the margin than for the safe votes within its core groups of traditional support. The equalitarian policies of economic austerity came under heavy pressure after 1949 and the government gave up its attempt to control in detail the wage and salary settlements between the unions and the employers' associations.[31] The stringent policies of investment controls were gradually relaxed, and there were even some adjustments in

31. Wages were settled through a system of compulsory arbitration up to 1952. For an account of problems of union–government relations during this period see W. Galenson, *Labor in Norway* (Cambridge, Mass., Harvard University Press, 1949), Chs. 12–13. For further developments see M. W. Leiserson, *Wages and Economic Control in Norway 1945–1957* (Cambridge, Mass., Harvard University Press, 1959), Chs. 4, 5, and 10. For partisan analyses see A. Berglöff, *Trenger vi en funksjonær-bevegelse?* (Oslo, FSO, 1952), and "6 års historie," *FSO-nytt* (June 1958), pp. 4–6, and Aake Anker-Ording, *Funksjonæren i går, i dag og i morgen* (Oslo, Funksjonærs-ambandet, 1962).

the steeply progressive taxation schedules.[32] Taxation proved a vexing area of policy pressures: the rural and the industrial wings of the party were concerned to maintain the high tax levels for the middle- and upper-income brackets while the salaried and professionals within the party pressed forward their claims for increased rewards for their training, skills, and responsibilities. With continuing inflation a number of better-off industrial workers came within the reach of progressive taxation, and adjustments were reluctantly made, but taxation still remained a core issue within the party.

Survey analyses of voter positions on crucial issues between the parties may help us to pinpoint this process of change. Unfortunately we do not have at hand any time series data for stands on policy issues, but an analysis of responses from a nationwide survey carried out in 1957 may at least help us to map the major dimensions of conflict and consensus within the system. Table 3.4 gives estimates of the range of differences in positions between the supporters of the governing Labor party and the voters for the four "established" opposition parties. To guard against overinterpretation each party clientele has been divided into an "active" group of members and campaign participants and a "passive" group of citizens who reported no political activity beyond voting. The results tell us a great deal not only about the divisions within the Labor Party but also about the conditions for a coalition of the opposition parties.

On all the issues of income distribution and government-enterprise conflict we find a distinct polarization between Labor and the Conservatives. Whatever the level of Labor discontent with the government, the Conservatives tend to unite in outright opposition against its equalitarian and *dirigiste* policies. There is one significant exception, however: only 50 per cent of the Conservative "actives" and 37 per cent of the "only-voters" find fault with the rigidity of the tax controls for independents reporting their own incomes. On this score the Agrarians take the clearest stand against the government: almost without exception they are self-employed or employers and consequently oppose measures designed to ensure detailed controls of income statements. The Conservative Party also speaks for a clientele of independents but in addition counts a large wing of

32. Detailed comparisons between rates of income tax progression for a number of countries are given in *Innstilling om progresjonen og andre spørsmal i forbindelse med statsskatten* (Olso, Finans- og tolldept., 1964), Tab. III, 1–4. The following extract illustrates the extreme equalitarianism of the Norwegian system of taxation:

Marginal taxation for family with two children
(percentages of added income of Nkr. 1000)

Income level in Nkr.	Denmark	France	Netherlands	Norway	Great Britain	Sweden
20,000	25.8	12.0	21.9	27.3	23.3	26.4
50,000	47.3	20.0	47.5	66.3	30.1	47.6
100,000	50.4	30.0	59.2	77.3	34.4	56.0

Table 3.4. Differences in Policy Positions Among the Voters for the Five Major Parties: "Active" vs. "Only-Voters" (survey data for 1957)

Policy area Direction of statement	Ranking of parties from lowest to highest per cent opposed to government policy									
	Actives					Only-voters				
	Least opposed to govt. policy				Most opposed to govt. policy	Least opposed to govt. policy				Most opposed to govt. policy
Taxation	Lab.	Lib.	Chr.	Agr.	Cons.	Lab.	Lib.	Chr.	Agr.	Cons.
Taxes too high	58	67	77	78	93	66	80	82	90	91
Too much control of income reports (independents)	Lab. 4	Lib. 17	Chr. 24	Cons. 50	Agr. 60	Lab. 4	Chr. 18	Lib. 23	Cons. 37	Agr. 46
Control of economy										
Too much restriction of house building	Lab. 23	Chr. 37	Agr. 50	Lib. 67	Cons. 78	Lab. 29	Agr. 48	Chr. 51	Lib. 67	Cons. 67
Too much interference with enterprise	Lab. 5	Chr. 57	Lib. 67	Agr. 78	Cons. 83	Lab. 12	Agr. 38	Chr. 44	Lib. 60	Cons. 69
Too little to encourage private saving	Lab. 18	Chr. 70	Lib. 70	Agr. 78	Cons. 89	Lab. 29	Agr. 60	Chr. 65	Lib. 76	Cons. 79
Too little done to stop inflation	Lab. 12	Chr. 43	Lib. 55	Agr. 66	Cons. 80	Lab. 15	Chr. 44	Agr. 50	Lib. 56	Cons. 62
Protection of primary economy										
Too little support for agriculture	Cons. 7	Lab. 9	Chr. 23	Lib. 33	Agr. 63	Lab. 11	Cons. 12	Chr. 17	Lib. 19	Agr. 62
Religion										
Too little done to strengthen Christian faith and morals	Lab. 18	Lib. 44	Cons. 56	Agr. 59	Chr. 97	Lab. 26	Cons. 42	Lib. 44	Agr. 65	Chr. 90
Defense										
Military budget too high	Cons. 33	Chr. 50	Agr. 53	Lab. 66	Lib. 72	Cons. 49	Agr. 63	Lab. 63	Chr. 71	Lib. 71
N	Lab. 164	Lib. 18	Chr. 30	Agr. 32	Cons. 54	Lab. 407	Lib. 75	Chr. 68	Agr. 52	Cons. 120

readily taxable salaried employees, and these tend to resent the income deductions of the self-employed and the employers just as much as the middle-class Labor voters.

To put it very schematically, Labor and the Conservatives will be at opposite poles on issues within the advanced corporate economy of the cities but will tend to take their stand on the same side in the territorial-cultural conflicts within the system. They take very similar positions on the level of support for the primary economy, and they do not differ much in their reactions to the religious activism of the Christian People's Party. These are the basic issues of conflict within the "established" opposition: the Agrarians defend the rural economy against the industrial and commercial interests in the cities and will therefore often conflict with the Conservatives; the Christians fight the tolerant secularism and tepid Lutheranism nourished in the urban bourgeoisie and will therefore often find it difficult, if not impossible, to cooperate with the Conservatives. The third of the Middle parties, the core group of Liberals still sticking to the old Left standard, is much more difficult to place in the political landscape of the 'fifties. The party is split in several wings, but the average positions registered through the analysis of survey data place its voters in the middle range on almost all issues. The one exception is defense: on this issue the Liberals rank first in the proportion expressing outright opposition to the policies of the government. But this is not a very distinctive reaction. There was widespread rank-and-file resentment against the heavy burden of the defense budget in all parties, and on this score the governing Labor Party had as much of a problem controlling its clientele as any of the other parties.

If we compare the stands taken by Labor voters toward the policies of their government we find remarkably low levels of disaffection on all issues but two: taxation and defense. These two exceptions tell us a great deal about the problems of electoral strategy facing the party. Labor leaders have not only had to cope with increasing pressures for a recognition of income differentials and hierarchies of economic status but have also found themselves in a great quandary over their commitment to pursue the foreign and the military policies agreed on with the "established" opposition parties in 1949. Their concern to attract the middle class softened their ideological stands and brought them closer to the "bourgeois" opposition, but this very détente, and especially the cross-party agreements on a common policy of defense within the Western alliance, triggered off articulate splinter movements and endangered the majority position of the party. The events of 1963 forced an agonizing reappraisal of this dilemma: how could the party crush the left splinter and still retain its appeal to the rising middle class?

The Swedish Social Democrats had pointed to a possible solution. They had seen the dangers of a "soft" strategy in the mid-'fifties and found a powerful alternative: instead of continuing a policy of general détente they were gradually driven to accentuate a new line of potential conflict in the system and made a major effort to polarize the electorate over this conflict. They came to the conclusion that it was time to break down the old status division between manual wage earners and salaried employees and to try instead to establish a joint platform for the defense of the employed against the employers and the economically independent. Their strategy was to focus on issues that united the workers and the new middle class against the employers and the owners. They found a perfect answer in the proposal for publicly administered retirement pensions based on average earnings during the peak period of the work career. This plan met a widely felt need for improvements in old age benefits and at the same time recognized the principle of a hierarchy of rewards reflecting differences in training, skills, and responsibilities. The issue was fought out in a national referendum in 1957 and later in the Riksdag, and there is a great deal of evidence that this strategy actually paid off. The Social Democrats strengthened their overall position and broadened their appeal to the new middle class.[33]

The Norwegian Labor Party took much longer to make up its mind. There was no urgent need for a change in strategy before 1961, and the Common Market issue delayed the effect of the elective defeat of the government that year. The decisive change came in September 1963: in its radical counterprogram the Labor Party not only proposed a system of state-administered service pensions along Swedish lines but at the same time put forward a comprehensive plan for investments in the backward peripheries of the nation from the huge capital fund to be established through employer and employee contributions toward the pensions. Whether economically defensible or not, this program revealed a deliberate strategy of electioneering: its ambitious aim was to secure the party's position on all its difficult fronts in one move. The pension plan was designed to strengthen the appeal to the new middle class (the *L-B* front in Figure 3.3); the investment plan was designed to secure the rural wing of the party (the *L-F* front); and the whole program was designed to strengthen the role of the state in the national economy, and might therefore help mend the fences to the left of the party.

To many observers this program indeed appeared to be a master stroke of electoral strategy. In the first round, the strategy clearly paid off: in moving leftward the Labor Party clearly kept the dissidents at bay without seeming to lose any of its middle-class appeal. Whether the gains registered at the local elections in 1963 heralded an upward swing for

33. Details of the policy discussions and strategic considerations behind these developments will be found in the forthcoming dissertation by Björn Molin at the University of Gothenburg. A lively, but obviously subjective account of the pensions issue is given in Herbert Tingsten's autobiography *Mitt Liv*. (Stockholm, Norstedts, 1964), 4, 221–59. For survey statistics on the resultant changes in electorial alignments see Bo Särlvik, "The Role of Party Identification in Voters' Perception of Political Issues: a Study of Opinion Formation in Swedish Politics 1956–1960," paper, Fifth World Congress of the International Political Science Association, Paris, 1961.

Labor or simply reflected a short-term success in the mobilization of marginal voters it is still difficult to say: the opposition parties, possibly guided by the Swedish experience, have not offered outright battle over the pension issue, and Labor leaders seem unlikely to be able to polarize the electorate over this issue as their Swedish counterparts did. What is certain is that the new situation will force continued reappraisals of party strategy and prompt a variety of efforts to break the deadlock between government and opposition.

Numerical Democracy and Corporate Pluralism: Votes Count but Resources Decide

By 1965 the four parties of the "established" bloc will have been in opposition for 30 years. They had a brief spell in office in the summer of 1963, but that was poor consolation for so many years in the wilderness. Such protracted opposition raises a series of problems in a political system: How can citizens opposed to the government keep up their partisan enthusiasm when their votes seem to make so little difference? How can the parties recruit dynamic leaders when the chance of ever gaining office appears so remote? How can the interests and values seen to be threatened by the government be defended when the opposition parties are continuously outnumbered in the fight for electoral votes?

These questions have not yet been subjected to detailed research in Norway. Survey data for 1957 give evidence of widespread defeatism among the voters for the opposition parties: When asked whether they thought Labor would lose its majority in the election that year only 10 per cent of the Middle parties and 20 per cent of the Conservatives saw any such likelihood. Only a minority of the voters for the opposition in fact seemed motivated by a desire for a change in the government. When asked whether they would vote for the nearest party if the chances of their own proved very small, only about one-third of the voters in the middle and about half of the Conservatives declared themselves willing to pool forces. To large masses of citizens in the "established" bloc, elections clearly were not occasions for choosing between alternative governments but simply opportunities for registering loyalties to particular parties—elections were held to decide on territorial representation in the legislature, not to make a choice between competing teams of potential governors. The only opposition party seriously concerned to establish a basis for an alternative government was the Conservative Party: it took the lead in the campaign for a united opposition front and showed great willingness to join in electoral alliances against Labor. Even in this party, however, the drive for government office was rarely a dominant motive among party workers and candidates. It is perhaps significant that when the Labor government, after its return to power in September 1963, offered high positions in the civil service to two Conservative leaders they did not hesitate to accept: they knew that this might take them out of politics, but they preferred the certainty of appointive position to the uncertain prospect of ministerial power.

There has been much talk, particularly among the right-wing activists, about the possibility of setting up a "shadow cabinet" of representatives of the four parties of the nonsocialist opposition, but this has not come to anything: the middle parties have been wary of any such commitment and have been anxious to keep doors open to other alternatives. One wing of the Liberal party has indicated potential willingness to join in a coalition with Labor if the government should not regain its majority. This has caused a great deal of worry and resentment within the other parties of the opposition and has made the prospects for a clear-cut solution of the parliamentary situation very dim indeed.

How can rights be defended and interests protected in such a halfway system? Clearly if voters in the "established" bloc really felt oppressed by the Labor regime they would forget their traditional differences and rally to the defense of their cause in a broad antisocialist front. But so far there have been few signs of such a development. The explanation is very simple: the opposition may have been losing in the fight for votes but the interests it represents and the causes it stands for can still be defended through other channels of influence on government decision-making. Votes count in the choice of governing personnel but other resources decide the actual policies pursued by the authorities.

The extension of the franchise to all adults and the maintenance of a strict majoritarian rule of decision-making in the legislature made it possible for a movement of the hitherto underprivileged to rise to power. But the parallel growth of a vast network of interest organizations and other corporate bodies made it impossible to rule by any simple "50 per cent plus" principle. To understand the strategies and counterstrategies of government and opposition we have to analyze the bargaining processes between the giant alliances of such associations and corporations. The vote potential constitutes only one among many different power resources brought to bear in these bargaining processes: what really counts is the capacity to hurt or to halt a system of highly interdependent activities. In the triangular conflict between labor, the farm interest, and business no single group dares to rely exclusively on its electoral machinery. The efforts on the electoral front are paralleled at the level of organizational action and at the level of the mass media. The workers and employees rely on their capacity to call strikes and to paralyze recalcitrant industries and service sectors. The farmers and fishermen have given top priority to the establishment of an efficient machinery for the control of production and marketing: one obvious purpose has been to increase their ability to withhold needed primary goods from the consumers and to force decisions on prices and subsidies. The managers, owners, and financial interests rely on their power to call off investment plans, to withhold skills, and to channel their initiatives to areas beyond the control of the unions and the national government. We have seen how these groups of organizations constitute the major poles in the system of electoral alignments and how the fates of the parties tend to be decided at the fronts between these poles (Figure 3.3). But none of the groups can rely exclusively on the verdict of one citizen, one vote contests. Even if they lose out in the competition for votes and seats they can still bring their organizational resources to bear on the actual policy decisions of the government. They need not actually use the weapons at their disposal, but the very fact that they can claim a measure of control over central factors in the national economy acts as a deterrent in the bargaining process. The crucial decisions on economic policy are rarely taken in the parties or in Parliament: the central area is the bargaining table where the government authorities meet directly with the trade union leaders, the representatives of the farmers, the smallholders, and the fishermen, and the delegates of the Employers' Association. These yearly rounds of negotiations have in fact come to mean more in the lives of rank-and-file citizens than the formal elections. In these processes of intensive interaction, the parliamentary notions of one member, one vote and majority rule make little sense. Decisions are not made through the counting of heads but through complex considerations of short-term or long-term advantages in alternative lines of compromise.

This two-tier system of decision-making places the Cabinet in an intricate position: it stands at the top of the electoral hierarchy but it is only one of four corporate units at the bargaining table. The Labor leaders *could* of course decide to throw all their weight behind the claims of the trade unions, but this could hurt them electorally—they need votes beyond the households of the unions to stay in power. Despite the close organizational ties between the unions and the party, the Labor Cabinet has consequently been anxious to divorce itself from the triangular conflict in the national economy. The responsible ministers have of course not tried to conceal their sympathies with the wage earners and the employees, but they have had to balance these interests against their stake in the electoral resources in the primary economy and their concern as employers of a major sector of the nation's labor force. The Cabinet has increasingly had to take on the role of mediator between the conflicting interests in the national community. At least in matters of internal policy it can rarely if ever force through decisions solely on the basis of its electoral power but has to temper its policies in complex consultations and bargains with the major interest organizations. To guard against diffi-

culties and reversals in these processes of bargaining the government has
over the years built up a large network of consultative boards and councils
for the representation of all the relevant interests.[34] This has worked very
well at the lower level of sectoral interest representation, but an attempt
to establish a Board of Economic Coordination on the lines of the Dutch
Sociaal-Economische Raad (SER) failed miserably in the early 'fifties:
the partners felt that such a formal body made them hostages of the
government and committed them to policies they could not defend within
their constituent organizations.[35] The bargaining at the top still takes
place in a constitutional vacuum. There is an efficient government machinery of mediation and there is also the possibility of instituting compulsory arbitration in cases of deadlock and of threatened strikes or
lockouts, but no serious attempt has as yet been made to establish anything approaching a corporative framework for decisions on the distribution of incomes between the three principal sectors of the economy.

The Labor Party has clearly lost a great deal of leeway for its policies
through the development of this two-tier system, but perhaps for this
very reason has strengthened its position in the nation. At least in private,
many business leaders will express relief that there is a Labor government
to keep the unions in check: if the Labor Party were to lose power,
strikes might become a major weapon of political struggle. Whether this
argument is realistic or not, it points to an historically important dilemma
of Labor strategy. In the doctrinal controversies of the 'twenties the
revolutionary wing advocated the development of a strong organization
for direct action against the established economic system, while the reformists wanted to mobilize for power through the existing electoral and
parliamentary channels. When the first Labor government was voted out
of office in 1928, there was evidence that the decisive opposition move
had originated not within the parties but in the financial circles concerned
to protect the currency and the position of the banks.[36] The revolutionaries concluded that parliamentary action was futile; the reformists concluded that everything would change once the party had won its majority.
Events proved both wrong: parliamentary action was not futile, but even
when Labor had a clear majority it could not introduce major changes
in the structure of the economy. The labor movement has throughout its
history kept up its two fronts: it has mobilized for industrial action
against employers and for political action against other parties. The
strategies chosen on the two fronts could not always be reconciled: the
very success of the movement on the electoral front restricted its freedom

34. See J. Moren, *Organisasjonene og forvaltningen*.
35. For an analysis of the reasons for the dissolution of the early Board of Coordination and of the arguments for its reestablishment in the form of an Economic
Planning Council see S. Lindebrække, "Samarbeid mellom staten og det private
næringsliv." *Næringsrevyen Norges Handel, 12*(29) (August 1964), 470–74, 479.
36. See Roset, *Det norske Arbeiderparti*, pp. 134–37.

of action on the industrial front. Whether losses on the electoral front would make for increasing industrial unrest is difficult to say: it seems likely that the many years of uneventful bargaining will have set precedents that will be hard to break.

Whatever happens in the electoral and organizational channels of decision-making will again be affected by the balance of influences in the third channel—the mass media. During the crisis in the summer of 1963 the Prime Minister stated in one of his speeches that the press, not the other parties, was the real opposition in Norway. There is a great deal of evidence of the importance of the newspapers in Norwegian politics.[37] The burgeoning press played a crucial part in the early partisan struggles between the Right and the Left. Newspapers speaking for each of the parties were established in practically all the urban localities and in many rural centers. The papers became the principal organs of public debate and established links of close communication between the parties and the articulate citizenry and between the politicians and the local and national authorities. The press acquired a number of community functions beyond the purely political, however, and many newspapers became economic enterprises of great strength and independence. When the Labor Party rose to power it was rarely able to challenge the power of the established Liberal or Conservative press. With the help of the local trade unions it managed to establish some 40 dailies throughout the country, but these have never reached more than about one-quarter of all households. Survey data for 1957 [38] indicate that only about 30 per cent of the Labor voters read the party press exclusively while practically one-third are completely unexposed to Labor newspapers. This means, of course, that loyalty to the Labor Party is more likely to be maintained through primary group channels and in unions and other organizations, but it also means that a sizable proportion of the voters come under regular cross-pressure between their party spokesmen and the newspapers they read. Newspaper reading may not convert them from their basic Labor allegiance, but it does expose them to the arguments of the opposition. It is not possible to trace in any detail the effects of this exposure, but survey data indicate more agreement with government positions among the party-loyal readers than among the party-indifferent. To what extent this openness to opposition pressure finds direct reflection in decisions at the top of the party hierarchy is of course difficult to estimate, but the very lively debates in the newspapers indicate a great deal of awareness of counter-arguments to policies proposed.

The disproportionality between votes and newspaper copies simply

37. See S. Rokkan and P. Torsvik, "Der Wähler, der Leser und die Parteipresse," *Kölner Zs. Soziol.*, *12* (1960), 278–301, and S. Høyer, "Pressens økonomiske og politiske struktur," *Tss. for samfunnsforskning*, 1964 (4), 221–42.

38. Rokkan and Torsvik, "Der Wähler," p. 293.

reflects the lag between the two crucial moves of mobilization: the press flourished after the mobilization of the peasantry and was too firmly entrenched to be affected by the subsequent mobilization of the workers into politics. The development of the electronic mass media—radio and TV—came after the second wave of mobilization and took place under the exclusive sponsorship of the government. The Broadcasting Corporation has tried to adhere to strict rules of neutrality in politics and has adopted very rigid principles of time allocation among the parties. In a multiparty system, however, this means that more time is allocated to the opposition than to the government. Even the provision for double time for Labor—one unit for the government and another for the party—does not change this. There is no proportionality between the voting strength in the electorate and the share in the total mass of political messages sent out. This party-parity rule is not seen as an injustice but again functions to counteract the effects of strict adherence to the majoritarian principle in the choice of government.

Are There Alternatives?

Are there any realistic alternatives to the current deadlock between government and opposition?

Changes might come about through a variety of internal strains and external pressures, but whatever their origins the changes would have to be channeled through one or the other of the two channels of decision-making: the electoral-legislative and the organizational-corporate. Fluctuations in the electoral fates of the parties open up a variety of alternative futures for the regime, but changes in the electoral procedures may increase or decrease the possibility of each alternative. Much of what happens in the electoral-legislative channel will depend, however, on the outcome of decisions within the "second tier" of the system, at the level of corporate bargaining. To map all these possibilities of change is impossible within the present context, but it may help us gain perspective on the conditions of opposition in one Western democracy if, by way of conclusion, we review some of the major alternatives to the current arrangements. Let us look first at the alternative electoral outcomes and their likely consequences for the regime.

1. *Labor returns to the majority position in Parliament.* This would break the current deadlock but face the nonsocialist parties with the bleak prospect of another spell of protracted opposition. There would be increasing bitterness among the frustrated aspirants to power and a real danger of widespread alienation from a system offering so few hopes for the opposition.

2. *Neither Labor nor the nonsocialist bloc gains a majority of the seats and the balance of power is held by left-wing splinters.* This would mean

a continuation of the current deadlock: a repeat of the 2–74–74 situation
in the current Storting or some equivalent situation without a workable
positive majority but with a constant threat of negative majorities against
any government based on one of the competing blocs. Variants of this
situation tend to occur with increasing frequency in Scandinavia: the
Swedish election in September 1964 produced the constellation of 8
Communists, 113 Social Democrats, and 112 nonsocialists, and the Danish
election a week later produced 10 Left Socialists, 76 Social Democrats, 10
Radicals, and 81 outright nonsocialists. Several solutions are possible in
such situations. One may opt for a minority government and keep it afloat
on tactical majorities varying from issue to issue; one may prefer a
minority government based on a longer-term agreement with one supporting party; or there will be a coalition government. In the current
situations in the three countries the Social Democrats have all opted for
the first solution: minority government without direct ties to any other
party. The Swedish Social Democrats used to enter into bargains with
the Agrarians, but this so-called "Red-Green" agreement broke down in
1956. The Danish solution was for a number of years a coalition between
Social Democrats and Radicals, but this did not work after the 1964
election. If future elections in Norway continue to produce deadlocked
situations, the only likely alternatives are two: Labor will decide to stick
to the minority government arrangement or it will strike a bargain with
one of the Middle parties, most likely the Liberals, either for parliamentary
support or for a share in the government. An arrangement or coalition
with the Left Socialists seems very remote and a broader coalition toward
the right is not very likely except in a situation of national emergency.[39]

3. *The nonsocialist bloc gains a majority.* If this were to happen, the
alternative nearest at hand would be a coalition of the four "established"
opposition parties—a continuation of the experiment made in the summer
of 1963. How long such a coalition could be kept together is anyone's
guess. Difficulties over incomes policy might soon make for strains between the Agrarians and the Conservatives and so would any proposal
to enter into European agreements on primary products. A Labor-Liberal
coalition might prove an alternative, but how far the two parties would
be willing to go in agreeing on a joint policy would depend on a number
of factors.

The majority-minority situation in the electorate is very tight, and no
amount of sociological trend analysis could generate reliable predictions
of the outcome. The fate of the last seat hangs on a few hundred votes

39. The possibility of a Norwegian *Proporz*, or all-party government, is discussed
in D. Flem, *Det sveitsiske demokrati* (Oslo, Aschehoug, 1945); L. S. Oftedal, "Stort-
ingsmakt og regjeringsmakt," *Samtiden*, 62 (1953) 169–76; G. Garbo, *Samregjering. Et
parlamentarisk alternativ* (Oslo, Norges Venstrelag, 1960); and P. Stavang, *Parlamentarisme og maktbalanse*, pp. 212–17.

in most of the constituencies and very small movements in the electorate could bring one bloc or the other over the 75-seat mark. In this situation, changes in the electoral law may make for a great deal of difference and have therefore been much discussed. The crux of the situation is this: the nonsocialist parties have an interest in increasing the likelihood of a split in the Labor Party and may therefore propose to lower the 1.4 threshold to 1.3 or 1.2, but this very move will of necessity also make it highly unprofitable for the four opposition parties to merge. The largest of the opposition parties, the Conservatives, has an inherent strategic interest in higher thresholds but seems ready to forego this advantage in order to encourage splinters from Labor. The Swedish proposal [40] to ensure greater parliamentary stability through a provision for moderate overrepresentation of the largest party has been received with little enthusiasm in Norway. Several proposals have been made for the addition of members-at-large for each region, but the stated purpose has in this case been to increase overall proportionality, not to ensure a premium for the near-majority party. The Labor Party has on occasion ventured to suggest a switch to the Anglo-American system of plurality decisions, but this would give it such overwhelming majorities in the first phase and cause such bitter quarrels among the opposition parties that even the party most likely to gain from it in the long run, the Conservatives, have shown no inclination to accept the idea. The Sainte-Laguë procedure fits the party system very well: it favors the one-seat Middle parties in the multimember constituencies and discourages mergers of party lists.[41] Any

40. See Författningsutredningen, *Sveriges statsskick. Del 2. Motiv* (Stockholm, SOU, 1963), *17*, 57–80.

41. An example from the Bergen elections of 1957 and 1961 illustrates this very clearly:

List	Candidate votes	Seat allocation				Votes per seat
	(5 candidates)	Divisors			Total	
1957		1.4	3	5		
Labor	146,871	104,907 = I	48,957=III	29,374=V	3	48,957
Conservative	75,653	54,037 = II	25,217		1	75,653
Liberal	47,658	34,041 = IV			1	47,658
Christian	29,440	21,028			0	
Communist	12,921	9,229			0	
1961						
Labor	154,753	110,537 = I	51,584=III	30,950	2	77,376
Joint Conservative-Christian	97,043	69,316 = II	32,347=V	19,408	2	48,521
Liberal	50,752	36,251 = IV			1	50,752
Communist	12,250					

The joint Conservative-Christian list produced a gain of one seat for the nonsocialist front despite a decrease in the relative voting strength of this bloc. This happened change toward a strengthening of the chances of the larger parties at the poles of the system would disturb the current equilibrium. It would increase the likelihood of a return to clear-cut Labor majorities, and it would threaten the survival of the Middle parties as separate units in many constituencies. The success of the joint "Bourgeois Front" list in one of the Southern Swedish constituencies in 1964 strengthened the arguments for closer electoral cooperation among the four opposition parties, but there is little likelihood that this solution will be uniformly adopted in the near future. Considerations of electoral tactics will force different solutions in different constituencies.

All these speculations concern arrangements within the electoral-parliamentary channel of influence. What happens in this channel, however, will in great measure depend on the tensions, conflicts, and solutions in the other channel, the corporate-organizational. So far there has been no tendency to fuse the two channels. The Finnish attempt to bring union representatives directly into the Cabinet would not make sense in Norway. There has been a great deal of discussion of the possibility of establishing a policy coordination body along the lines of the British National Economic Development Council, but no question of developing a corporate chamber on the lines of the Dutch SER.[42] The protagonists in the triangular conflict over incomes do not want to bind themselves within a common framework and prefer to take their chances in an uncertain bargaining market. The corporatism of the "two-tier" system of decision-making is implicit and latent, not formal and institutionalized. The Constitution recognizes only one type of representation: the territorial. Functional representation is channeled implicitly through the parties and explicitly through boards and councils under the central administration, but there is no instituted procedure of legitimation for such representatives —no constitutional provision for the definition of functional electorates, for rules of nomination, and for procedures of election. Any move toward explicit corporatism would require some such regularization of the government of private organizations and associations and, at least at present, this seems to be too high a price to pay for the uncertain gains in stability and accountability to be achieved through a merger of the two "tiers." The overlap in personnel, the criss-crossing of role relationships, the interdependence of strategies at the two levels all create complex

---

because the below-threshold votes for the Christians could be added to the Conservative surplus. If all three nonsocialist parties had presented one joint list, however, the result would have been a clear-cut loss (147,795 for the joint list vs. 154,753 for Labor): the first seat for the Liberals cost much less than the third seat for a joint list.

42. See J. Moren, *Staten og næringslivet* (Bergen, Chr. Michelsen Institute, 1962); S. Rostoft, *Samarbeidet mellom staten of næringslivet* (Bergen, Norges Handelshøyskole, 1963); and S. Lindebrække, "Samarbeid."

constraints on the actions of the participants, and these may be more effective in integrating the system than any formal framework of institutional arrangements.

The great danger of these complex systems of interdependent decision-making is that representatives get tied into charmed circles of negotiators and administrators and become immune to communications from their rank and file. The loose and informal two-tier system may leave them more exposed to backbench pressure than formal provisions for functional representation in a corporative assembly. Whatever the institutional setting, this is a problem of crucial importance in advanced mass societies. The survival of democratic pluralism may depend as much on provisions for effective channels of opposition and protest within the private associations and the corporate bodies as on the chances for a regular alternation of governments at the top.

Postscript September 1965

This attempt at an analysis of forces and counterforces in Norwegian politics was written under the impact of the deadlocked constellation created in 1963: the first draft was written at the University of Manchester in May 1964, and the final version was completed in October of that year (a few footnotes were added later).

At the time the chapter was written it was expected that the volume would appear shortly before the next contest of forces in Norwegian politics: the election of representatives to the Storting scheduled for September 12–13, 1965. Instead, this analysis is now destined to appear a number of months *after* what turned out to be a major upheaval in the affairs of an otherwise stable and circumspect polity: Labor lost out after thirty years of near-continuous government and the four cooperating parties of what we have termed the "established opposition" were finally confronted with the task of forming a regular majority cabinet. Time and space will not allow any detailed discussion of the background and the implications of this dramatic change in political fortunes but the reader is at least entitled to a quick summary of the new situation.

By American standards the 1965 election could hardly qualify as a "landslide" but with so many lists so close to the thresholds of representation even minor defections from Labor could produce significant changes in the majority-minority balance.

The decline of the Labor Party can be seen in this comparative table for the last general elections:

Party	% of electorate	1961 % of votes cast	Total seats won	% of electorate	1965 % of votes cast	Total seats won
CP	2.3	2.9	0	1.2	1.4	0
SP	1.9	2.4	2	5.1	6.0	2
Labour	36.8	46.8	74	36.7	43.1	68
Liberal	7.0	8.9	14	8.8	10.4	18
Christian	7.6	9.6	15	6.9	8.1	13
Agrarian	7.3	9.3	16	8.4	9.9	18
Conservative	15.7	20.0	29	17.9	21.1	31
Turnout	79.1			85.4		

Comparing 1965 and 1961 we see that the Labor Party retained its share of the *electorate* (36.7 vs. 36.8%) but lost out in the contest for *votes* (down 3.7 points to 43.1%). The net losses flowed leftward as well as rightward: the Socialist People's Party had lists in all the 20 multimember constituencies and nearly tripled its strength while the Liberals, the Agrarians, and the Conservatives all made significant progress. The balance in the system was disturbed but not quite disrupted: the three competing Socialist parties still polled 50.5 per cent of all votes cast and the four cooperating parties of the old opposition had not quite reached the magical 50 per cent point.

But the Socialist majority of votes was again without political significance: what counted was the fate of each list and this time as many as 34 Socialist lists (16 CP and 18 SP) did not reach the threshold. The result was a clear victory for the cooperating nonsocialist parties: they gained six more seats and could command a clear-cut majority of 80 over 70.

Could the four parties actually pull together and make effective use of this majority? This was the question asked among politicians and analysts throughout the Nordic countries the day after this "turn of the tide." The four parties had shelved their differences during the campaign: would they be able to reach workable compromises when confronted with the longstanding policy issues of the Norwegian system? Our analysis has pointed to the principal sources of strain and *malaise* among the four parties, but it is very difficult to predict how far it will prove possible to keep these tensions within bounds under the paramount pressure for unity in the face of embittered opposition. Much will depend on external forces. Will the European issue come up again? Will the negotiations over the continuation of NATO strain the established unity in matters of alliance policy? Whatever the outcome, aficionados of comparative politics will watch with fascination the behavior of this curious system at the half-way point between straight Anglo-Saxon "ins–outs" alternations and mixed Continental coalition and *Proporz* manipulations.

4

SWEDEN:

STABILITY OR DEADLOCK?

Nils Stjernquist

In Sweden the Social Democratic Party has been in power almost without interruption since 1932. To the right of the government are three nonsocialist parties, often called the "bourgeois" parties; the Conservative Party, the Liberal Party, and the Center (until 1959, the Farmers') Party. To the left of the government is the Communist Party with only a few members in the Riksdag. The Center Party has sometimes collaborated with the Social Democrats on the governmental level. During the Second World War there was a coalition government consisting of all parties except the Communists.

The nonsocialist parties sometimes comment that the opposition is, or soon will be, without importance. As the Conservative leader, Gunnar Heckscher, stated in 1963:

> In fact the concentration of power in the government and in the governing party is the most characteristic feature of Swedish politics just now. We are rapidly moving away from the politics of compromise based on reciprocal concessions which was typical of our country from the mid-thirties to the mid-fifties. The Social Democratic government is more and more impatiently dictatorial, and the Social Democratic Party is concentrating on an unceasing and indisputable possession of power . . . The chief risk is that we really might end up by having a kind of one-party system by which the opposition is allowed, in principle, but care is taken to see that it never has any political importance.[1]

Even some Socialists have said that the opposition finds it difficult to carry out its function. As early as 1951 Prime Minister Tage Erlander asked what would happen to "an opposition that represents almost half of the citizens but which never has an opportunity of trying its strength

1. G. Heckscher, *Trygga folkstyret!* (Stockholm, 1963), pp. 12 ff.

For comments and criticism I wish to acknowledge my debts to Pär-Erik Back, Robert A. Dahl, Agne Gustafsson, Val R. Lorwin, Hans F. Petersson, Stein Rokkan, Bo Särlvik, Torbjörn Vallinder, and Ernst Wigforss.

as the government and which never has practice in assuming the responsibility which this involves." [2]

Other observers, however, argue that the opposition *is* worthwhile and does have influence. The Liberal leader, Bertil Ohlin, said in 1963:

> The opposition, as we all know, has had a great influence on the development of society in Sweden since the war by putting an end to the Socialist "harvest-time" before it began, by speeding up and influencing a number of reforms, and, furthermore, by criticizing the government's mistakes and bringing about corrections.[3]

Some spokesmen even suggest from time to time that the Socialist government gets its ideas from the opposition.

These diverse opinions are not academic evaluations but part of a national political debate. They may therefore represent tactical moves and appeals to various electorates as well as candid observations or fears.

What really is the role of the opposition in the present political system?

Constitutional Provisions [4]

The Swedish Constitution, dating from 1809, provides for a distribution of power between king and Parliament (called the Riksdag). According to the Constitution the king has the executive power, Parliament the powers of taxation and budget-making. The legislative power is divided between king and Parliament. Parliament also has control of the executive power.

The Constitution did not lay down the parliamentary system. When this system was decisively accepted in 1917, the change took place without any alteration in the constitutional provisions, which still give the king, not the ministers, the governmental power and still permit the king to choose his ministers without regard to party support or majorities in Parliament.

The Swedish Parliament has been divided since 1866 into an Upper House and a Lower House, which in all matters have equal competence and powers. If the houses disagree on legislative matters and their opinions cannot be reconciled, the question is dropped. If they differ on matters concerning state expenditure or taxation, each house has to vote on the different decisions. Then by the method of "joint division" the votes of the two houses are put together and the opinion that receives a majority of the aggregate number of votes constitutes the decision of the Riksdag.

---

2. *Reformer och försvar. En bok till Per Edvin Sköld* (Stockholm, Tidens förlag, 1951), p. 172. Cf. *Tiden* (1963), pp. 449 ff.

3. B. Ohlin, *Liberal utmaning* (1963), p. 18.

4. See N. Andrén, *Modern Swedish Government* (Stockholm, Almqvist and Wiksell, 1961). See also L. Frykholm, "Swedish Legal Publications in English, French and German 1935–60," *Scandinavian Studies in Law*, 5 (1961), 196 ff.

If the aggregate number of votes is evenly divided, the issue is finally decided by drawing lots.

Universal and equal suffrage for men in the elections to the Lower House was introduced in 1909. At the same time proportional representation came into being. In 1918–21 universal suffrage was introduced for women too and for both sexes in municipal elections. The members of the Lower House are elected directly, the members of the Upper House indirectly by the county councils and, in the largest cities which are not represented on the county councils, by the city councils. The term of members of the Lower House is four years; that of members of the Upper House, eight years; every year one-eighth of the memberships in the Upper House are renewed.

The bicameral system has been and still is effective, even though some people argue occasionally that the Lower House should be more influential than the Upper House.[5]

The Socioeconomic Structure

A century ago Sweden was largely agrarian. Almost 75 per cent of the total population was engaged in agriculture and only about 13 per cent lived in the towns. Today the situation has changed completely. In 1960 only 13.8 per cent of the economically active population was occupied in agriculture and forestry, and people have at an increasing rate since 1945 moved into urban areas, especially to the three largest cities.

During the process of industrialization, which began slowly in the 1870s and increased rapidly in the 1890s, both the total and relative number of wage earners increased. In contrast, one of the most important changes in the last few decades has been the increase in the number of salaried employees, chiefly as a result of new methods in industry and the expanding activity of state and local government. In 1960 salaried employees constituted about 35 per cent of the economically active population, wage earners about 51 per cent, and employers about 14 per cent.

The occupational groups have built up local and national organizations with far-reaching influence. The wage earners are organized in trade unions with the LO (Landsorganisationen) at the top, the farmers in producers' associations with the SL (Sveriges Lantbruksförbund) at the top. For most of the salaried employees the TCO (Tjänstemännens Centralorganisation) is their top organization. Salaried employees with a univer-

5. In 1963 a royal commission presented a draft for a new constitution to replace the constitution of 1809. The commission proposed that the parliamentary system be incorporated in the written constitution. The majority of the members of the commission preferred a unicameral system. (See *Statens offentliga utredningar* [1963], No. 16–18.) At the beginning of 1965 two special commissions were appointed, one to examine technicalities of the electoral procedure and one to investigate the interdependence between national politics on one hand and regional and local politics on the other. In the meantime the party leaders continued their discussion of basic features of a new constitution. Cf. n. 62, below.

sity degree have built up the SACO (Sveriges Akademikers Central-organisation), some public servants' groups the SR (Statstjänstemännens Riksförbund), while a large group of low-salaried employees have joined the LO in a section of their own (Statstjänarkartellen). On the other side, employers in the private sector are organized in the SAF (Svenska Arbetsgivareföreningen).

By the time the bicameral Parliament came into being in 1866, the division of the population into the Four Estates (nobles, clergy, burghers, and peasants) was outmoded. Instead the population could be divided in a rough way into three social groups: the upper, middle, and lower classes. To the upper class belonged the senior bureaucracy and the big indus-trialists, to the middle class the small businessmen, salaried employees, and farmers, to the lower class the wage earners and farm laborers (over-whelmingly the largest part of the population at that time). Although the distribution has been changed by the urban shift mentioned above, the division into these social groups is still used.

The Cleavages and the Party System [6]

Sweden covers a vast area (450,000 sq. km.) but has a population that is small (about 7.7 million in 1965) and highly homogeneous. Regional differences for the most part are not of real importance in politics, and religion has not played a role in politics comparable with that in the Catholic countries. The overwhelming majority of the population belongs to the Lutheran State Church. Friendly relations exist today between the State Church and nonconformists. The nonconformists have generally supported the Liberals, while a majority of the active members of the State Church vote with the Conservatives or the Center Party. The Socialists were, to begin with, opponents of the State Church. By and large, however, as they began to assume responsibility as the government, their attitude became more neutral.[7] Among the Socialists there is an organized group that is actively religious, and religious interests today are probably protected by a majority in Parliament. In the 1964 elections to the Lower House a new party appeared, called the Christian Democratic Union (KDS), to a large extent supported by the Pentecostalists. It got about 75,000 votes mainly at the expense of the Liberals and the Socialists, but did not win a seat.

THE OLD SOCIETY   As early as the eighteenth century, during the so-called Era of Liberty, Sweden had a highly developed parliamentary system with two parties, the Hats and the Caps. They were mainly or-

6. I. Andersson, *A History of Sweden* (2d ed. Stockholm, Natur och Kultur, 1956); D. A. Rustow, *The Politics of Compromise: a Study of Parties and Cabinet Govern-ment in Sweden* (Princeton, Princeton University Press, 1955); D. Verney, *Parlia-mentary Reform in Sweden* (Oxford, Clarendon Press, 1957).

7. C. A. Hessler, *Statskyrkodebatten* (Stockholm, Almqvist and Wiksell, 1964), with an English summary.

ganizations inside Parliament, which at that time consisted of the Four Estates. This old parliamentary system was abolished by a coup d'etat by the king in 1772.

After the parliamentary reform of 1866 the cleavage between the two well-established classes on the one hand and the lower class on the other was for a long time not a real political problem, because the lower class was excluded from the suffrage. The dominant cleavage was between the farmers and the bureaucracy.

In accordance with the provisions of the Constitution of 1809, Parliament for a long time had no influence upon the king's choice of ministers, and they were recruited from the ranks of the senior bureaucrats. It was impossible, however, to avoid opposition to the government in Parliament and quite naturally a party system developed inside Parliament. Suffrage restrictions made it possible for the upper class to control the Upper House and for the middle class to control the Lower House; in the latter the farmers won a majority. The Agrarian Party in the Lower House formed the opposition to the government. In appointing ministers, the king was eventually obliged to take into consideration how Parliament would react, although in 1887 he still characterized parliamentarism as a foreign practice unknown to the Constitution.[8]

In the 1880s the tariff question deeply involved all interests in economic life and led to large cleavages both inside and outside Parliament and also among the farmers. As a result, politics began to interest the voters as well as those who were not entitled to vote, and from then on real election campaigns took place.[9]

In the 1890s a new political issue, the move for universal suffrage, came to the fore.[10] At the end of the nineteenth century only one-quarter of the men over 21 had the vote. The question of universal suffrage deepened the cleavage between those who were comfortably off and the poor. People with a liberal ideology demanded universal suffrage. The adherents of this ideology in the Lower House formed the Liberal Party in 1900, and two years later this party started a national organization. The Socialist Party had come into being as early as 1889, when a national organization was started, and the Socialists too demanded universal suffrage, which offered them their only hope of gaining a strong representation in Parliament. In 1897 the first Socialist representative, Hjalmar Branting, entered Parliament. On the opposite side the Conservatives, in defense of their position, organized a national party in 1904 and then organized themselves in

8. Letter from Oscar II to his ministers, Nov. 21, 1887, published in T. Petré, *Ministären Themptander* (Uppsala, 1945), p. 296.

9. E. Håstad, "Tullstridens val och folkmeningen," in *Festskrift till Axel Brusewitz* (Uppsala, 1941), pp. 105 ff.

10. T. Vallinder, *I kamp för demokratin: Rösträttsrörelsen i Sverige 1886–1900* (Stockholm, Natur och Kultur, 1962), with an English summary.

Parliament.[11] The demand for universal suffrage was in fact a demand for a change in the fundamentals of the existing society and for a transfer of political power to new strata. The main lines of the present party system were established during the struggle for universal suffrage.

Universal suffrage was introduced gradually from 1909. At the same time, to protect the interests of the established classes, the PR system came into being. Closely allied to the suffrage question was the issue of parliamentarism and ministerial responsibility. The Liberals demanded parliamentarism and were supported by the Socialists. The king and the Conservatives were against parliamentarism. After the elections to the Lower House in 1917, when the two parties on the left got a strong majority, the king finally had to accept the parliamentary system and appoint a government consisting of both Liberals and Socialists. The Conservative Party still held a majority in the Upper House, until the democratization of the county councils in 1918 changed this situation.

The PR system made it possible for more than two parties to compete effectively in elections. Thus from 1911 a real three-party system—Conservatives, Liberals, and Socialists—developed.

MINORITY PARLIAMENTARISM, 1920–32   Universal suffrage and the growing number of wage earners made it possible for the Socialists to become the largest party. One problem for them was that for a long time the lower class did not participate as actively in elections as the other classes. Another problem was that the left wing of the Socialists had in 1917 formed their own party, from which different Communist parties developed in the 1920s. The Liberal Party declined in size and between 1923–34 was split into two factions. In 1921 the Farmers' Party, now called the Center Party, was formed.[12] Thus when democracy was fully established Sweden had a multiparty system with five parties which are still represented in Parliament. Appendix Table 4.1 shows the distribution of seats in the Riksdag since 1922.

Universal suffrage and parliamentarism were soon accepted in the 1920s by those who had previously opposed them. Having realized their constitutional program, the Liberals and the Socialists found it no longer possible to continue their collaboration in the government, for they had contrary views on how society ought to be constructed from the socioeconomic point of view. The Socialists demanded nationalization in principle, while the Liberals together with the Conservatives and the Center Party, all following their own ideologies, acted as guardians of the prevailing system. Nationalization now created the deepest cleavage

11. There was in the beginning one Conservative group in the Upper House and one in the Lower House.

12. The party was formed by the amalgamation of two smaller parties originating from the 1910s.

between the parties, and it was obvious that the dividing line on the party scale was between the Socialists and the Communists on the one side and the nonsocialist parties on the other.

During the period of minority parliamentarism from 1920–32 no party held a majority position (Appendix Table 4.2). A coalition between the Socialists and one of the nonsocialist parties was hardly possible,[13] nor could the nonsocialist parties collaborate with each other in the government. Sometimes, indeed, all the political parties actually preferred to be out of power. Each election to the Lower House led to a defeat for the governmental party and to a change of government. During this period Sweden changed its government at least every other year. Since the government was without a parliamentary majority, political issues were solved in each separate case by compromises by at least two parties. Political power was concentrated in Parliament, especially in the committees, where the political compromises were made. The Liberals were no doubt in the best position to control the situation and to form a stronger government than could be formed under the leadership of the Socialists or the Conservatives. Sometimes a Liberal government tried to find support from the right, sometimes from the left, but sometimes the Conservatives and the Socialists made a united stand against this system of fleeting majorities.[14] Socialists and Conservatives, but not Liberals, today quite naturally have unhappy memories of minority parliamentarism.[15]

MAJORITY PARLIAMENTARISM FROM 1933   In the development of the parliamentary system the year 1933 forms a dividing line. Since that year one party has been dominant—the Socialist Party. A main feature of its policy has been collaboration with the Center Party. In elections to the Lower House the distribution of votes for the Socialists and Communists on the one hand and for the three nonsocialist parties on the other has been very stable, oscillating since 1940 between 58–42 per cent (1940) and 49.6–50.3 per cent (1956).[16] Among the three nonsocialist parties, however, there have been considerable fluctuations (Appendix Table 4.3).

The Socialists took over the government in the autumn of 1932 when the depression and unemployment were at their worst. In this situation the majority of the party had decided to drop the demand for nationalization and instead concentrate on a social welfare policy.[17] Thus the most im-

13. At the end of the 1920s negotiations between the Socialists and the Liberals took place but without result.

14. A Conservative review could boldly characterize the Liberal government as a dictatorship. See *Svensk tidskrift* (1929), p. 327.

15. See G. Andersson, "Regeringar utan riksdagsmajoritet," in *Ekonomi, politik, samhälle; en bok tillägnad Bertil Ohlin* (Stockholm, 1959), pp. 15 ff.

16. In the 1958 elections the figures were 49.6–50.4 per cent. At that time, however, the Communists were active in only a few constituencies.

17. H. Tingsten, *Den svenska socialdemokratiens idéutveckling, 1–2* (Stockholm, Tidens förlag, 1941).

portant cleavage between the Socialists and nonsocialists was eliminated. However, to say that the Socialists accepted the socioeconomic structure of society would not be correct. Social welfare programs were seen as another means of leveling incomes.[18] Furthermore, influenced by Keynes, the Socialists wanted a higher level of state activity and an economy planned by the state. The Conservatives and the Liberals still acted as protectors of the structure of society and opposed state regulation. The Center Party, however, was able to accept state regulation in agriculture. This explains to a large extent why it was possible in 1933 for the Socialists and the Center Party to work out a common program for economic policy. As a result of the agreement the government was able to rely on a majority in both houses. Thus the period of minority parliamentarism came to an end and was succeeded by a system that can be called majority parliamentarism, although the Center Party had not yet entered the government. Political power moved from Parliament to the government.

In 1936 the defense question caused an open cleavage in Swedish politics. For a short time the Socialists let the Center Party take over the government. After the elections to the Lower House in the autumn of 1936, the Socialist leader, P. A. Hansson, formed a new government, this time in coalition with the Center Party.

The nonsocialist parties, taken together, held a minority position in the Lower House in 1937. In 1941 the Socialists acquired a majority in the Lower House and in 1942 also in the Upper House. During the war political power was highly centralized in the Cabinet, which at that time also included representatives of the Conservatives and the Liberals. Only the Communists remained outside the government. As in other countries in wartime, the government was given far-reaching authority, and Parliament functioned only as an apparatus for registering what the government had already decided. A prerequisite for the all-party government, however, was an understanding that nothing be decided in matters involving internal cleavages.

After the peace in Europe in 1945 the all-party government was dissolved and the Socialists formed a new government. They were still in a strong position, with almost half the votes in the Lower House and a majority in the Upper House and in joint divisions. In 1944 they had made their party program more radical, and the cleavages between them and the nonsocialist parties were now more sharply emphasized. When Sweden's foreign exchange position became difficult in 1947, the nonsocialist parties criticized the government for its economic policy and what they called "misrule." In the 1948 elections to the Lower House, the Liberals more than doubled their seats, though this was mainly at the expense of the

18. E. Wigforss, *Ha vi råd till sociala reformer?* (1937), pp. 17 ff.

Conservatives and the Center Party; the Socialists lost three seats. The nonsocialist parties did not succeed in gaining a majority in the Lower House.

The Socialists found it troublesome, however, not to control the majority in the Lower House and for that reason the Center Party was invited to enter the government after the elections of 1948. After some hesitation it declined the invitation. In 1951 new negotiations resulted in a coalition government of the two parties. They had a common program concerning economic policy and agriculture. The issues between the government and the opposition now involved primarily economic and tax policies. By this time the extensive social welfare program, which was passed from 1946 to 1950, was supported as energetically by the non-socialist parties as by the Socialists. On defense policy,[19] foreign policy,[20] and educational policy, there was almost complete unanimity.

In the elections to the Lower House in 1956 the government parties both suffered setbacks. The situation seemed especially dangerous for the Center Party, which lost about one-quarter of its seats. Its supporters were mainly farmers, and the agrarian population was decreasing rapidly. Furthermore, many of the party's supporters were dissatisfied with its collaboration with the Socialists. As a result of the elections, the three nonsocialist parties together obtained a majority in the Lower House. The coalition between the Socialists and the Center Party continued, however.

In 1957 the pension question became a major political issue. The Socialists were planning a general supplementary pension that would be compulsory and involved building up large funds. The nonsocialist parties opposed the plan, but they did not express their opposition in joint action. The Conservatives and the Liberals sponsored a voluntary system of agreements between employers' organizations and employees' organizations; the Center Party's attitude was that the system had to be founded on "personal voluntariness." In the autumn of 1957 the electorate was asked to help settle the question by a consultative referendum. About 46 per cent of those who participated preferred the Socialist approach, about 35 per cent the plan of the Conservatives and the Liberals, and—the most interesting development—15 per cent supported the Center Party. The problem was not solved by the referendum. Immediately afterward the Center Party declared that it could no longer remain in a coalition with the Socialists, and as a result the entire coalition government resigned. The King first explored the possibility of forming a government consisting of all parties except the Communists, a solution recommended by Conservative leader Jarl Hjalmarson and Liberal leader Bertil Ohlin. After discus-

19. Cf. T. Erlander, "Försvaret över partierna," in *Fred och försvar under 60-talet* (Stockholm, 1961), pp. 11 ff.
20. Cf. H. Tingsten, "Issues in Swedish Foreign Policy," *Foreign Affairs*, 37(1959), 474 ff.

sions with the leaders of the nonsocialists parties, Socialist leader Tage Erlander, who had already said that the Socialists were against this solution, refused to join an all-party government. Ohlin and Hjalmarson were then asked by the King to investigate the possibility of forming a government supported by the nonsocialist majority in the Lower House. However, the leader of the Center Party, Gunnar Hedlund, said that he did not want to enter into a government with the other two nonsocialist parties or to support a Liberal-Conservative government. He underlined the fact that the Socialists still had the majority in the Upper House and that from a political point of view it was impossible for him to start collaborating with the Conservatives and the Liberals immediately after having left a coalition with the Socialists. Erlander then formed a government consisting only of Socialists.

In the spring of 1958 the nonsocialist majority in the Lower House rejected a pension proposal made by the Socialist government, which then ordered elections to the Lower House. The Socialist Party won five more seats and the nonsocialists lost their majority. The most striking fact was that the Liberals lost 20 seats and the Center Party won 13. The pension question gave the Center Party an opportunity to reestablish its strength and appeal to groups other than the agrarian population.

The pension question was solved in 1959 mainly along the lines advocated by the Socialists. But neither the Socialists nor the nonsocialist parties controlled a majority in the Lower House or in joint divisions. At the end of 1959 a government proposal for the introduction of a general sales tax brought harsh criticism from the opposition and could be put through only with the help of the Communists, who abstained from voting in the joint divisions.

After the elections to the Lower House in the autumn of 1960 the Socialists had one seat more than the three nonsocialist parties together and still controlled a majority in the Upper House. But because of the Communist members they were one seat short of a majority in the joint divisions. The municipal elections in 1962 strengthened the position of the Socialists in the Upper House, and in 1964 they regained their majority in joint divisions. On the eve of the elections to the Lower House in 1964 it was generally expected that the Socialists would win a stable majority; in the municipal elections in 1962 they had received 50.5 per cent of the votes, an increase of 2.7 per cent in comparison with the elections to the Lower House in 1960. But in fact they did not win more than 47.3 per cent of the votes; they lost one seat in the Lower House, and lost their majority in the joint divisions.[21]

21. The number of Socialist seats in the Upper House will increase by one in both 1966 and 1967, hence from 1967 the Socialists will regain the majority in joint divisions.

Two new parties participated in the 1964 elections—the Christian Democratic Union (KDS), which did not receive a sufficient number of votes to be represented in Parliament, and the Citizens' Union (MBS), which appeared in only one constituency (Malmö) and won three seats. The purpose of the MBS was to unite the three nonsocialist parties and overthrow the Socialist government. It acted against the national organizations of the nonsocialist parties and was supported primarily by people who had previously voted Conservative and by two big Conservative newspapers. It was successful in that one of its representatives was a Conservative, one a Liberal, and one a member of the Center Party. Each one tried to join his original party in Parliament; the centrist, however, was not accepted by his parliamentary group. Although the Socialist Party lost a little ground—both absolutely and relatively—the three nonsocialist parties and the MBS taken together also lost ground. The Liberal Party, it is true, won two seats and the Center Party one, but the Conservatives lost seven seats and all three parties received relatively fewer votes. As a result of the efforts of their new leader, Carl-Henrik Hermansson, the Communists won three seats and increased their percentage of the electorate from 4.5 (in 1960) to 5.2.

The margins between the Socialists and nonsocialists have been small since 1960, and illness or refusal to follow the party line can unexpectedly change the situation. This nearly equal balance has invited agreements behind the scenes. A far-reaching agreement of this type was made on the taxation question in the autumn of 1961 between the Socialist government and the Center Party. The policy of the Center Party shows that it prefers to have contacts both with the Socialists and inside the nonsocialist sector, especially with the Liberals, and to utilize the advantages of being the balancer (see below).

PARTY AFFILIATION   There is an obvious correlation between party affiliation and occupational group and, on the whole, socioeconomic status. Table 4.1 shows the 1964 voters by party affiliation and nonvoters in different occupational groups. Table 4.2 shows them by occupational groups.[22]

The majority of the wage earners support the Socialists and the majority of the farmers the Center Party, while the salaried employees are split up, primarily among the Conservatives, the Liberals, and the Socialists. It may, however, be emphasized that actually among the Socialist voters the relative number of lower-salaried employees is increasing while the

22. The tables and figures are from a Political Science Institute of Gothenburg Survey by B. Särlvik, published in *Official Statistics of Sweden, The Elections to the Riksdag During the Years 1961–1964, 2* (Stockholm, 1965). See also B. Särlvik, "Politisk rörlighet och stabilitet i valmanskåren," *Statsvetenskaplig tidskrift, 67* (1964), 185 ff.

Table 4.1 The 1964 Voters by Party Affiliation in Occupational Groups
(in percentages)

	Cons.	Lib.	Center	KDS	MBS	Soc.	Comm.	No answer	Non-voters	Total	N
Larger employers, higher-salaried employees	42	27	3	2	6	7	—	4	9	100	160
Farmers	12	11	58	2	0	6	0	2	9	100	297
Smaller employers	12	28	14	2	1	20	1	4	18	100	255
Lower-salaried employees, shop assistants	13	22	5	1	2	41	2	3	11	100	740
Farm and lumber workers	3	12	17	1	—	42	3	4	18	100	171
Other workers	3	6	7	1	0	64	4	2	13	100	1226

Table 4.2 The 1964 Voters by Occupational Groups in the Political Parties
(in percentages)

	Larger employers, higher-salaried employees	Farmers	Smaller employers	Lower-salaried shop employees, assistants	Farm and lumber workers	Other workers	Total	N
Cons.	25	13	12	36	2	12	100	265
Lib.	10	8	18	40	5	19	100	408
Center	1	48	10	11	8	22	100	359
KDS	10	12	12	30	5	31	100	41
MBS	29	3	7	45	—	16	100	31
Soc.	1	1	4	25	6	63	100	1248
Comm.	—	1	3	18	9	69	100	67
No answer	8	6	13	30	9	34	100	77
Nonvoters	3	8	13	23	9	44	100	353
Total	6	10	9	26	6	43	100	2849

Table 4.3 *The 1962 Voters by Their 1964 Votes*

	Voting in 1964										
Voting in 1962	*Cons.*	*Lib.*	*Center*	*KDS*	*MBS*	*Soc.*	*Comm.*	*No answer*	*Non-voters*	*Total*	*N*
				(in percentages)							
Cons.	74	8	3	1	7	1	0	1	5	100	254
Lib.	4	77	4	4	2	1	1	1	6	100	372
Center	2	1	88	1	0	2	0	0	6	100	290
Soc.	0	1	2	1	0	88	2	1	5	100	1155
Comm.	0	0	3	3	0	12	76	0	6	100	34
No answer	9	10	6	1	1	18	2	33	20	100	154
Nonvoters	7	10	8	2	0	31	2	2	38	100	459
Not entitled to vote	5	15	8	2	2	37	0	4	27	100	131

Table 4.4 *The 1964 Voters by Their 1962 Votes*

	Voting in 1962									
Voting in 1964	*Cons.*	*Lib.*	*Center*	*Soc.*	*Comm.*	*No answer*	*Non-voters*	*Not entitled to vote*	*Total*	*N*
					(in percentages)					
Cons.	71	6	2	2	0	5	12	2	100	265
Lib.	5	71	0	3	0	4	12	5	100	408
Center	2	4	71	7	0	3	10	3	100	359
KDS	7	32	7	21	3	5	20	5	100	41
MBS	55	19	3	3	0	3	7	10	100	31
Soc.	0	1	1	81	0	3	11	4	100	1248
Comm.	2	3	2	37	39	2	13	0	100	67
No answer	3	3	0	10	0	66	12	6	100	77
Nonvoters	3	7	5	16	0	9	50	10	100	353

relative number of workers is possibly decreasing. In the 1930s and 1940s it might have been possible for the Liberal Party to be transformed into a party for salaried employees. In the old days and even in the 1950s all parties appealed to the farmers; the percentage of farmers among the members of Parliament has always been higher than among the electorate.

Stability within the electorate is generally rather high. There has been more mobility among the nonsocialist parties than between these parties on the one hand and the Socialists on the other. The net fluctuations between the two blocs were (at least from 1954 to 1962) chiefly due to fluctuations in participation in elections. Table 4.3 shows voters and non-voters in the 1962 municipal elections distributed by voting behavior in the 1964 election. Table 4.4 shows voters and nonvoters in the 1964 election distributed by voting behavior in the 1962 municipal elections.

About 70 per cent of those interviewed voted in both elections for the same party, while 7 per cent of those entitled to vote in both elections did not participate either in 1962 or in 1964. About 8 per cent of those entitled to vote both years changed over from one party to another—4.3 per cent from a nonsocialist party to another nonsocialist party, 0.6 per cent from a nonsocialist party to a socialist (Socialists and Communists) party, 2.1 per cent from a socialist to a nonsocialist party and 1.1 per cent from one socialist to another socialist party.

FROM CLEAVAGES TO CONSENSUS AMONG THE PARTIES   The two most widely discussed issues in recent years, the pension question and the sales tax question, were solved in a manner not endorsed by the opposition. The solution to the pension question, however, was soon generally accepted, although in the 1964 elections the Conservatives criticized the funds for being too large. The sales tax alignment was astonishing, for in a reversal of traditional roles the Socialists introduced the tax while the nonsocialists opposed it. On the whole the cleavages between the parties have decreased since the beginning of the 1930s, for many reasons.

Before the introduction of universal suffrage the socioeconomic and ideological cleavages were very deep, and the society was in fact a class society.[23] As democracy was gradually accepted these differences were modified. Considerable further leveling took place when the Socialists abandoned their demand for nationalization and all the nonsocialist parties accepted a social welfare policy. Universal suffrage gave political power, in principle, to the "little man," whose interests, by and large, the non-socialist as well as Socialist parties tended to look after. To a large extent he achieved the same income and the same standard of living as the middle class. It is significant that while 2.5 per cent graduated from secondary school (gymnasium) in 1932 [24] and 6.5 per cent in 1950, the figure had

23. Cf. S. M. Lipset, *The First New Nation* (New York, Basic Books, 1963), pp. 235 ff.
24. The average age of graduation is 20.5.

increased to 17.1 in 1964 and is, according to the secondary school reform
of 1964, expected to increase to 30 per cent by the end of the 'sixties, a
figure that is probably too low.[25] The concept of class is in fact not very
useful in politics today. The Socialists do not appeal only to wage earners,
nor does the Center Party appeal only to farmers. The Conservatives have
used the idea of "the common citizen" as a political slogan. The political
parties often appeal to all groups in society, and modern mass-media have
certainly made people feel less like members of a particular class.

Swedish society today is highly pluralistic.[26] The organizations favor
compromises; they try to avoid state regulation and strikes and to come to
terms with each other by bargaining. Since 1947, there have been practically no strikes. The top organization of the employers and the top
organization of the industrial workers came to a major agreement at
Saltsjöbaden in 1938; labor relations are now said to be characterized by
"the spirit of Saltsjöbaden." There are channels between political parties
and socioeconomic organizations, for instance between the Socialists and
the trade unions and between the Center Party and the farmers' organizations. But the fact that the interest groups are not organized along party
lines has caused overlapping memberships and cross-pressures, so cleavages
are not polarized and political parties are inclined to compromise. Interest
groups in many fields bargain directly with the government; in matters
such as salaries and wages for state employees the agreements between the
government and the organizations result in the Riksdag being presented
with a fait accompli.[27] The organizations and not the political parties
actually deal with problems of distribution of income. It has been said that
cooperation between the government and the big organizations—which
has been characterized as "Harpsund-democracy"[28]—means that the opposition is passed over, and this is dangerous for the parliamentary system.[29] On the other hand it has been stressed that the organizations are of
vital interest to individuals and give them channels to political decision-
making other than voting on election day.[30]

25. The percentage of members of the Lower House with a university degree increased from 10.9 to 20.3 (in the Socialist group from 7.7 to 11.4) from 1933 to 1963.

26. See G. Heckscher, "Interest Groups in Sweden," in *Interest Groups on Four
Continents,* ed. by H. W. Ehrmann (Pittsburgh, University of Pittsburgh Press, 1958),
pp. 154 ff.; H. Zetterberg, "National Pastime: Pursuit of Power," *Industria International* (1960), pp. 105 ff. Zetterberg overestimates the role of the organizations.

27. In order to strengthen the position of Parliament, a parliamentary salary delegation was introduced in 1965. The delegation will follow the bargaining process and
be able to accept an agreement concerning salaries for state employees on behalf of
Parliament.

28. Harpsund is the summer residence of the Prime Minister, where top-level meetings between politicians and leaders from big business and the organizations take
place.

29. N. Elvander, "Organisationerna och statsmakterna," *Industriförbundets tidskrift*
(1963), pp. 424 ff.

30. B. Östergren, "Organisationsväsen och demokrati," *Tiden* (1962), pp. 206 ff.

The main aim of Swedish economic policy has been to secure social welfare and full employment and to raise the standard of living. Democracy has become equated with social services.[31] To realize this aim it has been necessary to give priority to actions that can lead to an increase in production.[32] On this point the government, the opposition, the organizations, and big business are united. Another important factor is that a country like Sweden, which is greatly dependent upon its exports and imports, cannot act independently of big business or independently of other countries. It can be argued that a Socialist government is advantageous for big business, since it is best fitted to put pressure on the trade unions in the bargaining process. All these considerations taken together have many times made the nonsocialist parties and the Socialists accept the same policy. In the process ideological differences have been pushed aside.

Up to 1933 the great political issues—universal suffrage and nationalization—were easy for the electorate to understand. But the issues of economic policy since 1945 have been very complicated for politicians and more so for the man in the street. Both from the economic and the technical points of view modern society is so complicated that the power of the bureaucracy and technocracy[33] has increased at the expense of politicians and political parties. The decisions on principle, the long-term planning, and the far-reaching authority now in the hands of the government have in fact restricted the power of Parliament and thus the power of the political parties. This has been a problem for the opposition parties in particular.

The electorate has become more apolitical because of the complicated structure of modern society and the decrease in cleavages. Depoliticization must not be overestimated, however. Party identification is still rather strong, and about one-quarter of the adult population are members of a political party.[34] Moreover participation in elections has increased rather than decreased (see Appendix Table 4.4).

Compromises between the parties and their bargaining tactics have no doubt helped to decrease the cleavages.

The present parliamentary situation invites the parties to concentrate on groups in the middle, on people who are likely to be among the floating vote—at one time primarily farmers but today more often salaried em-

31. J. Westerståhl, *Dagens Nyheter,* Aug. 4, 1956.
32. A specific problem is that further rises in the standard of living would become more and more expensive, relatively speaking. Cf. Prime Minister Erlander, *Upper House Minutes* (1956), 2, 23 ff.
33. The civil service is on the whole traditionally not appointed according to party lines and neutral on political issues.
34. Cf. U. Himmelstrand, "A Theoretical and Empirical Approach to Depoliticization and Political Involvement," *Acta Sociologica, 6* (1962), 96 ff.

ployees. Because they must appeal to identical interests, the proposals the parties put forward to each such group must therefore be similar.[35]

The parliamentary situation has long been one of an almost even balance between the Socialists on the one hand and the nonsocialist parties on the other. The Socialists have as a rule had a majority, but even a slight shift in the electorate has been and still is enough to alter this. The 50-50 balance makes both blocs and all the four parties cautious, and therefore has a leveling effect.[36]

Do cleavages no longer exist? The development just mentioned has led to the opinion, especially underlined by Herbert Tingsten,[37] that ideological cleavages have disappeared. Cleavages of today, it has been said, are restricted to the question: Which persons ought to be in power? The cleavages are certainly latent or potential, however, to a greater extent than is often recognized. For example Socialists and the nonsocialist parties still differ concerning the role of the state in economic life. But such differences are not generally brought before the public.

Cleavages sometimes occur *within* the parties. During the last few decades, however, the parties have been so well established and party identifications among the electorate so strong that new political issues have not produced changes in the party system. The emergence of the KDS and the MBS in the 1964 elections is interesting from this point of view. The MBS may be seen as a protest against the party system on the nonsocialist side.

The Conditions of the Opposition

In the debate within Sweden on parliamentarism and the role of the parliamentary opposition one school of thought has taken the English parliamentary system as a model, calling it the pure form of parliamentarism.[38] Characteristic of this form, as it has been understood in Sweden, are majority elections and hence a two-party system consisting of one majority party, which forms the government, and one minority party, which forms the opposition and is entirely out of power. The aim of the opposition party is to replace the government party by presenting alternatives with which it hopes to win the confidence of the majority of the electorate in the next election. It has often been maintained that the

35. In 1948, 3 per cent of the private members' proposals in the Lower House were signed by members from all parties except the Communists. In 1964 the figure had increased to 8.3.

36. It may be added that the members of both houses are seated by constituency, not party affiliation.

37. A leading Swedish political scientist, Tingsten was chief editor of the Liberal newspaper *Dagens Nyheter* from 1946 to 1960.

38. See e.g. C. A. Hessler, "Parlamentarismens begrepp," in *Studier tillägnade Fredrik Lagerroth* (Lund, 1950), pp. 172 ff.

English form of parliamentarism also implies alternations in office between the two parties, which presupposes a considerable proportion of floating votes among the electorate. In recent years Conservatives and Liberals have emphasized that alternation in office is necessary so that a one-party system will not emerge de facto and so that democracy can function in a satisfactory way.[39] A very long period of one-party rule would lead to a process of degeneration in the governing and alienation in the governed. The party in power would find it increasingly difficult to resist the temptation to regard itself as the *only* party able to serve society.[40] The primary task of the party system, it has also been said, is to facilitate a transfer of power from the incumbents to the opposition.[41] In rejoinder it is argued that the rules of the game in democracy positively presuppose a good chance of a change; but this again presupposes a lively opposition with a well-defined policy which it is prepared to put into effect should it come into power.[42] Obviously a democratic system cannot in itself guarantee alternations in office from one party to another.[43]

In this view of the English system, the function of the government is to govern, the function of the opposition is to oppose the government exclusively by criticizing government policy and presenting alternatives. Criticism provides in fact a most valuable and necessary brake on the government.[44] With all the efforts of the opposition directed toward victory in the next election, its strategy might be called an electoral strategy.

On the opposite side in the Swedish debate on parliamentarism and the role of the opposition, there has been another school of thought which has argued in favor of another system, also called a pure one. Fundamental to this system are PR elections and hence a multiparty system. The basic justification for PR is a belief that each party ought to be represented in Parliament in proportion to its strength among the electorate. In a democratic system, it is argued, this principle ought to be applied, too, in forming the government. Thus the government ought to be an all-party government, and the ministries and political power should be divided among the parties in proportion to the number of their seats in Parliament. The main aim of an opposition in a system of this kind would be to influence the policy-making process. The means available to the opposition would be compromises; its tactics, bargaining. But this aim is incompatible with the basic aim of the opposition in the English approach. For partici-

39. Cf. B. Ohlin, *Liberal utmaning* (1963), p. 18; G. Heckscher, *Trygga folkstyret!* (1963), pp. 12–14; *Svenska Dagbladet*, Aug. 4, 1964; *Dagens Nyheter*, Aug. 23, 1964.
40. S. Wedén, *Samhällsåskådningar och partier* (1963), p. 59.
41. *Dagens Nyheter*, July 16, 1963.
42. Cf. H. Adamsson, *Industritjänstemannen*, December 1963.
43. Cf. K. C. Wheare, *Legislatures* (London, Oxford University Press, 1963), p. 120.
44. Cf. O. Dahlén, *Stärk demokratin* (1964), pp. 46 ff.

pation in the policy-making process means that the opposition assumes a share of responsibility for government policy. By entering an all-party government the opposition would attain its goal of influencing the policy-making process, but it would weaken not only its claim to replace the government but also its role as the parliamentary opposition as such. With an all-party government there would be no alternative, no shadow government—indeed ought not to be any opposition at all among the parties. Instead the opposition would have to come from inside the parties and from groups outside the parties. The electorate would be stable. The fundamental structure of society could hardly be changed or attacked. The system could not function without a general sharing of common fundamental values.

The idea of joint work by all "good" parties has had a strong appeal in Sweden, and the all-party-government system, like the PR system, has been called just. Proponents of a permanent all-party government often emphasize that the English approach only increases dissatisfaction among the electorate and the politicians.

The two forms of government mentioned here are both "pure," ideal types at opposite ends of the scale.[45] However, facts have only in exceptional cases corresponded to either of the extremes on the scale. Generally there has been a mixture or a combination of the two systems. How then has the opposition functioned?

In the last few decades of the nineteenth century the opposition cannot be characterized as an opposition in the parliamentary sense. It had no desire either to replace the government or to collaborate with the government. Its main aim was to cut down state expenditure.[46] But the method of solving great political issues through compromise laid the basis for a political tradition.

In the period 1900–20, irrespective of which party formed the government the Liberals in fact acted as an opposition against the prevailing structure of society, while the Conservatives served as guardians of that structure. The Liberal Party, and especially its leader Karl Staaff,[47] believed in the English concept of the role of the opposition. Thus, when they were out of power the Liberals tried to replace the Conservative government, and when they were in power they were in principle not

45. The arrangement in the beginning of the 1920s, when no party wanted to be in government either alone or in coalition with another party and the government was therefore composed of high officials, is also the opposite of the all-party government but is antiparliamentarian. It was never considered a normal solution.

46. See N. Stjernquist, "The Swedish Constitution and the Budgetary Principles," *Scandinavian Studies in Law*, 6 (1962), 222.

47. See L. Kihlberg, *Karl Staaff, 1–2* (Stockholm, Bonniers förlag, 1962–63).

open to compromises with the Conservatives. In the beginning the Socialists were against any collaboration with a nonsocialist party on the government level, and among them were many who preferred revolutionary to electoral tactics. At the end of the period, however, the Socialists found it possible to collaborate with the Liberals even on the government level.

The crucial decisions, however, when universal suffrage for men and the PR system were introduced in 1907–09, were a typical political compromise. The PR system removed the real basis for the English system, though politicians did not embrace the idea that any other concept of an opposition party should be adopted. By the 1920s the main goal of the Socialists was not revolution but nationalization, the changing of the economic structure of society. From then on their opposition was entirely parliamentary, but they were still in opposition to the socioeconomic structure of society, while the nonsocialist parties tried to maintain this structure. The Socialists, however, did not hold sufficient power to achieve their objective.

Independent of whatever party formed the government, the opposition was in practice directed toward influencing the policy-making process. But the opposition parties sometimes hesitated to seek office. Generally it was assumed that it was undesirable to be in power during elections. The government party lost every election in the 1920s. The tactics of the opposition parties were electoral, but at the same time directed to a high degree toward bargaining with the government party or with other parties. Thus a system of majorities changing from question to question was developed. Government power was weak. On the other hand, because there were several opposition parties, each was weak. Politics was characterized by compromise between the parties, not primarily between the government and the opposition. Thus the system diverged markedly from the English one.

During the period of minority parliamentarism, when the political system was discussed the discussion generally started from the weakness of the government, not from the role of the opposition. The remedies proposed, however, would all have affected the role of the opposition. One remedy proposed by some Socialists was to change the electoral system to a majority system.[48] Tage Erlander, then a student at Lund University, argued in favor of the American system with a directly elected president.[49] Nils Herlitz, later a Conservative member of the Upper House and a lead-

48. See especially Motion No. 239 (1930) in the Upper House by G. Möller, R. Sandler, and K. Schlyter. P. A. Hansson, however, was in favor of the PR system.
49. *Arbetet*, July 4, 1928; reprinted in *En verklig folktidning, Arbetet 1887–1962* (Malmö, 1962), pp. 126 ff. As a comment, Erlander declared in the reprint that after 1932 parliamentarism had functioned well, on the whole, in Sweden.

ing authority on constitutional law, recommended in 1929 a system with an all-party government.[50]

The position of the government was strengthened by the collaboration between the Socialists and the Center Party from 1933. Instead of occasional cooperation between two or more parties in order to solve special issues, as the practice had been in the 1920s, an organized and permanent collaboration took place between two parties with a common program and control over a majority in both houses. Neither one opposition party nor all opposition parties together could any longer meet the government party as an equal.

Did the new situation change the aims, the tactics, and the role of the opposition? In principle, the opposition parties still wanted to replace the government party. They still criticized government policy and the trend to increase the state sector, and they still acted as guardians of the socioeconomic structure of society. But in fact the aims and tactics of the opposition did change. After the coalition government came into existence in 1936, the opposition parties had to face openly the new situation of a majority government. The Liberal leader, Gustaf Andersson, then made the following declaration for his parliamentary group:

> Our conduct toward the government and its majority in the Riksdag can of course have various forms. One way is to sit back and let things take their course. Another is to oppose at every turn just for the sake of opposition. Finally, the third way is to take an active part in dealing with and deciding on the matters in hand to the best of our ability, and on every occasion act as if we had a part in the responsibility for what happens. Obviously we ought to take the last-mentioned course.[51]

The Conservative leader, Gösta Bagge, also offered collaboration and said that his party was delighted at each real decrease in party cleavages.[52] Prime Minister Hansson compared the statements from the Conservative and Liberal parties with statements from these parties during the election campaign in 1936 and said that he was somewhat astonished. But

> an opposition that wants to come and cooperate with us in order to make the parliamentary decisions as good as possible, and as a basis for these make opinion in the Riksdag as wide as possible, this kind of opposition can always count on its points of view receiving a good deal of consideration.[53]

50. N. Herlitz, "Regeringsproblemets svårigheter," *Svensk tidskrift* (1929), pp. 177 ff.
51. *Svenska Dagbladet*, Jan. 12, 1937.
52. *Lower House Minutes* (Jan. 20, 1937), pp. 1 ff.
53. Ibid. p. 25.

Obviously the opposition had now adopted a new policy: in election campaigns, the English approach; in parliament and elsewhere, collaboration with the government in order to influence the political decision-making as much as possible.

The period of all-party government in World War II, when there was no place for a parliamentary opposition, was important for the development after the war. Prime Minister Hansson, it is said, would not have disliked having the all-party government continue after the war, but what he really wanted has been open to discussion.[54] What is certain is that the leaders of the Conservative and Center parties were against the dissolution of the all-party government at that time.

Since 1945 the Conservative and Liberal parties have said in each election campaign that it was time for a change, that the Socialists should be out and the nonsocialist parties in. To this extent they have clearly accepted the English approach. This pursuit of office was especially conspicuous in the 1948 elections, in the pension campaigns in the 1950s, and in 1957, when the Center Party left the government. The recent efforts to unite the nonsocialist parties in one party (see below) are motivated by the hope of getting a nonsocialist government.

The acceptance of the English approach has been clearer in the Conservative Party than in the Liberal Party. In an article in a weekly journal in 1962 Conservative leader Gunnar Heckscher underlined the fact that the opposition had two tasks: keeping a guard on the government and presenting alternatives. He also argued for real opposition which in his opinion often gave better results than going along with the government. In the same journal Liberal leader Bertil Ohlin stated, in words reminiscent of the period of minority parliamentarism, that the most important thing was that in critical situations no party should have a majority (including votes from supporting parties). Thus all parties would be obliged to take into account the views of different groups of people.[55]

On the other hand, spokesmen from all three nonsocialist parties have often made statements in favor of an all-party government.[56] Since 1946, the most prominent advocate of this system has been Herbert Tingsten. But, it has been asked, would the result not be the disappearance of parliamentary opposition? Who would take on its task of criticizing? Effective opposition is as important as effective government. In answer to this objection, it has been argued that if an all-party government were to come about, party discipline would have to be slackened, opposition

54. See for instance E. Wigforss, *Kan dödläget brytas?* (Stockholm, Tidens förlag, 1959), pp. 16 ff.
55. *Vecko-Journalen* (1962), No. 31. Cf. Ohlin in *Dagens Nyheter*, Oct. 22, 1964.
56. Conservative Party leader Gunnar Heckscher did not recommend the system. G. Heckscher, *Trygga folkstyret!* (1963), p. 22.

would have to be released inside the parties, and the electorate would have to be revitalized by use of the referendum.[57] The Socialists have been against all-party government except in times of crisis.[58]

In Parliament, however, the opposition parties are still anxious to look after their "right" to proportional influence in the political process and to see that the government is in contact with them in all important matters and really takes their interests into consideration. To a large extent there has been consensus, collaboration, and compromise between the government and the nonsocialist opposition parties. The opposition, however, has not had an influence proportional to its relative strength in Parliament. And, further, it is significant that the Center Party, even when out of government, has been more influential than the Conservatives and the Liberals. When an opposition party has been left out, it has protested. Thus the Conservatives and Liberals reacted against the agreement between the Socialists and the Center Party on the taxation question in 1961.

The tactics of the opposition in Parliament have to a high degree been those of bargaining. The opposition parties have often made proposals that would increase state expenditure, yet they have also been eager to reduce taxes and hence have restricted their proposals for higher state expenditure. But universal suffrage and the widespread acceptance of social welfare programs have resulted in Parliament's abandoning its nineteenth-century tradition of trying to cut down state expenditure. Today this job is primarily a duty of the government and especially of the Minister of Finance. Only the Conservative Party—in opposition to the claims of the Socialists that the government ought to have "sufficient" resources—has sometimes upheld the old tradition but at the same time abandoned the tactics of bargaining. As the Conservative leader, Jarl Hjalmarson, said in 1960, "The government and the Riksdag must have so little money that they are always obliged to live according to the stern principle of scarcity." [59]

The comments made here all have to do with opposition from the nonsocialist parties. The opposition from the left, from the Communist Party, has been carried on mainly inside the trade unions. On the parliamentary level the Communists have not played a significant part. Between 1945 and 1951 and from 1961 onward they held the balance between the nonsocialist opposition and the Socialists in the Lower House and between 1958 and 1963 and between 1965 and 1966 in joint divisions. But not being in the middle of the party scale they could not join the nonsocialist parties in

57. H. Tingsten, *Argument* (Stockholm, Bonniers förlag, 1948), pp. 196 ff. Cf. T. Vallinder in *Modern demokrati* (Lund, Gleerups förlag, 1963), pp. 73 ff.
58. Prime Minister Erlander in *Radio*, Oct. 28, 1957. E. Wigforss, *Kan dödläget brytas?* (Stockholm, Tidens förlag, 1959), pp. 16 ff.
59. *Svenska Dagbladet*, Aug. 14, 1960.

any action that would have overthrown the Socialist government. As previously mentioned, they abstained from the final vote on the sales tax question in 1960 and in this way helped the government. They did not dare to act in the same way as the People's Socialist Party in Norway did in 1963.[60]

Why Has Compromise Become So Important in Politics?

With the decrease in the cleavages between the parties and the increase in consensus, better conditions for compromise and agreement have, on the whole, been created. The effect has often been cumulative: every compromise probably tends to reduce existing cleavages.

Compromise is traditionally considered the Swedish technique in politics,[61] and the word "compromise" evidently sounds pleasing to Swedish voters. Even when the cleavages were deepest at the beginning of the century, the great political issues of universal suffrage, the election system, and the bicameral system were solved by compromise. The days of minority parliamentarism in the 'twenties necessitated cooperation and compromise between at least two of the parties. The periods of coalition government—despite the conflicts that arose toward the end of the war—helped to cement this tradition.

The proportional representation system fixed the multiparty system and laid the institutional basis for compromise politics. This trend has been strengthened by the fact that the political parties are proportionally represented on the parliamentary committees. Moreover, in a multiparty system the middle party—in Sweden the Liberals in the 1920s and the Center Party after 1932—has a key position since it can act as a balance, and it is generally inclined to make compromises.

National politics have been influenced by local politics. Entry into national politics and into membership in the Riksdag is normally by way of local politics. The member of Parliament often retains his membership on local commissions. Moreover, the members of the Upper House are elected by local bodies.[62] In local politics compromise is the normal way of dealing with differences of opinion, and the practice is institutionalized by proportional representation in the local authorities and the local committees.

National politics have been influenced by the politics of the large

60. Cf. Ch. 3.
61. Cf. F. Lagerroth, "Staaff eller De Geer? *Statsvetenskaplig tidskrift, 46* (1943), pp. 1 ff.
62. In the present discussion concerning a change-over to a unicameral system, Prime Minister Erlander has emphasized the importance of the connection between national politics and local politics. To maintain this connection and to keep participation in the local elections at a high level it is necessary in his opinion that local elections influence the composition of Parliament and thereby national politics. Cf. n. 5.

organizations: the trade unions, employers' associations, and so on. Bargaining and compromise are the tactics of these organizations, and "the spirit of Saltsjöbaden" has spread to the relations between political parties.

The opposition's desire to cooperate in the decision-making process leads it toward compromise. The opposition, to quote Hedlund, wants to have a policy of results, e.g. a policy that gives it a reasonable influence. Moreover, the expansion of state activity and long-range planning during the last few decades means that it is now more important for a political party to be in the government than it was in the 'twenties.

The government, wishing to act for all classes and interests and to have a wide following when solving great political issues, is usually inclined to compromise.

The party leaders' strong position and the increased discipline within the parties have facilitated compromises. Particularly interesting are the party leaders' conferences. They have been used for making agreements on issues that are troublesome from the political point of view, for instance on defense and the budget [63] and on the question of driving on the right.[64] It is believed that conferences and agreements help the parliamentary system to work smoothly. The contrary view, however, is that questions are taken out of politics.

All this evidence suggests the difficulty that parties have today in presenting the electorate with clear alternatives. When they seek to persuade the electorate in election campaigns that there *are* important differences among parties, they often go back to the cleavages of the old days. They carefully watch the proposals of the other parties in order to make it clear to the electorate that they are eager to look after the interests of the people. This is especially conspicuous in the field of social welfare.

The Influence of the Opposition

Although the opposition parties ordinarily have close to half the votes in Parliament, their influence on the conduct of government is relatively small. How can we account for the fact that their influence is so disproportionate?

63. See I. Amilon, "Partiledarkonferenserna, en studie i parlamentarisk praxis," *Statsvetenskaplig tidskrift, 66* (1963), 278 ff

64. Parliament decided in 1963 to change over from left-hand traffic on the roads to right-hand traffic. In a consultative referendum in 1955, about 83 per cent of the participants had said "no" to a change. The pressure from those who were in favor of a change continued, with support on the whole from all the newspapers. The political parties were afraid that the issue would come up as a political issue. It was therefore taken out of politics by a party leaders' agreement in 1963 in favor of a change. In this process the party groups in Parliament were consulted, and guarantees were given of a majority in each group for a change. It was further guaranteed that no new referendum would be demanded.

In trying to criticize the government in order to replace it and at the same time collaborate with it in order to participate in the decision-making process, the opposition has fallen between two stools. For the two objectives are incompatible.[65]

The opposition has been divided. For this very reason, however, some claim, it has been able to win more votes in elections (see below).

Because of the increasingly complicated structure of society, the party that acts as the government has a superior position. The government has all the ministries, agencies, and royal commissions at its disposal. It may be stressed that the Center Party, with its special interest in agricultural policy, when in a coalition government has always held the Ministry of Agriculture. The opposition's resources for working out alternatives to the government's proposals or for taking the initiative are greatly inferior to the government's. The fact that the opposition parties are represented on the more important royal commissions certainly guarantees that they have some opportunity for observation and control, but they can by no means neutralize the government's advantage. The opposition parties, particularly the Liberals and the Center Party, lack economic resources to build up a sufficiently big party secretariat of their own.

Long-term planning, broad decisions on principle, the delegation of authority, and the government's own negotiations with the great organizations have all pushed the Riksdag to one side with the result that real decisions are made in the Riksdag less frequently than previously. Thus opportunities for observing and taking action have diminished for the opposition parties.

In some cases, in the opposition's view, the government has acted without due reference to the Riksdag or to the opposition.

Finally, an unproved and subjective observation offered by some critics is that the opposition has not been able to attract peeople of talent and ability because it has little hope of ever being in power.

Why No Change?

Why has the opposition not managed to oust the Socialists from their position? In other words, why has the parliamentary majority not swung over to the nonsocialist side?

This can be explained partly by the reasons just given as to why the opposition has not obtained more influence. The opposition has fallen between the two stools of opposing and participating. It has been divided

65. U. Himmelstrand ("A Theoretical and Empirical Approach," p. 93 ff.) states the hypothesis "that the opposition parties in Sweden, particularly the Liberal Party, are more depoliticized than the Socialist Party in the sense that they have more clearly dissociated ideology and practical politics. Being caught on the horns of this dilemma, ideological faithfulness and political effectiveness both being sought, a dissociative solution . . . is ready at hand for a permanent opposition party."

and thus weak. It has insufficient resources. In addition, with the expanding economy since World War II there has been prosperity and practically no unemployment. This situation favors the government party, especially insofar as the Communists have got only a few seats.

The opposition has not been able to present alternatives that would give it a distinctive character of its own in the opinion of the electorate. Neither have their alternatives been attractive enough in comparison with those of the Socialists to make the majority of the electorate support the opposition parties. The Socialists have also done a better job of organizing their election campaigns.

The Center Party has not wanted to overthrow the Socialist government. This party prevented a change in 1957, when the nonsocialist parties together held a majority position in the Lower House.

The Communists have not wanted and have been virtually unable to vote against the Socialist government in crucial decisions.

Toward Better Conditions for the Opposition?

There is a strong feeling in Sweden that the opposition is too weak. On the other hand, it is emphasized, especially by the Socialists, that in these days when society has a complex economic and technological structure a strong government is essential; the electoral method ought to be such that it favors the formation of a strong government. In general discussions of the means of governing, it has been pointed out that the political parties taken together are too weak in relation to the socioeconomic organizations and bureaucracy, and that political discussion and consequently the vitality of the democracy are too weak.[66]

The problem put here is basically insoluble. There is no way of getting an electoral system which at the same time would result in a strong government and a strong opposition. But it may be of interest to try to analyze the measures that have been proposed to strengthen the opposition.

An improvement in the financial resources of the opposition parties would undoubtedly help them. The Center Party has proposed that each opposition party should be granted money to finance a secretariat for parliamentary and research work in order to create a better balance between the government and the opposition.[67] The royal commission on the Constitution has proposed that every party should have a government appropriation for one full-time secretary. The commission has also called for reorganization of the working conditions of the Riksdag, which would favor the opposition parties in particular.[68] In the recent debate there has

66. Cf. H. Tingsten, "Stability and Vitality in Swedish Democracy," *The Political Quarterly, 26* (1955), 140 ff.
67. Lower House, 1961, Motion No. 58.
68. *Statens offentliga utredningar* (1963), No. 18, pp. 211 ff.

been a call for considerably more aid to the political parties.[69] In fact, however, a real reorganization of the opposition's resources and the formation of a "shadow secretariat" that can match the ministries presupposes a two-party system.[70]

Another topic that has aroused lively discussion is the suggestion that an amalgamation of the nonsocialist parties would strengthen the opposition's position and in fact give it a chance to come to power. Since the nonsocialist parties have been out of power for a long time, two of them for a very long time, there is today, quite naturally, a tendency toward unification of the opposition. Those adherents of the Center Party and the Liberal Party who feel close to the Socialists would probably dislike such an amalgamation and to a large extent abstain from voting or change over to the Socialists.[71] Whether an integration would in the long run help the nonsocialist bloc has been widely discussed. Interest is higher among the Conservatives than among the Liberals and the Center Party, and higher in the newspapers and among the general public[72] than inside the political machines.

In October 1962 a Swedish weekly journal asked the three nonsocialist party leaders: Is organized collaboration among the nonsocialist parties to be desired and is such collaboration possible? Conservative leader Heckscher answered that collaboration was to be desired and perhaps possible. Liberal leader Ohlin replied that the forming of a nonsocialist bloc was the best help the Socialists could receive, because then the Liberals and the Center Party could be suspected of condoning the sins of the Conservatives. Center Party leader Hedlund said that unification was unrealistic and that a nonsocialist bloc would only favor the Socialists.

---

69. L. Andersson, I. Carlsson, A. Gustafsson, *Författningsreform—nytt alternativ* (Stockholm, Tidens förlag, 1963), p. 82; O. Ruin, "Kanslihusets ställning," in *Morgondagens samhällsproblem* (Stockholm, 1963), p. 94; P. Ahlmark, *Vår fattiga politik* (Stockholm, 1964), pp. 121 ff.

70. Cf. O. Ruin, "Kanslihusets ställning," p. 94.

71. Cf. *Idun-Veckojournalen* (1965), No. 2.

72. Public opinion polls (Svenska Institutet för Opinionsundersökningar, SIFO) taken in 1961 and 1963 show that interest in a united nonsocialist party was greater among electors who voted for these parties than among the Socialists. But the interest seems to have declined somewhat on all sides in the intervening period.

Voted in the last election for

	Socialists		One of the nonsocialist parties	
	1961 %	1963 %	1961 %	1963 %
Prefer 2 parties	31	18	59	48
Prefer 4 parties	44	49	25	29
Doesn't matter	13	9	4	4
Doubtful	12	24	12	19
Total	100	100	100	100

For that reason the three parties ought to be independent of one another.[73] On later occasions Hedlund has repeatedly said "no" to an amalgamation of the opposition parties. It is obvious that such a move would make it impossible for the Center Party to keep its position as the balancer. The Socialists have asked from time to time why the opposition parties do not get together and agree on *one* alternative. In July 1962, when Prime Minister Erlander was asked which he preferred—a single opposition bloc with a clear alternative or three divided small parties—he answered:

> A single nonsocialist bloc would probably give Swedish politics a firmer contour, and it is possible that the formation of a bloc of this kind would make it easier for the Socialists to convince the electorate of our political advantages. Therefore, a bloc of this kind would probably bring about some advantages of a tactical and propaganda nature for Social Democracy. From the point of view of the nation the nonsocialist parties can be divided as long as they form the opposition. If they are aiming at taking over the government, then they had better work out a unanimous program.[74]

The amalgamation issue and the best way to realize the amalgamation were widely discussed in the 1964 elections, when the MBS Party competed in the Malmö constituency with both the Socialists and the three nonsocialist parties. The Malmö constituency is entirely urban, has a strong Conservative Party, a weak Liberal Party, and a diminutive Center Party. The leaders of the new party emphasized that the MBS was the first step toward an amalgamation. People who were in favor of an amalgamation in principle argued, however, that the first step should not be taken on the local level. The discussion continued after the elections. More probable than an immediate amalgamation of the nonsocialist parties may be a more intimate collaboration or an amalgamation of the Liberal Party and the Center Party.

A unification of the nonsocialist parties can be arranged by changes in the electoral legislation. One method proposed is a change-over to the system of a simple majority in elections, which might automatically create a two-party system. Within the royal commission on constitutional reform there was a majority in favor of such a system in principle.[75] But the introduction of a two-party system would not in fact bring about a

73. *Vecko-Journalen* (1962), No. 40. The nonsocialist party leaders made the same statements in the Lower House, Jan. 22, 1964.

74. *Stockholms-Tidningen,* July 15, 1962. See also Erlander, *Upper House Minutes* (1956), *2,* 18. Gunnar Myrdal, who was a member of the Socialist Cabinet in the 1940s, criticized, in a speech of May 1, 1964, the inability of the opposition to amalgamate and said that it would be useful for the "strong, conservative" Socialist Party to compete with a united opposition.

75. *Statens offentliga utredningar* (1963), No. 16, pp. 51 ff.

change in the fundamentals of the present situation—the tug of war for the marginal votes—and hence the same policies would remain.

A return to the proportional method (d'Hondt) which was applied up to 1952 would make it necessary for the nonsocialist parties to cooperate in elections as they were obliged to do before 1952. Such cooperation, however, would be inconvenient for the Center Party in its role as balancer. The d'Hondt method was abandoned when the Center Party entered a coalition government with the Socialists in 1951, and it was then replaced by the present proportional method (Sainte-Laguë), which makes it possible for the nonsocialist parties to stand alone in elections. It is characteristic of the attitude of the leader of the Center Party, Gunnar Hedlund, that he is said to have described the Sainte-Laguë method as "a miraculous formula." [76]

A change-over to a permanent all-party government would probably give the opposition parties greater influence.

A weakening of the position of the interests groups would strengthen that of the parties.

If the cleavages were more clearly distinguishable, there would be more intense political discussion.[77] It would make compromise politics more difficult and would therefore decrease the opposition's influence, but at the same time it would give the opposition a chance to strengthen its position in the electorate. It is in fact a problem for the political parties to find new issues that emphasize the cleavages and stress the differences between one party and another. On the other hand, it is of vital importance to a party that its stand on a new political issue does not antagonize marginal groups. From all these points of view, the pension question was a successful one for the Socialists.[78]

How can the present situation of the opposition best be described? Some representatives of the nonsocialist opposition will certainly characterize the situation as a stable deadlock, as there are no changes in the government. Other representatives will probably say that the 50–50 balance between the Socialists and the nonsocialist parties is a good thing, as it obliges the two blocs to respect each other and especially the groups in

76. *Sydsvenska Dagbladet,* June 18, 1963.

77. Cf. H. Meijer and O. Ruin, "Ny författning?" *Tiden* (1963), p. 336.

78. According to S. M. Lipset, "Class Structure and Politics," *Daedalus* (Winter 1964), p. 287, the Socialists introduced the pension reform largely because their electoral research had suggested that such a proposal would be popular not only with their traditional supporters, the manual workers, but with many white-collar workers. This statement can be argued. Cf. B. Särlvik, *The Role of Party Identification in Voters' Perception of Political Issues: a Study of Opinion Formation in Swedish Politics, 1956–1960* (mimeo., paper for the International Political Science Association Congress, Paris, 1961). See also B. Molin, *Tjänstepensionsfrågan* (Gothenburg, 1965), with an English summary.

the middle. The Socialists, on the other hand, will probably emphasize the stability, since they have been in power practically since 1932, but at the same time underline the instability that results from their not being able to command a majority either in the Lower House or in the joint divisions and from the fact that small fluctuations in the electorate can change the situation.

The viewpoints described here are largely a part of the political debate among the various parties. The idea that a proportional election is a fair election is deeply rooted, and the same is true of the attitude toward compromise. Moreover, the present party organizations act as built-in stabilizers in the system. Institutional changes are therefore difficult to achieve. The socioeconomic organizations are so consolidated that they too have a stabilizing effect in the present situation. Finally, it could probably be said that in many circles even outside the government party people are more pleased than displeased with the present arrangements. From those points of view the situation is best characterized by "stability" or, if you wish, "a stable deadlock."

This stability or deadlock, however, is promoted by a number of contributory factors. An alteration in one or several of these could bring about changes. Shifts in the structure of society and in the composition of the population could transform the party system. A deterioration in the economic situation or in the international situation could result in an all-party government. A further expansion of the influence of interest groups or of technocracy will probably make it necessary for the political parties to reconsider their situation. A change-over to a two-party system, however, with one Socialist and one nonsocialist bloc, or an amalgamation of two of the nonsocialist parties will, as previously mentioned, hardly alter the basic feature of the present political system, as the parties will still appeal to the floating votes in the middle of the party scale. A considerable increase in the number of Communist votes and seats would be more important. It would oblige the Socialists to conduct a war on two fronts, which is always difficult, and to make their program more radical, thereby emphasizing the differences between their views and those of the nonsocialist parties—but at the risk of neglecting the floating votes in the middle.

5

BELGIUM:
RELIGION, CLASS, AND LANGUAGE
IN NATIONAL POLITICS

Val R. Lorwin

An energetic Belgian Prime Minister described the policy of his Catholic-Socialist coalition government in 1962 as an attempt at "dialogues" between Catholics and anticlericals, between labor and employers, and between the two linguistic-cultural communities of the nation.[1] If Théo Lefèvre did not mention a dialogue between the government and the parliamentary opposition, it was not forgetfulness or disdain for a numerically small formal opposition. It was a recognition of the way in which the chief cleavages in Belgian society have cut across government and party lines more often than they have divided government from formal opposition.

The three dialogues that Théo Lefèvre sought recall the three oppositions which have dominated Belgian political life. The oldest opposition arose from differences over the relationships of Church and State and the role of Catholic and public schools. This is the only form of dialogue in which each party has spoken with a single voice. It is the only one in which a sort of two-party system has existed, pitting the Catholics first against the Liberals and later against the Socialists as well.

The second opposition is that which brought into being a Socialist Party and the labor wing of the Catholic Party. Strong employer associations and well-organized trade unions carry on a continuing dialogue, with an occasional assist or call to desist from the government. The dialogue of these "social partners" is paralleled by the political dialogue be-

---

1. Senate, *Compte-Rendu Analytique*, June 13, 1962, p. 480.

I gratefully acknowledge the help of the Center for Advanced Study in the Behavioral Sciences, the Social Science Research Council and its Committee on Comparative Politics, the Graduate School of the University of Oregon, the Rockefeller Foundation Constitutional Democracy Program, and the Ford Foundation. To friends and acquaintances in Belgium and elsewhere, I am so deeply (and happily) indebted that I must wait until a full-length book on Belgian politics permits me, however inadequately, to thank them.

tween the Socialist Party and the Catholic left wing, on the one hand, and the Catholic right wing and the Liberal Party, on the other.

The third opposition to which Lefèvre alluded, that of the "cultural communities," has not been essentially party-forming. It has confronted the Flemish-speaking and French-speaking ethnic-linguistic communities, and now also the regions of Flanders and Wallonia, sometimes with Brussels as a third interlocutor.

The system of parties has been remarkably stable for eight decades. It has withstood two world wars and two enemy occupations, changes in social structure, the rise of regional-linguistic movements, the introduction of universal suffrage and of proportional representation, the Great Depression, the tides of international communism, the surge and collapse of European fascism, the shifts from Belgian neutrality to international commitment and back and forth again, the acceptance of the welfare state, the forced abdication of a monarch, and the loss of a vast colony. It has withstood changes of name and structure by each of the parties. (For simplicity, I shall sometimes speak of the "Catholic Party" in a context that includes the years since 1945, when it was reborn as the Christian Social Party; of the "Socialist Party" to signify what was until 1940 called the Belgian Workers Party; and of the "Liberal Party" to denote the group which in 1961 reorganized as the Party of Liberty and Progress.)

On the surface the party system has been simple, stable, and even logical. There have been only three national parties since the 1880s, each associated with one of the nation's "spiritual families," and each with its network of socioeconomic organizations. There has been a fairly stable balance of voting strength among the three parties since the introduction of universal equal suffrage. Obligatory voting has almost done away with fluctuations in electoral participation. A large measure of proportional representation has caused voting strength to be fairly well reflected in parliamentary representation, with a rather close correspondence in party balance between the two houses of Parliament. And—oh, miracle for the American beholder—there have been frequent readjustments of parliamentary representation to reflect population changes.

The loyal oppositions appeared early in national history. Oppositions of principle appeared much later, but they did not long challenge the legitimacy of the regime. The Constitution slowed the process of democratization of the suffrage, but this prevented such shocks as France experienced with the sudden acquisition of universal suffrage.

The regular course of constitutional government has been stimulated or deflected by an occasional general strike. But it has been suspended only by enemy occupation. Only islands of disadvantaged groups remain alienated from the community, and most people share its essentially middle-class values. The rapid pace of industrialization has had a slower reflection in social structure, because many villagers have been able to become industrial workers without losing their attachment to the soil, thanks to the dispersion of factories and subsidized low railway fares for workers.

The regime has never suppressed the right of the opposition to oppose, except in the wake of wartime treason. Parliament invests, formally controls, and occasionally even overthrows cabinets. In both houses, the outs confront the ins and, except for a few minor parties, can look forward to sharing power. The parties aggregate the demands of social groups and bargain them out in Parliament and government. Political and ideological oppositions pervade voluntary associations as well as all of public life. They are even projected into education and the bureaucracy, but does that not again show how logical, or at least consistent with cultural reality, the system is?

The reader will of course have understood that the political system of Belgium is more complex, and the political history richer, than these orderly appearances suggest. But first let us see the political system as it emerged in the critical early years of national existence.

The Union of Oppositions

The Belgian state was born parliamentary, and with the concept of opposition as legitimate. It was a self-conscious "union of the oppositions" which made the national revolution of 1830 against William I, king of the Dutch-Belgian "amalgam" created by the Congress of Vienna. These "oppositions" were groups—not yet parties—which thought of themselves as Catholics and as Liberals. They went back to the experience of an earlier national uprising, the Brabant Revolution of 1789, in which the Austrian Netherlands momentarily shook off the rule—and the reforms— of Joseph II. The Statists, or Van der Nootists, opposed the reforms of Joseph II; they sought to maintain the customs and privileges of the established Catholic Church and the narrowly based oligarchy of landowners, masters of urban crafts, and nobles who dominated the sclerosed provincial assemblies or Estates. For a moment they worked with the followers of François Vonck, members of the higher business and professional classes and intellectuals, who welcomed the rationalization Joseph II sought at the expense of the Church and the provincial Estates, but upheld Belgian autonomy against the aloof and impolitic, if enlightened, Habsburg despot.

Together the Statists and the Vonckists swept out their Austrian rulers and tried to establish a decentralized, oligarchic, federal republic. But they soon set upon each other; chiefly, the Statists set mobs upon the Vonckists as enemies of the Church. In this civil strife, the Habsburgs easily reconquered the "United Belgian States."

It was the successors of these two groups who found themselves, for different reasons, in opposition to Dutch King William. The Catholics rallied to defend the Church and its educational system against the lay, centralizing hand of William I, whom they saw as a Dutch-speaking Protestant version of Joseph II. The Liberals, although in sympathy with the anticlerical and centralizing measures of William, felt threatened by his restrictions on freedom of the press, his favoring of Dutchmen over Belgians in appointments, and his promotion of the Dutch language against the French which was by now the language of almost all the Belgian elites.

In an unusual effort of tolerance and comprehension, Belgian Catholics and Liberals agreed in 1827–28 on a "union of the oppositions" against William's innovations. This union of the oppositions launched the constitutional protest that preceded the sudden revolt that won national independence. Then the Unionists went on, in the "National Congress" of 1830–31, to write a constitution with freedoms of speech, press, and religion liberal indeed in the Europe of Metternich and Wellington. The suffrage provisions were less ungenerous than those of Britain or France at the time. But a minimum direct-tax requirement for voting left room within the constitution for only a modest expansion of the national electorate.

To avoid the chaotic decentralization of the Brabant Revolution, the Constitution created a unitary state. But it left place for extensive local autonomy and thus for the communal (municipal) politics which soon produced vigorous party oppositions. The members of the National Congress had in their minds, as their president said, "the hatred of the last king and the fear of the next one." Not free to set up a republic, which would have alarmed the Great Powers too much, they created a "republican monarchy." The monarch was restricted to specified powers, and his ministers were declared responsible to Parliament. All powers were identified as emanating from the nation.

The Constitution did not separate Church and State, as many Belgians like to say. But it set new patterns of freedom for both. There would be no established Church, but all recognized religions would be supported by the State. The State would not intervene, however, in the operations of the churches or their appointments. With Protestants and Jews no more than one per cent of the population, the Catholic Church thus obtained a rare combination of material support and freedom from state control. The guaranties of freedom of education and of association left the Church free to carry on its educational efforts, its training of the priesthood, its charities and social services.

If for Catholics the Church was to be free of control by the State, for Liberals the State had to be free of control by the Church. The Constitution set forth a number of the liberal freedoms that were anathema in other Catholic lands, where error was not permitted to compete with revealed truth. Rome grudgingly recognized the "liberal hypothesis" of the special "Belgian case" as the best it could obtain.[2] Not until Leo XIII, however, did Rome fully accept the Belgian constitutional charter and its modern liberties.[3]

From Unionism to Party Government

The principle was soon established that a cabinet had to have the support of a majority not only in the House of Representatives, the predominant chamber, but also in the Senate, an elected body with a highly restrictive direct-tax qualification for membership. If there was doubt about the government's ability to govern or about its still representing a majority of the enfranchised minority (the *pays légal*), one or both houses were dissolved, and the voters were called upon to decide. There might also be a dissolution in the event of serious differences between the two houses.

Leopold I promoted "unionism," or government that declared itself impartial—above party and without reference to parties. In unionism he saw the best hope of protecting the new nation's existence from evident external threats and potential internal threats. It also gave him the largest personal role under a constitution written, as he grumbled, "when the King was not there to defend the monarchy." Grumble he did, but he was too shrewd to flout the Constitution openly or clash head on with a parliamentary majority. From 1831 to 1847, Leopold presided over unionist cabinets. Most were mixed cabinets of Catholics and Liberals; a few were one-party cabinets, but based on unionist majorities in Parliament.

Unionism was conservative. It was better for business, its advocates thought, than "sterile discussions" of "vain ideological questions."[4] The example of France was always there to show how dangerously such discussions might agitate the masses. Anyway, social and economic issues hardly intruded yet upon that organized political life which a leading moderate Liberal termed "the diplomatico-juridico-Catholico-baroquo-political fracas."[5] Even before Parliament began to vote on party lines, there was considerable awareness of political group identification. Local

2. See the admirable and fascinating series of books and articles by Msgr. A Simon on the relations between Church and State, between the monarchy and the Vatican, in the nineteenth century, especially *Le Cardinal Sterckx et son temps* (2 vols. Wetteren, Scaldis, 1950); *La Politique religieuse de Léopold I*, Brussels (Goemaere, 1953); *Catholicisme et politique: Documents inédits (1832-1909)* (Wetteren, Scaldis, 1955); and *L'Hypothèse libérale en Belgique: Documents inédits, 1839-1907* (Wetteren, Scaldis, 1956); *Le Parti Catholique Belge, 1830-1945* (Brussels, Renaissance du Livre, 1958); *Le Cardinal Mercier* (Brussels, Renaissance du Livre, 1960), and *Léopold I* (Brussels, Renaissance du Livre, 1963).

3. K. Van Isacker, S.J., *Werkelijk en Wettelijk Land: De Katholieke Opinie tegenover de Rechterzijde, 1863-1884* (Antwerp, Standaard Boekhandel, 1955), pp. 248-50.

4. Quoted by Colette Lebas, *L'Union des catholiques et des libéraux de 1839 à 1847* (Louvain, Nauwelaerts, 1960), p. 38.

5. Joseph Lebeau, quoted by Carlo Bronne, *Joseph Lebeau* (Brussels, Renaissance du Livre, 1944), p. 60.

electoral associations, many of them run by the Masonic lodges, opposed the clergy in local elections, many of which were more partisan than national elections.

In 1838 the Belgian bishops forbade the faithful to be Masons any longer. This brought the Vatican condemnation of Freemasonry onto the Belgian scene for the first time, and it created a crisis of conscience for many hitherto obedient Catholics. As the Masonic lodges had not yet become anti-Catholic, the crisis of conscience was not in all cases resolved in favor of the Church. This was the first, but far from the last, time the Church was to drive out believers in the name of the political unity of Catholics. To the bitterness of ideological difference was now added fear of international secret organization, which the Liberals saw in the Church of Rome and the Catholics saw in Freemasonry.

The bishops' action gave a powerful impetus to the formation of the Liberal Party in 1846 and its move toward homogeneous one-party cabinets. The Liberals who broke with unionism were among the moderates, not the extremists, of the party. Offering both alternative personnel and alternative policies, they put forth cogent views of the role of parties in government and in opposition. Said Paul Devaux in 1839:

> A practical opposition . . . tries not only to destroy, but knows what it will put in place of what it overthrows. This opposition has its extremes, its agitators, but they constitute neither its essence nor its base . . . In a state organized like ours, the real and lasting alternative is not between the existence and the absence of an opposition, but rather between a violent, exaggerated opposition and a practical, moderate opposition, a friend of order; or even between parliamentary opposition and an extraparliamentary opposition.[6]

With the passing of the foreign threat to the nation's existence, unionism had lived its hour. The King had to recognize the impossibility of unionist cabinets or even unionist majorities for cabinets of a single party. The Liberal Joseph Lebeau affirmed the need for party government:

> The inauguration of one-party cabinets is the end, and the irrevocable end, of an overly long political hypocrisy which not only altered the principles of representative government, but struck unfortunate blows at the morality of the administration . . . Mixed ministries are the exceptional state of power; they are never its normal state.[7]

But he promised that if Belgian peace was threatened from without or from within by "a frantic demogogy menacing public order and our institutions," the nation would go back to "mixed cabinets." It was not to

6. Quoted in Lebas, *L'Union des catholiques et des libéraux*, pp. 241–42, note.
7. Bronne, *Joseph Lebeau*, pp. 92–93.

do so until the German invasion of 1914, except for a few years in the 1850s.[8]

If party government was ineluctable, Leopold I hoped at least to prevent a division of the nation's conservative forces. He had always seen the union of throne and altar as natural and necessary.[9] Now he tried to build up a party of "dynastic men and religious men" to support the political and social order against the threats of democracy. In this hope the old king was disappointed. To conservatives, the threat of political democracy was remote, and the threat of social and economic democracy even more remote. The very ease with which the monarchy survived the European storm of 1848—at the small price of extending the suffrage to its modest constitutional limits—lessened the force of Leopold's argument. The division between Liberals and Catholics had hardened.

Liberals and Catholics: The Classic Model

In his plea for moderate and responsible opposition, Paul Devaux had not foreseen the bitterness that would come to characterize the opposition of the two conceptions of public life and of the roles of State and Church. To Catholics the liberty proclaimed by the Constitution was the liberty to build certain of the nation's institutions, notably of education and welfare, aided by a "mutual benevolence" between Church and State.[10] (While a national system of public education was only slowly and painfully being organized, Catholic educational institutions were functioning at all levels. To this day, they have continued to have more students at every level than the public system.) [11] In these Catholic aims, and in the pressure of the hierarchy and parish priests to produce "good elections," the Liberals saw a threat to the independence of the State and to the diffusion of Liberal notions among future generations of Belgian voters. Liberalism took on an anti-Catholic tone absent in its early years. Pressed by the now-embattled Masonic lodges and the rationalist societies, the Liberals moved on after mid-century to an even more anticlerical posture and sought not only independence of the State from the Church, but its supremacy: the neutralization—that is, the laicization—of all education, welfare work, and even burial grounds.

What was neutral or secular to the Liberals, especially in education, was antireligious to Catholics. As the contest waxed more bitter, many priests

---

8. Of De Decker, head of the unionist ministry of 1855–57, it was said by some fellow Catholics that he was like "a double-barrelled gun, which went off by itself, one barrel against the enemy and the other against his friends." Frans van Kalken, *La Belgique contemporaine (1780–1949)* (2d ed. Paris, Colin, 1950), p. 87.

9. Largely indifferent to religion, Leopold himself remained a Protestant, shrewdly judging that he could be of more use to the Church, and the Church to him, if he did not become a converted Catholic. All his successors have been Catholics.

10. The phrase is that of Simon, *Le Parti Catholique Belge*, p. 73.

11. For numbers of students in the two systems in 1960–61, see Appendix Tables 5.1 and 5.2.

led the faithful in the prayer: "From schools without God and from teachers without faith, deliver us, O Lord." [12] Not indolently leaving all the work of deliverance to the Lord, the clergy urged the faithful on to political activity and, after 1863, to political unity within the Catholic Party.

The pattern of opposition emerged in the debate over the school law of 1850, and reached its zenith after the Liberals' 1879 school law. The clergy literally drove out of the Church many of those who tolerated the public schools. The Catholic parliamentary delegation (far more reasonable than the clergy, the violent Catholic press, and most of the faithful [13]) implored the new Pope to restrain the hierarchy and through it the parish clergy. But this was more than Leo XIII and his Nuncio could do.

The extremes of opposition were not in electoral tactics but in attacks on the intimate beliefs and social relationships of Liberals and Catholics. The rationalists ridiculed religious ceremonies and sometimes attacked funeral corteges. Priests used their spiritual powers to enforce—or so they thought—the political unity of the faithful: from the pulpit they attacked Liberals present in church and denied the sacraments to public school teachers and parents of their pupils.[14]

Religious and antireligious manifestations were thus not only sources of cleavage, but also forms of propaganda and constraint. As in other old Catholic countries, believers confronted unbelievers with no third choice that might diffuse hostilities. The appearance of the Socialist Party only reinforced this dichotomy. For the one thing about which the Socialists long remained sectarian was their opposition to religious sectarianism.

These tactics of opposition did not attack the regime. But they poisoned the atmosphere of social life and political discourse in many communities. The Dreyfus case in France and the Ulster issue in England perhaps cut more deeply and polarized opinion more sharply. But both were shorter-lived, and neither involved so many people's daily lives for so long a period as did the church-school issue in Belgium.

The Liberal-Catholic opposition produced a classic alternation in national government between 1846 and 1884, with the Liberals dominant most of the time. In 1884 the Catholics began an unparalleled 30 years in control of the central government. The balance of strength among the taxpaying voters was fairly close. But the small number of voters and the quirks of the electoral system before proportional representation made for occasionally sharp swings in electoral results.[15]

12. Henri Pirenne, *Histoire de Belgique*, 7 (2d ed. Brussels, Lamertin, 1948), 234.
13. Van Isacker, *Werkelijk en Wettelijk Land*, passim.
14. Simon, *Le Parti Catholique Belge*, and Van Isacker, *Werkelijk en Wettelijk Land*.
15. On the electoral system, see John Gilissen, *Le Régime représentatif en Belgique depuis 1790* (Brussels, Renaissance du Livre, 1958). For the electorate and results of elections under the *régime censitaire*, see Appendix Table 5.3.

Despite the ideological alignment, there were floating voters. Ideological lines might be broken—or reinforced—by economic-interest appeals, social pressures or fraud. Even after the secret ballot act of 1877, electoral irregularities were widespread among those happy few whose fiscal contributions marked them as independent, intelligent, and interested enough in the commonweal to rate the franchise.[16]

The depth of opposition did not reflect polarization along lines other than Church-State issues. Social and economic issues hardly appeared as yet on the political agenda. There was some difference, but no polarization, in the parties' social bases among the voters and among the voteless masses whom they brought onto the stage in mob scenes from time to time. The Catholics could call upon the rural masses more than upon the city masses, upon Flemish more than upon Walloon or Brussels crowds. Catholic voters comprised the largest part, though far from all, of the great landowners, including those of the hereditary nobility. The Liberals' chief strength was in the industrial, commercial, and professional bourgeoisie.

Neither of the two "spiritual families" was monolithic in opinion or in electoral behavior. No sooner did the Liberal Party achieve a precocious national structure in 1846 (31 years before England's National Liberal Federation) than splits developed. The Progressives favored suffrage extension, which the Doctrinaires heartily opposed. This and other conflicts —over the degree of antireligious action and over personalities—often produced competing Liberal electoral slates, notably in the capital.

The Catholics, served politically by the structures of the Church, began to build a special party structure only in the 1860s and firmed it up only in 1884. Meanwhile they were divided in their attitudes toward the liberties protected by the Constitution. The ultra-right Catholics criticized the parliamentary Catholic Party for taking part in the governance of a state that tolerated error and evil impartially with truth and good. These "Ultramontanes"—the sense of this word in Belgian history is different from its meaning elsewhere—formed no party or organization and elected no one to Parliament. At no time did they attack the political regime as such. There was no such hopeless pursuit of an outworn system as the French Catholic devotion to a royal restoration. But they harried the Catholic M.P.'s—the parliamentary Right.

The Ultramontanes had a very large following because of their support in the lower ranks of the clergy, their press, and the social or intellectual eminence of a number of their spokesmen. Leo XIII felt that the divisions in the Catholic community and the opposition of some Catholics to the Constitution had contributed to Liberal political victories. No sooner did he become Pope than he told the Belgians that even

16. In 1890–91, almost 23,000 votes were challenged. That was the record year for election appeals. Gilissen, *Le Régime représentatif*, p. 111.

if their Constitution, like all man-made works, was imperfect, half a century's experience showed that "in the present state of modern society, the system of freedom in Belgium is favorable to the Church. Belgian Catholics must not only refrain from attacking, they must also defend, the Constitution." [17]

The "social question" came to be an issue in Catholic political circles only slowly. Despite the efforts of the socially conscious Catholic politicians, many of them aristocrats, of the "New Right" after the turn of the century, the demands of Christian Democracy [18] did not become urgent until the Flemish masses had votes equal to their numbers.

The Socialist Party

Church-State issues had prevented a concentration of the possessing classes in the conservative party which Leopold I had wanted. Religious differences prevented the socialist political organization, formed in 1885 and prudently named the Workers Party, from representing more than one section of the working class. Within that section, the Socialists created a subculture—"a state within the State," their leader Emile Vandervelde called it—of consumers' cooperatives, friendly societies (mutual insurance groups), trade unions, and party which set a pattern for Catholic, and even Liberal, organizations.

The party settled down to the role of a loyal opposition even more rapidly than most other so-called Marxist parties. It concentrated on winning universal suffrage rather than fighting the class war. The Belgians were almost all revisionists, and showed little taste for the doctrinal debates that raged in other continental parties. "They have nothing to revise, for they have no theory," sneered Karl Kautsky in the typically un-Marxist statement of an orthodox Marxist.[19]

The strategy of universal suffrage called for the tactic of alliance with the Progressive wing of the Liberal Party. To the electoral and parliamentary fight, the Socialists added the thrust of the general strike.[20] The French syndicalists of the pre-1914 generation made a fetish of the revolutionary general strike, but never tried it. The Belgian Socialists carried out four general strikes before 1914 to advance political democracy.

The grant of universal manhood suffrage, although with plural voting,[21]

17. Speaking to a delegation of the Belgian Catholic press, 1879. Van Isacker, *Werkelijk en Wettelijk Land*, p. 249.

18. This term refers in Belgian history only to the labor, socially progressive currents within the Catholic community and the Catholic Party.

19. Kautsky to Victor Adler, May 23, 1902, in Adler, *Briefwechsel mit August Bebel und Karl Kautsky*, ed. Friedrich Adler (Vienna, Weiner Volksbuchhandlung, 1954), p. 400.

20. For an excellent discussion, see Carl Landauer, *European Socialism* (2 vols. Berkeley, University of California Press, 1959), *1*, 478–80.

21. The new constitutional provision gave all men the vote at age 25, with supple-

brought the Socialists into the parliamentary arena with a rush in 1894.[22] There they fought for equal manhood suffrage and for other reforms, notably universal free primary school education and equality in military service. The effect of all these would be to help integrate the industrial working classes and the peasantry into the social and political order.

The Liberals were the great victims of the enlargement of the franchise, for they were unable to compete with the Socialists for the votes of industrial workers and with the Catholics for the votes of the Flemish masses. Proportional representation, introduced in 1900, saved them from the sort of parliamentary catastrophe that later struck the British Liberals.[23]

The Catholic Party introduced proportional representation to avoid a government–opposition duel with the Socialists alone. The Liberals represented substantial political traditions in the cities and in some rural areas, and a middle-class and upper-middle-class political temperament which could not be accommodated either in a confessional party or in a workers' party. Proportional representation did not lead to a multiplication of small parties; except for a brief period in the 1930s and in 1946, the three-party system endured.

Compulsory voting was instituted along with universal male suffrage. Abstentions immediately dropped from an earlier 20–30 per cent to the 5 or 6 per cent customary since then (with spoiled ballots a smaller percentage). The performance of the duty has entered into the customs of the nation.

In 1890, at a great mass meeting of Socialists, 70,000 manifestants had vowed that they would struggle "with neither rest nor relaxation till the day when, by the introduction of universal suffrage, they had in truth won a fatherland." [24] The weighted voting of the universal suffrage they had obtained a few years later, after the general strike of 1893, was a reminder of inequality and inequity still to be overcome. Paradoxically, it was the German conquest of the fatherland in the First World War that finally won the workers their full political membership in it.

In the common suffering and opposition to the occupying Germans, conservatives acquired a new respect for the patriotism and good sense of the Belgian Socialists. Cardinal Mercier was only the most illustrious

mentary votes for heads of families over 35, for property owners, and for those with certain educational attainments. The new electorate of 1894 numbered some 1,371,000 men with 2,111,000 votes. About 850,000 voters cast only one vote; 290,000 had two votes; 220,000 had three votes, the maximum permitted. For the voting system, see Gilissen, *Le Régime représentatif*, pp. 119–32.

22. For results of elections to the House from 1894 to 1914, see Appendix Table 5.4.

23. Maurice Duverger, *Les Partis politiques* (1st ed. Paris, Colin, 1951), Fig. 29.

24. Julien Kuypers, *Bergop!* (Antwerp, Ontwikkeling, 1957), Plate XLII. The famous "oath of St. Gilles."

example of this new attitude. King Albert had long shown tolerance toward the party and sympathy with workers' problems.

With liberation, this remarkable monarch showed that he knew when to depart from strict constitutionalism. The long-mounting pressures for equalization of the suffrage had been pent up during the war. If the constitutional amending process had been followed, a Parliament with amending powers would have been elected under the old plural voting system. Workers and peasants who had suffered in the trenches or in deportation could have cast one ballot each, while war profiteers could have cast two or three. Instead the King and the government called the voters to the polls on a one man, one vote basis. The Parliament they elected legitimized the change by constitutional amendment. Conservatives grumbled that it was not legal, and indeed it was not. But any other course would have been a flagrant, needless injustice straining the constitutional and civic consensus far more, at a time when moderates and conservatives all over Europe (and the United States) feared revolution.

In Belgium alone of the belligerent nations, Socialists continued in the Cabinet after the war. Well could King Albert tell a friend, "I made of Socialism a party of government." [25] That governmentalism was confirmed by the extensive reforms of three years of post-war national union government. By 1921, when Belgian Socialists were ready to go back into opposition, they could contrast the realization of all their old minimum demands with the political reaction and social conflict in postwar Britain and France, and promise a constructive opposition.

It is high time, now, to go back to the third of the dialogues of which Théo Lefèvre spoke—that of the two communities which we may call linguistic or ethnic or regional.

The Flemish Question

The nation born in 1830 was bisected by an internal linguistic frontier which had hardly shifted since the fifth century A.D., running from west to east just south of Brussels. It separated the French-speaking southern provinces (which also spoke French dialects, chiefly Walloon) from the Flemish-speaking northern provinces. But within Flanders itself there was a more complex and provocative frontier, a linguistic-social barrier between the Flemish-speaking masses—peasants, workers, and lower middle classes—and their French-speaking native elites, some of whom hardly even knew Flemish.[26] "French in the parlor; Flemish in the kitchen," ran the telling, scornful phrase.

25. Tschoffen, in Institut Belge de Science Politique, *Aspects de la Société Belge* (Brussels, Librairie Encyclopédique, 1958), p. 23.

26. A single example: Msgr. Dechamps, cardinal-archbishop of Malines from 1867 to 1883, did not know Flemish, the language of the majority of his diocese. A. Simon, *Catholicisme et Politique*, p. 64.

This could pass as long as "one spoke as sang the bird." [27] Then came the linguistic patriotism of national or regional consciousness, in Flanders as in so many parts of Europe in the nineteenth century. The advocates of the Flemish cause first saw it only in linguistic and sentimental terms. "The language is the whole people," was their slogan. "Language is more than an instrument; it is the soul of a people. To outrage it is more than a misdeed; it is a sacrilege." [28] The Flemish people must be free to learn and to use their own language; their language must have equal standing with French. But the protagonists of Flemish had to define and to spread the language of cultured speech, for the rich tongue of medieval literature had fallen into a degraded and divided state. Most Flemings spoke one of a number of often mutually incomprehensible local dialects. Only a tiny minority spoke a correct Flemish, or *Nederlands* (Dutch), the name by which it is now legally called. And first its defenders had, as Jan-Frans Willems said, literally to "teach their people to read."

The cultural backwardness of the Flemish masses reflected the economic backwardness of Flanders. After the heyday of its medieval communes, after the glory of sixteenth-century Antwerp, Flanders had fallen far behind Wallonia. While Wallonia paced the continent's industrial revolution, Flanders had only its agriculture, its textiles, and the port of Antwerp. In its overpopulated villages, a wretched peasantry long tried to keep cottage industries alive, while many of its sons went off to work in Walloon coal mines and steel mills, in Brussels, in France, and the United States. The Flemings had the doubtful consolation of being more numerous [29] —and more Catholic.

Differences in the pace of industrialization accentuated regional contrasts. In Wallonia, as in many other industrializing areas of Europe, most of the new working classes turned away from, or grew up outside, the church of their fathers. Not until well into the twentieth century did a modernized Catholicism stay the loss of workers' support brought on by industrialization, displacement, and urbanization.

In the Belgian self-image, Wallonia has become dechristianized while Flanders has remained Catholic. The reality is more nuanced, although the self-image is one form of reality. The contrast is chiefly between industrial-and-urban and rural-and-small-town populations. Walloon rural areas have retained their Catholicism but in the large Flemish cities the Church has lost most industrial workers.

The dominance of French reflected the political and social dominance of the French-speaking property holders and professional elites of nine-

27. Godefroid Kurth, *La Nationalité belge* (Namur, Picard-Balon, 1913), p. 196.
28. Alfons Willems, in *Beschryf van de Betooging en Het Banket van den 25 April 1859, ter Eere der Vlaamsche Tael-Commissie* (Brussels, Verbruggen, 1859), p. 14.
29. The first census, in 1846, showed 2,471,000 Flemish-speaking and 1,827,000 French-speaking Belgians.

teenth-century Belgium. Naturally they carried on the national government and most local government in their own tongue. Some, moreover, saw the French language as a vehicle of national unification and centralization. So Parliament and all but three city councils debated in French; the army commanded in French; the courts judged in French. For several generations, education in Flemish stopped with the primary schools; secondary schools and universities taught exclusively in French. Only in French could one make a professional or civil service career. "To be Belgian," complained Flemish intellectuals, "we have to cease being Flemish."

The first leaders of the Flemish movement came chiefly from modest strata of the intelligentsia—lower civil servants, school teachers, priests. To many of these, especially the lower clergy, the tide of godlessness that threatened pious Flanders was peculiarly associated with the French language and literature, which "oozed crime and demoralization." [30] It was associated with the French nation, persecutor of the Church, with French-speaking industrial Wallonia, where Flemish immigrants lost their faith, and with the *francophone* (French-speaking) Liberal bourgeoisie of Flanders itself.

The emphasis on language diverted the attention of the Flemish movement from the social and economic bases of Flemish inferiority in Belgian life. "The myth that 'the language is the whole people' " for a long time dominated the thinking of leaders of the Flemish movement.[31] That movement took form first in literary and cultural associations. There were occasional political forays at the municipal level, notably in Antwerp, where they were associated with antimilitaristic activity. But no regional political parties appeared before the First World War.

Among the national parties, the Liberals were the most nationally minded, including as they did in Flanders so many of the French-speaking bourgeoisie of the region *(Fransquillons)*. Individual Liberals, however, were among the leaders of the early Flemish cultural movement. The Socialists at first insisted on seeing in Flanders only the same economic and social evils they saw in Wallonia, accentuated by the economic backwardness and clerical domination which they associated with each other. The Catholic Party showed some interest, but the democratic side of the Flemish movement clashed with the conservatism that long dominated the party. In the immediate prewar years, Flemish representatives of all three parties began some concerted action, notably in favor of a Flemish-language [32] university. Meanwhile, as all aspects of public life tended to

30. M.J.J. van der Voort, *Coup d'oeil sur la langue et la littérature flamandes* . . . (Antwerp, 1837), p. 18, cited by Pirenne, *Histoire de Belgique*, 7, 274.

31. Telemachus, "De Spanning tussen de Taalgroepen: een sociologische benadering," *De Maand, 6* (1963), 332.

32. The "proper" language of cultivated usage is referred to variously as Dutch ("Nederlands") or Flemish; the dialects as Flemish.

become politicized the Flemish cultural movement split into Liberal and Catholic and Socialist organizations.

Only at the very end of the century had the government come around to requiring an official text of its laws in Flemish as well as French. By the First World War it had made some place for Flemish, alongside French, in secondary education, administration, and criminal justice in Flanders.

The war gave new dimensions and new urgency to the Flemish problem. If it deepened national feeling among many Belgians, it also deepened the opposition between the Flemish and "the others." Military sacrifice was glaringly unequal, by the direction of invasion and the nature of Belgian social structure. The Germans overran the country too fast for the Walloon contingents to be mobilized as fully as the more distant Flemish. When skilled workers were taken out of the lines and sent to jobs in French industries, most were necessarily Walloons. Remaining in the trenches were mostly Flemings, with a majority of their officers French-speaking. Serious incidents in some units in the trenches and in punishment camps behind the lines pitted Flemish soldiers against often uncomprehending commanders.

The Germans encouraged Flemish separatism, leaving a train of political booby traps for the Belgian nation after the war. The Flemish "activists," as they were called, who accepted measures of autonomy from the occupation authorities, were not political leaders for the most part, but literary and cultural figures. Only the national government's long indifference to their just cause was responsible for their collaboration with the enemy, they claimed; it was "now or never."

After the years of suffering in the trenches, in occupied Belgium, and in deportation, the old demands for Flemish equality could no longer be put off. Equal suffrage, moreover, gave a new political weight to the masses of Flemish peasants and workingmen. But the war had also called forth a surge of Belgian nationalism, which brought a stiffening against Flemish claims. The prosecutions of the activists after 1918 caused some French-speaking Belgians, consciously or unconsciously, to identify not only the men on trial, but the entire Flemish movement, with treason. By a comparable reflex many loyal Flemings felt resentfully that not just the "activists" but the entire Flemish people were being put in the dock.

The Interwar Years

The prewar government-versus-opposition relationship disappeared with the first elections under universal equal suffrage. The 1919 elections produced a balance of voting strength which, *grosso modo*, has continued to the present: the Catholics in the lead, with their chief strength in Flanders and rural Wallonia; the Socialists a very close second and occasionally overtaking the Catholic Party vote between the wars, strongest in

Wallonia, Brussels, and the largest Flemish cities; the Liberals, the victims of equal suffrage, a distant but significant third, strongest in Brussels and holding some traditional "fiefs" elsewhere. Flemish nationalist parties and, soon, a Communist Party became permanent minor actors on the national scene.[33]

Since there was no backing for minority governments or cabinets made up of nonparliamentary figures, coalition cabinets became the rule. Between the wars, the most frequent combinations were Catholic-Liberal and tripartite cabinets. The term "tripartite" should not conjure up an impression of anything like unanimity. With party discipline poor in Catholic and Liberal ranks, all cabinets faced serious oppositions within their own parliamentary delegations, even on their votes of investiture. Most often they received what Emile Vandervelde called "a vote of short-run confidence or of delayed no-confidence."[34]

One government was unique—formed in 1925 by the Catholic Party's Flemish laborite wing with the Socialists. It fell in less than a year because of a threatened monetary crisis. But it gave the Socialists the tantalizing hope, not to be realized, of a breakup of the Catholic Party on socio-economic lines, whereby the Socialists would emerge as the largest party, allying with the Catholic labor wing or absorbing some of it.

The Catholic Party's internal difficulties encouraged such hopes. With the growth of its allied social movements, it had become a *standen-organisatie*, to use the Flemish term, a party of corporate membership of its several "estates." It held together, in loose and quarreling federation, the organized *standen* of Catholic labor, Flemish farmers (the Boeren-bond), the "middle classes,"[35] and the party's original political circles, primarily aristocratic and bourgeois in composition, and now of steadily declining importance. By 1936, under the pressures of Flemish nationalism, the party also reorganized in two nearly autonomous regional wings.

Despite the repeated crises of parliamentary government in the 1930s, the three traditional parties surmounted their rivalries sufficiently to meet several of the nation's hardest challenges. In 1935 they formed the tripartite Van Zeeland Cabinet which, despite some Catholic and Liberal defections in Parliament, set the nation on the way to economic recovery.

The parties also suspended their oppositions long enough to fight the

33. For election results since 1919, see Appendix Tables 5.5 (votes for the House) and 5.6 (seats). For electoral system, Gilissen, Ch. 6. Women did not receive the vote in national elections until 1949. For regional distributions of votes and of party support, see Tables 5.7 and 5.8.

34. *Annales Parlementaires, Chambre,* Feb. 21, 1933, p. 370, cited by Carl-H. Höjer, *Le Régime parlementaire belge de 1918 à 1940* (Uppsala, Almqvist, 1946), p. 341, n. 5.

35. Following Belgian usage, I use the term "middle classes" here to mean self-employed business and professional people, artisans, and small employers.

one successful flash party in Belgian history, the Rexists of Léon De-grelle.[36] In the 1936 elections, six months after its birth, this nationalist, anti-Marxist, anti-Semitic party won a ninth of the nation's votes (and a sixth of those of French-speaking Belgians). Degrelle had dropped the specific Catholic appeal of "Christus Rex" to summon all Belgians to the good cause. Along with its negative aspects, Degrelle's whirlwind oratory and writing stirred many people, especially young Catholics and some young Liberals, with its appeal for a purer, radiant Belgium. For all its demagogic vagueness and ugly menaces, his appeal was not quite fascist until the war.

Degrelle himself did not run in 1936. A year later, with his deputies revealing Rexist ineptitude and emptiness in Parliament, the leader him-self stood for the House in a Brussels by-election which he forced[37] as a sort of national plebiscite. In the face of the clear and present danger, the three national parties united behind the candidacy of the Prime Minister, the Catholic Paul van Zeeland. On the eve of the vote, the Cardinal-Archbishop of Malines spoke out against Degrelle as a "danger to the country and to the Church." The alternatives stood forth with rare clarity: Rex or the regime. Van Zeeland received 80 per cent of the vote. Rex was a punctured balloon; in the 1939 elections, it sank from 21 to 4 House seats.

The Linguistic Laws of the 1930s

It was a long time before Parliament enacted the equality for the Flemish language King Albert had promised from the throne on the liberation of the country in 1918. The Flemish showed increasing bitterness at the delays in giving effect to solemn promises, while the *francophones* showed irritation at the aggressiveness of Flemish leaders.

Specific Flemish parties had made their appearance in 1919, rising to a modest peak in 1936 and 1939, when they elected 16 and then 17 members out of 202 members of the House. In the Flemish cantons alone, however, they reached 15 per cent of the votes cast in 1939. Their threat to the established parties, especially to the Catholic Party, moreover, was much greater than their percentage of the electorate. They functioned in effect mostly as pressure groups attempting to affect action by the government and by major parties.[38]

The Flemish movement had been essentially democratic in style, with

36. See essay by Jean Stengers on the extreme right in Belgium, in Hans Rogger and Eugen Weber, eds., *The European Right: A Historical Profile* (Berkeley and Los Angeles, University of California Press, 1965).

37. By having a Rexist deputy and all the Rexist alternates resign.

38. Jan Dhondt, "De evolutie van de partijen tussen de twee wereldoorlogen," *Res Publica, 4* (1962), 370–80; A. W. Willemsen, *Het Vlaams Nationalisme, 1914–1940* (Groningen, Wolters, 1958), and Willemsen, "Sociologie als Therapie?" *De Maand, 6* (1963), 493.

important elements of social radicalism and pacifism. In the 1930s, however, its extremists took on a totalitarian style, in two movements (to which we cannot devote space in an essay concerned with the "legitimate opposition"): the Dutch-speaking National Solidarity League (Verbond van Dietsche Nationaalsolidaristen, Verdinaso) and the Flemish National League (Vlaams Nationaal Verbond, VNV).

The main Flemish agitation, however, went on outside the extremist groups. Though even the loyal opposition often overflowed peaceful channels, the riots and bloodshed were far less than in any one of a large number of strikes in the United States at the time. But preoccupation with linguistic issues in the 1930s kept Parliament in a state of recurring turmoil. It rendered laborious the formation of cabinets and made their maintenance difficult. It took the attention of parties, governments, and electorate from the challenges of the Depression and European fascism.[39]

A series of laws in the 1930s finally enacted a long-delayed equality for the Flemish language in education, administration, justice, and the army. As it turned out, the laws were implemented only partially, most successfully in the courts, where there were sanctions for noncompliance. By this legislation Flanders and Wallonia would be unilingual; only in Brussels would there be some attempt at bilingualism. There would be instruction in the second national language in the schools, but that language would be a foreign tongue to almost all. Many Flemings, and a few rare *francophones*, would be more or less bilingual, but only as the result of personal effort or family circumstances. The hopes for French as a national unifying factor had failed. But it continued in national economic life and in the higher ranks of public administration to hold a predominance which, diminishing and precarious as it was, roused the opposition of many Flemings.

The Communist Party

History denied the Belgian Communists opportunities such as their brethren in less fortunate lands exploited. The first years were critical. In the political democracies where a left opposition failed to win a strong position in the Socialist movement before the rise of international communism, the Communist Party never became a major force on its own. The entering wedge in the major continental belligerents was the reaction against Socialist and trade union support of the war. But in the long-neutral little nation which, as King Albert said, had been "driven to heroism," revolutionary defeatism and postwar recrimination against social patriotism were absurd.

39. In 1939, for example, a tripartite government fell and Parliament had to be dissolved in a dispute over the government's naming a convicted and amnestied activist to the Flemish Academy of Medicine—this within half a year of the outbreak of war.

The political and social reforms of the immediate postwar government justified Socialist participation in it against criticism from the extreme left. Among the working class, the tightly meshed organizations of the Socialist world supported each other against Communist penetration. Even in the Depression, the Communists failed to emerge from political isolation. The Socialists rejected Popular Front proposals—which would not have made sense anyway, given the positions of the Catholics and Liberals. Instead the Socialists joined with the other two major parties in national union cabinets, as they had in previous emergency situations.

The Aftermath of World War II: Class Relations

The Second, like the First, World War diminished certain oppositions, created new ones, and sharpened others. If the First War marked the full acceptance of the Socialist Party, the Second marked that of the labor unions. Under the Nazi occupation, clandestine personal contacts among leaders of industry and Catholic, Socialist, and Liberal trade unionists produced a "pact of social solidarity" of symbolic and practical importance. The pact was implemented after the Liberation by wide advances in social legislation and collective bargaining. Leaders of employer associations and trade unions developed the habit of periodic meetings, with government leaders and without them, to regulate the labor market and consider national social policies. Wages, relatively low before the war, were raised more above prewar levels than in any other Western country. Social generosity was possible because of the relatively fortunate state of the national economy. Meanwhile, the government's vigorous currency contraction and stabilization measures kept the money wage increases meaningful and saved Belgium from the social tensions of galloping inflation.

Employers as a group were not discredited as they were for a time in France and Italy. The transition to a welfare state was made with their cooperation and hence without the resentments and conflicts of postwar industrial relations in France and Italy.[40]

Union and industry representatives came to exercise powers of administration in a number of quasi-public social welfare agencies. They sit together in advisory councils on national social and economic policy and on the boards of public and semi-public industrial and financial institutions. A few leading figures of the employer associations and Socialist and Catholic unions now frequently decide social policies in face-to-face contacts remarkably close for an otherwise stratified society. Sharing power in social affairs with labor unions, the employers have preserved

40. For a comparison of this and earlier historical experience with that of France, see Val R. Lorwin, "Labor Organizations and Politics in Belgium and France," in E. M. Kassalow, ed., *National Labor Movements in the Postwar World* (Evanston, Ill., Northwestern University Press, 1963), pp. 142–68.

most of their economic power and gained a high degree of social peace. Industrial conflict has been of mild proportions since the war; the two big general strikes were both directed at the government, not at employers.

The Parties

The postwar scene has been dominated by the three traditional parties. They broke with traditional names and structures, however. The Catholic Party was reborn as the Christian Social Party (Parti Social Chrétien, PSC [41]). It declared its "deconfessionalization" and its intention to be less conservative and more social-welfare-minded. In structure it was to be unitary, based on individual membership instead of the prewar federation of "estates" (*Standen*), and national instead of a federation of Flemish and francophone wings.

So it looked in the new dawn of 1945. The party did indeed become more "social." It soon forgot about "deconfessionalization," however. It avoided the head-on oppositions of the interwar *Standen*, but found new methods of informal recognition and even rather formal aggregation of the claims of its "estates." [42] While recognizing the regional wings in the party, it has been a force for national unity. At the war's end, the party found itself in the opposition for the first time in 61 years. Several experiences of opposition only confirmed it in its "governmental calling." But that "calling" it shares with the other two national parties; since 1918, all three have spent much more time in government than out (see Appendix Table 5.9).

The old Workers Party was reborn too in 1945, resuming the Socialist name (Parti Socialiste Belge, PSB) its forebears had prudently laid aside six decades earlier. The party adopted individual membership instead of the old collective affiliation of unions, cooperatives, and friendly societies.

The Communist Party represented a significant opposition only—paradoxically—when its tactics were those of cooperation and identification with the national interest in resistance and reconstruction. In 1944, for the first time, it had members in the government, a sizable labor union following, and much public sympathy or at least friendly curiosity. Even though national elections were postponed until 1946, when the party was already

41. Each national party obviously has both French and Flemish names. I have used only the French name and French initials.

42. There is no space here to discuss some of the interesting methods of reconciliation of divergent socioeconomic groups within the Catholic political community. One is the Agenda Committee, a body not even provided for in the party statutes, which has brought together leaders of the social groups (the old *Standen*) and the political heads of the party in periodic meetings of great policy importance. Another is the balancing of candidates from, or acceptable to, interest groups in the various constituencies. Multimember constituencies facilitate such slate-balancing. Agreed slates may be submitted to the party primaries for expected confirmation. Disagreements may be fought out in the primaries or finally decided by national leaders.

in decline, it obtained one-eighth of the total vote. For the first and last time since universal equal manhood suffrage, a fourth party surpassed the Liberals in votes and House seats.

The Socialists had fused their unions with those which emerged under Communist leadership at the liberation. Contrary to widely accepted opinion, trade union fusion was possible without suffocation by the Communists. The conditions were a vigorous Socialist leadership, Socialist union ties with other Socialist working-class organizations, and freedom from the myth of "no enemies to the left." There were enemies to the alleged left, but they seemed less dangerous as an internal minority than as an external opposition.

Eliminated from the Cabinet early in 1947, the Communists staged unsuccessful strikes against the government and the Marshall Plan a year later. Their popular vote dwindled steadily to a postwar low of two per cent in 1958, recovering slightly in 1961. The party retained some following in Walloon industrial centers and among Brussels white-collar and public service employees. Weak in numbers, leadership, press, and intellectual support, the Communist Party was almost pathetically mild and colorless. It shuffled along in the wake of the Socialist Party, halfheartedly claiming to be in advance of it.

The Liberal Party merged in 1961 with a few minuscule right-wing splinter parties to create the Party of Liberty and Progress (PLP). The PLP's chief innovation was an explicit repudiation of historic Liberal anticlericalism.

Immediately after the war, an attempt was made to break out of the mold of religious and antireligious opposition. A group of Catholics and Socialists, influenced during the war by the British experience, attempted to launch a Labor Party form of political action. They hoped for a realignment of parties, more modern and less emotional, primarily on social and economic issues. But the old parties reaffirmed themselves too soon for that. Especially among its original Socialist sponsors, old loyalties and calculations were too strong for the new Belgian Democratic Union (Union Démocratique Belge, UDB). When the UDB entered the election campaign of 1946, it was chiefly a mildly left and laborite Walloon Catholic group. To many, therefore, it looked like only a dissident Catholic formation. Perhaps it had too high a percentage of intellectuals. Certainly it lacked the mass base its orientation required, for the Catholic and Socialist trade unions returned to their old party affinities. The UDB went into its first and last election with two Cabinet ministers. It came out with a mere 2.2 per cent of the vote and a single deputy. The experiment came to an abrupt end. Its failure confirmed the confessional character which Catholic political action once again assumed.

The Royal Affair

The first great cleavage of postwar national life arose from the passionate debates over the constitutionality and wisdom of Leopold III's wartime behavior: his refusal to follow his Cabinet into exile after his surrender of the army in May 1940, his own and his entourage's hesitating or hovering attitude toward the German occupants, and the circumstances of his wartime remarriage.

At the end of the war Parliament declared the sovereign "unable to reign." While the King's brother Charles efficiently and discreetly performed the functions of regent, governments comprising both the pro-Leopoldist PSC and the anti-Leopoldist PSB and/or Liberal Party agreed to disagree on the issue. In 1950 a PSC parliamentary majority was able to carry through an advisory national referendum.[43] With some 10 per cent of the ballots blank or invalid, some 52 per cent of the eligible electorate pronounced for the exiled King's return. Taking account only of valid ballots, as most favorable to the King's cause, he had a 58 per cent majority. But was there a national majority or only a conflict of regional majorities? Flanders showed a Leopoldist majority (of valid ballots cast) of 72 per cent. But Wallonia gave him only 42 per cent, and Brussels 48 per cent.

The Leopoldist cause was strong enough to prevent any Flemish nationalist or dissident Catholic tickets in the national election of 1950, and the PSC won a majority in both houses, the only such majority since universal equal suffrage. Parliament ended the King's "inability to reign," despite Socialist threats of a general strike. When the monarch set foot on Belgian soil again, the Socialists launched a determined strike movement. It ended quickly, with the first victims—upon the death of several strikers at the hands of gendarmes, the King and the PSC government gave in, and the King made way for his young son Baudouin.

Once again the Socialist labor movement, with considerable middle-class support, had used the general strike for a political purpose, with complete victory for the first time. An hereditary sovereign and a duly constituted cabinet with an intact parliamentary majority had given way to avert further bloodshed and perhaps civil war. Their restraint at the eleventh hour preserved both the monarchy and national unity.

Why had this limited and sentimental issue provoked such violent opposition? The long debate kept alive opposing wartime memories. It gave a dramatic new, personal emphasis to the existing regional and party and religious divisions. (For a picture of the Catholic political pre-

43. The referendum was not sanctioned, but it was not specifically prohibited, by the Constitution. This was its first and only use; it was thinly veiled as a "consultation of the people." As in elections, voting was compulsory. On the votes, see E. R. Arango, *Leopold III and the Belgian Royal Question* (Baltimore, Johns Hopkins Press, 1963), pp. 189–90.

dominance in Flanders, and the Socialist predominance in Wallonia and Brussels, see Appendix Tables 5.7 and 5.8.) Only a class alignment was lacking to make polarization complete. There was no compromise possible, only postponement, and—Leopold's health being good—the issue would not die down. The referendum had merely exacerbated regional antagonisms, for it reopened the disagreement on whether the unit of decision was the nation or the region. A Liberal had asked before the referendum, "What will happen to the unity of the country when the Walloons can say that the Flemings imposed a king on them or the Flemings can say that the Walloons kept them from having a King?" [44] As it turned out, the Walloons said the first, and then forced the Flemings to say the second.

The School Issue

Five years later the Catholic political leaders, who in 1950 had yielded to force, themselves threatened force against a parliamentary majority, this time on the school question. After World War I the old issue of government support had been settled in favor of the Catholic primary schools. Now the issue that flared up, once the royal question had been settled, involved the secondary schools. The PSC majority legislated in favor of the Catholic secondary schools in 1952. A few years later (1955) a Socialist-Liberal government reversed that policy. Thereupon the Catholic opposition attempted a series of extraparliamentary pressures. The party president's call to boycott the government's postal savings and checking accounts and its bond issues was ineffective. In a march on Brussels— classic tactic of national protest—Catholics had their heads clobbered by tough gendarmes. With sporadic hooliganism by schoolboys and some acts of violence by adults, the Catholic protests were a long way in both style and aims from the Socialists' general strike.

Catholics were too wedded to tradition and order to feel at home in this kind of opposition activity. Moreover, unlike the Socialists in 1950, they knew they had another remedy. Indeed, at the next general election they won in the conventional political arena the victory they had failed to win in the streets.[45]

The dialectic of government-opposition-new government did produce a temporary and perhaps a permanent synthesis. After their electoral success in 1958, largely on the school issue, the PSC leaders took the initiative to get agreement with the two national parties supporting the public schools. The heads of the three parties negotiated the "school pact" of 1958, a 12-year truce that hopefully offered to take the school question out of

44. Blum, *Annales Parlementaires, Chambre des Représentants,* Jan. 18, 1950, p. 3.
45. The 1958 victory did not give them a majority: there are no landslides in Belgian politics. Its gains permitted the PSC to turn out the Socialist-Liberal Cabinet and to form the next government.

politics at last. The Catholics accepted the principle that where neither the communes nor the provinces (nor private initiative) organized nondenominational elementary or secondary schools, the national state should do so. The Socialists and Liberals accepted the principle that public subsidies should cover teachers' salaries for private (i.e., Catholic) schools. In good collective bargaining manner, the pact provided for a permanent tripartite panel to settle the conflicts of interpretation and implementation bound to arise under any such long-term accord.

All opposition over schools did not abruptly dissolve. There were thorny questions of allocations of funds to the competing educational systems, appointments to teaching positions in the public institutions, and the meaning and observance of "religious and philosophical neutrality" in public schools, questions the tripartite panel has so far settled.

Each party had reasons for wanting the pact, but it was the PSC that risked most, for it gave up the issue that had so often cemented the political unity of Catholics of different regions and classes.

The Flemish Problem Again

The occupation authorities had not deliberately favored Flemish autonomism in World War II as they had a generation earlier.[46] Contrary to the belief of many Walloons and Bruxellois, the *francophones* had no monopoly on resistance to the Nazis nor the Flemings on collaboration. Contrary to the belief of many Flemings, the widespread and perhaps excessive purge after the war struck many French-speaking as well as Flemish Belgians.[47] But as after the First World War, the demand for an amnesty came from the Flemish, and again aroused long and heated debate.

Flemish nationalist action resumed slowly, at first only under the cautious form of cultural and youth movements. From 1949 on, the Flemish Volksunie (People's Union) showed that a Flemish regionalist party had a permanent, if small, place in national politics. By 1961, with six per cent of the vote in Flemish districts, it elected five (out of 212) House members. Its importance was less as an opposition party than as a pressure group, weighing especially upon the PSC's action.

Unlike the VNV and the Verdinaso, neither the Volksunie nor the related Flemish People's Movement (Vlaamse Volksbeweging) is authoritarian, let alone totalitarian, in structure or style. In Parliament, the Volksunie has conducted itself generally as a loyal opposition. Its members are too few to practice any serious obstruction, but they do not even vote in systematic opposition.

Outside Parliament, Flemish organizations are not above troubling the

46. The Germans did release Flemish prisoners of war soon after the surrender, while holding most Walloons to the bitter end.

47. John Gilissen, "Étude statistique sur la répression de l'incivisme," *Revue de Droit Pénal et de Criminologie,* 31 (1950–51), 513–628, especially summary 624–26.

public order now and then. The Flemish Action Committee for Brussels and the Language Frontier organized marches on Brussels and other demonstrations whose force impressed public opinion. For a time the Volksunie maintained a paramilitary youth organization. But whatever the latent threat to democratic processes from some "hard" elements, in the early 1960s they did no more than interrupt services in the several Antwerp and Ghent churches having French-language sermons, deface French-language highway markers and business signs on Flemish soil, and rough up bystanders in occasional "border incidents" around Brussels.

Meanwhile, the course of economic development was slowly eliminating some of the old Flemish disadvantages. An overwhelming percentage of postwar investment in new industries, especially by foreign capital (notably American), was in Flanders. The structural unemployment which had so long plagued Flanders was finally being absorbed by the region's and the nation's demands for labor. With submarginal old Walloon coal mines being shut down, more productive new seams were opened up in the Flemish Campine. These changes would naturally take time to produce their social and psychological and political effects among Flemings. Walloons, however, soon regarded them as marking the irrevocable passing of control to the once-backward northern provinces.

The Walloon Problem

There has never been a Walloon consciousness as strong as the Flemish consciousness. Walloons have thought of themselves in local terms—as Liégois or men of the Borinage, as people of Namur or Charleroi—more than in regional or linguistic terms.

As long as Wallonia prospered and *francophones* ran the nation, there was no "Walloon problem." A few people manifested inquietude about the region's prospects even before the First World War, but until recently the only regional interest groups were small sentimental movements of a literary or folklore character and minor economic-interest organizations.

With the end of World War II, the shift in the relative position of Wallonia began to alarm an area once confident of its economic destinies. To the continued experience of demographic decline (see Appendix Table 5.10) was joined the newer, more harrowing experience of economic stagnation due to superannuated coal mines, old factories and equipment, and an industrial structure still reflecting the first industrial revolution.

Frustrations and fears came to a head in a general strike of 34 days' duration in December 1960 and January 1961, which broke out despite the opposition of the national leaders of the Socialist unions and party. The stoppages began as a protest against the PSC-Liberal government's omnibus economic retrenchment bill after the loss of the Congo. Then they turned into a violent protest against government policies toward Wallonia. For in the heat of the strike, as their immediate national demands were getting nowhere, some Walloon Socialist leaders—chiefly of a left orientation—launched federalist demands and a regional organization. With the founding of the Walloon People's Movement (Mouvement Populaire Wallon, MPW), Walloon federalism for the first time had a mass backing.

Flemish federalists sought regional autonomy for its own sake or chiefly for cultural reasons. Walloon federalists sought regional autonomy to improve their region's economic prospects and to carry out the economic and social reforms they could not win on a national basis. The MPW called itself a pressure group—not afraid of a term that disturbed many citizens—but it represented a threat of independent political action that could come only at the expense of the Belgian Socialist Party.

Walloon Socialists might optimistically foresee an absolute majority for themselves in their own region. But the Flemish Socialists opposed a federalism that would leave them so clearly a minority in their region. The national PSB leadership responded vigorously and (so far) successfully to contain the MPW threat by their less disciplined Walloon comrades. But the general strike and the MPW had exacerbated divisions between Walloons and Flemings. Even more it had exacerbated divisions between the right-wing majority (Flemish and Walloon) and the small but significant left minority (Walloon and Bruxellois) which has been a permanent feature of the Socialist trade unions and party.

The Problem of Brussels

Brussels and its environs supply the leading issue of Flemish-Walloon contention. Here is a special form of the metropolis–provincial opposition to be seen in many nations. A pole for Flemish immigration and the center of the nation's French-speaking dominance, Brussels became for *Flamingants* (militant pro-Flemish elements) both an obstacle to overcome and a *terra irredenta* to recover.

Near the capital the fifteen-centuries-old language frontier has shifted visibly and significantly. The once-little Flemish city in the last century became a French-speaking metropolis. Here not even Dutch, let alone the Flemish dialects, could compete with French. The culturally stronger language was also the language of upward social and economic mobility in the capital. Most Flemish immigrants, or at least their children, were lost to Flemish culture. The 1932 language law seeking to make Brussels bilingual was honored in the breach by the authorities of a number of communes of metropolitan Brussels. Flemish citizens, more numerous in the nation than their *francophone* compatriots, complained that they did not feel at home in their national capital.

Another dimension of the problem was the migration of Brussels families to the suburbs and rural communes of surrounding Flemish Brabant. Naturally they wanted to use their own language and have their children taught in it. *Flamingants*, however, could not view this merely as a local manifestation of a universal urban–suburban migration. Some called it a "robbery of Flemish soil." For the proximity of French speech brought an increasing, intolerable competition for Flemish. In other ways too they saw an "oil stain" spreading out from Brussels over the Flemish countryside. Some of the newcomers were indifferent Catholics at best, and some freethinkers, and they disturbed the political balance in hitherto overwhelmingly Catholic Flemish communes. Even when the newcomers were good Catholics there were conflicts—often within parishes—with old settlers.

By the early 1960s, language and regional issues again dominated national politics. In 1962 and 1963, the Lefèvre-Spaak (Catholic-Socialist) government managed with the greatest difficulty to put through a series of laws on these issues, some giving greater force to old principles and some enacting new principles.

The new principle was that of fixity of the language frontier. The law scrapped the 1932 principle of administrative conformity, in various communes along the language frontier, to language practices as determined by a periodic language census. The census had become something of a referendum of preferences rather than a finding of facts about existing linguistic knowledge and use.[48] The new law fixed the existing language frontier [49] and administrative practices along it, in theory permanently. Here was a long step toward an undeclared federalism.[50]

In behalf of Flemish rights, another law sought to give more reality to official bilingualism in the Brussels metropolitan area by creating sanctions and a mechanism for enforcement. In behalf of the *francophones*, it recognized some of the facts of migration out of the capital to its outskirts by concessions in administrative practices in certain Flemish communes with large French-speaking minorities.

The third in the triptych of language laws confirmed the principle, accepted in the 1930s, of unilingualism in the schools of Flanders and Wallonia. But it made a greater effort to improve quality and augment the amount of instruction in the second language in each area, and in metropolitan Brussels to provide more Flemish schools in *francophone* communes, while making it harder for Flemish parents to send their children to French schools.

48. See Paul M. G. Lévy, *La Querelle du recensement* (Brussels, Institut Belge de Science Politique, 1960); Vlaams Aktiekomitee voor Brussel en Taalgrens, *Geen talentelling* (Brussels, 1959).

49. A few administrative transfers were made (with considerable political furor) to give homogeneity of language to each of the two language zones and to each province except bilingual Brabant.

50. Cf. Lode Claes, "Het federaliseringsproces in België," *Streven* (April 1963), and in English in "The Process of Federalization in Belgium," *Delta* (Winter 1963–64), pp. 43–52.

Why Linguistic-Regional Opposition Remains So Intractable

The linguistic-regional conflict appears more intractable than class conflict or the religious-ideological conflict. For this there are many reasons.

1. The sentimental and practical interests of the two linguistic communities are not effectively organized, and the geographical regions have
no administrative or formal political existence. There are no recognized
representatives qualified to formulate demands, to negotiate, and to fulfill
commitments.

2. Flemings know little of Walloon thinking; the Walloons know less of
Flemish thinking. People on each side therefore tend to see and to resent
the others as a solid bloc arrayed against them.[51] Actually each linguistic
community, each region, is far from monolithic on any relevant issue.

3. Inequality—bane of the relations between man and man—poisons the
relations of the two cultural communities. Flemings are aware of *francophone* snobbishness toward the Dutch language,[52] a snobbishness still
touched with old assumptions of social superiority.

French-speaking Belgians, always a numerical minority, now fear that
they will become a sociological minority. They are aware that they lack
the feeling of community (some would say "national" feeling) of their
Flemish-speaking compatriots. Neither Walloons nor *francophones* have
any concept or—significantly—any phrase comparable to the powerful
Flemish *"ons volk"* ("our people"). And *"ons volk"* embraces the Flemish-speaking people of Brussels as well as those of Flanders. There is no
such identification between Walloons and French-speaking Bruxellois.

4. Many of the Flemish elite pass their days in an environment that
keeps linguistic sensitivities raw. If they work in, or deal with, national
institutions in Brussels, they find French still the dominant language. They
may assert the rights of their own language to equality, at the cost of
friction with *francophones*. Or they may, as good fellows, carry on in a
language few of them command as they do their mother tongue,[53] and at
the cost of friction with more punctilious Flemings.

5. In the arguments over the Brussels area, the thorniest complex of
linguistic opposition now, Flemish and *francophone* spokesmen keep appealing to different values. The contrast is classic. The Flemish appeal to
the rights of the collectivity; the *francophones* to those of the individual.

---

51. Differences in ways of thinking and feeling are at least as important as differences in language. For difficulties of understanding by people speaking more or less
the same tongue, see Anton van Duinkerken, "Two Ways of Looking at Flanders:
A Dutch View," *Delta* (Winter 1963–64), pp. 39–42.

52. The "Walloon View" of Flanders, in ibid., pp. 33–39, is an example of the
persistence of stereotypes and snobbery, culminating in an oft-repeated joke (sic) at
the expense of Flemings comparable to some of the unfunny "darky" stories in the
United States.

53. Common parlance calls people "bilingual" if they have a fair working knowledge of the second national language. If bilingualism means perfect command of the
two tongues, there are few bilingual people even among Flemings.

The former, socially still at a disadvantage in Brussels, ask the state to protect their language and the continuity of their culture even against members of their own community who wish to be assimilated, at least through their children, into the other linguistic community. The socially dominant group wants the state to protect the individual's right to choose his cultural medium, but does not recognize the social and economic pressures and "silent intolerance" [54] weighing upon the Flemish in the Brussels environment.

6. There is an incongruity between many of the grievances and the remedies sought. Legal equality for the Dutch language cannot of itself make up for a lack of precision, uniformity, and style in Flemings' use of their own language. No official policy can preserve for the Walloons an equal share of responsible government posts when their numbers are so much fewer than those of the Flemish and when comparatively few of them make the effort to learn the other national language. Official policy alone cannot restore the Walloon birthrate. In fact, the Flemish birthrate has been falling, with a generation's lag, to meet that of Wallonia.

7. The Flemish still see themselves as oppressed, despite the political weight of their numbers, the progress in use of the Dutch language everywhere except in the Brussels area, and a recent economic growth in Flanders that is much more rapid than that of Wallonia. What Michael Balfour might call "the reflexes of underdogs" [55] continue far beyond the conditions that created them. So do the reflexes of "overdogs" or former overdogs. The Walloons look backward too, but only to contrast past security with fears for the future. They forget that the Walloon economy, even if relatively unprogressive, still yields wage rates and incomes well above those of most of Flanders. If Dutch is advancing, the French language still dominates in the higher echelons of the economy, finance, and administration.[56]

The *francophones* have a far higher percentage of students at university-level institutions than their percentage of the university-age Belgian population (See Appendix Table 5.11), even when allowance is made for foreign students taking courses in French. Although Brussels still determines and administers much, perhaps too much, of the nation's life, many Bruxellois feel threatened between Flemish aggressiveness and Walloon indifference to their special interests. In this unique national triangle of one oppressed majority and two oppressed minorities, rational and tolerant discourse is not easy.

8. Local and regional leaders and interest groups compete for public

---

54. The phrase is that of Telemachus, "De Spanning tussen de Taalgroepen," p. 334.
55. Michael J.L.G. Balfour, *States and Mind* (London, Cresset Press, 1953), p. 97.
56. On the latter, see Edw. Van Leuven, *De Evolutie van de Personeelseffectieven in Overheidsdienst* (Brussels (?), 1962 or 1963), pp. 25–27, offprint of two articles from the *Tijdschrift voor Bestuurswetens-chappen en publiek Recht*, 1962, nos. 4 and 5, pp. 230–37, 304–19.

and private investment and for other advantages in public policy. Too often these normal clashes of local or regional economic interest are intensified because they are seen in the sentimental light of ethnic-linguistic conflict.

9. Money has met many of the historic demands of the working classes. More money has made the school pact acceptable to Catholic and public institutions. Money helps to meet regional economic demands. But it can do little to solve the linguistic demands and counterdemands.

10. The national sentiment that might offset centrifugal tendencies is weaker—for good or for ill—than in any other European nation. Political socialization in most cases emphasizes the particularistic, not the national. Belgians know a Flemish culture and a Dutch culture, a French culture and in folklore a Walloon culture—but hardly a Belgian culture. Except for the king, few national symbols [57] have power to move or to hold. And the monarchy, though generally accepted, is far from universally popular. The army suffers as a symbol from the antimilitarism traditional among the Flemish in general and among the Socialists in Wallonia. Each culture has its own historic memories, and those of Flanders are regional rather than national. In Flanders the anniversary of the Battle of the Golden Spurs in 1302 is more lively than the national holiday, and the Flemish lion evokes more enthusiasm than the national flag. In what other capital of a democratic nation would federalists give the unfurling of the national colors as an excuse for assault and battery? [58]

The Factors of Unity

We should examine consensus as well as conflict.

1. The Constitution is, to be sure, no longer venerated as once it was. But except for the federalist proposals its institutions are accepted with little question. If there is a "crise de régime," as Belgians frequently say, it is in the demands for modernization, for greater efficiency and authority, more participation by citizens in civic life, and forms of decentralization in the working of the existing institutions—fine but often contradictory demands—which are the staples of discussion in Western democracies.

In the royal question, both sides appealed to the Constitution, while taking opposing views of the constitutionality of the king's acts. In the school conflict, neither side questioned the constitutional provision for

---

57. Among the rare discussions see Roger Mols, *Bruxelles et les Bruxellois* (Louvain, Société d'Etudes Morales, Sociales et Juridiques, 1961), pp. 121–33; Léo Moulin, "Les Liturgies nationales," *Revue Générale Belge* (January 1962), pp. 21–34.

58. In Wemmel, Flemish suburb of Brussels, in June 1963, Flemish nationalist demonstrators assaulted some citizens who flew the national colors from their windows. A Volksunie leader did not hesitate to say, publicly and privately, that the flags had been "a provocation" to the demonstrators.

freedom of education, while each asserted that only its own approach could realize that freedom in practice.[59]

2. Born with the nation, the monarchy is a symbol of its existence and unity. Except for the decade of the 1940s, the kings have been not only symbols, important as that role is, but mediators. The royal function has had "some of all three of Max Weber's ideal types of power: the traditional, the charismatic, and the rational." [60] That function is more important in a multi-ethnic than in an ethnically homogeneous state. Even in the heat of the fight against the return of Leopold III there was relatively little attack on the institution of a monarchy which, said the Socialist Achille Van Acker, "the nation needs as it needs bread."

3. Communal politics, on the whole, is a factor of unity. The commune is the normal ladder to national political office, and a high percentage of M.P.'s continue to hold communal office. Communal councils are elected by proportional representation. Electoral arithmetic requires administration by coalition in most of the larger communes. Municipal coalitions form and fall apart, most often with scant reference to ideology, and generally (at least before 1964) with little reference to national coalition patterns. Politicians thus are likely to have considerable experience of alliance at one level of government with people they oppose at another level. On balance, this experience tends to diminish hostilities by making the reasons for opposition seem relative rather than absolute.

4. Brussels has a "national vocation." Its very existence as a metropolis depends upon the performance of national political, administrative, commercial, financial, and cultural services. Out of interest and sentiment, Brussels wants (even if it fails to show the necessary linguistic tolerance) to maintain the unitary state. Conversely, advocates of regional separation *à deux* find Brussels a stumbling block.

5. Economic life reflects the national experience and helps to shape it. Most large industrial and financial enterprises are national. Exports and the transit trade, upon which Belgium is so heavily dependent, call for national action. The highly structured system of collective bargaining is essentially on a national, industry-wide basis.

6. Most social and economic interests, except those of a specifically local or regional character, are organized nationally. National organizations preserve their unity by recognizing diversity. Almost all of them have either formal bifurcation or informal recognition of the two linguistic communities or of the two (or three) geographic regions.

7. If all the lines of cleavage ran in the same direction, the tensions in the nation might become unbearable. Comparisons with Austria and

59. See the excellent discussion in André Mast, "Une Constitution du temps de Louis-Philippe," *Revue de Droit Public et de la Science Politique* (November-December 1957), pp. 987–1030.

60. "La Couronne et le Pays," *Revue Nouvelle, 30* (July 15, 1959), 57.

France may be helpful. The Fourth Republic collapsed in part because, in what Maurice Duverger called a "superposition of dualisms," [61] its many divergent lines of cleavage made impossible any continuing or cohesive majority in public opinion or Parliament. In Belgium the "superposition of dualisms" has not led to anything as paralyzing as the political fragmentation of the Third or Fourth Republics. On the other hand, further polarization along the same lines as those of ethnic-linguistic differences in Belgium might disrupt a territorial unity less deeply rooted than that of the French nation.

In *Austria infelix* between the wars, polarization was the prelude to civil war. To be sure, the oppositions of ideologies, social groups, and regions in Belgium (or in the Second Austrian Republic) are not of the armed ferocity of those of the First Austrian Republic. Some Belgians, with emotion or coolly, envisage a dissolution of the national state. But they do not envisage civil war for regional independence.

Each great factor of division—religion, class, party—is also a factor of national cohesion across regional and language boundaries. The leaders of the Church and the national labor and employer organizations are conscious of national responsibilities. In the political parties, although secondary leaders defend chiefly Flemish or Walloon or Brussels interests, the top leaders are highly conscious of their role in the aggregation of regional claims. In their own ways, and no doubt generally in their own interests, all these organizations work to surmount the tendencies toward further polarization.

Opposition Style

Between the wars, most governments were either Catholic-Liberal coalitions or tripartite. The Liberals were not ready to join with the Socialists except in the presence of the Catholics. Since the war, there have been no more "national union" cabinets. All possible coalitions of two major parties have governed. Any combination remains politically possible, although arithmetically, most of the time, only a coalition of the PSC with one of the other two has been possible.[62] This general availability for cabinet coalitions we might, for the sake of a short and catchy name, call *Allgemeinkoalitionsfähigkeit*. It contributes elements of stability and of instability.

The possibility of a reshuffling of partners in the coalition dance leads to some instability, which is not always dysfunctional. There is no single pattern of majority-minority relations. But on balance a certain stability results from the interchangeability of majority and minority roles and the

61. *Les Partis politiques*, p. 262.

62. Since the Second World War the Socialists and Liberals together have had a majority in both houses only in the 1954–58 legislature. On the recurrence and duration of various combinations, see Appendix Table 5.7.

continuity of personnel [63] and of role expectations. As a Liberal Vice-Premier remarked, "We have all had the experience of being in the government and that of being in the opposition." [64] The considerable stability of cabinets since the war, as compared with the troubled interwar years, also reflects a greater cohesiveness of all three parties.

Shifts in the weight of the various Catholic social groups in differing government combinations help make *Allgemeinkoalitionsfähigkeit* possible. As the largest party (in all but two legislatures since 1918), the PSC has most freedom in the choice of coalition partners. But the very existence of choice may heighten internal strains. Each coalition formula is identified with different social and regional groups and leading personalities within the party. Switches from one partner to another, or from government to opposition and vice versa, extend those strains from party cadres to social constituencies.[65]

Within the Socialist Party the duration of national government participation tends to bring protest from a left opposition based on doctrine, temperament, and—most recently—Walloon restiveness. To this tension the party contributes by the special socialist form of ancestor worship which consists of intoning ancient slogans believed to keep the ghosts of departed leaders from haunting the scenes of a briefly revolutionary youth.

The Socialists have been pulled by contradictory hopes and strategies. Most have ceased to nourish the old confidence, supported by Marxist analysis and the disaffection of industrial workers from the Church, that continuing industrialization would give them an absolute majority. Never since 1925 have they even reached the 39.4 per cent of the vote they won that year. Unless the PSC breaks up, they cannot expect a majority, perhaps not even a plurality.

Prime Minister Spaak announced his coalition with the Catholics in 1947 as one to last a generation. The royal affair blew it up two and a half years later. In 1954, Prime Minister Van Acker announced his coalition with the Liberals as the "alliance for a generation." During that generation, his coalition's school policy was to reduce what was regarded as a

63. The latter is based in part on the many safe seats in multimember constituencies and on party cooptation in the Senate.

64. A. Lilar, *Annales Parlementaires, Sénat,* Nov. 18, 1958, p. 15.

65. One switch will illustrate these problems. Its 1958–61 coalition with the Liberals gave weight to the PSC's conservative social groups and its Walloon constituency. In the 1961 electoral campaign, the PSC defended its government by attacking the Socialists for violence and lawlessness in their recent general strike. The election returns in, the PSC invited the "Reds" it had just been denouncing to replace the Liberal Party as its coalition partner. The PSC loss of votes made it quite natural, under the rules of the game, for it to change its coalition partner. But many conservative PSC activists and voters felt betrayed by the sudden shift after 12 years of frequently hard opposition between their party and the PSB. The outgoing Prime Minister was naturally bitter about his successor's public appeals for a change of coalition partner.

major source of Catholic political recruitment. Such a policy put economic reform on the shelf, for the Liberals had all the economic ministries. The coalition collapsed with the voters' rebuke in the election of 1958.

The current "grand alliance" of the two mass parties adds to the weight in the PSC of the Catholic Labor Movement and of the party's Flemish wing, of which labor is the chief component. In the present constellation of Belgian politics, this alliance gives the maximum possibilities of social and economic reform. Yet it is acceptable to many influential business people.[66] For it minimizes the incentives for either Socialist or Catholic unions to outbid the others in militancy of industrial tactics or political demands, and maximizes the interest of their leaders in government stability.

National leadership having passed from them, the Liberals have long consoled themselves with the role, in their self-image, of "balance wheel of the nation's politics." [67] But their participation in governments led by the Socialists and the Catholics failed to prevent the bitter dualistic confrontations of the royal affair and the school fight.

In creating the new Party of Liberty and Progress, the Liberals (for there is still no other name for the men and women of the PLP) modernized and centralized a traditionally loose political organization. Where the UDB had failed to surmount religious cleavages on the left, the PLP sought with considerable success to surmount them on the right. By the municipal elections of 1964, the PLP had attracted enough candidates of known Catholicism to cover up the old Liberal image of anti-Catholicism.

Like the Liberal Party, the PLP seemed to find its chief support among middle-class business and professional people, who as individuals and in their interest groups are for the most part less effectively organized and less committed politically than workers or Flemish peasants. In opposition since its formation in 1961, the PLP could combine the frankest "catch-all" economic-interest appeals in all sections of the country [68] with uninhibited *francophone* linguistic appeals in Wallonia and Brussels.

Whatever the outgoing majority-minority alignment, parties fight national elections alone and not in tandem.[69] The direction and relative

66. Of course many business leaders, quietly or openly, have supported measures of recent reform, e.g. of the tax system.

67. Others have applied harsher terms, including that of the world's oldest profession, to the Liberals' ability to bargain for much more than their proportionate share of Cabinet posts in any coalition they enter.

68. Said a Liberal Minister of the Middle Classes (a Ministry which may be a Belgian Liberal contribution to the science of public administration), in laying down the burdens of a long public career: "In my first political speech, I said that my ambition was to become a 'merchant of happiness.' And this is what I have tried to be all through my career." L. Mundeleer, *Le Soir*, Brussels, Jan. 29, 1958.

69. Joint Socialist-Liberal slates were of importance in the pre-World War I days, when both were in semipermanent opposition. Of small consequence have been such joint slates in some overwhelmingly Catholic provinces since 1946. See Appendix Tables 5.5 and 5.6.

weight of any leading campaigner's attack on his opponents reflect his postelection coalition preferences. (The vocabulary of coalition possibilities runs: "My coalition is a marriage of reason. Your coalition is an unstable combination. His coalition is an alliance against nature.")

In Parliament, members of the opposition, even the Communists, have the right of the floor, including the (unwritten) right of interruption. They can usually have items placed on the agenda, although the government has priority for its business. Their verbal and written interpellations impress constituents more than cabinets.

Effective scrutiny of the budget, classic locus of the opposition, is difficult now in any parliamentary democracy. Yet Belgian budget debates are often the occasions for meaningful expositions of policy by ministers and criticism by various oppositions, including those within the majority.

In general, however, the opposition does not exercise most of its formal rights in budget matters, for lack of time and competence or out of a feeling of hopelessness.[70] Budgets are often submitted late; functional divisions of ministerial allocations are in many cases inadequate and confusing; supplemental budgets come in after expenses have been incurred, sometimes including expenses rejected in regular budgets. The reports to Parliament by the Court of Accounts on the legality of past expenditures are years behind. The important public activities carried on by the quasi-public or "parastatal" agencies are beyond parliamentary budget control.

The chief aim of party opposition is dislocation of the governing coalition. Dislocation tactics seek to increase the strains between the two partners of any coalition and within each of the governing parties. Each party out of office can focus special appeals and electoral threats on those elements of a party in government which chafe at their own party's choice of coalition partner. The Liberals can threaten the PSC right wing and vice versa. The Catholic trade union wing can embarrass the Socialist unionists and vice versa. These dislocation tactics we might see as "negative bargaining."

The Socialists face a special paradox in their relations with the PSC as a coalition partner. In the long run, they would like to see the PSC fall apart on socioeconomic issues. But in the short run, they can have the legislation they want only if their PSC partners prevent too many of their right-wing M.P.'s from breaking party ranks in committee and floor votes. If they fail to show legislative gains, the Socialist managers of the coalition face criticism within their own party.

When the two mass parties are together in the "grand alliance," the official opposition is small in numbers. In the legislature chosen in 1961, the recognized opposition in the House mustered only 20 Liberals, plus 12

---

70. An informal group may use its power not by pruning a budget but by holding it up entirely to get a policy or administrative change, as Flemish deputies did in 1962 with the education budget in order to obtain a measure of federation in the Ministry of National Education and Culture.

from the minor parties, against the government's 180. For part-time M.P.'s, with no staffs of their own, this makes a heavy burden for the opposition, especially as committee meetings may go on simultaneously with floor debates, interrupted only for votes on the floor.

The larger the nominal majority, however, the more safely may the oppositions within the governing parties manifest themselves in debate, committee action, and floor votes without bringing down the government. Usually they wish to avoid doing that, and that is a government's strength.[71]

Public employment has been an arena of opposition. Employment and promotion in national, provincial, communal civil service and the quasi-public bodies have reflected party, religious, regional and linguistic cleavages and competition. A reduction of partisanship in national civil service hiring after the war brought an increased political pressure on promotions. This is, however, an old and civilized society, which respects vested interests. The rules of the game do not permit political dismissals; in fact, they hardly permit dismissals at all. But responsible officials are often sidetracked when a minister of a different party takes over a department.

Does it make the civil service more representative, more in tune with the rest of society, to have it reflect the religious and political and linguistic affinities of Belgians? The reflection is not candid, however. Everyone pays lip service to politically neutral professional competence, and each successive Cabinet's declaration of policy deplores the politicization of the bureaucracy. But it is always necessary to repair past inequities. Always in the name of restoring equilibrium, therefore, the balance in the civil service reflects the changing of partners in the saraband of coalition formation and opposition. But alternations of favoritism and discrimination do not secure anything recognized as equilibrium by the contending political, religious-ideological, and linguistic groups. For a long time, the contrasts between principle and practice have diminished public esteem for the public service, adversely affected work and personal relationships within the service, and discouraged initiative among all but the boldest.[72]

71. In 1963 Flemish PSC opposition to a major language bill caused the PSC Prime Minister to tender his government's resignation. Only when the King had refused it (as no doubt Lefèvre expected) was the Prime Minister able to hammer out a compromise among the members of his own party and the majority, enabling the government to carry on.

72. Among the few discussions in the literature, see especially the admirable essay by André Molitor, "L'Administration dans la société belge," in Institut Belge de la Science Politique, *Aspects de la société belge*, pp. 113–34; J. Vandendries, "L'Influence de la politique dans la vie de l'administration en Belgique," *International Review of Administrative Sciences*, 24 (1958), 512–22; Victor Crabbe, "Les Commissions de réforme administrative en Belgique," ibid., 20 (1954), 869–903, and the reports of the commissions of inquiry cited in that article: Edw. Van Leuven, *De Evolutie van de Personeelseffectieven in Overheidsdienst*; also Val R. Lorwin, "The Politicization of the Bureaucracy in Belgium" (Stanford, Center for Advanced Study in the Behavioral Sciences, 1962).

In 1964 the Lefèvre government proposed the most serious and comprehensive steps in a generation toward a reform of the civil service. But it was unable to achieve much of its program in its own weakened state at the end of the term of the legislature.

The courts are not a channel of policy opposition. There is no judicial review of parliamentary action. The Constitution bids the courts enforce only those administrative regulations (royal decrees) which are in conformity with the laws, but the courts have not used implied power much. Appeals are often taken to the Council of State against specific arbitrary acts of administration—for example allegedly political promotions made without due regard for the forms of civil service procedure. But such appeals constitute only a minor form of political opposition.

A party out of power or a locally entrenched interest may use its control of communal or provincial government to counter national policies. Most frequently it works within the law, though at times it operates beyond the law's margins. Many Socialist burgomasters and police chiefs gave support to strikers and condoned violence in the general strikes of 1950 and 1960–61. They were following the tradition of the Liberal burgomasters of large communes who in the nineteenth century abetted anti-Catholic manifestations and riots. Most significant in its continuing consequences, perhaps, was the refusal in 1960 of several hundred Flemish burgomasters, of all parties, to administer the government's bilingual forms for the national census. (Their disobedience reflected their concern that the responses would show the progress of French in some communes.) The government yielded to this defiance and sent them only Flemish forms.

In this nation of extensive commercial publicity efforts, appeals to general public opinion by both government and opposition are surprisingly bland and ineffectual. The principle of a party press is accepted, but neither of the two mass parties has a press comparable to its numerical importance, especially among *francophone* readers.

Newspapers in many lands are farther to the right than the voters. The Belgian phenomenon of the continuing opposition of the *Libre Belgique* may be almost unique. This well-informed, well-written but heavily slanted Brussels French-language daily has a national circulation which even includes many thousands of *bien-pensant* Flemish. Nominally very Catholic but with no spirit of charity, it is also aggressively conservative, nationalistic, and *francophone*. Its insistence on treating the Socialists as the "enemy brothers" of the Communists has helped keep alive Socialist anti-Catholicism. It directs its biting criticism at the progressive wing of the PSC as much as at the party's rivals. In a small country, the opposition of one such powerful journal is equal almost to that of another opposition party.

The Brussels boulevard press (especially *Pan* and *Pourquoi Pas?*) plays a minor but occasionally significant opposition role by its revelations. The weekly *Pan* is a Belgian analogue of the Paris *Canard Enchaîné.* It is notably well informed about the Court and about the law courts. It is one of the few French-language sheets to mock *francophone* as well as Flemish excesses, and was courageous enough to defend the Lefévre-Spaak government in its most unpopular hour. The Liberal-oriented *Pourquoi Pas?* meanwhile has moved toward the right and engaged in bitter anti-Flemish and antigovernment diatribes.

The public corporation that runs the nation's radio and television networks allocates equal time in campaigns to each of the three national parties, but in driblets. To recognized minor parties it gives some, but much less, time. None of the parties has yet made effective or significant use of such time as it has had. The corporation fills positions in terms of the proportional representation so widespread in Belgian life. Its job allocation among the parties leaves out the minor parties in favor of the exclusive rights of those a Volksunie deputy called "the Holy Trinity." [73]

Congo

In what was perhaps the nation's greatest responsibility—its vast colony— the opposition had not fulfilled its role for four decades. There had been strong and often well-informed and thoughtful criticism of Leopold II's Congo administration. After the nation acquired the King's former personal domain,[74] the Socialists at first continued a vigorous opposition which gave reality to parliamentary control. After the First World War, however, by indifference and by more or less common consent, the Congo was insulated from the scrutiny of the Belgian political process. Congo policies were decided by a paternalistic administration, the Church, and large industrial and financial interests. All parties shared responsibility for it; if only Catholics and Liberals held the ministerial portfolio of colonies, Socialists were also responsible as prime ministers. No party in opposition turned the light on the nation's imperatives and choices in the Congo. Belgians knew little about the colony, naturally, and neither parliamentary debates nor election campaigns enlightened them. The task would have been difficult. And indifference made it easier to release the Congo—but too suddenly, once the decision was taken.

The internal rivalries of the homeland were, however, projected onto the screen of the Congo: the school fight, the competition of the trade unions, and the linguistic issue. The latter created a final echo in the parliamentary discussion of the organic statute giving the colony its

73. Daniel Deconinck, *Annales Parlementaires, Chambre de Représentants,* June 6, 1961, p. 16.
74. For a fascinating description of the political process of that acquisition, see Jean Stengers, *Belgique et Congo: L'élaboration de la charte coloniale* (Brussels, Renaissance du Livre, 1963).

independence. A leading Flemish Socialist deputy protested against the undue importance of the French language and the slight to Flemish: he saw it as "intolerable that the two languages should not leave the Congo on an equal footing."

Eppur Si Oppone

As I hope the preceding pages have indicated, there are still lively oppositions in Belgian life. They are not what they were in the classic system of an ideological two-party taxpayers' suffrage elite, nor are they those of the three-cornered party stage onto which the Socialists first advanced the cause of the working classes. As for the opposition of principle, it has receded almost beyond sight or sound. Politics have settled down chiefly into an opposition of center-right and center-left, capable of regrouping in response to old ideological concerns, to bursts of general antigovernmental feeling, and especially to linguistic fears and resentments.

The ideologies are largely *Privatsachen*, to be sure. But they have left their structures of institutions and attitudes. The heritage is clearest in the institutions of Catholicism, whose renewed vitality may be due as much to the tensions among the different social groups within the Catholic community (which a more socially homogeneous Socialist community does not experience) as to the renewal of Catholic social doctrine and the advent of Catholic lay action.

A great complex of organizations asserts the positive values of Church and school, of Catholic social and political action. But also, complain some earnest Catholics, it minimizes "dangerous outside contacts." It is possible to live most of one's life in a Catholic world: parish, school, youth movement, trade union or farmers' league or other occupational group, family association, consumer cooperative, friendly society, clinic and hospital, cultural organization, women's movement, and pensioners' organization. There are few meaningful personal contacts between most Catholics and non-Catholics. As the Catholic Center of Socio-Religious Research said in one regional study, "People of each group know people of the other groups only through stereotypes. These are usually simplified and deformed images of reality, of which a chief aim is to disparage the people of the other group." [75]

The old phenomenon of *Verzuiling*, or compartmentalization of life within "spiritual families," is in some ways decreasing. There are many more contacts among the elites of the Catholic, Socialist, and Liberal worlds. Ideologies have been losing their thrust and their rancor. But the organizations based upon them have become increasingly well established in most of organized social life. In the United States, multiple

75. Jean Remy, *Charleroi et son agglomération, 1: Unités de vie sociale* (Brussels, 1961?), 494.

memberships in voluntary associations may tone down hostilities. In Belgium, they reinforce them, as the memberships are all ordinarily within one spiritual family and one language group.

A thoughtful writer in the lively journal of a Catholic "ginger group" finds the old idea of "philosophical and religious barriers" laughable—"as if Belgium were peopled with philosophers and theologians!" [76] And one might add that philosophers and theologians have advanced beyond the structures their predecessors created. But people remain conditioned by those structures. "These ruins are inhabited," as the American boy discovered in running about Oxford.[77]

Most interest groups are not free to shop around from one political party to another because they are tied to a single spiritual family. But they may be more or less active during a political campaign, depending both on the care shown for their interests and even more on the threat to their sentiments. The Catholic unions have been most active politically in response to the threat against the Catholic schools. To be sure, interest groups usually do not have to shop around. Each mass party will meet the offers of the other party. Thus the PSB and the PSC competed with each other through the 1950s, election after election, in promises (and performance) to raise old-age pensions and to reduce the term of military service.

The major interest groups ordinarily have rather good access to decision-making centers, whoever is in office. A dramatic clash in April 1964 between the doctors and the government was in part due to the almost total inexperience of the former in lobbying and bargaining on economic, as distinct from purely professional and ethical, concerns. Despite the close powers of regulation of the profession by the Ordre des Médecins, with its compulsory membership, the doctors had almost no organizations for bargaining with the government and the friendly societies under the revised health insurance law. That inexperience was a major cause of the breakdown in negotiations which resulted in the doctors' strike. An immediate result of the conflict was the new, modern, and exigent organization of this small but strategically placed interest group. If its members sympathized with the party in parliamentary opposition at the moment, they seemed to recognize the advantages of maintaining a nonpartisan stance.

Most Belgians do not yet accept the full implications of pluralism, despite the slackening of anticlerical passions and the growth of tolerance and ecumenical feeling in the Church. Partisans of public and parochial

76. *La Relève*, March 7, 1964, p. 2, untitled article on Guy Cudell, unsigned (by F. Coupé).

77. Muriel Beadle's book by that name (concerned with other matters) (Garden City, New York, 1961).

schools may tolerate each other; not many yet fully accept the other system's legitimacy. Catholics and non-Catholics have similar reservations in their attitudes toward each others' hospitals.

Governments, wiser than their constituents, have enshrined pluralism in a representation for all recognized interests in every aspect of life affected with a public interest or expenditure, from elected local and national political assemblies, the Central Economic Council and the joint collective bargaining commissions, down to the three brass bands—Liberal, Catholic, and Socialist—which sound forth, with the aid of public subsidies, in any large city.

The institutionalization of all these particularisms helps to maintain the attitudes to which they once gave more militant expression. The attitudes may remain long after the ideologies have lost their force, as in Austria. In Belgium in normal times the attachments and antipathies of the spiritual families are pervasive but not virulent, brooding rather than aggressive. If meaningful personal contacts with people of other subcultures are few, so are the occasions for personal hostility. Normal man will not be political man much of the time. Joining a trade union or even a party may be—rather than an act of commitment and participation—merely conformism to a social milieu, an insurance policy for a career, a key to a housing project. For many, organizational membership is a dull gray rather than a militant Red or a faithful Black.

Listen to the advice to civil service aspirants by the leader of a Flemish nationalist organization, which has no trade unions of its own: "Join the union connected with the party of the Minister in whose department you want a job." For other limiting cases, look at some commuting Flemish workers who join a Catholic union to have peace in the Flemish village where they live and a Socialist union to have peace in the Walloon mill where they work.

Yet even the antiheroes of these limiting cases respond to demands for support of an opposition, on the set occasions of political balloting or occupational elections, or on the unpredictable occasions when a royal affair or a regional strike sends gusts of new passion flooding through old canals. The classic opposition has indeed waned, as Otto Kirchheimer has so well demonstrated.[78] But the waning of that opposition has left the attitudes and the institutions of many oppositions, manifest and latent. *Eppur si oppone.*

78. Otto Kirchheimer, "The Waning of Opposition in Parliamentary Regimes," *Social Research, 24* (1957), reprinted in R. C. Macridis and B. E. Brown, eds., *Comparative Politics* (Homewood, Ill., Dorsey, 1961), pp. 216–27. Cf. Gabriel A. Almond, "A Comparative Study of Interest Groups and the Political Process," *American Political Science Review, 52* (1958), 270–82.

6

THE NETHERLANDS:
OPPOSITION IN A SEGMENTED SOCIETY

Hans Daalder

Legal parliamentary opposition has been a permanent feature of Dutch political life for over a century. By definition, it could not have arisen earlier: there was plenty of opposition previously, but no parliament. One could argue that there was not even a Dutch state until 1795. The Republic of the Seven United Provinces which existed from around 1579 to 1795 was merely a loose confederacy of practically sovereign polities, so much so that even at the end of the eighteenth century the States of Holland still addressed the States of Zeeland as: "Honorable High Mighty Gentlemen, Favored Friends, Neighbors and Allies." A parliament proper was only introduced in 1814 when central authority was securely established. Direct elections for the lower house did not come until 1848.

Neither the rise nor the role of oppositions could be explained adequately, however, without careful attention to the enduring effects of previous experiences. Pluralism and certain kinds of legitimate opposition predated parliamentary government and democracy in the Netherlands. Older elite characteristics and traditional modes of interelite conflict and accommodation have had a lasting influence. Even present-day social cleavages, between classes and masses and between latitudinarian Protestants, orthodox Protestants, and Catholics have their roots in sixteenth and seventeenth-century divisions.

Roughly speaking, Dutch experience with opposition can therefore be summarized as follows:

First, medieval traditions successfully resisted central authority. Political power thus remained highly dispersed in the seventeenth and eighteenth centuries, if strictly oligarchical. There was no recognition of opposition as a justifiable attempt on the part of the outs to replace existing rulers. But factionalism was a well-understood phenomenon. The need

---

I am much indebted for criticism to Robert A. Dahl, Hans Daudt, Robbert P. van den Helm, Val R. Lorwin, Ivo Schöffer, and Ed van Thýn.

to adjust conflicting interests fostered a tradition of compromise and an acceptance of disagreement and diversity.

Second, the imposition of central government after 1795 provoked a conflict about the scope of government. Slowly, a democratic, reformist opposition developed in Parliament which successfully enforced ministerial responsibility after 1848.

Third, a dominant liberal elite became confronted with policy-oriented and even democratic structural opposition from orthodox Protestants and Catholics. This led increasingly to mass politicization. Shortly afterward, a Socialist opposition developed which was at first in total conflict with the society, then became a democratic structural movement, then turned increasingly toward policy-oriented or even office-seeking opposition. Neither of these successive emancipationist groupings achieved an independent majority. Rather than destroying the previously established political order, they came to form highly segmented subcultures which strengthened the pluralist character of Dutch society.

Fourth, the main political parties have learned to operate within a system of political bargaining in which separate ideological traditions are carefully respected and protected, but in which a considerable measure of practical cooperation is achieved. Most articulate interests have an opportunity to make themselves felt. But the effective foci of decision-making have tended to become rather centralized (though remaining collegial and pluralist). All parties engage in policy opposition and in office-seeking opposition. But while opposition is thus continuous, it is often fluid. While there is no strong opposition of principle to the system, there appears to exist a considerable gap between leaders and led. Survey and other data reveal a high degree of satisfaction with living standards and little interest in politics. While the ground plan of the party system has changed little since World War I, the modern electronic mass media subject the prevailing segmentation to increasing strains.

Throughout the last centuries there has been comparatively little violence in public life. Governments have been relatively secure and comparatively seldom repressive, while oppositions have been on the whole moderate if persistent. Both rulers and ruled have jealously insisted on their own autonomy. Governments have tended to enjoy a rather free hand, but have used authority on the whole in rather responsible fashion. Otherwise, the words of a British minister at the Hague, written over a hundred years ago, would still seem pertinent:

The Dutch are little disposed to take a busy and sustained part in politics. They enjoy their liberties rather than exercise their rights. Some vital question must be at stake, affecting the conscience, the heart, or the purse of the nation, to rouse them to exertion. The Pope, or the

House of Orange, the finances, or the colonies, must be in question; then the masses are stirred to an active participation in public affairs.[1]

Central Government and Persistent Pluralism

As Robert Dahl observes in the introduction to this volume, a formal opposition is likely to be permitted in a political system if (1) the government believes that an attempt to coerce the opposition is likely to fail, or (2) even if the attempt were to succeed, the costs of coercion would exceed the gains.[2] Both circumstances have prevailed in the Netherlands from an early date. The Dutch political community itself was born of successful resistance against attempts at coercive centralization by the Burgundian and Hapsburg overlords in the fifteenth and sixteenth centuries. In the *Placaet van Verlatinge* of 1581, the Dutch States-General solemnly renounced their legal prince, Philip II, justifying their opposition on two grounds: "the liberties of men, wives and children and of future descendants, for which the Law of Nature bade them to sacrifice even goods and blood" and the circumstance that of old princes had ruled in the Low Countries, "after recognition of privileges, customs and ancient traditions, on condition, contract and agreements breaking which a Prince is deprived by right of the rule of the land." [3]

For a while the States-General looked around for a new sovereign. But before long they came to be satisfied with the peculiar construct of the United Provinces of the Netherlands established in the *Unie van Utrecht* in 1579 as little more than a temporary alliance. Thus at a time when absolutism and the divine right of kings came to dominate in most European countries, Dutch particularist interests successfully sought to arrest the further growth of central government.[4]

What emerged was a highly pluralist, decentralized political society. The States-General stood technically at the pinnacle of the political hierarchy. But this assembly was itself made up of strictly mandated delegates

1. Report from Lord Napier to the Foreign Secretary (1860), published in full by J. C. Boogman in *Bijdragen en Mededelingen van het Historisch Genootschap,* 76 (1957) 213.

2. This volume, p. x.

3. The last Orange Stadholder, William V, greeted the American Declaration of Independence as "a parody of the document which our ancestors made public against King Philip II of Spain." See P. Geyl, *Geschiedenis van de Nederlandse Stam, 5* (Amsterdam, Wereldbibliotheek, 1962), 1203. His statement was, of course, highly anachronistic; even Madisonian democracy would have been far too progressive for a man of his small caliber, who was himself at one time reinstated in power with the aid of Prussian troops.

4. For full treatment in English, see especially G. J. Renier, *The Dutch Nation: An Historical Study* (London, Allen and Unwin, 1944), and Pieter Geyl, *The Revolt of the Netherlands, 1555–1609* (2d ed. London, Benn, 1958), *The Netherlands in the Seventeenth Century,* Part I (London, Benn, 1961), Part II (London, Benn, 1964), and *History of the Low Countries: Episodes and Problems* (London, Macmillan, 1964).

from the seven provincial states who were in turn dependent on the various nobilities and cities that composed them.[5] What resulted was a curious amalgam, in which central authority was severely restricted. Althusius and others provided the new structure with a suitable political formula based on the concept of sovereignty from below through a pyramid of freely established *consociationes*. Authority was thus theoretically circumscribed by the prior claims of ancient privileges and contractual undertakings. Aristotelian preferences for the mixed state and natural law theories of legitimate resistance to unlawful authority thus came to solidify what was in fact a highly oligarchical, loosely jointed confederacy.[6]

Within the Republic, the most powerful and richest province, Holland, tended to play a paramount role. Holland alone paid more than half the confederal budget. Its Grand Pensionary tended to be the most powerful official in the Republic, apart from the Orange stadholders. But Holland was at the same time extremely jealous of its independence. Its maritime and commercial interests often conflicted with those of the other provinces which it tended to regard mainly as protective bastions against invasion on land. Consequently Holland had an interest in maintaining the confederacy, but preferably at minimal strength.[7]

The Orange stadholders, too, provided something of a central focus in the Republic. They inherited some of the truncated functions of the traditional princely overlords and enjoyed a very high social and political prestige. Their main immediate powers were of a military nature. They occupied the offices of Captain-General and Admiral of the United Provinces. But they never succeeded in obtaining absolute control over the armed forces, even though they sometimes used them to promote political purposes by methods little short of those of a coup d'état. Administrative control over the Admiralty was divided among five Admiralty Boards, residing in different maritime cities. As to the army, the States-General appointed the highest officers and sent their own political deputies with the Captain-General to determine joint strategy. Army control was further decentralized by the so-called repartition system: each of the provinces was made directly responsible for financing the troops garrisoned within its boundaries. Troop movements were subject to approval

5. See I. Schöffer, in *500 Jaren Staten-Generaal in de Nederlanden* (Assen, Van Gorcum, 1964), pp. 64–98.

6. See E. H. Kossmann, "Politieke Theorie in het Zeventiende-eeuwse Nederland," *Verhandelingen der Koninklijke Nederlandse Akademie van Wetenschappen*, Nieuwe Reeks, 67 (Amsterdam, 1960). For a shorter version in English see Kossmann, "The Development of Dutch Political Theory in the 17th Century," *Britain and The Netherlands*, papers delivered at the Anglo-Dutch Historical Conference, 1959 (London, Chatto and Windus, 1960), pp. 91–110.

7. J. C. Boogman, "Achtergronden en Algemene Tendenties van het Buitenlands Beleid van Nederland en België in het Midden van de 19e Eeuw," *Bijdragen en Mededelingen van het Historisch Genootschap*, 76 (1962), 50 ff.

of the provincial states concerned. Individual cities, which often claimed a measure of direct control over parts of the army, could normally rely on their own *schutterijen*, armed guards of independent burghers who gave substance to the strong independent stand many cities chose to take. Thus the tradition of divided control remained strong enough to prevent the development of a strong autochthonous military establishment. Most troops were mercenary soldiers from abroad. Toward the end of the eighteenth century there was only one factory in the Dutch Republic that could make rifles.[8]

The confederal structure of the United Provinces also militated against the establishment of a powerful central bureaucracy. All the more important bodies of the Generaliteit were filled by delegates from all the provinces under a rotating chairmanship. They were served by only a handful of permanent officials who might attain considerable personal influence,[9] but had no means to coerce. Effective political power at the center depended therefore on the ability to balance carefully widely varied particularist interests. Within the restricted circle of effective decision-makers each man took part in the discussions as the representative of a quasi-independent province or city. All therefore learned to live in a climate of constant reciprocal opposition, which fostered the habit of seeking accommodation through slow negotiations and mutual concessions. This also caused a measure of public debate. Within each city or province, citizens were usually prevented from criticizing their rulers. But at the same time these rulers might well see profit in strengthening their case through a public airing of their views and a deliberate attack on the opinions of potential adversaries elsewhere in the Republic. Throughout the life of the Dutch Republic an unending stream of pamphlets and books on controversial issues (so-called *libellen* or *paskwillen*) poured forth from the printing presses.[10]

International considerations tended to further the growth of a spirit of laissez faire in the spiritual as in the economic field. The city oligarchs

8. S. J. Fockema Andreae, "De Nederlandse Staat onder de Republiek," *Verhandelingen der Koninklijke Nederlandse Akademie van Wetenschappen*, Nieuwe Reeks, 68 (Amsterdam, 1960), 117. Since 1848 the Dutch Parliament has dismissed 28 defense ministers (out of 63 ministers who lost their jobs over a conflict with Parliament), usually over trivial financial matters. Dutchmen accord high professional military officers a rather low prestige; according to a recent study generals and colonels are ranked 15th among 57 possible professions, below veterinarians, mayors of small communities, clergymen, and high school teachers; see F. van Heek and E.V.W. Vercruijsse, "De Nederlandse Beroepsprestigestratificatie," in *Sociale Stijging en Daling in Nederland, 1* (Leiden, Stenfert Kroese, 1958), 25–26.

9. In addition to Fockema Andreae's thorough study (see n. 8), see also A. M. Donner, "De Geschiedenis van het Bestuur," in *Nederlands Bestuursrecht* (Algemeen Deel, Alphen, Samson, 1962), pp. 11–42.

10. G. J. Renier used these writings as the basis for his interesting *The Dutch Nation*, passim.

were particularly well aware of the economic benefits which emigré groups brought to the country by promoting industry and trade. They were also highly conscious of the unfavorable effects of ideological partisanship on international trade. Consequently they deliberately sought to de-emphasize ideological conflict at home. A "political" preparedness to live with existing cleavages has ever since gone hand in hand with a relatively peaceful outlook in international affairs. International law and political neutrality enjoyed widespread support as providing a happy combination of high ethics and economic profit. To quote John de Witt, one of the foremost leaders of the Dutch Republic: "The interest . . . of this State [is] posed in this that calmness and peace be everywhere and that commerce may be carried on unhindered." [11]

Does all this mean that pluralism made opposition a recognized feature in Dutch politics as early as the seventeenth or eighteenth century? The answer depends on the way one defines the word "opposition." There was considerable regional conflict which found institutionalized expression in the complex deliberative procedures that prevailed at the center of the Republic. There was ample strife on many issues: international, constitutional, economic, financial, social, and religious. There was often an attempt made to build up partisan support throughout the territory of the Republic, in order to carry special decisions through the cumbersome confederal organs. In addition, more or less lasting groupings tended to coalesce around the Orange dynasty and the *Staatsgezinden* (the leading city oligarchs, called *Heeren* or *Regenten*) respectively. As neither of these groupings were strong enough to completely subjugate the other, they were forced to live with one another, enjoying at most a temporary predominance at any given period. But what was lacking was a view on either side of accountability toward a sovereign people. Active politics was carefully reserved to small, privileged, generally hereditary segments of the population. "Ins" and "outs" were not thought of as complimentary forces that might both contribute to good government, but at most as self-seeking factions. A changing of political personnel only occurred through political intimidation, such as the high-handed *wetsverzettingen* (literally, changing of the laws) by which various Orange stadholders replaced too independent *regenten* by more congenial ones, or through manipulated or spontaneous rebellions by the multitude in time of war or economic depression. If it is true that the Dutch Republic knew comparatively little political violence, it is yet well to remember that two of its leading statesmen, Oldenbarnevelt and John de Witt, died in conditions little short of judicial murder. Grotius, the able advocate of Dutch particularism, was himself forced into exile. For considerable periods of time, the regents did without stadholders. And toward the end of the eighteenth century, domestic conflict

11. Cited by Boogman, "Buitenlands Beleid," p. 51.

reached such tension that it was only temporarily restrained by Prussian arms.

The Dutch Republic lasted until the country was overrun by French troops in 1795, long enough to have a profound and lasting influence on political behavior. Dutch *Unitarissen* and French administrators then laid the administrative framework for a unitary state which was retained by the first Orange king, William I (1813–40). William's activist regime was the nearest experience to royal absolutism the Netherlands ever had. Since then the country has had a relatively strong central administration. But the imposition of new central government machinery on what had hitherto been a highly particularist society did not destroy the effect of earlier political styles. Some older regent groups continued to take a fairly independent stand, and regional diversities retained considerable importance. Centralization did induce a change in the site of opposition, however. Whereas oppositions had formerly tended to be restricted to particularist bases even when they fought on the national scene, activist centralization now caused them to shift their attention almost entirely to the center itself. Henceforth political oppositions perforce addressed a national audience and carried their battles into the national arena. Unlike the old Republican days, oppositions could no longer agree to differ, being relatively secure in their quasi-independent sovereignties. They could only achieve their aims through changes in the personnel, the policies, and even the structure of government. Organized political opposition, in the sense of regular endeavor to change the rules of the game, and with it the persons and policies pursued, must therefore be dated in the Netherlands from this period.

Dissatisfaction with the King's expensive mishandling of the Belgian Separation (1830–39), among other things,[12] led to increased political activity, both in Parliament and in the country at large. Liberal opposition gained increasing force, while simultaneously Calvinists and Catholics came to protest against the Josephist attitude of William I in matters of church organization. In 1840 the King abdicated, unwilling to rule after a mild constitutional change. Eight years later his successor, William II, agreed to a much more drastic constitutional revision. It restrained royal power and made possible a considerable extension of political activity to all groups and areas.

Since 1848 central government and a rejuvenated system of local self-government have existed side by side. While improved communications have led to a relatively peaceful interpenetration,[13] regional factors have

12. See Lorwin, this volume, pp. 149–50.
13. For a fuller discussion of the relevance of this factor to problems of general political development, see Hans Daalder, "Parties, Elites and Political Development(s) in Western Europe," in J. LaPalombara and M. Weiner, eds., *Political Parties and Political Development* (Princeton, Princeton University Press, 1965).

remained of considerable importance for the working of opposition in the Dutch system.

Distinct regional interests have clashed, for instance, in matters of central government expenditure. In the nineteenth century in particular, various governments fell because they did not placate articulate regional interests in Parliament on matters of railways, canals, or even the physical location of courts of justice.[14]

Later opposition parties partly owed their chance to develop to continued social and geographic diversity. Elements of peripheral protest played a substantial part in the rise of Liberal, Catholic, Calvinist, and Socialist opposition. D. Hans and M. Litten [15] have shown how both Liberals and Socialists drew most of their earliest strength from the northeastern provinces. Similarly, the rise of a separate Catholic movement was greatly encouraged by the circumstance that most Dutch Catholics live in two quite heavily Catholic southern provinces; they almost invariably elected Catholic deputies long before there was a Catholic Party. The orthodox Protestants, too, owed much of their electoral strength and social stamina to attitudes of protest in clearly defined orthodox regions against the nonfundamentalist influences from the nation's cultural centers. Differences within the orthodox Protestant camp can to some extent be traced to deep-rooted historical factors, such as the particular way in which the Reformation struck root and variations in the challenges which local Protestants faced from other confessions, and from special social and economic situations.[16]

Finally, the persistence of strong local government traditions has eased the pressure from nationally dominant elites.[17] New social groups have

14. There have always been a considerable number of judges and mayors and other local government officials in the Dutch Parliament, reminiscent of the days before 1795 when the States-General was nothing but an assembly of local interests. (For the period 1848–79, see S. J. Fockema Andreae, *500 Jaren Staten-Generaal in de Nederlanden*, pp. 217 ff.) This has continued to be true, although there were no residence requirements during the period of the district system and even though proportional representation has made the arrangement of party lists a highly centralized affair since 1917. The percentage of representatives actually living in the two provinces, North and South Holland, has declined from three-fourths in 1913, to two-thirds in 1933, to two-fifths at the present time; see N. Cramer, "Portret van de Parlementariër," *Het Parool*, September 19, 1964.

15. D. Hans, *Het Nederlandsche Parlement* (Amsterdam, Van Kampen, 1911), pp. 146–48 and M. Litten, "De geografische verdeeling der politieke partijen in Nederland vóór den wereldoorlog," *Mensch en Maatschappij*, 12 (1936), 50–59 and 126–39.

16. Generally speaking, the militant *Gereformeerden* tend to be concentrated more heavily in the maritime provinces and in the cities, the *Orthodox-Hervormden* who form the backbone of the Christian Historical Union in the traditional rural areas of the center and east of the country, and the theocratic supporters of the Staatkundig-Gereformeerde Partij in rather isolated regions like Zeeland and the Veluwe.

17. See Robert L. Morlan, "Central Government Control of Municipalities in The Netherlands," *Western Political Quarterly*, 30 (1959), pp. 64–70. Fear of particularism has resulted in central government appointment of burgomasters for over a

been able to acquire positions of responsibility in local and provincial government long before they have acceded to power at the center. All manner of coalitions between rival groupings have proved practicable at the local level without immediate reference to the political situation in the national capital. The existence of various levels of government has thus widened the opportunities for positive political action and participation by different groups. This has facilitated cooperation among all kinds of political groups within one constitutional order. While governments have been far from all-powerful, oppositions have rarely been completely without power.

To conclude: persistent pluralism has been a powerful factor in allowing the rise of formal oppositions without violent reversals of the constitutional order. Central power developed relatively peacefully and gradually and became an integral and accepted part of society, not its alien overlord. This facilitated the transfer of older traditions of compromise and the continued recognition of the value of diversity to the modern state. Regional variations in turn came to fit relatively easily into the new political system, becoming sufficiently part of the whole so as not to fragment the political order.

Classes and Masses

THE ENDURING IMPACT OF OLDER CLASS RELATIONSHIPS   Until late in the nineteenth century Dutch politics tended to be the exclusive domain of the classes rather than the masses. The styles of older elites have therefore exerted a substantial influence on present-day political behavior.

At an early date in Dutch history the more important provinces came to be dominated by burgher elements. Both in Holland and in Zeeland, towns formed the backbone of government in the time of the Republic: in the states of Holland the nobility had only one vote, against 18 votes for the cities; in Zeeland, too, the towns had all the votes but one. Within the towns political power was concentrated among self-contained and self-recruiting oligarchies consisting, in the words of an old city charter, of the "richest, most honorable, notable and peaceful." [18] These oligarchies became more exclusive in the eighteenth century and adopted all the styles and titles of an hereditary aristocracy. But if the city regents became, in the words of Renier, more and more "bourgeois gentilhommes," intermar-

---

century. But though central government appointees, burgomasters have in fact often become the champions of local government against the central government itself; mayors are frequently elected to Parliament where they readily criticize their nominal superiors.

18. These words are taken from the *Privilege* of Delft, 1445; see Renier, *The Dutch Nation*, p. 17. The supreme bodies in Dutch cities were called *vroedschappen*, the "wise men." To this day *vroede mannen* are often considered capable of settling painful political conflicts.

riage between newer and older aristocracies at the same time made the latter more and more into "gentilhommes bourgeois." [19]

This pervasiveness of bourgeois values has had important consequences. It saved the Netherlands from the bitter antagonism between the nobility and the *tiers état* which had such explosive effects in France. The Dutch elites retained considerable political, social, and economic prestige. This tended to help them in maintaining their legitimacy; it also dampened working-class militancy, and eased the integration of the working class into the national political community.[20]

Political security made it easier for the ruling classes to permit considerable social freedom to the citizens at large. Mass interference with politics was not permitted; on several occasions in Dutch history rebellious actions by the masses have been quelled by arms and rather heavy-handed "justice." The Dutch regent class did not consider itself in any way responsible to the population at large; affairs of state have traditionally been settled in considerable secrecy.[21] But at the same time, city folk were left a fairly wide autonomous sphere in which they could privately shrug their shoulders over their rulers.[22] This has fostered a rather peculiar mixture of both deference and indifference which has tended to characterize the attitude of most Dutchmen toward authority.

Further, the self-reliance of the regent class has tended to be a factor in the preservation of political liberties. Even after the arrival of central government, the Dutch elites were never completely absorbed into the state apparatus. Memories of old freedoms have helped to ward off autocratic government. Representative government was obtained in 1848 long before the full effects of the Industrial Revolution and rising pressure on the part of the masses were felt.

Finally, the Dutch political elites have never identified completely with one state church. Calvinist pressure in the sixteenth century ensured that the Dutch Reformed Church was officially recognized as the "true religion," and offices were in principle reserved to its adherents. But even in the time of the Republic the city fathers tended to be fairly permissive toward dissenters, Jews, and Catholics. Since 1795 all citizens have formally enjoyed equal civil rights irrespective of religious allegiance. In other

19. Renier, *The Dutch Nation*, p. 104.

20. See Val R. Lorwin, "Working Class Politics and Economic Development in Western Europe," *American Historical Review, 63* (1958), 338–51 and S. M. Lipset, "The Changing Class Structure of Contemporary European Politics," *Daedalus, 93* (1964), 271–304, for general analyses along these lines.

21. I have elsewhere attributed the comparatively little interest of Dutchmen in politics (and the displacement of political studies by legal studies which took place in the nineteenth century) to this special relationship between relatively secure ruling elites on the one hand and rather free citizens on the other; *Leiding en Lijdelijkheid in de Nederlandse Politiek*, Leiden inaugural address, 1964, pp. 10 ff.

22. Renier, *The Dutch Nation*, pp. 180 ff., and 253 ff.

words, the ruling elites, divided themselves in their religious sympathies, have tended to be relatively tolerant. Orthodox Calvinists and Catholics consequently have had to fight an uphill battle against latitudinarian traditions. Rather than upholding a reactionary status quo, they have represented emancipationist movements.[23]

From the end of the eighteenth century, the monopoly of the regent class slowly waned. But upper-class elements retained considerable influence, and even after the introduction of full parliamentary government and ministerial responsibility in 1848 the franchise remained highly restricted. Parliamentarians owed their selection for a long time mainly to small coteries of local patricians, and party organization was practically absent.[24] The power of Parliament thus tended to be somewhat negative. The *Grand Bourgeois* deputies were usually satisfied to hold cabinets and ministers accountable. They used legislative and budgetary powers to ensure adequate consideration for their private rights and interests, but rarely sought to force a particular ministerial *équipe* on the Crown. The king thus maintained substantial influence on ministerial appointments, and many ministers continued to be chosen from outside the parliamentary circle. The influential Liberal leader Johan Rudolf Thorbecke, himself often a minister but also a redoutable opposition leader in Parliament on other occasions, thus characterized the resulting system:

> A free and independent monarchical government with unlimited parliamentary responsibility of ministers, a freely elected representative assembly, independent, deciding according to its own views and judgment, without any link with the voters; exercising general legislation jointly with the monarchical authority, but without participating in the executive power, whose working it controls through the means of ministerial responsibility.[25]

This careful equilibrium was broken up from the 1870s onward by a series of issues that led to more intensive mass participation: the school issue, the conflict about franchise extension, and what an earlier generation termed "the social problem," i.e. the relation between the state and the new industrial proletariat. These issues broke the practical autonomy of the upper classes and gave rise to the establishment of well-organized opposition parties.

23. The failure to grasp this point has faulted Duverger's analysis of Dutch experience on almost every point. It may also account for the fact that the Netherlands does not really fit Almond's typology of a continental European political system; Gabriel A. Almond, "Comparative Political Systems," *Journal of Politics, 18* (1956), 391–409.

24. See S. J. Fockema Andreae, in *500 Jaren Staten-Generaal*, pp. 215 ff. and J. C. Boogman, "De Britse Gezant Lord Napier over de Nederlandse Volksvertenwoordiging (in 1860)," *Bijdragen en Mededelingen van het Historisch Genootschap, 71* (1957), 189 ff.

25. J. R. Thorbecke, *Parlementaire Redevoeringen, 10*, xii–xiii.

THE SCHOOL ISSUE AND THE FORMATION OF RELIGIOUS PARTIES   From the early part of the nineteenth century on, both orthodox Protestants and Catholics had felt uneasy about the increase in secular influences in the Netherlands. But they had tended to find themselves at opposite political poles. The orthodox Protestants were for long practically indistinguishable from the Conservatives, who shared their abhorrence of the French Revolution and, to some extent, their belief in the natural Protestantism of the Dutch nation. The Catholics, on the other hand, resented the Protestant habit of linking together God, Calvinism, the Netherlands, and the House of Orange. After their long condemnation to practical oblivion in the seventeenth and eighteenth centuries, they tended to be hesitant in political action, and at most to expect favorable consideration from the Liberals, whose secular outlook made for a comparatively tolerant attitude toward Catholic demands.

For a long time neither orthodox Protestants nor Catholics were very militant in politics, though for different reasons. The orthodox Protestant elite was so much a part of the upper-class Establishment that most leaders hoped to reverse the "modernist" trends in church and state from the inside.[26] They pointed to past history as witness to the need to return to the ways of the fathers, and generally expected the Orange dynasty to be sympathetic to this cause. Had not the Orange stadholders traditionally been the champions of the Calvinist masses against the latitudinarian regents? Against a predominantly non-orthodox Parliament, they often put their trust in executive privilege.[27] They denied the representativeness of the Liberal *pays légal* and appealed over the head of Parliament to the "people behind the electorate" who had preserved Calvinist orthodoxy with greater purity. But when lower-class elements walked out of the Dutch Reformed Church in fundamentalist protest in 1834, the orthodox

26. Orthodox Protestants divided into roughly three religious groups around the middle of the nineteenth century: (1) the *Ethisch-Irenischen*, who stressed individual conscience and direct missionary activities from one believer to another; (2) the *Confessionelen*, who wished to restore orthodoxy by stricter church organization, and (3) the later *Gereformeerden*, who put great stress on freedom for the local churches; they wished to maintain strict adherence to established doctrine among like-minded individuals but rejected state enforcement. Although Ethical Irenicals and Confessionals were opposed to each other's methods, they usually agreed on the value of preserving a national church, in contrast to the *Gereformeerden*, who did not hesitate to break up the Dutch Reformed Church in the name of true doctrine. The *Gereformeerden* organized partly as a subdivision of the Dutch Reformed Church where they enjoyed local preponderance, partly in separate Gereformeerde Kerken; they have formed the backbone of the Anti-Revolutionary Party, while Ethical Irenicals and Confessionals have associated on the whole with the Christian Historical Union.

27. Anti-Revolutionary spokesmen sought to make a clear distinction between "counterrevolutionaries" who would wish to reverse history and "antirevolutionaries" who, while rejecting the entire spirit of 1789, would yet recognize change. Groen van Prinsterer was strongly influenced by the German political theorist Friedrich Julius Stahl.

elites had sympathized rather than followed suit. Catholics, on the other hand, were afraid to jeopardize their newly gained legal freedoms and thus treaded very carefully and timidly, preferring the safety of isolation to active political participation.[28]

This situation changed, however, from about the 1860s as a result of various factors. Improved communications made for more intensified central government action. The outlook of the dominant Liberals (as well as a number of Conservatives) came to be more secular, and in some cases even frankly anticlerical. Events abroad, such as the German *Kulturkampf* and the conquest of the Papal State in 1870, added further fuel. The smouldering conflict finally broke into the open over the control of education, which assumed increased importance in the wake of social and economic modernization. Schools were vital to religion, culture, and political power. The issue touched not only the elites, moreover, but parents in all walks of life. It thus contributed to a thorough politicization of the still disenfranchised masses.

This new situation had different effects on orthodox Protestants and Catholics. The latter for a time withdrew further into isolation, severing such tenuous links as had previously existed with the Liberals. The orthodox Protestants, on the other hand, found themselves faced with the question whether to break away from what were after all influential positions within the elite. Many hesitated or even refused, preferring compromise to the doubtful pleasures of the political wilderness. But others reasoned as the first prominent orthodox Protestant political leader, Guillaume Groen van Prinsterer, a former private secretary to the king, who held: "In our isolation lies our strength" or, to use a Dutch word: "In our *onafhankelijkheid* (independence), our firmness of principle, lies our force." Opposition to the Liberals thus reduced the Catholics to a fairly passive isolationist stand under the protection of the newly established church hierarchy, while the orthodox Protestants became increasingly activist and even mass-oriented.[29]

The architect of the Calvinist mass movement was a clergyman, Abraham Kuyper.[30] Within a score of years he organized (or helped to organize) a militant daily newspaper (1872); an Anti-School Law League (1872) consciously modeled on the British Anti-Corn Law League; a

28. Catholic emancipation in all its aspects has been brilliantly analyzed by N. de Rooy and L. J. Rogier, *In Vrijheid Herboren* (The Hague, Pax, 1953).

29. Unlike the Catholics, the orthodox Protestants could not rely on a church organization to fight their battles; this partly explains the much greater and earlier development of the Anti-Revolutionary Party as compared to the Roman Catholic Party. Only in 1896 did Catholic deputies underwrite a common program; a federation of constituency parties was not formed until 1904; not until after the arrival of proportional representation and universal suffrage was an articulate national party organization developed (1926).

30. See D. Jellema, "Abraham Kuyper's Attack on Liberalism," *Review of Politics*, *19* (1957), 472–85.

massive petition movement against a new Liberal School Bill (1878) which obtained over 300,000 signatures at a time when the electorate was only a little over a third of this figure; a political party, the Anti-Revolutionary Party (1879), which proclaimed resistance against the world of 1789 and pioneered modern mass-party organization techniques in the Netherlands; an independent Calvinist University (1880) which provided the new movement with its future intelligentsia; and finally a separate church organization, the Gereformeerde Kerken, formed in 1886 after a walk-out of Calvinist fundamentalists from the Dutch Reformed Church, which then merged six years later with most of the earlier separationists of 1834. Through the aid of careful electoral and parliamentary organization, the Anti-Revolutionaries soon came to replace the Conservatives as the main anti-Liberal opposition party.[31]

Their organizational onslaught nothwithstanding, the Anti-Revolutionaries were too weak numerically to destroy the Liberal domination without Catholic support. It took Catholics quite a while to realize that they shared with the Calvinists, as Groen had phrased it, "community of injustice, of faith, and of danger." But a common oppositional stance in Parliament, and common interests in the school issue, slowly led to increased cooperation, first in parliamentary tactics, then at the ballot box, and finally after a constitutional revision of 1887 (during which the religious groups threatened a policy of noncooperation unless the Liberals agreed in principle to the constitutionality of school subsidies) in a joint cabinet (1888–91). From then on, until 1913, Dutch politics witnessed an almost classical alternation between Liberal and (religious) coalition cabinets (see Figure 6.1).

The line between government and opposition became clearly drawn. Though parliamentary bargaining between the parties remained of some importance, ultimate power was increasingly shifted to the constituencies that gave fairly clear verdicts about personalities and policies. The religious parties used their power, first and foremost, to obtain recognition of their common claims on matters of school subsidies, fully accepted in a great national compromise between all parties in 1916–17 during the First World War. Ever since 1918, the religious parties have jointly obtained a majority of seats in Parliament.

Several features of the opposition campaign of the religious groups between 1870 and 1916 should be noted.

Their impact made itself felt only gradually. For a long time their leaders hoped to achieve their aims by action within the elite, through persuasion, petition, and protest. They sought to convert existing authority rather than challenge it. This slow pace was made possible on the one

31. Conservative seats in the lower house declined from 1868 to 1888 as follows: 19, 16, 9, 6, 1, 1; during the same years the Anti-Revolutionaries rose from 7, 16, 9, 15, 19 to 27.

Figure 6.1. Alternating Governments in the Netherlands: The Lower House of Parliament, 1888–1913

Note: *Religious coalitions governed from 1888–91, 1901–05, and 1908–13; Liberal cabinets of somewhat different shades from 1891–1901, 1905–08, and 1913–18. The last two Liberal cabinets were minority governments relying on support from the Socialists and/or one or more religious parties. The 1905 Cabinet was dismissed by Parliament over a defense budget, and was followed by a new minority cabinet of the religious parties which subsequently obtained a majority in the 1909 elections.*

hand because of the diversified character of the governing elites, on the other because the existing social pluralism tended to soften grievances and for a long time kept the masses from political action.

The movement assumed dimensions of real political importance only when the dichotomy of classes and masses was broken. Yet the entry of the masses also took place only gradually and resulted as much from proselytizing activities by existing elite groups downward as from the organization of new counterelites upward. For a long time, moreover, mass action was carefully tempered by a strong insistence on the need to respect public authority and to follow leadership. Toward the end of the nineteenth century, this situation even forced a break between two wings of the orthodox Protestant movement. Kuyper was willing to make all-out use of the organizational weapon to capture government power, but the leader of the Anti-Revolutionary parliamentary group, A. F. de Savornin Lohman, insisted on the need for the extraparliamentary party to leave government and Parliament alone so that it could work out the necessary compromises free from mass pressure. This led to a breakup of the party in 1894, and the continuous existence since then of two orthodox Protestant parties: the more highly disciplined mass organization of the Anti-Revolutionary Party and the more loosely organized Christian Historical Union, formally established in 1908.

The coalition of the religious parties proved mainly a *mariage de raison* in favor of the parallel promotion of minority interests. Catholics and orthodox Protestants shared the desire to promote their own subcultural freedoms against the strong cultural dominance of the Liberals. But in the last analysis this was not so much a claim for exclusive power as a demand for equal rights and social recognition. Catholics, Anti-Revolutionaries, and Christian Historicals disagreed with one another in paradoxical ways, moreover. The Christian Historicals came nearest to wanting the restoration of orthodoxy as the official state religion. They derived their support almost exclusively from adherents of the Dutch Reformed Church who were angered at Kuyper's exodus of 1886.[32] But this church traditionally also organized a very large number of nonfundamentalists Protestants. Consequently, the Christian Historicals tended at one and the same time to identify the Dutch nation with Protestantism (which made for strained relations with the Catholics) and to assume a relatively conciliatory attitude to less fundamentalist elements. The Anti-Revolutionaries, in contrast, preferred the subcultural isolation of true believers, if necessary, to what they feared would at most be an empty official theology. Kuyper rejected all thought of theocratic compulsion and put great store on the independence of local churches. The more militant and mass-based orthodox Protestants, in other words, consciously opted for the lesser evil of a permanent minority position. From this vantage point they found it easier to use hard political tactics, including cooperating with the Catholics against the Liberals. The Catholics, finally, were the most numerous but at the same time most passive supporters of the religious coalition. Afraid to expose themselves to antipapist reaction, they were generally satisfied to be a follower rather than a leader in the religious coalition.

The minority position of each of the religious groupings within the nation as a whole strengthened the introverted orientation of each of them. The lines of political division came to coincide roughly with denominational boundaries. This gave the Dutch party system considerable stability, especially after proportional representation was introduced. But the potential automatism of the expression of electoral opinion led at the same time to some degree of dissociation between electorate, Parliament, and government.

THE IMPACT OF THE ELECTORAL SYSTEM AND OF SUFFRAGE EXTENSION   The potential mass mobilization effect of the school issue was diminished by

32. From 1889 to 1960 the Dutch Reformed Church declined from about 48.7 per cent of the population to 28.3 per cent while the number of those belonging to no church rose from 1.5 per cent to 18.4 per cent. During the same period the number of *Gereformeerden* remained a fairly steady 9 per cent of the population. (See Appendix Table 6.5.) About half the members of the Dutch Reformed Church must be assumed to belong to the various orthodox groups, including those *Gereformeerden* which for local reasons stayed within the Dutch Reformed Church (see n. 26). The latter group appoints roughly a quarter of Dutch reformed ministers.

certain features in the electoral system which existed until 1917: a district
system requiring an absolute majority on the first ballot, with a second
ballot between the two top candidates in case no candidate won in the
first round.[33]

The geographic element in electoral representation worked to the disadvantage of the more militant sections of the religious opposition groups.
As shown by Hofstee,[34] social modernization has tended to spread from
the more internationally, commercially oriented north and west of the
country to the more traditional regions in the east and south. Among the
restricted electorate of the north and west, the Liberals for a long time
obtained a majority, so that relatively few Catholics and Anti-Revolutionaries were elected from these regions. The religious groups thus drew most
of their earliest strength from more traditional areas where a strong measure of paternalism tended to dominate.[35] Differences in the franchise between urban and rural areas tended to reinforce this situation. Generally
speaking, the franchise requirements were considerably higher in the cities
than in the rural districts. But they were kept high enough in both to give
an advantage to the upper classes, which were disproportionally Liberal in
orientation. Gerrymandering further strengthened this overrepresentation
of Liberals. The religious groups were thus reduced to their more conservative bastions. They did not fully profit from their massive pluralities
in the Catholic south nor could they derive proportionate strength from
their sizable minorities in the north and northwest and in the larger cities
generally. They only slowly overcame this handicap when Catholics in
mixed areas learned to vote for orthodox Protestant candidates.[36] But not

33. Until 1887 members were usually elected in two-member districts, each member
being elected at large for a four-year period at alternate two-year elections. From
1887 most members sat for single-member districts, which were also introduced for the
larger cities in 1897. For details, see chapter on the Netherlands in Stein Rokkan, ed.,
An International Guide to Electoral Statistics (forthcoming), and M. Albrecht, *De
Invloed van het Kiesstelsel op de Samenstelling van de Volksvertegenwoordiging en
op de Vorming van de Regering* (Amsterdam, De Arbeiderspers, 1960). It is a pity
that the inaccurate interpretation of Dutch electoral experience by Enid Lakeman and
James D. Lambert, *Voting in Democracies* (London, Faber, 1955) has been given a
wider circulation in Harry Eckstein and David E. Apter, eds., *Comparative Politics:
A Reader* (New York, Free Press, 1963), pp. 292-95.

34. E. W. Hofstee has documented this hypothesis with a careful study of the
Dutch birthrate; see his "De Groei van de Nederlandse Bevolking," in *Drift en Koers:
een halve eeuw Sociale Verandering in Nederland* (Assen, Van Gorcum, 1962), pp.
13-84. See also Litten, *Geografische Verdeeling*, passim.

35. Between 1848 and 1870 Catholic districts of the south were often represented by
Liberal Catholics from the West, dubbed Papo-Thorbeckianen. This was no longer
possible after 1870 when a highly conservative Catholic Electoral Association *Noord-
Brabant* captured the nomination process for local candidates.

36. It proved easier to persuade Catholics to vote for Protestant candidates than
vice versa. Profits from electoral cooperation thus accrued almost exclusively to the
Anti-Revolutionaries, which strengthened their leadership posture in Dutch political
life.

until the introduction of proportional representation in 1917 was this disadvantage fully overcome.

The franchise itself was extended slowly. (See Appendix Table 6.1.) Until 1887 it remained at the same level, effectively restricting the suffrage to one in eight adult males. In 1887 the electorate was expanded to about a quarter of the adult male population; it was doubled to about half in 1896. For the next twenty years no further changes in the electoral law proved politically possible. But the electorate slowly grew from about 52 per cent in 1897 to about 68 per cent in 1913 as a consequence of automatic enfranchisement through economic prosperity.[37] Universal suffrage was only obtained in 1917 as part of the national compromise which also resulted in equal subsidies for religious schools. This slow expansion of the electorate prevented the sudden inrush of the masses in the *pays légal* and facilitated the careful elaboration of compromises.

Mass influence made itself felt even more slowly in Parliament and in government than at the ballot box. Between 1850 and 1870, no less than 66 per cent of the Anti-Revolutionary parliamentary group in the lower house [38] were members of the nobility (as against a much lower 36 per cent for the Conservatives, 15 per cent for the Catholics, and 10 per cent for the Liberals). This percentage declined to 63 per cent for the period 1871–87, and 45 per cent from 1888–96. Even after Kuyper broke with De Savornin Lohman and "all the men with the double names" in 1894, the number of Anti-Revolutionary deputies belonging to the aristocracy remained comparatively high (17 per cent, as against 53 per cent for the Christian Historicals and 23 per cent for the Catholics for the period 1896–1917).[39] Similar tendencies prevailed in ministerial recruitment.[40] Obviously even noblemen could be activist politicians, and some were. But at all times potential Anti-Revolutionary militancy was further restrained by the need to govern with the support of the much less activist Catholics and Christian Historicals and to keep the confidence of the constituencies. Figure 6.2 shows that the religious coalition gained or lost power mainly through votes for or against Anti-Revolutionary candidates.

---

37. See Appendix Table 6.1 and *G. M. Bos, Mr. S. van Houten* (Purmerend, Muusses, 1952), pp. 117–18.

38. Until 1917 the provincial states (which elect the upper chamber in Holland) were constitutionally bound to make their choice from a list of those who paid the highest direct taxes (until 1887 this list contained at most one name for every 3,000 people living in a province, and from 1887 to 1917 one name for every 1,500). From 1887 to 1917 eligibility was extended to those who had served in high political or administrative office. See J. Th. de Ruwe, *De Eerste Kamer der Staten-Generaal* (Dissertation, Nijmegen, 1957), pp. 4–6.

39. Calculations by J. J. de Jong, as published by A. Hoogerwerf, *Protestantisme en Progressiviteit* (Meppel, J. A. Boom, 1964), p. 176–77.

40. See the excellent study by Mattei Dogan and Maria Scheffer-van der Veen, "Le Personnel Ministériel Hollandais," *L'Année Sociologique* (1957–58), pp. 95–125, in particular pp. 103 ff.

Kuyper might harangue the unprincipledness of the *kleurloze middenstof* (the colorless floaters); he could not obtain a majority at the ballot box without their support.

Figure 6.2. Number of Seats for the Three Religious Parties in the Lower House of Parliament, 1888–1913 (total number of seats = 100)

The slow process of franchise extension thus blunted the edge of the religious opposition groups. But it had considerable influence on the internal structure and relative strength of the parties. Generally speaking, the religious parties handled the participation crisis with more success than the Liberals. Perhaps the most crucial date in Dutch politics is 1894. A fairly radical Liberal Cabinet had proposed extending the franchise to all men who could read and write and did not live on charity (this would have amounted in practice to about 74 per cent of all adult males). The proposal met with serious parliamentary resistance. It was first whittled down and then provoked a dissolution of Parliament in which the Cabinet was defeated and all parties split. The Catholics recovered their unity with little difficulty. As we saw above, internal conflict led to a lasting separation between Christian Historicals and Anti-Revolutionaries, but the need for electoral and government coalition-building tended to hold these parties fairly closely together even so. The Liberals, however, who had only barely achieved a measure of party organization, were split into no less than three groups: a right, a center, and a radical left. The latter actively propagated universal suffrage, sometimes in direct cooperation with Socialists who were campaigning for the same end inside and outside Parliament. This stand of the Radicals must have strengthened reformist tendencies among the Socialists. But as a whole the Liberal movement was too elitist and too little organized to manage the demands of the rising working classes. This inevitably reduced it to a relatively small, mainly upper- and middle-class party once universal suffrage was introduced in 1917.

Universal suffrage was accompanied by proportional representation and the compulsory vote. This was decided partly as a matter of abstract justice: it seemed the natural corollary of the principle that each vote should have equal value. But at the same time it also had practical political meaning. It was thought right that Parliament should present a perfect mirror of the different groups that composed the nation. This fitted in well with the isolationist tendencies of the various minority cultures. It also underlined the historic separation of government and Parliament. While Parliament represented the nation, and government was fully responsible to it, as a more "national" institution the government yet stood somewhat apart from particular cleavages.[41] But it followed from this that future elections were mainly to choose parliamentary representatives, not governments.

THE CHALLENGE OF THE WORKING CLASSES   The potentially alienating effect of the long-delayed extension of the franchise was partly offset by the circumstance that the full effects of the Industrial Revolution were felt comparatively late in the Netherlands. This affected the development of the Dutch labor movement in a number of ways.

First, the lesser orders of society had for a long time been the passive objects of paternalism and philanthropy. The position of the existing elites seemed invulnerable, and they ruled with considerable confidence. The poor thus lived under strong outward and inward social control and in such poverty that little energy was left to raise themselves out of this position.[42]

Second, the growth of a modern labor movement was preceded by the emancipation movement of Calvinists and Catholics. For a considerable time, both Calvinist and Catholic reaction to the "social problem" tended to be one of moralization and negative antisocialism. Initially, many lower-class people outside the more traditional areas were thus lost to the churches, especially in certain parts of the rural areas in the north and west where the churches themselves had become highly rationalistic, and in the industrializing cities to which many workers from the more traditional countryside emigrated. But at the same time a sense of historic grievance and political and ecclesiastical organization tended to keep many other

41. See C. W. de Vries, *Cort van der Linden: de visie van een groot staatsman,* (The Hague, Nijhoff, 1952).

42. See in particular I. J. Brugmans, *De Arbeidende Klasse in Nederland in de 19e eeuw* (3d ed. Utrecht, Het Spectrum, 1958), and L.G.J. Verberne, *De Nederlandse Arbeidersbeweging in de Negentiende Eeuw* (Amsterdam, Van Kampen, 1950).

would-be proletarians within the religious groups. Within both the Calvinist and the Catholic subcultures, effective working-class organizations soon developed. Though these may have been instruments of continuing social control, they also eventually helped to democratize the religious parties from the inside and to force them to take a more positive attitude toward the claims of the new working classes.[43]

Third, as a consequence of late industrialization the first working-class movements did not stem from an industrial proletariat. Roughly speaking, three early groups may be distinguished.

Artisans were first in establishing crafts unions, which sought mainly to provide their members with a measure of social security and intellectual enlightenment. Their political orientation tended to be either Radical-Liberal or Anti-Revolutionary according to their religious outlook. They helped to strengthen the more radical wings of both movements and thus to prevent their too close identification with the existing social order. They did not resort to revolutionary action, but put their trust in suffrage extension, for which they campaigned actively.

In the second place, the agricultural depression of the latter part of the nineteenth century, led in certain parts of the country (notably in Groningen, Friesland, and Noord-Holland) to a highly radical outlook among impoverished farmers and agricultural laborers. The earliest Radical and Socialist deputies were elected from constituencies in these areas, which have preserved a fairly left-wing voting record to this day.

Finally, some manual laborers acquired an early socialist consciousness, due to a special combination of religious and socioeconomic factors. Some of the older cities, especially Amsterdam, had an autochthonous proletariat, eking out a precarious living in the harbors, warehouses, and inland transport. In some other regions, sweatshop industries (textiles, potteries, etc.) provided an easy target for socialist propagandists. Finally, canal- and peat-digging led to unusual working conditions that tended to nourish both rebelliousness and a strong sectarianism. Most of these groups devel-

---

43. See R. Hagoort, *De Christelijk Sociale Beweging* (Franeker, T. Werer, 1956); W. G. Versluis, *Beknopte Geschiedenis van de Katholieke Arbeidersbeweging in Nederland* (Nijmegen, Dekker and Van de Vegt 1949); and M. Ruppert, *De Nederlandse Vakbeweging* (2 vols. Haarlem, De Erven F. Bohn, 1953).

In both Calvinist and Catholic circles considerable conflict broke out between those who considered the "social problem" above all a moral issue and those who demanded effective working-class organization. For a time, militant elements in both camps combined to form an antisocialist, but interconfessional union. The Catholic Bishops eventually permitted the establishment of autonomous working-class unions on the condition that these would be exclusively Catholic. From then on the *Christelijk-Nationaal Vakverbond* (CNV) became a purely orthodox Protestant organization. Oddly enough, the word *Christelijk* is now often used interchangeably with orthodox Protestant in the Netherlands. Membership in the (overwhelmingly Socialist) CNV was until recently forbidden to Catholics; but the controversial pastoral letter *De Katholiek in het Openbare Leven van deze Tijd* (Utrecht, 1954) was rescinded on this point in 1965.

oped an anarchist outlook, which was easily fostered by the absence of the vote, and a belief in the possibility of a drastic reversal of the socio-economic system through spontaneous revolutionary action which tends to be typical of small-scale economic organization.[44]

Fourth, late industrialization exposed the Dutch working-class movement to considerable influence from abroad where socialist ideologies and union organization had developed much more strongly. The influence of French syndicalism, German Marxism, and British New Unionism are all easily traced. They led to a certain amount of fragmentation of political action, to highly doctrinaire debates among socialist intellectuals, and to various organizational splits in both the political and union wings of the working-class movement.

The first effective Socialist leader was an ex-clergyman, F. Domela Nieuwenhuis. He had great oratorical influence, and was elected to Parliament in 1888 (after a short imprisonment for *lèse-majesté*). Once there, he was completely cold-shouldered by his bourgeois opponents. After that he turned increasingly anarchist. When he committed the first Socialist Party, the Sociaal-Democratische Bond, to a rejection of parliamentary methods, a number of his followers broke away and established the Sociaal-Democratische Arbeiderspartij (SDAP, 1894).[45] It adopted an orthodox Marxist line, taking its program almost literally from the Erfurt Program of the German Social Democratic Party. Marxism provided a particularly useful formula: it helped to foster the class consciousness of the Dutch workers, so exposed to diverting political traditions; it "scientized" hope, and thus made life more bearable in what was otherwise a relatively weak social and political position; and it vindicated concentration on the immediate political battle, seemingly sanctified by long-term revolutionary ideology.

Participation in electoral and parliamentary battles soon led the SDAP to acquire a vested interest in the existing regime. Had not the old Socialist slogans: "The Vote or Revolution!" and "Voting Right or Fist Right!" been a fitting portent? Franchise restrictions led the party into a highly un-Marxian wooing of poorer but enfranchised farmers in the north. Conscious of the need to attract Calvinist and Catholic workers, the party went on record as early as 1902 that it did not oppose in principle the granting of subsidies to religious schools. It entered into informal electoral agreements with the Liberals to promote the common cause of

44. See Lorwin, "Working Class Politics," and Lorwin, "Syndicalism," in the forthcoming *Encyclopaedia of the Social Sciences*. The relation between syndicalism and small-scale economic organization has been stressed particularly by H. B. Wiardi Beckman in his excellent study, *Het Syndicalisme in Frankrijk* (Amsterdam, Em. Querido's Uitg.-mij., 1931).

45. See D. J. Wansink, *Het Socialisme op de Tweesprong—de geboorte van de S.D.A.P.* (Haarlem, Tjeenk Willink, 1939).

universal suffrage. Participation in Parliament gave ample opportunity for informal pressures and coalition building on specific issues. In 1913 the Socialists were even offered some seats in a Liberal government; the parliamentary leaders were tempted, but the offer was rejected by a more militant party congress. World War I, in which the Netherlands remained neutral, nevertheless led to a further rapprochement with the bourgeois parties and to the critical assumption of a measure of executive responsibility, notably in local government. The Socialists fully shared in the great national compromise of 1916–17 in which full parity for the religious schools, universal suffrage, and proportional representation were accepted by all the major parties.

Full integration in the political system took much longer, however, than these developments seemed to forecast. This was due partly to continuous opposition from the left, but mainly to the continued powerful position of the religious and Liberal parties.

The decisive break with the anarcho-syndicalists had come in 1903 after a somewhat lukewarm attempt at a general strike had foundered on a resolute stand by the (Kuyper) government.[46] This led to bitter recrimination within the working-class movement. The anarcho-syndicalists accused the Socialist officials of having betrayed proletarian solidarity. The Socialists countered with the argument that there was little value in badly organized action in behalf of unclear political and economic goals. Some of the better organized industrial unions went on to establish a new Trades Union Congress (NVV, 1906) as a rival to the earlier, mainly syndicalist Nationaal Arbeids Secretariaat (1893). The new federation was given a powerful lift by the now fast-arriving large-scale industrialization. The NVV unions concentrated on effective organization and collective bargaining, and soon became part of the system rather than a threat to it.[47]

In 1909 a group of left-wing Marxists were expelled from the SDAP for having published an opposition journal within the party. For a number of years they remained a minor sect. But during World War I they made common cause with pacifist, anarchist, syndicalist, and other revolutionary groups who jointly organized Revolutionary-Socialist Committees against Mobilization, High Prices, and Rationing. In 1918 the party renamed itself Communistische Partij Holland. It obtained a small but fairly constant vote, notably in those regions which had acquired an anarchist outlook before the workers were given the right to vote.

But the SDAP's greatest setback came in 1918. Its hope for a large increase in votes under universal suffrage was dashed when it obtained only

46. For a model analysis, see A.J.C. Rüter, *De Spoorwegstakingen van 1903* (Leiden, Brill, 1935).

47. See Fr. de Jong Edz., *Om de Plaats van de Arbeid* (Amsterdam, De Arbeiderspers, 1956).

22 per cent of the national vote (against 2.3 per cent for the Communists). Revolutionary rumblings in Germany and in some Dutch army camps then led the Socialist leader, P. J. Troelstra, into an impromptu statement that the revolution would not stop at the Dutch border, and that the time had come for the Socialists to take over the reins of government. No effective steps were taken to carry out this threat, but the Cabinet (composed mainly of the religious parties) reacted by mobilizing its religious and bourgeois supporters in a clamor of national indignation which culminated in a mass demonstration around the Queen in the Hague. Troelstra's rashness was strongly criticized by other Socialist leaders, and he tried to retreat as far as possible from the implications of his statement. Nevertheless, the Socialist movement was again effectively isolated from the other political parties.

Between the wars, the SDAP tended to live a fairly lonely life in Parliament. Conflict among other parties might occasionally give it a chance to influence proceedings and even to help defeat a Cabinet. But its strength never rose above a quarter of the national vote. None of the other parties (with the sole exception of a small radical party) seriously considered forming a governing coalition with the Socialists. Although the party opposed the government, it was not an opposition that could seriously hope to replace it. On both sides relations were somewhat strained: for a considerable time the Socialists refused to attend the opening of Parliament and to cheer the Queen; the bourgeois parties retaliated by continuing to exclude the Socialists from certain official posts. Inevitably the Socialist movement assumed a somewhat introverted character. The party built up a large number of ancillary organizations and gave its supporters the fullness of life which their estrangement from the churches prevented them from getting elsewhere. The movement succeeded in raising the cultural level and political consciousness of Dutch labor to a considerable degree. But it added to the characteristically strong ideological segmentation of Dutch social life. The party found itself in a kind of ghetto, from which it could not free itself without outside help.

Not until the Depression of the 1930s and the rise of Nazism sapped erstwhile democratic certainties did a change occur. In the early 1930s some left-wing elements in the SDAP attempted to steer the movement back into revolutionary channels. They proposed to organize mass campings of the unemployed outside the cities and to engage in active street demonstrations. The SDAP leadership rejected these schemes and the leftist opposition was ejected from the party in 1932. After this the SDAP turned increasingly to Plan-Socialism. In 1935 it put forward an elaborate national plan that sought to relieve unemployment by large-scale public works and other injections of purchasing power in the slack economy. The *Plan van de Arbeid* signaled the wish of the Socialists to cooperate with other classes and political groups for the rehabilitation of the existing economy. A similar attitude developed in other parties and facilitated a slow rapprochement. At the same time, Nazism turned most Socialists away from their earlier pacifist leanings. National defense and national symbols, including the monarchy, were more readily accepted. Finally, the long-standing coalition of Catholics (who had moved to the left under the pressure of universal suffrage and new economic insights) and the Anti-Revolutionaries (who had assumed a very conservative position under their leader H. Colijn in the 1930s) broke up in 1939. The Socialists were invited to enter a Cabinet composed of Catholics, Christian Historicals, and assorted Liberals. The Socialist leader, J. W. Albarda, advocated entering the Cabinet in a confidential memorandum to the party executive that throws a clear light on the party's quandary.[48] Albarda argued first that Socialists had traditionally overestimated the numerical significance of the proletariat by wrongly including in it small peasants, petty bourgeois, officials, and so forth:

> These groups live on economic and social bases different from those of the working classes; they also have other social ideologies and ideals, to a certain extent anticapitalistic, it is true, but not socialist.
>
> Secondly, many of our old theses and dogmas, which had unrivaled value in bringing the working class to consciousness and organization, have now become a liability for further growth of the socialist movement.

Albarda pointed particularly to the need to abandon dogmatic insistence on the class struggle and on the conflict between religion and socialism, which he called "a liberal prejudice garbed in Marxist dress." If such a change did not occur he prophesied doom for the party, because traditional allegiance alone would not suffice and would inevitably lead to eventual demoralization. The only hope, he argued, was to penetrate the traditional clienteles of the religious parties:

> It is quite understandable that all bourgeois parties, not least the Catholics, are afraid of the arrival of a Cabinet with Social Democrats. . . . For from the very day that the SDAP becomes a governing party (provided this is on a firm footing), its position changes. Then a bridge will have been built over the abyss that now yawns between the religious and the socialist part of our nation. Then traffic will begin over this bridge . . . A new growth will start for our movement, and this growth will not be easily halted. The hitherto impregnable voting masses of the religious part of the nation will become potentially available for our efforts.

48. This memorandum has been printed in full in the otherwise highly unsatisfactory dissertation of H. M. Ruitenbeek, *Het Ontstaan van de Partij van de Arbeid* (Amsterdam, De Arbeiderspers, 1955), pp. 249–54.

Two Socialist ministers entered the government in 1939, later than in any other Western European country. The new government was soon to be the Dutch government in exile.

During the occupation many Socialists hoped for drastic changes through a complete restructuring of the party system. In 1945 the SDAP merged with the Radical Party, a number of left-wing Catholics and Christian Historicals, and some independents in a new Partij van de Arbeid (Labor Party). But the 1946 elections killed its extravagantly high hopes: it won only 28.3 per cent of the vote. Catholics, Christian Historicals, and Anti-Revolutionaries remained on the whole faithful to the traditional parties, and a Communist upsurge nibbled away at the Socialist Left. From 1945 to 1958 the Socialists nevertheless formed a leading element in coalitions otherwise composed of Catholics and, after 1948, also of some representatives of the smaller parties. For ten years, the popular Socialist leader, W. Drees, was Prime Minister. The party edged slowly upward, thanks to gains from both Communists and the religious parties, until it reached its all-time high of 32.7 per cent in 1956, for a while outranking the Catholics in size. Its electoral fortunes turned again in 1958, however, and the party was excluded from the government. It did not do very well in opposition and fell back in 1963 to its 1946 level. (For full data see Appendix Table 6.1.) But the Socialists returned to the Cabinet after an interim crisis in the spring of 1965.

Cleavages and Consensus in the Dutch System

The simultaneous emancipation of minority groups resulted in an exceedingly rigid segmentation of Dutch society. At least three distinct subcultures coexist: an orthodox Protestant one (comprising some 20–25 per cent of the nation); a Catholic one (numbering over a third); and a "general" one. The latter comprises less than half the population and, being composed mainly of Dutchmen who are neither orthodox Protestant nor Catholic, it tends to assume a rather special place on the political continuum. The "general" subculture is moreover further subdivided into various groups. On the religious side it contains more or less latitudinarian Protestants, humanists, and agnostics. Politically, it is divided between Liberals on the one hand, and various Socialist groups on the other. The latter form in many respects a special subculture of their own. It should be stressed that the religious subcultures hardly answer to Gabriel Almond's description of "significant survivals, 'outcroppings,' of older cultures and their political manifestations," remnants that are attributable only to "uneven patterns of development" and "failure on the part of the middle classes in the nineteenth century to carry through a thorough-going secularization of the political culture." [49] On the contrary, far from being traditionalist remnants, they themselves pioneered modern political tech-

49. Almond, "Comparative Political Systems," pp. 405 ff.

niques and have on the whole adjusted well to the processes of modern industrial development. The threat of secularization has been countered by a large number of burgeoning social organizations *within* each sub-culture that seek to cope with the complex social problems of the modern industrial era and do so successfully on an explicitly religious basis.

The pattern of subcultural isolation comes out most clearly in the educational field. Since the school pact of 1916–17, churches and parent organizations of every religious outlook have been entitled to full state subsidies (determined on the basis of the cost of normal public schools), provided they meet certain legal requirements as to qualified teachers, curriculum, and number of pupils. Whereas two-thirds of Dutch children still went to government schools in 1900, the proportion today is only a little over one-fourth. (See Appendix Table 6.6.) Separate schooling has spread from elementary to secondary and technical education, and for some years both the Calvinist and Catholic universities have been subsidized practically on a par with the older national universities. Organizations for recreation and culture are generally split along denominational lines. Unions, employers, workers, farmers, and *Middenstanders* reflect a tripartite division, of general, Catholic, and Calvinist organizations, while hospitals, old people's homes, and to a lesser extent government-subsidized cooperative housing projects show even greater pluralist divisions. A Dutchman can live an isolated life within a homogeneous ideological environment from the cradle to the grave, meeting people of different outlook only in the street, the army, and perhaps in factory or office and more recently on television screens. The technical term used for this segmentation is *Verzuiling*. The image is one in which the national state is supported by a variety of pillars (*zuilen*). The word has become slightly pejorative, however, as if "pillari-zation" inevitably meant "compartmentalization" or, in another metaphor, as if "columnization" meant in practice "colonization" by a tight ideological cadre.

J. P. Kruijt, a Dutch sociologist who is the recognized elder statesman of *Verzuiling* studies, has constructed a table (Table 6.1) to indicate the extent to which segmentation has moved forward in different social spheres. The interpretation of this table is complicated by the fact that the Dutch Reformed Church continues to organize both fundamentalist and non-fundamentalist elements; since there are many shades of both it is difficult to quantify the real degree of *Verzuiling* within this denomination.[50]

From all available data it appears that the extent of segmentation is still increasing both with respect to the number of formal organizations on

50. Although most orthodox Protestants within the Dutch Reformed Church have been drawn into separate organizations, some groups have resisted this trend on principle; they have not wanted to see the nation and the church surrendered by default to the less fundamentalist or agnostic elements of the population.

Table 6.1 Degree of Segmentation (Verzuildheidsgraad) in the Netherlands (percentage of persons belonging to different churches, or to no church, organized in subcultural associations or participating in subcultural activities)

	Catholic	Calvinist (Gereformeerd)	Dutch Reformed	Other [a]	No church [a]
Census (1960)	40.4	9.3	28.3	3.6	18.4
Elementary school (1957)	90 [b]	90 [b]	50 [b]		10 [b]
Farmers unions (1953)	95 [b]	90 [b]	37 [b]		practically nil
Labor unions (1958)	90 [b]	90 [b]	30 [b]		practically nil
Membership in Radio Association (1955)	89	94	32	18	4
Party vote, lower house (1959)	84.3	95 [b]	32 [b]	very few	very few
Newspaper reading (exclusively religious dailies) (1955)	79	58	9	8	1
Active membership associations (1955) religious, plus other	77	80	43	40	14
exclusively religious	71	73	36	33	13
Book reading (last book read exclusively religious) (1955)	16	39	19	18	15

a. For Other and No church, the figures represent percentages of membership in Catholic or Protestant organizations or activities in a Catholic or Protestant context.

b. Approximate figure.

Source: J.P. Kruijt, *Verzuiling* (Zaandijk, Heynis, 1959), p. 40.

explicitly ideological lines and the hold of Catholic and Protestant organizations, as contrasted with "general" ones, on their members.[51] This trend is strengthened by the current practice of distributing government subsidies indiscriminately to organizations of all three subcultures and carefully balancing government advisory bodies in all walks of life with representatives from each.

In view of these sharp divisions, what have been the factors that have prevented the social system from flying apart? What has restrained any subculture, or any two subcultures in coalition, from destroying potential adversaries by political weapons? The answers must be sought partly in historical factors, partly in certain system-sustaining forces still at work to this day. The following historical explanations seem to me suggestive.

To reiterate a point made previously: throughout Dutch history the leading political groups have tended to occupy a strong position. None of the fundamental opposition movements have been able to displace the existing power holders in one stroke. The ruling groups have had little fear that this might happen. Consequently, they have tended to adopt a relatively permissive attitude toward political opposition. There have been little violence and little political repression in Dutch public life. There have also been practically no attempts at conspiratorial activity, which would have seemed somewhat ridiculous in the face of certain failure and also somewhat superfluous because less violent means were generally available for the expression of political discontent.

At no time have the Dutch ruling circles been completely closed or homogeneous. Power resources have usually been spread so widely that single groups have had little chance to impose their will without serious friction. This has nurtured a feeling of mutual tolerance, strengthened a mutual willingness to seek accommodation, and made people ready to leave others alone provided they were left alone themselves.

This natural pluralism caused differences of opinion to generate relatively little heat, strong reciprocal prejudices notwithstanding. Protest groups tended to become politicized only slowly. Political militancy was tempered at all times by those sympathizers who wished to work from within rather than against the existing regime, while even the more militant thought in terms of increased influence rather than of actual monopoly of power. Consider a typical passage from that great mass organizer, Abraham Kuyper, addressing the party faithful of the Anti-Revolutionary Party on the eve of the election that was to carry him into the prime ministership (1901):

More than a quarter of the Chamber, we [that is, the Anti-Revolu-

51. See J. P. Kruijt and W. Goddijn, "Verzuiling en Ontzuiling als Sociologisch Proces," in *Drift en Koers*, pp. 227–63.

tionaries, without Catholic support] can never win; in this situation all the clamor for a ministry of our own can make no other impression on insiders or outsiders than foolhardiness, rooted in nothing, which we as Christians should resist. It is easy to blind ourselves to the question where to find men prepared and able to solve the big questions which our policy, based on our principles, faces . . . In practically all bureaus, in all organs of the state, in all prominent posts, the leaders are able and influential, I readily admit, but not given to our principles.[52]

Slow accommodation made for a gradual domestication of opposing groups in the pre-existing pluralist system and facilitated a transfer of older traditions of compromise to political newcomers.

The strong divisions into which the successive waves of emancipationist action by Calvinists, Catholics, and Socialists split Dutch society never extended to all government institutions. The electorate and Parliament came to be divided much more than the Cabinet, the judiciary, and the bureaucracy.

If elections and political conflict drove parties apart, the need for government forced them together. Government cooperation could be achieved only on matters of common concern, not on behalf of too particularist demands. Once in government, former opposition groups could not always convert their nominal powers into concrete action; lack of experience and internal dissension might give older government groups the opportunity to continue to exercise power even when they were reduced to a minority position in Parliament. Between 1848 and 1887, for instance, domestic squabbles often forced the Liberals to leave the reins of government to Conservative statesmen even though the number of Conservative deputies dwindled rapidly. The Liberals, in turn, could still form cabinets in the first decades of this century, although their forces were by then on the decline, because the remaining seats in Parliament were divided between the rising Socialists, on the one hand, and the religious parties on the other. When the coalition of Anti-Revolutionaries, Catholics, and Christian Historicals broke up in 1925, statesmen from these parties continued to preside over quasi-national "extra-parliamentary," "business," "personality," or *intermezzo* (caretaker) governments because they at least agreed on the undesirability of entering into a coalition with the Socialists.

Similarly, the bureaucracy has tended to be a political stabilizer. For a long time educational advantage made the Dutch bureaucracy something of a Liberal cum Christian Historical reserve; Anti-Revolutionaries, Catholics, and Socialists initially found it easier to secure specific concessions

---

52. Cited by P. A. Diepenhorst, in *Schrift en Historie—gedenkboek bij het vijftigjarig bestaan der georganiseerde Anti-Revolutionaire Partij* (Kampen, Vitg.-mij. J.H. Kok, 1929), p. 255.

from it than to try to take it over. More recently a political element seems to have become more prominent in appointments and promotions. But a spoils system has at no time been desired or countenanced in Dutch administration. Newcomers, even from partisan milieus, have generally accepted the view that the national interest should prevail over party concerns. Party appointments have therefore not led to increased bitterness among the various groups, but rather to new forms of brokerage and collaboration among them.

The monarchy, too, has tended to play a substantial integrating function. For a considerable time Liberals (in the nineteenth century) and Socialists (until well into the twentieth) thought the Crown too much a part of the Conservative Establishment. Catholics have often resented the habit of orthodox Protestants of claiming the House of Orange as their private property. But as each subcultural group became more fully emancipated, it found less difficulty in accepting the Crown as a symbol of political community above party—a development made easier by the long tenure of Queen Wilhelmina (1890–1948), who deliberately broke away from the Court ghetto in which she found herself immured [53] to become eventually the great personal symbol of national resistance in 1940–45. More recently certain personal developments in the royal family jolted the complacency of those who thought the Crown could retain its earlier symbolic value while the members of the "national family" still had complete freedom to live their lives according to their own ideas and wishes. But these events do not seem to have lessened the confidence of the great majority of the nation in the value of monarchy as an institution. The Netherlands Institute for Public Opinion found a drop in expressed preferences for monarchy from 86 per cent in favor in February 1964 (after the first intimation of difficulties in connection with the intended marriage of Princess Irene), to 74 per cent in June 1965, when the engagement of the Crown Princess to a German commoner, Claus von Amsberg, was announced. But at the same time the number who favored a Republic remained practically stationary at 9 per cent, the difference being made up of an increased number of "don't knows." Disenchantment with the monarchy seemed to be increasing, however, in intellectual circles and may acquire political significance in the long run. But even there, and much more so among political leaders, there was considerable reluctance to lose the Crown as a symbol of Nation above party.

But perhaps the greatest contribution of the past has been the effect of accumulating experience. Even staunch isolationists have learned that a strong insistence on subcultural rights need not prevent day-to-day cooperation with representatives from rival groups. Each subculture has

53. See Queen Wilhelmina's Memoirs, *Lonely, but Not Alone* (London, Hutchinson, 1960).

gained considerable recognition for its special claims and has obtained practically all that can be had through state action. All groups are reasonably certain that future claims will be honored as far as possible through a compromise sharing of state benefits. They have learned from painful experience that other issues are not negotiable and hence not enforceable through state action. Unfulfilled demands (like special Sunday legislation for the Calvinists or permission for public processions throughout the country for the Catholics) may be brandished as signs of party identification, but they have proved to be so much *hors concours* that they no longer block practical cooperation on other matters.

All these historical factors would count for little, however, if there were no contemporary forces sustaining the system. Of course there are.

The divisive effects of segmentation are softened by the circumstance that none of the subcultures has much chance of acquiring an independent majority, while there is at the same time little advantage to any two of them in forming a lasting coalition against the third. Calvinists and Catholics have been united in their demand for separate schools and recognition of other common subcultural interests, but many historical sentiments and contemporary issues divide them. Both may well silently acknowledge the value of the "general" subculture as a potential counterweight against rival religious groups. Calvinists and "generalists" combine to resist too explicitly Catholic wishes, while Catholics and "generalists" share a distaste for too puritan attitudes on the part of the more outright orthodox Protestants and together reject their claim that Calvinism is (or should be) the foundation of Dutch national life.

This circumstance is reinforced by tactical considerations on the parliamentary scene. For many years now numerical relations have been such that neither the combined religious groupings nor the nonconfessional ones have had an adequate working majority in the lower house. Ever since 1939 the Netherlands has therefore been governed by cabinets of a mixed religious-nonreligious character. This has tended to lessen old antagonisms. Anticlericalism has practically disappeared from Dutch politics for reasons of both conviction and political expediency. Both Liberals and Socialists learned long ago that they are individually and jointly powerless. They can obtain a share of government power only by the grace of one or more of the religious parties. They are also well aware that their long-term electoral chances depend on their ability to gain votes from traditionally religious quarters. Ever since the war, they have therefore consciously sought to de-emphasize their earlier restrictive *Weltanschauung* traditions. Both have recognized publicly the positive value of Christianity. The Labor Party has even arranged for explicitly Catholic, orthodox Protestant, and humanist working groups within its fold.

Coalition politics has in the same way contributed to a lessening of socioeconomic tensions. The three religious parties have a much more heterogeneous social following than either Liberals or Socialists. This has tended to draw the religious parties toward a centrist position and to make them natural brokers between conflicting interests, first within their own ambit, but indirectly also in society at large. Tactical and electoral considerations have simultaneously pushed the Socialist and Liberal parties in the direction of what Otto Kirchheimer has called the catch-all type of political party.[54] A recent study has documented the observation that party programs of the main Dutch parties have increasingly converged on some points since 1946; it appears that elite groups tend to be in closer agreement on policy issues than potential party clienteles.[55]

Interest group politics have made for many links across ideological boundary lines. So far the more specific industrial associations, as well as individual enterprises, have most successfully resisted the *Verzuiling* trend. But even where interest groups have themselves been subject to ideological divisions, the need for effective promotion of joint interests has usually made for frequent confederal contacts among them. This has kept communications between the *zuilen* more open than they might otherwise have been. At the same time, it has had a significant influence on the way policy is made in the Netherlands. On any one matter there are usually a great number of interest groups involved. This leads to very complex consultations and maneuverings. To operate in this complex situation with any chance of success usually necessitates considerable discretionary authority for the leaders of the interest groups involved. This encourages strong centralization of power at the top. But such leaders are therefore also able to take the responsibility for far-reaching decisions (which may be of strategic importance to the government). Complex compromises usually emerge from these deliberations. To make them digestible for widely different ideological groupings, they are often couched in highly abstract, quasi-scientific terms. Thus many issues are consciously depoliticized, paradoxically as a result of ideological divisiveness, but also as a means to offset its centrifugal tendencies.

Government, the Five Main Parties, and Policy Opposition

GOVERNMENT AND PARLIAMENT   With the exception of the Catholic Party, all parties have been outside the government for some period since 1946 (the Liberals from 1946 to 1948, from 1952 to 1958, and again since 1965; the Anti-Revolutionary Party from 1946 to 1952; the Christian Historical Union from 1946 to 1948 and since 1965; and the Socialists from

54. See Otto Kirchheimer, "The Transformation of the European Party System," in LaPalombara and Weiner, eds., *Political Parties and Political Development.*
55. A. Hoogerwerf, "Sociaal-Politieke Strijdpunten: Smeulend Vuur," *Sociologische Gids, 10* (1963), pp. 249–63.

1958 to 1965). (See Appendix Table 6.2.) Whether parties have been inside or outside the government has obviously made for substantial differences in their influence and political attitudes. Yet the importance of this circumstance has been reduced by certain factors: first, even when a particular party has not been in the government, this has not prevented its allied subcultural interest groups from being closely involved in the making of government policy; second, although a party may have been outside the government, this has not necessarily induced it to engage in hard opposition tactics against the government; and conversely, when a party has been a member of a government coalition, this has not necessarily implied warm support. The explanation must be sought in the peculiar historical nature of Dutch Cabinet–Parliament relations and in the intricate coalition politics that have maintained these.[56]

As we saw earlier, the Dutch Parliament has never insisted that ministers be chosen exclusively or even chiefly from among its members, even though it has held ministers at all times fully accountable to it. The complexities of coalition politics and the withdrawal into subcultural isolation have made Dutch parties often willing to compromise on persons who are experts in a particular field rather than strong political personages. Since 1848 almost two-thirds of Dutch Cabinet ministers have assumed their posts without previous parliamentary experience.[57] Only in two or three cases have ministers combined ministerial portfolios with parliamentary seats, and since 1938 this has not been permitted by the Constitution. Even one-time "politicos" readily assume a posture of "above party" once they have attained ministerial office. The government as a whole tends to preserve some detachment from Parliament. Ministers have access to Parliament and are in charge of their own bills. They may be dismissed by a simple adverse vote, and many individual ministers as well as entire cabinets have indeed been sent from office in this way.[58] But the exceeding complexity of the process of Cabinet-making in the Netherlands has made Cabinet crises highly unpopular. Few parties see an easy

56. See H. Daalder, "Parties and Politics in The Netherlands," *Political Studies, 3* (1955) 1–16; Daalder, *The Relation Between Cabinet and Parliament in The Netherlands*, report to the International Political Science Association, Rome, 1958; E. van Raalte, *The Parliament of the Kingdom of The Netherlands* (London, Hansard Society, 1959).

57. Dogan-Scheffer, "Le Personnel Ministériel Hollandais," p. 100.

58. Since 1848 (not including the period 1939–46) the average Dutch Cabinet lasted for somewhat over two years and eight months. Between 1848 and 1888 no less than nine cabinets resigned after conflicts with Parliament. But of twenty-four cabinets between 1888 and 1963, fourteen served during the entire session of a Parliament, while only six ended prematurely through internal dissension or an adverse parliamentary vote (often the same thing!). The dismissal of individual ministers, too, has become much less frequent in recent times: whereas some forty-three ministers resigned over parliamentary conflicts between 1848 and 1922, only four have done so since then.

way to replace a Cabinet once it has been formed, and they have generally
allowed it to live out the four-year parliamentary period (not infrequently
after an intermediate crisis, "solved" by a return of the old *équipe*). In only
a few cases has a real *renversement des alliances* taken place, as in 1939,
1958, and 1965. The Netherlands is therefore in the paradoxical situation
that complex party relations make for protracted periods of Cabinet-
making, but that this very long duration of Cabinet crises reinforces the
stability of governments once formed.[59]

But if cabinets enjoy considerable discretion, so does Parliament. Their
nominal participation in the government does not prevent Dutch parties
from acting like Pontius Pilate toward any specific government proposal.
Parliamentarians like to give the impression that they can treat Cabinet
proposals entirely as objective matters on which they are still free to make
up their minds. No one party adopts the posture of all-out government—
or all-out opposition—party. Each seeks to reserve its opinion, and to
make it dependent on a careful assessment of the specific situation or proposal at hand. If particular government proposals are the immediate outcome of a Cabinet program which was negotiated when the Cabinet was
formed, participating parties usually, if at times grudgingly, feel bound to
honor their obligations. If it is evident that an adverse vote would lead to
an undesired ministerial crisis, these parties also tend to comply in Parliament, if often only under protest and not until after some give and take
between ministers and parliamentary groups. In all other matters, the
outcome remains an open question. Parties may more readily oppose if
they know for certain that other parties will see a particular bill through.
Issues that would arouse too strong a protest from any five of the bigger
parties, or at least from one whose participation in the government is
indispensable, are touched upon quite hesitantly. Certain issues are held as
long as possible in cold storage, and are removed only by *force majeure*.
A long delay may not make the matter easier to handle, but if necessary
Dutch parties will act jointly, though belatedly, to remove a matter from
political debate by arriving at a mutually acceptable solution. They
usually find it easier to compromise than to make a final and definite
choice among alternatives.

To a considerable extent, opposition in Dutch politics tends therefore
to dissolve inside the system rather than to assume a distinct character.
There is often hidden conflict between ministers, whether on party, departmental, or personal grounds. Individual ministers know that they are
linchpins in a carefully constructed Cabinet structure; they are sometimes

59. Even when party relations were relatively simple, as they were between 1888
and 1913, only one Cabinet was formed in *less* than one month. The record so far
has been the period of 117 days taken up by the formation of the 1956 Cabinet. For
full data on the length of Cabinet crises, see Georg Geismann, *Politische Struktur und
Regierungssystem in den Niederlanden* (Frankfurt, 1964), Appendix, p. 289.

not beyond exploiting their positions for highly individualistic policies. There may be a fairly steady *Nervenkrieg* between such ministers, or the Cabinet as a whole, and significant sections of Parliament. There is considerable rivalry among the parties, both in debate and at the polls. But they also bargain continuously, and often a nominal opposition party has helped to save a government from its own "friends."

THE MAIN OPPOSITION PATTERNS   What are the usual opposition patterns within this general framework? As the three main religious parties are tied rather closely to specific denominational groups, there is relatively little electoral competition among them. There is much talk of Christian Democratic affinity and cooperation i.e. between the Catholics and the two orthodox Protestant parties, and at times there has been definite nostalgia for the good old days of an exclusive coalition of the religious parties. The sharpest opposition tends to be between the Liberal and Socialist parties, which represent the greatest polarization on the socioeconomic scale. Since 1952 these parties have not sat in the same government, and both have at various times indicated that this is as it should be. Of decisive importance are the relations between the religious parties and their nonconfessional rivals, because these will determine the specific orientation of the government. Both Liberals and Socialists eye the religious parties with something of a love–hatred complex. They should like to make further inroads on their rather steady electoral clienteles, and both stand to profit if they can polarize political conflict in such manner that left-wing elements in the religious parties find it necessary to move over to the Labor Party and more conservative groups toward the Liberal Party. But the necessity of coalition-building forces them at the same time to tone down their most explicit demands. Hard electoral tactics may jeopardize their future bargaining position, while their present bargaining position is weakened by awareness on all sides that it is possible for the religious parties to govern without Liberals or Socialists, but not for Liberals or Socialists to govern without the religious parties.

Internal relations among the religious parties are therefore of decisive importance for Dutch politics. Their members and various elite groups tend to disagree among themselves about which nonconfessional party is the more eligible partner for a *mariage de raison*. Too close identification with any one of them might in the long run prove to be the worst choice, for those most in sympathy with the specific policies advocated by the nonconfessional ally might decide next time to go all the way and vote for the latter which, by virtue of government participation, is now apparently respectable and certainly offers more clear-cut choices on socioeconomic issues. At the same time, religious supporters on the other wing may bolt the party and join the nonconfessional opposition party in order to force a future coalition of a different character. Consequently, the religious parties attempt to keep the nonconfessional parties at arm's length, and to prefer friendly relations with both but intimacy with neither. To effect this, they stress the ideological differences that separate all of their followers from those in the nonconfessional camp.

The outcome is a curious paradox, which may be best illustrated by the specific position of the Catholic Party. Since 1918 the Catholic Party has been invariably represented in all regular cabinets. Its numerical importance (a third of Parliament, at its center!) is such that it can prevent the formation of any other coalition, but cannot escape government responsibility (unless it wishes to provoke an anti-Catholic coalition against itself, which it does not). But at the same time it is faced with a non-Catholic majority that prevents it from exploiting its political position for too specifically Catholic demands. On matters on which it is internally united it therefore tends to lack power, and on matters where it has power it is not united. This results in a very special position. Catholics have tended to be more outspoken and active in Parliament, where they can be fully themselves and use their voting strength as they think fit, than in the Cabinet, which is likely to have a non-Catholic majority and where even Catholic prime ministers have to tread carefully.[60] This dual position has tended to widen the division between Cabinet and Parliament, and thus to allow for a wide range of carefully played opposition tactics all round.

The historic separateness of Dutch parties has strengthened their unity at the parliamentary level; they have usually achieved a fair measure of success in maintaining a common front, even without formal disciplinary action. Reasonably strong group cohesion has facilitated interparty bargaining and enhanced Cabinet stability. The detachment of Cabinet from Parliament lessens the scope for personal ambition. Parliamentarians are far from certain that they will ever be called to ministerial office. They are therefore often as much, or perhaps even more directly interested in successful policy opposition than in the displacement of government personnel.

The wish to maintain external unity shifts the burden of policy decision to consultations *within* each of the parties, where the center of gravity tends to lie with the parliamentary group and to a lesser extent with the extraparliamentary party organization. The intensity of intraparty conflict may be considerable. But it is lessened by at least three factors: the desire not to offer hostages to competing parties; the considerable leverage which central party authorities can wield through the highly centralized nomination procedures (encouraged by the list system of proportional repre-

60. Comparatively few Dutch prime ministers have been Catholic. On the other hand the most prominent Catholic Party leaders have generally stayed outside the Cabinet in strong control of their parliamentary group. The first two great Catholic leaders, Schaepman and Nolens, were priests; typically this was thought to rule them out for ministerial appointment, unlike their Protestant counterparts such as Abraham Kuyper.

sentation); and the widespread awareness of the need to preserve a working relationship among all groups within the party and its potential electoral clientele if total parliamentary strength is to be maintained intact.[61]

At the same time the system offers considerable opportunity for special interest groups to make their weight felt. The attempt to balance electoral slates has led to direct representation in Parliament of a host of interest group executives (whether employers, farmers, workers, or *Middenstand* organizations). These representatives gravitate toward specialized parliamentary committees, where they cooperate easily with representatives of similar interests in other parties. This situation seems to invite a degree of tacit collusion between such specialized parliamentary committees, extra-parliamentary interest groups, and special bureaucratic interests, and tends to strain the resources of those who are responsible for welding a coherent policy under disparate pressures: the Cabinet, the Prime Minister, the Minister of Finance, party leaders, budget officials, etc. Their efforts are not facilitated by the strong particularist strands in Dutch political and bureaucratic life, where individual ministers insist jealously on their autonomy and where civil service recruitment is practically entirely in the hands of individual departments, or even of department sections.

The Strains of Segmentation

Strong segmentation and sharp political divisions provoke certain dysfunctional strains in the system. One can distinguish these in three categories: first, the occurrence of small splinter parties that carry the logic of segmentation to organizational extremes; second, mounting criticism of the *Verzuiling*, which according to some is symptomatic of a deeper-lying political malaise; and finally, the (admittedly somewhat marginal) existence of explicit antisystem groups.

INTEGRALISM AND OVERLAPPING   Strong segmentation has fostered the establishment of small parties which unwittingly confirm its basic pattern. On the one hand, certain integralist groups within each *Zuil* have adopted an extreme ideological position, in isolationist opposition to what they regard as the unprincipled attitudes of their larger subcultural brethren. Sometimes such groups have been satisfied to operate within the ambit of the larger party and merely to sermonize the official leadership. But especially in the case of the Calvinists, the Socialists, and to a lesser extent the Liberal Party, such groups have also often gone beyond and established separate political parties. Besides the Anti-Revolutionary Party and

---

61. There has been little systematic study of intraparty relations, but see J. J. de Jong, *Politieke Organisatie in West Europa na 1800* (The Hague, Nijhoff, 1951) and I. Lipschits, "De Politieke Partij en de Selectie van Candidaten," *Sociologische Gids*, *10* (1963), 273–81.

the Christian Historical Union, there are now two sectarian Calvinist parties represented in Parliament (with three seats and one seat respectively). They are supported by small denominational groups and tend to favor an undiluted, at times even theocratic Calvinism. The larger Staatkundig-Gereformeerde Partij has been represented in Parliament since 1922, and has become a nationally cherished antiquity. Some revolutionary socialist groups falling between the Socialists and Communists occasionally secured parliamentary seats between the wars. They have not done so since, but a Pacifist Socialist Party emerged in 1957 and successfully sought representation: the PSP secured 3 per cent of the national vote in 1963 and now has as many deputies in the lower house as the Communists (four seats). On the far right, a host of disparate anti-dirigiste movements have formed and reformed, usually with little success; two of the more important ones will be mentioned later as antisystem oppositions.

These integralist movements have not been very strong in the aggregate. But they have served as gadflies, forcing the larger parties not to stray too far from their ideological positions lest they lose votes. They have reinforced the tendency of Dutch party leaders to honor their subcultural traditions, if not in deed then at least in word. And the ever-present threat they have represented has been a constant element in the determination by the main parties of long-term strategy, restricting possible tendencies to seek closer forms of collaboration among them.

Integralist parties are the logical opposite of *overlapping* parties. I use this term to describe groups that seek to combine otherwise distinct forces in the political system. Attempts to straddle existing political boundaries have historically occurred particularly on the following fronts:

1. *Between orthodox Protestants and Socialists:* From the early days of the twentieth century there have been numerous groupings that sought to deduce a more radical program from Christian principles than either the Anti-Revolutionary Party or the Christian Historical Union has done. Some of these obtained occasional seats in Parliament. The most prominent example was the Christian Democratic Union (1926–40; two seats in 1937), which merged with the Socialists in the Labor Party in 1946. The orthodox Protestant working group within the Labor Party and the Pacifist Socialists continue to cater specifically to this clientele;

2. *Between Catholics and Socialists, on the one hand, and Catholics and Liberals, on the other:* Dissident groups sometimes arose out of either wing of the Catholic Party to give expression to progressive and conservative programs, respectively. They have always disappeared again under the combined pressure of history and the bishops. The most important recent example was the Catholic National Party (one seat in 1948, two seats in 1952), a conservative movement that originated in protest against the government's policies over Indonesia and did much to wean the Catholic

Party away from the explicitly progressive stand it had adopted after 1945.

3. *Between Liberals and Socialists:* Between 1901 and 1940 a radical party maintained itself with a steady strength of 5–7 per cent of the national vote and a highly articulate intellectual leadership. It, too, fused with the Socialists in the Labor Party in 1946 (its most prominent leader, P. J. Oud, was soon to bolt to the Liberals, however). Left-wing Liberals continue to have some nostalgic feeling for it, and occasionally reach a measure of organizational unity trying to offset right-wing pressures within the party by a threat of reviving the old radical separateness.

4. *Between two or more religious parties:* There have been some movements which have sought to bridge the gap between Anti-Revolutionaries and Christian Historicals, or, more ambitiously, all three religious parties. So far this drive has led only to further splintering in the name of unity. Public opinion polls suggest a considerable measure of grass-roots support for the idea of amalgamation (though not for any special party that has yet appeared).[62] Political expediency has so far militated against such moves, however. Long ago a wise Christian Historical argued that one could catch more fish with two nets than with one. A CDU on the German model would seem likely to get fewer votes than the present three parties separately. The electoral system provides all possible encouragement to those who might wish to resist such an amalgamation by the establishment of new parties, and many present supporters of a religious party might well bolt to a nonreligious party once tight historical and denominational links were broken.

CRITICS AND CRISIS? The *Verzuiling* phenomenon has recently come under increasing attack. In all camps there are strong pleas for a more "open" attitude toward other subcultures and for greater cooperation across traditional dividing lines. But "national" solutions rather than organized ideological pluralism are more confidently advocated by Liberals and Christian Historicals than by Catholics and Anti-Revolutionaries, while the Socialists tend to be somewhat split between isolationist memories and a desire for "national" assertion.

These underlying attitudes have recently come to an open test over the control of radio and television. At present, radio and television time have been carefully proportioned among four large associations (of Catholic, Calvinist, Socialist, and "general" members respectively), and a much smaller latitudinarian Protestant one. The five organizations are in addition

62. According to investigations of the Netherlands Institute of Public Opinion (NIPO), around 90 per cent of those who indicated support for either ARP or CHU declared recently in favor of one unified Protestant party. This view is not shared by the CHU leadership, which has consistently rejected Anti-Revolutionary overtures over the last twenty years. Relations were further embittered when the two parties went different ways in the Cabinet crisis of 1965.

jointly responsible for some broadcasts and special time is reserved for the government, political parties, and some specialized cultural organizations. This pluralist structure has been criticized from various sides. Some Liberals and Socialists, as well as latitudinarian Protestants, have advocated a more "national" system on the B.B.C. model. Others have pleaded free access for independent commercial stations. The expansion of television facilities, and the question how to finance them (whether by advertising or increased levies on the public), have made the issue more and more urgent during the early sixties. But it only came to a head in the summer of 1964 when a private company erected an artificial platform in the North Sea, just outside Dutch territorial waters, and began broadcasting both radio and television programs. The company attempted to increase its popular appeal by floating a large number of small shares which found a willing public. Although in opinion polls some 70 per cent of the Dutch people declared themselves opposed to government measures against this new station, and although opposition also came from the Liberals, who were at that time represented in the government, the Dutch Cabinet and the majority of Parliament passed special legislation declaring Dutch laws applicable to artificial installations on the so-called continental plateau outside territorial waters. In December 1964 officials of the Department of Justice accordingly silenced the station.[63]

The issue caused lively political debate. Whereas Catholics, Calvinists, and Socialists tended to lean toward a defense of the existing system (supplemented by carefully controlled television and radio advertising that would benefit the existing organizations), this was much less true of the Dutch press. The attitude of the press is easily explained. "Neutral" newspapers (i.e. newspapers that are not Catholic, Socialist, or strongly Calvinist, hence are generally apolitical, Liberal, or vaguely Protestant) have long had a disproportionate influence in the Netherlands, partly because they were first in the field, partly because strong adherents of any subculture find it easier to read a so-called "neutral" newspaper than one strongly identified with an alien ideology. Some newspaper interests have looked with covetous eyes on the possibility of extending their sway in the new electronic mass media, whereas others have at least wished a measure of newspaper influence on television to offset feared losses in advertising income. It looked for a time as if a typical Dutch concert composed of some quasi-ecumenical elite groups, both high-toned and strident newspaper interests, candidates for commercial television, and assumed mass pressure for less ideology and more pop programs might break through the existing radio and television organization.

63. But when the government did silence the station, 43 per cent expressed approval, only 33 per cent continued disapproval, and 24 per cent no opinion. NIPO data, January 1965.

But in March 1965 disagreement between Liberals and Christian Historicals on the one hand, and Catholics and Anti-Revolutionaries on the other, led to a breakup of the nonsocialist coalition which had been in office since 1959. The Liberals demanded access for independent companies, and attacked the alleged *Zuilen* monopoly. Catholics, Anti-Revolutionaries, and soon the Socialists too resisted this Liberal drive. They rejected all forms of commercial television and demanded as a condition of entry for newcomers not unsubstantiated "nationalist" or "populist" claims, but a hard numerical following consisting of dues-paying members adequately registered. They jointly formed a new government in April 1965, the Liberals and Christian Historicals reverting to opposition. All clamor notwithstanding, there were no signs of a popular uprising against the new coalition in local elections for the Rijnmond authority in June 1965, when some 10 per cent of the Dutch population went to the polls: the Labor Party gained slightly, but the Liberals actually lost some votes as compared with 1963. It remains to be seen, however, whether the coalition of subcultural groups can permanently resist the leveling influence of an increasingly general culture and the decline of ideological certainties on the part of large masses of the population.

There is much talk about political malaise, generally, in the Netherlands. Frequent complaints are uttered against the existing government system: Parliament is thought to be no longer in a position to control the Executive; ministerial and civil service recruitment is believed to have declined in quality; parties are accused of oligarchy and rigidity; interest groups are said to be too prominent; elections are felt to be insufficiently meaningful; mass apathy is thought to be spreading, etc.

It is difficult to disentangle fact from fancy in these discussions. Underlying value judgments are not always made clear. Opinions are freely expressed without much hard evidence. Available evidence seems to be somewhat contradictory, and fundamental data are often lacking. But the following indications may be given about the stability (or instability) of the political and social system:

1. *Electoral participation.* In spite of indifferently enforced compulsory attendance at the ballot box, both the number of people voting and the number of people casting valid ballots has increased fairly steadily over the past forty years (see Table 6.2).

2. *Aggregate strength of the five main parties.* Increased electoral participation notwithstanding, the share of the combined vote for the five larger parties has, on the whole, increased since 1945 as compared with the interwar period. The Dutch electoral system provides every encouragement for splinter parties: the entire country is for all practical purposes treated as one constituency; financial deposits required of new

parties are low; and the threshold for representation in the Parliament has at no time been higher than 1 per cent of the valid national vote (since 1956 when the membership of the lower house was expanded from 100 to 150 members it has been only two-thirds of 1 per cent). Even so, all other groups *combined* (whether integralist, overlapping, or antisystem parties, or just ephemeral oddities) have at no time obtained more than 16 per cent (in 1933) of the valid national vote. In only a few cases have the five main parties had less than 90 per cent of the seats in the lower house (i.e. in 1918, the first year of universal suffrage; in 1933 and 1937 during the Depression; and in 1946 and 1948 when the Communists obtained a sizable share of the national vote, see Table 6.2).

3. *Increasing electoral mobility.* The fairly stable distribution of votes among the main parties since 1918 (see Appendix Tables 6.3 and 6.4) is, in fact, somewhat deceptive: it is a result not of stable electoral preferences but rather of the circumstance that certain crosscurrents have tended to cancel one another out. The apparent stability of the Catholic Party, for instance, masks a secular loss to both Labor and Liberals, compensated for by the advantage the party derives from the increasing number of Catholics in the electorate.[64] The Anti-Revolutionary Party has lost a third of its strength since 1950, apparently to the Christian Historical Union as well as to the Liberals and Socialists. The number of votes for the Liberals, Socialists, Pacifist Socialists, and Communists combined has increased from 36 per cent in 1937 to a postwar record of 47.3 per cent in 1959, while the total vote for all religious parties declined from 56.4 per cent to 52 per cent in the same period, despite their differential advantage in the birthrate. (See Appendix Table 6.4.) These facts attest to an increased electoral mobility in the Dutch electorate, as does the appearance of strong crosscurrents between the Liberals and Socialists, and of more incidental borderline traffic between the religious parties on the one hand and the non-religious parties on the other.[65] It is difficult to say whether this increased sensitivity points to heightened political awareness on the part of the electorate or to alienation from the existing party system. There is no doubt that the leaders of all parties are becoming more concerned with the images of their parties and tend to rely less on traditional clientele relationships. Yet the movement is not yet of such dimension that a breakup of the traditional alignments seems at all likely (whether through a reorientation from the top down or from the grass roots up).

64. Actual Catholic voting records are better measured by the so-called Index of Political Orthodoxy, i.e., the percentage of recorded Catholics who actually vote for the Catholic Party. According to data from the Catholic Institute for Social Research, this index has declined from 92 in 1948, to 88 in 1952, 87 in 1956, 85.9 in 1959, to 84.9 in 1963 (albeit with considerable regional variations). See for an interesting analysis W.J.J. Kusters, "Stembusgedrag en Maatschappijstructuur," *Sociologische Gids, 10* (1963), 226–38.

65. Cf. the discussion between Kusters and Van Thijn, ibid., pp. 228–48.

Table 6.2 Extent of Electoral Participation and Share of Large and Small Parties in National Vote and Seats for Lower House of Parliament (1918-1963)

	1918	1922	1925	1929	1933	1937	1946	1948	1952	1956	1959	1963
Electoral participation												
Percentage of eligible voters voting	Data not available		91.4	92.7	94.5	94.4	93.1	93.7	95.0	95.5	95.6	95.1
Percentage of valid votes	Data not available		95.3	95.4	95.4	96.3	96.9	96.9	97.0	97.9	97.7	97.5
Valid votes in % eligible voters	88.6	88.8	87.1	88.4	90.2	90.9	90.2	90.8	92.1	93.5	93.3	92.8
		(estimates)										
Share of Large Parties												
Percentage of valid votes [1]	87.2	87.8	88.4	89.1	83.9	84.6	86.2	87.0	86.7	91.5	91.6	87.5
Number of Seats [1]	87	94	94	92	87	89	88	89	90	94	142	135
											(95%)	(90%)
Share of Small Parties												
Percentage of Religious splinters [2]	2.0	4.1	5.1	4.6	6.2	5.8	2.8	3.7	5.8	2.9	2.9	3.1
Percentage of left-wing socialists and communists [2]	3.6	2.2	2.4	3.0	5.2	4.1	10.8	8.1	6.5	4.8	4.8	5.8
Percentage of right-wing and interest parties [2]	7.2	5.9	4.1	3.3	4.7	5.5	0.2	1.2	1.0	0.8	0.7	3.6
Number of seats [1]	13	6	6	8	13	11	12	11	10	6	8	15
											(5%)	(10%)
Percentage of votes cast for parties that did not obtain representation [3]	2.2	7.1	4.9	3.3	4.0	3.9	1.1	1.6	2.0	1.4	2.0	1.5

1. Number of seats in lower house: 1918–56, 100; 1956 to date, 150. Allocation of remainder of seats: 1918–33, largest remainder (Roget system); 1933 to date, highest average (d'Hondt system).

2. The assignment of political groups to categories (religious parties, left-wing socialist parties, and right-wing and interest parties) is necessarily somewhat arbitrary; percentages are therefore approximate only.

3. Threshold formulas: 1918, 50% of electoral quotient; 1922–33, 75% of electoral quotient; 1935 to date, electoral quotient (1% of valid national vote between 1935–56, and two-thirds of 1% of national vote since 1956).

Source: Central Bureau of Statistics and calculations by R. P. van den Helm.

4. *Survey evidence.* The evidence from such surveys as have been published is also somewhat unclear.[66] Interest in and knowledge of the field of
politics are apparently at a low level, yet for lack of comparable data for
historical periods it is not clear whether this situation was really much
different, say, forty years ago. Many people feel that they have little
influence on politics, but they do not seem very anxious to become actively
involved in political life. The image of politicians is not always flattering,
and quite a few respondents regard them as mainly self-seekers. At the
same time, many seem to think that party politics are not overly important
for government policy; quite a few seem to consider it relatively unimportant whether a particular political party is in the government or not,
and many opine freely that parties should quarrel less and cooperate more.
The suggestion that small parties complicate the workings of government
finds frequent assent, but most people think it undemocratic to raise the
threshold for representation. Most respondents say that they regard parties
and party principles as more important than personalities, but they often
reveal an uncritical admiration for particular ministers, which if not expressed in party votes then at least shows up in public opinion polls.[67]
Does all this point to fundamental dissatisfaction? Other data reveal a very
high degree of satisfaction with present living standards and future economic prospects. Younger people sometimes seem to take a more positive
attitude toward politics than older ones, and rising educational levels tend
to make for greater knowledge of political affairs. Perhaps the best conclusion one can draw is that most people are neither much worried nor
much interested at the present time, and many realize that Dutch politics
is not actually so important in view of the overwhelming role of international factors.

ANTISYSTEM OPPOSITIONS   It was mentioned earlier that the total electoral strength of antisystem opposition groups has tended to be low
in the Netherlands. Both Communists and National Socialists scored their
best results, moreover, when they offered a moderate, "national" image,
and they declined greatly in importance when events abroad cast a dark

66. The most convenient collections of data are in: Wiardi Beckman Stichting,
Verkiezingen in Nederland (Amsterdam, 1951); *De Nederlandse Kiezer, Een Onder-
zoek naar zijn gedragingen en opvattingen*, with English summary (The Hague,
1956); J. J. de Jong, *Overheid en Onderdaan* (Wageningen, Zomer and Keuning, 1956);
L. van der Land a.o., *Kiezer en Verkiezing* (mimeo., Amsterdam, 1963) also in a much
shortened English version: *Voting in The Netherlands, A Panel Study in an Amsterdam Suburb*, report to the International Political Science Association, Geneva, 1964;
H. Daudt and H. Lange, "Welvaart in Nederland," *Ariadne, 18* (1963), 360–65; Hans
Daudt and Henk Lange, *Youth and Politics in The Netherlands*, report to the International Political Science Association, Geneva, 1964; and A. Hoogerwerf, *Protestantisme en Progressiviteit*.

67. When NIPO pollsters asked Dutchmen recently what man (living or dead)
they most admired, by far the largest number (about a quarter of all respondents)
spontaneously named Joseph Luns, the Dutch Minister of Foreign Affairs, who can
admittedly be very amusing in TV broadcasts.

shadow over them. Yet their existence has some importance, both as a measure of potential dissatisfaction in the system and as a yardstick with which to judge the attitude of democratic government to fundamental oppositions of principle.

The Communist Party [68] has represented the oldest and steadiest opposition of principle, having had seats in the Dutch Parliament ever since 1918. The hard core of its strength is found among alienated groups in Amsterdam and some other regions where, as we saw, a rebellious, mostly anarchist kind of socialism crystallized very early in Dutch social history. The party obtained its largest following in 1946, when its vote temporarily soared above 10 per cent, mainly under the influence of Russian victories, a strong resistance record, and the simultaneous refashioning of the SDAP into the Labor Party. At the same time the Communists also seemed to ride high in the trade union field. They became the chief sponsors of an Eenheidsvakbeweging (EVB, later EVC) that was established in 1945 to unite workers whatever their religious or political allegiance in one common union organization. But the Socialist and religious unions soon struck back, and the government and employers refused to deal with the EVB. When a few political strikes petered out, it soon declined in importance. Communist strength has gone down ever since, both at the ballot box and in union organization. Rock bottom was touched in 1959 when internal divisions destroyed the remnants of the EVC, and the Communist Party received only 2.4 per cent of the national vote, almost entirely in its most traditional areas.

Ever since its inception, the Communist Party has remained completely isolated in politics.[69] Known Communists are disqualified for most types of government employment. Since the Prague coup of 1948 other parties have refused to accept Communists as partners in local government executive organs. Communists were excluded from certain parliamentary committees, notably in defense and foreign affairs. Although they could publish and campaign freely, they were not allotted radio or television time. It is a moot question whether this discrimination was effective or superfluous. In any case, the new 1965 Cabinet decided to change this practice and to admit the Communists to radio and television on a par with other parties represented in Parliament. Generally speaking, the Communist movement has remained a sect in a sectarian country. True to this tradition, it has done itself considerable harm through internal heresy hunting.

68. Cf. F. Kool, "Communism in Holland—A Study in Futility," *Problems of Communism, 9* (1960), 17–24. The most convenient, though inadequate, data in Dutch are in W. van Ravesteyn, *De Wording van het Communisme in Nederland, 1907–1925* (Amsterdam, Van Kampen, 1948), and M. Perthus, ed., *Voor Vrijheid en Socialisme, Gedenkboek van het Sneevliet Herdenkingscomité* (Rotterdam, Gramo, 1953).

69. The Communists were invited to nominate one of their leaders for Cabinet membership in 1945; they demanded the Ministry of Agriculture and Food but were only offered the post of Minister Without Portfolio, which they refused.

Fascist groups were formed from the early 1920s onward, followed later by National Socialist groups that sought their inspiration in Germany. Most of these movements were exceedingly small and hardly worth attention but for the role which some of their members were to play later during the German occupation.[70] The most important group was the Nationaal-Socialistische Beweging of Anton Mussert. It won an unexpectedly large victory during the provincial elections of 1935, when it secured almost 8 per cent of the national vote, mainly at the expense of the nonconfessional bourgeois groups. (During the same period the Communist Party never rose much above 3 per cent.) Originally a somewhat petty bourgeois protest movement, it turned increasingly radical. In competition with some other fascist groups, it attempted to organize the beginnings of a private militia. This in turn provoked similar militant behavior from Communists and left-wing Socialists. The government of the time (under the Anti-Revolutionary leader Colijn) reacted by banning uniforms and public insignia on public streets and by other measures relating to public order. After that the NSB dwindled in strength, and received only 4 per cent of the vote in 1937 and slightly less in 1939.[71] Its decisive hour was to come only with foreign invasion.

Since 1945 extreme right-wing parties have been even less influential than they were in the interwar period.[72] Small financial interest groups, veterans and repatriates from the colonies, authoritarian orthodox Protestants and old-fashioned reactionary Liberals have sometimes formed fleeting political parties that never succeeded in passing the very low threshold for representation. The only movement that has done so is a more Poujadist-oriented Boerenpartij (Peasant Party) that obtained three seats in Parliament in 1963. Its main strength lies with small peasants and small shopkeepers who cannot keep pace with the impersonal forces of economic rationalization in both agriculture and retailing. In addition, it may have received a certain popular support for its efforts to stand up to the dominant political and administrative system. Its ideology is a curious mixture of authoritarianism, individual self-reliance, direct interest appeal, and considerable demagogy. Its fame is partly dependent on the earthy appeal of its leader, H. Koekoek. Interestingly, when Dutchmen were asked in 1964 to give the names of Dutch politicians, the names most

70. See W. Warmbrunn, *The Dutch Under German Occupation, 1940–1945* (Stanford, Stanford University Press, 1963), passim.

71. For an attempt to investigate the social roots of National Socialist strength and its consequent decline in the Netherlands, see G. A. Kooy, *Het Echec van een 'Volkse' Beweging—Nazificatie en Denazificatie in Nederland, 1931–1945* (Assen, Van Gorcum, 1964).

72. National Socialist parties have been proscribed in the Netherlands since 1945. The courts stopped one attempt to refound a National Socialist movement in 1954. After 1945 most Quislings lost both the active and passive franchise, usually for a period of ten years. The return to the electorate of a number of former Nazis may have been a factor in the increased vote for the extreme right in 1963.

frequently given were those of the then Socialist opposition leader, A. Vondeling, and of Koekoek, who symbolizes opposition to the system as a whole.[73]

GOVERNMENT AND OPPOSITION   The Netherlands is now, as it always was, a small but highly pluralist society. There is considerable friction and opposition whether from explicitly political groups or others. Ministers, parliamentarians, bureaucrats, interest groups, mass media, promotional associations, individual capitalist enterprises, and independent academic experts all seek to influence specific government policies. Tactics are equally varied: they comprise public criticism, propaganda campaigns, formal and informal petitions, threats to withhold services, informal pressure on strategically placed persons or groups, consultation, bargaining, legislation, and what not. The central objects of such pressures are ministers, parliamentarians, and bureaucratic agencies, the key means the securing of regular access, especially via representation in advisory bodies and party slates.

These processes have been little studied in the Netherlands, partly because of their fugitive quality, partly because a legalistic tradition has long preempted attention for the more formal institutional elements of policy-making. This same tradition has made for considerable secrecy about affairs of state, which in turn complicates the problem of gaining true insight.

Even without further inquiry it seems likely, however, that the situation would bear out Stein Rokkan's statement:

> a proliferation of sectional and functional organization . . . tended to soften the overall strains in the system and to reduce the level of polarization. What we tend to find is a cumulation of forces making for a narrowing of the alternatives for national politics, a fragmentation of the networks of policy-influencing organizations, and a consequent decline in the importance of the decisions of the electorate-at-large. This may tend to lower the level of general political participation and to alienate from politics sizeable sections of the once-enfranchised citizenry, leaving the basic decisions to a bargaining process between interest organizations, parties and agencies and departments of the national bureaucracy.[74]

If this is true, the question whether opposition is distinct or dissolves into the system assumes a new importance. Presumably the complexity of modern society automatically produces enough countervailing forces to make for a considerable amount of intergroup opposition on all policy matters, whether highly specialized or not. Yet it seems that only a definite

73. See Daudt and Lange, *Youth and Politics*, p. 10.
74. Stein Rokkan, "Mass Suffrage, Secret Voting and Political Participation," *European Journal of Sociology*, 2 (1961), 152.

and powerful Opposition in Parliament can secure regular accountability and guarantee the openness of the system. It is on this point that the Dutch situation seems most vulnerable. The need to defer to many interests, the tradition of collegial rule, the constant quest for compromise, encourage careful consideration of policy questions. But they lead at the same time to some measure of deliberate depoliticization,[75] which makes it difficult for the common man to identify himself with particular policies or with the somewhat transcendental game of general politics. The presence of many oppositions is therefore not a real substitute for the absence of a strong Opposition that challenges government wherever possible— on the basis of its own strength, not from the need to ingratiate itself with future coalition partners. The absence of a real Opposition potentially weakens every government. A strong Opposition can provide a government with strength as it increases the confidence of the citizenry at large that government actions can bear scrutiny and can be challenged in specific instances. Even if this may not increase the measure of direct citizen participation, it may lessen the danger that government becomes too distant for the ordinary citizen, leaving him a helpless object of diverse pressures and possibly even of what Gabriel Almond termed "a Caesaristic breakthrough" from above.[76]

75. A former Clerk of the First Chamber drew the "logical" conclusion from the Dutch situation when he proposed the inclusion of all democratic parties in every government as a matter of course; he argued that the traditional detachment between government and Parliament would guarantee a sufficient measure of opposition on specific issues. See A. L. De Block, *Samenwerking in Nederland als Staatkundig Vraagstuk* (The Hague, Centrum voor Staatkundige Vorming, 1955). For a highly critical analysis of the Dutch situation, see J. F. Glastra van Loon, "Kiezen of Delen," *Nederlands Juristenblad* (1964), pp. 1133–42 and 1161–67. Glastra van Loon attributes the simultaneous existence of a tepid conformism and an irresponsible criticism of all politics and all politicians to the absence of a strongly articulated Opposition. He would like to see this changed by a system of direct popular election of the Prime Minister.

76. See Almond, "Comparative Political Systems," p. 409. The closest experience to a movement against the old party system was the Nederlandse Unie in 1940–41. Led by a triumvirate of younger men who had been quite critical of prewar politics, the Unie sought to present a national platform. It called for the cooperation of all Dutchmen in a new movement toward regeneration of Dutch society. Though boycotted by most old party leaders who thought or found political action during the German occupation impossible, it attracted a very large mass following, mainly because of its strong stand against the Dutch National Socialists. The Germans proscribed the movement in 1941 when it no longer served any purpose for their occupation politics. See Warmbrunn, *The Dutch Under German Occupation*, pp. 133–36.

Some of the Unie's leaders were later active in the Nederlandse Volksbeweging, a movement of a relatively large number of politicians from all parties which called for a reorientation of the party system in 1945. But old party ties soon reasserted themselves so that the NVB left little trace in Dutch politics; it did however provide a catalytic effect on the fusion of a number of left-wing forces into the Labor Party.

7

GERMANY:
THE VANISHING OPPOSITION

Otto Kirchheimer

In the particular context of the German experience, the terms with which we are concerned may be defined as follows:

1. We shall refer to "political competition" if political jobs are filled by selection from candidates whose number is in excess of the places to be filled.

2. We shall speak of "loyal opposition" if the political competition involves some form of goal differentiation between available candidates in harmony with the constitutional requirements of a given system.

3. We shall speak of "opposition of principle" if the competitor's behavior indicates the desire for a degree of goal displacement incompatible with the constitutional requirements of a given system.

Any form of political opposition necessarily involves some kind of competition. The reverse does not hold true: political competition does not necessarily involve opposition.

Our problem, in German terms, is about 100 years old. The Bismarck constitution functioned in a society split into two major camps. On the one hand was the military-bureaucratic complex which dominated Prussia, monarchic in principle; on the other, the up-and-coming bourgeoisie. While the monarchy represented the state, officially identified with the moral order, the bourgeoisie stood for the sum total of what the Germans would call *die bürgerliche Gesellschaft*. Executive power remained concentrated with and at the disposal of those in control of the state, while legislative power had become a joint enterprise of those controlling the state and the forces of the *bürgerliche Gesellschaft*. Since Bismarck's grant of federal universal suffrage in 1868, the urban proletariat had been brought to political notice as an independent and rapidly swelling section of Germany's *bürgerliche Gesellschaft*. Bismarck had not meant to integrate the working class into the official order as both the Liberal and Conservative parties had done in England. Rather he thought to keep the liberal bourgeoisie at bay in its own bailiwick, the parliamentary assembly, by utilizing the working-class franchise. But, as with so many of his domestic political schemes, he was unsuccessful. Through Bismarck's grant of federal universal franchise, the long-standing cleavage between the official state power and the *bürgerliche Gesellschaft* acquired more disturbing dimensions as Social Democratic Party (SPD) opposition of principle increased.

This opposition of principle grew by leaps and bounds during the halcyon days before the First World War. It was both a political party and a chapel. Some of its leaders were intent on nudging out the incumbents gently from the seats of both social and political power. Yet these tacticians, who were concerned with the parliamentary impact of tomorrow's elections, had to contend with fervent adherents certain of an impending millennium and scornful of any compromise that might obtain only a bit of daily progress. Yet, kept at arms' length and intermittently harassed by an official state organization which rejected the SPD as unpatriotic, the SPD's executive body could comfortably straddle the issue of tomorrow's policies by dilatory formulas.

The Weimar Period

The Weimar settlement presumably eliminated the cleavage between the state and the *bürgerliche Gesellschaft,* between the executive and parliament. Can we then, for the lifetime of the Weimar regime, speak of political competition beginning to develop along lines in any way familiar in America or England? Could the Weimar system be understood as a political game played by alternating leadership groups with the tolerance, acquiescence, and electoral consent of the population at large? Such a description would cover only a segment and not the most important one of the Weimar political reality.

There was rather a threefold system of political competition in this severely transfigured heritage of the previous constitutional period. There was the struggle between those parties which, half by inclination, half by political necessity, had become upholders of the constitutional order (most important of them, at least in numbers, the SPD), and the parties of opposition of principle, divided into Communist and nationalist components (including the Nazis), digging in for a siege of the establishment from two directions.

Opposition of principle had undergone mutations of thought and action as a consequence of and reaction to several developments. The left revolution which had failed at home had succeeded abroad to the East. There were drastic changes in conditions of existence among proletariat and bourgeoisie. Opposition of principle was no longer characterized by a state of mind patiently waiting to take over society's accumulated store of resources in the fullness of time but by the spirit of conquest here and now. The parties of opposition of principle were now very different from the half-political, half-chapel opposition of the benign pre-World War I days. They considered elections a ready-made battleground, where they might integrate and exploit their gains and then proceed to more far-reaching political action.

Between the parties operating within (or at least not clearly outside) the parliamentary system, there was a certain amount of political competition, genuine though slack and sporadic. These competitors were more intent on picking up pieces of disintegrating parties than in competing for each other's more or less well-established clientele. This intrasystem competition did not lead to clear-cut positions of majority versus minority, government versus loyal opposition.

The SPD had from the outset contributed to the frustration of such solutions by opting for proportional representation in January 1919. Whether a majority election system would have led to a much different outcome is unclear, because the heritage of the Empire had left strong traditional and religious cleavages superimposed on social class differentiations in German society. The SPD option for proportional representation was probably only partly due to loyalty to an outdated party program, only partly inspired by the battles of yesteryear's lopsided imperial election districts. A more important motive was probably the SPD leaders' fear of facing undivided governmental responsibility and their incapacity for making any attempt at implementing the central core of their party program.

At any rate the results were clear enough. There was never a chance to establish a government–loyal opposition relationship during the decade in which, in constitutional theory at least, a sort of parliamentary government existed. The difficulties of a multiparty regime, the job interests of each party's members, the socioeconomic interests of each party's clientele, and above all each party's urge for self-preservation as a political unit in the face of the precarious existence of the whole republican state machine almost forced the major parties, loyal to the system, to try to hang on to some pieces of the central state apparatus, or at least to some strategic administrative positions in the strongest political component, Prussia.

Yet if elections were also a means to determine to what pieces of the executive and the administrative machine a loyal party could manage to hang on, the total amount of and the structure of executive and administrative power accessible to the parties were scarcely determined by shifting election results. This power depended (memories of the previous regime) on the relative strength of the military and civilian bureaucracy and the political apparatus proper. And here we face a certain level of highly significant political relations involving little competition: the interrelation between all military and certain bureaucratic power holders and those officeholders emanating from and legitimized by the confidence of

Parliament. Certainly the military considered itself an independent establishment willing to negotiate contracts with rival sovereignties but otherwise serving the political establishment only on its own terms.

Therefore, from the very outset, opposition of principle against the existing constitutional system and the power of the bureaucratic and especially the military officeholders narrowed down the significance of electoral competition as a political basis for the determination of policy. There was little room left for the development of a concept of loyal opposition resting on alternative policy choices propounded by parties working within the constitutional framework.

Toward the end of the regime a continuing process led to the rapid disappearance of both political competition and loyal opposition. First, any attempt of the parliamentary establishment to contest the military-bureaucratic power of decision ceased to exist. Then the parliamentary establishment was ignored during the bureaucratic and military rearguard action against the growing forces of the opposition of principle of the Right. Finally, after Hindenburg's death in 1934, any idea of the military establishment's continuation as an independent factor in possible opposition to the National Socialist power was eliminated.

Nazism and the Occupation

The Third Reich permitted shared sovereignties as well as some sort of intrasystem competition. In the economic realm competition went on surreptitiously by quality differentiation or battle for administrative preference. In the political realm the system used an amount of intensive subleadership competition for the favor of the supreme leader. This intrasystem leadership competition might sometimes be artfully exploited to enlarge the interstitial space for opposition. Yet, and this is decisive: there was otherwise no bridge or easy communication between both competition and opposition. Opposition had to shed the purely competitive garb, and it became the banned and hunted opposition of principle, the only form of opposition meaningful or possible under the conditions of that regime.

The immediate afterwar and occupation period, 1945–49, brought an interesting separation of the functions of competition and opposition. There was a certain amount of competition among the various groups admitted to the classes for political reeducation put up by the Western Allied authorities, which included trial-run elections. The programs of these parties did not have much relation either to government decisions of the day, which were monopolized by the occupiers, or to the parties' own policies two or three years later, determined as they were by the swiftly changing political realities. Yet these programs served as posters for reassembling the various prewar party general staffs, reestablishing communication lines with old clienteles, and giving prospective recruits for political jobs a chance to look around. In addition they opened up to the public at large devices for getting reacclimatized to a sort of competitive politics, allowing them to show some innocuous preference for one or the other duly licensed competitor.

To the extent that there did exist an element of opposition it had nothing to do with the incipient German party or governmental structure but was opposition without any element of competition. This was an abnormality to be explained by the distorted focus of responsibility in occupation government; General Clay's customers were the Germans, but his responsibility and responsiveness ran to Washington. Opposition consisted of the open or subterranean resistance which indigenous leaders, most effectively those without jobs in the occupation-installed governments, such as Kurt Schumacher, put up to some of the policies of the occupation authorities. This opposition rested on different vistas of Germany's future role and organization, all related to the divergent national interests that separated foreign occupiers and incipient German political operators. The opposition became more effective as more discord between Western and Eastern occupiers necessitated close attention to German susceptibilities.

Social Democratic Opposition

The end of the Western occupation regime shades over into the beginning of the Bonn establishment. The new regime was put into the saddle by the Western occupation powers after the American authorities in early summer 1948 had taken the decision that was to determine much of the future course of German politics: to carry through a drastic currency reform without tying it in any way to a change in the distribution of property or in the ownership of the means of production. The new political regime, whose political viability was vouched for by the continued presence of the occupiers (now turning protectors and allies), rested on the acceptance of periodic elections carried on by competing parties. The whole apparatus was in the traditional Western style. It was tied up with and constitutionally answerable to a Parliament whose activities, in the long run, became at least as problematic as those of similar European institutions. The 1949 elections had given no party anything approaching a majority. But the future perennial chancellor, Konrad Adenauer, the leader of the catch-all Christian Democratic Union, managed to squeeze into office with a one-vote majority.

Both the narrowness of the government coalition's original parliamentary basis, the contrasting personalities of the two leaders involved (Konrad Adenauer and Kurt Schumacher), and the initially sharply drawn issues made it appear that Germany now for the first time had a parliamentary opposition, performing in the classic parliamentary tradition. Kurt Schumacher characterized his party's role in this sense when he opened the debate after the first government declaration by Chancellor Adenauer on September 20, 1949: "The essence of opposition is a permanent attempt to force the government and its parties by concrete proposals tuned to concrete situations to pursue the political line outlined by the opposition." [1] Such opposition seemed grounded on both domestic and foreign policy issues.

On the domestic front the SPD had already lost the first round in 1948 before the establishment of the Bonn government. After the currency reform, Ludwig Erhard, the economic delegate in the bizonal governmental structure who became the indefatigable propagandist of the so-called "social market economy," had his policy of doing away altogether with economic restrictions and rationing adopted, over the protest of the Social Democratic Party, which was representative of the urban consumer at large. Under the new establishment, Schumacher would come back to the same charges with increased vigor, becoming the sharpest critic of what he called the authoritarian state defending the interests of the property owners.

In foreign policy Schumacher tried to fight a two-front war. As a participant witness of Weimar history he wanted above all to avoid having his party again labeled defeatist and unpatriotic. First and foremost, therefore, he was firmly set against the slightest attempt to compromise with the regime in the Eastern zone. But at the same time he initiated the fight, persevered in by his party for only a short while after his death in 1952, against making Western Germany a partner of the various initial European integration endeavors. He described them not as praiseworthy efforts at a union of all democratic European peoples, but as the suspicious and undesirable enterprise of the momentarily ruling capitalist and Roman Catholic forces of little Europe. To his mind European integration was not only a conspiracy against the revival of the German nation but also against the people of the largely socialist-oriented nations of northern Europe. Instead, his policy stood for a conscious effort to reunite Germany at the earliest conceivable moment as an independent national community outside the framework of Eastern domination or Western mortgages.

Both by the choice of its leaders and the orderly, not to say conservative, background of its party members, this Schumacher policy of opposition was, however, to be exercised only within the strict limits of parliamentary procedure as prescribed by the Basic Law which the Social Democratic Party had prominently helped to shape. Opposing the present administration the SPD would steadfastly stand by the Bonn setup as established

1. *Bundestag Stenographische Berichte, 1,* (1949), 32.

under the Basic Law. From the outset it might have looked as if the chance of unfolding such a type of loyal opposition was to be enhanced not only by the tenuous parliamentary hold of the government, but also by the insignificance of any element of opposition of principle.

Under the harsh climate of economic deprivation prevailing in 1949, both the left- and right-wing oppositions of principle had managed to return to the first Bundestag a small band of followers, in spite of the recent experience with National Socialism and the current unfolding of the Communist regime in East Germany. But, totaling in the first Bundestag only about six per cent of the membership, these groups at no time had any appreciable influence on the work of assembly or government. Even at that early time, there was at no point a need for the parties loyal to the Basic Law to suspend their government–opposition battle in order to repulse the onslaught of destructive forces. Later, after the first apparent success of the Erhard economic policy, which was materially helped by the Korean boom, the opposition of principle disappeared completely from the Bundestag. It dwindled to a trickle among the public at large, even before the government read it completely out of the circuit of official party competition by courtesy of two Constitutional Court decisions.

But the disappearance of the Communist and rightist opposition of principle, which might have enlarged the scope for a loyal SPD opposition within the democratic framework, had no such invigorating effect. We might rather be tempted to say that disappearance was one element among others in the steady erosion of the potentialities of loyal opposition. Schumacher's initial attempt to force the will of the opposition on the government revealed itself through the years as a complete fiasco on all fronts. Two successive electoral defeats were instrumental in the SPD's ardent desire long before the start of the 1961 election campaign to disentangle itself clearly from any notion of opposing major governmental policies. The SPD consciously strove to eliminate parliamentary opposition as a desirable pattern for the conduct of political business.[2]

Let us first look at the stages of this breakdown of parliamentary opposition before trying to assess its reasons and its impact on the larger political scene. In 1947 suspicion was general against the German entrepreneurial class—a consequence of its support of the rising Hitler regime and its close association with it during the war. Even the Christian Democratic Union (CDU) had to make some genuflection, in its Ahlen program exercise of 1947, to public ownership. Scarcely more than six years later the tables had turned. The seeming success of the Erhard brand of eco-

2. I am intentionally dealing here mainly with the SPD because it stood, at least for some time, for alternative policy goals. The smaller parties, including the still fully operative third party, the Free Democratic Party, never had anything but a tactical motivation to enhance its competitive position, at no time making the slightest discernible attempt to sponsor alternative policies.

nomic liberalism, proudly acclaimed at the 1953 Hamburg pre-election congress of the CDU, served to rehabilitate the image of the German entrepreneur.

The SPD, after its first election defeat in 1953, started the long road of retreat on all fronts. Immediately the SPD relegated the socialization of the means of production to an inconspicuous place. By 1959, when redrafting its program in Godesberg, its social and economic clauses had become a collection of vistas and projections for an expanding society designed, à l'Américaine, to play up to nearly all segments of society by the proper insertion of strategically chosen, yet vague enough recognitions of group positions. If somewhat greater concern was given to the party's traditional labor clientele, great ingenuity was exercised to refrain from recommending any definite form of societal organization. Explicit condemnation hit only those systems restricting the free development of the human personality. Attitudes regarding the government of the day became a matter of purely tactical concern.

In such a tactical exercise, interparty competition still has an important role. On the domestic front, for example, the party continues to make a special effort to gain the ear of groups whose sympathies may be in relatively easy reach, such as Protestants in general and Catholic workers in particular. Both are supposed to be attracted by the unconditional shelving of the last vestige of the traditional "religion is a private affair of the individual." In the 1959 program, collaboration with the churches comes before a short reference to freedom of thought. Yet the 1959 program still took the view that children should be educated in common rather than in separate denominational state schools; three years later, in the light of modified tactical needs, such a clear-cut position had already again become outdated.[3] Catholic workers, for whom the party competes with the CDU, are also to be attracted by the heavy emphasis on the regressive character of government fiscal policy. The demand for exten-

---

3. See the instructive discussion at the Cologne SPD Parteitag (Protokoll, Bonn, 1962, pp. 391–92, 405–12), and the recent pamphlet, "Katholik und Godesberger Programm Zur Situation nach *Mater und Magistra*," published by the SPD party executive in March 1962; the pamphlet tries to show the similarities of approach between the Papal encyclical and the Godesberg program of the SPD. However, in the guise of interpretation, it offers the Catholic Church compromises on the school question which would not be smaller than those promised by other parties (pp. 47–51, esp. p. 51). The first postwar *Konkordat* concluded in February 1965 between the Vatican and the SPD-led Lower Saxony state government kept this promise. It is, as a matter of fact, more favorable to the church in regard to educational policies than the provisions so far applying in areas under CDU-led state governments. What is relevant from our viewpoint is the intent. It matters little that an element of self-deception is involved in such tactics of accommodating the churches at any price. At any rate, the *Konkordat* aroused a certain amount of resentment, especially among teachers. It also led to the withdrawal of the FDP from the Land government and the substitution of the CDU.

sion of existing social welfare and pension schemes is also an ever recurrent theme.

All this then remains on the purely competitive level. The same social policy themes and suggestions will recur in the propaganda of the CDU's labor wing. The economic and social organization (in the form it has taken since the early '50s) is no longer challenged in principle. The present interplay between economic liberalism and oligopolistic power of individual firms, and between various economic and social groups may not work out satisfactorily. In that event, the SPD, along with other parties, might be glad to accept changes suggested by experts to meet the new conditions. Yet the SPD's present program is an attractive sales prospectus for desirable group futures, and is neither designed to provide concrete answers for special contingencies nor, in contrast to the discarded old formulas, a total scheme for societal development.

The SPD not only shuns any frontal attack on the economic system but through the mouth of its 1964 convention keynote speaker on economic affairs paid special tribute to "the dynamics of market economy as an inalienable part of a libertarian economic order." [4] At the same time, however, in good catch-all party platform style the acceptance of the market economy is counterbalanced by an affirmative nod toward all those dirigiste policies required by modern industrial society. With an eye on the competitive advantages to be obtained it will press with a more lusty voice the claims of an actual and potential clientele. It has urged the continuation of a publicly sponsored housing program in spite of an overheated economic situation, and upheld, to a certain degree at least the job interests of miners threatened by cheaper fuel resources.

In matters of economic policy, then, the SPD simply yielded to the overwhelming success of the German economy of the '50s. But the foreign policy picture is by no means as clear-cut. In spite of the SPD's initial resistance, a measure of Western economic integration came off as planned. Rearmament too has been carried through within the framework of the Western alliance. This policy has paid off in economic terms and has enhanced German status within the Western community. Yet the policy has brought Germany no nearer the goal proclaimed by the SPD and echoed by the government: reunification in freedom. Nevertheless, the SPD's policy of opposition has caved in on this front more unconditionally than on any other. Until the middle '50s the SPD fought a rearguard action to delay Western integration. Under Schumacher's initial impetus it opposed the Schuman Plan and the setting up of the Council

---

4. See, e.g., Dr. Karl Schiller in SPD Parteitag, 1962 Protokoll, pp. 256–58, and his statements on the need for "cautious accommodation of the coal industry to the changed consumption structure" in the 1964 Karlsruhe party convention, quoted in *SPD Parteitag Arbeitsgemeinschaft B*, November 24, 1964 (uncorrected Protokoll, pp. 12–13).

of Europe. With the full support of its adherents and other large groups it fought in Parliament and in the Constitutional Court against the incipient rearmament effort. Its line faltered in the mid-'50s when it started to uphold the need for national defense and fully collaborated in implementing defense policies. In 1957 and 1958, however, it used the general abhorrence of atomic war for a vigorous parliamentary action. In 1959 it sponsored a so-called "German Plan" of foreign policy. To the need for accommodation with the Soviet Union to obtain a Western-style unity of Germany it tied a form of acceptance of a demilitarized zone in Europe. Yet by mid-1960 it had dropped the attempt at developing an independent foreign policy line. It solemnly abjured any thought of forcing the will of the opposition on the government; it now became its task "to find a common understanding to see what can be done, both in concrete situations and as a long-term proposition." [5] It condemned the idea of a third way between freedom and Communism which was still inherent in the "German Plan." To show their prospective political partners the seriousness of their intentions, the SPD leadership, dragging along the reluctant party chairman, Erich Ollenhauer, rammed a resolution through the 1960 Hannover party convention which whittled down the blunt rejection of German production, stationing, or use of atomic weapons contained in the otherwise tame enough Godesberg program of the previous year.[6]

By 1964 there were too few clear-cut foreign policy lines and initiatives left to allow one to speak of "the SPD foreign policy." A few distinctive emphases are still discernible—some continued opposition to the unnecessary dependence on nuclear weapons for European defense and vigorous resistance to the further spread of strategic nuclear weapons (in line with American strategy concepts) and special concern for both the needs and the propaganda possibilities inherent in the party's predominant position in Berlin. Yet none of these emphases is far from the tactical line of a broadly based interparty foreign policy, and none offers either basic criticism or alternative positions.[7]

The concept of opposition as a framework for presenting policy alternatives was officially abandoned in the speech given by the SPD's candidate-designate for the chancellorship, Willy Brandt, with the 1961 elections in mind: "In a sound and developing democracy it is the norm rather than the exception that the parties put forward similar, even identical demands in a number of fields. The question of priorities, of the

---

5. Herbert Wehner as official speaker in the foreign policy debate on June 30, 1960, *Bundestag Stenographische Berichte, 46,* 7055.

6. The Hannover debate was a tactical exercise. Two years later the same leaders were to emphasize a maximum of restraint concerning independent Western European atomic weapons.

7. See, e.g., Fritz Erler in the foreign policy debate of October 12, 1962, in *Bundestag Stenographische Berichte, 51,* 1773–80.

rank order of tasks to be solved, and of methods and accents thus becomes ever so much more the content of opinion formation." [8] This statement sees the reduction of opposition to its purely competitive elements as both necessary and desirable.

The basic factors in this change of political style, which have operated in most advanced industrial societies, have in recent years been discussed extensively.[9] They may be summarized as follows: the modern welfare state can now provide solutions to problems of many social groups without in this process worsening the situation of competing social groups. This weakens the old clashes of immediate interests and converts them into mere conflicts of priority in the time sequence of satisfactions. This has freed political parties of the necessity of concentrating their electioneering efforts on specific groups while antagonizing others. It allows them now to compete simultaneously for the electoral allegiance of a great variety of social strata. This situation allows their policies to be determined by tactical requirements of the moment, relegating ideologically determined long-range goals to a remote corner.

Foreign policy considerations work in the same direction. An opposition party may tactically exploit unpopular government decisions, especially those whose full meaning is slow to unfold. But first, such tactical advantage is balanced by the authority and prestige which the conduct of foreign policy bestows on the responsible statesman. Secondly, the interstitial changes which an opposition party operating within a framework of national consensus may propose are either too technical and complex or too vague and general to have an appreciable impact on the voter's attitude. By the same token, the revolutionary social implications of technological progress—the threat of mass unemployment—are cushioned by major power competition with the corresponding armament efforts of the big and medium-sized powers. Such "prophylactic" expenditures prevent the pressures on major parties both from the outside and from within their own ranks for new and radical solutions of major foreign and domestic problems. They allow them to avoid raising the more important problems of our time (threat of universal atomic destruction, dispropor-

8. Willy Brandt, *Plaidoyer für die Zukunft* (Frankfurt, Europaisch Verlags Anstalt, 1961), p. 17.

9. See, for an early succinct statement, Herbert Tingsten, "Stability and Vitality in Swedish Democracy," in *Political Quarterly*, 26 (1955), 140–51; for my own views, see "The Waning of Opposition in Parliamentary Regimes," in *Social Research* (Summer 1957), pp. 128–56, reprinted in John W. Wahlke and Heinz E. Eulau, *Legislative Behavior* (Glencoe, Free Press, 1960). Most recently the point has been taken up in considerable detail in Manfred Friedrich, *Opposition ohne Alternative* (Cologne, Verlag Wissenschaft und Politik, 1962), and with an added request for a revision of political style in "Politik ohne Alternative? Zur Profilneurose der Parteien," in *Neue Zuercher Zeitung*, April 21, 1963, p. 7. See also the articles by Karl Dietrich Bracher and Seymour Martin Lipset in "A New Europe?" *Daedalus, 93*, No. 1 (Winter 1964).

tion between the living standards and the expectations of advanced and former colonial countries, impact of technological change on social and economic structure of advanced nations), or, to the extent they cannot be disregarded, to handle them in vague, carefully modulated and, above all, noncontroversial ways, thus barring them from the field of national party competition. Major interparty differences lose their raison d'être when overriding technological, international, and military problems are not debated among the parties.

In modern industrial societies, the parties loyal to the regime in addition carry on a certain amount of competition with each other. The wider and more diversified the appeal they try to make, the greater their competition; the more they restrict their appeals to specific social groups, the less their competition. If the potential clientele is as broad as the electorate, there will be a more concerted effort than if it is known in advance that the structure and goals of the organization militate against reaching more than a regional, religious, or occupational segment. But as long as comparative electoral standing in the population is by common consent a yardstick for allocating spheres of political influence, some competition has to go on. The verdict may not actually be related to the performance of the competitors, as the electoral outcome is likely to depend mainly on the voters' reactions to events outside the control of the political actors. But political convention has sanctioned this yardstick in preference to more complicated and less clear-cut ones.

Now in a figurative sense this competition involves some element of opposition, if for no other reason than that the party representatives take their places on opposite sides of the moderator in their TV contests. To what degree their competition involves an actual element of opposition in the sense of our definition—sponsoring differential goals in one or the other major field of political contention—is a different question. Different historical backgrounds, traditions, and ideologies and varying objectives of their leaders and their clienteles may lead to variations in emphasis in the vague proposals on how to face tomorrow's still undecipherable reality. At any rate, opposition and competition timetables do not necessarily jibe. The more closely the dates of elections correspond to a prearranged constitutional schedule, the less the likelihood that interparty competitive pressures will coincide with situations crying out for alternative political solutions. The candidates' fights may be more in the nature of a collision between people obliged to squeeze through the same narrow thoroughfare to punch the clock before 8:45.

Competition and opposition are related techniques for obtaining political power. Competition performs a sort of selection among those eager to arrive, unless the candidates take their precautions. They may come near to distributing the prizes beforehand by a combined operation, depriving the public of the essence, though not the fun, of its role of selection. An element of opposition makes a collusive agreement less likely. Goal differentiation may transcend the mere accumulation of personal, organizational, or social-status defense positions.

In democratic politics competition and opposition easily intertwine. Political practitioners may shuffle back and forth between competing and coalescing, refurbishing traditional goals to look like new ones and putting up new signposts while trying to minimize the shock of goal displacement.

To these general reasons for the waning of opposition in advanced industrial societies should be added at least one German phenomenon unknown to any other European nation—the imposed division of the country into two parts. There is the all-pervasive fact that what used to be the Communist opposition of principle has now become a hostile state organization, which is master of a considerable part of Germany's former territory. From the German Democratic Republic's offices flows an uninterrupted stream of criticism—always prejudiced, often inane, and on rare occasions revealing—of West German institutions, policies, and personalities. This criticism is coupled with attempts to exploit every false step of the West German antagonists both in Germany and the world at large, but especially to set the West German population against its political establishment. The reaction in West Germany has been to play down divisive elements and internal criticism and to look with suspicion on any type of criticism which is parallel with, even if organizationally independent of, that coming from East Germany. The mere fact of the existence of two mutually exclusive regimes transforms any opposition into opposition between the two regimes, emptying strictly domestic conflict of much of its substance and meaning.

This overriding conflict has had an abiding effect on the internal structure of the SPD. Both Communist foes and domestic competitors of the SPD, each for their own propaganda reasons, like to point out the common root of Communism and Social Democracy in nineteenth-century Marxism. Naturally, then, the SPD seeks in thought and action to make clear its radical departure from these suspect origins, even if this leads to the opposite result of making it look nearly indistinguishable from its main domestic competitor, the CDU. The SPD endeavors to eliminate the picture of the political party as a community of true believers.[10] It substitutes the image of an association of people who have banded to-

10. The Cologne 1962 SPD party convention was presented with a motion (55–56) asking it to abandon the habitual form of greeting, "Comrade" (*Genosse*), and substitute "party-friend" (Protokoll, pp. 466, 648). This motion might have arisen from the acute embarrassment caused the party when the late Chairman Erich Ollenhauer was not firm enough in his response to Khrushchev, who, upon meeting Ollenhauer said, "We call each other 'comrade,' don't we?" While the motion was tabled without discussion, it seems symptomatic that the issue was raised.

gether for the pursuit of goals lying exclusively in the political field and left themselves complete freedom in all other fields. This development, officially emphasized at all times, is in line with the disappearance of intra-party debate. As long as alternatives to official policy persisted, internal party discussion and the democratic party structure played a significant role in policy elaboration. This party democracy was safeguarded not only by tradition, but by the realities of the political process. Under Weimar, many voters shifted back and forth between an extreme party, such as the Communists, and a party which worked within the constitutional frame-work, such as the SPD, each of which promised satisfaction of partly identical claims. (The same situation prevailed between the German Nationalist Party and the National Socialist Party.) The very possibility of such a switch gave the internal party opposition some leverage in com-batting the official party line. The demise of the Radical Left has thus become one element in the change of the internal style of the SPD. There are scarcely any remnants of such internal opposition left.[11]

Another element is the nature of present discontent and ensuing internal party discussion. Discontent now does not lie principally within the socio-economic sphere; no crying needs of important segments of the popula-tion clamor for immediate action. Discontent revolves around more abstract problems of foreign policy and German unity. These generate a flood of professional and subprofessional comment, but neither heat nor popular pressure for immediate solution. This situation allows the party executive to ride roughshod over deviationists—mostly violators of reso-lutions which declare participation in other organizational activities, such as anti-atomic bomb marchers or support of left-wing student organiza-tions, incompatible with party membership—and to carry out swift policy shifts with a minimum of intraparty fuss and friction.

The reduction of the opposition to its competitive element does not determine whether such competition will emphasize electoral or bargain-ing elements. Electoral and bargaining tactics are not mutually exclusive but the two opposite poles of a continuum. Bargaining strength will, to a degree varying with the democratic propensities of a given polity, be underpinned by electoral success; on the other hand, electoral tactics may be modulated by interest in striking political bargains.

The SPD, exactly like its Austrian sister party, only so far less success-fully, has laid more stress on bargaining than on electoral tactics. This may be due simply to a lack of self-confidence evidenced by its still holding on to a slightly modified system of proportional representation.

11. Some of these problems have been perspicaciously treated by a meanwhile ejected academic representative of the intra-SPD party minority, Wolfgang Aben-droth: *Aufstieg und Krise der deutschen Sozialdemokratie* (Frankfurt, 1964), pp. 50 ff., and "Innerparteiliche und Innerverbandliche Demokratie als Voraussetzung der politischen Demokratie," in *Politische Viertel-Jahresschrift*, 5, No. 3 (1964), 307–38.

While PR makes it more difficult for the party to hope ever to obtain a clear-cut majority, it does serve as a guarantee against electoral reverses taking a catastrophic turn. However, its conversion into a catch-all popular party organization has produced some second thoughts in SPD ranks on this point. During the December 1962 coalition negotiations the SPD turned down tentative advances by the CDU in the direction of adopting a straight majority electoral system. Yet the feeling of having successfully engineered the transition to a multiclass organization is making the SPD slightly more hospitable to the idea of a majority system as perhaps an additional, though by no means exclusive, approach toward gaining governmental positions.

The importance of the election system as a factor influencing the preference for electoral versus bargaining tactics should not be overrated. The political style of a country's elite may be equally if not more significant. Unlike the British situation, the fate of a German politician is influenced only mildly by his party's ability to obtain a majority or a plurality at election time. Due to the ways of access to politics in Germany, neither his livelihood nor his social standing will depend on the outcome of the electoral battle. Some major and middle-level politicians, irrespective of whether they want to escape the frustration of the intra-party politics of the CDU or the dampening of their ambitions through the SPD's prolonged failure to gain federal office, have a good chance to find berths with financial and status rewards in the top echelons of the state governments. The switch will allow them still to share some of the political limelight and perhaps make a comeback on the federal level. More important, political personnel on the intermediate level more often than not has entered Parliament as major officeholders of semi-autonomous public or private organizations (cities, counties, employer or trade union groups, agricultural associations, etc.); in other instances they may have status as civil servants or judges. In a handful of cases their party's hold on the reins of the federal government may give such men a chance at federal office. Neither their professional standing nor their financial security depend upon such preferment. In view of the relatively limited number of top political officeholders on the federal level (about 20) and the slow turnover in Cabinet jobs, such careers would anyhow be rare. Major federal political office is at the same time only a mildly attractive prize in a country which provides for its professional, intellectual, and civic elite many comfortable berths requiring less exertion and furnishing sufficient pay and security. Hankering for the spoils of government by impatient politicians is not a major element in political party life, nor does it force what one may call an electoral style on political competition.

A major element in the prevalence of bargaining-type politics is the country's federal structure. From the outset no single party has ever been able to dominate all state governments. Consequently the federal and state administrations must be prepared to work with each other on a close and continuous basis in all matters pertaining to finance, legislation, and administration irrespective of the particular administration's political complexion. Even if the effect of election victories—never spectacular under proportional systems—were not diffused by the staggering of the dates of the federal and state elections, the permanency of different interest constellations as between the states and the federal government deprives the party label of much of its meaning. Any federal government must periodically try cajoling the states into abandoning part of their constitutionally sanctioned hold over income and corporation taxes. Conversely, any state wants to keep maximum administrative and financial powers against the expanding claims of both the federal intruder and the formally subordinate cities and counties. This situation puts a constant premium on bargaining tactics.

Such conflicts are in most cases handled through purely bureaucratic channels. While the professional skill and experience of one or the other politician or administrator-politician may be decisive for the outcome of such a bargain, such activity has low political visibility and little value for electoral debates. The parties function as one element, and not necessarily the most important one, in an interbureaucratic equilibrium in which central, state and, local bureaucracies all play their roles.[12] As a rule state politics and even state–federal relations are crowded out of voters' minds at the time of state elections by issues or sentiments of a more general nature. This makes it easy for all participants in the political game to keep many subjects exclusively within bureaucratic channels. In cases of patent inability to reach an agreement, the terms of the federal–state bargain may be redefined [13] by a *deus ex machina* decision of the Constitutional Court. Electoral expectations or results figure only at infrequent intervals as determinants of action in this wide area of financial and administrative policy.

Another, and final, point on the decline of the opposition concerns the popular understanding of the concepts of party and state. The Bonn establishment was designed as an antidote to an adventurous and disorderly one-party government. In this establishment Adenauer himself— and this is part of his success story—embodied both the pragmatic virtues

12. Related viewpoints might be found in Edward L. Pinney, *Federalism, Bureaucracy and Party Politics in Western Germany: The Role of the Bundesrat* (Chapel Hill, University of North Carolina Press, 1963).

13. As happened in the 1962 television controversy, when a number of Land governments successfully sued the federal government for its attempt to put up a federal television station with privately financed programs. See *Entscheidungen des Bundesverfassungsgerichts, 12* (1962), 205.

of an interest-compromise-oriented party politician and the traditional type of state authority, functioning above and beyond the day-to-day struggles and firmly directed toward national goals.

Thus there have been two political images operative in German minds. The one perceives the turning of the German political parties from ideologically oriented gatherings of loyal adherents into bureaucratic machines soliciting individual votes and the assistance or benevolent neutrality of interest congeries. The party here is a machine for receiving and sorting out claims on the state; it is thus one more instance, belated but significant, of the turn of Germany into a Western-style business society. The party that performs these functions of processing claims most efficiently is then rewarded with office by a perspicacious electorate.

The competing image of the state as an objective value structure above and beyond all interest organizations and all parties has not disappeared, however. It is vivid not only as a somewhat idealized description of their own social functions among bureaucrats and members of the academic profession, but among the population at large. The near-general acceptance of the welfare state—in spite of the official German trappings of the so-called "social market economy"—involves a community obligation to take care of the citizens' minimum needs. This mental climate reinforces already existing inclinations to stress administrative continuity behind the gyrations of the players on the political scene. It is more than likely that the expectation of orderly and continuous government performance was held against the Adenauer regime, once the prolonged uncertainties and incessant rivalries of the succession crisis had become public knowledge.

The parties themselves are by no means averse to looking on their own role in administrative-bureaucratic terms rather than in competitive-electoral terms.[14] To some extent this tendency rests on apparent or real

14. Here is an example of bureaucratic-type state authority in the practices of what, in federal terms, is still the "opposition" party. The Socialist majority of the Diet of the city-state of Bremen in December 1957 passed a bill referring differences between a legally instituted personnel representation and the state government over personnel policies, including appointments and dismissals of less than top-ranking state officials, to an arbitration board. The board was to be manned by representatives of both state employees and the state government, and the decisive vote would lie with the chairman, the Social Democratic President of the City Assembly. The state government, also headed by a perennial Social Democratic Lord Mayor, unwilling to tolerate such diminution of state authority, first took its grievance to the state Constitutional Court. After having narrowly lost the case in the Bremen jurisdiction, it resorted to the federal Constitutional Court, which promptly vindicated its position and voided the law. (*Entscheidungen des Bundesverfassungsgerichts, 9* [1959], 268.)

Nobody will be astonished that a German Constitutional Court manned by people with judicial, bureaucratic, and university professors' backgrounds would look with jaundiced eyes at an attempt to treat the state as an employer exactly on the same level as any other party to a collective contract. The court would see in such a law necessities of relations between the Federal Republic and East Germany, which, e.g., has led Federal Republic jurisprudence to assimilate party documents and papers to state secrets. This tendency also appears in the patterns of party financing, which recently has been shifting from exclusive reliance on membership fees (mainly in the SPD) and business contributions (mainly in the CDU and Free Democratic Party, or FDP) to federal treasury financing. At present the federal government distributes 38 million DM a year to the parties mainly according to the electoral strength of the federal party organizations.[15]

It is only logical that under such circumstances the SPD visualizes the goal of interparty competition more as that of universalizing bargaining practices than removing the stronger competitor from office.[16] That goal

---

only the possibility of diminishing state authority beyond the critical point rather than visualizing the potentiality that a compromise effected by a strategic person with a position midway between the interest groups and the formal state authority could maintain the uninterrupted functioning of public services. What is revealing, however, is that a socialist-led state administration felt an irresistible urge to go to such pains to teach its own majority the sanctity of the principle that state authority transcends groups claims.

15. As the law stands now 20 per cent of the total sum is distributed in equal shares to the CDU, Christian Social Union (CSU), FDP, and SPD; the other 80 per cent is allocated to the various parties according to the number of seats they hold in the Bundestag, which presently nets the SPD slightly over 13 million DM. The total election outlay for the 1961 Bundestag election may have come to 70 to 80 million DM. See Ulrich Dübber, *Parteifinanzierung in Deutschland 1962* (Cologne, Westdeutscher Verlag, 1962) and Ulrich Dübber and Gerard Braunthal, "West Germany" in *Comparative Political Finance*, ed. R. Rose and A. J. Heidenheimer (*Journal of Politics*, 1963). However, under a three-party agreement concluded in January 1965 *central* expenditures for the 1965 elections will be both supervised and kept to a prearranged maximum level of 16.5 million DM for the CDU-CSU and 15 million DM for each of the other two parties. The SPD has protested the increasing reliance on state financing for political organizations—more favorable to the CDU and FDP with low membership receipts than to the SPD which in 1963 received 14 million DM in membership fees. It has therefore been able to spend part of the federal bonanza, which is augmented by various similar outlays in the individual states, for educational rather than for straight political purposes. The whole institution of official party finance underlines the degree to which German parties turn increasingly into quasi-official machines.

16. Recently Wolfgang Kralewski and Karlheinz Neunreither (in *Oppositionelles Verhalten im ersten Deutschen Bundestag, 1949–1953* [Cologne-Opladen, Westdeutscher Verlag, 1963]) have studied in detail SPD participation in federal legislation during the first legislative period. We reprint part of an instructive tabulation which shows how many bills, at the time of the final vote, were passed against SPD opposition. The percentage relates to the number of total statutes passed in the respective fields during the first legislature (page 92):

Budget—78.9%   Internal affairs, police, culture, etc.—14.8%
Foreign affairs—55%   Labor, social legislation—11.8%
Agriculture—19.4%   Economics—7.4%
Finance—15.4%

In evaluating these percentages it has to be taken into consideration that SPD rejection of the budgets of most individual ministries is a pure matter of form, indiis in accord with popular ideas. An early 1963 poll indicated that a majority of those expressing an opinion considered a coalition of the two major parties, CDU and SPD, "a favorable solution in the interest of the Federal Republic." [17] What does this approval mean? As the poll did not ask how many people would have preferred clear-cut majority party rule, its meaning is open to doubt. But in conjunction with other inquiries (see Appendix 7.1) it may signify some popular knowledge of the declining level of interparty controversy as well as some popular groping for orderly and steady government performance under conditions of maximal popular consent. A broad interparty compact may fulfill the same psychological function as the objective and independent state power for which people still hanker. Thus the enlarging of case-to-case, interstitial, and administrative bargains to the level of permanent political bargaining in the form of a major party coalition government might seem just a question of time.[18] Before it happens, however, the CDU, which still has a national plurality, has to be convinced that such a coalition would be both desirable and profitable for it.

The circle is nearly complete: the SPD now shuns the very idea of an opposition role, and multiplies both demands and offers of unconditional participation. All the government can do to protect itself from this impetuous urging is curtly to recall that no way exists to force the government to accept the SPD as a partner.[19] Such rebuffs only make the

---

cating the official opposition status of the party. The rather substantial number of rejections in the foreign policy field is, as explained in our text, a matter of the past. The removal of foreign policy from the field of party politics, so much desired by the authors (pp. 93, 99) has long since taken place. On the other end of the scale we find the field of economics indicating that most reconstruction legislation, even at the height of SPD opposition under the Schumacher regime, was noncontroversial from the outset or mutually satisfactory compromises had been obtained before the final vote. Interestingly enough the book, which contains among other things exhaustive studies of the legislative process in regard to three particular subject matters (boundary police bill, bill protecting youth against obscene literature, and the Constitution Court bill), comes to the conclusion that the effectiveness of the opposition in the legislative process has depended mainly on the varying quality of the opposition experts in the respective committees (p. 213). The substance of the policy differences seems to have played a much smaller role.

17. *Emnidinformationen*, No. 13 (1963) of March 25, 1963, p. 2, lists 36 per cent favoring an SPD-CDU coalition, 23 per cent favoring a CDU-FDP coalition, 9 per cent an SPD-FDP coalition, with 32 per cent uttering no clear-cut preference.

18. The details of the German variants of the demise of political opposition have recently been described, though with some ideological somersaults, in Waldemar Besson, "Regierung und Opposition in der deutschen Politik," in *Politische Vierteljahresschrift*, *3* (September 1962) 224–41.

19. See the explanation of the CDU speaker, Von Brentano, in the debate on the government declaration of December 6, 1961, *Bundestag Stenographische Berichte*, *50*, (1961) 65–73. The argument proffered by the same speaker that if the SPD were to join the government no controller would exist seems a bit tortured. The SPD had already on its own volition abandoned any thought of exercising a control function.

SPD strategists redouble their efforts to minimize their differences with the government and follow what is now commonly referred to as the "embracement" strategy. SPD energies are all bent to enhancing the chances for a permanent cut-in on the governmental organization.[20]

Competition with the goal of participation in the competitor's enterprise can make only marginal allowance for criticism. Conduct in Parliament must be modulated to express identity of thought patterns in all major affairs, but allow enough for small-scale needling to keep the advisability of joining forces steadily before the competitor. It may not be easy to keep about 200 M.P.'s always in line with the tactical requirements of the hour. Yet following both the listless general debates and the mass of trivia which the backbenchers pour out during oral questioning time impresses one with the lack of controversial issues or their studied avoidance. At question time there is universal eagerness to plead local and special interest group causes dear to the individual member or, at times, to prove one's loyalty and patriotic eagerness, to publicize German concerns and grievances throughout the world. The oral question remains by and large in the realm of the backbencher's title to recognition; it becomes an auxiliary weapon for political criticism only on special occasions.

One such rare flareup happened in 1962 when the question period was utilized for ventilating the *Spiegel* affair.[21] But one must immediately note the self-imposed tactical restrictions. Neither at that time nor in its written interrogatories submitted to the federal government did the SPD venture to raise the problem of freedom of critical opinion versus treason legislation which has aroused public concern. Instead it sought, successfully, to trip Minister of Defense Franz Josef Strauss on his inconsistent and incomplete statements and his unwarranted assumption of powers outside his own jurisdiction. The CDU's tactical retort—publicizing SPD members' irregularities in handling army committee material—was apparently sufficient to restrain the SPD from taking major parliamentary initiatives. Thus the SPD tacitly agreed to have the whole problem settled in the political no-man's-land where the judicial branch tries to figure out how to handle pernicious political dissent. It remains to be seen to what extent the quite recently introduced "currents events hour," during which members may speak extemporaneously on recent events for five minutes up to

20. All arguments for cooperative government by all parties may be found in endless variation in W. Brandt's keynote speech at the Cologne 1962 party convention. *Protokoll*, pp. 56–86; see also the characteristic discussion "Es hätte auch Schlimmer werden können" between party boss H. Wehner and some *Spiegel* editors in *Der Spiegel*, September 25, 1963.

21. Bundestag session of November 7, 8, and 9, 1962. *Bundestag Stenographische Berichte*, pp. 1949–2091; see also Otto Kirchheimer and Constantine Menges, "The Spiegel Case," in *Politics in Europe*, ed. G. M. Carter and E. F. Weston (New York, Harcourt Brace, 1965)

a total of one hour, will relieve the boredom pervading the entire institution.[22]

This, then, is a society which started out to practice party government and at first attempted to make it work within the grooves of the government–opposition system. The trappings of party government are there. They may be used to establish government formulas ranging from government by the strongest party alone, via interstitial stages of coalition between a major party and satellite parties, to the so far unrealized aim of the SPD—an Austrian-type combined operation of the two great parties. Whatever the particular form of party government, both those forces operating everywhere in advanced industrial societies and those forces arising out of the specific contemporary German situation have led to the steady erosion of goal-oriented opposition. What remains is a certain level of interparty competition, whose edges are blunted by all-pervasive bargaining carried through on a bureaucratic rather than a political level. Permanent institutionalization of such a bargaining style on the political level would mean an interesting attempt to stabilize political relations. In the last analysis such an endeavor at a watertight political cartel can be successful only if every outside or potential competitor is eliminated.

This raises the question: To what extent does the German political system allow for legal opposition outside parliamentary and party channels? The question coincides with the problem of constitutional limitations on extraparliamentary opposition. The Bonn Basic Law has privileged the parties as organizations that take part in the creation of the political will. It has penalized parties that want to impede the working of the free democratic order or endanger the existence of the Federal Republic. It allows the Constitutional Court (Art. 21, para. 2) to ban them altogether. The same rule holds for any other organization whose activity is in contradiction with "the Basic Law, the constitutional order or the idea of peaceful understanding between nations" (Art. 9, para. 2). With this exception, so far applied to the Socialist Reich Party and the Communist Party, and that of the impractical rule of Article 18, allowing an individual to be divested under the same conditions of some specifically mentioned basic rights, extraparliamentary opposition is legal. It is fully protected by the freedom of conscience, freedom of opinion-forming, and freedom of association provisions (Arts. 4, para. 1, Art. 5, para. 1, and Art. 8) of the Basic Law. If the Basic Law narrows freedom of opinion by adducing the limitations of the general laws,[23] "those which protect youth and personal

22. The first current events discussion of February 10, 1965, is reported in *Das Parlament*, February 17, 1965, together with the introductory remarks of Bundestag Vice-President Carlo Schmid.

23. According to the interpretation of the Constitutional Court, these "general laws" have to be interpreted from the "value-creating impact of the free democratic order and therefore themselves be restricted again in their effectiveness as limits on

honor" (Art. 5, para. 2), this does not create any government prerogative for supervising questions of political style.[24]

Boundary-line cases may, as they do in the United States, involve weighing priorities between freedom of opinion and protection of the interests of either the individual or of state security. This task devolves in the main on a federal Constitutional Court, inclining in a number of situations toward preferred freedom doctrines. Beyond such areas of possible conflict and choice there exists a guaranteed area for legal, yet extraparliamentary, opposition. The boundary-line cases, however, demonstrate that there may exist a considerable gap between constitutionally sanctioned legal extra-parliamentary opposition and widespread public assumptions as to the legitimacy of such extraparliamentary opposition. Due to the increasing desiccation of parliamentary opposition, this question of the boundary lines of legitimate opposition has increased in importance. There is no doubt that uninvited suggestions, memoranda, and public discussion policy statements, emanating from academic or loosely church-connected groupings, on atomic policy, foreign affairs, inter-German policy, or social policy problems are considered appropriate even though they may often be considered unwelcome and inopportune in official circles. More and more general policy debates are taking place these days within the framework of such extraparliamentary groups rather than within political party organizations. Beyond this arena there is a grey zone of doubt.

There exists some tendency to look at systematic deviationism from official policies, especially in the field of East–West or inter-German relations, as illegitimate. This does not always involve condemnation of an advanced or deviant viewpoint, but simply a not uncommon conviction that such difficult problems should be handled by experts officially selected for the purpose. Consequently a television producer or a deviant press organ, like *Der Spiegel*, which does not observe these invisible boundaries may run into hostility. To what extent such hostility can be translated into action depends both on the legal situation and on community support for the attacked person or institution. The deviant producer's show may be put off the air by the public broadcasting corporation, as recently happened in the Panorama case. Putting legal impediments in the way of *Der Spiegel*, as the authorities found out too late, is much more involved and difficult. On the other hand, if it can be alleged with some degree of plausibility that the person or group involved

---

the basic right" (of free opinion formation). *Entscheidungen des Bundesverfassungsgerichts,* 7 (1957), 198, 208, and Professor H. Ehmke in his arguments in support of the constitutional complaint of the Spiegel Publishing Company filed with the federal Constitutional Court on May 1, 1963, pp. 66–79 (Verfassungsbeschwerde 1 BvR586/62 privately printed, Hamburg, 1963).

24. See A. Hamann, "Das Recht auf Opposition und seine Geltung im ausserparliamentarischen Bereich" in *Politische Vierteljahresschrift,* 3 (September 1962), 241, 255.

not only wants to exercise unhealthy influence on the general opinion-forming process but also strays into the field of political organization proper, both the established competitors—the parliamentary parties and the administrative organs of the state—will scan the records of the new-comers with magnifying glasses to discover improper motivations and unconstitutional connections. While deviant opinion is to some degree tolerated, legitimacy is not easily granted to movements and parties moving outside recognized channels in a country where the devastating memories of the '20s and '30s are still vividly in the minds of the older generation and where present conditions do anything but invite radical reorientation. Legality and legitimacy are not altogether identical in the German order of things. But prevalent legitimacy notions have a tendency to narrow down the radius of action left for legal, but extraparliamentary, opposition.[25]

25. The best introduction to this vast theme may be found in *Bestandsaufnahme Eine Deutchse Bilanz,* ed. H. W. Richter (Munich, Kurt Desch Verlag, 1961). For the most typical recent case see R. Schmid, "Auf dem Weg zum Überwachungsstaat" in *Die Zeit,* March 19, 1965, p. 3.

8

AUSTRIA:
THE POOLING OF OPPOSITION

Frederick C. Engelmann

The Prerepublican Background

Prior to 1889, the Austrian half of the Austro-Hungarian monarchy had neither a politically organized urban proletariat, nor widespread suffrage, nor responsible government. The Emperor had granted basic political freedoms in the 1860s, and in 1873 an unrepresentative Parliament was created, to which deputies were sent by landowners, burghers, chambers of commerce, and villagers. The Emperor continued to reign quasi-absolutely through ministers responsible to himself. The strongest political group was the German Liberals, who governed until 1879; after that the Emperor preferred to trust the advice of elements of the German and Polish nobility, the high clergy, and the high bureaucracy. The Germans formed only one-third of the population of "their" half of the monarchy, and the Emperor chose to give governmental responsibility to those who were not as intent on promoting a German hegemony as were the Liberals. The regime was not truly multinational, however, as the interests of Czechs, southern Slavs, and Ukrainians met with relative neglect. After 1879 the German Liberals formed the principal opposition. Soon they split into several groups, ranging from aristocrats to moderately progressive intellectuals (many of them assimilated Jews). Because of these splits, liberalism disintegrated organizationally and survived as an attitude rather than as a movement. Some former Liberals formed a German nationalist movement, which included even racist anti-Semites.

Organized legal opposition in Austria[1] dates from 1889. In that year, the Social Democratic and Christian Social parties were founded. The former was a typical party of the urban proletariat; the latter began as a movement of small tradesmen and soon developed into a party of the lesser non-class-conscious population, especially the smaller peasantry. Between them, these parties preempted the support of the not as yet enfranchised elements of the German-speaking population. In 1896 about

---

1. For the period prior to 1918, the term Austria denotes the western half of the Austro-Hungarian monarchy.

one-fifth of the parliamentary seats were given to representatives elected by universal suffrage, and a few Social Democrats and Christian Socials entered the Parliament. The Christian Socials achieved a notable success one year later—the capture of Vienna's municipal government.

In 1907 the Emperor granted universal and equal manhood suffrage, and the Social Democratic and Christian Social parties became the leading German-speaking parties. The Christian Socials formed the strongest single parliamentary party in the ensuing election. The next election (1911) brought a Social Democratic plurality. But because of the absence of responsible government neither party became an influential opposition. Obstructive parliamentary tactics, originally used by German radicals against Czechs, became the order of the day as the nationalities struggle drowned out any normal government–opposition dialogue. During these years, the Emperor did most of his ruling by decree, and Parliament became increasingly impotent. The monarchy disintegrated under the impact of the First World War, but the two young German mass parties—Christian Socials and Social Democrats—maintained their identity and were ready to play their roles in the future small republic of German-Austria.

The First Republic—Institutions, Parties, Cleavages, and Opposition

The establishment of the First Republic in 1918 brought representative government with a responsible executive to Austria. Only from this point on did Austria have true parliamentary opposition—an opposition legitimately capable of replacing the government. While the First Republic lasted from 1918 to 1938, the period of normal operation of opposition extended only from 1920 to 1933. From 1918 to 1920, the two major parties, Christian Socials and Social Democrats, formed a government coalition. The last five years of the First Republic were taken up by the Patriotic Front [2] dictatorship of Dollfuss and Schuschnigg.

German-Austria—the lands that were, according to Clemenceau, "left over" once the other nationalities had carved their states out of the Habsburg monarchy—adopted a constitution in 1920. There was responsible government, with the Cabinet elected by the Parliament, and a weak President. Amendment in 1929 provided for a strong President elected by popular vote (the first actual popular election took place only in 1951), who appoints the Chancellor and his government, who in turn must enjoy the confidence of the Parliament.

The country was left with its prewar political forces. The major ones, in terms of electoral support, were the Christian Socials and the Social Democrats. The German Liberals and Nationals, both weak ever since the introduction of universal suffrage, were further handicapped by the

2. The Patriotic Front consisted of Christian Socials, Catholic and fascist paramilitary organizations, and assorted anti-socialist elements.

severing of their heartland, the Sudeten areas, from German-Austria. They survived in two rather weak political organizations: the largely urban petit-bourgeois Pan-German People's Party, and the anticlerical Agrarian League. The only other political group, the Communists, never even achieved parliamentary representation in the First Republic. Their weakness was due to the organizational and ideological efforts of the Social Democrats, who successfully prevented the political splitting of the workers that took place nearly everywhere else.

The three major groupings—clerical-Catholic,[3] Marxist-socialist, and Liberal-National, true representatives of Almond's three subcultures [4]—were more than political organizations. They were veritable subcultures, with their own ideologies, interest groupings, and manifold ancillary party organizations. The strong involvement in the politics of these subcultures of hundreds of thousands of individuals made for inflexible voting behavior, resulting in a static electoral picture. The use of paramilitary organizations by the groupings made particularly apt the Austrian term used to designate them: _Lager_ [5] (armed camp). Instead of giving their political energies to the young and frail state, Austrians squandered them on their respective _Lager,_ which provided spiritual guidance, economic representation, and avocational direction. The young state was, in fact, not wanted by most of its citizens. The Liberal-National _Lager_ was of course dedicated to union with Germany. Even many Social Democrats desired _Anschluss_ to the Weimar Republic; and postwar plebiscites indicated that some of the provinces with strong Christian Social majorities wanted it too. Many Austrians continued to feel that the state, proclaimed in 1918 to be part of Germany, was nothing but the product of a dictated peace settlement.

In 1919 and 1920 an attempt was made to make the weak state viable by having it governed jointly by its two main political groups. But Christian Socials and Social Democrats were too hostile to one another to permit this coalition to succeed. The Social Democrats, confident that some day they would be voted into power, unburdened themselves of governmental responsibility and went into opposition. Until the elimination of Parliament in 1933 they remained the principal opposition group.[6] Some Liberal and agrarian groups, mainly splinters, temporarily joined them in opposi-

3. During the First Republic, the Christian Social Party expanded its base, adding to Catholic artisans and shopkeepers larger business interests that cannot be called clerical.

4. Gabriel Almond, "Comparative Political Systems," _Journal of Politics, 18_ (1956), 391–409.

5. The first systematic discussion of the _Lager_ is contained in Adam Wandruszka, "Oesterreichs Politische Struktur," in Heinrich Benedikt, ed., _Geschichte der Republik Österreich_ (Vienna, Verlag für Geschichte und Politik, 1954), pp. 289–485.

6. See Appendix Table 8.1.

tion, but their presence did not at any time affect opposition strategy and tactics. The government was formed from 1921 to 1930 by the *Bürgerblock* (bourgeois bloc) consisting of the dominant Christian Socials and their allies, the Pan-Germans, and operating on the basis of an agreement entered into in 1921. Schisms in the bourgeois camp after 1930 reduced the government majority to one seat and strengthened those Christian Socials who eventually decided that the way to fight Hitler was to subdue the Social Democrats and abolish democracy.

The nature of Social Democratic opposition in the First Republic was democratic-structural.[7] The Social Democrats accepted the political institutions of representative democracy and the rules of free party competition—in fact they were the only party to do so consistently—but they were committed to bring about structural changes in the socioeconomic order. Some of these had been achieved prior to 1920. Tenants' protection had been granted by the Imperial government during the war, and the Social Democrats had utilized the short-lived coalition to place basic social security legislation on the statute books. In these fields, the main role of the opposition was to fight a holding operation, particularly against rent increases. The main policy achievement of the *Bürgerblock* government—currency stabilization through a deflationary loan from the League of Nations—met with heavy Social Democratic opposition throughout the period.

Much of the opposition of the Social Democrats was waged territorially. The city of Vienna, made a province early in the First Republic, had the first socialist government west of Russia, and the party made it a laboratory and showcase for socialist policies of welfare, housing, and taxation. These policies themselves formed the main, and certainly the most publicized, aspect of the Social Democrats' structural opposition. As policy objectives realized in Vienna, they were constantly before the Austrian voter as a set of policy alternatives.

Policy and territorial opposition was heavy enough; but its weight was increased by other factors. The Social Democrats integrated all of their opposition in their Austro-Marxist ideology, which took the place of religion with most Austrian workers. They also preempted political control of workers' economic representation: on the side of formalized policy advising through control of the Chamber of Labor, on the side of labor organization through control of the free trade unions. They achieved a degree of political organization unequaled in free parties through their

7. Charles A. Gulick, *Austria from Habsburg to Hitler* (Berkeley, University of California Press, 1948), is a monumental catalog of the nature and tactics of First Republic opposition (with a strong socialist bias). A concise summary of party warfare is contained in Mary MacDonald, *The Republic of Austria, 1918–34* (London, Oxford University Press, 1946), pp. 63–81.

system of cadres (*Vertrauensleute*). Finally they controlled the workers' leisure time by providing them with a full set of avocational organizations for everyone from cyclists to antialcoholics.

Throughout this period, opposition tactics were hard. Only twice did bargaining between opposition and government succeed. In 1927 education laws with mild social reforms, barely acceptable to the Social Democrats, were passed, and structural changes in the Constitution were agreed upon by both parties in 1929. The normal relationship between the parties was much less friendly. In Parliament the Social Democrats occasionally made use of walkouts or other obstructive tactics. Elections were fought with hard slogans. Some of the leaders felt that the party could hope to capture workers' votes only, but that victory would be theirs if it could capture virtually all of them.[8] A notable exception to class-based electoral tactics was the rent control issue; it appealed to many non-home-owners among the petit-bourgeois.

Outside Parliament, the Social Democratic opposition made use of a paramilitary organization, the Republican Defense League (Republikan-ischer Schutzbund). Born in the days of postwar free corps activities, the Defense League had the mission of protecting the Republic and the position of workers in the society. It was a useful counterweight to fascist groups (politically allied to the government) as long as it remained under the discipline of the party executive. But uncontrolled mob action after a typical class-justice situation (the acquittal of murderers of demonstrating workers in 1927) did irreparable damage to the Defense League's reputation among the uncommitted part of the population. The 1927 riots were the beginning of continuous paramilitary warfare between government and opposition. The rise of National Socialism after 1930 made this warfare three-cornered.

Hitler's rise to power united the Social Democrats in opposition to the *Anschluss* and made them staunch defenders of Austria's integrity. However, the Christian Socials, in facing the rising "brown" tide, turned not to them for aid, but to Mussolini. Exasperated by its one-vote majority in Parliament, and lacking a basic faith in democratic institutions, the government allowed itself to drift into the elimination of Parliament in March 1933. Dollfuss, the Christian Social Chancellor, subsequently founded the Patriotic Front and made clear that he was setting up a dictatorship. Terror activities of the tolerated *Heimwehr* (progovernment paramilitary organization) against the now outlawed Defense League led to resistance by the latter, bringing on the brief civil war of February 1934. The result was the "capture" of "red" Vienna and the outlawing of the Social Democratic Opposition. On May 1, 1934, a corporatist constitution was proclaimed,

8. Robert Danneberg, *Die Entwicklungsmöglichkeiten der Sozialdemokratie in Österreich* (Vienna, Verlag der Wiener Volksbuchhandlung, 1924).

and legal opposition, in fact any political organization outside the Patriotic Front, was at an end. Four years later the country itself ceased to exist, becoming a part of Hitler's *Reich*.

The Second Republic

INSTITUTIONS, PARTIES, CLEAVAGES   In 1945 the reconstituted Republic was governed initially by an antifascist concentration in which the People's Party (ÖVP), Socialists (SPÖ), and Communists were equally represented. There were no other legal parties, and therefore there was no legal opposition. The Constitution of 1920, with its 1929 amendments, was put in force once again. The country was divided into Russian, U.S., British, and French zones of occupation.[9] A free election, held in all zones, for a central parliament resulted in a parliamentary majority for the People's Party, a strong Socialist delegation, and only four Communist deputies. This election reduced the Communist government delegation to one member, who resigned in 1947. The government was left in the hands of the People's Party and Socialists, whose coalition is still in office.

Under this coalition the makeup of the government, and the representation of the two coalition parties within it, is decided in negotiations following each parliamentary election. Changes in the electoral picture in the elections of 1949, 1953, 1956, 1959, and 1962 have been slight.[10] Despite the fact that negotiations have become increasingly long (two months in 1959, four and one-half months in 1962–63), few portfolios have ever changed hands in these negotiations. The coalition operates on the basis of a coalition pact; these pacts are ratified by the two partners after each renegotiation of the coalition. The pacts of 1949 and 1953 were kept secret, though the latter has since been published. The pacts of 1956, 1959, and 1963 were made public. According to each of the pacts, decisions arrived at in the coalition committee (consisting of the top leaders of the two partners) are enacted by the unanimous vote of the parliamentary delegations of both partners. A complex clause of the pact of 1963 allowing some exceptions to this unanimity rule soon became the subject of controversy between the partners, but no legislation has been passed as yet by means of this clause. The *Proporz*—a system of two-party patronage exercised in proportion to the most recent election results—is used in government corporations and nationalized industries only. Within the regular departments of government, the party controlling the particular department has the major voice in bureaucratic appointments. The conventional stories according to which every government job in Austria is held by

9. An official at headquarters of one of the coalition parties emphasized to the writer that until the end of the occupation in 1955 much of the potential opposition energy was diverted into opposition to the occupation.
10. See Appendix Table 8.2.

three people—one "black," one "red," and one doing the work—are inaccurate.[11]

The coalition regime operates under the Constitution of 1920, as amended in 1929. Coalition pact and coalition committee (called "working committee" since 1963) are extraconstitutional institutions. The pact, with its provision for mandatory parliamentary support for bills on which the coalition committee agrees, has been attacked by leading constitutional authorities as contrary to the constitutional guarantee of the free exercise of the parliamentary mandate.[12] This particular issue, pitting the realities of the party state against a constitutional provision of dubious meaning, need not be resolved here; at any rate, the coalition practice cannot in fact be contested by any agency in a position to overrule the coalition committee.

Another provision of the Constitution however is of supreme importance in the operation of the coalition, and particularly in the exercise of intracoalition opposition (*Bereichsopposition*). This provision, Article 76, makes individual ministers responsible to Parliament. The authoritative interpretation of this provision, by both constitutional authorities and the Council of Ministers, has been that this individual responsibility imposes the unanimity rule on the Council of Ministers. On the policy-making side this means that a coalition government can act only on proposals cleared by the leaders of both coalition partners, i.e. the coalition committee. As regards opposition the interpretation means that either partner can render effective his opposition to policy proposals to the point of preventing their enactment. The requirement of unanimity prevents the coalition regime from adopting the Swiss model of decision-making by majority vote of the executive, also in use in the Austrian provinces.[13] Under this scheme, all or most parties are represented in the executive—in Switzerland by arrangement, in most Austrian provinces by right.

The parties of the Second Republic were fathered by the three *Lager* of the First Republic. The Liberal-National *Lager*, already weak in the First Republic and then bloated by National Socialism, is definitely of modest significance in the Second. Its party, the "Fourth Party" admitted by the Allies in 1949, was originally called League of Independents, and became known in 1955 as the Freedom Party. It not only lacks a common ideology, but, more importantly, the allegiance of a major interest group.

The coalition parties are of course the successors of the political representatives of the two major *Lager*. The chief reasons for continuation of the coalition beyond Austria's liberation from foreign occupation by the

11. John MacCormac, "The Improbable Coalition That Governs Austria," *Reporter*, January 23, 1958, pp. 33–37.
12. *Bundes-Verfassungsgesetz*, Art. 56.
13. Despite this constitutional difficulty, elements in the ÖVP favored the adoption of the provincial system on the federal level in 1963.

State Treaty of 1955 are (a) an inertia brought on by nearly two decades of multifaceted collaboration of the two parties and allied interests, and (b) the heritage of the *Lager* situation. The latter expresses itself in the fear of both subcultures of being governed by the other. This fear was—until 1962 at least—greater on the part of the Socialists who constituted the opposition *Lager* of the First Republic.

In the Second Republic, the subcultures have maintained their political as well as their socioeconomic bases. The Socialist Party was rebuilt quickly after 1945 and soon reached its First Republic membership strength. The organizational cadres have lost some verve, but they continue to exist; the ancillary organizations show less intensive activity, but they maintain their membership. The People's Party has a looser federal organization; yet its aggregate membership is as numerous as that of the Socialists. Such *dépolitisation* as has taken place, then, affects party life but not party membership. The latter maintains itself through spoils; there are on both sides *Proporz* jobs and *Proporz* franchises; in addition, membership in the Socialist Party is the easiest way to a municipal apartment.

The tie-up within each subculture among party, socioeconomic chambers, and interest groups reflects the rigidity of the First Republic nexus. The overwhelming majority of business and agriculture is in the camp of the ÖVP, and a very substantial majority of labor with the SPÖ. A system of compulsory membership in the chambers of commerce, agriculture, and labor, and partisan elections within all three of these chambers, gives conclusive evidence of the continued party-interest tie-up.[14] Among the voluntary interest organizations, the business and peasants' leagues of the ÖVP dominate in business and agriculture; on the labor side there is a suprapartisan Trade Union Congress, but all of the major unions, and therefore most Congress offices, are under Socialist control.

Ideological differences between the subcultures have subsided. In 1945 the church left politics. Clericalism has played a continually diminishing role in the People's Party. The Socialists found themselves after the war without their chief ideological element. In 1958 they adopted the largely de-ideologized Vienna program. Austrian society shows some of the conditions on which Kirchheimer bases his theory of the waning of structural differences,[15] and Austria is of course the home of Bednarik's shallow youths.[16] Yet despite all these developments, the two major subcultures remain socially and psychologically separated. *Lagermentalität* (*Lager* feeling and identification) persists. It has lost much of its philosophical basis, but retains its psychological reality; having lost much in ideology, it

14. See Appendix Table 8.3.
15. "The Waning of Opposition in Parliamentary Regimes," *Social Research, 24* (1957), 127–56. See also his chapter in this volume.
16. Karl Bednarik, *Der junge Arbeiter von heute* (Stuttgart, Gustav Kilpper Verlag, 1953).

yet remains as mentality.[17] Most individuals' identification with their party remains strong.[18] The mutual distrust engendered by *Lagermentalität* goes far in explaining the persistence of the coalition, as well as the continuing peculiar condition of opposition under the Second Republic. Paradoxically, the second major explanation for the persistence of the regime is the convenience that the collaboration, so well established in years of coalition practice, has for parties, chambers, and interest groups.

NATURE OF THE OPPOSITION   Legal opposition in the Second Republic dates from 1947, when the Communist Party left the government. The Communist Party has remained as an organized opposition party, never surpassing its initial strength and losing its parliamentary representation in the aftermath of the Hungarian Revolution. It continues as legal but rather ineffectual opposition, and its few remaining islands of support are some of the industrial plants that had been under Russian control prior to 1955.

In 1949 the Socialists, intent on breaking the parliamentary majority of the ÖVP, persuaded the Allies to license a fourth party, which they hoped would split the non-Socialist vote. The licensing coincided with the enfranchisement of one-half million minor Nazis, most of whom supported the new party initially. The fourth party is now in its second incarnation. Having been variously called League and Electoral League of Independents, it has been the Austrian Freedom Party since 1955.

While it is unable to transcend the national subculture, it must share it with the major parties. ÖVP and SPÖ, identified with postwar reconstruction and aided by the *Proporz*, have gained the allegiance of many nationalists. The Freedom Party has been interested more in the representation of interests excluded by the coalition than in opposing coalition policies. These excluded interests are varied. First of all, there are those

17. The writer is indebted to Juan J. Linz ("An Authoritarian Regime: Spain," paper delivered at the 1963 Annual Meeting of the American Political Science Association, New York City, pp. 9–11 and notes) for the suggestion of Theodor Geiger's distinction between ideology and mentality (*Die soziale Schichtung des deutschen Volkes*, Stuttgart, 1932, pp. 77–79). Linz quotes "Mentality is *subjektiver Geist* (even when collective), ideology is *objektiver Geist*. Mentality is intellectual attitude, ideology is intellectual content. Mentality is psychic predisposition, ideology is reflection, self-interpretation, mentality is previous, ideology later, mentality is formless, fluctuating—ideology however is firmly formed . . . Ideology is a concept of the sociology of culture, mentality is a concept of the study of social character."

18. In a 1962 poll of the Sozialwissenschaftliche Studiengesellschaft (Vienna), respondents were asked to identify the three policy positions to which they objected most strenuously. They were then asked to say what they would do if the party with which they identified were to adopt these three policy positions. 38 per cent of the Socialists questioned said they would vote for the SPÖ anyway, while 23 per cent said they would consider voting for a different party. These figures show nearly as much inflexibility as those obtained from Communist respondents (49 per cent would vote Communist anyway, 27 per cent would consider voting for a different party). People's Party voters showed more flexible attitudes (26 per cent would vote ÖVP anyway, 28 per cent would consider voting for a different party).

ex-Nazis who did not find a ready home in either of the major parties. There are also some academic groups, some minor groupings that are anticlerical as well as anti-Socialist, and some interests based on war events; the latter includes those people who were bombed out and not properly compensated and prisoners of war who returned years after the end of the war. While the party does show staying power, it has some similarities with the German Refugee Party (BHE): as the excluded interests become assimilated to the major parties, the Freedom Party has diminishing appeal. The lack of expandability of the Freedom Party's electorate can be seen when it is recognized that it steadily commands only a small vote in the face of the fact that voting for the Freedom Party is just about the only way in which an anticoalition vote could be cast by a non-Communist. A possibly expanded role open to the party under the slightly looser coalition pact of 1963 may enable it to help one partner to outvote the other on some issues in Parliament (as it actually did during the Habsburg crisis of that year), but it will hardly strengthen it as an opposition party.

Yet the Freedom Party does maintain a monopoly of parliamentary partisan opposition. Another party, the European Federalists, has been in evidence only in the parliamentary election of 1962 and the presidential election of 1963. The new party was launched by liberal intellectuals, a tiny group in Austria. It received only a minimal vote in 1962. The four per cent it gained in the presidential election of 1963 does not seem significant when it is realized that the European Federalist candidate was the only candidate not nominated by a coalition party.

More important than the opposition parties are elements of opposition to the coalition found either within the realm of the coalition parties themselves or at least close to one of them. Among these elements is, first, the so-called independent press. In addition to the so-called "boulevard" press we find included here two of Austria's major newspapers, the Vienna *Presse* and the *Salzburger Nachrichten*. Both of these papers occasionally flirt with the Freedom Party, but they consider themselves bourgeois papers and recognize the ÖVP as the major bourgeois party. They find fault, however, with the organizational leadership of the ÖVP, and with those elements in the ÖVP who give voice to their sympathy with the coalition regime.[19] The second anticoalition element within the general framework of the coalition is much of Austria's remaining private in-

19. The independent press has one continuous field day in opposing the coalition. Its main rival, the party press, is interested more in attacking the coalition partner than in upholding the cause of the coalition. The latter is done only in infrequent editorials in the *Wiener Zeitung*, the dry official gazette, and was done occasionally in the daily *Neues Österreich*, under suprapartisan management until 1963. On the other hand, the government is not generous toward this type of opposition where it controls the situation. When it took over operation of the radio from the occupation powers after the State Treaty, the first victim was the "*Watschenmann*," a freewheeling program of public criticism previously produced by the U.S. radio station.

dustry.[20] Industrial circles feel that in their representation both in the Business League of the ÖVP and in the Chamber of Commerce they are outnumbered by small business interests, which are generally friendly to the coalition. Much of private industry therefore, though its leaders are often identified with the ÖVP, will oppose the coalition regime, which it considers stifling to the development of large-scale free enterprise. Third and most important, there is the anticoalition wing of the ÖVP. This wing, which calls itself liberal or "reformist," is only partly opposed to the coalition. Most of the members insist only on major reforms in the mode of policy-making, hoping that a less rigid coalition will remove the Socialist veto over economic policies. It is linked closely with the industrial interests just mentioned and finds support also among originally anticlerical groups within the ÖVP. This wing is therefore particularly strong in the anti-clerical province of Styria. However, not everybody in the wing is anti-clerical; its chief exponent, Hermann Withalm, the ÖVP's general secretary, comes from the Catholic fraternity world. Finally there are anticoalition elements in the SPÖ. These came to the fore only in 1963 in the wake of the Habsburg crisis (the proposed return of the pretender). Since the SPÖ is more tightly organized than its partner, these elements had not been easy to locate. Even before the Habsburg crisis, they had flirted with the notion of forming a "small" coalition with the Freedom Party. Since the fall of Franz Olah as Minister of the Interior and his ex-pulsion from the SPÖ (late 1964), the Socialist anticoalition elements have lost most of their strength.

The main opposition in the Second Republic is still the opposition be-tween the two major parties. Within the coalition regime, it has taken the shape of *Bereichsopposition*—the opposition of one partner to those aspects of the regime governed by the other partner, and vice versa. Every department of government is subject to this *Bereichsopposition*. Its most prominently visible means is the institution of the secretaries of state. A secretary of state holds the constitutional position of a parlia-mentary secretary whose ostensible function is to assist his minister in parliamentary business. In reality however the secretary of state is a spy of one party implanted in a ministry administered by the other party. Secretaries of state are not provided for in every department. In fact, secretaryships of state are prizes the parties contend for in the postelection government negotiations.

The two coalition parties hold vastly different views of *Bereichsoppo-*

20. In 1962 Alexander Vodopivec (*Wer regiert in Österreich?* [2d ed. Vienna, Verlag für Geschichte und Politik, 1962, p. 255]), a hostile but knowledgeable ob-server of Austria's nationalized industry, reports: "A recent investigation has shown that 75 per cent of the total corporate capital is directly or indirectly in the public domain" (i.e., nationalized; "indirect" nationalization is administration by nationalized banks).

sition. To the People's Party, *Bereichsopposition* is a Socialist trick enabling the SPÖ to try its hand simultaneously at playing government and opposition.[21] The Socialist view of *Bereichsopposition,* on the other hand, is that it is the function of the party not holding a portfolio to oppose those in charge of its administration.[22] There are at least two reasons for these differing points of view. The first is historical. As the successor of the Christian Socials, the ÖVP continues to see itself as the party of government and the SPÖ as the party of opposition, despite the coalition. Secondly, in every coalition government so far the ÖVP has held the chancellorship and the Ministry of Finance. The holding of these portfolios has meant that the party has been concerned more than the Socialists with overall management and policy initiative. In the eyes of the ÖVP, *Bereichsopposition* in the realm of the chancellorship and the Ministry of Finance is outright opposition, irresponsible on the part of a cogoverning party.

While on the positive side the coalition regime constitutes a pooling of policy-making, *Bereichsopposition* amounts to a pooling of opposition. Policy initiatives are taken by the party holding the portfolio. Even the government declaration following the formation of each government—the Austrian equivalent to the Speech from the Throne—is an uneasily coordinated amalgamation of departmental policies, originating with the party controlling the department in each case. All policies are bargained over in meetings of the coalition committee. The policy veto of the coalition partner enables him to make effective a good part of his opposition to a policy. The unanimity rule in the committee, coupled with the fact that the real leaders of the coalition partners are present on the committee, means that bargains arrived at in the coalition committee can normally be made to stick. It should be noted here that the SPÖ, with better internal discipline, is in a better position to commit itself to a policy than is the ÖVP with its federal structure dividing it into business, agriculture, and employees and with its vociferous anticoalition element. The administration of every department is under constant attack from the party press, the parliamentary group, and organizational spokesmen of the coalition

21. Statements on this by ÖVP leaders and publicists are legion. For the classic version, see Wilhelm Boehm, "Koalition als Problem," *Österreichische Monatshefte,* July-August 1950, pp. 479–83. Julius Raab blamed the defeat of 1959 on this alleged Socialist duplicity (*Österreichische Monatshefte,* May 1959, p. 1).

22. The leading Socialist writer on this point is Friedrich Scheu (*Zukunft,* February 1956, pp. 36–39; October-November 1956, pp. 305–08; April-May 1959, pp. 99–102). See also the statements by Oscar Pollak (*Zukunft,* February 1952, pp. 33–36) and Franz Olah (*Forum,* June 1959, pp. 211–13). Several party leaders impressed the virtues of *Bereichsopposition* on the writer in interviews in 1960. Before his retirement from active politics, Adolf Schärf presented the position of vice-chancellor, which he held for 12 years, as that of a virtual leader of the *Bereichsopposition* (SPÖ, *Bericht an Parteitag, 1956,* p. 21).

partner. While all this *Bereichsopposition* takes place, the anticoalition press and the other anticoalition elements listed above carry on a continuous opposition to the coalition itself, and to many of the bargains that have been arrived at in the coalition committee.

Parliamentary elections, which must be held at least once every four years and may be held earlier only by mutual agreement of the coalition partners, feature the employment of electoral tactics primarily between the two coalition partners, *who are the chief antagonists in every election.* These tactics will be described briefly in the next section. What should be emphasized here is the fact that the electoral efforts of the opposition parties proper (Freedom Party, Communists) involve only a minor part of the total campaign effort—the campaign looks to the observer, quite properly, like one which is fought between ÖVP and SPÖ. Throughout the campaign, the continuation of the coalition after the election is assumed by nearly everyone, though the anticoalition elements in the ÖVP make this assumption most reluctantly (especially in 1956, 1959, and 1962). In 1959 the mode of policy-making within the coalition was made a major issue by the ÖVP.[23] In the ensuing negotiations, however, the issue was once again resolved by the maintenance of the status quo, the rigid coalition.

The continuation of the coalition is favorable to the organizations of both coalition parties and to at least two of Austria's three major interests. The *Proporz* system is and continues to be a convenient patronage vehicle for both major parties. It is of course deleterious to the organizational workings of the opposition parties. The labor-socialist subculture prefers (or preferred at least until 1962) political codetermination to the risk of an alternation between government and opposition. Agriculture and small business, though before 1963 they would have had a better chance than labor to be on the government's side in a system of alternation, have come to prefer the social peace of the coalition to the potential hazards of the alternation pattern. On the other hand, large business and private industry at least consider taking chances with the potentialities of the alternation pattern in preference to a coalition with what amounts to a built-in labor veto.

Until 1963 ÖVP reform circles were the only ones that publicly discussed the possibility of forming a "small" coalition with the Freedom Party in preference to the existing "great" coalition. The Habsburg crisis spurred intentions on the part of some SPÖ leaders to form such a small coalition with the Freedom Party, without the People's Party. As might be expected, the chambers and interest groups on both sides responded to

23. For the fate of the issue in campaign and negotiations, see Frederick C. Engelmann, "Haggling for the Equilibrium," *American Political Science Review*, 56 (1962), 656, 660–61.

the worsening coalition climate with pleas for continued collaboration. Certainly the 1963 crisis shows that mutual feeling between the partners continues to be poor, and that distrust and tension between them is real. The growing together of the coalition parties seems out of the question —there is no reason to believe that Austria will ever be governed by one "black-red" coalition party. After 20 years of coalition, one of the salient facts of Austrian political life is the continuing opposition attitude between the two major parties.

OPPOSITION STRATEGY AND TACTICS   Because of the coalition, opposition in Austria is sui generis. The nature of its strategy differs among the various opposition elements. Communist opposition, no longer revolutionary, is a structural one. The opposition of the Freedom Party, and of anticoalition elements within the coalition parties, is of the policy opposition type. But the facts of life in the coalition make it difficult to express this policy opposition clearly. No one has stated a set of alternative policies should the coalition cease to govern.

Opposition of one partner to the other can, within limits, be termed an office-seeking opposition. The two coalition parties are clearly vying for the presidency and the chancellorship (which goes to the party with the parliamentary plurality). Up to 1965 the SPÖ invariably won the former,[24] the ÖVP the latter (twice with fewer votes, though one more seat, than the SPÖ). Electoral competition is also reflected in the distribution of other executive offices. Any advantage gained in an election is registered in the redistribution of these offices after the election (though the extent of the shift indicates not only the magnitute of the electoral success, but also the relative negotiating skills of the delegations of the two parties). During the first 20 years of coalition, competition for office has involved only foreign affairs, nationalized industries, and the secretaryships of state. Education, finance, commerce, agriculture, and defense have always been "black." Justice, interior, social welfare, and transport have always been "red."

In general, the coalition has brought about a softening of opposition; yet statements about policy opposition in Second Republic Austria are difficult because the makeup and intensity of the opposition vary from issue to issue. The majority of issues is dualistic, yet the parties do not always oppose one another on them. In the period 1955–62, the main antagonists, in varying constellations, have been the following four elements: the SPÖ, the ÖVP, anticoalition elements (primarily the independent press, industrial interests, and anticoalition segments of the ÖVP), and the Freedom Party.

Externally, Austria was faced during this period with the twin prob-

24. See Appendix Table 8.4. President Schärf having died in office, a presidential election was held on May 23, 1965. Franz Jonas (SPÖ) won narrowly.

lems of its own neutrality and of European integration. Both parties have been backing a strict observance of the obligations of the State Treaty of 1955 (the SPÖ with greater enthusiasm). Anticoalition elements and the Freedom Party have been pursuing a pro-Western (primarily pro-German) policy, presumably to the degree of jeopardizing neutrality.

In regard to Austrian symbols and coalition styles, the main issues have been the proposed return to Austria of the pretender to the former throne, Otto von Habsburg, and the numerous scandals of the coalition regime. In the former case, ÖVP and anticoalition elements supported the Administrative Court ruling permitting Otto's return to Austria (1963); SPÖ and Freedom Party outvoted the ÖVP on the issue in Parliament, while Socialist ministers issued orders nullifying, at least temporarily, the effect of the court ruling. The scandals of the 1955–62 period aroused strong antagonism between the partners; the recurring charge against the ÖVP is shady dealing to finance the party; against the SPÖ, mismanagement of nationalized enterprises.

In the internal policy field the main economic issues, collectivism and fiscal management, have been clouded for want of a definite ÖVP position; in regard to these issues, there has been pronounced hostility between Socialists and anticoalition elements. On rent control the SPÖ, defending the status quo, has been facing all the other elements. In such noneconomic fields as agriculture, education, and church-state relations, the coalition has succeeded in substituting some consensual policies for earlier, usually heavy, opposition between the partners. Compared to the First Republic, the coalition has definitely brought about a softening of issue-opposition between the two major parties.

To the issues should be added another factor responsible for a general softening of the objective aspects of opposition: the *Proporz*. The civil service in the First Republic was made up of Imperial holdovers, of Nationalists (especially in the judiciary), and, as a major group, of members of Catholic fraternities. Socialists had been barred from the conventional recruitment channels, and very few were in the federal service between 1918 and 1934. The main sociopolitical effect of the *Proporz* has been the assignment of part of the recruitment channels to the SPÖ. In the Second Republic, difficulty in finding enough qualified Socialists was encountered at first. The League of Socialist Academicians, founded by Karl Waldbrunner (Minister for Nationalized Industries, 1949–56), initially took in academicians who were not members of the CV (overall organization of Catholic fraternities), whether Socialist or national. After nearly two decades of *Proporz*, the Austrian bureaucracy is no longer the conservative force it was prior to 1938. There is no more need for socialists to engage in structural opposition to the civil service and thereby to the apparatus of the state.

In regard to opposition tactics, the Communists tried violent tactics at first, but the failure of their 1950 *Putsch* reduced them to rather in-effectual electoral tactics. The Freedom Party uses electoral tactics primarily. Since 1953 it has been approached regarding collaboration by one or the other coalition party, more often by the ÖVP. Neither party ever held out much of a bargain to them until a confidential offer by the Socialists in 1963 reputedly envisioned giving electorally lucrative ministries (commerce, agriculture) to the Freedom Party if there were a "small" coalition with the SPÖ. In Parliament, the Freedom Party engages in the electoral tactics normally employed by an opposition party with a greatly limited constituency.

The coalition itself is of course a grand effort to replace the hard tactics of the First Republic with bargaining. The effort has not been without success; after all, bargains between the partners are the sine qua non of policy-making. But these bargains come about only in the confidential arena of the coalition committee. Public discourse between the parties, whether in Parliament, in the party press, between the two party headquarters, or at the hustings, continues to be hard. Parliamentary debate easily slides into name-calling between ÖVP and SPÖ, often involving civil war memories of the First Republic. The writer witnessed how these memories were evoked in 1960 during a trivial patronage incident. Anyone observing the chamber in session is bound to feel that he is witnessing two hostile party blocs. Positive feelings between the delegations of the coalition parties are evoked only when Freedom Party deputies launch their regular, though hopeless, attacks on the coalition. Many of the editorials in the party press are devoted to attacks on the coalition partner. Such editorials—assailing leaders, organization, and policy stands of the other party—are by no means restricted to election campaigns. The party press services invariably place sharply diverging interpretations on current internal events, and statements emanating from party headquarters tend to be hostile to the coalition partner.

Parliamentary election campaigns bring hard opposition tactics between the parties to a peak. The tone of the campaigns, while not as ideological as during the First Republic, is hostile, more so than in a number of countries in which it is not known beforehand which parties will form the next government. In substance, however, Austrian elections differ from those in alternation countries. Only in Austria does it make sense for parties openly to purport to aspire to an electoral equilibrium with the opponent, and to accuse the opponent of desiring to rule by himself.[25]

The move to bargaining tactics has been and continues to be slow because of the lag in perception of the diminishing socioeconomic differences between the two subcultures. It is this lag in perception which helps

25. For the equilibrium theme in the 1959 election, see U. W. Kitzinger, "The Austrian Election of 1959," *Political Studies, 9* (1961), 119–40; Engelmann, "Haggling for the Equilibrium."

to perpetuate *Lagermentalität.*[26] So far there has been a vicious circle here: Many Austrians fail to perceive diminishing socioeconomic differences because they were born into a *Lager.* They continue to identify with their subculture exactly because they fail to perceive diminishing socioeconomic differences. Thus these subcultures continue to persist despite progressing de-ideologization, and they continue to be reinforced by belief. Some Socialists become managers, but they continue to be known and to identify as *Socialist* managers. Switches in party allegiance occur primarily when workers who become employees are switched to a Catholic union, or when villagers begin to commute to an industrial job and become members of a Socialist union.

Sizable elements in each subculture feel that the other subculture is solidifying. Some Socialists feel quite seriously that a new form of *Bürgerblock* is in the making. This time presumably the bourgeois elements would form *one* political organization, combining the clerical and liberal camps as they are defined by Almond.[27] There is some evidence that this development is taking place; just as in the German CDU, national and capitalist elements in the ÖVP exist next to clerical ones. On the other hand, groups in the ÖVP and anticoalition elements close to the ÖVP continue to see the specter of a Marxist unity front consisting of Socialists and Communists. They point out correctly that Communists have consistently supported Socialist presidential candidates, though of course outside support from Communists alone could not have elected these candidates. It is true that even after de-ideologization the Socialist subculture continues its efforts to maintain organizational rigidity. For proof of such rigidity in the Socialist camp, critics like to point to the much-discussed disciplinary cases within the movement. These however are now more than a decade past, and the most striking, the Erwin Scharf case, dealt with Communist infiltration.[28] A more relevant example of organizational rigidity is the case of the weekly paper *Heute.* Since all but the official Socialist party publications were essentially anti-Socialist, it had been felt by groups within the party that the party ought to subsidize an independent-looking weekly. *Heute,* the weekly so launched, occa-

26. S. M. Lipset writes: "nations that have experienced a continuing long-term conflict among social classes may take much longer to recognize the declining need for ideology." ("The Changing Class Structure and Contemporary European Politics," paper delivered at the 1963 Annual Meeting of the American Political Science Association, New York City, p. 3). As noted above, in the case of Austria "mentality" should be substituted for "ideology."

27. Almond, "Comparative Political Systems." For the Socialist view mentioned here, see Norbert Leser, *Begegnung und Auftrag* (Vienna, Europa-Verlag, 1963), pp. 224-32.

28. Franz Olah was expelled in 1964 because of clear indications that he was placing personal ambition above party interest; the official reason for his expulsion was breach of party discipline.

sionally also *acted* independently. Under repeated attacks from some quarters within the party, its life was snuffed out at the age of three and one-half years, and Austrian papers once again were either officially Socialist or anti-Socialist.[29] The fact that the Socialists still organize their subculture as though it were a First Republic *Lager* continues to have a tendency to unite all those outside it. This tendency in turn provides a bit of a true ring when the independent press continues to call "bourgeois" everyone who is not a Socialist or a Communist.

Elites and Opposition

The leaders of the major *Lager* in the First Republic did not differ in socioeconomic position as sharply as the populations of these two *Lager*. Few of the political leaders on the side of the Christian Socials were former aristocrats or leaders in business or industry, and few of the leaders of the Social Democrats were workers. Most of the Social Democratic leaders, among them a number of Jewish intellectuals, equaled or bettered their political opponents in education, and few leaders on either side were wealthy. They were however fundamentally different in two ways: (a) in their belief systems, and (b) in their religion (most Social Democratic leaders, whether from Catholic or Jewish families, were militant Free-thinkers). The parties' principal leaders were an actual "black" priest, Ignaz Seipel, and a virtual "red" priest, Otto Bauer. The elites conceived of their roles as leaders of armed camps, which needed to be completely mobilized. Seipel felt that all potential allies needed to be kept on the side of the anti-Marxist; not just shopkeepers, peasants, and intellectuals with a distinct Catholic orientation, but all anti-Marxist business groups, and of course the *Heimwehr*, the fascist paramilitary organization. The Social Democrats, having reduced the Communists to a negligible force, felt they were the masters of the workers' *Lager:* if only all workers could be mobilized there would be a Socialist government. The attitude of both elites hardened the discourse between government and opposition.

In the Second Republic, socioeconomic similarities between the two major elites are more pronounced, and their ideological differences are not as great. If anything, elites were more similar, certainly friendlier, prior to the ÖVP reform of 1951, when the party was dominated by concentration camp victims who felt a strong affinity with those Socialist leaders who had been concentration camp victims themselves.[30] From

29. The fact that the daily "boulevard" paper *Express* is now owned by the Socialist publishing concern hardly constitutes an exception; *Express* does not usually editorialize.

30. Of the elites in the Second Republic, an acute anticoalition journalist writes: "The oligarchy is still a fairly homogeneous circle. Observers at receptions, cocktail parties, and other official functions by no means have the impression that representa-

the beginning, both parties have come under the control of interest spokesmen. These interest spokesmen, used to interest bargaining, transferred their skills to the chief policy-making arena, the coalition committee. To this body the parties send their five or six principal leaders. In this way the keeping of bargains is assured, for the committee consists of the real leaders of the parties' constituent groups. Also, the work of the committee, although often hampered by an unfriendly atmosphere and by real differences of interest, is facilitated by the habituated bargaining ways of its members.[31]

Robert Dahl has suggested that incumbent elites, once industrialization is accomplished, try to minimize differences among the voters, while opposition elites try to emphasize them.[32] During the First Republic, both sides emphasized these differences precisely because the Christian Social elite was not truly an incumbent one, but one whose place at the seat of power dated only from 1921. Today both elites attempt to work along the lines suggested by Dahl for the advanced industrial stage —by seeking electoral support from all quarters—yet the shackles imposed by continued *Lagermentalität* and by the static party-interest nexus keep them from doing so singlemindedly.

There are clear examples of depolarizing efforts by both elites. The very founding of the ÖVP symbolizes the effort to create a true people's party. The founders set up a federation in which workers and employees were to be equal in influence with businessmen and peasants—a far cry from the Christian Social Party of the First Republic. The party began its role in the coalition by agreeing to the nationalization of key industries and banks. The Catholic Church withdrew from politics, and efforts to construct a new Catholic ideology were all but abandoned. On the Socialist side, it became obvious immediately that the party was no longer in the hands of the Austro-Marxist followers of Otto Bauer, but of Karl Renner and his moderate associates. Yet until Adolf Schärf exchanged the leadership of the party for the federal presidency (1957), there was hesitation in abandoning a basically anticlerical stand. The new party program (1958) and Bruno Pittermann's leadership are depolarizing agents. After some initial anguish,[33] the party has done its share to take

---

tives of two hostile camps are facing one another. They mix easily like acquaintances with similar income, equal prestige, the same cars, and basically not too strongly opposed interests." Vodopivec, *Wer regiert in Osterreich?*, p. 321.

31. Several former members of the coalition committee told the writer that they had perfected their bargaining skills in negotiations with the Russian occupiers.

32. In an unpublished memorandum prepared for the Bellagio conference.

33. For a brief flare-up of antireligious feelings, see SPÖ, *Parteitag 1959, Protokoll*, pp. 121–29. The ideological front against the church has crumbled. Josef Hindels, one of the leading neo-Marxists in the SPÖ, wrote in 1963: "The deep and far-reaching changes in Catholicism demand an unprejudiced reexamination of our relations with the Catholic Church." (Quoted in *Furche*, July 6, 1963, p. 6.)

religion out of politics, and it is wooing the votes of churchgoers. The new policy is aided by the progressive and nonpartisan attitude of Cardinal König, Austria's chief prelate since 1956.

But there is also resistance to depolarization on both sides. When leadership of the ÖVP moved from the peasants to the Business League (1951), there began to be talk of re-ideologization in an economic direction. Reinhard Kamitz, Minister of Finance from 1952–60, followed the "social market economy" of his big cousin Erhard. Efforts were made to reestablish a bourgeois camp under the principle of a socially tempered economic individualism. These principles were emphasized in the ÖVP's successful 1956 campaign. Among the loosely connected leaders of the new direction are Kamitz, a national liberal himself, the clerical Hermann Withalm (who became the ÖVP's general secretary in 1960), Josef Klaus, first governor of Salzburg, then Minister of Finance, who became federal chairman of the ÖVP in 1963 and Chancellor in 1964, Josef Krainer, governor of anticlerical Styria, and Fritz Molden, former editor of the independent Vienna *Presse*. Some of the driving forces are organized in the anti-Socialist *Akademikerbund*. Spokesmen permeate the independent press (*Presse, Salzburger Nachrichten, Berichte und Informationen*); among them is the author of the only up-to-date book on Austrian politics, Alexander Vodopivec.[34] On the Socialist side there has been less resistance to depolarization. However, pressure from the cadres persuaded the leaders that it would be unwise to give up the annual May Day parade in Vienna. Also, the noisy stand taken by Bruno Pittermann and Franz Olah, the chief party leaders, in the Habsburg crisis indicates that the elite is not beyond resorting to an old-fashioned class appeal. Paradoxically, this one was accompanied by a flirtation with the Freedom Party.

The historical sequence of the genesis of opposition in Austria follows the German pattern. The urban proletariat developed first, dating from before 1848 (as an organized political movement from 1889), general suffrage dates from 1907, and representative government from 1918. During the coalition of 1918–20, the "opposition," i.e., the Socialist element within the coalition, gained several achievements by bargaining, especially in the fields of social welfare and housing; but because of the establishment of the *Bürgerblock*, the attractiveness of strong opposition and hard tactics was not reduced, and there was in fact a recurrence of them after 1920, leading eventually to civil war and the breakdown of the system.

Austrian Socialists have learned from their First Republic experience that they cannot hope to obtain and sustain a political majority on the basis of a class appeal. If the party they oppose, though the bonds of the coalition "marriage" now unite the two, were led by the old ruling group

34. Vodopivec, *Wer regiert in Osterreich?*

from Imperial days, a Socialist class appeal might be more successful. But the ÖVP is the party of peasants, shopkeepers, and white-collar workers—segments of the population whose political power was as dependent on the grant of universal suffrage as was that of the industrial workers. Because of the persistence of the national subculture, the ÖVP also cannot hope to gain a majority on a static group appeal. The coalition is of course reinforced by the probability that *each* partner will remain in a permanent minority situation (though the ÖVP had 82 of 165 seats from 1956–59). Therefore both parties use electoral tactics to gain a plurality which puts them into a favorable position for bargaining within the coalition. In the interelection period the parties bargain within the coalition for the enactment of policies and for the protection of interests. In this bargaining process, the parties pool both government and opposition.

Opposition tension within the coalition is outliving the objective conditions that make for such tension in these days when advanced industrialism and the Cold War tend toward a lessening of opposition.[35] The circular nature of *Lager* structure and subjective perceptions accounts for this lag. At the same time there are lingering psychological inequalities between the partners, all favoring the ÖVP: (a) the ÖVP is identified (though hardly in fact) with the pre-1918 state; (b) the ÖVP is identified with the government of the First Republic; (c) the ÖVP is identified with such high-ranking elite groups in the Austrian society as the former nobility, the owners of private industry, and leaders in the professions (though it is not *led* by members of these elites); (d) the ÖVP is identified with the holding of the chancellorship and the Ministry of Finance. These factors appear to justify the party in referring to itself as the "state-bearing party." This self-appellation in turn brings on a continued identification of the Socialist party with opposition, and continued demands by the Socialists to gain recognition as an equal partner within the coalition.

Socialists in turn have taken advantage of this psychological inequality within the coalition. Since those thinking of discontinuing the coalition have been thinking of an ÖVP or an ÖVP-Freedom Party government, the SPÖ has been holding on to the coalition as a guarantee of codetermination for labor. Alternation, Socialists say, would mean the recurrence

35. In view of the great extent of nationalization of Austria's industry, the blunting of issues in advanced industrial societies (see Otto Kirchheimer's chapter in this volume; also Kirchheimer, "Waning of Opposition") is partially counterbalanced by the issue of nationalization itself. Yet this issue should not be overemphasized. Socialists do not appear to be greatly concerned with further nationalization. A 1962 poll made available privately to the writer indicates that 40 per cent of the Socialist respondents expected further nationalization in case of a Socialist victory, while 21 per cent expected no changes. However, 67 per cent of ÖVP respondents expected the Socialists to nationalize further, and only 6 per cent did not.

of a *Bürgerblock;* to borrow from Orwell's *Animal Farm:* "Jones would come back." Only the Socialist negotiating success after the electoral defeat of 1962, and the overwhelming Socialist victory in the presidential election of 1963 (the first clear victory ever won in any election since free elections have been held in Austria) made it appear to the SPÖ that *it* might be able to govern without the ÖVP. The Habsburg crisis, following President Schärf's reelection by only one month, provided the opportunity to present to a baffled Austrian public the possibility of a "small" coalition of Socialists and Freedom Party.

This development did not come about; but the coalition, an external and internal necessity during the occupation and an internal necessity since 1955, may yet be moving toward a third stage, one of at least partial loosening.[36] Such a loosening would run counter to the continuing party-interest tie-up. If it could be accomplished (which no longer appears likely) by pushing the ÖVP into opposition, or by at least outvoting it in Parliament, it would not violate the maxim: no government against the industrial worker. The cavalier position taken by some Socialist leaders toward the coalition in 1963 may actually have reduced the psychological inequality between the partners and thus weakened even further the lingering *Lagermentalität.*

Speculations about the future of the coalition are particularly hazardous in the post-1963 situation;[37] they are also unnecessary for an evaluation of the nature of opposition under the Austrian coalition regime. Such an evaluation can be undertaken on the basis of the experience of the coalition's first 18 years.

In a different chapter of this book, Nils Stjernquist points to the tension between two basic opposition aims: displacing the government and influencing the policy-making process. If there were an all-party coalition, the opposition could realize the second aim at the expense of the first,

36. The loosening of the coalition, long a demand of the ÖVP, was implemented by the 1963 coalition pact in the following fashion: If the partners fail to agree on a specific policy, either partner may introduce a motion regarding it three months after the date of disagreement. Parliament is to vote five months later. The losing party may demand a plebiscite. Not the ÖVP, but rather the SPÖ threatened to make use of the above provision in early 1964. Motions were then in progress amending the electoral law and proposing a law against corruption. Efforts to enact either measure, with the aid of the Freedom Party, against the votes of the ÖVP were subsequently abandoned.

37. In September 1963 Josef Klaus, a "reformer" who earlier in the year had resigned as Minister of Finance because he refused to enter into further (and to him unsound) bargains with the Socialists, replaced Alphons Gorbach, the Federal Chancellor, as leader of the ÖVP, and in April 1964 as Chancellor. The Socialist attitude toward the ÖVP hardened in early 1964, and threats to form a "small" coalition between SPÖ and Freedom Party became more frequent. However, the "small" coalition idea apparently died with the dramatic purge of Franz Olah, Socialist Minister of the Interior, by his party in the fall of 1964.

and indeed at the expense of its opposition role proper. Has Austria solved Stjernquist's dilemma by, on balance, doing away with opposition?

The argument of this chapter has been that the duopolistic construct known as the Austrian coalition does maximize opposition influence without giving up the aim of displacement entirely. There is, to be sure, no complete replacement. As long as the coalition continues in its present form, neither ÖVP nor SPÖ will capture the government in its entirety, neither will be pushed out entirely, and no third party will be admitted. But displacement remains a constant operational aim. The People's Party attempts every six years to displace the Socialist President (unsuccessfully so far), and the Socialists have so far made five attempts, equally unsuccessful, to displace the People's Party's Chancellor. The presidential election of 1957 and the parliamentary elections of 1953 and 1959 came very close to achieving this displacement. Displacement has in fact occurred in the Foreign Ministry, the Ministry for Nationalized Industries, and indirectly through the creation and abolition of secretaryships of state. It is the knowledge that displacement is a realistic possibility which makes real struggles out of Austrian elections, despite the limited risk imposed by the coalition regime. Thus the electoral tactics employed are real opposition tactics, as are the bargaining tactics on which all policy-making in the coalition is based.

Even at the bargaining stage, the coalition does not hopelessly comingle the functions of government and opposition. Opposition goes on constantly as the delegates of one party veto some of the policy proposals of the other. True, both sides share the responsibility of government. But no one is truly responsible for the government as a whole. The Constitution, as noted earlier, makes each minister responsible directly to Parliament. But each minister only carries out such policies as have been approved by his party. Thus the functions of government and opposition remain separated in coalition bargaining. No one needs to accept governmental responsibility for what he opposes. Opposed policies simply are not enacted. Enacted policies reflect mutual consent of the parties; that is at best, though rarely, true agreement, but at least opposition that has been given up voluntarily in the bargaining process. This opposition is of course cast in a peculiar shape by the coalition regime. Everyone opposes: the Communists, the Freedom Party, the independent press, the anticoalition factions and interests, and, most importantly, the coalition parties themselves. The partners have not given up their mutual distrust. Neither wants to give up his share in the government, and neither wants the partner to govern freely and uncontrolled within his sphere. Therefore opposition is and remains pooled, along with government.

While everyone opposes, everyone is opposed. Every policy and every officeholder faces opposition. Except for impurities in the system, nothing and nobody goes unexamined. Through its secretaries of state, and through its probing into policy and administration in the process of coalition bargaining, the examining party has access to information going beyond that available to opposition parties in systems with normal government and opposition parties or coalitions.

The comingling of government and opposition functions within Austria's limited liability coalition has not been particularly conducive to policy-making. The *Junktim (do ut des* horse trading in policy-making) is not an Austrian invention nor an Austrian monopoly; yet its formalization and frequent use has made it impossible to govern Austria according to any kind of integrated program. The *Proporz*—as a system of patronage also hardly an Austrian monopoly—increases partisan emphasis in personnel matters when the interest of the country calls for less partisan emphasis. In contrast, *Bereichsopposition*, while not conducive to responsible opposition, gives to opposition a fullness, strength, and mode peculiar to Austria. Of the various aspects of this stormy marriage of convenience, here is one where a virtue has been made of necessity.

9

FRANCE:
NOTHING BUT OPPOSITION

Alfred Grosser

As Bertrand de Jouvenel in *The Pure Theory of Politics* distinguishes between *potestas* and *potentia*, between "Authority" and "authority," so in principle it is desirable to distinguish between Opposition and opposition. The first implies a rather precise role in a pluralistic political system, clearly defined by constitution or custom. The second suggests a variety of attitudes and behavior of which the only common characteristic is hostility to power. Unhappily this distinction, useful as it may be in other countries, is without much utility for studying opposition in France. Answers to apparently simple questions, such as "Who opposes?," "To whom is one opposed? to the government? to the regime? to the state?," "How is opposition carried on?" require so many careful distinctions that the question whether Opposition with a capital "O" has meaning in France must be reserved for the conclusion of our inquiry.

What we must do, then, is to study all the methods of opposition in French politics to the extent that these are employed in ordinary political life. Coups d'etat, civil wars, techniques of subversion are not in our domain, even though we shall have to try to specify what the limits to the existence and legal action of opposition are in France.

Legality and Legitimacy

THE LIMITS OF LEGALITY   In France, opposition is scarcely restricted at all by legislation. Until 1958 the political parties were not covered by any special statute and were, in general, ordinary associations defined by a law (1901) which provides that: "Every association founded for the purpose or aim of an illicit object, contrary to the laws or to decent practices, or which would have the aim of weakening the integrity of the national territory and the republican form of government, is null and void."

The Constitution of the Fifth Republic carries an article (Article 4), rather directly inspired by a provision in the Constitution of West Germany, of which the last sentence, obscure in itself, has never had to be given precise meaning since no party has been accused of violating it: "Political parties and groups assist in the expression of the franchise. They are formed and conduct their activities freely. They must respect the principles of national sovereignty and democracy."

Although radio and television are largely under government control,[1] the free exercise of opposition by the press is without doubt better respected than in a large proportion of the other pluralistic democracies, since the right to question the validity of the regime, and even the values on which the political society rests, is completely accepted. The law on the liberty of the press (1881), however, makes it punishable as a crime or misdemeanor to provoke various illegal actions by public utterances, whether oral or written. Thus it is punishable to provoke by public utterances, crimes of murder, pillage, incendiarism, sedition, and various crimes against the security of the state; to dissuade members of the armed services from performing their duty; to utter seditious cries or songs in public places; to publish false news if it is done in bad faith and disturbs the public peace; and (Article 26) to give offense to the President of the Republic in various ways.

Illegal seizures of newspapers stopped with the end of the war in Algeria. However, because of the ambiguity of the constitutional situation under the Fifth Republic, the application of Article 26 continues. Whoever displays his disapproval when the head of state passes by can be condemned for "offense to the President of the Republic." Article 26 makes this a misdemeanor and is rather frequently applied. The President of the National Assembly interrupts any deputy who attacks General de Gaulle; for the members of Parliament must not call the President of the Republic into question, since he is not responsible to Parliament. The courts and the President of the Assembly are perfectly right, since General de Gaulle embodies the collectivity and assures the continuity of state, like the Queen of England or the President of the Republic in Italy and in Germany. The difficulty is, however, that General de Gaulle is also the President of the Republic in the American sense, that is to say, the real head of the executive. But the President of the United States can be hooted at by any ordinary citizen and attacked by any member of Congress.

Tolerance with respect to the opinions and even the attitudes of opposition has remained much the way it was under the preceding republics. Thus the recruitment of future high officials is based solely on their capacities. To be sure, the government has the right to determine the list of candidates competing for entrance to l'Ecole Nationale d'Administration. But it cannot invoke the political opinions of a candidate in order to prevent his access to the public service. By a decision of 1954, annulling

1. See below.

a refusal to admit five supposedly Communist candidates, the Council of State affirmed that the administration could not invoke adherence to any political party that has a legal existence, much less refer to the opinions of the candidate. In 1962 the simultaneous admission to l'Ecole Nationale d'Administration of the one-time president of the National Students Union (Union Nationale des Étudiants Français, UNEF) who had been criticized by the government for having had contacts with the Algerian Nationalists, and of a student who had been interned for his activities on the extreme right, symbolized a liberalism for which one scarcely finds an equivalent in other countries, even in those generally supposed to be the most democratic. It has happened in France, but in what other Western democracy would an anti-Communist government impose on reluctant colleagues a university professor who is a member of the central committee of the Communist Party?

RECOURSE TO VIOLENCE   Opposition must not, however, resort to violence. The principle is simple to formulate; its application is more difficult. Certainly a coup d'etat is not permitted, at least when it fails, and the attempts of the Organisation d l'Armée Secrète have normally mobilized against their authors the forces of the police and a virtually unanimous opinion among the public.

But these are extreme cases. What is normal is a rather broad acceptance of pressures exercised by the most diverse means on the institutionalized authorities. The police and the courts have been indulgent toward gatherings of Poujadists who have mauled tax inspectors, merchants who have prevented the seizure of the furnishings of a fellow merchant condemned for fraud, peasants who have barred roads or surrounded prefectures. All these forms of violent opposition to legislative, judicial, or administrative decisions an indulgent opinion regards as demonstrations rather less extreme than the right to strike.

The right to strike was guaranteed by the preamble to the Constitution of 1946, which was reaffirmed in the Constitution of 1958: "the right to strike may be exercised within the framework of the laws that govern it." Such laws are practically nonexistent. The most recent (1963) and the most discussed is a law "relative to certain forms of the strike in the public services." This mainly imposes a strike notice of five days. But while this law regulates striking, it nonetheless affirms the legality of strikes on the railroads and in the electric power industry (which are publicly owned), and by teachers, whereas a half-century ago Briand considered that he had both the right and the duty to break a railroad strike by mobilizing the railroad workers. The total defeat of the procedure of requisition utilized against the miners in 1963 has shown that the right to strike has practically no limits, whether it is a question of opposing the state in its role as an employer, or the state as a representative of the general interest, or even the application of a law voted by Parliament, that is, by representatives of the whole peeople.

There are several reasons why resort to means not foreseen by the classical rules of liberal democracy has to some extent become normal. In the first place, organized groups are numerically and financially rather weak in France. The power to mobilize supporters constitutes an essential criterion of their representativeness: many strikes and demonstrations are undertaken solely to exhibit the influence and therefore the representativeness of the group that organizes them. Furthermore, the use of threats is the commonest form of group action. How is it possible to establish a precise boundary between a peaceful threat and a violent threat? During election periods a group will demand that candidates and parties take a position on questions that interest the group. While Parliament is in session, a group will threaten the parliamentarian that it will oppose his reelection if he does not satisfy their demands. Faced by the government or by the chief of state, a group will more or less overtly tie its "yes" on a referendum to the satisfaction of an occupational or regional demand. In an even more specific way, a group that is financially or economically powerful can obtain results by affecting the finances and credit of the state. In the case of open threats, as in demonstrations by peasants or strikes by employees, it is a matter of seeking satisfaction for the demands of a group by threatening disorder or slowing up or impeding the functioning of the economy or the public services.

For a great many years, two aspects of the strike have led to impassioned discussions: their "politicization" and the right of employees of the state to strike. What is a political strike? The answer is difficult even if one puts to one side the question of the legitimate or illegitimate character of a purely political strike. A work stoppage designed to obtain safer and healthier working conditions is assuredly not political. A strike that has as its avowed end stopping the war in Indochina is without question political. But there are many shades between these two extremes. Is a strike "political" if it seeks to bring pressure to bear on Parliament at the moment of a vote on a law? The conceptions vary according to the climate of the times.

In West Germany, for example, the law on workers' codetermination in the steel and coal industries was obtained in large part by a threat to strike. Some years later the dominant tendency in Germany was to speak retrospectively of *Parlamentsnötigung*, or "violence to Parliament." In France one tends to distinguish between pressure exercised on the government and on Parliament in relation to a social or economic decision and in relation to a political decision. But where is the boundary between the two? Doubtless one would regard as political any attempt to mobilize opinion against a decision made by political institutions. However, that is one of the aims of a strike: for a strike will fail if opinion is sharply hostile to it. It seems clear that disorder flows as much from the weakness, the poverty, the internal divisions of a trade union, from its inability to impose respect for its agreements on its own members, from unions out-bidding one another for support, from the need to strike in order to prove that the union is strong, and from the difficulty of arbitrating among the divergent interests of members, as from obstacles to a reasonable and organized use of the threat to strike.

In any case, the trade unions will always resort to the threat that a strike constitutes as long as two elements in public life continue. The first is the fact that half the workers are blocked from an effective voice in government by the existence of a strong and isolated Communist Party. Since these workers normally express an attitude of opposition, why would the majority or the government take into account peaceful pressure they might try to exert on a particular issue? In the second place trade unions are not on a footing of equality with financial or busi-ness groups in negotiating with the administration. Whatever the orienta-tion of top officials may be, between them and managers in banking and industry there is a community of background, language, and intellectual attitudes that creates a certain amount of understanding and sympathy for the managers.

To the conviction (in our view justified) that the various social groups are not on a plane of equality in influencing the decisions of power, and that a strict respect for the rules of classic democracy favors the most powerful, another consideration should be added. Political life has changed in content since the rules of pluralist democracy were enunciated. This change has posed a problem which constitutional law and political science have not yet clearly considered. Today law serves more and more as a means for transforming the society; that is to say, the majority has the right to decide the future of a minority group and the right to change radically the conditions of life of a socially or geographically determined group. The traditional democratic rule required that such a minority group should yield without complaint after having sought to make its own point of view prevail. But can one realistically expect a group that feels itself to be victimized by a change not to resort to violent forms of oppo-sition if its members feel themselves deprived of rights to which they are deeply attached? The strike of the Belgian doctors in 1964 constitutes the most spectacular case. It is deplorable that nowhere, as little in France as in Belgium, has the basic issue been adequately debated: what changes in social conditions can the collectivity impose on individuals and on groups in the name of the common good? As long as that question has not been frankly attacked, one cannot really examine *au fond* the problems presented by peasant demonstrations or even the Poujadist actions of merchants.

CONFLICTS OF LEGITIMACY   In any case, however, it is not a question of the nonclassical forms of "bargaining opposition" nor even of "policy opposition." Ever since 1789, French political history has known oppositions much more profound than these, since the oppositions in France challenge the legitimacy of the regime itself.

One can speak of legitimacy only in countries and periods where it is contested. In Switzerland, in the United States since the Civil War, in Great Britain for an even longer time, it is enough that a government respects the law. As long as it does not transgress the law, its legitimacy is not questioned: the obedience of citizens is founded on the common belief that it is their duty to consent to the exercise of governmental authority. It is entirely different in France. We do not need to go back to the Revolution and to the attempt to replace royal legitimacy by the legitimacy of popular rule, for you may recall that the Third Republic was challenged for a very long time, notably by many Catholics and workers.

In 1940 the drama unfolded. Was the Vichy regime legitimate? If legitimacy is founded on the adherence of a large majority of citizens, reinforced by the legal character of the transmission of power and the act of formal recognition by foreign states, the answer should be in the affirmative. But the legitimacy of Vichy was contested from the outset in two distinct though related ways. The appeal on June 18, 1940, by De Gaulle opposed the legitimacy of the nation to the legitimacy of the majority. That the adversary was called Hitler and that the French government was exposed to the possibility of contamination by Nazism mattered little at the beginning. For other opponents, on the contrary, the challenge was above all moral: first the arbitrariness, then the impress of Nazism disqualified Vichy even more than the signing of the armistice.

The Fourth Republic witnessed a multiplicity of denials of legitimacy. In the long quarrel over German rearmament, one part of the Left denied at the outset the legitimacy of any regime that would accept the European Defense Community, which was held to be immoral: the majority decision, it was said, would not bind the citizens. On the Gaullist side, the same conclusion was based on the abandonment of sovereignty which the treaty entailed. Again, the wars in Indochina and Algeria were challenged on a moral ground: a regime that tolerated tortures and summary executions, that violated its own principles in opposing the liberty of other peoples, unquestionably lost its own legitimacy and no longer enjoyed the right to be obeyed, even if its governments issued from a majority of the elected representatives of the people. With respect to Algeria, a challenge on national grounds was particularly important: no government, no majority, it was asserted, has the right to abandon one piece of the national patrimony or to expel from the national community those who wish to remain within it. It was in the name of this challenge that the Fourth Republic was overthrown. The "week of the barricades" in January 1960, the "putsch of the generals" in April 1961, the terrorist action of the OAS in 1962, all invoked the same principle in order to overthrow the Fifth Republic.

There are other ways of denying the legitimacy of the majority. The distinction, which everyone admits in theory, between the *pays légal* (the majority that expresses itself through electoral and institutional devices) and the *pays réel* (a true but invisible majority) is very old. Formulated in these terms on the extreme right by *L'Action Française*, it has often been utilized by others: occasionally by the anticlerical Left against the laws involving government aid to Catholic schools; as a doctrinal matter by the Communist Party, which holds itself to be a minority solely because the people have not yet been liberated from "alienation"; finally, in an entirely personal fashion by General de Gaulle. In a speech on radio and television which constituted the turning point of the "Algérie Française" revolt (January 19, 1960), he declared: "By virtue of the mandate which the people have given me and of the national legitimacy which I have embodied for 20 years . . ." He has often returned to that simple idea: the majority only represents the *pays réel* if it is faithful to him.

It is worth reflecting for a moment on the persistence of conflicts over legitimacy in the political society of France. To say that it is a question of a "conflicted" society, while American society is "consensual," is to distinguish but not to explain. It seems to me that there are several contributing causes. For one thing, in France the Constitution, lacking age and that prestige which quasi-sacred texts like the Constitution of the United States possess, is considered only a procedure of government. Political society in France is defined not by the rule of law but by the rule of the majority. It is here, in the rule of the majority, that some of the most characteristic aspects of French life are revealed: absence of respect for the minority, refusal of a dialogue, identification of the current government with the state. And also the confusion between the current government and the regime: the minority finds it easy to attribute to the institutional system the defects it thinks it finds in the attitude or in the actions of the majority. Under the Fourth Republic, General de Gaulle found fault with the "system." Under the Fifth Republic, the opponents find fault with the "regime." If the Constitution is only a mechanism, why in fact establish a clear distinction between the institutions and the majority? This question is even more pertinent when the absence of a distinction allows you to escape from the very rule which you had previously claimed for yourself. You can be favorable to the rule of the majority, but to denounce the "system" or the "regime" allows you to challenge the legitimacy of any majority you oppose.

In addition, from a taste for language and a pleasure in ideas, political conflicts are so thoroughly rationalized and ideologized that compromises are rendered nearly impossible. Finally, the fact that the economic and social structures are subjected to constant critical examination, to basic questioning, means that the power of the state, if not indeed the law, appears even in the eyes of many non-Marxists as the reflection of a power situation which it is perfectly normal to contest. These last two phenomena are inseparable from a set of opposition attitudes which we need to examine in detail.

Opposition—A Principle of Political Life

THE CITIZEN AS OPPONENT   For a very long time, the typical French citizen has considered his participation in political life as a means of weakening the state. The title of Alain's book, *The Citizen Against the Authorities*, nicely expressed, between the two world wars, a fundamental attitude. Noted by sociologists and humorists, the distrust of Frenchmen for authority—evidenced by everything from verbal criticism to refusing statistical information to the government—is real and profound.

This attitude has at least two causes, one historical, the other pedagogical. For hundreds of years one regime after another in France has had one common feature: centralization. Decisions are taken in Paris even on local matters. Even today, a loan made to the mayor of a village by the state savings bank of the neighboring city must be approved by a government bureau in the capital. Thus the state, the Power, has never been looked on with a sense of belonging, with the idea that one participates in it, but as a distant power from which one has to demand advantages and to which one has to be opposed. Since participation even in the most local decisions is limited, how can one conceive political life as participation in shaping the future of a community?

Moreover, education in the primary school in France rests on two essential principles: it is authoritarian and it appeals to the individual qualities of the students. The school child and the student at the lycée are never called upon to participate; the infallibility of programs and teachers is an axiom; but the ranking of the individual student is the basic pedagogical stimulus, and from his first compositions to his dissertation for the baccalaureate, the student is invited to express his personal reactions. The combination of the absence of participation and individualism necessarily gives birth to a spirit of criticism, of opposition.

Le civisme du refuse has its advantages. Under both the German occupation and Vichy, the spirit of rebellion was the most elementary and the most widespread form of resistance. Even under a regime presenting some authoritarian characteristics like those of the Fifth Republic, respect for the state is limited. In October 1963 the Council of Administration for the Franco-German Office of Youth (a product of the treaty of January 22, 1963) met for the first time. To the surprise of the German participants, the representatives of the French youth movements continued throughout the conference to object to all of the proposals of the minister who had appointed them. It was the Germans, who live in a regime that seeks to be completely liberal and founded on citizen participation, who did not dare go too far against their *Obrigkeit*. One should not push this analysis of the spirit of opposition too far, however, for the French have always gladly granted to their country what they have refused to the state.

The unfortunate consequences are nonetheless numerous. The most evident is the systematic vote of opposition. Neither the ephemeral success of Poujadism nor the permanent implantation of the Communist Party can be explained without taking into account this attitude of a general denial of Power. And even the claims of legitimacy, even the ideological structures of noble facade, are only disguises for that denial.

Another consequence is something of a paradox: the opposition of principle results in a confusion between state and government, a confusion from which the largest beneficiary is the governing majority of the moment. In that respect the case of the French radio and television network is particularly significant. In France this network is the monopoly of the state. Private chains cannot broadcast on French territory even if (as with Radio-Luxembourg and Europe I) they are allowed to install their principal offices in Paris. This monopoly has been established, like the other nationalizations, by virtue of a conception which is expressed in the preamble to the Constitution of 1946 reaffirmed in that of 1958: "All property and all enterprises that now have, or subsequently shall have, the character of a national public service or of a monopoly in fact, must become the property of the community." The importance of radio and television in matters of information is such that the formula can be applied to them, the principal objective being to avoid the influence of money, notably by means of advertising. The doctrine of every French government since 1945 has been that "community" and "government" are synonymous. However, in Great Britain or in Germany the government is taken to mean the majority of the moment, while the national community comprises all of the tendencies which are expressed in public life. In France it was necessary to wait until 1964 for a statute on radio and TV, still imperfect, that reduced the confusion born indirectly from the wholesale hostility of citizens to the state.

PARLIAMENT AND THE PARTIES AS COLLECTIVE OPPONENTS   In most pluralist countries, to speak of opposition is to evoke the idea of parliamentary opposition, a provisional minority facing the government majority. Under the Third and Fourth Republics, the French situation was that only in appearance. In reality the principle of parliamentary sovereignty was so firmly implanted in the minds of the French that the Parliament, one might say, constituted very nearly a sort of permanent and collective opposition to the government of the moment. Its distrust of the Cabinet was a measure of citizen distrust of Power. The role of the parliamentary committees was thought of largely as a technique for weakening government authority. Both houses were masters of their own proceedings, a fact that prevented the Cabinet from ensuring that bills would be discussed in the form in which it presented them. The principal preoccupation of the government was not to fall; thus the Chamber or the National Assembly found itself solidly established in its function of sovereign—a judge nearly always malevolent toward the executive. It was all the more malevolent because the majority of parliamentarians perceived themselves as having the right in turn to become ministers which, even in the hearts of members of parties in the government, made them opponents in part, impatient to see a new ministerial combination give them the chance to obtain or to regain a portfolio.

Another factor helps to make the deputy or senator a demanding interlocutor of the government. Even more than in other countries, the parliamentarian in France is not only a representative of the people in the noble sense but a veritable solicitor, charged with obtaining specific advantages for the individuals and groups in his constituency. In this case the centralism of France exercises a particularly unfortunate influence. Since decisions on local affairs most often have to be taken in government offices in Paris, it is in Paris that one has to intervene in order to make sure that the slow movement of the relevant papers is accelerated. And who is better charged with this task than the parliamentarian? Rather indifferent to Parliament as an institution, full of distrust for parliamentarians as a collective group, the French citizen tends to appreciate his representative insofar as he is an intermediary between himself and Power, insofar, that is, as the deputy serves as a spokesman for his own special claims. The deputies of the majority have no less work; they must negotiate and solicit as much as the others. They simply have a better opportunity to get results for their clients who thus have their initial ideas reinforced: the state is an enemy from which you must seize whatever advantages you can.

Under the Third and Fourth Republics the nature of relations between Parliament and government, combined with the multiplicity of parties and the frequency of changes in the majority coalition, also had a particularly important repercussion on the idea of opposition in France. In Great Britain, the United States, and present-day Germany, elections constitute in large measure less a designation of representatives than the ratification or the rejection of the policies practiced by the incumbent government, by the dominant party. One might say that the French situation is the inverse of the Austrian. In Austria the voter, in going to the polls, virtually has a choice only between two parties which have been jointly in power for several legislatures. In France every party takes up, during the electoral campaign, the language of opposition.

Take for example the last elections of the Fourth Republic, those of January 1956. Naturally the Communists, out of power since 1947, and the Poujadists criticized the total activity of a legislature that had begun in 1951. The Socialists had been in opposition since the preceding election, but they had sustained the Mendès-France government in 1954–55. The MRP had violently fought this last government for two-thirds of its term and had participated in eight other cabinets during that period. Radicals, moderates, and Gaullists were often divided, some participating in, others opposing the same government. But all the parties presented themselves before the electors deploring the overall balance sheet of the legislature. The mildest oppositional language consisted in saying for a party: "Excellent things were done, at such and such a moment, thanks to the action of our ministers. But I recognize that the net result was not brilliant, even for the cabinets in which I participated: but after all I was not alone in office." The speaker ought then to have added: "I cannot tell you if, after the elections, I shall be in power or in opposition, nor with whom. What I ask of you, dear voter, is to give me your vote and leave the rest to me." How can the voter avoid having his spirit of systematic opposition reinforced when no one asks him to approve the balance sheet of the legislature or any one cabinet with its credits and debits?

TRADE UNIONISM AS OPPOSITION OF PRINCIPLE   In the United States as in Germany the trade unions, like other groups, accept the common ideology and take as given the fundamental principles that govern the political, economic, and social organization. It has never been thus in France, nor is it now. As a recent example one could take the new draft of rules which the leaders of the Confédération Française des Travailleurs Chrétiens (CFTC), the most important trade union organization after the Communist-dominated Confédération Générale du Travail (CGT), had adopted by their congress on November 7, 1964, when the CFTC became the Confédération Française et Démocratique du Travail (CFDT). Among other things the draft states that:

> Every struggle of the workers' movement for liberation and collective advancement of the workers is based on the fundamental notion that every human being is endowed with reason and conscience and that he is born free and equal in dignity and in rights.
>
> In a world in evolution marked by the progress of techniques that should serve his fulfillment, the worker is more than ever threatened by

dehumanizing or technocratic structures and methods which make him an object of exploitation and subjection . . .

The Confederation unites trade union organizations open to all the workers resolved—in mutual respect for each other's personal, philosophical, moral, and religious convictions—to defend their common interests and to battle to establish a democratic society of free and responsible men . . .

The Confederation challenges every situation, every structure, every regime which ignores these demands. It therefore challenges every form of capitalism and totalitarianism . . .

It intends to carry out this action not by erecting into a system the principle of the development of class antagonisms, but rather by favoring the growth of the consciousness by the workers of the conditions for their emancipation.

The key word is "challenges" (*conteste*): The unions never cease to reaffirm the importance of the function of "challenging" or "contesting." And to challenge is to oppose not merely the government of the moment but the very economic and social foundations of the political system.

However the time has long since passed when the trade unions refused to enter into the slightest relationship with the state. On the contrary, the unions participate more and more in consultative organs. From the Planning Commission and the Social and Economic Council to the departmental technical committees, the councils (national or lower), committees, offices, and bureaus, the consultative organs are innumerable. Their real audience varies enormously, as does the role played by the representatives of the unions. But to what extent does participation in one of these councils render the unions accountable for a decision or a policy of which they disapprove? Is not consultation basically in conflict with the function of "challenging" which the unions attribute to themselves? Can they simultaneously participate in organs established in and by a given society and challenge the overall structure of that society? Today the trade unionists tend to deny that this presents them with a dilemma: they speak of a permanent tension between challenging the system and participating in it. In reality, however, the second gradually seems to overtake the first in the unions not Communist-dominated. The result is a noticeable change in the conduct of the trade unions as systematic opponents. For them as for the other organized groups a process of integration is taking place which is clearly transforming the nature of opposition in present-day France.

The Forms of Present-Day Opposition

REFERENDUMS AND ELECTIONS   The Fourth and Fifth Republics were born under conditions that were almost exactly inverse. While all the parties in power that jointly submitted a constitution to the country in

1946 represented more than 70 per cent of the voters and 55 per cent of the registered voters, the constitution was accepted by only 53.5 per cent of the voters, and only 36 per cent of those who were registered to vote. In September 1958 on the other hand, 78 per cent of the voters (66.4 per cent of the registered voters) adopted the constitution proposed by the government headed by General de Gaulle, while in the elections that followed two months later candidates who claimed his exclusive support obtained only 20.4 per cent of the votes (15.2 per cent of the registered voters).

Two conclusions can be drawn from this comparison. On the one hand, the dominant parties were more legitimate in 1946 than the regime, whereas in 1958 General de Gaulle was more popular than his party, which was about to constitute the axis of the majority. On the other hand, citizens clearly made a distinction between the different methods of voting. We need therefore to distinguish the nature of approval and opposition which the votes under the present regime reflect.

Excluding the vote on the Constitution, the Fifth Republic has experienced three referendums: on January 8, 1961, on the policy of self-determination in Algeria (75.2 per cent yes); on April 8, 1962, on the agreements of Evian giving independence to Algeria and the delegation of the power to execute them (90.6 per cent yes); October 28, 1962, on the adoption of a proposed law providing that the President of the Republic be elected directly by universal suffrage (61.7 per cent yes, or 46.4 per cent of the registered voters.) In the eyes of many of the opponents of General de Gaulle, these three referendums and the adoption of the Constitution have been no more than plebiscites. The reality is much more complex.

The personal element has obviously played a large role. How many voters had read the Constitution in 1958? The President of the Republic has done everything to assure that the referendums would take on the appearance of votes of confidence in him personally. But it would be inexact to say that the partisans of the General have each time hoped for a "yes" vote and his adversaries for a "no" vote, and even less correct to say that the vote was independent of the stated purpose of the referendum. In fact, even if the chief of state maneuvered for a long time to lead public opinion to the point of accepting a change in Algeria, in the minds of the electors the referendums of January 1961 and April 1962 turned quite as much on the Algerian policy itself as on General de Gaulle's personal qualities; hence many citizens who opposed the idea of charismatic power nonetheless voted "yes." And in October 1962 both the content of the question posed and the procedure itself were subject to lively debate.

That referendum, however, had a quite special character. In the three preceding referendums various parties had campaigned in behalf of a "yes" vote. In April 1962 the only appeal for "no" came from the extreme Right. Thus in order to separate the good Gaullist wheat from the chaff of the "partisans," General de Gaulle with considerable skill provoked the conflict of October which put all the parties in the "no" camp, with the single exception of those who claimed unconditional fidelity to his person, even though an appreciable part of the "yes" vote finally did come from men who simply approved the direct election of the future President or who considered that the camp of the "no's" represented a return to a detestable past.

Four examples are insufficient for arriving at definitive conclusions on the procedure of referendum, even if one adds the three constitutional referendums of 1945–46. However, they permit one to make some specific points. The French citizen values direct consultation and submits himself to it with discernment, as witness the variety of results. In a referendum, even the Communist voter largely loses the systematic oppositional behavior that traditional analysis tends to attribute to him. The referendum appears largely as a means of fostering positive participation in large part because it simplifies the consultation. At the same time, all the risks of excessive personalization of Power are increased by the referendum procedure. The duality Power/Opposition tends to reduce itself to the duality approval/disapproval of a man. But the exceptional historical character of General de Gaulle allow one to think that this danger is smaller than the advantage gained in France by an evolution toward a conception of political life founded more on participation than on refusal.

It will doubtless be the same for the election of the chief of state. A typical voter will doubtless vote *against* certain candidates in casting his ballot, but at least in 1965 the citizen will have the impression of giving a mandate directly to the future chief executive, once it is taken for granted that even without De Gaulle the precedent he has created as a President who wields power and employs the Premier as an assistant will be imposed on his immediate successor.

The desire of the electoral body for a homogeneous unity among President, government, and parliamentary majority clearly appeared in the election of November 1962. To be sure, the Gaullist party (Union pour la nouvelle République, UNR) obtained only 31.9 per cent of the votes on the first ballot. But this was the greatest percentage ever obtained by any French party; and what is more, the triumph on the second ballot completely demonstrated the decline of the opposition vote. Nothing demonstrates, however, that this situation will last beyond General de Gaulle, although it does throw a totally new light on electoral phenomena.

THE FALSE TRIANGLE   The Assembly elected in November 1962 had the composition indicated in the following table. Because the UNR/UDT benefited from a disciplined vote, and because the Pompidou government received the united support of this group and of the independent Republicans, France finally arrived at the situation which, in principle, all its political theorists had dreamed of: a disciplined and stable majority consistently supporting a government which, in principle, lasts through a whole legislature.

Union pour la nouvelle Républic, Union Democratique du Travail,[a] and affiliates	233
Independent Republicans and affiliates [b]	35
	268
Communists	41
Socialists and affiliates	66
Rassemblement Démocratique and affiliates [c]	39
Centre Démocratique [d]	55
Deputies not belonging to any group	13
	194
Total	462

a. Somewhat left- and labor-oriented Gaullists.

b. Friends of M. Giscard d'Estaing, Minister of Finance.

c. Radicals and Union Démocratique et Socialiste de la Résistance (U.D.S.R.) of M. Mitterrand.

d. Movvement Républicain Populaire (MRP) and UDSR of M. Pleven.

Unhappily the very real progress toward a solution of the French problem of government stability which this state of affairs constitutes is considerably attenuated by three deviations that keep the present mechanism from truly resembling either the British or German system.

First, the "corset" that M. Debré wanted to impose on Parliament with the constitutional mechanisms of 1958 is too tight. Made in order to compel an Assembly with an inclination toward permanent opposition to allow the government to survive and to work, these mechanisms tend to render parliamentary life uninteresting by preventing the minority from actually controlling the Cabinet's action. The mechanisms include the principle of the "blocked vote," which permits a government to avoid putting troublesome amendments to a vote, limitations on the domain of the law (the Constitution specifies what belongs to the Parliament, all other issues belonging to the executive), the possibility of having a text that has not had a favorable vote adopted by making it a question of confidence [2]—all of them means of reducing the normal role of Parliament.

2. Under Article 49 the Premier can, after the Council of Ministers has deliberated, take the existence of the government before the National Assembly on the vote of a text. In this case the text is considered as adopted unless a motion of censure, put down within the following 24 hours, is voted in the conditions set forth in the preceding paragraph. An example of the application of Article 49, taken from the con-

Second, both the opposition and the majority have great difficulty getting used to the existence of a stable situation. In Great Britain, the opposition understands that its role in Parliament excludes the possibility of making the government fall. The most it expects to do is to modify the actions of the government, possibly by giving publicity to the positions taken by the opposition. At the Palais-Bourbon, the opposition benches are generally empty because debates that cannot result in the overthrow of the Cabinet do not interest the deputies. The oral questions on Friday, which in principle are a means of controlling the government (at Bonn, it was the play of this mechanism that forced Franz Josef Strauss to resign because of the *Spiegel* affair) generally have no weight and attract only a few members. For its part the majority does not yet understand that democracy also consists of a dialogue with the minority. "Since we can do what we wish, what good is it to discuss the matter?" The majority benches therefore are also deserted.

Third, the major reason why the game is not played by the British or German rules is this: In appearance France exhibits today the normal situation of parliamentary regimes with a dominant party: tension among the three points of a triangle formed by the government (drawn from the dominant party) the leadership of the party, and the majority in Parliament. But the fact is that these three points all depend on the same force outside the triangle: General de Gaulle. This in large part explains the malaise that troubles relations between the majority and opposition: the first is never certain whether the position it defends today may not change tomorrow; the second tells itself that it is not very useful to attack the government or the parliamentary majority since they simply reflect a will that is not under parliamentary control.

THE OPPOSITIONS   If one neglects for a moment the social forces of opposition, what today are the political opposition forces in France? In our view, it is convenient to distinguish three kinds:

First, the opposition desiring to share in government: These are all the parties which extend from the Socialists of Guy Mollet to the Independents, whose great man remains M. Pinay. Even if one part of this opposi-

---

clusion of the debate on the French nuclear striking force, the famous *force de frappe:*

> *The Speaker.* Here are the results of the votes on the motion of censure:
>
> | Majority required for the adoption of the motion | 277 |
> | For adoption | 214 |
>
> (Applause from the Right and extreme Left)
> The required majority not having been attained, the motion of censure is not adopted. (Applause from the Left and the Center)
> In consequence the bill for the program relating to certain military projects is considered adopted ...

(*Journal Officiel, Assemblée Nationale,* November 23, 1960, p. 3972.)

tion—Socialists or Radicals—sometimes speaks in opposition to the regime, they all voted yes in 1958 and since then have sometimes been in power, sometimes in opposition. Tomorrow Socialists, Radicals, MRP, and Independents could participate anew in a government without changing their basic inclinations or habits.

Second, the opposition of sheer protest: On the extreme right, this comprises those who are nostalgic for Vichy and those who are nostalgic for "Algérie française," two categories composed often but not invariably of the same persons. Despite the existence of several particularly violent weeklies, this opposition no more represents an effective political force under the Fifth Republic than it did under the Fourth, which was not overturned by it. It was only the decolonization (Indochina but mainly Algeria) that led to an alliance between this extreme right and part of the Army.

Badly organized after the frequently ephemeral regroupings of which the PSU (Parti socialiste unifié—even though hardly at all *unifié*) has, since 1961, been by far the most representative, the importance in the electoral body of the left opposition of protest is almost negligible, but it exercises a certain influence on the minority of Frenchmen who seek a militant cause or who are searching for a political commitment. It is situated between the Communist Party, which it regards with a mixture of blame, envy, and optimism and which disdains it, and the Socialist Party, which it considers opportunistic and a traitor to the people's cause. Its pleasure in political rigor and doctrinal purity produces a rather distinct behavior: courage and clarity of analysis have led its militants, notably in the matter of decolonization, to protest, to bear witness in the name of values neglected by the great majority of Frenchmen and by their representatives. And often the respect for these values has constituted its political wisdom. But at the same time a certain incapacity to think of themselves as governing, to understand the demands of reality, has always pressed the largest proportion of its members to condemn even the men to whom they feel closest.

Third, the Communist Party: One should reserve to the Communists a special place, not only because since 1945 they have gathered more votes than any other party of alliance in every election except those of June 1946 and November 1962, but also because the behavior of the voters and of the non-Communist parties is in large measure determined by its existence: because its very presence contributes a certain number of particular characteristics to the political game in France. Even if since 1947 a gulf has existed between the Communist Party and other political groups, one should not forget that the party does not appear in the eyes of French opinion as a systematic and eternal opposition force, as a permanently destructive element. Even if one were to ignore its important role in the Resistance from 1941 to 1944, the Communist Party held an important place in the two greatest periods of social progress that France has known in the twentieth century: the Communists supported the Popular Front government in 1936–37 and they participated in the governments of the Liberation under the direction of General de Gaulle from September 1944 to January 1946, and under governments headed by the Socialists or the MRP until May 1947. During that second period, the mobilization of energy by the Communist Party for the reconstruction of France was extremely effective. The party itself maintains a deep nostalgia for the period when it participated in power. Even today, when it wishes to describe how political life might be better in the future, what it refers to is the model of tripartism of 1946.

Although the de-Stalinization in the U.S.S.R. and the atmosphere of international détente facilitate its tasks, the party scarcely knows how to profit from its advantages. Despite the great mass of its adherents, the devotion of its militants, the skill of its propagandists who know how to tie the everyday difficulties of the housewife to the great world problems, the Communist Party appears old and sclerotic. Maurice Thorez became secretary general in 1930 at 30 years of age and kept his post until shortly before his death in 1964. The numerous internal purges, the refusal, incapacity, or inability to support an intellectual life analogous to that of the Italian party, the absence of precise political ends—all these have weakened the party. Its power to attract young people with a sense of social justice has diminished. Its power of mobilization has become insignificant in relation to the number of its members and its voters, even when it is a matter of acclaiming Mr. Khrushchev on an official visit to Paris. Contrary to the expectation of many observers, the arrival of General de Gaulle in power caused it to lose a good share of its clientele, for it declined from 5.1 and 5.5 million votes in 1951 and 1956 to 3.9 and 4 millions in 1958 and 1962.

The Communist Party remains nonetheless an essential factor in French political life. Its very presence transforms the nature of the problems to be solved. Until 1958 the existence of a powerful parliamentary group sometimes withdrawn into a shell, sometimes kept to one side, falsified the political game: the axis of the governmental majorities necessarily passed to the right of the arithmetical center of the Assembly. With the return of voting in single-member districts, the idea of constructing a barrier against the Communists at the run-off election also favors the Center-Right, to the detriment of a Left destined never to become a majority in the absence of the Communists—or to be dominated by them should they enter into the majority.

On the one hand, then, one might foresee the decline of conflicts (the end of decolonization, the effects of the détente between Washington and Moscow), the evolution of social groups toward participation in a bargaining opposition, the acceptance by the parties, since De Gaulle, of the necessity to confine themselves to a "democratic-reformist" opposition and even to a "policy opposition." France, pressed by technical civilization, moves toward the pacification of its political society. Yet one may also foresee the permanence of the Communist Party as a center of disturbance, uncertainties and confrontations in institutional matters, the pronounced pleasure of groups and even of parties in challenging the government and "democratic structural opposition," and so no "normalization" of French political society.

Each of these two forecasts has about an equal chance of being realized. This is why it is not ultimately possible to discover in the past or in the present or in the future an Opposition in France. There always has existed, there will exist in the foreseeable future, a variety of oppositions, diverse in type and perpetually intertwined.

10

ITALY: OPPOSITIONS ON LEFT, RIGHT, AND CENTER

Samuel H. Barnes

Parliamentary opposition in Italy reflects general patterns present in other Western democracies plus some uniquely Italian characteristics. Analysis must begin with the following factors which condition the operations of the Italian parliamentary system:

the complex multiparty system

the historical experiences and institutional framework which have influenced Italian expectations and conceptions of opposition

the various cleavages in the body politic and their relation to political parties

the search for governmental stability in a system in which the opposition ranges from competition for office to the revolutionary alternatives of communist or fascist systems.

Opposition and the Party System

The Italian Republic is the sole remaining major European state with a classic multiparty parliamentary political system. Burdened like the French Fourth Republic with a Communist Party which receives almost one out of every four votes, the Italian system, unlike the French, is dominated by a powerful Christian Democratic Party which has received from just under half the votes cast in 1948 to a low in national elections of 38 per cent in 1963 (see Appendix Table 10.1). The position of the Christian Democratic Party near the center of the political spectrum, its long hold on office and deep penetration of the machinery of the state, and its firm doctrinal and organizational base—all these make it the governing party of Italy and the chief target of political opposition.

This opposition has been fragmented and largely unconstructive. The evolution of modern Italy has given rise to the typical socioeconomic cleavages of an urban industrial society without obliterating preexisting socioeconomic, regional, and historical divisions. Furthermore, ideological differences divide groups and regions which are otherwise similar. The present structure of political conflict reflects these various cleavages.

On the formal parliamentary level, Italian parties can be placed on a left-to-right continuum.[1] While such a continuum is inadequate for the analysis of many political systems, it does not greatly distort the realities of Italian politics; furthermore, it is a useful way of viewing Italian parties. On the left of the spectrum is the PCI. Although its functional role may be somewhat different, Communist espousal of an "Italian way to communism" still leaves it far from playing the formal role of a democratic opposition. Its neighbor on the spectrum and former ally, the PSI, has wavered between revolution and accommodation; the majority under Pietro Nenni accepted the existing democratic state and sought to work within it while the minority faction preferred a working alliance with the PCI. Opposition to Socialist participation in the Cabinet led to a withdrawal of much of the PSI left wing and the formation of the Italian Socialist Party of Proletarian Unity (PSIUP) in 1964. The PSDI differs from the majority in the PSI largely on the issue of the nature of its opposition: under the leadership of Giuseppe Saragat, the PSDI often supported and participated in postwar cabinets, while the PSI remained in opposition from 1947 until 1963. The tiny PRI likewise supported several postwar governments. The DC is in the center of the spectrum. The right is composed of the PLI, which is a constitutional conservative party of the "economic right," the monarchist PDIUM, and the neofascist MSI.

The parliamentary division of the parties simplifies reality, giving the parties a monolithic appearance which they do not in fact possess. The several dimensions of conflict which separate the parties also divide them internally, giving rise to factions which are continually subjected to the influence of wings of the other parties nearest them on the continuum. These factions are of importance in almost all of the parties, and particularly so in the governing parties, for they have often functioned as an internal democratic opposition. Thus the formal opposition and the real opposition must be distinguished, and an analysis of the latter must take into account the internal party factions.

1. The following abbreviations (taken from the parties' Italian initials) are used in this chapter:

DC	Christian Democratic Party
MSI	Italian Social Movement (neofascist)
PCI	Italian Communist Party
PDIUM	Italian Democratic Party of Monarchical Unity
PLI	Italian Liberal Party
PRI	Italian Republican Party
PSDI	Italian Social Democratic Party (Saragat Socialists)
PSI	Italian Socialist Party (Nenni Socialists)
PSIUP	Italian Socialist Party of Proletarian Unity (Vecchietti Socialists)

The PCI is the most monolithic of Italian parties. Its internal political divisions, while intriguing in themselves, are seldom relevant to the party's external politics. As already mentioned, the PSI was divided into a majority that wished to end its intransigence and play the parliamentary game and a procommunist minority which, while not opposing this in principle, set such a high price on Socialist cooperation that it was difficult for the Center parties to pay it. The departure of most of the minority into the PSIUP strengthened the unity of the PSI even though it weakened the party in Parliament. The evolution of the PSI greatly influenced its relations with the PSDI; indeed, a faction of the latter party returned to the former on the ground that Socialist acceptance of representative democracy rendered the PSDI unnecessary. While groups within both parties favored unity, bitter memories and personal ambitions hindered reconciliation. Even the small Republican Party is divided into factions that differ in their attitudes toward the "opening to the left" and clericalism.

Perhaps most important of all are the factions within the Christian Democratic Party. It contains a trade union faction, a reformist faction, an office-oriented majority, a traditionalist conservative faction, and several personal cliques operating both within and without these factions. The internal unity of the Liberal Party was enhanced by the schism of its radical members following the 1953 elections, leaving it in the hands of its more conservative members. The monarchist movement was long the toy of wealthy Southerners whose personal feuds led to the formation of rival monarchist parties, then the merger of the two, and, finally, in 1963 an electoral defeat which reduced the party to a fraction of its former parliamentary strength. The monarchist PDIUM represents no significant socioeconomic group or doctrine, and its decline is perhaps evidence of the growing rationalization of the Italian party system. The neofascist Italian Social Movement, like the Communist Party, opposed the constitutional system; but its 1963 national congress revealed a badly divided party, with one faction favoring intransigence and another accommodation with the system. So deep were the differences over the party's future role that the unity of the party was placed in jeopardy.

There are thus several levels of parliamentary opposition in Italy. There is the opposition of the parties which reject the constitutional order, such as the PCI and MSI. There are also often constitutional parties left outside the coalition, as has several times been the fate of the PLI. And there is the opposition within the governing parties of the factions that oppose the programs of the moment. This policy opposition differs from the internal maneuvering common to all political parties in the high degree of formal organization and recognition achieved by Italian party factions. Some single-party (*monocolore*) Christian Democratic minority cabinets accepted support where they could find it, from the Monarchists and even the MSI; and of course in this case the very concept of "opposition" becomes confused. While there has been some variation in the pattern of opposition, since 1947 the Christian Democrats have dominated the government and the PCI has been the largest of the opposition parties.

It is obvious that such a multiparty system with alternatives ranging from the PCI to the MSI differs greatly from the multiparty systems of most of northern Europe. Only France is perhaps roughly comparable to Italy, where the "monstrous trinity" of "disillusionment, skepticism, and indifference" have left a heritage of civic alienation.[2] Opposition in Italy taps a dimension of intensity not present in most of the other countries discussed in this book. These political divisions have deep roots in Italian history. Before we turn to a consideration of the contemporary saliency of these divisions in the polity and in Parliament we must examine this historical dimension.

Opposition in Perspective

PREFASCIST EXPERIENCES   In few countries of the Western world is the past so much a part of the present as in Italy. Its landscape, its cities, its monuments, its people are visible reminders of the continuity and change, the invasions and divisions, the greatness and decline which have made Italy both the museum and the laboratory of human achievement. In the arts the Italian past is a goad, a glorious and live tradition, a yardstick; in politics it is largely a burden, something to be overcome, a fountain of disunity and bad habits.

Italy was politically unified in the 1860s; its social and economic unity is still in the making. As a consequence of the hegemony of Piedmont, the achievement of unity seemed to many Italians merely the substitution of one alien, if Italian, rule for an Austrian, or Bourbon, or Papal one. The Liberal leaders of the new state imposed the constitution, the administrative machinery, and the debts of Piedmont on all of Italy. The South and the islands in particular, having known the harsher aspects of feudalism with few of its humane features, were to feel that liberalism was but a more modern—and more efficient—form of exploitation. The Liberal response to the South's opposition was centralization and force, soon supplemented by corruption: Liberal governments came to terms with the area and adopted its habits of buying off and frustrating opposition through the use of the machinery of the state and its local agent, the prefect. A career official responsible to the Minister of the Interior, the successful prefect produced votes for the friends of the government through the judicious exercise of discretion in awarding governmental

---

2. The phrase is from A. William Salomone, *Italian Democracy in the Making* (Philadelphia, University of Pennsylvania Press, 1945), p. 9.

favors and local improvements, the bribing and intimidation of opponents, the rigging of elections, and the careful cultivation of the local notables who organized the limited electorate as "clients." These practices, used mostly in the South, regularly provided the government with pliable majorities. They also left a heritage of cynicism, highly politicized administrative machinery, corruption, and the absence of civic pride and of vital local government.

On the national level the intrigues of the prefect, local notables, and leading parliamentarians made possible from the 1880s until the First World War a type of parliamentarianism known as *trasformismo*. This was a system in which prime ministers and cabinets remained in office by altering policies and personnel, when necessary, to fit the parliamentary majority. But this majority was itself largely the creation and creature of the Cabinet, thanks to the manipulation of elections as described above and of deputies through favors and, sometimes, outright bribery. Cabinets took their support where they could find it, whether right or left, thus making a coherent opposition impossible. These practices were facilitated by the small size of the electorate. In 1880 only the 2.2 per cent of the population which paid taxes or was educated could vote.[3] Due to the long withdrawal of Catholics from politics and the disenfranchisement of the lower classes, there was remarkable unanimity on socioeconomic questions in Parliament. Coupled with the practice of *trasformismo*, this agreement prevented the young state from developing a coherent parliamentary opposition.

The influence of Parliament on government policies varied greatly in the Liberal period. The king often exercised considerable influence, especially in foreign and military affairs. In addition, several leaders— Agostino Depretis (1881–87), Francesco Crispi (1887–96), and Giovanni Giolitti (1903–14)—so mastered the game of *trasformismo* that they were subjected to little meaningful parliamentary control. There were, of course, deputies who were in opposition to the government and the system. Radicals, reactionaries, and Mazzinian Republicans provided a steady flow of criticism. But they were few in number, divided among themselves, and repeatedly demoralized by defections to the majority. Moreover, they lacked a coherent social base. Only with the rise of socialism did a large opposition of principle emerge capable of withstanding the temptations of *combinazione*, of intrigue for personal advancement.

The genius of parliamentary politics after the turn of the century was Giovanni Giolitti. Cagy, experienced, open-minded, Giolitti appreciated the historical significance of the socialist movement and improvised a

3. Giovanni Schepis, "Analisi statistica dei risultati," in Alberto Spreafico and Joseph LaPalombara, eds., *Elezioni e comportamento politico in Italia* (Ivrea, Comunità, 1963), Tavola I, p. 384

strategy for dealing with it. The socialists were to be domesticated by being incorporated into the parliamentary system through the expansion of the suffrage.[4] Their numbers were to be balanced by the cultivation of the Catholic masses who would also be enfranchised by the extension of the suffrage. The Catholic Church, likewise frightened by the growing strength of socialism, cooperated: the *non expedit* (the Papal prohibition on Catholics voting or holding public office) was relaxed in 1905 and 1913, and was abandoned following the First World War. There had been independent militant Catholic deputies for some time, and in the 1913 elections, in the absence of a Catholic party, a compact between Giolitti and the president of the Catholic Union, Count Gentiloni, promised Catholic support for those liberals who would favor religious schools and orders and oppose divorce.

Catholics and Socialists were not alone in opposing the Liberal system. The first Nationalists appeared in 1913; and just before the outbreak of the war, the Liberal era seemed to be coming to an end. With changes in the times and the electorate, the old techniques of manipulation and corruption no longer worked effectively. Gaetano Salvemini, calling Giolitti *il ministro della mala vita*, the minister of the underworld, bitterly denounced his hand in the corruption and intimidation of the 1913 election: "confronted not with a mere two or three thousand voters, but with ten thousand or more voters in a constituency to be 'managed,' he was forced to increase the dose of violence to ensure success."[5] Hence the Fascists were not the first to introduce violence into Italian politics: but with the advent of mass parties, mass violence was to be needed, and the Fascists were to be better organized for this than the Liberals.

By the elections of 1919, the transition from the Liberal system of *trasformismo* to the multiparty system was complete. In the Parliament chosen in that year the Socialists were the largest party (156 seats), followed by the Popular Party, a new reformist constitutional democratic party of the Catholic rank-and-file (100 seats). Universal manhood suffrage, proportional representation, and Catholic participation had produced, for the first time in Italian history, disciplined mass parties in Parliament which would not play the parliamentary game of *trasformismo*.

4. As early as 1903 Giolitti had invited a socialist leader to take a portfolio in his Cabinet, but he refused. See Salomone, *Italian Democracy*, p. 49. The Reform Act of 1882 gave the vote to literate males over 21 with no taxation requirement; the 1912 Reform Act added males under 30 who had served in the armed forces and all males over 30, including illiterates (i.e., quasi-universal manhood suffrage). Female suffrage was adopted in 1946. Proportional representation was first used in the 1919 elections.

5. "Introductory Essay," in Salomone, *Italian Democracy*, p. xiv. Salvemini's pamphlet, "Il ministro della mala vita," subtitled "Notes and documents on the Giolittian elections in Southern Italy," was written in 1909. Although conceived as propaganda and not scholarship, it nicely captures the essentials of the elections in the South in the Giolittian era. It is reprinted in a volume with the same title edited by Elio Apih (Milan, Feltrinelli, 1962), pp. 73–141. See also Robert C. Fried, *The Italian Prefects* (New Haven, Yale University Press, 1963), pp. 120–62.

For the extension of the suffrage and the participation of Catholics greatly increased the size of the electorate, and proportional representation enabled the parties to discipline their representatives by placing them lower on the list or eliminating them entirely. This had been difficult to accomplish in a single-member district where, in order to be assured of repeated reelection, the deputy had merely to retain the allegiance of the few hundred voters necessary for a majority of the restricted electorate.

There was now an opposition, or rather, there were several oppositions, for among the Socialists, Populists, Fascists, Nationalists, and Liberals in Parliament, only the Liberals had the experience and attitude of a governing party, and they were in a minority and divided among themselves. The Socialists, excited by the example of the Russian Revolution, vacillated between trying to duplicate it and settling down to parliamentary democracy. During the crucial year of 1919 the party seemed to do neither; it succeeded merely in frightening the middle classes and antagonizing its potential allies.[6] In 1921 the revolutionary wing broke away and formed the Italian Communist Party. The Populists were in a position in Parliament to be the arbiters of the system, but fear of socialism within the Catholic hierarchy cost the party first its independence and eventually its existence.

Fascist violence was viewed by many moderate Italians as a mere continuation of past practices by more effective means against a Socialist enemy which had first begun to employ mass violence. The role of fascism in the downfall of Italian democracy is well known. The errors of tactics and judgment committed by Socialist, Catholic, and Liberal politicians are also well documented. Why did the Italian political system fail to come to terms with its opponents? While no definitive answer can be given, some relative factors can be examined.

The unification of Italy was achieved under the guidance of the liberal aristocracy and the upper middle classes, and these groups continued to dominate politics for the remainder of the nineteenth century. These were without doubt the most enlightened groups in the country, and their relative unity made it easier to pursue coherent policies of centralization and economic development. Furthermore, the manipulation of elections, especially in the South, was a considerable improvement over an alternative device—force. Given the general poverty of Italy, its uneven modernization, and its divided loyalties, the achievements of the liberal state should be viewed with understanding and charity. If the liberal system was inadequate, it was no more inadequate than most other European political systems of the age. Neither France nor Germany, for example, really dealt satisfactorily with the claims of Catholics and Marxists during the

6. Daniel Horowitz has written that "the Socialist Party, with a choice between a policy of revolution and a policy of reform, chose the verbiage of revolution and the substance of neither." *The Italian Labor Movement* (Cambridge, Harvard University Press, 1963), p. 133.

period preceding the First World War. In the Giolittian era the Italian
political system made great progress toward overcoming its weaknesses,
and it is today often viewed as the golden age of Italian democracy. Its
weaknesses were judged severely by an age which combined high ideals
with an ignorance of what was to follow.[7] But the liberal system failed to
come to terms in time with the two major forces of present-day Italy—
Marxism and Catholicism. These two mass movements, and especially the
former, matured outside of and in opposition to the liberal state.

Despite late industrialization and the dominance of agriculture, Italian
civilization has been an urban civilization. Even the landowning aristocracy
has been oriented toward the cities. Consequently the urban proletariat
was not the creation of industrialization and Italian socialism has not been
dependent on the industrial worker. Some predominantly agricultural
regions have been radical strongholds and agricultural workers have provided many of the militants and voters of the left. Italian socialism has a
romantic strain perhaps traceable to its anarchist origins. It has historically
wavered between a maximalist program for a revolutionary reconstruction of society and a minimalist reformism often bordering on oppor-
tunism. The weakness of Italian trade unions and the low level of political
skills within the lower classes have robbed the movement of stability.
From Turati and Bissolati to Nenni, leaders who have moved toward
accommodation with the system have repeatedly found themselves out-
flanked on the left. Only after the turn of the century did the liberals
seriously study the *possibility* of coming to terms with the socialist
opposition: the extension of the suffrage (1912) and the adoption of
proportional representation (1919) were belated recognition of the *necessity* of coming to terms. Given the sharp cleavages between social classes
in Italy plus the traditional regional divisions and individualism, the task
of making a loyal parliamentary opposition out of a revolutionary movement was a formidable one. No country with a similar social structure
seems to have succeeded, even under much more favorable circumstances.
It is thus noteworthy that this seemingly indigestible electorate showed
signs of eventually becoming absorbed into the parliamentary system before fascism relegated the effort to the "might-have-beens" of history.[8]

7. Salvemini, who was a bitter foe and critic of Giolitti before the rise of fascism,
was to write in 1945: "I would have been wiser had I been more moderate in my
criticism of the Giolittian system. My knowledge of the men who came after
Giolitti in Italy as well as of countries in which I have lived during the last twenty
years has convinced me that if Giolitti was not better, neither was he worse than
many non-Italian politicians, and he was certainly less reprehensible than the Italian
politicians who followed him." "Introductory Essay," in Salomone, *Italian Democracy*,
p. xv.
8. H. Stuart Hughes suggests that Giolitti had succeeded in "domesticating" the
Socialists only to have them later regain "their revolutionary militancy." *The United
States and Italy* (Cambridge, Harvard University Press, 1953), p. 59.

The nature of the Catholic opposition to the liberal state was considerably different. It derived more from the Vatican's temporal politics than from the alienation of Catholics as such. To be sure, legitimists in the South, the Black Aristocracy of Rome, and pro-Austrian conservatives in the North continued their formal intransigence well into the twentieth century. On the other hand, many Catholics, the lower clergy included, applauded national unity and tried to lessen the impact of the *non expedit*. The prohibition on Catholic participation was not always respected, but it did prevent the organization of a Catholic political party. Catholics were active on the local level, however, first with the toleration and later with the approval of the hierarchy. With the rise of socialism and the expanding political activities of Catholics the need for national coordination was evident and gave rise to the Popular Party. While representing an opposition group in Italian society, the party was by no means committed to parliamentary opposition, and it formed with the Liberals and Socialists a potential large democratic majority in the Chamber. But the Catholics were internally divided, inexperienced, and lacking in self-confidence. The three democratic groups saw each other—not the Fascists and Nationalists—as the chief enemy.

It is not necessary here to assign responsibility for the failure of liberal democracy in Italy. But it should be noted that blame cannot be restricted to any single group. The Liberals made many mistakes. The Catholic withdrawal from politics deprived the system of a stabilizing force of potentially immense importance. The indecision of Italian Socialists likewise contributed to the disaster. And, finally, the madness of nationalism rampant in the first half of the twentieth century poisoned the system. In the tragedy of errors that destroyed Italian democracy there are many *personaggi*.

REPUBLICAN INSTITUTIONS AND THE LEGACY OF FASCISM   A widely read history of Italy tends to see fascism as a natural development out of weaknesses existing in the liberal state.[9] Certainly the interpenetration of party and state, corruption, elitism, violence, militarism, and absence of opposition characteristic of fascism all find their precedents in the earlier system. A more kindly interpretation would view fascism as a mere parenthesis in the evolution of liberal democracy in Italy. Perhaps the two points of view are not irreconcilable. The political system which emerged after the Second World War exhibits many characteristics of the prefascist system. The formal institutional structure has changed more than behavioral patterns. The Chamber of Deputies resembles that of the prefascist monarchy; the Senate, on the other hand, is now elected, not appointed, and is roughly similar in composition and powers to the lower house. Elections to the

9. Denis Mack Smith, *Italy: A Modern History* (Ann Arbor, University of Michigan Press, 1959), p. vii.

Senate and Chamber are by proportional representation. The Cabinet is similar to the earlier one, but has lacked the stability of some prefascist cabinets. A president has of course replaced the king. Several innovations in the new constitution—the Constitutional Court, the High Judicial Council, and the Economic and Labor Council—were implemented only slowly, and 15 years after the constitution went into effect only five of the proposed 19 regions were functioning. The Italian bureaucracy remains highly centralized, and political considerations are likely to enter into any administrative action at any level. Interference by both the Christian Democratic Party and the hierarchy of the Church in the administration reinforces the feelings of many Italians that the Republic is a Christian Democratic *political system*, as previous ones were Fascist or Liberal. The state machinery, in other words, is still viewed not as the instrument of the collectivity but of the ruling party.

The most important difference between the Republic and the prefascist constitutional monarchy lies not so much in institutional structures or behavioral characteristics as in the lineup of political forces in Parliament. The Catholic opposition, reinforced by economic conservatives and others afraid of communism, has come to power. The descendents of the old Socialists are now divided among the PCI, PSI, PSDI, and PSIUP. Unable to find a mass base in an age of universal suffrage, the forces that provided the old Liberal majority are divided among several parties. The old clientele relationships of the South remain but the votes no longer go exclusively or even predominantly to the PLI. The PRI survives precariously from election to election, but its future is not bright. The Monarchists have no prefascist equivalent, although they are a primarily clientelistic party not unlike the prefascist reactionary Southern cliques. The MSI is a nostalgic reactionary party with more in common with fascism in its early years and in its "purified" form under the Italian Social Republic than with the long years of power and accommodation. This revised lineup of parliamentary forces perhaps suggests greater changes in the Italian political culture than have actually occurred. In fact, most of the same groups which dominated the Italian economy, society, and polity under the Liberal state and the Fascist state still occupy commanding positions under the Republic. The range of groups participating in power, however, has broadened, and the range represented in Parliament has broadened even more.

Among the many legacies of fascism were two of great significance to our discussion. One was the discrediting of most of the groups and institutions formerly associated with legitimacy. The monarchy, the aristocracy, the bureaucracy, the judiciary, the business community, the military, the educational system, and most of the old political groups had compromised with fascism in various degrees. The Roman Catholic Church stood alone among the symbols of order at the end of the war. The Lateran Treaties of 1929 completed and formalized the reconciliation between the Church and unified Italy, and they did much to legitimize fascism. Religion and fascism, however, came increasingly in conflict, and at the end of the war the Church reaped a not completely deserved harvest of goodwill and prestige. It became the rallying point for the forces of order and conservatism, and, soon, of constitutional democracy itself. The Christian Democracy which emerged as the dominant force in Italian politics in the 1940s was considerably more than the prefascist Popular Party. While many Christian Democratic leaders had been active in the earlier party, the new party recruited from a much wider segment of the population. In the atmosphere of crisis and threatening revolution of the postwar period, the choice was often posed as being between God and Communism, and the Christian Democrats became the chief beneficiaries of the panic of conservative and middle-of-the-road voters.[10] As a result the party contained many disparate elements held together by fear, and the decline in its electoral appeal evident in the 1963 elections was perhaps due as much to the general relaxation of tension and the relative depolarization of Italian politics as to anything else.

The second political legacy of fascism was the myth of the Resistance. The Communists maintained the best underground organization during the Fascist years. Their discipline and sense of direction enabled them to exploit the Resistance movement better than the other parties. The Italian Resistance was almost exclusively a Central and Northern phenomenon, for the South was liberated quickly and was never under German control. This separate experience during a crucial moment in Italian history has greatly contributed to the political differences between North and South. The Resistance was not a Communist-led or -inspired movement; leaders and sympathizers of all the Center and Left parties participated in it. But the Italian Communist Party, like its French counterpart, had more than its share of martyrs, provided more than its share of the personnel and conspiratorial skill, and reaped more than its share of the material and symbolic rewards of liberation. The material rewards were dominant positions in local government and trade unions, and real property in the form of equipment, offices, weapons, and money. The symbolic rewards included the myth of Communist leadership of the great movement for

10. Gabriel Almond and Sidney Verba, using data from attitudinal surveys, have concluded that "Italy presents us with the curious anomaly of a political system in which the formal democratic constitution is supported in large part by traditional-clerical elements who are not democratic at all, and not even political in a specialized sense of the term. Opposed to the constitution is a left wing, which, at least in part and at the rank-and-file voter level rather than among the party elite, manifests a form of open partisanship that is consistent with a democratic system." *The Civic Culture* (Princeton, Princeton University Press, 1963), p. 160.

the regeneration of Italian society. The Resistance, in the areas where it existed, constituted one of the few genuinely popular mass political movements in the history of Italy, a country whose history has been made by its elites. It is unfortunate that its exploitation by the Left has forced the Christian Democrats to play down its significance, a policy that tends to reinforce the identification of the Resistance with the Left in the popular mind. Thus a legacy of fascism was the emergence of the Communist Party as a well-organized and -financed political machine, benefiting from the prestige of Russia, its own antifascism, and its role in the Resistance, all of which have given it a peculiar legitimacy even among many non-communists.

Opposition and the Polity

It is a truism of political science that different socioeconomic groups tend to be disproportionately represented in different political parties. How parliamentary opposition is related to the socioeconomic composition of the parties is one of our major interests. Regional, class, and ideological differences loom large in Italy; and of these differences, the class cleavage is probably the most important. For poverty makes mere survival a struggle and politics a grim zero-sum game in which the gains of one group correspond perfectly with the losses of another. Italy is experiencing rapid economic growth and social change at the moment, and the objective socioeconomic differences show signs of decreasing; but psychological attitudes change slowly and objective changes in differences are not immediately reflected in political behavior.

Gabriel Almond and Sidney Verba have written the following:

> The picture of Italian political culture that has emerged from our data is one of relatively unrelieved political alienation and of social isolation and distrust. The Italians are particularly low in national pride, in moderate and open partisanship, in the acknowledgement of the obligation to take an active part in local community affairs, in the sense of competence to join with others in situations of political stress, in their choice of social forms of leisure-time activity, and in their confidence in the social environment.[11]

This is undoubtedly a fair, if exaggerated, characterization. For a more detailed discussion we must note the political importance of regional, ideological, and social differences. Then we will examine the Italian political culture in general.

REGIONAL DIFFERENCES   Both economic and political considerations have led to the concentration of Italian industry in the North, especially in the

11. *The Civic Culture*, p. 402.

triangle formed by Milan, Turin, and Genoa. The North was closer to European markets and influences and more progressively administered at the time of unification; protective tariffs and government subsidies compounded this initial advantage. The standard of living is much higher in the North. The wages of industrial workers in the North approach those of the average Dutch worker. Moreover, the existence of alternative employment in an expanding economy has raised overall wages and led to a rapid influx into urban areas, into the provincial capitals as well as the large cities. In addition, Northern Italy has some of the nation's richest agricultural land; and there are many efficiently run large farms and smaller farms operated by owners and sharecroppers. The latifundia system of the South is absent. Many marginal farms have been abandoned; rural cooperatives and other self-help organizations have been developed; and educational possibilities have been extended. Among the political ramifications of these developments are reduced apathy, a higher degree of party and interest organization, less corruption in politics, and greater political sophistication and rationality.

Much of Southern Italy is still dominated by *la miseria* and a sense of hopelessness, alleviated only by emigration and remittances from abroad. Here the misfortune of poor land is compounded by the abundant population attempting to live off it. Fascist legislation which remained in effect until the mid-1950s made it legally difficult for most Southern peasants to leave their communes. Until the fall of fascism the situation of the South was largely hidden from the world and, indeed, from most Italians.[12]

Several coastal cities of the *Mezzogiorno*, such as Naples and Palermo, have long been administrative, commercial, and cultural centers. These and other areas have recently felt the impact of industrialization and economic development. Even the more developed areas of the South, however, suffer from poverty and overpopulation, while the interior of the lower part of the peninsula and of the islands remains barely touched by the economic boom, except for a loss of its males to the factories of Italy and Northern Europe.[13] Despite the beginnings of land reform and industrialization, the South remains economically backward. The political consequences are apathy, electoral volatility, and cynicism.

The interior is an area of large estates and small subsistence plots. The population lives in crowded hilltop towns and works the surrounding

12. Since the Second World War the plight of the Southern poor has been widely publicized by Carlo Levi, Ignazio Silone, Danilo Dolci, the studies published in *Nord e Sud,* and numerous other scholarly works.

13. It has been calculated that 2,235,000 persons left the South between 1952 and 1962. Half migrated abroad and half to Piedmont, Lombardy, Liguria, and, in lesser numbers, Latium. Some four-fifths of industrial investments are in the North, and almost four-fifths of investments made in the South are in agriculture or public works. *Annuario politico italiano, 1963* (Milan, Communità, 1963), pp. 225–26.

land. Some farm scattered plots which they themselves own; others till the soil as sharecroppers; still others hire themselves out as day laborers. But the man who owns his land may be poorer than a sharecropper, and all are susceptible to economic and political pressures at election time. The middle class is limited to professional men, civil servants, some agricultural managers, and some middle-sized landholders. As a group the Southern middle class has proved unprogressive and subservient to the small upper class, and efforts to create a prosperous rural middle class on owner-operated farms through land reform and government technical assistance have been disappointing.

Political parties in the South tend to be more individualistic than in the North; patron–client relationships are extremely important, and electoral shifts may reflect merely the change in loyalties of a local notable. Personalities are often more important than programs,[14] sentiment than reason, food baskets on holidays than year-round schools. Parties differ greatly in this respect, but they all are affected. The Left is somewhat less, and the Christian Democrats and Monarchists somewhat more, involved in this peculiar play of personalities and favoritism. Party organization is embryonic, associational life poorly developed or nonexistent, and political ignorance and apathy widespread. Regional parties sometimes take a line independent of the national party, as did the Sicilian Christian Democrats, and historic suspicion of outsiders applies equally to party organizers.

Central Italy, which starts north of Rome and extends to the Po Valley, is in the middle in behavioral as well as geographical terms. It is in general much poorer than the North and agriculture remains of great importance, although the balance is rapidly shifting to industry. Its poverty, however, has not been as demoralizing as in the South, and workers and peasants have long experience with political and other organizations for self-help. Central Italy contains the Tuscan, Emilian, and Romagnan strongholds of the Left. Moreover, the middle class is more numerous and progressive, and the upper class less reactionary than in the South. Consequently, Central Italy more closely resembles Northern than Southern Italy in its political behavior.

IDEOLOGICAL DIFFERENCES   The ideological divisions of Italian politics should be approached with considerable caution. Certainly they are overtly among the greatest in Western Europe, surpassing even those of France in their range and depth. Italian voters choose among a bewildering variety of ideological and political commitments—Marxist (communist

---

14. For example, Southerners are more than twice as likely to cast preference votes than Northerners (i.e., to vote for particular individuals on the party's list, rather than merely to vote for the party's slate as a whole). Schepis, "Analisi statistica," Tavola XXVI, p. 398 f.

and three socialist), liberal, fascist, traditionalist, integral Catholic, and social Catholic. These labels mask a variety of basic issues which crosscut the parties, such as democracy or totalitarianism, clericalism or laicism, Catholicism or secularism, laissez faire or government planning, the status quo or social change. It is probable that these policy choices are more fundamental than the ideological assumptions from which they are seemingly derived. For there is evidence accumulating that mass publics everywhere have extremely limited ideological perceptions; and, given the low level of education and political sophistication of the average Italian voter, it would be surprising if these findings did not also apply to Italy.[15] The role of ideology in Italian politics is consequently difficult to evaluate.

A tentative and preliminary analysis of the role of ideology should begin with social stratification and the educational system. Relatively few Italians receive a secondary education and even fewer attend a university. The potential audience for sophisticated ideological appeals is limited. The political elite, however, is well educated and, except for Communists (who are heavily lower class in origin), party leaders are not greatly dissimilar in educational and social background.[16] Italian higher education heavily emphasizes legal studies and the humanities, the manipulation of ideas and symbols, which encourage a tendency to view politics in abstract terms. Skill in the manipulation of symbols is an important source of influence for party elites in a country with traditional respect for learning combined with limited diffusion of it. But the importance of ideology can be exaggerated. For in all of the parties to the right of the Communists (and on the local level they too often "play the game"), ideological considerations do not prevent leaders who are secure in their party posts from entering into *combinazioni* inconceivable from the ideological viewpoint. Ideology is a weapon of particular importance in inter- and intraparty struggles, and is also a useful analytical tool in discussing some aspects of Italian politics; but it can easily confuse rather than clarify the reality of the Italian situation.

15. See Angus Campbell, Philip E. Converse, Warren E. Miller, and Donald E. Stokes, *The American Voter* (New York, Wiley, 1960), Ch. 9; and Philip E. Converse, "The Nature of Belief Systems of Mass Publics," in David E. Apter, ed., *Ideology and Discontent* (New York, Free Press, 1964), pp. 206–61. Little data is available for Italy on this point, but a study of the ideological perceptions of a group of PSI *members* by the author strongly reinforces the suspicion that Italians will conform to the patterns found by Converse.

16. Differences among leaders are in the direction one would expect, however: Monarchists tend to be higher in social class, Socialists lower, and Christian Democrats in between, although most are from the middle classes. For data on the background of Italian deputies (almost all top party officials are in Parliament, and most are deputies) see Luigi Lotti, "Il parlamento italiano, 1909–1963: raffronto storico," pp. 141–200; and Giovanni Sartori, "Dove va il parlamento?" pp. 312–46; both in Sartori et al., *Il parlamento italiano, 1946–1963* (Naples, Edizioni scientifiche italiane, 1963).

SOCIAL STRATIFICATION / Social class is a very important explanatory variable in Italian politics. Objective social differences are perhaps the greatest in democratic Europe, and the sense of social inequality is very strong. Moreover, the strength of the family plus economic stagnation have made social mobility difficult. As elsewhere, education is the key to social mobility, and higher education has been largely limited to those of means. Economic development is undoubtedly leading to an upgrading of Italian society as a whole, but the political results are not yet apparent.

The socioeconomic basis of Italian parties is blurred by two factors, the interclass nature of Christian Democracy and the division of each class's vote among several parties. The Christian Democratic party is truly an interclass party: in 1958 it received about 23 per cent of the votes of industrial workers, sharecroppers, agricultural workers, and other low income groups, according to estimates of Mattei Dogan.[17] But of these same groups, some 7 per cent voted for rightist parties and 70 per cent for the PCI, PSI, and PSDI. Moreover, a high proportion of the Christian Democratic working-class voters are women.[18] The PCI and PSI get about half their votes from the industrial working class alone. In the most heavily industrialized zones, however, the Communist portion of the industrial working-class vote falls to 38 per cent; thus the Communists are not necessarily stronger in the more industrialized areas.

There is further evidence of the association between communism and class in the Red Belt across Central Italy. Here a declining sharecropping system and the beginning of industrialization combine with a radical tradition to form the heaviest concentration of leftist voters in Italy. There seems to be a great income differential between Christian Democratic and leftist voters in agricultural categories, with the former coming from the higher income groups. According to the estimates of Dogan, large farmers vote overwhelmingly for the rightist parties; small and middle-sized

17. Taken from Dogan, "La stratificazione sociale dei suffragi," in Spreafico and LaPalombara, eds., *Elezioni*, pp. 407–74; and Dogan, "Les bases sociales des partis politiques en France et en Italie," paper presented at the Fifth World Congress of Sociology, Washington, D.C., September 2–8, 1962. These figures are estimates derived from a variety of sources and should be accepted with caution as indicative rather than definitive. Italian polling data are inadequate as a source of this kind of information because of the extremely large portion of respondents who refuse to divulge their party identification or vote to interviewers. See Almond and Verba, *The Civic Culture*; Pierpaolo Luzzatto Fegiz, *Il volto sconosciuto dell'Italia: dieci anni di sondaggi DOXA* (Milan, Giuffre, 1956); Alberto Spreafico, "Orientamento politico e identificazione partitica," pp. 689–732, and Paolo Ammassari, "Opinione politica e scelta elettorale," pp. 733–84, both in Spreafico and LaPalombara, eds., *Elezioni*.

18. Dogan, "La stratificazione sociale dei suffragi," p. 420; see also Dogan, "Le donne italiane tra il cattolicesimo e il marxismo," in Spreafico and LaPalombara, eds., *Elezioni*, pp. 475–94.

farmers support the DC; sharecroppers (very important in Central Italy) and farm workers provide the PCI and PSI with a strong agricultural following.[19]

The nonagricultural middle-class vote is likewise divided along social class lines, with about half the votes going to the DC and most of the rest being divided among the PLI, PRI, MSI, and PDIUM. Only the salaried lower middle class votes PCI and PSI in substantial proportions (30 per cent).[20]

The number of women in the Christian Democratic electorate should also be noted. In 1958 slightly over half the female electorate voted Christian Democratic, and they provided 63 per cent of the votes received by that party. As there are a million more women than men in Italy, this tendency assumes considerable importance.[21] Dogan attributes the Christian Democratic vote of women to religious and traditionalist impulses, rather than to economic or ideological conservatism.[22] He concludes that if only men had voted in 1958, the Communists and Socialists together would have received more votes than the Christian Democrats.[23]

POLITICAL CULTURE   The foregoing discussion has focused largely on the electorates of the various parties. The continuing relationships between parties, their members, and auxiliary organizations form another important source of information about the relationship between parliamentary opposition and social structure. The concept of political subculture is sometimes used as a form of shorthand to suggest the interconnected network of party, trade union, press, club, youth, recreational, and other organizations which cater to the associational needs of the party member from youth through old age, integrating him into the party, satisfying his needs for comradeship, and isolating him from contact with members of rival subcultures. The concept is useful in the Italian situation. The major parties and, with less success, the minor ones too are membership parties with extensive auxiliary organizations providing material and symbolic benefits to their members, ranking from the imposing formal structure of integral Catholicism to the individualistic emphasis on economic interests among the Liberals. The concept of subculture is useful— but it can be misleading. For the most important subcultural divisions of

19. Mattei Dogan, "Les bases sociales des partis politiques en France et en Italie" (note the limitations of these figures discussed in footnote 17).

20. Ibid.

21. *Annuario statistico italiano, 1962* (Rome, Instituto Centrale di Statistica, 1963), p. 15.

22. "Le donne italiane tra il cattolicesimo e il marxismo," p. 492.

23. Ibid., p. 478. However, this viewpoint is challenged by Joseph LaPalombara and Jerry B. Waters, "Values, Expectations, and Political Predispositions of Italian Youth," *Midwest Journal of Political Science*, 5 (1961), 54.

Italy are not primarily political, nor do the lines of cultural cleavage necessarily correspond to the party divisions. They are, however, related in interesting ways.

Perhaps politically the most important cultural heritage in Italy is that of the peasant. Largely cut off from opportunities for advancement and self-improvement, but living an essentially urban life, he has shaped the attitudes and expectations of the Italian form of communal individualism. In its extreme form this individualism has been labeled by Edward Banfield "amoral familism": "Maximize the material short-run advantage of the nuclear family; assume that all others will do likewise." [24] In areas where extreme poverty has not reduced the range of charity to the nuclear family, the extended family, godparent relationships, and associations have in various ways operated to reduce the uncertainty of a precarious existence. Increasingly, political organization is being adopted as a weapon in the struggle, and it is not surprising that those parties such as the Christian Democrats and Communists which have been most successful in exploiting face-to-face relationships and inserting themselves in the existing social fabric have been most successful in gaining loyal members.[25] This peasant heritage has important behavioral consequences. The industrial worker may still live in an agricultural zone, even in the North; he undoubtedly has relatives who remained behind to till the land; and he is at best only one or two generations away from the peasant state.[26] Many of the differences in Northern and Southern political behavior are to be explained by the greater advances made in the North in altering this peasant culture.

The traditional Italian middle class is a small, cultivated group which has proved capable of defending its class interests but has been less successful in carrying through either a thoroughgoing secularization of public life or a deep revolution in Italian social structure. It has oscillated between respect for clerical and aristocratic privilege and a vague liberalism. Like the lower classes it divides its vote between confessional and lay parties, the latter being the PLI, PRI, and PSDI rather than the PCI and PSI. The small aristocratic upper class has little political power, but it has greatly influenced the social and political attitudes of the insecure middle class. The numerically important subcultures are therefore those of the middle class and the lower class (industrial and agricultural, both largely

24. *The Moral Basis of a Backward Society* (Glencoe, Ill., Free Press, 1958), p. 85.
25. For claimed party membership (which should be treated with caution) of the Christian Democratic, Communist, and Socialist parties in 1960–62, complete with geographical and other breakdowns, see *Annuario Politico Italiano, 1963*, pp. 1262–69.
26. In 1936, 48.4 per cent of all employed Italians worked in agriculture, hunting, or fishing. The figure for the South was 57 per cent, rising to 75 per cent in the Abruzzi and in Basilicata. *Statistiche sul Mezzogiorno d'Italia, 1861–1953* (Rome, SVIMEZ, 1954), p. 46.

urban-based and peasant in background). The electorates of the parties to the left and right of the Christian Democrats fit more or less neatly into one of these political subcultures. But every party must share a subculture with at least one other party. And the Christian Democrats are firmly established in both subcultures.

For some purposes it might be convenient to view Christian Democracy as associated with a separate, nonclass-based subculture. But there is no evidence of great differences in outlook between one businessman who supports the PLI because of its economic conservatism and his colleague who votes Christian Democratic for business reasons and out of fear of communism, nor of differing basic attitudes between a landowning farmer who votes Christian Democratic to protect his farm and the sharecropper who votes Communist because he does not own land. The differences lie in perceptions of interests and how best to further them—not in *Weltanschauungen*.[27] This is not to deny the existence of a specifically Catholic subculture in Italy which would prefer an integral Catholicism, but it is far from being coterminous with Christian Democracy. Nor is the Communist Party, despite its size, able to isolate its members organizationally, except in some rural areas and some urban neighborhoods where the party has a virtual monopoly in lower-class milieux. But this is a monopoly over culturally deprived and socially isolated groups rather than over "true believers" in a competitive situation. And most PCI voters are doubtlessly not ideological communists. Finally, it should be noted that the level of political subcultural identification which exists, for example, in the Netherlands requires a degree of organization and politicization simply not present in Italy.

Although the level of associational activity in Italy is perhaps lower than in several other European countries, Joseph LaPalombara has discovered groups covering roughly the same fields of activity which would be found in the United States.[28] A major difference between Italian and American groups is the former's fragmentation along party or ideological lines. Thus there are Communist-Socialist, Christian Democratic-Republican, Social Democratic, and neofascist trade unions. Similar duplication is found in women's, students', veterans', and other types of organizations.

---

27. Hadley Cantril suggests that matched pairs of Christian Democratic and Communist voters differ in the relatively better fortune of the former: "Those who do *not* vote Communist are, by and large, people who in one way or another have had some breaks in life so that they have managed in their own eyes to get along well enough and more or less on their own." *The Politics of Despair* (New York, Basic Books, 1958), p. 125. For a study of *ex*-communists in Italy (and France, the United Kingdom, and the United States) see Gabriel Almond, *The Appeals of Communism* (Princeton, Princeton University Press, 1952).

28. "The Utility and Limitations of Interest Group Theory in Non-American Field Situations," *Journal of Politics*, 22 (1960), 29–49.

Several of the most important interest organizations, however, speak for a relatively united segment of the population. Confindustria, the peak organization of industry, and Catholic Action, the lay affiliate of the Church, have no significant competitors in their fields. This is true also of a third organization, the Christian Democratic-oriented Association of Direct Cultivators (independent farmers), which has outdistanced its leftist and other rivals by more than nine-to-one in representation elections.

Catholic Action is of course wholly Christian Democratic in politics. With the party deeply indebted to the clergy and to the Civic Committees of Catholic Action for electioneering and propaganda, representatives of the Church and Catholic Action have long been able to count at least upon excellent channels of access and sympathetic consideration by the ministries and administration at all levels. With the growth of a more effective organization in the past decade, the party has been more independent. The importance of Catholic Action has also been reduced by the less aggressively partisan attitudes of the Vatican since the death of Pius XII, as well as the altered atmosphere under the opening to the left.[29]

The party alignment of Confindustria has been more complicated. During the De Gasperi era it was assured of good personal contacts with the government even if it seldom seemed very influential. Under his successors, however, the organization felt stifled and frustrated, and in 1958 it made an "incredibly amateurish and abortive" attempt to intervene in the elections on behalf of the Liberals.[30]

The historic identification of the Italian political system first with the Liberals, then with the Fascists, and today with the Christian Democrats has important ramifications for the operations of interest groups, and the feedback in turn reinforces the bitterness of opposition and the intensity of the political struggle. For the Christian Democrats largely exclude non-Christian Democratic-affiliated groups from influence on government. In general, those groups which can claim a "kinship" *(parentela)* relationship with Christian Democracy are granted favored access to decision-makers, whether in the party or in the ministries; others are largely excluded. Thus the Christian Democratic-oriented trade union, the Association of Direct Cultivators, and Catholic Action have privileged relationships which they assiduously cultivate and exploit. Interest groups not affiliated with Christian Democracy or one of its minor party allies are usually

29. Marcello Vigli, "I comitati civici nella nuova situazione politica," *Tempi moderni, 10* (1962), 57–72. For a study of Italian Catholic Action by an American-trained sociologist see Gianfranco Poggi, *Il clero di riserva* (Milan, Feltrinelli, 1963).

30. LaPalombara, "The Utility and Limitations of Interest Group Theory in Non-American Field Situations," and "La Confindustria e la politica in Italia," *Tempi moderni, 7* (1961), 3–16.

unable to participate meaningfully in the governmental process. They feel that only changing the system will alter this situation, hence the bitterness and negativism of opposition. It is not so much that significant *interests* go unrepresented in contemporary Italy; rather, the government determines who will be permitted to represent those interests vicariously. This is of course quite different from the model pluralistic society with a neutral state and free competition of interests.

This discussion of the bases of political conflict in Italy might be summed up as follows: Italian society is fragmented along a number of lines of cleavage. It is changing from the shape of an elongated pyramid common to developing countries to the normal curve characteristic of industrial society with most units clustered close to the midpoint. Some areas of the country still resemble the pyramid in social structure; others approach the normal curve. But attitudes still reflect the extreme class divisions of the earlier society, and only the Christian Democratic Party has substantial strength at most social levels. Other parties are largely tied to particular classes. However, no party is able to monopolize the voice of a class, as the classes themselves are fragmented along ideological and other lines. But there is little evidence that ideological considerations are foremost in motivating party choice within the mass electorate; rather, perceived interest and local considerations seem more important in choosing between parties. Interest organizations follow the lines of class and/or party, and those representing the opposition are largely blocked from the governmental process. The parties in Parliament are separated by the classes and ideologies they represent, the resulting gulf between their programs, and their mutual intolerance.

Opposition and Parliament

THE PROBLEM OF A MAJORITY   The Italian parliamentary system strongly resembles that of the Fourth French Republic, but the dominance of a single party makes the Italian system in reality quite different in a number of important particulars.[31] The absence of a strong democratic opposition party or parties eliminates the possibility of a democratic alternative government, while the strength of the extreme Left makes it impossible to rule out an undemocratic alternative.[32] And the interclass

31. The political process in Italy has received little attention. An important beginning based on extensive field work is LaPalombara's *Interest Groups in Italian Politics*. See also Norman Kogan, *The Politics of Italian Foreign Policy* (New York, Praeger, 1963); and A. Predieri, "La Produzione legislativa," in Sartori et al., *Il parlamento italiano*, pp. 205–76.

32. For a discussion of this and related issues, and a warning against simplistic single-cause explanations of parliamentary and electoral behavior, see Joseph La-Palombara, "Political Party Systems and Crisis Governments: French and Italian

nature of the dominant DC enables it to shift from one position to another as the mood of the electorate changes. Furthermore, many Christian Democratic leaders exhibit pragmatism, flexibility, willingness to compromise, and instinct for the politically popular and useful. The Christian Democratic Party thus in many respects forms half of a two-party system.

Although the PCI could provide the other half, its ideological and class bases make it an extremely unlikely candidate for the alternative government in a two-party system. It is possible that the changes in outlook implicit in the acceptance of the opening to the left by the DC may combine in the long run with the revisionist tendencies of the PCI to alter basically the role of the PCI in the system. It seems certain, however, that the intent of the architects of the opening to the left was rather to isolate and weaken the PCI, not to accommodate to it. The reasons for the opening to the left require attention.

The Christian Democratic Party is more than just another party, albeit a large one, which plays the parliamentary game of coalition building. Its size, its position at the center of the political spectrum, its close ties with dominant ecclesiastical, business, and interest group elites, and its long domination of the machinery of state give it a predominant position in Italian parliamentary politics. It is the center, the pivot of Italian politics, and for all practical purposes there is no majority possible without it. Consequently, the basic question of parliamentary politics in the Italian Republic has been: Who will support the Christian Democratic-dominated coalition? Parliamentary arithmetic dictates how many parties are necessary to a majority and the marginal utility of their votes, hence also the price that can be set as the outer limit to be considered; bargaining determines the concrete policies and personnel. A caveat should be entered here, however, in order to avoid misrepresentation: ideological barriers limit the range of parties which effectively engage in negotiations. Although some single-party Christian Democratic cabinets have tacitly depended upon the support of the rightist parties, the Monarchists and MSI have never been in the Cabinet. The PCI has not been represented in the Cabinet since 1947, and the PSI was likewise excluded from 1947 until 1963.

In the first legislature under the Republican Constitution (1948–53) the parliamentary majority of the Christian Democrats made coalition technically unnecessary; rather, De Gasperi's desire to strengthen the new Republic led to his inclusion of all the Center parties in the Cabinet. This

Contrasts," *Midwest Journal of Political Science*, 2 (1958), 117–39. For an excellent analysis of the Italian party system see Giovanni Sartori, "European Political Parties: The Case of Polarized Pluralism," in Joseph LaPalombara and Myron Weiner, eds., *Political Parties and Political Development* (Princeton, Princeton University Press, 1965).

Center coalition included the PSDI, PRI, and PLI in addition to the Christian Democrats. In 1950 the PLI dropped out; and in 1951 the PSDI also departed, leaving only the PRI still in the Cabinet with the DC. Following the elections of 1953, which resulted in a loss of seats for each of the coalition partners, the search for a majority became a paramount issue. The De Gasperi era had ended, and attempts by De Gasperi to form a single-party minority government failed. Giuseppe Pella succeeded in this for four months, but Amintore Fanfani failed in his bid to succeed him. A new Center was eventually formed with the PSDI and PLI which lasted through the ministries of Mario Scelba and Antonio Segni (January 1954–May 1957). A single-party DC Cabinet under Adone Zoli governed for the year before the elections of 1958.

The 1958 elections witnessed a mild revival of all the Center parties except the PRI. However, the difficulties of finding a majority increased. In particular, it was no longer possible for the Center-Left parties to cooperate with the PLI, which therefore went into opposition. Consequently, Fanfani began to speak openly of the need to enlarge the Center majority by seeking to woo the Socialists away from the Communists and into a new Center-Left coalition. But his government had the support of only the PSDI and *some* Christian Democrats: he resigned because of lack of support from members of his own party on secret ballots. A Christian Democratic *monocolore* Cabinet under Antonio Segni lasted 13 months, to be replaced by an unfortunate Christian Democratic government under Fernando Tambroni. Lacking a clear majority in Parliament, these governments were forced to court the favors of parties, or at least factions, outside the Cabinet. Tambroni depended upon the support of the Monarchists and MSI, and was forced to resign by violent antifascist demonstrations by Communists and Socialists. The extremists could accomplish in the streets what they could not accomplish in Parliament— the overthrow of a government—but only by capitalizing on the antifascist sentiments of the population. Tambroni was replaced in July 1960 by Fanfani, who began, or accelerated, an historic shift in Italian politics.

This new course, the opening to the left, had been long maturing in the thoughts and actions of several politicians of the Left-Center. In addition to Fanfani and other Christian Democrats, leading Social Democrats under Saragat and the Republican La Malfa led the campaign for the opening to the left. Its actual implementation was dependent upon the convergence of three separate but related developments. One of these, the weakening of the strength of the Center parties in Parliament, was largely a result of the other two—the changes in the policies of the Kremlin and the Vatican and their impact on Italian politics. Significantly, these developments were outside the Italian political system proper.

The succession of Christian Democratic *monocolore* cabinets resting

upon the toleration of other Center and sometimes rightist parties served
to dramatize the deterioration of the parliamentary situation. Not only
did the DC not have a majority in Parliament: even with the PSDI and
PRI there was no majority and these latter two parties would not enter
into a coalition with the PLI. The Christian Democrats had dominated
Parliament and the Cabinet since 1945. High office came naturally to their
leaders; the skills required to maneuver between the demands of the
masses, clergy, and conservatives equipped them well to face the challenge of new opportunities; if it proved necessary to shift to the left in
order to retain office, the shift could and would be made.

This shift was facilitated by changes in the policies of the Catholic
Church and in the organization of the party itself. Under the leadership
of Pope John XXIII, the Vatican began to accommodate to some of the
changes of the century. This led to a recognition of the strength of the
Marxist parties in Italy. By no means did the Church either within or
without Italy cease its opposition to Communism or leave Italians spiritu-
ally free to vote as they pleased. But an inevitable result was to reduce
considerably the polarity of Italian politics and to facilitate a rapprochement between the PSI and the Center parties. Furthermore, the new
Vatican policy involved something of a withdrawal of the Church and
Church-related organizations such as Catholic Action from some of their
more exposed positions in Italian public life. This withdrawal was
paralleled and even preceded by the development of a Christian Democratic organizational structure based on a mass membership and forming
a moderately effective electioneering machine which freed the party from
its complete dependence on the Civic Committees of Catholic Action at
election time. While leading Christian Democrats were not controlled by
the apparatus of the party as was the case with some of the leftist parties,
the party secretary, Fanfani, and his successor, Aldo Moro, were able to
use the apparatus on behalf of the opening to the left in internal political
struggles.

The crucial Christian Democratic Naples party congress of January
1962 approved the experiment of the opening to the left. Most Christian
Democratic leaders bowed to the seeming absence of alternatives. They
had extracted several guarantees, some public, some merely implicit.
Antonio Segni, a moderately conservative Christian Democrat, was elected
president in 1962 over the Social Democratic leader Saragat.[33] The new
government had to be a programmatic one, that is, it was restrained by
the coalition agreement, which provided for strict adherence to Italy's

---

33. Segni subsequently became very ill and eventually resigned; Saragat was named
president in late 1964 after a long and bitter election. These events had important
ramifications for the internal unity of the Christian Democratic Party and the survival
of the coalition.

international agreements (the Atlantic alliance, in particular), limiting nationalization to the electric industry, and the establishment of the regions provided for in the Constitution but never authorized by Parliament. A start was made by the Socialist-supported Center-Left government of Fanfani before the elections of April 1963. But the anticipated entry of the PSI into the Cabinet following the election was delayed until the end of the year, for at the last minute some of the Socialist leaders got cold feet. The reason is related to the other development—changes in Soviet Communism.

Paradoxically, the PSI moved away from the PCI as the U.S.S.R. became more conciliatory and the Italian Communists "softer." Socialists suffered greatly from the memories of working-class divisions and ineffectualness which preceded the rise of fascism. The mystique of the Resistance and the hope of a working-class victory led them into an electoral agreement with the Communists in 1948. The PSI went into the election the equal of the PCI and emerged the junior partner. Following a period of recriminations and confusion, unity was restored under the leadership of Pietro Nenni, a popular prefascist leader who favored continued close ties, but not electoral alliances, with the PCI. A period of monolithic rule within the PSI began. Even during this period, however, Nenni spoke of the "Socialist Alternative," and his later espousal of autonomy for the PSI was but an extension of trends evident before the crucial year of 1956.[34] In that year Soviet intervention in Hungary and Khrushchev's denunciation of Stalin had a traumatic effect on Italian Socialism. Nenni returned his Stalin Peace Prize and strongly denounced Russian actions in Hungary. The party resolved that socialism was not possible without democracy and, further, that acquiring power democratically also involved a willingness to give it up when defeated in elections. Italian Communists have acknowledged the possibility of the working class coming to power peacefully; they have never suggested that political power, once attained, would ever be peacefully relinquished by Communists. The PSI majority thus values constitutionalism for its own sake. This was reflected also in the reestablishment of democracy within the party. The majority faction supported Nenni in his slow and sometimes agonizing journey from the "People's Bloc" to the Center. A minority faction favored retention of close ties with the PCI and feared a rapprochement with the PSDI and DC. Nenni's majority was not large, and from either necessity or choice he moved very cautiously.

The success of the PCI, the stagnation of the PSI vote, and the decline in the DC vote in the elections of April 1963 were variously interpreted as approval and rejection of the opening to the left. Nevertheless, following the elections Aldo Moro attempted to form a government which

34. See Zariski, "The Italian Socialist Party."

included the Socialists. At the last minute, Nenni's majority divided and
the decision had to be postponed until after the PSI congress in October.
This congress supported Nenni, and in December the long-gestating DC-
PSI-PSDI-PRI government took office. The desertion of 25 PSI deputies
and 13 senators (most of whom joined the PSIUP) did not prevent the
government from securing a majority; and their departure indeed strengthened the position of Nenni in the PSI.

The coalition resolved for the time being the problem of a government
majority. But it brought to the majority a party which was itself badly
divided on the issue of participation and considerably different in outlook
and size from the minor parties of the old Center coalition. The PSI
continued to cooperate with the PCI in trade unions and numerous local
governments; in many of these areas of activity it was extremely difficult
for the Socialists to desert their long-time allies and to cooperate with
Christian Democrats. The importance of personalities and face-to-face
relationships at the grass-roots level added to their difficulties in this regard. In alliance with the PSDI and PRI (which reduced its conservative
wing to impotence), the PSI was in a position to make demands which
were difficult for moderate and conservative Christian Democrats to accept. Yet the PSI had to produce tangible results from participation or
be cut down by leftist competitors. While relations between government
and opposition entered a new phase with the opening to the left, by no
means was a stable relationship between government and opposition
worked out.

THE TACTICS OF OPPOSITION   The tactics of opposition in Italy range
from very mild bargaining to semirevolutionary activity, and in Parliament from scholarly discourse within committees to obstructionism and
even violence within the Chamber. The primary distinction to be made
is, of course, between the Center opposition and that of the extremes.

The Center parties—and these generalizations apply equally to factions
within a party—rely primarily upon the pressures they can bring to bear
upon the majority to get what they want. They agree among themselves
on many questions, especially in foreign affairs and constitutional matters,
but agreement is a matter of convergence, rather than identity, of viewpoints. And on some of these basic issues there are disagreements, as on
the implementation of the Constitution. The existence of several dimensions on which there is an underlying basic antagonism or even incom-
patibility of viewpoint results in a seeming conspiracy to ignore the issues
completely as the price to be paid for government stability.[35] As a result,

35. This reflects an old tradition of Italian politics: Denis Mack Smith wrote of the
late nineteenth century that, "Every government was a coalition, for no group was
ever powerful enough of its own. This usually meant that when any real division or
clash of principle emerged, it was driven underground in order to prevent the majority breaking up." *Italy*, p. 203.

some of the most pressing and obvious problems of Italian life are ignored, or treated ad hoc and without the attention they deserve.[36] Thus a basic conflict between the Christian Democrats and the lay Center parties exists in the field of church-state relations, but the issue is played down and sensitive related areas such as education, divorce, and clerical privileges get little attention. Anticlericalism pays no political dividends, and even the PCI treats the Catholic religion and the Papacy—though not all their representatives—with a peculiar respect. More important differences lie in the field of social and economic policy and in the competition for office, and it is of course difficult to separate these matters completely. The officeholding rather than policy orientation of much of the Christian Democratic leadership reinforces this tendency.

The classic Center stretching from the PSDI through the PLI left no constitutional opposition outside the Cabinet. Consequently, bargaining and the encouraging of outside support from business or farmers or Catholic Action or unions were among the principal tactics available to the internal factions within the coalition. Conservative Christian Democrats could bring pressure on the coalition through the Church and Catholic Action, the Liberals were supported by much of the business community, the Left by noncommunist unions, etc. Each party ran its own candidates separate from the others, so policy differentiation for electoral purposes was, in effect, an opposition tactic even within the coalition.

Anticommunism made it virtually a coalition *against* something rather than *for* something: the slightest relaxation of the sometimes hysterical tension of the era led to the disintegration of the alliance. First the PLI departed; although it returned for a short period, its electoral aim of uniting conservatives made participation unwise. Repeatedly, the other two parties also declined Cabinet positions. But the DC alone lacked a majority and had to depend upon the occasional support of other parties, occasionally including the extreme Right. In this situation, the distinction between government and opposition became confused. Cabinets sometimes resigned because of opposition by Christian Democrats on secret ballots. This was the fate of the first two Fanfani cabinets, for example. Thus the opposition from within the coalition had a wide range of tactics to employ, ranging from bargaining to the withdrawal of support on secret ballots and, sometimes, open revolt in Parliament and on votes. In Italy the outcome of parliamentary balloting cannot always be anticipated, and the absence of a formal majority often makes the results even more problematical. Italian parliamentary life consequently has a certain vitality seemingly lost by the assemblies of less volatile lands. Whereas administrative politics tends to replace parliamentary politics in countries which have achieved considerable consensus on basic issues, Italians feel that they are *governed* not *administered*. Basic decisions are made by the party

36. See A. Predieri, "La produzione legislativa."

leaders rather than Parliament as such. The outcome of votes can *usually* be precisely predicted. The individual deputy or senator counts for very little. But it would be a mistake to consider insignificant what goes on in Parliament.

While the extremist parties can seldom influence government policy through the more peaceful channels of bargaining, other possibilities are open to them. Parliament provides an excellent platform for these groups, as their spokesmen find a national audience and personal immunity provided them. Both government programs and government shortcomings—scandals in particular—provide the subject matter. Debate frequently becomes heated, and violence has at times broken out in the Chamber, especially involving Communists and neofascists. It is sometimes difficult to distinguish honest criticism from obstructionism, and the opportunities abound for the latter. The rules of procedure of committees, the Chamber, and the Senate do not, and probably cannot, completely eliminate the possibility of obstructionism in the legislative process.

The opposition can also exercise influence on the government from outside the formal structure. It has already been related how the Tambroni Cabinet resigned because of demonstrations of the extreme Left. Following the attempted assassination of Communist leader Palmiro Togliatti in 1948, the demonstrations reached an almost insurrectionary peak. Neofascists too have been involved in street violence. Labor disputes and protests have often been manipulated by the Left opposition to embarrass the government. It is increasingly difficult for the Communists to manipulate the unions for purely political aims, but there are sufficient economic issues which are political dynamite to make union activity a rewarding field for the opposition. Consequently, despite the absence of communication between government and opposition, the latter is not without means for influencing the former.

With the opening to the left, the Italian parliamentary system entered a new phase. The reduction of tension and the electoral decline of the DC made possible and necessary a modification of the old centrist formula. Ten years of instability had shown that even with the support of the PSDI, PRI, and PLI the parliamentary majority of the DC and its allies was intolerably slim, and also that the PSDI and PRI would not serve with the PLI. The DC consequently had to choose its allies either to its right or to its left.

The rightist solution appealed to many conservative Christian Democrats, and even to some moderates who saw Italy sliding into the instability of the French Fourth Republic. The stability of the systems of De Gaulle or even Salazar served as examples to some, and the possibility of a similar fate for Italy cannot be casually dismissed. Other Christian

Democrats, concerned with democracy and aware of some long-range trends in Italian society, rejected the rightist alternative in favor of a long-term effort to strengthen the constitutional system by incorporating the PSI into it. These leaders won a victory in 1962–63 with the maturation of the opening to the left. It is less certain that they won the war.

The Center-Left government isolated the PCI (and PSIUP) in opposition on the left, with the PLI, PDIUM, and MSI also opposing the government. Several factions within the coalition were not pleased with the 1963 formula. While the departure of most of the PSI minority into the PSIUP in 1964 strengthened the hand of Nenni, an important group of his followers preferred a more innovative program; and these policy preferences were shared by many Christian Democrats. Other important Christian Democrats also were not in sympathy with the experiment, for opposite reasons. Thus, as in the past, the outcome of factional struggles within the governing parties had great influence on the course of events. Equally important, as in the past, were the attitudes and behavior of the Vatican and the Communists, both Italian and Russian. The evolution of Italian politics was therefore only in part controlled by Italian politicians themselves.

11

PATTERNS OF OPPOSITION

Robert A. Dahl

If one reflects on the differences in the patterns of opposition in the ten countries examined here, the first, the most obvious, and yet the most striking conclusion is likely to be a new awareness of the great variety of different patterns of opposition in democratic systems. The answer to one of the questions posed in the first chapter is clear and unmistakable: there is no single prevailing pattern of opposition in Western democracies.

Can we make order out of the variety we have discovered? The patterns of opposition in the countries discussed in the preceding chapters —not to mention those in the score of democratic countries we have had to ignore—are too complex to repose easily within any classification scheme. Nevertheless, the simplification provided by a typology will prove useful in exploring some of the other questions set out in the first chapter. The present chapter will be devoted, therefore, to a search for a helpful way to classify the patterns of opposition revealed in this volume.

Oppositions, it appears, differ in at least six important ways:

1. The organizational cohesion or concentration of the opponents.
2. The competitiveness of the opposition.
3. The site or setting for the encounter between opposition and those who control the government.
4. The distinctiveness or identifiability of the opposition.
5. The goals of the opposition.
6. The strategies of opposition.

Let us examine each of these.

Concentration

Opponents of a government may display varying degrees of organizational cohesion; they may all be concentrated in a single organization, for example, or they may be dispersed in a number of organizations operating independently of one another.

Probably in no country, and certainly in no democratic country, are all the active opponents of government ever concentrated in one organization. If we concern ourselves with political parties, however, the situa-

tion is rather different. Because a political party is the most visible manifestation (and surely one of the most effective forms of opposition in a
democratic country, it is this particular form with which we have been
most concerned in this book.) However, the extent to which opposition is
concentrated depends on the party system of a country. Although genuine
one-party systems probably cannot exist and certainly do not now exist
except where governments prohibit opposition parties, in a few countries
where key civil liberties are by no means wholly impaired, as in Mexico, a
single party has enjoyed a near monopoly of votes, or, as in India, of parliamentary seats. In each of these countries, although some opposition is
concentrated in small parties, a good deal of opposition operates as factions within the dominant party. The highest degree of concentration of
opposition exists in two-party systems, where the out-party has a substantial monopoly of the opposition. In multiparty systems, opposition is likely
to be dispersed among several parties.

In the English-speaking world, all thought about opposition has been
dominated, at least in this century, by simple two-party models—to which
multiparty systems are a kind of unsatisfactory and probably temporary
exception. And this view, so confidently held in Britain and the United
States, has often been accepted even outside the English-speaking world.

Yet the facts themselves are enough to discredit such a parochial notion.
To begin with, the system of two dominant parties has not been much
imitated outside the English-speaking world and its zones of influence. Of
30 countries having in 1964 opposition parties, widespread suffrage, and
governments based on relatively recent elections, only 8 would be considered "two-party systems" in the usual sense.[1] Of these 8 countries, all
but 2 (Austria and Uruguay) are either English-speaking democracies or
were launched politically under the influence of Britain or the United
States.

Moreover, as our essays on Britain, the United States, and Austria make
clear, even where there are only two dominant parties the patterns of
opposition are often radically different. Indeed, in the English-speaking
world, the British two-party system as we now understand it seems to

1. The eight countries are Australia, Austria, Panama, the Philippines, New Zealand,
United Kingdom, the United States, and Uruguay. Even Australia is a highly doubtful
case, since it can be included in the two-party class only if the coalition of the Liberal
and Country parties is treated as a single party. The tests used to distinguish the two-
party systems were somewhat arbitrary, but defensible. Two of the 30 countries, India
and Mexico, were excluded because of one-party dominance. The other 21 countries
were excluded because the proportion of third-party seats in one popularly elected
chamber of the national legislature totaled more than 5 per cent. South Africa, which
would have qualified as a two-party system by this test, was excluded from the list
of 30 democratic countries because of its suffrage restrictions. A more carefully developed classification of party systems could not possibly change the size of the two-
party category by much.

exist only in Britain and in New Zealand. In Australia, one of the two major "parties" is actually a coalition of two parties, while in Canada third parties have been much more significant than in either the United States or Britain.[2] The United States is a paradoxical case. The relative weakness of third parties throughout American history makes the United States an even more clear-cut example of two dominant parties than Britain; yet within this framework of two parties, as we have seen, (the American pattern of dispersed opposition has nearly as much in common with some of the European multiparty systems as it does with the "concentrated" British pattern.)Finally, as Allen Potter indicates in his essay, the British two-party system as we know it today has not existed for much more than the last four decades. Thanks first to the Irish Nationalists and then to Labor, Britain could scarcely be classified as a genuine two-party system for the 40-year period from about 1880 to 1920; while in the middle decades of the nineteenth century, the British pattern was rather similar to that of the United States: two heterogeneous parties with an executive drawing support from sympathetic elements in both parties.[3] Hence even in British experience the recent pattern is somewhat abnormal.

2. "In the thirteen elections to the Canadian Commons between 1921 and 1963, third parties (that is, parties other than the Liberals and Conservatives) secured over ten per cent of the total popular vote eleven times, and over 25 per cent five times. The low point was six per cent in 1930, and the high point 32 per cent in 1945. Although third parties have not been represented in the Commons in the same high proportion as they have in total votes, they have had enough M.P.s to keep either of the major parties from a legislative majority in six (including the two most recent) of the thirteen parliaments elected since 1921. These six parliaments, however, have sat for only 12 of the 43 years from 1921 to 1964, and during several of these 12 years the Liberals, as at present, have been just short of majority status." Leon D. Epstein, "A Comparative Study of Canadian Parties," *American Political Science Review, 58* (March 1964), 49.

3. *The Economist* observed on April 2, 1864:
The real danger of the present day is that which was pointed out by the great and gifted De Tocqueville. "There are no great topics now to divide parties. There is a concurrence almost unanimous between men of all parties. In consequence, men dispute on small subjects. The old contests of principle become faction fights, mere questions of persons. Governments are turned out perpetually upon questions of no intrinsic importance, just because the Opposition contrive to obtain a temporary and casual majority." Such in substance were the opinions of the great thinker, but they have not been borne out by the recent experience of this country. We have remarked with interest and pleasure that, during the last years of Lord Palmerston's Government, such passions and petty interests as De Tocqueville spoke of have never become predominant, that they have never even obtained substantial influence. The state of things has been most remarkable. The difference between the moderate supporters of the Ministry and its moderate opponents is of the very faintest kind; many men on opposite sides could as a wit has said, "change heads without its being noticed." No great question has arisen to divide or excite them. The Government has been maintained in office by a substantial coalition of the moderate men of both parties. Mr. Bright hates the Government; Mr. Newdegate hates it. But the Liberals who do not go as far as Mr. Bright, the Tories who do not go so far as Mr. Newdegate, by a tacit and informal alliance, have banded to-

In sum, it might be reasonable to consider multiparty systems as the natural way for government and oppositions to manage their conflicts in democracies, while two-party systems, whether resembling the British pattern or the American, are the deviant cases. It is conceivable, of course, that the deviant cases represent superior forms; yet multiparty systems exist in Denmark, Norway, Sweden, the Netherlands, and Switzerland, countries widely thought to have handled their political, social, and economic problems with at least as much skill, justice, and social peace as any other democracies.

In addition to the number of important parties, concentration has yet another dimension. Parties themselves vary enormously in internal unity, as measured, for example, by the way their members vote in parliament; what is formally a single opposition party may in fact disintegrate into a number of factions. Since there are variations in the degree of unity and factionalism among parties even within a particular country, it is difficult to characterize whole systems; in Italy and France the Communists have been highly cohesive in their voting in the parliament, whereas in both countries the other parties are much more divided among themselves.

In order to consider the bearing of concentration on patterns of opposition in the ten countries treated in this volume, it is helpful to combine these two dimensions into four simple categories: [4]

1. Two-party systems with a high degree of internal party unity, as in Britain.

2. Two-party systems with relatively low internal party unity, as in the United States.

3. Multiparty systems with relatively high internal party unity, as in Sweden, Norway, and the Netherlands.

4. Multiparty systems with low internal party unity, as in Italy and France.

To the extent that an opposition takes the party system of the country into account in selecting the strategy it will pursue, different party sys-

---

gether and maintained the Government. Lord Palmerston is in power because sensible persons of average opinions think he ought to be in power. The selection of a Prime Minister by what we may call the common element in the two opposing parties is a new improvement in representative government. It is the only mode in which a strong administration can be upheld in times when parties are equal—when no great question divides them. It is the only mode by which the great dangers which De Tocqueville spoke of can be eluded or escaped.
(Quoted in *The Economist*, April 4, 1964, p. 45.)

4. This scheme would be inadequate for many purposes, but it is sufficient to provide a rough guide to the degree of concentration of opposition in the countries treated in this volume. For a sophisticated treatment of the problem of classifying and analyzing party systems, see Giovanni Sartori, "The Theory of Parties Revisited," in L. Binder and D. Easton, eds., *Theory and Method in Comparative Politics* (Englewood Cliffs, N.J., Prentice-Hall, 1965).

tems should be associated with different strategies. Thus an opposition confronted with a party system of the first type is likely to behave somewhat differently from an opposition confronted with one of the other kinds of party systems. I shall return to this point in a moment.

Competitiveness

How competitive an opposition is depends partly on how concentrated it is. In this case "competitive" does not refer to the psychological orientations of political actors but to the way in which the gains and losses of political opponents in elections and in parliament are related. On the analogy of an equivalent concept in the theory of games, two parties are in a strictly competitive (or zero-sum) relation if they pursue strategies such that, given the election or voting system, the gains of one will exactly equal the losses of another.[5] Because in any given election the number of seats in a legislative body is fixed, whenever only two parties run competing candidates in an election they are necessarily engaged in a strictly competitive contest, since the seats gained by one party will be lost to the other. Applying the notion of strict competition to a legislative body presents some problems; but we can get around most of these by stipulating that two parties are strictly competitive in a legislature if they pursue strategies such that both cannot simultaneously belong to a winning coalition. As an empirical fact, of course, no legislature is strictly competitive all the time; some measures gain overwhelming or unanimous approval, while on others party leaders deliberately permit their followers to vote as they choose. In some legislatures, however, key votes are usually strictly competitive; votes on the formation of a government, votes of confidence, votes on the major legislative and budgeting measures submitted by the government, etc. We can regard parties as strictly competitive in parliament, then, if they are strictly competitive on key votes.

It might be conjectured that in a parliamentary or presidential system monopolized by two highly unified parties, competition would always be strictly competitive. The salient example is, of course, Britain. Yet the parties *could* deliberately decide to collaborate either in parliament or in elections, or in both. During most of two world wars the major parties in Britain agreed to substitute collaboration for competition: coalition cabinets were formed, and elections were delayed until after the end of the war. In Austria from 1947 onward, the People's Party and the Social-

5. This definition puts stress on the strategies of the parties rather than, as in the theory of games, on the objective characteristics of the game or contest itself. For a comparison, see R. D. Luce and H. Raiffa, *Games and Decisions* (New York, Wiley, 1947), Ch. 4; and A. Rapoport, *Fights, Games and Debates* (Ann Arbor, University of Michigan, 1960), Ch. 7.

ist Party formed a coalition government that left virtually no opposition in Parliament; yet at each election the two parties vigorously fought one another for votes. The most extreme displacement of competition by coalition has occurred in Colombia, where the two major parties deliberately entered into a pact to eliminate competition not only in Congress but in national elections; the agreement was intended to last through four elections and four terms of office for a total of 16 years.

Even in a system with two unified parties, then, strict competition is not inevitable. Yet the temptation to shift from coalition to competition is bound to be very great, particularly for the party that believes it could win a majority of votes.[6] Hence coalition in a two-party system imposes severe strains and probably tends to be an unstable solution. Whether, given these strains, the arrangement in Colombia will run the full 16 years therefore seems rather dubious.

In the United States, the two major parties are strictly competitive during presidential elections and for the most part during congressional elections; but in Congress party cohesion is weak as compared with Britain, and elements within one party enter into winning coalitions with elements of the other party even on key votes. In multiparty systems strict competition is unlikely; in fact unless one party can form a majority by itself, strict competition is actually impossible; for unless two parties are willing to enter into a coalition, no majority can be formed. Moreover, parties may not be strictly competitive even during elections, for they may enter into electoral alliances that limit competition in various ways, for example by uniting in some districts around a single candidate, as in runoff elections in France.

Thus the competitiveness of opposition (in the sense in which the term is used here) depends in large measure, though not completely, on the number and nature of parties, i.e., on the extent to which opposition is concentrated. The possibilities we have discussed, and for which examples actually exist, extend from a system in which the opposition is concentrated in a party that is strictly competitive both in elections and in parliament, through various systems in which opposition strategies are both cooperative and competitive, to systems in which the minority party that would ordinarily constitute the opposition coalesces with the majority party both in elections and in parliament (see Table 11.1).

6. One of the rare instances in the modern history of British parties when parliamentary party members revolted and displaced their leader occurred in 1922 when Conservatives turned against Austen Chamberlain because of his determination to continue the wartime coalition with the Liberals through the forthcoming election. (R. T. McKenzie, *British Political Parties* [London, Heinemann, 1955], pp. 83 ff.) In 1940, however, Neville Chamberlain resigned as Prime Minister because he was *unable* to form a wartime coalition; a few months later he gave up the leadership of the party (Ibid., pp. 47–49).

Table 11.1   Competition, Cooperation, and Coalescence:
Types of Party Systems

Opposition in

Type of system	Elections	Parliament	Examples
I. Strictly competitive	Strictly competitive	Strictly competitive	Britain
II. Cooperative-competitive			
A. Two-party	Strictly competitive	Cooperative and competitive	United States
B. Multiparty	Cooperative and competitive	Cooperative and competitive	France, Italy
III. Coalescent-competitive			
A. Two-party	Strictly competitive	Coalescent	Austria, wartime Britain
B. Multiparty	Cooperative and competitive	Coalescent	
IV. Strictly coalescent	Coalescent	Coalescent	Colombia

Site

Because it seeks to bring about a change in the behavior of the government, an opposition will employ some of its political resources to persuade, induce, or compel a government to alter its conduct. The situation or circumstances in which an opposition employs its resources to bring about a change might be called a *site* for encounters between opposition and government.[7]

All ten of our systems offer oppositions the opportunity to challenge the government by influencing public opinion in order to increase support for themselves, by winning votes and parliamentary seats in elections, by entering into an executive coalition, by gaining support in parliament for legislation, by negotiating with other officials, and by negotiating with unofficial or quasi-official organizations.

The relative importance of these sites varies from one system to another. In some systems one site is relatively decisive: victory in that encounter entails a rather high probability of victory at the rest. But other systems may not offer a decisive site; an opposition may win an encounter at one site and lose at another.

In one sense, to be sure, public opinion is a decisive site in every democracy; for each democracy it would be possible in principle to specify some amount and distribution of opinions that would be decisive. Moreover,

7. Or an "arena"; cf. H. D. Lasswell and A. Kaplan, *Power and Society* (New Haven, Yale University Press, 1950), p. 78.

aside from the question of "decisiveness," influencing public opinion is highly important because success in that undertaking creates capital that can often be converted into influence at the other sites. Conversely, even if microscopic public backing is by no means always a fatal weakness, it is always a severe handicap, while outright public hostility greatly magnifies the difficulties of gaining influence at any site.

Nonetheless, the amount and distribution of public support required for an opposition to gain victory vary even among different democracies, and specifically among those analyzed in the preceding chapters. Unfortunately, the theoretical and empirical patterns have not, as far as I know, been at all worked out, and I shall not attempt to do so here. However, among the countries described in this volume it is possible to distinguish, in a rough way, four somewhat different patterns of "decisiveness."

First, in Britain, which is unique in this respect, parliamentary elections are relatively decisive. For a political opposition to succeed in changing important government policies, a condition that is ordinarily both necessary and sufficient is for it to win a majority of seats in a parliamentary election. By winning a parliamentary majority, the opposition is able to select the executive; and because of party unity the onetime opposition, now the new government, can count upon its majority in the House of Commons to support its policies. The consequences for opposition strategies are obvious. Ordinarily an opposition will concentrate on winning public opinion to its cause and its candidates so that it can win a future parliamentary majority. Every other use of its resources must be subordinated to this controlling purpose. Parliament itself is not, then, a site for genuine encounters so much as it is a forum from which to influence the next election. Parliamentary debate is not intended to influence Parliament as much as the public—and hence future elections; negotiations to enter into the Cabinet would, on the whole, be futile; and everyone knows it.

Second, in some countries where, unlike Britain, elections are not decisive (even though they are important) the formation of the executive is relatively decisive: an executive coalition is moderately sure of gaining the necessary parliamentary support for the policies the coalition agrees on; a group not in the executive coalition is much less likely to gain support for its policies. This pattern exists in countries with multiparty systems where the parties are cohesive in parliamentary voting, as in Holland and Italy, and also in the unusual Austrian two-party coalition system. In these countries the parties attempt to influence public opinion and win parliamentary seats in elections, but they take it more or less for granted that they cannot govern except as part of a coalition. Hence, unlike the British parties, they shape their strategy to take advantage of opportunities for bargaining their way into the current coalition, replacing it with a different coalition, or forcing new elections that are expected to improve their bargaining position.

Third, some countries that might be placed in the second category because of the working of their parties and the regular governmental institutions have in fact moved closer to a system in which elections and the selection of the executive coalition are decisive only with respect to other *official* sites—parliament, the bureaucracies, local governments, and so on. But on a variety of key issues bargaining has been displaced from these official sites to "bargaining processes between the giant alliances of . . . associations and corporations," as Stein Rokkan says of the "two-tier system" in Norway. So important has this bargaining become in the Scandinavian countries that parliamentary democracy in the conventional sense has been to some extent replaced by a kind of democratic corporatism—or, if one prefers terms less tainted by undemocratic connotations, by a pluralistic democracy with highly organized associations.

The fourth group of countries bears some similarity to the third category because of the dispersed or pluralistic character of key decisions; what distinguishes these countries, however, is the fact that even among official sites none is decisive. For the absence of a decisive site has been produced by a deliberate dispersion of legal authority through constitutional devices such as federalism, separation of powers, and checks and balances. The United States and Switzerland are probably the extreme cases, though West Germany also falls into this category.

Distinctiveness

The distinctiveness of opposition in a political system is largely a result of the three factors we have just discussed: cohesion, competitiveness, and the relative importance of different sites.

In the classic model, the opposition is clearly identified. The principal sites for encounters between opposition and government are the national parliament, parliamentary elections, and the communications media; hence parliament enjoys a virtual monopoly over official, day-to-day encounters. There are only two major parties, both highly unified; hence the opposition is highly concentrated in a single party. Finally, the two parties are strictly competitive in parliament and in elections. As a result of all these conditions, opposition is so sharply distinguished that it is possible to identify unambiguously *the* opposition. In Britain, which has at various times most closely corresponded to this classic model, the distinctiveness of the opposition is symbolized by its very name, "Her Majesty's Loyal Opposition."

The United States and Switzerland both lie close to the opposite extreme. In the United States the sites at which conflict occurs between supporters and opponents of the conduct of government are scattered among the two houses of Congress, the bureaucracy, the White House itself, the courts, and the 50 states, to mention some of the main official sites. The two parties are decentralized; and in Congress they pursue cooperative–competitive strategies. Hence it is never easy to distinguish "opposition" from "government"; and it is exceedingly difficult, if not impossible, to identify *the* opposition. In Switzerland the opposition is perhaps even less distinctive, for in addition to the features that lessen the distinctiveness of opposition in the United States, the Swiss add a multiparty system, referenda, and a plural executive (the Federal Council), the members of which are drawn from all the major parties (including most recently the Socialists), and by tradition conduct themselves in a nonpartisan fashion.

Goals

Although it is obvious that oppositions differ in their goals, it is exceedingly difficult to reduce differences in goals to a manageable analytical scheme. Political actors, as we all know, have long-run aims and short-run aims, and their short-run goals are not necessarily deduced from their long-run goals; the short-run goals may so much dominate their choice of strategies that their "long-run" goals are, realistically speaking, nothing more than the outcome of their short-run goals. Everyone knows too that the ostensible goals of a political actor may not be his real goals; his public objectives may differ from his private objectives. There is no simple way to get round these complexities in the notion of aims or goals. The solution I have chosen is a deliberate oversimplification. I simply postulate that certain goals, whether long-run or short-run, public or private, are "dominant" or "controlling"; and I distinguish between (a) aims or goals and (b) strategies.

In the case of an opposition, the *controlling goals* are the objectives that the opposition seeks to arrive at by changing the conduct of the government. The *strategy* of opposition consists of the means it chooses to obtain these goals.

As to goals, an opposition may oppose the conduct of government because it wants to change (or to resist a possible change in) (1) the personnel of government; (2) the specific policies of government; (3) the structure of the political system; or (4) the socioeconomic structure. Although these are by no means sharply distinct categories, for the sake of simplicity we shall speak of them as if they were more clearly distinguishable than in fact they are. The seven most relevant patterns are shown in Table 11.2.

The fourth type exhibited in Table 11.2—political reformism that is not policy-oriented but is concerned with changes in the political struc-

Table 11.2 Patterns of Opposition: Goals*

Types of opposition	Opposition to the conduct of government in order to change (or prevent change) in				Example
	Personnel of govt.	Specific policies of govt.	Political structure	Socio-economic structure	
NONSTRUCTURAL OPPOSITION					
1. Pure office-seeking parties	+	−	−	−	U.S. Federalists 1815–30
2. Pressure groups	−	+	−	−	U.S. Farm Bureau Federation
3. Policy-oriented parties	+	+	−	−	U.S. Republican Party
LIMITED STRUCTURAL OPPOSITION					
4. Political reformism (not policy-oriented)	+ or −	−	+	−	Britain: Irish Nationalists; U.S.: Women's suffrage movement
MAJOR STRUCTURAL OPPOSITION					
5. Comprehensive political-structural reformism	+	+	+	−	France: RPF
6. Democratic social-structural reformism	+	+	−	+	Dem.-Socialist parties
7. Revolutionary movements	+	+	+	+	Communist parties

Symbols: + = yes
        − = no

* Note that number 4, limited structural opposition, includes two subpatterns: i.e., either the presence or absence of opposition to the personnel of government. There are 16 theoretically possible patterns. The remaining 8 do not appear in the table because they were felt to be irrelevant or highly unlikely.

ture and perhaps in the personnel of government—has been, historically, a somewhat transitory kind of opposition in the Western democracies. The most important distinction is between systems that have relatively little structural opposition and those that have a great deal.

The United States has been something of a deviant case. As we saw in Chapter 2, opposition in the United States has been pretty much limited to the nonstructural varieties because of a rather widespread acceptance of the major political, economic, and social structures. By about 1815, the

Federalists had little left to quarrel with even on matters of government policy; their views became more and more indistinguishable from those of the leading Democratic-Republicans. A recent study of Federalism argues that

> the single most compelling motive for Federalists to engage in political activity after 1815 was the lure of public office both for its own sake and because it meant that they would once again participate in the day-to-day actions of government. Federalists had always believed themselves peculiarly fitted to rule and their exclusion from office was perhaps more noxious to them than their defeat on public issues.[8]

Although the Democrats and Republicans have not been, most of the time, purely office-seeking (despite their well-known reputation for being as alike as Tweedledum and Tweedledee), in opposition they tend to be policy-oriented and to avoid any challenge to the basic structures of American politics and society. And a great deal of opposition to the conduct of government in the United States manifests itself not in the parties but in the activities of pressure groups, which usually direct their energies to highly specific questions.

Is the United States, then, a gigantic unique case? Or is it the prototype which other stable democracies will tend to emulate? A good case can be made for both points of view. As the preceding chapters have shown, where major structural opposition exists it is for all practical purposes a monopoly of the Communists together with a much smaller element on the extreme Right. Whatever their "ultimate aims," the socialist parties (if we except the small left-socialist groups) have become essentially policy-oriented—in some cases with strong hankerings after the pleasures of office. This is most clearly evident in Germany, as Kirchheimer has shown in his essay, and in the Scandinavian countries, where the socialists, after more than a generation in office, have either carried out or renounced their major structural reforms and hence, like the Democratic Party in the United States, emphasize policies that would leave the major social, economic, and political structures of the country substantially intact or subject only to evolutionary transformations not directly induced by socialist policies.[9]

8. Shaw Livermore, Jr., *The Twilight of Federalism* (Princeton, N.J., Princeton University Press, 1962) p. 266. A contemporary, Edward Everett, said in 1828 that the lure of office in the United States was much greater than in England. "We have nothing to which the ambitious can aspire, but office . . . Office here is family, rank, hereditary fortune, in Short Everything, out of the range of private life. This links its possession with innate principles of our Nature; and truly incredible are the efforts Men are willing to Make, the humiliations they will endure, to get it."

9. See also Kirchheimer's pioneering contribution to this question, "The Waning of Opposition in Parliamentary Regimes," *Social Research* (Summer 1957), pp. 128–56.

Of the countries examined here, only in Italy and France is there today
a relatively large structural opposition represented in parliament—or, for
that matter, outside it. (The decline of structural opposition in the other
countries brings them, at least temporarily, closer to the situation that has
prevailed in the United States throughout most of its national history.)

Strategies

The specific strategies used by opponents in order to change (or to prevent possible change) in the conduct of government are of almost infinite
variety. For they are the product of man's enormous capacity for ingenuity, including the special ingenuity of ambitious and unscrupulous men.
Even if we confine our attention to democracies, with which we are ex-
slusively concerned here, strategies that have been used at various times
defy tidy classification.

Nonetheless, some patterns do emerge from our analysis so far. The
strategy an opposition is likely to select depends, in part, on all of the
characteristics that have been examined up to this point. Thus strategies
obviously depend to some extent on goals: a revolutionary opposition is
not likely to follow the same strategy as a pressure group. But as we have
seen, given roughly similar goals a strategy that might make a good deal
of sense in one system would be inappropriate in another. Putting goals
momentarily to one side, then, one might deliberately oversimplify the
actual variations in order to formulate the strategic imperatives of our
various systems as follows.

Strategy I. Opposition will concentrate above all on strict competition
by seeking to gain enough votes in elections to win a majority of seats in
parliament and then to form a government (cabinet or executive) consisting only of its own leaders. This strategy is encouraged by a system
characterized by two unified parties, where opposition is highly distinctive, and elections are decisive. The only system of this kind among our
ten countries is Britain, where the strategy is in fact usually pursued by
the opposition party.

Strategy II. An opposition will try to convert additional voters and to
gain additional seats in parliamentary elections, but it will assume that it
cannot win a parliamentary majority; hence it will concentrate heavily
on entering into a governing coalition and gaining as much as it can by
intracoalition bargaining. This strategy is encouraged by a system with
more than two major parties that have a high degree of party unity, and
where the selection of the government (i.e. cabinet or executive) is relatively decisive. This strategy is usually followed by oppositions in Belgium,
France, Italy, and Holland.

Strategy III. An opposition will adopt all of Strategy II, but in addition
it will assume that many important decisions will be made in quasi-official

bargaining among giant associations; hence failure to get into the cabinet need not prevent it from gaining some of its goals by hard bargaining in these quasi-official encounters. This strategy is encouraged by multiparty systems in which Strategy II is appropriate but in which in addition there exists a rather highly developed structure of democratic corporatism. Strategy III is followed most notably in Norway and Sweden, perhaps, but also in the Netherlands and, to some extent, in a good many other countries as well.

Strategy IV. Oppositions will assume that gaining public support and winning votes in elections are both important but neither is always necessary or always sufficient, since any one of a great variety of sites may prove decisive in a specific case and none will prove generally decisive. Hence an opposition will adapt its specific tactics to its resources and to the most vulnerable site or sites. It may concentrate on pressure group activities, intraparty bargaining, legislative maneuvering, gaining favorable judicial decisions, actions at state and local levels, winning elections, or any combination of these. This kind of strategy is encouraged by a system in which constitutional rules and practice prevent any site from being decisive and where opportunities for preventing or inhibiting government action are numerous. The most notable examples of this strategy are provided by the United States; however, among our ten countries, West Germany also seems to approach it.

These, then, are four rather general strategies encouraged by the characteristics of the system in which opposition finds itself, or, more specifically, by what I have described as other elements in the pattern of opposition (concentration, competitiveness, distinctiveness, and sites) without respect, however, to the influence of goals.

Although the goals of an opposition influence its choice of strategies and tactics in ways too various to examine here, two additional strategies (or sets of strategies) may be encouraged in any democratic system where the opposition is motivated by certain kinds of goals.

Strategy V (really a set of strategies) is pursued by an opposition committed to the survival of the political entity when the opposition and the government believe that survival is seriously threatened by severe internal crisis, subversion, war, or the like. A great threat to the political entity encourages overtures by the government to opposition groups to enter into a broader coalition for the duration of the crisis; it encourages all oppositions committed to preserving the political entity (usually, therefore, all the nonrevolutionary oppositions) to adopt coalescent strategies. Coalescent strategies may vary somewhat from one system to another, but in general an opposition tries to enter into a coalition government on the most advantageous terms, seeks to confine conflicts within the cabinet and to prevent them from breaking out in parliament or in public, and keeps open the possibility of reverting to strict competition when the crisis has passed, or at the next election. This is the strategy pursued in Britain in both world wars, by the Swedish parties in the Second World War, and in Italy during the immediate postwar period. Austria is the most interesting example, however, for the coalescent strategy has been pursued by both the major parties long after the dangers that initially encouraged that strategy have declined; what now seems to preserve the strategy is a fear by both parties of the consequences, not so much for the survival of the polity as for the immediate benefits to the parties themselves should the arrangement give way to a competitive pattern.

Strategy VI (also a set of strategies) is often pursued by revolutionary oppositions committed to the destruction of the political entity or the main features of its constitutional system. The essence of this strategy is to use whatever resources the revolutionary opposition has available in order to disrupt the normal operation of political processes, to discredit the system, to impair its legitimacy, and, in general, to increase the vulnerability of the polity to seizure of power by the revolutionary opposition. This was the strategy pursued by the Nazis and the Communists in Weimar Germany. The failure of this strategy for the Communists and its success for the Nazis, the exigencies of Soviet foreign policy created by the threat of Nazi Germany, the wartime Allied coalition and postwar efforts to preserve that coalition all induced the Communist parties at various times to subordinate their revolutionary strategy to cooperative and coalescent strategies. In the intervening years since the end of the Second World War, the failure of revolutionary oppositions to gain or hold power in any European country without outside military assistance, the discrediting of Stalinism since Khrushchev's famous revelations at the Twentieth Party Congress in 1956, the increasing independence of European Communist parties from Soviet control, and the declining importance of the classic proletariat in expanding economies have evidently generated doubts within the two major Communist parties of Western Europe, those of France and Italy, as to the superiority of the revolutionary strategy over strategy II. Publicly, at least, the French and Italian Communist parties have come to emphasize strategy II—without, so far, yielding the advantages of a revolutionary strategy when it suits their purposes. Conceivably, the European Communist parties—the only important revolutionary oppositions now remaining in the Western democracies, even in Italy—may be undergoing a fundamental transformation of both goals and strategies, a change that will lead them to abandon revolutionary strategies in Western democracies. Yet it is much too early to leap to that facile conclusion. And even should the present Communist parties do so, it seems likely that a rival "Chinese" variety of Left-Communist would continue in both France and Italy to adhere to a revolutionary strategy, probably as a separate party.

To conclude, therefore, that the strategy of revolution is for all practical purposes dead in the Western democracies is, at the very least, premature.

Some Conclusions and Unsolved Problems

The main conclusions from the discussion in this chapter are, then, these:

First, there exist a great variety of different patterns of opposition in democratic systems.

Second, patterns of opposition differ, among other characteristics, in concentration, competitiveness, relative decisiveness of site, distinctiveness, goals, and strategies.

Third, a choice among strategies is partly determined for an opposition by all the other characteristics of the pattern. The influence of these other characteristics on strategies can be represented schematically as in Figure 11.1.

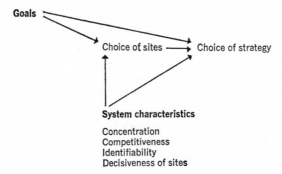

Figure 11.1. A Schematic Representation of the Influence of Various Characteristics of Opposition Patterns on the Choice of Strategies

Fourth, although this offers some explanation for the selection of opposition strategies, our analysis so far leaves the other characteristics pretty much unexplained. Evidently, then, a fuller explanation of differences in strategy would require some explanation of the differences that exist with respect to goals, concentration, competitiveness, identifiability, and site. Moreover, ideally one would want to account not only for present differences in these characteristics among our ten countries but also for any significant changes that have occurred, such as a decline in structural opposition.

These are formidable tasks. In the present state of knowledge, explanations will have to remain highly incomplete and conjectural. The aim of the next chapter is nevertheless to sketch out some explanations.

12

SOME EXPLANATIONS

Robert A. Dahl

To the question whether a standard pattern of opposition has developed in Western democracies, the answer is, as the preceding chapter shows, a confident no. Is there, however, one major factor that "causes" the variations in patterns from one country to another? Can we, to put the question a little differently, relate the differences in patterns to variations in some single factor? Here again the answer appears to be definitely in the negative.

It is possible to identify at least seven factors or conditions that help to account for differences in the patterns of opposition. The interplay of the seven factors is, unfortunately, doubly obscured, for not only is the relation between each of these conditions and patterns of opposition a complex one, but to complicate matters further the relations among the seven conditions themselves are unclear. As a start toward clarifying some of these relationships, therefore, I propose to advance several preliminary hypotheses:

1. Five primary conditions that help to explain patterns of oppositions are
    constitutional structure and electoral system;
    widely shared cultural premises;
    specific subcultures;
    the record of grievances against the government;
    and social and economic differences.
2. Two intervening factors that help to account for variations in patterns of opposition are highly (but perhaps not completely) dependent on the primary conditions. These are
    the specific patterns of cleavage, conflict, and agreement in attitudes and opinions;
    and the extent of polarization.
3. Within some limits that cannot be specified, each of the five primary conditions can vary independently of the others.
4. However, no one of the primary conditions (nor, of course, either of the intervening factors) can vary independently of the others without

limit. That is, if a change in one of those conditions is sufficiently great, it will occur only in association with changes in one or more of the other conditions.

5. Within a given country, a large change in one of the seven conditions increases the likelihood that the existing pattern of opposition will change in a specifiable way. As between two countries, a large difference with respect to one of these conditions is likely to be associated with a difference in patterns of opposition in the two countries.

6. Within a given country, two or more of these conditions may reinforce one another by promoting the same pattern of opposition; they may offset one another by promoting conflicting patterns; or they may be independent of one another. Differences in the patterns of opposition in two countries may therefore be accounted for by the way two or more factors interact with one another.

Constitutional Structure and Electoral System

Constitutional frameworks and electoral systems, it might be objected, have nothing to do with the characteristics of opposition; we must look instead to social, economic, cultural, or psychological factors. This kind of objection reflects a "reductionism" that seeks to reduce political factors to something more "basic," just as biophysicists seek to explain biology by evoking the "more basic" laws of physics. Yet just as biophysicists have encountered severe difficulties in reducing biology to physics,[1] to ignore the effects of constitutional and electoral institutions leaves one in serious difficulties. (The American constitutional system, it was pointed out in Chapter 2, provides a complex array of positions from which a minority coalition can check presidential policies favored by a majority coalition in Congress.) The constitutional framework thereby inhibits a high degree of concentration of all opposition groups, encourages diffusion, helps prevent clear identifiability, and reduces the prospects of strict competition. All these characteristics, in turn, favor the use of bargaining strategies. To take another case, if the present electoral system in Britain were replaced by one of the continental systems of proportional representation, the present degree of concentration, identifiability, and strict competitiveness of the opposition party surely would not continue to exist. For in the last half-century, no party in Britain has ever received a majority of popular votes.[2] Hence under most PR schemes, no one party could ever have formed a government during this period; all governments would necessarily have been coalition governments; in these circumstances strategies

1. Michael Polanyi, *The Study of Man* (Chicago, University of Chicago Press, 1959).

2. For 1910–51 see E. Lakeman and J. D. Lambert, *Voting in Democracies* (London, Faber and Faber, 1955), p. 35. For the period 1945–64, see the table in Potter, Chapter 1, p. 11.

of parliamentary bargaining (Strategy II) would have had a great deal more utility for parliamentary opposition and the government than they can possibly have under the present system, which, as we saw, strongly promotes strict competition and concentration on elections (Strategy I). To take a final example, the abrupt change in the pattern of opposition from the Fourth Republic to the Fifth can be accounted for mainly by the changed position of the chief executive. Indeed, there is good reason to think that a return to the Constitution of the Fourth Republic would to a considerable extent restore the previous pattern of opposition.

Several kinds of institutional arrangements seem to have a bearing on patterns of opposition: the extent to which constitutional arrangements effectively allocate independent political resources (sources of power) to the chief executive, the legislature, and the courts (separation of powers), and to geographical units (federalism); the relative magniture of the political resources allotted to chief executive and legislature for influencing one another; and the system of elections, whether single-member district or some form of proportional representation. It is impossible to show that any of these or any combination of them *totally* determines patterns of opposition even in the short run, for to every plausible generalization of this kind there seems to be an exception. Moreover, in the long run, constitutional and electoral arrangements themselves respond to other factors: the pattern of opinions in a country may render some system of proportional representation far more acceptable than a single-member district, winner-take-all system of elections.[3]

Yet the evidence does strongly suggest that different constitutional and electoral arrangements raise or lower the likelihood of a particular pattern.[4] Thus constitutional separation of powers and federalism both create a variety of alternative sites and reduce the possibility of an all-or-nothing victory through elections; hence both tend to decrease the relative importance of electoral encounters as compared with encounters at other sites. They also encourage decentralization in the control of parties[5] and

3. Giovanni Sartori, "The Theory of Parties Revisited," in L. Binder and D. Easton, eds., *Theory and Method in Comparative Politics* (Englewood Cliffs, N.J., Prentice-Hall, 1965); see also his "European Party Systems: The Case of Polarized Pluralism," in Joseph LaPalombara and Myron Weiner, eds., *Political Parties and Political Development* (Princeton, Princeton University Press, 1965), and John Grumm, "Theories of Electoral Systems," *Midwest Journal of Political Science, 2* (November 1958), 357–76.

4. S. M. Lipset, "Party Systems and the Representation of Social Groups," *European Journal of Sociology, 1,* No. 1 (1960), 50–85.

5. For a comparison of party organization in Australia (federalist) and New Zealand (unitary), see Gwendolyn M. Carter, "The Commonwealth Overseas: Variations on a British Theme" in S. Neumann, ed., *Modern Political Parties* (Chicago, University of Chicago Press, 1956), pp. 58–105, especially at pp. 92–97. For a comparison of two federal countries with substantially different party systems, see Leon D. Epstein, "A Comparative Study of Canadian Parties," *American Political Science Review, 58* (March 1964), 46–59.

thereby decrease the distinctiveness of the opposition and the chances for a strictly competitive contest between government and opposition. As a result of all these factors, both separation of powers and federalism confront an opposition with the alternative of carrying out a revolution to sweep the whole fragmented structure away, or else adopting a strategy for gaining goals by influencing the existing personnel of government rather than relying exclusively on winning elections and displacing the governing party or coalition. To increase the relative magnitude of the political resources available to the president, prime minister, or cabinet operates in the opposite direction. The more the power of the chief executive is increased relative to the power of legislators, the more an opposition will have to concentrate its efforts on the chief executive. This in turn increases the importance of winning elections in order to replace the executive. All three factors taken together generate pressures to concentrate the oppositions into a single coalition which, by its unity, has a chance to win the election; this in turn will emphasize the distinctiveness of opposition and push the system closer toward strict competition.

As to electoral arrangements, it is unnecessary to recapitulate that extensive controversy. The view that PR is a necessary condition for multiparty systems, and that single-member districts with plurality elections are a sufficient condition for a two-party system, is definitely untenable. Yet PR does seem to be a sufficient condition for more than two parties; none of the nations using a complete PR system for national elections has a two-party system, and if the reasoning about the United States and Britain employed a moment ago is correct, then both these countries would in all likelihood move toward multiparty systems if they were to adopt PR for national elections. PR decreases the concentration and distinctiveness of opposition; reduces strict competition and increases the need for cooperation; and thereby increases the rewards to be gained from bargaining strategies of various kinds. The argument of these paragraphs is summarized in Table 12.1.

Thus if constitution-makers wished to concentrate the opposition and encourage the existence of two distinct and strictly competitive parties each employing a strategy of winning elections in order to form a powerful one-party executive, they should recommend a parliamentary system without marked constitutional separation of powers; an executive with relatively great political resources in comparison with the legislature; a unitary rather than a federal system; and election of members of parliament by a relative majority of votes in single-member districts. However, constitution-makers in some countries would be well advised, as we shall see, to hesitate about adopting such a constitution because of its explosive potentialities if political attitudes were to become highly polarized. Conversely, if constitution-makers wished to diffuse the opposition into a

Table 12.1. *The Influence of Constitutional Structures and Electoral Arrangements on Patterns of Opposition*

·Effects of:	Decisiveness of one site	Concentration	Distinctiveness	Strict competition	Concentration on Strategy 1 *
I. Separation of powers	—	—	—	—	—
II. Federalism	—	—	—	—	—
III. PR	—	—	—	—	—
IV. Increase in relative power of executive	+	+	+	+	+

+ = increase
− = decrease

* Strict competition, winning elections, and forming a one-party, noncoalition executive. See above, p. 344.

variety of different sites and parties and to encourage cooperative–competitive strategies with a strong emphasis on gaining entry into parliamentary coalitions, they should recommend proportional representation, a relatively weak executive, constitutional separation of powers, and federalism. However, the price of such a constitution might be a certain paralysis in the executive except in a country with rather high consensus —which, since it would have nothing to fear from a concentrated opposition, would have no great need to employ these constitutional devices in order to diffuse and fragment the opposition.

Widely Shared Cultural Premises

That we are examining the products of historical developments should serve as a warning. Our ten countries have had different histories: even Swedes and Norwegians do not share the same past. The history of a country is in this one respect analogous to the past of an individual: behavior at any given moment is a product of interplay between the present situation and what has already been learned from responses to earlier situations. In an individual, the sum total of these learned orientations is his personality; in a nation or a country, its culture.

Both notions are diffuse, and we are barely past the threshold of scientific knowledge about personality and culture, particularly as they bear on politics. Nonetheless, few students of comparative politics doubt that certain countries do have different political cultures: that leaders and a great part of the people differ from one country to the other in their orientations toward politics. For example, as Alfred Grosser suggests, underlying attitudes about opposing the government are rather different in France from what they are in, say, Britain or the United States. A

Frenchman, typically, is more disposed to oppose, less disposed to support the government—any government.[6]

Despite the slender evidence, the conjecture that patterns of opposition may have something to do with the widely shared cultural premises of a country is much too important to ignore. Our data—indeed, all existing data—do not permit one to do justice to the conjecture. We do not even know what weight to assign cultural factors as compared with others. But we cannot ignore them. What follows, then, is not a summary of findings but a sketch for a theory.

Four kinds of culturally derived orientations toward politics seem to have a bearing on patterns of opposition:

1. *Orientations toward the political system.* These orientations may be classified as allegiance, when attitudes, feelings, and evaluations are favorable to the political system; apathy or detachment, when attitudes, feelings, and evaluations are neutral rather than positive or negative; and alienation, when attitudes, feelings, and evaluations are unfavorable.[7] In the United States, Great Britain, Sweden, Norway, and (in a more complex way) Holland, the political culture evidently generates widespread allegiance. In West Germany (and perhaps Austria), it seems to generate detachment. In Italy and France, and possibly to some extent in Belgium, it generates alienation [8] mixed with a large measure of apathy.

2. *Orientations toward other people.* Beliefs that one can have faith and confidence in others, or conversely that one should exercise distrust and suspicion toward others, seem to be culturally rooted to some extent, even if there are great individual variations around the cultural norm. Though comparative evidence is scanty, Almond and Verba found sizable variations in "faith in people" among their samples in five countries: "the Americans and British tend to be consistently most positive about the safety and responsiveness of the human environment, the Germans and Italians more negative, and the Mexicans inconsistent." [9]

---

6. That the difference is one of degree and is subject to long-run changes is suggested by Bagehot's comment that "The natural impulse of the English people is to resist authority." *The English Constitution,* (New York, Dolphin Books, Doubleday, n.d.), p. 306.

7. These concepts are derived from the first systematic empirical study of political culture on a comparative basis: Gabriel Almond and Sidney Verba, *The Civic Culture,* (Princeton, Princeton University Press, 1963), pp. 21–22. The concept of allegiance was in turn derived from Robert Lane, *Political Ideology, Why the American Common Man Believes What He Does* (New York, Free Press, 1962), pp. 170 ff.

8. For Britain, U.S., Germany, and Italy, see Almond and Verba, *The Civic Culture,* Ch. 14, p. 402, and passim. For the others, the classification is a purely qualitative judgment based primarily though not exclusively on the essays in this volume.

9. Ibid., p. 268. For example, the percentages agreeing that "most people can be trusted" were: U.S., 55 per cent; U.K., 49 per cent; Germany 19 per cent; Italy 7 per cent (Table 4, p. 267). Whether the expression in quotation marks has precisely equivalent meanings in the different countries is uncertain.

3. *Orientations toward cooperation and individuality.* Some cultures emphasize the virtues of cooperating with others, conciliating opposing views, compromise, willingness to submerge one's own special ideas in a larger solution. Other cultures stress the value of maintaining one's individuality, distinctiveness, the integrity of one's personality and ideas, preserving personal integrity by avoiding compromises. The political culture may, of course, stress these attitudes more—or less—heavily than the "general" culture. Though concrete evidence of cultural differences among our countries is difficult to find, it hardly seems open to doubt that in Sweden, Britain, and the United States, the political culture strongly emphasizes the virtues of compromise and conciliation and the possibility of compromising without threatening personal integrity; indeed, in these countries compromise is widely hailed as virtuous. In France and Italy, on the other hand, the virtue both to individuals and to groups of maintaining personal integrity and distinctiveness, even at the price of conflict, seems to be relatively more heavily stressed both in the general culture and in political life.[10]

4. *Orientations toward problem-solving.* Sartori has emphasized the importance of looking "at the underlying cultural patterns if we want to understand the difference between democracies of the Anglo-American type and, let us say, of the French type." [11] Englishmen and Americans, he argues, tend to be characterized by an empirical or (in a loose sense) pragmatic approach to problems, whereas among the French, Italians, and Germans,[12] a rationalistic approach is more likely to dominate thinking about politics. Sartori sketches the two orientations as follows:

10. Direct evidence is hard to find. One indirect piece of evidence for "cooperation" versus "individuality" is membership in voluntary organizations. Almond and Verba found such memberships much more frequent among Americans and Britishers than among Italians and Mexicans, *The Civic Culture*, pp. 301–06. On Italy, see also Arnold Rose, "On Individualism and Social Responsibility," in *European Journal of Sociology*, 2, No. 1 (1961), 163–69. For insights on French "individualism" see François Bourricaud, "France" in Arnold M. Rose, ed., *The Institutions of Advanced Societies* (Minneapolis, University of Minnesota Press, 1958), pp. 498 ff.

11. Giovanni Sartori, *Democratic Theory* (Detroit, Wayne State University Press, 1962), p. 233.

12. While a weakness in empirico-pragmatic styles of thought is often ascribed to Germans, other observers might not agree that their style is "rationalistic" in quite the sense of French and Italian "rationalism." Thus Deutsch and Edinger speak of "the two underdeveloped traditions of empiricism and equality: two muted themes in German culture . . . The mercantile traditions of empiricism, rationality, adaptability, and ease of compromise seem markedly underrepresented . . . German culture thus offers its members two quite different roles for imitation: on the one hand the obedient, dependable craftsman, and on the other, the bold, romantic knight and his intellectual cousin, the daring, demonic magician." Karl W. Deutsch and Lewis J. Edinger, *Germany Rejoins the Powers* (Stanford, Stanford University Press, 1959), p. 17.

While the empirical (empirico-pragmatic) mentality stays *in medias res*, close to what can be seen and touched, the rationalist mentality soars to a higher level of abstraction and hence tends to be far removed from facts. While the former is inclined to accept reality, the *raison* tends to reject reality in order to re-make it in its own image; while empiricism tends to be anti-dogmatic and tentative, rationalism tends to be dogmatic and definitive; while the former is eager to learn from experience and to proceed by testing and re-testing, the latter goes ahead even without tests; while the empiricist is not deeply concerned with rigorous coherence and distrusts long chains of demonstration, the rationalist is intransigent about the necessity for deductive consistency—and therefore, in the summing up, while the former prefers to be reasonable rather than rational, the latter puts logical rigor above everything and thus is rational even if it means being unreasonable. While the empirical approach takes the attitude that if a program does not work in practice there must be something wrong about the theory, the rationalist will retort that what is true in theory must also be true in practice—that it is the practice, not the theory, that is wrong.[13]

The extreme cases would then be represented in two hypothetical political systems:

Orientations to:	System I	System II
the political system	allegiant	alienated
other people	trustful	mistrustful
collective action	cooperative	noncooperative
problem-solving	empirico-pragmatic	rationalistic

13. *Democratic Theory*, p. 232. No better illustration of the "empirical" attitude toward political decisions could be found than Bagehot's description of the House of Commons:

it may seem odd to say so, just after inculcating that party organization is the vital principle of representative government, but that organization is permanently efficient, because it is not composed of warm partisans. The body is eager, but the atoms are cool. If it were otherwise, parliamentary government would become the worst of governments—a sectarian government. The party in power would go to all the lengths their orators proposed—all that their formulae enjoined, as far as they had ever said they would go. But the partisans of the English parliament are not of such a temper. They are Whigs, or Radicals, or Tories, but they are much else too. They are common Englishmen, and, as Father Newman complains, "hard to work up to the dogmatic level." They are not eager to press the tenets of their party to impossible conclusions. On the contrary, the way to lead them—the best and acknowledged way—is to affect a studied and illogical moderation . . . Nor indeed . . . are the leaders themselves of the House of Commons, for the most part, eager to carry party conclusions too far. They are in contact with reality . . . And the end always is, that the middle course is devised which *looks* as much as possible like what was suggested in opposition, but which *is* as much as possible what patent facts—facts which seem to live in the office, so teasing and unceasing are they—prove ought to be done.

Walter Bagehot, *The English Constitution*, pp. 181-83.

It seems reasonable to think that opposition in these two hypothetical systems would differ in the following ways:

In System I, opposition would stress the importance of:	*In System II, opposition would stress the importance of:*
maintaining a stable government	achieving goals, even if this leads to instability in government
adhering to the political and constitutional rules of the game	changing the rules if this is required by goals
making evolutionary changes by marginal adjustments	making major structural changes, possibly by revolutionary means
factual analysis rather than ideological consistency	ideological consistency rather than factual analysis

Perhaps the most interesting difference in these two contrasting cultural orientations is the extent to which they would encourage consideration by political elites and activists of major structural changes in society, economy, and polity. Because System I would deal only with marginal alternatives, proposals for major structural changes would receive slight attention. Thus System I might prove to be rigid if it were confronted by problems that could not be met satisfactorily by the existing structures. System II, on the other hand, would encourage political elites and activists to consider major structural changes; but the emphasis on deducing the program from an abstract ideology, and the willingness to violate or change the constitutional and political rules to achieve political goals, might so thoroughly fracture consensus that discussion—a "dialogue"— about the alternatives would, in practice, be impossible. The structural alternatives presented by different groups would not be analyzed and discussed as much as merely proclaimed: in the place of discussion, there would be a dialogue of the deaf.

The two systems, it should be said again, represent the extreme cases. In practice, concrete political systems, including the ten examined in this book, would fall short of the extreme types. Probably the United States comes closer than any of the other nine countries to our hypothetical System I; the orientations and the oppositional behavior ascribed to System I are, in fact, usually attributed to the United States. Present-day Britain, the Scandinavian countries, and Holland also seem to display the characteristics of System I. Italy and France, on the other hand, probably approach System II somewhat more closely than any of the other countries described in the preceding chapters.

Yet it bears re-emphasizing that while the evidence we have lends credence to these conjectures, our observations in this area are still mainly impressionistic. Much research remains to be done before we can be at all confident about the interplay between political cultures and patterns of opposition.

Subcultures

Almost any difference in behavior or beliefs can lead to the development of so many special patterns of thought, language, identity, and other forms of behavior that we can appropriately label these patterns as a subculture. Once it develops, a subculture often displays remarkable tenacity, for the levers of change cannot easily be manipulated by outsiders, and those inside the subculture are rewarded not for changing their way of life but for adhering to it.

Conflicts involving subcultures are likely to be especially intense, and therefore particularly difficult to manage, because they cannot be confined to single, discrete issues; to the person sharing the perspective of a subculture, conflict over a "single" issue threatens his "way of life," the whole future of the subculture. The historic conflict of anticlericals and Catholics over funds for parochial schools was surely not often perceived, on either side, as a simple, straightforward question of how to finance education: it was a matter of rival ways of life or fundamental notions about freedom. In the United States, the question of voting rights for Negroes has never meant simply whether Negroes should vote: the typical white Southerner has perceived this, or any other extension to Negroes of the rights and liberties enjoyed by whites, as a threat to "the South"—in short, to a way of life built directly upon the subjection of the Negro.

To some extent, all of the countries examined here are societies divided into subcultures. Occupation; social status; race, language, and ethnic group; religion; residence; size of community; and region—these are nodes, everywhere, around which cultural distinctiveness develops. But it is when the numbers who participate in a subculture are large, the differences sharp, and the subculture comprehensive that the effects on political conflict are greatest.

Not one of our ten countries has wholly escaped conflict exacerbated by differences among subcultures (or between a subculture and the dominant culture), and in six of the ten countries conflicts of this kind have—at least for a time—directly shaped the characteristics of opposition:

In *Britain*, the conflict over Ireland is now substantially ended, but while it endured it involved a subculture based on region, religion, and ethnic identity. The conflict proved to be incapable of solution within the framework of the British political system.

In *Norway*, the conflict, now diminishing, between "center" and "periphery," based on region, residence, occupation, language, and to some extent religion has been important in political life during much of this century.

In *Holland,* the conflict over religion has led to the division of Dutch society into three rather distinct communities.

In *Belgium,* the conflict between Walloons and Flemings reflects subcultures different in language, religious views in part, and region.

In *Austria,* the conflict between two *Lager* has dominated the political scene since the beginning of the Republic.

In the *United States,* the South has for nearly two centuries formed a distinctive regional subculture with profound effects on American political life.

Since opposition between a subculture and a government that represents a different subculture or the dominant majority culture is highly explosive, how have our countries responded to those conflicts?

In general, conflicts involving subcultures rarely seem to be handled— for long—by the normal political processes employed in other kinds of issues. For this sort of conflict is too explosive to be managed by ordinary parliamentary opposition, bargaining, campaigning, and winning elections. The chief ways in which these conflicts have been dealt with are these:

1. *Violence* and *repression.* This has been a response in Britain, in Belgium, and, most notably, in the United States, where violence has even erupted into a civil war. The possibility of violence and civil war always lurks as a special danger in countries with hostile subcultures; and this danger undoubtedly stimulates a search for alternative responses.

2. *Secession* or *separation.* This was the solution to the problem in Ireland. It was the solution sought by the South that eventuated in the American Civil War.

3. *Mutual veto* on government policies. In this case, each opponent can veto changes in the status quo involving his subculture. This is most clearly the system in Austria. But it is also characteristic of Holland and, to a considerable extent, Belgium and the United States.[14]

4. *Autonomy.* Autonomy may be granted to a regional subculture, as in the case of the South, which after about 1874–80 received, de facto, a grant of autonomy from Congress, President, and Supreme Court. Or, as in Holland, autonomy may be granted to subcultures that do not have a regional basis.

5. *Proportional representation* has been used to guarantee a subculture that it will be represented in parliament even though, as in Belgium, it does not receive much autonomy. And proportional representation in the broader sense of representing groups more or less in proportion to their numbers can be applied in all kinds of agencies and organizations, as in Belgium.

14. Passage of the Civil Rights Act of 1964 represents the first successful effort since the Reconstruction period to overcome Southern resistance in Congress to legislation protecting Negro rights.

6. *Assimilation.* This seems to be the evolutionary pattern in Norway. For a century and a half it was the characteristic response to ethnic group differences in the United States; but the process of assimilation has failed, so far, in the case of Negroes.

The Record of Grievance

The extent to which citizens of a country are allegiant or alienated depends in some measure on the way the government has responded to grievances in the past and is expected by citizens or subjects to respond in the future.

Reflecting on observations made during 1950–51 in the Provençal village of "Peyrane," Lawrence Wylie noted that

> there never has been a time since the beginning of Peyrane's history, when contact with organized humanity has meant anything but the exploitation and manipulation of the individual. The wandering hordes, the Romans, the feudal lords—including the neighboring papal rulers, the agents of Provençal counts and French kings, the nineteenth-century regimes set up by Paris, the twentieth-century bureaucracy centralized in Paris—all these form an unbroken past in the vague memory of the village. They all mean domination by a human power beyond the control of the individual. At best the domination has brought unsought modifications in living habits. At worst it has brought disaster. And so it has become conventional to think of human power as a plague to be classed with the plagues of nature: the odious government, the leveling mistral, the flooding Durance.[15]

If the citizens of the United States and Britain are much more confident than the citizens of Germany, Italy, and Mexico that they could do something to prevent the passage by the national legislature of a law they considered to be unjust or harmful, as Almond and Verba report,[16] surely these differences have something to do with the historic record of how grievances have previously been handled. To be sure, these differences in attitudes may now be embedded in the political cultures of these countries; but the political cultures themselves can be explained in part by the record of the past.

The burden of grievance is not, however, invariable in human societies. The institutions of a society generate a greater burden of grievance during some periods than in others; moreover, for a variety of reasons some societies evidently generate a smaller burden of grievances than others. Thus the accumulated burden of grievances may be low and allegiance high: either because the social and economic institutions of a country tend

15. *Village in the Vaucluse* (rev. ed. New York, Harper Colophon Books, 1964), p. 332.
16. *The Civic Culture*, p. 185, Table 1.

to generate a relatively small burden of grievance; or because, even though great grievances have been generated in the past, the government has responded to alleviate them.

Returning to the French village ten years later, Wylie was surprised to discover marked changes even in that brief period:

> As I went out into the country and talked to the farmers I realized the importance of the changed economic situation and state of mind of the farm people in the commune. They have a new awareness of their professional status and dignity, which is reflected in the growth of their professional organizations and in their sense of solidarity with farmers elsewhere . . . It was obvious that French farmers were in agreement that if they wanted action there was nothing to be gained by talking to elected officials . . . At last they had come to feel that their most effective political representatives were not the traditionally elected officers—deputies and senators—but farmers themselves who had been elected to office in professional organizations . . . Once there was no more hope of turning back, the inevitability of change was accepted, it at last became possible for people to devote their energy to seeking new solutions for their problems. People acquired a greater sense of freedom to act for their own welfare. The rejection of the old political system, the modernization of the farms, the tractor demonstrations, the development of farmers' organizations are, to a certain extent, manifestations of this changed spirit.[17]

For nearly a century the most insistent internal threat to the allegiance of citizens was the burden of grievance accumulated among the urban and (particularly in Italy) rural proletariats, a burden that threatened to alienate the working classes if the grievances were not heeded—or to alienate the middle classes if they were. The problem, then, was how to gain the allegiance of the working classes to democratic institutions without alienating the other social strata. This problem has not been solved in all ten countries: France and Italy in particular do not seem to have worked out a solution, though they may be in the process of doing so. In Germany (and perhaps in Austria) commitment to democratic institutions is untested by adversity and may still be somewhat weak; but working classes, at any rate, are as allegiant as other major social strata, and in this narrow sense a solution has been reached to the problem of political alienation among the working classes. In the remaining six countries, the problem has been solved, at least in the main. One of the significant developments of this century has been, then, the integration of the working classes into a large number of Western democratic systems and the decline in these countries of any serious threat to parliamentary democracy

17. *Village in the Vaucluse,* pp. 359, 362, 364.

generated by class conflict. The importance of this development for the future of oppositions can scarcely be exaggerated.

Even aside from France and Italy, however, the integration of the urban and rural workers into political life has not followed an identical pattern.[18] Despite the diversity of specific patterns, it is possible to clarify some of the major aspects of the process by drawing a simplified and abstract picture of how a political system might solve the problem of acquiring the allegiance of the working classes to democratic institutions without alienating the other strata, particularly the middle and upper strata. One might conjecture that the likelihood that this problem would be solved would be relatively high if the following conditions were met:[19]

1. As the urban (or rural) working classes increase in numbers and in demands on the political system, there already exists an operating parliamentary system supported by a large and allegiant middle class and led by an experienced and allegiant political elite.

2. These incumbents, the middle classes and their leaders, head off severe and prolonged frustration over the operation of the political system by peacefully yielding an increasing degree of participation in political life to the working classes by

the extension of the suffrage,

allowing the development of political leaders representing the working strata,

permitting the participation of these political leaders in political decisions,

and accepting their entry into the government.

3. Entrepreneurs and managers yield enough of the benefits made possible by more efficient technology and organization to reduce the frustrations that had been generated by social and economic conditions during early industrialism.

4. The government undertakes regulation or structural reforms in such a way as to reduce social and economic sources of frustration to people in working-class occupations, without, however, seriously alienating other social strata.

Six of our ten countries have, in varying degrees, satisfied these four general conditions: Britain, Belgium, Holland, Norway, Sweden, and the United States. Of these, the five European countries have followed a roughly similar development, while the United States has traced a different

---

18. Cf. Val R. Lorwin, "Working Class Politics and Economic Development in Western Europe," *American Historical Review*, v. *63* (January 1958), 338–51.

19. Although the formulation here is not identical with S. M. Lipset's, it has much in common with his. See his discussion of legitimacy and democracy in "Some Social Requisites of Democracy," reprinted in Nelson W. Polsby, Robert A. Dentler and Paul A. Smith, eds., *Politics and Social Life* (Boston, Houghton Mifflin, 1963), pp. 541–68, at pp. 554 ff.

path. In the five North European countries, a constitutional system with an elected parliament, middle-class support, and experienced leaders drawn from the middle classes or the aristocracy was already in existence when the urban and rural workers began to develop political consciousness and demands. In all these countries viable labor or socialist parties that drew increasing support from the working classes were formed in the years from about 1885 to 1905. By the end of this period or a few years later the right to vote was gained by most workers in all these countries.[20] Even the existing middle-class parties began to respond to the demands of the new strata, and they sometimes supported measures designed to eliminate, or at least to mitigate, the worst social and economic evils of unregulated capitalism: social security laws, legal support for trade unions, expansion of public education, and the like. These reforms did not, however, prevent the growth of the labor and socialist parties. During the First World War and after, socialist leaders began entering into coalition governments. Although the labor parties and their leaders participated initially only as junior partners in coalition governments, eventually they secured a large enough vote in elections and seats in parliament so that, as the largest or second largest party in the country, they were highly influential in the conduct of government—sometimes as the major opposition to the government, sometimes as a coalition partner, sometimes as the governing party. In the extreme cases, Norway and Sweden, the labor parties have governed for three decades; in Britain, their victory in 1945 enabled them to carry out most of their immediate program; in other countries, even when the labor parties are not currently participating in the governing coalition it is reasonable for them to expect that they may be able to do so within a few years.

Thus in these five countries the first two conditions mentioned a moment ago have been met, and in the process the working-class parties have acquired the sobering experience of governing their countries. Meanwhile, too, the third and fourth requirements have been met by both economic and social development and by government regulation and reform. In all five countries the labor parties have witnessed the attainment of a good many of their immediate objectives, while their ultimate goals for a socialist society have more and more become hypothetical and rhetorical.

In the United States the four conditions suggested earlier have been met—but according to a different timetable and in quite a different way. As in the five countries just mentioned, so too in the United States, well before rapid industrialization expanded the urban working class from a

20. On the development of political participation in Western Europe, see Stein Rokkan, "The Comparative Study of Political Participation: Notes Toward a Perspective on Current Research," in Austin Ranney, ed., *Essays on the Behavioral Study of Politics* (Urbana, University of Illinois Press, 1962), pp. 47–90.

tiny minority into a substantial proportion of the population, democracy was a going system of government, backed by a "middle class" (consisting predominantly of farmers) and operated by leaders skilled in the arts of managing the country's political institutions.

But the United States met the second condition by providing for participation of the emergent working classes in political life in a way that frequently leads European socialists to the conviction that this country has skipped "an inevitable stage of capitalist development" and that sooner or later (despite impressive and increasing evidence to the contrary) it will have to turn back and rerun its history according to the North European pattern. The essential difference is that unusual conditions in the United States permitted it to arrive at the same result—the integration of the working classes into the political system—without the mediating role of a specifically working-class party. The transition was far from peaceful. "American workers," Val Lorwin has said,[21] "had to fight bloodier industrial battles than the French for the right of unions to exist and to function." Nonetheless, in the United States the working classes have always been, on the whole, strongly allegiant to the political system;[22] and though many workingmen's or socialist parties have been created to appeal to urban workers, few have lasted more than a decade and none has ever attracted the continuing support of more than a small proportion of the working classes.

The reasons for this great difference between the United States and the European democracies with which it has much in common in other respects are complex. One was the fact that workers had already acquired full political rights long before an urban proletariat of any size came into existence; thus workers were never alienated from the political system as a result of being excluded from it. In addition, two national, "grass-roots" parties were already on the scene, ready, willing, and able to recruit workers or supporters. To call them "bourgeois" parties is to miss an important point. If they were "bourgeois"—American middle-class—in their orientations, they were by no means so in organization and recruitment. They were distinctly not elite parties of notables. Typically, they were organized all the way down to the poorest precincts of the large cities; and they had perfected techniques—in essence, rendering primitive social services—for gaining and holding the loyalty of their followers. A working-class party could offer distant collective goals; it could not compete in immediate individual palliatives for concrete grievances. Finally, in a very large country with a decentralized federal system of government and parties, many of the most pressing legislative demands of

21. Val R. Lorwin, "Reflections on the History of the French and American Labor Movements," *Journal of Economic History* (March 1957), p. 37.
22. In this respect the 15 men studied in depth by Robert Lane seem representative. See *Political Ideology*, Ch. 10, "The Alienated and the Allegiant," pp. 161–76.

the trade unions had to be met not by Congress but by the state legislatures. As early as the 1830s (Philip Taft has shown) union leaders had learned the disadvantages of a workingmen's party in such a system and the advantages of working through existing parties.[23]

If the United States diverged from the North European countries in the ways in which the working classes entered into political life, it also diverged somewhat in relying more heavily on meeting the third condition by private action than by government intervention to reduce working-class frustrations. When one takes state laws into account, however, the difference is much smaller. But probably the burden of grievance generated among workers by the operation of American social and economic institutions was less in the United States than among European workers: relatively high wages, rapidly rising standards of living, free public schools, and less rigid status barriers kept down discontent, drained off working-class leaders, fostered middle-class values, and encouraged trade union leaders to concentrate on gains through collective bargaining.

Finally, two additional features of American society no doubt helped the country to evolve its own peculiar solution. The strong emphasis on a common liberal democratic ideology so characteristic of American life impeded the growth of ideologically divergent parties. In combination with this ideology, the ethnic diversity of the industrial working classes helped to fragment their opposition by providing ethnic identifications that weakened working-class cohesion.

Thus both the United States and the five North European countries substantially met the four conditions suggested earlier. By different paths they managed to maintain the earlier allegiance of the middle classes while they gained the allegiance of the working classes.

None of the remaining four countries has, however, fulfilled these four

---

23. Only a state legislature could compel defaulting employers to pay wages earned, impose safety rules on hazardous occupations, and define minimum sanitary standards in work places. The state legislatures prescribed standards for schooling, voting, and minimum ages for working, the employment of women, and limitations of hours of labor in certain occupations . . . Union representatives appealing for legislative concessions understood that frequently only a beginning in the reform of a given problem could be made, and they were usually confident that additional improvements could be subsequently introduced. They also knew that the great majority of legislators were not ideologically committed to or opposed to many pieces of legislation sought by organized labor, and the members of legislative assemblies would respond to the pleas and pressures at slow or rapid rates depending upon the problem and the forces arrayed against labor on a particular issue. Promotion of an independent labor party would have necessitated the severance of relations with many members of the legislatures, who, assured of organized labor's political hostility, would have been more reluctant to support the bills labor annually or biennially presented to the legislatures.
Philip Taft, "Labor History and the Labor Issues of Today," *Proceedings of the American Philosophical Society, 106,* (August 1962), 306. See also the same author's "On the Origins of Business Unionism," *Industrial and Labor Relations Review, 17* (October 1963), 20–38.

conditions. In Germany and Austria the first condition was not met; and because it was not met the whole problem was far more difficult to solve than in the United States and the five North European countries.

In Germany, as the working classes increased in numbers and in demands on the political system they were confronted not by a parliamentary system supported by a loyal and substantial middle class but by a recently created and almost powerless imperial legislature subservient to the Emperor and his Chancellor. A parliamentary system had to await the collapse of the Empire after the First World War; thus neither the middle classes nor the working classes underwent a sufficient period of tutelage in the politics of parliamentary democracy before the responsibilities of operating a republic were abruptly thrust upon them.

Since the first condition was not met, the second could not be. But in Germany the possibility of peaceful integration of the working classes was even more badly botched by the nature of the suffrage that was granted them. For although universal manhood suffrage was introduced in the Reich in the same year that Disraeli enfranchised a large part of the British urban working classes, Prussia itself maintained the three-class system introduced in 1849, which made a cynical joke out of working-class participation in public life. As Stein Rokkan has observed, "It would be difficult to devise an electoral measure more calculated to alienate the lower classes from the national political system than the one promulgated in Prussia in 1849." [24] Moreover, in granting universal manhood suffrage in elections to the imperial legislature, Bismarck's motive "was patently not to create a channel for the articulation of the interests of the economically dependent strata; the objective was to strengthen the policies of centralization by enlisting the support of the least articulate classes in German society . . . There is a wealth of evidence," Rokkan concludes, "to show that this constellation of institutions was highly dysfunctional: the extension of the suffrage appeared to encourage the participation of the lower classes, but the contrast between the two systems of elections made for widespread resentment and helped to isolate the workers in permanent opposition to the regime." [25]

In better circumstances, perhaps the Weimar Republic could have triumphed over this unpropitious past. But under the series of strains to which it was subjected, the task of solidifying the allegiance not merely of the working classes but (what proved more difficult) of the other strata as well was altogether too great, and it is not surprising that the Weimar Republic collapsed under the accumulated weight of postwar crises. The political and social origins of the First Austrian Republic were only slightly less foreboding, and its life almost equally short.

Today the working classes of Germany and Austria appear to be about

24. "The Comparative Study of Political Participation," p. 76.
25. Ibid., pp. 73, 76.

as fully integrated into, and as allegiant to, their democratic institutions as the other strata. In Germany, as Otto Kirchheimer indicates, class antagonism no longer serves as much of a political stimulus; and what was for generations considered the leading socialist party of Europe is now barely distinguishable in goals and strategies from the Christian Democratic Union. In Austria, coalition government and *Proporz* have provided the old enemies, the two *Lager*, with a very great stake in maintaining the system. The commitment to democracy may not be strong in either country; but allegiance is no weaker among the working class, evidence suggests, than among other major strata. It is not so much that the battle for allegiance has been won as that it has not been lost. The evidence of Almond and Verba seems to indicate that in Germany—and the same may be true in Austria—the population is neither alienated from nor allegiant to democratic institutions but rather indifferent or detached.[26]

Like Germany and Austria, the political development of France and Italy did not fulfill the four conditions suggested earlier. In both countries, the last two conditions were, at least until recently, met badly. In addition, Italy scarcely even fulfilled the first condition during the 60-year period of parliamentary government before fascism, for it failed to build up a large and allegiant middle class. Meanwhile, an extraordinary record, probably unparalleled in Western Europe, of violence and repression by the state against socialists, anarchists, trade unionists, and other workingmen's organizations must have strengthened the suspicion and hostility of the working classes toward parliamentary institutions. What is more, Italy arrived at the second condition rather late by maintaining a highly restricted suffrage until universal manhood suffrage was introduced in 1912: the result was an abrupt threefold swelling of the electorate. The First World War following upon the elections of 1913 and the rapid collapse of parliamentary government after the war meant that in Italy, as in Germany and Austria, the struggle for allegiance really began only two decades ago. So far, as Samuel Barnes' essay makes clear, the outcome remains in doubt.

Let me now draw this discussion together with three conclusions:

First, in seven of our nine European countries the politics of the working strata has converged toward a situation that has much in common with the traditional position of the American worker. An American is likely to consider desirable any change that brings European systems into conformity with his own. But the problem is not quite so simple.

For, in the second place, one cannot simply ignore the plain fact that, up to now, in Italy and France history has taken a different path. It is not yet clear, particularly in Italy, how the largest group of working-class voters, those who have voted for the Communists, are to be integrated peacefully into a viable political system.

26. *The Civic Culture*, pp. 428 ff.

Third, when the Left parties acquire a durable majority of votes, the problem of allegiance shifts from the working classes to the white-collar strata: lower middle classes, professional groups, businessmen. The problem would arise in Italy in its most extreme form if there were ever a coalition government in which the Communists participated. And for how long can a nation's second largest party, with the largest following of manual workers, be excluded from participating in the government? The problem is posed in much more moderate form in countries where the Left parties have become the largest parties and normally in control of the government: most notably Sweden, Norway, and the United States, where the parties representing the conservative middle classes have not been able to control the national government for the better part of the last three decades. To what extent will conservatives (whether in the Scandinavian or the radically different American sense) become politically alienated by their continuing exclusion from governing their countries? Certainly the American Right appears to be fully as hostile to the dominant tendencies in current American politics as the working classes of the United States ever were. And the strike of the Belgian doctors in 1964 shows to what length a professional group may go in opposing government policy.

Social and Economic Sources of Political Cleavage

An alternative though not necessarily contradictory way of describing and explaining these historical changes in the patterns of opposition in our ten countries is to attribute the changes in politics to long-run changes in social and economic factors, using these terms very broadly to include not only class, social status, and occupation but also such social factors as religion, ethnic group, and language. The political affiliations, loyalties, and attitudes of an individual, it might be said, are heavily dependent on his durable social and economic roles, functions, and affiliations: political cleavages are, according to this hypothesis, the expression of social and economic differences.[27] If the political behavior of various strata has become more alike in recent years, then this is because these strata have also become less distinct in their social and economic characteristics.

There is, surely, a great deal of truth in this explanation. The core of truth is to be found in the twin assumptions that social and economic differences usually are associated with differences in rewards and deprivations, in relative advantages and disadvantages; and that these differences in rewards and deprivations stimulate cohesion among those who are socially similar and conflict with those who are different. The difficulty with the explanation and the axioms on which it is founded is not so much

27. A special problem implicit or explicit in this kind of explanation, the relation of social and economic cleavages to "polarization," is dealt with below, at pp. 380–86.

that they are false as that they oversimplify a highly complex matter and thereby leave a great segment of political behavior unaccounted for.

To begin with, in the countries examined in this volume, the political affiliations, loyalties, and attitudes—in short, the political behavior—of individuals and groups cannot be traced to any single social or economic characteristic. Quite the contrary, political behavior is evidently influenced by a great variety of different social and economic characteristics.

The most important of these are differences with respect to economic position (in a broad sense), social position, religion, language or ethnic group, and region. Differences in economic position, ordinarily allied to differences in social position, are sources of conflict in all our countries. Religion is usually an important source of differences in political behavior in countries with sizable Catholic populations, because religious commitments generate differences in political attitudes between Catholics and Protestants or between Catholics and anticlericals, as in France, Italy, and Belgium. Differences in language or ethnic identification have been critically important in Belgium and the United States. And regional differences—associated often with some of the others—have been significant in the United States, Norway, Belgium, and, to some extent, Italy.

Second, some social differences are associated with differences in relative advantage, and hence with political behavior, in some countries but not in others. Differences in language are one of the commonest sources of cleavage in all parts of the world. In Belgium, as Lorwin points out, the bitterness between Walloons and Flemings arises not only from the language difference but also from the fact that language has been associated with a pattern of inequalities in occupations, education, social class, prestige, and opportunities to rise in Belgian national life. In Switzerland, on the other hand, although there are often abrasive relations at the cantonal level, conflict between German- and French-speaking Swiss has been largely avoided in national politics, evidently because few persons in either language group feel that they have been unfairly treated in Swiss national life as a result of their language.

Third, the ways in which different socioeconomic factors are related to one another do not produce a single pattern of cleavage in the different countries, but a great profusion of patterns. In a rough way it is possible to distinguish three patterns:

a. *Countries highly homogeneous except for social standing and economic position (which are highly correlated).* Among our countries these are Protestant nations where religious differences have ceased to be salient, and where ethnic, language, and regional differences have left only slight traces. Britain and Sweden fall most clearly into this class; Norway is a somewhat marginal member because of the declining but not insignificant influence of region, religion, and loyalty to the rural language. Because these differences are at a minimum, the most salient differences are those in occupations, incomes, and social standing—socioeconomic status. As a consequence, in countries like Britain and Sweden the political parties reflect more clearly than in other countries the differences in the class composition of their followings; the labor-socialist party draws the bulk of its strength from blue-collar workers, while the middle-class parties (or party) receive considerably more votes in the middle or upper strata than does the labor-socialist party. In this sense there is a higher degree of "status polarization" in politics than in other countries. But, as we shall see, this polarization is probably statistical rather than psychological.

b. *Countries in which several kinds of socioeconomic differences coincide and thus reinforce one another.* One of the surprising results of our inquiry is that this pattern does not exist in anything approaching a pure form in any of our ten countries. This may well be because a pattern of this kind would lead to such severe conflicts that a parliamentary system would founder. In each one of our countries where several different kinds of socioeconomic differences stimulate political conflicts, the planes of cleavage in one conflict do not coincide exactly with those in other conflicts—fortunately for the survival of the system. However, some countries approach this pattern more closely than others.

Belgium falls most clearly—even if imperfectly—into this category, for there, as we have seen, two of the three main planes of socioeconomic cleavage do coincide to some extent. The explosive nature of the question of the Negro in the United States also stems in considerable part from the fact that the most pronounced line of cleavage, that between North and South, goes hand in hand with differences in ideologies, economic issues, social systems, and regions.

c. *Countries in which several kinds of socioeconomic differences cross-cut one another.* It is in this case that the effects of "overlapping memberships," "conflicting identifications," and "cross-pressures" so much discussed in the literature of American political science may occur.[28] Thus a Dutch Catholic worker may have a strong sense of his identity both as a Catholic and as a member of the working class. Potentially, then, he is in conflict with non-Catholics on religious matters and with nonworkers on economic issues. Both his class and his religion are durable features of his life. As a worker living in a working-class ambience he finds common ground with other workers, be they Catholic or non-Catholic; as a Catholic living among Catholics he feels solidarity with other Catholics,

28. For a summary and critique as of 1958 see Robert E. Lane, *Political Life* (Glencoe, Free Press, 1959), pp. 187–203. The overlapping membership model particularly as it applies to the United States is examined by William C. Mitchell in "Interest Group Theory and 'Overlapping Membership,'" a paper prepared for the 59th Annual Meeting of the American Political Science Association, New York City, September 1963.

whether bourgeois or workers. He therefore has an incentive, particularly if his identification with each group is strong, to seek (or to accept at the behest of his leaders) ways of reducing conflict within each group. His desire for group solidarity may stem from psychological needs, from a fear of the collective consequences of internal divisions, from a strategy of influence in politics and economic life, or from all of these and other reasons. Whatever the reasons, though responses other than compromise are possible, he is likely to be receptive to compromises on questions involving religion or economic matters, for conflict threatens to divide a group whose solidarity he wants to maintain.

Although socioeconomic differences help to account for patterns of opposition, they leave a good deal unexplained. Even in a country with such sharp social and economic differences as Italy, political conflict is by no means purely a matter of conflict among different social and economic groups. Industrial workers evidently divide their votes among Communists, Socialists, and Christian Democrats. Even in a homogeneous country like Britain, where socioeconomic status has greater influence because of the weakness of other kinds of social distinctions, a third of the workers vote Conservative. Or again, compare the fate of the labor parties in Britain and Sweden. In Britain, the most urbanized and industrialized of our countries, the Labor Party has spent most of its history in opposition; while the middle classes are rather solidly united in a Conservative Party which, thanks to the support of its working-class voters, managed until the election of 1964 to remain in office for all except 6 years out of the previous 30. In Sweden, less urban and industrial than Britain, the Socialist Party not only wins the support of two-thirds or more of the working class, as the Labor Party does in Britain, but also gains a quarter of its votes from nonworking-class groups.[29] Thanks to middle-class support it has been in office for 30 years, and it is the bourgeois parties that have formed the opposition.

Why do socioeconomic factors account for only a part of the variation in patterns of opposition? Principally, it seems, because the causal chain from one's socioeconomic position to one's overt political action is long and tenuous; and each link in the chain may be weak enough to be broken by the pull of other forces. A pure social determinist might postulate a causal sequence in which one's overt political acts are completely determined by one's socioeconomic position.

$$\left\{ \begin{array}{c} \text{Objective} \\ \text{s-e position} \end{array} \right\} \xrightarrow{\ a\ } \left\{ \begin{array}{c} \text{Subjective} \\ \text{identifications} \end{array} \right\} \xrightarrow{\ b\ } \left\{ \begin{array}{c} \text{Political} \\ \text{opinions} \end{array} \right\} \xrightarrow{\ c\ } \left\{ \begin{array}{c} \text{Overt political} \\ \text{acts} \end{array} \right\}$$

But we know that each of these links can be so weak that it cannot bear the weight of the others. Whenever objective differences in socioeconomic

29. Above, p. 127, Table 4.1.

positions are blurred and ambiguous, as they are, for example, among clerical workers, then there may be only a weak correlation between socioeconomic position and subjective identification; hence while a majority of white-collar workers might identify themselves as middle class, a sizable minority might see themselves as working class. Moreover, for a variety of reasons subjective identifications vary in strength; and if one's identification with one's occupational group is weak, they may not have much to do with one's political opinion—as was probably the case with the wirer in a California radio factory who said: "Well, I work for a living so I guess I'm in the working class." [30] Finally, political opinions may be weakly related to overt political acts, particularly among people who are uneducated, who are unable to conceptualize abstract political ideas, or who are not interested in politics.

The link at *c*, between political opinions and overt political acts, is usually stronger among educated persons, intellectuals, and political activists than among the general population; conversely, however, among these very groups, the links at *a* and *b* connecting objective position, identifications, and political opinions are somewhat weaker than among the general population. Thus with the general population the breakdown in the hypothetical causal chain of the social determinist is likely to occur closer to the terminal end, at *c* or *b*; but among the political elites, the break is more likely near the beginning, at *a*.

The determinist's chain of causation is thus rather easily broken by the intrusion of factors that he assumes are irrelevant or extraneous. The British middle classes may not agree in their ideas more than the Swedish middle classes; but in Sweden PR encourages the middle classes to distribute their votes among several parties, whereas in Britain the single-member district and plurality elections make it simple for them to concentrate their votes on the Conservative Party. Other factors also have an opportunity to express themselves, as we shall see in a moment.

Specific Patterns of Attitudes and Opinions

I have already referred to attitudes and opinions in order to explain patterns of opposition. Widely shared cultural premises consist of attitudes, feelings, and evaluations held, presumably, by a substantial proportion of leaders and the general population. Subcultures are relatively distinctive sets of attitudes, opinions, and values that persist for relatively long periods of time in the life of a country and give individuals in a particular subculture a sense of identity that distinguishes them from individuals in other subcultures.

In this section, however, I am not concerned with the widely shared

30. V. O. Key, *Public Opinion and American Democracy*, (New York, Knopf, 1961), p. 141, n. 5.

attitudes that go into a general political culture nor with the *content* of political attitudes found in specific subcultures or other distinctive groups; I am concerned only with the *patterns* of cleavage and consensus formed by the ways in which political attitudes are distributed over the population of a country. What follows is an effort to draw together a tentative theory to explain how four factors may increase or decrease the incentives of political leaders to pursue conflicting goals and strategies (or, conversely, conciliatory goals and strategies).

These four factors are:

The *distribution* of opinions on political questions—specifically whether the distribution is single-peaked or bimodal.[31]

The *coincidence* of opinions among different individuals, that is, the extent to which individuals who agree on one question agree on others.

The *salience* or *intensity* of opinions on different questions.

The institutional means for aggregating opinions, and specifically the *party system.*

Let us begin with the last factor, for a belief widely expressed in the literature of political science is that a two-party system has a moderating influence on the selection of goals.[32] In a two-party system, it is often said, the government party and the opposition tend to converge toward common ground because both parties compete for the great mass of voters whose opinions on political questions differ only very little: the center. Yet this hypothesis assumes that there *is* a great mass of voters responsive to "centrist" ideas and proposals. But this might not be the case. If not, our hypothesis is that a two-party system would not necessarily lead to conciliation and compromise but might actually intensify political conflict. Suppose that opinion on some critical political question[33] were distributed along a continuum from the extreme left to the extreme right, as

31. Obviously there are many other distributions; but to add others not only increases the complexity of exposition but takes theory well beyond the limits of the data at hand.

32. Assertions about the moderating effects of a two-party system are surely among the oldest and most widespread in the modern study of political parties, and a number of writers on parties have provided explanations derived implicitly from the assumptions and argument in these paragraphs. See in particular A. Lawrence Lowell, *The Government of England* (2 vols. New York, Macmillan, 1908) and *Public Opinion and Popular Government* (New York, Longmans, Green, 1913); and E. E. Schattschneider's discussion in *Political Parties* (New York, Farrar and Rinehart, 1942) on "the moderating effect of the attempt to create a majority" in a two-party system (pp. 85 ff.). Lowell recognized the possibility that the distribution of opinion necessary for a two-party system to have a moderating effect might not exist: in this case, however, it was not a "true public opinion" and it would be impossible to conduct the government "by a true public opinion or by consent" (*Public Opinion and Popular Government*, p. 11).

33. I use the word "question" deliberately in this discussion to include issues, candidates, ideology, or any other matter on which political opinions exist.

in Figure 12.1.[34] Suppose, further, that the distribution were unimodal and similar to the familiar bell-shaped pattern (Figure 12.1); that political leaders were more or less familiar with the distribution of opinion; and that they were anxious to win elections by adopting a position on this

I. Moderation

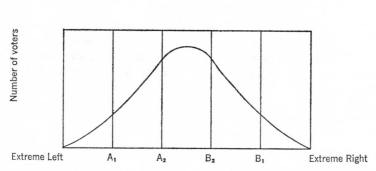

Figure 12.1. Effects of Distribution of Opinion on Two Parties

issue that would gain them maximum popular support. Suppose, now, that the ideologues of Party A were to advocate an extreme left-wing policy represented by the position A_1. The leaders of Party A would see that this extreme position would very likely cost them nearly all of the votes of people whose opinions were to the right of A_1, provided only that Party B were astute enough to take a position slightly to the right of A_1; hence if Party A were to take a position A_1, it might retain its extreme left wing but would probably lose votes catastrophically to Party B. In precisely the same way, if the ideologues of Party B were to advocate B_1, the party leaders would see how heavy a price they might ultimately pay in order to satisfy their extremists. Thus both parties would have strong incentives driving them toward positions close to the middle that have the support of the preponderant majority of citizens, say A_2 and B_2. If the parties were to adopt A_2 and B_2, most voters would feel that the policy adopted by the government was an acceptable one no matter which party were to win the election. And compromises between the two parties would not be par-

34. Spatial models, like those used in the exposition that follows, derive indirectly from Harold Hotelling, "Stability in Competition," *Economic Journal, 39* (1929), 41–57, but became an explicit basis for a theory of party competition in Anthony Downs, *An Economic Theory of Democracy* (New York, Harper, 1957). They were also employed in my *A Preface to Democratic Theory* (Chicago, University of Chicago Press, 1956), pp. 93 ff., which set out some of the argument that follows. The unrealistic character of some of the assumptions made in using spatial models has been severely criticized by Donald E. Stokes in "Spatial Models of Party Competition," *American Political Science Review, 57* (June 1963), 368–77. Stokes' criticisms are, I think, valid.

ticularly difficult, since positions A_2 and B_2 are not, after all, very far apart.

The effect of party competition in this situation would be to reinforce moderate or central opinion. By responding to the moderates and proposing moderate policies, the parties would help to strengthen moderate opinions and moderate leaders, which in turn would reinforce the tendencies of the parties to adopt moderate positions.[35] The moderating effects of party competition are likely to be particularly strong in a system under which legislators are elected in single-member districts by winning more votes than any single opponent. For in such a system, an extremist party advocating, say, A_1 might gain the votes of left extremists only to be swamped in the elections by the votes of the center. Moreover, an extreme left-wing party at A_1 might well cause enough defections to prevent a moderate left party at A_2 from winning the election; hence to vote for the extreme left party could produce policies even more intolerable to the left extremists than the policy advocated by the moderate left party. Consequently voters at the extreme left are confronted by the prospect that they will not only throw away their votes by supporting a party that advocates their views but they may well help to bring about a victory of a party on the right. Similar reasoning applies, of course, to the right.[36]

Even under a system of proportional representation with, let us say, four parties, dominant coalitions would tend to move toward moderation. For the moderate center parties would stand the best chance of winning the most votes; by winning the most votes they would acquire the most seats; and thus they would have the greatest influence in a governing coalition. Indeed the two moderate parties might well combine to form a governing coalition. But even a moderate party that considered the prospect of forming a coalition with the party on its extreme flank would hardly find it worthwhile to bargain away its own policies for those of its lesser partner simply to gain the support of the smaller party; for to do so would cause the moderate party to lose the bulk of its supporters to its moderate rival. Consequently the moderate parties would bargain from positions of strength, the extreme parties from positions of weakness.

The preceding analysis is probably correct, at least roughly. Yet it rests entirely on the assumption that opinions do in fact have a single mode. And there is no reason at all to rule out the possibility of radically different

35. In this discussion "moderate" means no more than being near the center of some distribution of opinions. In this sense, "moderation" has no intrinsic or necessary virtues and implies no psychological qualities in the "moderate" person or the supporters of a "moderate" party.

36. All these arguments were used, in less formal language, by moderate opponents of Senator Goldwater in their unsuccessful attempt to block his nomination by the Republican Party in 1964. The election demonstrated, I think, that their arguments were correct.

distributions of opinions. For example, some great question might divide
the opinions of citizens into two camps as in Figure 12.2. Now a center
scarcely exists; and the ideologues of moderation labor under the same
handicaps as the ideologues of extremism under the single-peaked dis-

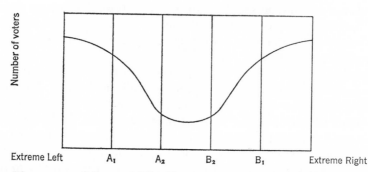

Figure 12.2. Effects of Distribution of Opinion on Two Parties

tribution. To the contention of moderates in Party A that they should
hold to position A_2, the left will argue that the great bulk of Party A's
support lies toward the extreme; and if Party A takes a moderate position
it might well see its support sapped by another party of the left. And so,
too, on the right. Once again, the single-member district system with
plurality elections reinforces the cleavage in opinion. If, for example, a
moderate left party were to adhere to its traditional position of centrist
moderation, it would run the risk that a new party would arise and advocate a position to the left of A_2. Such a party would be likely to swamp
the old moderate left party (as Labor in Britain did with the Liberals.) [37]
Thus when opinion is bimodal a two-party system based on single-
member districts and plurality elections is likely to intensify rather than
to mitigate conflict either by inducing the existing parties to shift to the
extremes or by generating a new extreme party (and thus ceasing, at least
temporarily, to be a two-party system). For a center party will, in time,
be reduced to a corporal's guard by the effects of the election system.
Indeed, it is altogether likely that with a bimodal distribution of political
opinions a two-party system may intensify conflict even more than a
multiparty system and proportional representation might do.

To be sure, a multiparty system cannot create moderation and conciliation where they do not exist. With proportional representation, the for-

37. Cf., for example, John Bonham, *The Middle Class Vote* (London, Faber and
Faber, 1954), pp. 149 ff., and Ivor Jennings, *Party Politics, The Growth of Parties*
(Cambridge, Cambridge University Press, 1961), pp. 250 ff.

mation of extreme parties would be inevitable; and by making it difficult for the center parties to form a viable coalition the growth of support for extreme parties would increase the chances for coalitions influenced by the extremes. This was the problem of Weimar Germany, and it is to some degree the situation in Italy. Yet where polarization is less than complete, proportional representation and multiple parties may help a center to survive as long as any significant number of left-center, center, and right-center opinions persist. Thus the center parties may manage to retain some bargaining power in the coalitions of government and opposition and thereby to weaken, at least partly, the strength of incentives to antagonism and conflict.

One must therefore qualify the hypothesis that two-party systems necessarily foster moderation and compromise while multiparty systems encourage antagonism and severe conflict. We conclude instead that *when voters' opinions are (and are thought to be) unimodal, both a two-party system and a multiparty system are likely to lead to moderation and compromise among the leading parties. When, on the other hand, opinion is strongly polarized in a bimodal pattern, two parties, each striving to retain the support of the extremists on its flank, will only exacerbate a conflict; and in multiparty systems the center parties will decline in votes and influence.*

So far in this discussion I have implicitly assumed that it is possible to characterize opinions on all important questions or conflicts by means of a single, summary distribution. Thus if Smith is to the "left" and Green to the "right" of Jones on one question, Smith will be to the left and Green to the right of Jones on other questions. But of course this is not necessarily the case.[38] The extent to which the opinions of individuals or groups coincide from one question to another may vary; and these variations are likely to encourage different patterns of opposition.

Thus the relative strength of incentives for conciliation and antagonism does not depend only on whether opinions are unimodal or bimodal, but also on the extent to which opinions coincide from one political question to another, that is, on the extent to which individuals or groups who agree (or are close to one another) on one question agree on other questions.

If there is a high degree of coincidence, so that individuals who agree on one political matter agree on others, then the effect is evidently quite straightforward: *high coincidence reinforces the effects of unimodal or bimodal distributions of opinion.*

If people who are moderate on one question are moderate on others, and if most people are moderate on every question, then the incentives of party leaders to engage in a search for moderate policies are, of course, very much increased. If, on the contrary, people who are at opposite

38. Cf. Stokes, *Spatial Models of Party Competition*, p. 370.

extremes on one question are likely to be at opposite extremes on all questions, and if most people are extremists, then moderate, conciliatory parties or coalitions will be even more likely to yield to intransigent political groups implacably at odds with one another.

If the effects of high coincidence seem clear, the effects of low coincidence are complex. To begin with, as compared with high coincidence, low coincidence of opinions increases the number of different clusters of persons with divergent opinions. Each of these "opinion-clusters" is potentially a separate political following—potentially, therefore, the basis of a separate political movement, whether pressure group, faction, or party. The point may be clarified by using Belgium as an example.

Belgians, as Lorwin has shown, have been at odds over three sets of questions. If we consider them as pro–con questions for ease of exposition, then in Belgium an individual might be characterized as:

> either pro-labor or pro-property;
> either anticlerical or pro-Catholic; and
> either pro-Walloon or pro-Flemish.

Because three dichotomous attributes can be combined in eight ways, in principle every Belgian might be located within one of eight possible combinations; for example, individual A, B, C, D, etc. might be:

> A: pro-labor/anticlerical/Walloon
> B: pro-labor/Catholic/Walloon
> C: pro-property/anticlerical/Walloon
> D: pro-labor/Catholic/Flemish
> etc.

At one extreme, coincidence among the opinions of Belgians might be maximally high. Individuals who agreed on one question would agree on the others; those who disagreed on one would disagree on the others. Thus by knowing how a Belgian stood on one of these questions one could predict perfectly how he would stand on the other two. Under the particular conditions of our example, this would mean that every individual would fall into one of two opinion-clusters. (Technically, one cluster might be empty, but we ignore that possibility.) For example, all Walloons might be pro-labor and anticlerical; and all Flemings Catholic and pro-property. In this case, the society, and presumably political life, would be polarized.[39] At the other extreme, coincidence among opinions might be at a minimum, so that if two persons agreed on one issue (if, for example, they were both Walloons) nothing could be predicted as to their opinions on the other issues. Hence all eight opinion-clusters might be

39. This result follows from the particular example. Conditions could be specified under which maximally high coincidence would mean complete unanimity.

represented in the population. Each would be a potential foundation for a separate political movement antagonistic to all the others.[40]

Yet low coincidence does not necessarily produce this kind of fragmented antagonism among opinion-clusters. In some circumstances, as we shall see, low coincidence may strengthen incentives for conciliation. The extent to which incentives for conciliation (or antagonism) are strengthened (reduced) appears to depend on two additional factors: the salience of a political question or intensity of opinions, and the available institutional means for aggregating opinions.

Suppose that in Belgium there were not only a low coincidence of opinions but that all three questions evoked extremely intense views on the part of everyone. In this case each opinion-cluster would tend to become a separate political movement, and it would be extremely troublesome for leaders to build political coalitions combining two clusters. For example, Catholics would split down the middle over labor and property and Walloon Catholics would split with Flemish Catholics. There would be four distinct Catholic parties, or four distinct factions within one Catholic party. If everyone held to all three of his opinions strongly, compromise would be impossible. Each question would involve a straight fight between a rigid majority and a rigid minority. And a majority that held together on one question would collapse completely on the next.[41]

It is quite possible, however, that one of the three questions in Belgium might be more salient than the others. In the simplest case, the same question would be salient to everyone, and therefore the other two would be less important to everyone. Suppose, for example, that everyone in Belgium believed that language was the overarching problem. In this case, the leaders of the Walloon community might profitably search for support among both socialists and pro-property Walloons, among both anti-clerical and Catholic Walloons; and so, too, with the Flemish leaders. Hence while conflict over language would doubtless grow more intense, the possibilities of conciliation on the other questions would increase, since everyone would have some incentive to reduce conflict on these questions.

But there is still another possibility: although everyone might believe that one of the three issues was the most important, different individuals might rank the importance of the issues in different ways. To one citizen,

40. This is equivalent to "the superposition of dualisms" of Maurice Duverger, *Les Partis Politiques* (Paris, Colin, 1954), pp. 260-65.

41. Discussions of the effects of cross-cutting cleavages in mitigating conflict usually ignore this possibility. The usual assumption, at least in recent American political science, seems to be that cross-cutting cleavages inevitably have a unifying rather than a disintegrating effect. But the analysis here indicates that unifying effects cannot occur if all the cleavages are felt with equal intensity. Conciliation is encouraged by cross-cutting cleavages *only* if some cleavages are less significant than others (as is shown in the paragraphs that follow).

the language question would be dominant; to another, Catholicism; to a third, socialism. When opinions are held in this fashion, the possibility of building coalitions of different opinion-clusters is evidently considerably increased. For example, it would now be easier to unite strongly pro-labor Walloons to whom anticlericalism is of secondary importance with fervent Catholic-Flemish workers who might otherwise support the Christian Social Party. Thus there would be a tendency for each opinion-cluster to yield somewhat on secondary issues in order to gain support on primary questions. Hence heterogeneous coalitions or parties might develop; and party leaders would exert great efforts in trying to conciliate their diverse followings.

The extent to which a nation with strong cleavages may be held together in part by its cleavages is perhaps best illustrated by the Netherlands. Abstractly considered, the Netherlands would surely be counted a prime candidate for political disintegration, since the country must bear not only some class antagonism but an even more profound cleavage over religion. Yet the very way in which the one conflict is superimposed on the other probably helps to reduce the potential for conflict. A Catholic party, as Hans Daalder shows, unties both working- and middle-class Catholics. The Protestant parties also cross class lines for their support. Although the Socialist and Liberal parties have had only modest success in gaining support among Catholics and orthodox Protestants, they do nonetheless persist in striving for votes among these religious groups and the liberal Protestants; consequently, less because of their actual support than because of the support they hope to acquire, Socialists and Liberals are a moderating influence on religious cleavages. Taken together, then, the efforts of the parties help to knit the community together.

As the Dutch example suggests, the effects of low coincidence cannot be explained simply by the salience of the questions among the various opinion-clusters, but also by the way in which political institutions encourage people in the different opinion-clusters to unite in coalitions. The most important of these institutions is, no doubt, the political party. If we assume that the number of important parties is not solely a function of the various patterns of opinion we have been describing but also of election systems, historical events, tradition, and the weight of institutions, then the effects of low coincidence of opinions (and hence the existence of a number of different opinion-clusters) will depend *in part* on the number of parties.

The matter, it must be admitted, is somewhat unclear. However, there is some reason for thinking that where political opinions do not coincide and are unequally salient, a two-party system strengthens incentives for conciliation and reduces incentives for conflict. The reasoning is often applied to the United States, which seems to meet the requirements for our hypothesis: low coincidence, unequal salience, and two major parties. Given low coincidence, the two parties are bound to be heterogeneous—as indeed they are in the United States. There, as we have seen, the co-incidence of opinions is too low to permit homogeneous parties. But these very circumstances create strong incentives for conciliation and com-promise. For party leaders have nothing to gain from yielding entirely to one opinion-cluster: They cannot possibly gain majorities in Congress or win presidential elections by that strategy. Hence they must devote un-remitting effort to building coalitions of different opinion-clusters not only in order to win elections but also to pass legislation. A major pre-occupation of the American politician is therefore to persuade any given opinion-cluster to give way on its secondary demands in order to gain—if only temporarily—the support of other opinion-clusters for its primary demands. Given the unequal salience of opinions on different questions among different opinion-clusters, politicians stand a fair chance of suc-ceeding in their efforts at conciliation.

How different are the effects of a multiparty system? Given the same conditions—low coincidence and unequal salience—the same process could, presumably, lead to similar results. Moreover, if a government is to receive the support of a majority in parliament, presumably the process must and will take place. Yet it does seem rather likely that the incentives for conciliation as compared with conflict are stronger if there are only two parties. For one thing, with two parties the process of conciliation is necessary not only in the legislature (as in a multiparty system), but also in nominations and elections. For another, in a two-party system a good deal of the process of negotiation takes place among politicians of the same party rather than among politicians of different parties; in this case the incentive to arrive at a viable compromise is strengthened, not weakened, by party loyalties.[42]

This somewhat abstract discussion of the effects of different factors on incentives for conciliation or conflict is summarized in Table 12.2.

Polarization

It is a common assumption, one by no means confined to Marxists, that urbanization, industrialization, the growth of national economies, and other features associated with social and economic modernization tend to result in a high degree of political polarization. A contradictory and more recent hypothesis is that, beyond some range, in Western societies mod-ernization leads to a decrease in political polarization.

42. This is a specific application of a familiar proposition. Drawing on George Simmel, Lewis Coser has formulated a number of propositions about conflict that are relevant to the discussion in this section. Thus "Conflict with another group leads to the mobilization of the energies of group members and hence to increased cohesion of the group." *The Functions of Conflict* (Glencoe, Free Press, 1956), p. 95.

Table 12.2 *Some Factors That Affect Incentives for Conciliating or Pressing Conflicting Opinions*

Factors that strengthen incentives for conciliating conflicting opinions	Factors that strengthen incentives for pressing conflicting opinions
1. All uni-modal distributions of opinions.	1. All bimodal distributions.
2. High coincidence of uni-modal distributions.	2. High coincidence of bimodal distributions.
3. Low coincidence, if of unequal salience.	3. Low coincidence, if of equal salience.
4. Two-party system: a. If opinions are uni-modal. b. If opinions have low coincidence but unequal salience.	4. Multiparty system: a. If opinions are uni-modal. b. If opinions have coincidence but unequal salience.
5. Multiparty system, if opinions are distributed bimodally with high coincidence.	5. Two-party system, if opinions are distributed bimodally with high coincidence.

To test either hypothesis is, unfortunately, difficult. To begin with, the term "polarization" is used in various ways. Typically, it is intended to refer to the extent to which a population is divided politically into two antagonistic camps distinguished by differences in socioeconomic characteristics.

Unfortunately, the concept is bristling with difficulties, for it combines at least three different notions that need to be distinguished.

1. It contains the idea of a dimension of bipolarity, dualism, a U-shaped distribution, the extent to which a population is divided into two categories. A measure of dualism might be the proportion of a population contained in the two largest categories.

2. It also contains the idea of a dimension of distance between the two largest categories. The greater the distance the more polarized the society.

3. Finally, it contains the idea of different characteristics with respect to which bipolarity or dualism might exist. The most important of these are:

a. Social and economic characteristics. Socioeconomic dualism, then, would be a measure of the extent to which a population is divided into two categories by class, status, language, religion, income, wealth, etc. A country where everyone considered himself a member either of the working class or the middle class would be completely dualistic with respect to these class categories.

b. Psychological, emotional, or affective characteristics. Psychological or affective dualism would require a measure of the extent to which a population is divided into two antagonistic or hostile groups.

c. Political characteristics. Political dualism would be measured by the extent to which a population is divided into groups distinguished by differences in political behavior—ideology, political goals and demands, party memberships or identifications, and voting. In the simplest case, a country where everyone voted either for Party *A* or Party *B* would be (by definition) completely dualistic with respect to voting.

Since the three main dimensions are logically independent, and the three types of characteristics are also logically independent of one another, managing the concept of polarization is inordinately difficult.[43] A moment's reflection will reveal the vast variety of different patterns that might be regarded as examples of polarization. Indeed, the concept is so complex that it has seemed advisable to avoid the term "polarization" wherever possible in the discussion that follows and to refer instead to some specific patterns. Among a very much larger number of theoretical possibilities, it is useful to imagine four different general situations in which a high degree of political dualism might exist.

1. *Political dualism unrelated to social or affective dualism.* To offer a hypothetical example, this would exist in the United States if everyone identified strongly with either the Democratic or Republican parties, or if everyone adhered either to a liberal or a conservative ideology, or to an isolationist or interventionist foreign policy; if, however, there were little antagonism between the two groups; and if there were little or no correlation between party loyalties or ideology and occupation, income, religion, etc.

2. *Political dualism closely related to a social dualism, but not to affective dualism.* This would exist in Britain if all manual workers were socialists and people in nonmanual occupations were conservative; and if there were little antagonism between the two groups.

3. *Political duality closely related to affective duality but not to any social dualities.* This would exist in France if everyone were strongly pro- or anti-De Gaulle; if there were very great antagonism between Gaullists

43. See, for example, *The American Voter,* where the concept of polarization is discussed at some length and used fruitfully in exploring American survey data without, however, escaping some ambiguity (pp. 338 ff.). The authors begin by defining polarization in psychological terms, i.e., in terms of antagonism: "The condition of active discord between social strata [is] *status polarization*" (p. 338, their italics). "Status polarization, then, refers to the degree to which upper and lower status groups in a society have taken up mutually antagonistic value positions" (p. 339). They then go on to suggest that status polarization (or, in terms of the distinction above, psychological dualism) is a function of a certain kind of social dualism, namely with respect to social class: "We can say in a rough way that *variation in the status polarization of a society reflects variation in the intensity and extent of class identification among its members.* When polarization is high most of the citizenry must have perceived a conflict of interests between strata and have taken on class identifications with fair intensity. When polarization is low, either few people are identifying or extant identifications are weak, or both" (p. 339, their italics). The measures they use do not, however, bear directly on the question of antagonism; for they measure "status polarization" by using indices of occupation in some cases (Figure 13-2, p. 347, and Figure 13-6, p. 358), and "subjective status" or class identification in others (Figures 13-3, p. 352; 13-4, p. 354; 13-7, p. 364; 13-8, p. 367). Thus while they define "status polarization" in psychological terms, they do not in fact measure antagonism. A. Campbell, P. Converse, W. Miller, and D. Stokes, *The American Voter* (New York, Wiley, 1960).

and anti-Gaullists; and if these differences were not correlated with social status, income, occupation, region, etc.

4. *Political dualism closely related to both social and psychological dualisms.* This is full-scale political polarization. It would exist in France if, in the example just given, the last condition did not hold and instead the middle classes and farmers were uniformly Gaullist while the working classes were uniformly anti-Gaullist.

It is obvious that each of these patterns of political dualism is significantly different from the others. What has been called "status polarization" sometimes refers to the second, sometimes to the last. Political polarization might refer to the third or fourth, but it might also refer to the first. Yet the consequences for oppositions, as well as for government, would surely be very different in each case.[44] Keeping these various possibilities in mind, what conclusions can we draw from the experiences of the countries examined in this volume? Although the data are hardly sufficient for solidly based generalizations, some tentative conclusions are suggested by the evidence at hand.

1. Objective status differences seem to be on the decline throughout Western Europe. Rising incomes, the redistributive effects of tax and welfare measures, increased consumption, standardization of consumer goods, expansion of white-collar occupations, and increased education (among other things) all contribute to a blurring of status differences and

44. The notion of political polarization is troubled by still other problems that we cannot pursue here. In particular, there are formidable problems of constructing satisfactory indices and measures. Since each characteristic—social, psychological, political—is a broad category, one problem is to choose a satisfactory attribute or set of attributes within that category. In discussions of social dualism, the attribute most frequently referred to is class or status, for which occupation, income, education, class identification, etc. are used as indicators. But status polarization is only one type of social dualism, though an important one; for a society may also divide along other lines—religion, ethnic group, region, for example. Indices of psychological polarity are difficult to construct. Gabriel Almond and Sidney Verba in *The Civic Culture* offer some highly interesting possibilities; how one political group views another—positive, negative, and neutral qualities (Tables 1-6, pp. 125 ff.); and psychological distance between parties as indicated by willingness to have one's son or daughter marry across party lines (Tables 7-11, pp. 132 ff.). Political duality is also broad; indicators might include party identifications or orientation to candidates, though these are all complicated by simple differences in the number of alternatives presented to voters in two-party and multiparty countries; by differences in policy preferences, ideology, and other attitudes.

In order to find the degree of relationship between political duality and social or psychological dualities, measures of correlation are needed. In principle, a wide variety of standard statistical measures of correlation might be applied. In practice, however, few are satisfactory because of limitations in the data. The authors of *The American Voter* suggest a simple straightforward Index of Status Polarization. Robert Alford uses the same index, calling it the "Index of Class Voting." Curiously, however, Alford objects to the index suggested in *The American Voter*, even though his own is identical to it in all but name (see *The American Voter*, Figure 13.1, p. 345, and Alford, *Party and Society* (Chicago, Rand-McNally, 1963), pp. 79 ff.) Alford uses his Index of Class Voting to compare Australia, Britain, Canada, and the United States.

the enlargement of middle strata who shade off into the skilled working class on the one side and the wealthy upper strata on the other.[45]

2. Political duality as reflected in political attitudes, aspirations, and loyalties varies a good deal among our countries; but once sharp differences in political attitudes also seem to be declining. Nearly all the essays in the volume emphasize the decline of socialism as a distinctive ideology; as Otto Kirchheimer has indicated in his essay, the change may have been greatest—it is, at any rate, the most remarkable—in Germany, the home of the classic European Social Democratic Party. Strong loyalties to different political parties do, of course, persist; but as the experience of the United States demonstrates, party loyalty may be strong and yet have little to do with differences in ideology or policy. While the United States is no doubt the extreme case, the essays in this book suggest that European democracies are moving toward a somewhat similar situation.

3. It would be hasty to conclude, however, that the same pattern is emerging in the United States and the European democracies: that is, the first pattern suggested a moment ago, where political duality, even where it exists, is unrelated to social differences or psychological antagonism. There are two difficulties with this hypothesis.

First, the relation between status or occupation and party preference does not seem to have declined in Europe. Indeed, Lipset concludes:

> A comparative look at the pattern of working-class voting in contemporary Europe reveals that with the exception of Holland and Germany, the leftist parties secure about two-thirds or more of the working-class vote, a much higher percentage than during the depression of the 1930's . . . The leftist working-class parties have increased their strength in most of Europe during the 1960's. It is clear, therefore, that the easy assumption made by many, concerning American as well as European politics, that greater national affluence would mean a weakening of electoral support for the left is simply wrong.[46]

Second, the English-speaking and European democracies exhibit no single pattern. Sizable differences occur from one country to another in the extent to which status or occupation is related to party preference. Alford, who applied an Index of Class Voting to voting surveys taken from 1952 to 1962 in the four major English-speaking democracies found that:

> Class voting is almost always above zero; only one Canadian survey falls below that mark. Great Britain is consistently higher than Australia

45. See particularly the essay by Otto Kircheimer, above. And the essays by R. Bendix, R. Dahrendorf, M. Crozier, D. Lockwood, and Raymond Aron in *European Journal of Sociology*, 1, No. 2 (1960), 181–282.

46. S. M. Lipset, "Class Conflict and Contemporary European Society, Daedalus" in S. R. Graubard, ed., *A New Europe* (Boston, Houghton Mifflin, 1964), pp. 337–69.

in the 1952–62 period . . . Australia is consistently higher than the United States . . . The United States is consistently higher than Canada, except for one 1948 Canadian survey . . . Canada always has the lowest level of class voting with the single exception mentioned.[47]

Moreover, there is no consistent pattern of change. In Britain, as Alford shows, the "electorate remains sharply divided along class lines. No decline of the differences between classes as such or of the political predispositions connected with occupational status has occurred." On the other hand, in Norway, as Rokkan has demonstrated, an interesting change has occurred since the 1890s, for the Labor Party has gradually increased its support among the lower manual strata at the expense of all other parties, and in this sense political behavior has become more closely related to social cleavage. But the Labor Party also receives a good deal of support from the middle and upper strata. In this respect, the pattern of incomplete polarization is the reverse of that in Britain.[48]

4. Yet if status polarization is not decreasing, most of our essays indicate that psychological dualism in political life—i.e., antagonism and hostility —has sharply declined since the interwar period. In this case, too, differences remain. The presence of large Communist parties in France and Italy produces (and doubtless is produced by) a higher level of antagonism between a large proportion of the population (and of political elites) than is true in the other countries.[49] And in the United States the level of hostility over racial issues obviously has remained high, although the antagonism has historically been sharpest between the Southern and Northern wings of the same party.

5. None of the countries examined in this book closely approaches the pattern described a moment ago as full-scale political polarization, where sharp political, socioeconomic, and psychological dualisms all coincide. In Italy, political antagonisms are probably higher than in any of the other countries; indeed, it is difficult to see how its parliamentary system could withstand much higher psychological voltages. But even in Italy, as Barnes points out, socioeconomic status is quite imperfectly correlated with political cleavages, and the political groups around the center have been able, so far, to prevent political life from turning into a straight conflict between Communists on the Left and anti-Communists on the Right. In

47. "The index of class voting was computed by subtracting the percentage of nonmanual workers voting for 'Left' parties from the percentage of manual workers voting for 'Left' parties. For Great Britain, the Labor party was used; for Australia, the Australian Labor party; for the United States, the Democratic party; for Canada, the CCF (or NDP) and Liberal parties" (p. 102, Table 5–2).

48. Above, pp. 89 ff. See also Stein Rokkan, "Geography, Religion and Social Class: Cross-Cutting Cleavages in Norwegian Politics," S. M. Lipset and S. Rokkan, eds., *Party Systems and Voter Alignments* (New York, Free Press, 1965).

49. Almond and Verba report that "Italian respondents show a far sharper (psychological) polarization between right and left than do the Americans, British and Germans" (*The Civic Culture*, p. 128).

Britain, Sweden, and Norway, where socialist and nonsocialist parties reflect differences in occupations, incomes, and status a good deal more strongly than the two major parties in the United States, the effects of socioeconomic differences on political life are, as we have seen, greatly attenuated because one of the largest parties in each of these countries has a socially heterogeneous following: thus in Norway the socialists draw as much as 40 per cent of the votes of the nonmanual workers, while in Britain a third or more of the manual workers support the Conservatives, and a quarter or more of the voters in nonmanual occupations have supported Labor. In these countries, moreover, psychological antagonisms appear to be exceedingly low.

How can we account for the absence of full-scale social-psychological polarization in these countries?

First there are the various factors, frequently mentioned in these essays, that are associated with economic "modernity," the growth of national communications, the blurring of class lines, etc.

Second, in some countries the effects of cross-cutting social characteristics have probably reduced both social and psychological dualities in political life.

Third, and paradoxically, it is in these countries, where political dualism along status lines has been most evident, that a long-run reduction in antagonisms and hostilities has been most notable. Political differences are most likely to reflect status differences, as we have seen, in highly homogeneous countries like Britain and Sweden where other differences—religious, ethnic, geographical—are comparatively slight. Yet this very homogeneity facilitates peaceful evolutionary reforms that blunt the edge of class hostilities.

Finally, it must always be kept in mind that our Western democracies, like other nation-states, are the products of an historical process during which extreme polarization has worked its drastic cures. In this book we have studied the survivors; we might have studied the casualties; we might, conceivably, be examining future casualties. Full-scale polarization is obviously an unstable condition for any polity, and particularly for a representative one. Extreme polarization of political life will be reduced somehow. Perhaps the strongest polarizing forces in modern times have been those of religion, language, and ethnic identity. If these forces do not polarize political life in most Western democracies today, this is only because they did so earlier. Typically they worked their drastic cure by destroying the political system: either by a separation into different countries, so that the cleavages became international rather than national, as with the separation of Ireland from Britain or Norway from Sweden; or by the creation of a one-party authoritarian or totalitarian states, as in the case of Fascist Italy, Nazi Germany, and Franco Spain.

13

EPILOGUE

Robert A. Dahl

To one who believes in the essential worth of a democratic polity, how much opposition is desirable, and what kinds? What is the best balance between consensus and dissent? Even among democrats there is not much agreement on the answers to these questions.

It is easy to see why. These questions seem to demand nothing less than a complicated assessment of democracy itself. Or to put the matter more precisely, one can judge the desirability of different patterns of political opposition only by employing a number of different criteria that would be used if one were appraising the extent to which a political system as a whole achieves what are usually considered democratic goals or values.

Eight of these standards seem directly relevant in judging different patterns of opposition. In comparison with other possible arrangements, one might ask, to what extent does a particular pattern maximize:

1. Liberty of thought and expression, including opportunities for dissenting minorities to make their views known to other citizens and policy-makers?
2. Opportunities for citizens to participate in political life?
3. When political conflicts occur, control over the decisions of government by majorities (rather than minorities) of citizens, voters, and elected officials?
4. Rationality in political discussion and decision-making, in the sense of increasing understanding by citizens and leaders of the goals involved and the appropriate means? [1]
5. Consensus in political discussion and decision-making, in the sense that solutions are sought that will minimize the size, resentments, and coercion of defeated minorities, and will maximixe the numbers of citizens who conclude that their goals have been adequately met by the solution adopted?

---

1. Cf. Bagehot, who refers to "one of the mental conditions of Parliamentary Government, by which I do not mean reasoning power, but rather the power of hearing the reasons of others, of comparing them quietly with one's own reasons, and then being guided by the result." *The English Constitution*, p. 44. See also p. 280.

6. The peaceful management of conflicts and the minimization of political violence?

7. Resolution of urgent policy questions, in the sense that the government directs its attention to any question regarded as urgent and important by a substantial proportion of citizens or leaders, and adopts solutions satisfactory to the largest number of citizens?

8. Widespread confidence in and loyalty to a constitutional and democratic polity?

A number of other criteria might be advanced, but these are enough to give an idea of the magnitude of the problem of evaluation. What is most obvious and most important about these criteria is that, like most standards of performance for complex achievements, they conflict with one another; if a political system were to maximize one of these ends it would probably do so only at considerable cost to some of the others. Moreover, because different individuals disagree about the relative importance of different goals, they disagree as to what is the best solution in general, and even for a specific situation. How then can one prescribe an optimal balance among competing goals, when the goals are nonquantitative and imprecise, and when one man's optimum may be another man's prison? Nor are these the only sources of disagreement. The eight criteria conflict with one another; there is a certain tension among them; we cannot maximize one goal beyond some range without sacrificing another goal.

In spite of all these obstacles to finding an "optimal solution," it is possible to clarify some of the costs and gains of different solutions, actual or proposed. Let me start by examining the tension created by wanting—as most good democrats do—freedom, dissent, and consensus.

Freedom, Dissent, and Consensus

The first criterion listed above emphasizes opportunities for dissent; and it is no doubt their concern for this goal that explains, in the main, why liberals and radicals have usually been keenly sensitive to problems of political opposition. For to look at any political system from the point of view of an opposition inclines one to stress the virtues of dissent, of *opposing.* Yet the last criterion in our list emphasizes the virtues of stability; and the penultimate criterion, the importance of resolution and dispatch, avoiding deadlock, paralysis, impotence in government. Sensitivity to these criteria leads one to be concerned with the high costs of unlimited dissent and to stress the importance of consensus, particularly if governments willing to protect dissent are to survive.

There are, we all know, many varieties of freedom. One variety of freedom exists to the extent that every citizen has opportunities to engage in political activities without severe social and governmental constraints. In all political systems this freedom—let me call it Freedom of Political

Action—is, like other freedoms, limited by government and society; yet it is the differences in these limits that distinguish libertarian from authoritarian systems. In libertarian systems (like the ten described in this book), the right to dissent from the views of government—to oppose the government—is a vital form of Freedom of Political Action. And political oppositions are a crucial expression of this Freedom.

Yet the very existence of dissent and political opposition is a sure sign that someone is constrained by government to do or to forbear from doing something that he would like to do and very likely feels he has a moral right, or even an obligation, to do. To feel politically free because one obeys laws one believes in, to obey a government one approves of, to obey governmental policies one wants or agrees with—here is a second variety of freedom. Since this variety, like the other, bears no accepted name, let me call it Freedom in Political Obligations.

Now if the existence of political opposition is evidence of Freedom of Political Action, it is also a symbol of the Unfreedom in Political Obligations[2] of those opposed to the government. I expect that some readers will now move a well-known objection. Even citizens who are opposed to the laws enforced by their government may nonetheless yield their implicit consent, provided these laws are adopted by procedures they regard as legitimate; in this sense, their Freedom in Political Obligations is not diminished by their need to obey specific laws to which they object. Let me recognize the force of this familiar argument and put it to one side as irrelevant here. I do so in order to distinguish (1) a polity in which a large and permanent minority accepts the constitutional procedures and arrangements, yet detests the policies of government, which seems to it tyrannical in what it does if not in the way it acts; from (2) a polity in which agreement is so extensive that minorities are microscopic and evanescent, and no one ever feels much injured by the laws he is obliged to obey. In the first case, members of the outvoted minority might accept the obligation to obey the laws because these were adopted according to legitimate constitutional processes, and yet feel constrained to obey laws they hold wrong. In the second case, they would feel no such constraint.

If you will allow me this distinction, it follows, I think, that in a democratic system where Freedom of Political Action is widely enjoyed, the less the dissent, the greater the Freedom in Political Obligations. In fact the only system in which every citizen would be completely free in his Political Obligations would be one in which political consensus was perfect; for no citizen would then feel constrained by government to do something he believed he should not do. The more extreme the dissent permitted, the greater the range of Freedom in Political Action; yet the

2. The notion of "unfreedom" is defined in Felix E. Oppenheim, *Dimensions of Freedom* (New York, St. Martin's Press, 1961), Ch. 4, "Unfreedom."

more numerous the extreme dissenters, the greater the number who are (at least temporarily and perhaps indefinitely) Unfree in their Political Obligations.

Let me try to make these abstractions more concrete by comparing a high-consensus system like Sweden with a low-consensus system like Italy. In a high-consensus system most citizens are only moderately opposed, if at all, to the character and conduct of government; by comparison, in a low-consensus system a great many more people are strongly opposed to the conduct and even the form of the government. The proportion of citizens who feel themselves coerced or constrained by government, and thus Unfree in Political Obligations is, naturally, much larger in the low-consensus systems than in the high-consensus ones.

Yet an extreme dissenter may enjoy more freedom to express his dissent in a low-consensus system like Italy than in a system with considerably more consensus like the United States. For (aside from any other reasons) the very magnitude of extreme dissent in Italy and France limits the extent to which dissent is coerced by social and governmental actions; in the United States, however, where extreme dissent is so small that it can be coerced at less cost, social and governmental constraints are rather powerful. Thus in the United States opportunities for discussing one's views with others, attending meetings, reading newspapers sympathetic to one's cause, joining in a like-minded party, and voting for like-minded candidates are extensive for most citizens—but not, often, for the extreme dissenter.

Thus a low-consensus country like Italy may actually provide more Freedom of Political Action (to Communists, Monarchists, and Fascists, for example) than a country like the United States where there is considerably higher consensus. Is low consensus a better guarantee of political freedom, then, than high consensus? Hardly, for a low-consensus system greatly increases the amount of Unfreedom in Political Obligations among its citizens. What is more, widespread Unfreedom in Political Obligations is inescapable as long as consensus remains low; for even if the Outs were to displace the Ins, their positions would only be reversed. The Freedom in Political Obligations of the one-time Outs would now be greater; but so would the Unfreedom in Political Obligations of the one-time Ins. Then, too, a low-consensus system is much more likely to impose other costs such as deadlock, political violence, constitutional instability, and destruction of democracy itself.

If, then, the most desirable long-run solution for a low-consensus country would be to increase consensus, surely the most desirable long-run solution for a high-consensus country would not be deliberately to foster extreme dissent! An obvious alternative solution would be to reduce the legal obstacles that limit the Freedom of Political Action among dissenters until they are legally on a par with all other citizens. This is, in fact, the solution adopted in a number of high-consensus countries. In this respect, the United States is a somewhat deviant case: most other stable democracies have not imposed as severe a set of legal and social obstacles to political dissent as exist in the United States.

Rationality, Dissent, and Consensus

If freedom of dissent is thought (by most libertarians and democrats) to be a desirable freedom in itself, advocates of libertarian democracy have usually contended, as John Stuart Mill did, that an opportunity for the expression of dissenting opinions is also a necessary (though definitely not a sufficient) condition for "rational" political action. The citizens of any country, in this view, need dissenters and oppositions in order to act wisely, to explore alternatives, to understand the advantages and disadvantages of different alternatives, to know what they want and how to go about getting it. Yet there is a certain conflict, one not always recognized, between the conditions required for a relatively rational consideration of alternatives, and the existence of extensive dissent or extensive consensus.

Where dissent is slight, the alternatives presented by political leaders for consideration among themselves and by the voters are likely to represent relatively small marginal changes. For in a society where nearly everyone is already rather satisfied with the conduct of government, alternatives profoundly opposed to existing government policy are not likely to be generated, proposed, or considered. Changes are likely to come about by paying attention to a relatively small number of marginally different alternatives to existing policies, examining a limited set of possible consequences, comparing the results of whatever changes are made, and making whatever further modifications are suggested by subsequent experience: in short, by incremental action.

Although incrementalism evidently seems to a great many people a less rational process than comprehensive and deductive approaches, in fact it offers great advantages as a process for relatively rational change.[3] The characteristics and effects of existing policies and institutions are more easily, more accurately, and more confidently known than for hypothetical policies and institutions. The effects of small changes are usually much easier to predict than the effects of large changes. Current processes generate information about effects, and since this information can be fed back to policy-makers, changes can be reversed, accelerated, or altered. In practice, moreover, peaceful change is usually highly incremental.

3. Cf. the discussion in R. A. Dahl and C. E. Lindblom, *Politics, Economics, and Welfare* (New York, Harper, 1953), pp. 82 ff., and the much more highly developed theory in C. E. Lindblom and D. Braybrooke, *A Strategy of Decision* (Glencoe, Free Press, 1963), Chs. 5 and 6, and C. E. Lindblom, *The Intelligence of Democracy* (Glencoe, Free Press, 1965).

Partly for this reason, no doubt, incremental change is the characteristic
method of democracies: liquidation of the Kulaks and the Great Leap
Forward would not have been carried out by parliamentary governments.

Yet if high-consensus societies can profit from the advantages of incremental change, they run an opposite danger. Where there is little dissent,
both political leaders and citizens escape the compulsion to weigh the
relative advantages offered by a comprehensive, large-scale change, even
when a large-scale change might prove less costly in the long-run than
either the status quo or a series of incremental changes. The history of
politics is writ large with the results of costly timidities that have produced
too little, too late.

Reflecting that incremental responses have frequently failed to match
the magnitude of a challenge, one is tempted to conclude that sharp political conflict, clashing ideologies, and even low consensus are needed for
a rational examination of alternatives. Yet the historical record seems to
offer little support for this view. For intense conflicts create their own
irrationalities, particularly when conflict is fortified by ideology. It is a
reasonable hypothesis that the greater the discrepancy between the goals
of the parties to a conflict, the more that problem-solving and persuasion
are likely to give way to bargaining and coercion.[4] The true believer does
not judiciously appraise the arguments of the infidel. Has the clash of
ideologies in France and Italy provided a more "rational" examination of
alternatives than the low-tension conflicts and unideological analyses
among Britons and Swedes?

In sum, high-consensus polities are able to give relatively rational consideration to small changes but they are prone to ignore the possible advantages of radical changes in the status quo. Low-consensus polities may
find it difficult to profit from the advantages of incremental changes; yet
posing radically conflicting alternatives to citizens and leaders is accompanied by the irrationalities of ideological controversy.

Is it possible to have the best of both worlds? A society where dissent is
low enough to encourage a relatively calm and objective appraisal of
alternatives, and yet sufficient to make sure that radical alternatives will
not be ignored or suppressed? Among our ten countries, if Italy lies at the
one extreme, the United States is at the other. Possibly some of the north-
European democracies come closer to the balance we seek. Yet if their
high-consensus endures and increases, will not they, too, suffer the disadvantages of weak dissent?

Dispersion, Concentration, and Majority Rule

Does the two-party system offer a solution? Probably no other cure is so
often proposed for the ailments of a sick polity. Does it not solve the

4. James G. March and Herbert A. Simon, *Organizations* (New York, Wiley,
1958), 129 ff.

problem of how to balance a large measure of consensus with a satisfactory amount of rational dissent? For cannot one party embody the values of stability and consensus, and the other the values of change and dissent?

The only country where a two-party system of this kind has ever endured in a relatively clear form is Britain, which does, I believe, exhibit many of the virtues claimed for the two-party system. Should it be more widely copied?

Unfortunately, the two-party system presents two imposing difficulties as a general solution. It is evidently not viable in many countries. And even if it were, it would not in all circumstances produce the results found in Britain.

The very rarity of the two-party system, a fact heavily stressed in an earlier chapter, argues that the existence of such a system requires an unusual combination of circumstances. The absence of one or more of these circumstances greatly reduces the likelihood that a two-party system will exist, or, if it does exist, that it will have the results expected of it.

The conditions under which a two-party system would provide an optimal solution for meeting the eight goals listed earlier probably include these:

1. The parliament is sovereign in law and in fact.

2. Within parliament, the principle of majority rule is applied to decisions.

3. Among citizens, and markedly among political activists, there exists a high degree of consensus on the desirability and legitimacy of the first two conditions; on the other characteristics of the constitutional system; on the rights, liberties, and duties of individuals and groups; and on a great many social and economic goals, institutions, and arrangements.

4. On all questions about which there are conflicting views, and for which governmental action is regarded by some people as desirable, most citizens divide into only two great clusters of opinion. These opinions, though stable for long periods, are not rigidly fixed but change with time, as does the size of the two opinion-clusters.

5. There are two political parties, and neither of these parties is, or expects to be, indefinitely out of office.

In these circumstances, two unified parties, each having a program and policies directed toward one of the two great clusters of opinion and competing actively for office, meet a great many of the criteria listed earlier. As long as most conflicting opinions fall into one of the two great clusters, the two-party system would provide an outlet for expressing views, including criticizing the government (Criterion 1), and opportunities for citizens to participate in political life (Criterion 2). Any fair system for apportioning parliamentary seats would insure that the government would represent the larger opinion-cluster rather than the smaller (Criterion 3). The existence of two divergent sets of public attitudes bounded by extensive consensus would facilitate rationality in political discussion and decision-making (Criterion 4), by insuring that alternatives would be posed, providing a reasonably clear choice to voters, and enabling a rather high degree of coherence of policies and programs. Rationality would also be enhanced because an opposition's past experience in office and its expectation of future responsibility as the governing party would encourage its members to avoid demagogic and irresponsible appeals for unworkable and unrealistic solutions. The existence of widespread consensus and the experience and expectation of governing would help to minimize the resentments of the opposition and the need for coercion (Criterion 5) and also to insure that conflicts would be peacefully resolved (Criterion 6). Policy questions uppermost in the minds of any large group of people would almost certainly be brought forward by one of the two parties; and in due time each party would have an opportunity to enact its own solution (Criterion 7). Finally, all these conditions taken together would surely go very far toward creating widespread loyalty to democracy and constitutional government (Criterion 8).

It is easy to see why the two-party model, especially in the idealized form in which it is often described, has charmed so many political observers. Yet the conditions I have just specified are an unusual combination; they have not always existed even in Britain.

In the first place, as we have already seen (Chapter 12), if a society is polarized into highly antagonistic camps, then the two-party system might actually increase the intensity of conflicts by wiping out the mediating center.

Second, opinions may fall into more than two clusters, as they generally do in Belgium, Holland, Italy, and the United States. In these circumstances, there would have to be more than two parties; or, as in the United States, the two parties would not be highly unified. Moreover, if a system of disciplined parties existed, it could produce flagrant contradictions with several of our criteria. Specifically, the application of the principle of majority rule and parliamentary sovereignty could lead to minority government, negate majority rule, and thus violate Criterion 3. For if a faction in one party, even if it were a majority faction, could use the instruments of party discipline to impose its policies on that party, and if that party had a majority in parliament, then the policies adopted by the government and agreed to by the parliamentary majority might well be policies preferred only by a minority and opposed by a majority of the whole country. When there are more than two large clusters of opinions it would be necessary, in order to satisfy our criterion, for different majority coalitions to form on different issues. Thus a multiparty system or two heterogeneous parties without strong discipline would be preferable.

Third, the government and the opposition parties might not alternate in office. In this case, an opposition might find demagogic and unrealistic appeals increasingly attractive. Even if, as Nils Stjernquist's essay shows, the problem of a permanent opposition is not at all peculiar to a two-party system, there is nothing inherent in the dynamics of a two-party system that guarantees an alternation between the two parties.

A system with two disciplined and strictly competitive parties, one controlling the government and the other providing a concentrated focus for opposition, is not always, therefore, a desirable solution. The circumstances under which it is the optimal solution may be, in fact, rather uncommon. The typical solution of democracies is not concentration but dispersion, not strict competition but bargaining and coalescent strategies. Given the conditions of political life in most countries, quite possibly this solution is preferable; for it is often possible where the other solution is not, and it may come somewhat closer to satisfying our various criteria.

Majority Rule, Minorities, and Organized Pluralism

Every solution to the problems of opposition that focuses upon party systems runs the danger of neglecting a palpable fact of political life: many important decisions are not made in parliament. To the extent that an opposition concentrates on elections and parliamentary action, it may be powerful in unimportant encounters and feeble or even absent when key decisions are made.

As the extent of governmental intervention and control in social and economic affairs has expanded, the work of parliaments has also multiplied. But even with the enormously increased work load of parliaments and the much greater weight and range of the effects that laws passed by parliament now have on social and economic behavior, the *relative* importance of parliaments in making important decisions has not increased in the same proportion; the "decline of parliaments" has become a familiar topic and a source of concern.

No single curve could summarize the historical changes in the power of various parliaments. But in a number of countries two kinds of developments have helped to increase the *relative* importance of other sites. One is a pronounced growth in many Western democracies in the power of a plebiscitary executive who acquires great political resources by winning a national election. Although this development is clearest in the United States and the Fifth French Republic, the rise of highly disciplined parties has led by a different route to similar results in Britain, Norway, Sweden, Austria, and a number of other democracies. In France and the United States, the Constitution, laws, and political practices grant extensive discretionary power and authority to an elected chief executive; in the other countries, if a party or coalition wins a majority of seats in parliament, party discipline insures that it will form a government whose policies cannot, for all practical purposes, be defeated by opponents in parliament. Although the development is highly uneven and the pattern is markedly different from one country to another, the importance of the legislature as a site for encounters between opposition and government is reduced to the extent that a plebiscitary executive (whether president or cabinet) has acquired the power to make key decisions without much restraint by parliament.

The other development that creates a powerful rival for parliament is the one stressed by Stein Rokkan in his chapter on Norway: the evolution of national bargaining among employers, trade unions, and other interests has led to a process for making decisions of great economic and social importance over which parliaments and sometimes even executives exercise scant control.

What these two developments have in common is the creation of highly strategic sites outside parliament—rivals to parliamentary power. Where they differ is in the importance of national elections. For if the rise of a plebiscitary executive has reduced the relative influence of parliament, that development has, if anything, made elections even more crucial. Yet because the concrete alternatives open to voters are few and simple in comparison with the great range of problems confronting a modern state, an election furnishes a vague mandate at best; and at worst it simply allows winners and losers to provide their own interpretations of the election returns.

Bargaining with the executive, bargaining among private and public bureaucracies, negotiations among the great national associations, all these provide ways of supplementing, interpreting, offsetting, and even negating the election returns. This is exactly the source of both the advantages and the dangers of organized pluralism and national bargaining.

Organized pluralism meets many of the criteria for opposition in a democracy that I proposed at the beginning of this chapter. For example, because it often enables key groups to arrive at decisions they find more acceptable than decisions imposed by legislature or executive order, bargaining is an instrument for gaining consensus and enlarging the area of Freedom in Political Obligations. It provides additional sites for effective expression of views, dissent, criticism. Often it insures that the specialized knowledge of the groups most deeply involved in some activity will be brought to bear on a solution. Yet if it has many advantages—and it is in any case inevitable in every modern libertarian industrial society—organized pluralism creates two problems that have not yet been solved anywhere. For one thing, since all resources except the vote are unequally distributed, some minorities (one thinks of the uneducated poor in the United States) may not have much in the way of political resources to bargain with: they have the ballot—and little else. In addition, to the extent that parliament is excluded from the process and elections provide only a vague and rather uncertain control over national leaders, there is no political institution in which majorities weigh heavily that can control the great bargained decisions by means of public review, appraisal, opposition, amendment, or veto.

Perhaps organized pluralism would weaken democracy in a small city–state, as Rousseau and his admirers would argue, for it encourages a citizen to take only a fragmentary view of his interests. And faction has always been the mortal disease of the city–state. Yet in the modern nation–state, it is difficult to imagine an alternative to organized pluralism that would not leave the plebiscitary executive and the official bureaucracies without effective oppositions, criticism, and control.

What is not yet perfectly clear, however, is how organized pluralism and national bargaining are to be reconciled with systems in which political equality and majority rule are major principles of legitimacy.

Oppositions in Western Democracies: The Future

There is a tension, then, among our goals, a tension that seems to be inescapable. The demands imposed by the values of democracy are extraordinarily severe.

To one who accepts these values, one perennial problem of opposition is that there is either too much or too little. The revolutionary parts of the world have a surplus of poverty and a deficit of order. The authoritarian countries have a surplus of order and a deficit of political freedom. Some of the Western democracies are achieving a mounting surplus of riches and consensus.

To be concerned over the decline of structural oppositions in most Western democracies may very well be an anachronism, a throwback to nineteenth-century styles of thought, on a par with a nonrational faith in the virtues of a balanced budget or the conviction that a seven-day workweek is indispensable if the working classes are not to become dissolute from having too much spare time on their hands. Should we not begin instead to adjust our minds to the notion that in the future—or at least in that short-run future into which it is not wholly senseless to extrapolate present trends—a great many Western democracies will have rather high levels of agreement and not much structural opposition?

That a large number of democracies have won the battle for the allegiance of their citizens among all social strata is, surely, a satisfying victory to anyone who believes in the values of a democratic polity. Yet it is difficult to disregard the sense of disquiet that follows hard upon one's awareness that severe criticism of social and economic structures has all but disappeared from the political life of many Western democracies— or else has become a monopoly of political forces like the Communists and the Radical Right whose allegiance to democratic values is, to say the least, doubtful. If the growth of extreme dissent can endanger a democratic system, universal but quite possibly superficial and irrational "consensus" may also be undesirable, for reasons I have just been exploring.

But is the trend evident in so many Western democracies over the past several decades toward greater consensus likely to continue? Might it level off, or even be reversed?

No way of conjecturing about the future, as Bertrand de Jouvenel has remarked, is more compelling than the temptation to project recent trends, "to suppose that tomorrow is going to differ from today in the same way that today differs from yesterday." [5] And as M. de Jouvenel also reminds us, it is the extrapolation of recent trends that has so often led men who understood their own time well to miss completely the large changes and abrupt reversals that transform the future into something radically different from the past. Suppose, then, that we make two assumptions about the future; that there will be no holocaust, an assumption without which it would be futile to speculate about the future of politics; and, that Western societies will continue to develop greater affluence, higher consumption, reduction of poverty, wider educational opportunities, and steadily increasing technical and technological resources. Under these conditions, what can we conjecture about the future of oppositions in Western democracies?

To begin with, even the growth of affluence does not automatically wipe out conflicts over the distribution of the national income and opportunities of all kinds. There is no reason to assume a decline in the familiar conflicts among different interest groups, each striving to insure that its members gain a satisfactory share. Indeed, since a just or satisfactory share probably cannot be defined so as to command general assent, and since any particular allotment reveals itself more and more clearly nowadays to be a product of political decisions and less and less an act of God, nature, or the inexorable operation of economic laws, conflicts over the distribution of income might, if anything, become more numerous even if less intense.

International policies will also remain, surely, subjects of conflict. Since there is small chance that international politics will diminish in importance and salience in the next half century, and since judgments of alternative policies and proposals will necessarily rest on highly controversial assessments of very great risks, gains, and costs, a variety of foreign policies, military affairs, treaties, regional and international organizations and alliances all promise a steady flow of internal conflict.

In many cases, conflicts over international politics and the distribution of national income and opportunities may not generate anything more

5. *L'Art de la Conjecture* (Monaco, Editions de Rocher, 1964), p. 82.

than the kinds of policy oppositions with which we are already familiar
in Western democracies. To this extent the future looks rather like the
immediate past that has been described in the essays here. Yet this may not
be the whole picture. For these two kinds of conflicts need not necessarily
entail only narrow group interests or technical matters. The more the
distribution of incomes and other opportunities is thought to be subject to
determination by government, the more relevant may become the ancient
and evidently inextinguishable controversies over the issue of equality
versus differential rewards. And conflicts over international affairs will
in some cases involve nothing less than alternative views of how the nation,
the civilization, even the species itself are most likely to survive or perish.

Yet neither of these kinds of issues inevitably entails structural oppositions. Are there possible sources of alienation in Western democracies
that might foster new structural oppositions? Since alienation has lately
become a fashionable topic, let me hasten to add that I do not mean to
imply anything about social or psychological alienation, whatever these
may be. I speak only of political alienation. A citizen is alienated from his
political system to the extent that he has unfavorable feelings, evaluations,
and attitudes toward it. I assume that a citizen might be alienated from
the political system in which he lives without necessarily being neurotic,
rootless, excessively anxious over his social standing, or otherwise much
different in personality and social characteristics from his fellow citizens.
In short, I wish to leave completely open the murky empirical question
of how political alienation may be related, if at all, to strictly social and
psychological factors.

Among the possible sources of alienation in Western democracies that
may generate new forms of structural opposition is the new democratic
Leviathan itself. By the democratic Leviathan I mean the very kind of
political system the chapters in this book have described, a product of
long evolution and hard struggle, welfare-oriented, centralized, bureaucratic, tamed and controlled by competition among highly organized
elites, and, in the perspectives of the ordinary citizen, somewhat remote,
distant, and impersonal even in small countries like Norway and Sweden.
The politics of this new democratic Leviathan, as we have seen so often
in the past chapters, are above all the politics of compromise, adjustment,
negotiation, bargaining; a politics carried on among professional and quasi-
professional leaders who constitute only a small part of the total citizen
body; a politics that reflects a commitment to the virtues of pragmatism,
moderation, and incremental change; a politics that is un-ideological and
even anti-ideological.

The traditional opposition to the new democratic Leviathan has come
from critics on the Right. In most European countries this traditional
opposition has been greatly enfeebled. In the United States, I suggested

in Chapter 2, a Radical Right has become alienated from the existing political system, for the principal leaders in the American system—whether in the Administration's coalition or nominally in opposition—accept policies, express views, and engage in conduct that the Right passionately rejects as evil; being a minority and unable to win national elections (and not many state or local elections) the Right has steadily suffered the humiliation of political impotence and rejection.

Is it likely that the wheel of history may make a full turn, that opposition to the democratic Leviathan may arise from a new quarter? There are already faint signs, not only in the United States but in high-consensus European systems like Sweden, Norway, and Britain, that many young people, intellectuals, and academics reject the democratic Leviathan—not because it is democratic but because, in their view, it is not democratic enough: this new Leviathan is too remote and bureaucratized, too addicted to bargaining and compromise, too much an instrument of political elites and technicians with whom they feel slight identification. Political isolation, alienation, and rebellion among youth, intellectuals, and academics are not, of course, new. Yet in the past half century the Left has, on the whole, sought to channel these feelings into support for policies and programs that have encouraged, not retarded, the development of the new democratic Leviathan. Is it not possible, however, that political alienation will increase, and that a new Left—if one can stretch traditional terms to cover the case—might channel these feelings into radical efforts (the shape of which we cannot foresee) to reconstruct the Leviathan to a more nearly human scale?

None of the three possible sources of future oppositions that I have been describing can be reduced, I imagine, to strictly technical questions. Although most issues involving the distribution of incomes and opportunities, international politics, and the democratic Leviathan have strictly technical aspects, few of them can be settled by strictly technical answers. The position one takes must depend in part on nontechnical factors—on values more implicit than explicit, psychological orientations and predispositions, identifications, feelings of hate, hostility, fear, jealousy, pride, self-confidence, respect, solidarity. If factors of this kind are to play a part, then there is good reason for expecting that political conflict will encourage the birth of new ideologies. For political elites and involved citizens alike will sense a need for broad, integrated views of the world to provide guidance, validity, and authority for their judgments on specific issues. And it will be surprising if these views of the world do not differ considerably in their perspectives, goals, evaluations, and assumptions about the nature of man and society.

Yet should these conflicting issues and ideologies develop it seems unlikely that they will be strongly associated, at least in the democracies examined in this book, with the familiar social and economic character-istics that have done such yeoman service in social theory in the recent past. For differences in political demands will probably become in large measure detached from general socioeconomic factors. At one end of the scale, new oppositions may reflect no more than conflicts among shifting coalitions of interest groups. At the other extreme, conflicting demands are likely to be attached to relatively durable orientations, perspectives, "mentalities," political philosophies, or ideologies that are related only casually to the kinds of social forces that have played such an important part in the political life of Western democracies in the past century.

In short, differences in basic political ideas and evaluations are likely to become more and more important in explaining differences in political behavior and therefore in patterns of opposition. Yet these crucial differ-ences in political ideas and evaluations will probably be less and less trace-able to differences in social and economic characteristics. In this sense, political ideologies, far from waning, will be ascendant.

To be sure, the traditional ideologies that have played so great a role in Western politics in the past century show every sign of being well on the way to ultimate extinction. But democracies have not eliminated all causes of political conflict; and if we agree with James Madison that "the latent causes of faction are sown in the nature of man," then democracies will not and cannot eliminate all causes of political conflict. If democ-racies cannot eliminate all the causes of conflict, is it not reasonable to expect that with the passage of time the clash of governments and oppo-sitions, indeed of one opposition with another, will generate—and will be generated by—new political perspectives that we cannot now accurately foresee?

APPENDIXES

Chapter 4. Sweden

Appendix Table 4.1. Distribution of Riksdag Seats, 1922–1965 According to the Election Results [1]

	1922 LH[2]UH[3]		1925 LH UH		1929 LH UH		1933 LH UH		1937 LH UH		1941 LH UH	
Conservatives	62	41	65	44	73	49	58	50	44	45	42	35
Liberals	41	38	33	35	32	31	24	23	27	16	23	15
Center Party	21	18	23	18	27	17	36	18	36	22	28	24
Socialists	93	50	104	52	90	52	104	58	112	66	134	75
Communists	7	1	5	1	8	1	2	—	5	—	3	1
Other	6	2	—	—	—	—	6[6]	1[6]	6[6]	1[6]	—	—
Total	230	150	230	150	230	150	230	150	230	150	230	150

	1945 LH UH		1949 LH UH		1953 LH UH		1957 LH UH		1959 LH UH		1961 LH UH		1965 LH[4]UH[4]	
Con.	39	30	23	24	31	20	42	13	45	16	39	19	33	26
Lib.	26	14	57	18	58	22	58	30	38	32	40	33	43	26
Cen.	35	21	30	21	26	25	19	25	32	22	34	20	36	19
Soc.	115	83	112	84	110	79	106	79	111	79	114	77	113	78
Com.	15	2	8	3	5	4	6	3	5	2	5	2	8	2
Other	—	—	—	—	—	—	—	—	—	—	—	—	—	—
	230	150	230	150	230	150	231	150	231	151	232	151	233	151

1. The years selected are those immediately following the years when elections to the Lower House were held. It may be observed that the distribution of Upper House seats generally fluctuates in some degree from year to year owing to the annual renewal of one-eighth of its membership. Underlined figures indicate a majority of seats.

2. LH—Lower House.

3. UH—Upper House.

4. The three MBS representatives are divided up into their original parties, i.e. one Conservative, one Liberal, and one Centrist. The last-mentioned was not accepted by his Parliamentary group in 1965.

5. One of the new Conservative members in the Upper House also belonged to the MBS.

6. Representatives of the Kihlbom group, which in 1929 was excluded from the Communist Party.

Appendix Table 4.2. The Parliamentary Support of the Government,
1922–1965

Year	LH [1]	UH [2]	JD [3]	Prime Minister	Party	Period
1922	92 [4]	50	142 [4]	Hj. Branting	Socialist	Oct. 13, 1921–
						Apr. 19, 1923
1923	92 [4]	50	142 [4]			
1923	62	41 [4]	103 [4]	E. Trygger	Conservative	Apr. 19, 1923–
						Oct. 18, 1924
1924	62	43 [4]	105 [4]			
1924	98 [4]	52	150 [4]	Hj. Branting	Socialist	Oct. 18, 1924–
						June 7, 1926
				(to Jan. 24, 1925)		
1925	103 [4]	52	155 [4]	R. Sandler		
1926	104 [4]	52	156 [4]			
1926	33	34	67	C. G. Ekman	Liberal	June 7, 1926–
						Oct. 2, 1928
1927	33	32	65			
1928	33	31	64			
1928	65	49 [4]	114 [4]	A. Lindman	Conservative	Oct. 2, 1928–
						June 7, 1930
1929	73	48 [4]	121 [4]			
1930	73	48 [4]	121 [4]			
1930	28	24	52	C. G. Ekman	Liberal [6]	June 7, 1930–
						Sept. 24, 1932
				(to Aug. 6, 1932)		
1931	28	23	51			
1932	28	22	50	F. Hamrin		
1932	89 [4]	55	144 [4]	P. A. Hansson	Socialist	Sept. 24, 1932–
						June 19, 1936
1933	103 [4]	58	161 [4]			
1934	101 [4]	61	162 [4]			
1935	101 [4]	62	163 [4]			
1936	100 [4]	65	165 [4]			
1936	37	22	69	A. Pehrsson-Bramstorp	Center	June 19, 1936–
						Sept. 28, 1936
1936	137 [4]	87	224 [4]	P. A. Hansson	Socialist/Center	Sept. 28, 1936–
						Dec. 13, 1939
1937	147 [4]	88	235 [4]			
1938	150 [4]	89	239 [4]			
1939	150 [4]	93	243 [4]			
1940	221 [4]	148 [4]	369 [5]	P. A. Hansson	Socialist/Center/Conservative/Liberal	Dec. 13, 1939–July 31, 1945
1941	226 [4]	148 [4]	374 [5]			
1942	226 [4]	148 [4]	374 [5]			
1943	226 [4]	148 [4]	374 [5]			
1944	226 [4]	147 [4]	373 [5]			

1945	214[4]	147[4]	361[5]			
1945	114[4]	83	197[4]	P. A. Hansson	Socialist	July 31, 1945– Oct. 1, 1951
				(died Oct. 6, 1946)		
1946	114[4]	84	198[4]			
1947	114[4]	86	200[4]	T. Erlander		
				(from Oct. 11, 1946)		
1948	114[4]	85	199[4]			
1949	111[4]	84	195[4]			
1950	111[4]	81	192[4]			
1951	111[4]	79	190[4]			
1951	141[4]	104	245[4]	T. Erlander	Soc./Center	Oct. 1, 1951– Oct. 31, 1957
1952	141[4]	104	245[4]			
1953	135[4]	104	239[4]			
1954	135[4]	104	239[4]			
1955	135[4]	103	238[4]			
1956	135[4]	103	238[4]			
1957	124[4]	104	228[4]			
1957	105[4]	79	184[4]	T. Erlander	Socialist	Oct. 31, 1957–
1958A	105[4]	79	184[4]			
1958B	110[4]	79	189[4]			
1959	110[4]	79	189[4]			
1960	110[4]	78	188[4]			
1961	114	77	191			
1962	114	77	191			
1963	114	77	191			
1964	114	78	192			
1965	113	78	191			

1. The Lower House had 230 members 1922–56, 231 members 1957–60, 232 members 1961–64, and 233 members from 1965. The Speaker was not allowed to vote before 1961. Thus in the period 1922–56 the government needed support from at least 115 members to command a majority, in the period 1957–60 from at least 116 members, and from 1961 from at least 117 members. Underlined figures indicate possession of a majority.

2. The Upper House had 150 members from 1922 to 1957 and 151 members from 1958. The Speaker was not allowed to vote before 1961. Thus in the period 1922–57 the government needed support from at least 75 members to command a majority, and from 1958 from at least 76 members.

3. JD = joint divisions. Needed to command the majority: 1922–57 at least 190 members, 1958–60 at least 191 members, 1961–64 at least 192 members, and from 1965 at least 193 members.

4. The total number was one more, but this member was the Speaker and as such not allowed to vote.

5. The total number was two more, but these two members were the Speakers and as such not allowed to vote.

6. One small group of Liberals stood outside the government.

Appendix Table 4.3. Percentages of Total Vote Cast for Each Party in the Elections to the Lower House, 1921–1964

	1921	1924	1928	1932	1936	1940
Cons.	25.9	26.1	29.4	23.5	17.6	18.0
Lib.	18.8	16.9	15.9	11.7	12.9	12.0
Center	11.1	10.8	11.2	14.1	14.3	12.0
Soc.	36.4	41.1	37.0	41.7	45.9	53.8
Comm.	4.6	5.1	6.4	3.0	3.3	3.5
Other	3.2	—	0.1	6.0[1]	6.0[1]	0.7

	1944	1948	1952	1956	1958	1960	1964
Cons.	15.9	12.3	14.4	17.1	19.5	16.5	13.7
Lib.	12.9	22.8	24.4	23.8	18.2	17.5	17.1
Center	13.6	12.4	10.7	9.4	12.7	13.6	13.4
Soc.	46.6	46.1	46.1	44.6	46.2	47.8	47.3
Comm.	10.3	6.3	4.3	5.0	3.4	4.5	5.2
Other	0.7	0.1	0.1	0.1	0.0	0.1	3.3[2]

1. Mainly voters for the Kihlbom group, which in 1929 was excluded from the Communist Party.

2. KDS 1.8% and MBS 1.5%.

Appendix Table 4.4. Participation in the Elections to the Lower House, 1921–1964 (in percentages)

1921	1924	1928	1932	1936	1940
54.2	53.0	67.4	67.6	74.5	70.3

1944	1948	1952	1956	1958	1960	1964
71.9	82.7	79.1	79.8	77.5	85.9	83.3

Chapter 5. Belgium

Appendix Table 5.1. School and Preschool Population by Sponsorship of School, Public and Private, and Level of Instruction, 1960–1961

	Public	Private	Total
Preschool	140,008	265,127	405,135
Primary	437,064	481,758	918,822
Secondary	209,801	316,931	526,732
University, higher technical institution, normal school	20,394	31,605	51,999
Total	807,267	1,095,421	1,902,688

Note: Almost all private elementary and secondary schools are Catholic institutions. Some nominally public primary schools (notably in Flanders) are Catholic institutions under municipal aegis. One major private university, the University of Brussels (5,047 students), is not Catholic.

Source: Ministry of Economic Affairs and Ministry of National Education and Culture, *Annuaire Statistique de l'enseignement, 1960–1961* (Brussels, 1962), pp. 20–21.

Appendix Table 5.2. School and Preschool Population by Sponsorship of School and Language, 1960–1961

	Public	Private
French	465,095	335,528
Flemish	336,141	759,324
German	6,031	569
Total	807,267	1,095,421

Source: *Annuaire statistique de l'enseignement, 1960–1961*, pp. 20–21.

Appendix Table 5.3. Membership of House of Representatives, by Party, During the Period of Taxpayers' Suffrage—Selected Years, 1847–1892

Year	Population (to nearest thousand)	Voters	Abstentions %	Seats Total	Catholics	Liberals
1847	4,338,000	46,000	27	108	53	55
1848(D)	4,359,000	79,000	33	108	25	83
1856	4,529,000	44,000	28	108	63	45
1857(D)	4,577,000	91,000	15	108	38	70
1864(D)	4,941,000	104,000	19	116	52	64
1870(D)	5,088,000	107,000	26	124	72	52
1878	5,477,000	92,000	28	132	60	72
1884	5,785,000	125,000	16	138	86	52
1892(D)	6,195,000	137,000	16	152	92	60

Note: Because of the difficulties in attributing party affiliations, there are no figures here for the years between 1831 and 1847. The House was renewed by half every two years, except when the entire House was dissolved. (D) indicates dissolution of the House. I have chosen the years in which there was a change of majority or a renewal of the whole House. Compulsory voting was not introduced until 1893.
Sources: Jean Temmerman, *Droit Public* (Brussels, École Royale Militaire, 1963), pp. 122–23, and John Gilissen, *Le Régime représentatif en Belgique depuis 1790* (Brussels, 1958), pp. 188–89.

Appendix Table 5.4. Election Results and Membership of House of Representatives, by Party, During the Period of Universal Suffrage with Plural Voting, 1894–1914 [a]

Year	Voters[b]	Valid Votes[b]	Seats, Total	Catholics Votes[b]	Catholics Seats	Liberals Votes[b]	Liberals Seats	Socialists Votes[b]	Socialists Seats	Liberal-Socialist (joint tickets) Votes[b]	Daensists[e] Seats
1894(D)	1,355,000	1,922,000	152	963,000	104	537,000	20	311,000	28	33,000	—
1896	694,000 [c]	928,000	152	489,000	111	202,000	13	34,000	28	174,000	—
1898	715,000 [d]	997,000	152	428,000	112	212,000	13	277,000	27	30,000	—
1900 (D)	1,473,000	2,053,000	152 [f]	994,000	86	502,000	34	461,000	31	—	1
1902	1,154,000	1,639,000	166	842,000	96	370,000	34	380,000	34	—	2
1904	774,000	1,115,000	166	487,000	93	283,000	42	301,000	29	—	2
1906	786,000	1,173,000	166	636,000	89	250,000	46	72,000	30	182,000	1
1908	814,000	1,201,000	166	518,000	87	223,000	43	272,000	35	149,000	1
1910	836,000	1,274,000	166	677,000	86	280,000	44	85,000	35	195,000	1
1912 (D)	1,746,000	2,622,000	186	1,337,000	101	306,000	44	243,000	39	693,000	2
1914	878,000	1,335,000	186	572,000	99	327,000	45	405,000	40	—	2

a. The House was renewed by half every two years, except when dissolution caused a renewal of the whole House. (D) indicates a dissolution.
b. Rounded off to nearest thousand.
c. Some 27,000 voters, with 41,000 votes, did not vote because the Catholic ticket was uncontested in one arrondissement.
d. Some 36,000 voters, with 54,000 votes, did not vote because the Catholic tickets were uncontested in two arrondissements.
e. The Daensists were Flemish Christian Democrats or leftish Catholics.
f. Proportional representation first went into effect in 1900.
Source: Gilissen, Le Régime représentatif, pp. 190–91.

Appendix Table 5.5. Votes for House of Representatives, by Party, During the Period of Equal Universal Suffrage, 1919–1961 [a]
(as percentages of total number of valid ballots)

Year	Soc.	Comm.	Lib.	Flem. Nat.	Rex	Cath.	Diss. Cath.	Misc.
1919	36.6	—	17.6	2.6	—	36.6	2.1	4.4
1921	34.8	0.05	17.8	3.0	—	37.0	4.3	3.0
1925	39.4	1.6	14.6	3.9	—	36.1	2.5	1.8
1929	36.0	1.9	16.6	6.3	—	35.4	3.2	0.6
1932	37.1	2.8	14.3	5.9	—	38.6	0.2	1.1
1936	32.1	6.1	12.4	7.1	11.5	27.7	1.1	2.0
1939	30.2	5.4	17.2	8.3	4.4	32.7	—	1.8
					UDB			
1946	32.6 [b]	12.7	9.5 [b]	—	2.2	42.5	—	0.5
1949 [c]	29.8	7.5	15.3	2.1	—	43.6	0.1	1.8
1950	35.6 [b]	4.7	12.0 [b]	—	—	47.7	—	—
1954	38.6 [b]	3.6	13.0 [b]	2.02	—	41.1	0.9	0.6
1958	37.1 [b]	1.9	11.8 [b]	2.0	—	46.5	—	0.7
1961	36.7	3.1	12.3	3.5	—	41.5	—	2.9

a. Abbreviations:

    Soc.—Socialist Party (Workers Party until 1940; Socialist Party after 1945)
    Comm.—Communist Party
    Lib.—Liberal Party (Party of Liberty and Progress since 1961)
    Flem. Nat.—Flemish nationalist parties (Flemish People's Union since 1954)
    Cath.—Catholic Party between the wars; Christian Social Party since 1945
    Diss. Cath.—Dissident Catholic tickets
    UDB—Belgian Democratic Union
    Misc.—Miscellaneous

b. In 1946, 1950, 1954, and 1958, the Socialist and Liberal parties ran joint tickets in Limbourg and Luxembourg provinces. I have assigned to each party a percentage of the joint vote based on the rather stable percentages obtained by their separate tickets in those provinces in 1939 and 1949. The possible error is unimportant, as the total involved each year is only about 2 per cent of the total national vote for all parties.

c. Women's suffrage introduced in national elections in 1949.

Sources: R. E. De Smet, R. Evalenko, and W. Fraeys, *Atlas des élections belges, 1919–1954* (Brussels, Institut de Sociologie, 1958), *Annexe*, pp. 10–11, for 1919–54, except for estimates referred to in footnote b and Ministry of Interior for 1958 and 1961.

Appendix Table 5.6. Seats in House of Representatives, by Party, During the Period of Equal Universal Suffrage, 1919–1961 (in number of seats immediately after each national election)

Year	Soc.	Comm.	Lib.	Flem. Nat.	Rex	Cath.	Diss. Cath.	Misc.	Total
1919	70	—	34	5	—	73	—	4	186
1921	68	—	33	4	—	76	4	1	186
1925	78	2	23	6	—	75	3	—	187
1929	70	1	28	11	—	71	6	—	187
1932	73	3	24	8	—	79	—	—	187
1936	70	9	23	16	21	61	2	—	202
1939	64	9	33	17	4	73	—	2	202
				UDB					
1946	69	23	17	—	1	92	—	—	202
1949	66	12	29	—	—	105	—	—	212
1950	77	7	20	—	—	108	—	—	212
1954	86	4	25	1	—	95	1	—	212
1958	84	2	21	1	—	104	—	—	212
1961	84	5	20	5	—	96	—	2	212

Abbreviations: See Appendix Table 5.5.
Sources: R. E. De Smet, R. Evalenko, and W. Fraeys, *Altas des élections belges, 1919–1954, Annexe,* pp. 14–15, for 1919–54, and Ministry of Interior figures for 1958 and 1961.

Appendix Table 5.7. Distribution of Votes Within Linguistic Regions, by Party, as Percentages of Valid Ballots for House of Representatives, 1961

Party	Total Vote (to nearest thousand)	PSC	Soc.	Lib.	Comm.	Flemish People's Union	Others	Total
Flanders	2,867,000	50.9	29.7	11.6	1.0	6.0	0.8	100
Wallonia	1,695,000	30.1	47.1	11.8	6.5	—	4.5	100
Brussels	668,000	28.0	41.6	17.0	3.6	1.7	8.1	100
German-speaking cantons	35,000	71.1	13.0	11.3	0.5	—	4.0	99.9
Belgium	5,265,000	41.5	36.7	12.3	3.1	3.5	2.9	100

Source: William Fraeys, "Les Résultats des élections législatives du 26 mars 1961," *Res Publica,* 3, No. 4 (1961), p. 394.

Appendix Table 5.8. Distribution of Electoral Support Within Parties, by Linguistic Region, as Percentages of Each Party's Total Vote for House of Representatives, 1961

Party	PSC		Socialists		Liberals		Communists	
	Votes	%	Votes	%	Votes	%	Votes	%
Flanders	1,460,000	66.2	852,000	44.1	332,000	51.1	28,000	17.3
Wallonia	511,000	23.4	798,000	41.3	199,000	30.7	110,000	67.9
Brussels	187,000	8.6	278,000	14.4	114,000	17.6	24,000	14.8
German-speaking cantons	25,000	1.1	5,000	0.2	4,000	0.6	—	—
Belgium	2,183,000	100.0	1,933,000	100.0	649,000	100.0	162,000	100.0

Source: Calculated from Fraeys, Table 5.7. All votes rounded off to nearest thousand.

Appendix Table 5.9. Party Experience in Government Coalitions and Opposition, 1918–1940, 1944–1963 [a]

	Duration (months)		
Duration of cabinet coalitions, by party of Prime Minister	Nov. 21, 1918– May 28, 1940	Sept. 26, 1944– Sept. 30, 1963	1918–63
Governments headed by:			
Catholic [b]	232	124	356
Socialist	9	104	113
Catholic and Socialist	11	—	11
Liberal	6	—	6
Total	258	228	486
Duration of cabinets, by party composition			
Catholic-Socialist-Liberal [b]	110	3	113
Catholic-Liberal	134	40	174
Catholic-Socialist	13	58	71
Socialist-Liberal	—	50	50
Catholic (one party)	1	50	51
Catholic-Socialist-Liberal-Communist	—	8	8
Socialist-Liberal-Communist	—	19	19
Total	258	228	486

Appendix Table 5.9. (Cont'd.)
Major parties in government and in opposition

	1918–40		1944–63		1918–63	
	Months	% of period	Months	% of period	Months	% of period
Catholic Party (PSC)						
In government	258	100	159	70	417	86
In opposition	—	—	69	30	69	14
Socialist Party						
In government	123	48	138	61	261	54
In opposition	135	52	90	39	225	46
Liberal Party						
In government	244	95	120	53	364	75
In opposition	14	5	108	47	122	25

a. Excludes the period of government in exile in World War II.

b. Including the Van Zeeland governments of 1935-37, whose Prime Minister, although of Catholic tendency, was not yet a member of the Catholic Party.

Source: Calculated chiefly from information in *Guide des Ministères, 1963–64* (Brussels, 1963), pp. 80–93 (which does not give party affiliations), and Carl-Henrik Höjer, *Le Régime parlementaire belge de 1918 à 1940*, (Uppsala, Almqvist, 1946).

Appendix Table 5.10. Population of Belgium, by Regions, 1910–1961

	1910		1920	
Region	Inhabitants (in 000's)	%	Inhabitants (in 000's)	%
Flanders	3,506	47.2	3,500	47.2
Wallonia	2,893	39.0	2,828	38.2
Brussels	1,023	13.8	1,078	14.6
Belgium	7,422	100.0	7,406	100.0

	1930		1947		1961	
Region	Inhabitants (in 000's)	%	Inhabitants (in 000's)	%	Inhabitants (in 000's)	%
Flanders	3,886	48.0	4,272	50.2	4,711	51.3
Wallonia	3,001	37.1	2,940	34.5	3,038	33.1
Brussels	1,205	14.9	1,300	15.3	1,439	15.6
Belgium	8,092	100.0	8,512	100.0	9,189	100.0

Note: Totals do not always add up due to rounding of numbers of components.
Sources: Conseil Economique Wallon, *Le Rapport Sauvy* (Liège, 1962), p. 7, for 1910–47, and census figures for 1961.

Appendix Table 5.11. School and Preschool Population by Language and Level of Instruction, 1960–1961

	French	Flemish	German	Total
Preschool	152,574	251,435	1,126	405,135
Primary (ages 6–12)	397,827	515,854	5,141	918,822
Secondary (ages 12–18)	222,058	304,341	333	526,732
University, higher technical institutions, normal schools	28,164	23,835	—	51,999
Total	800,623	1,095,465	6,600	1,902,688

Source: *Annuaire statistique de l'enseignement, 1960–1961,* pp. 14–15.

Chapter 6. The Netherlands

Appendix Table 6.1. The Franchise in the Netherlands, 1853–1963

Year	Number of enfranchised persons	Percentage of total adult population	Qualifications: age and sex
1853	83,561	11.0	Over 23; male only
1870	103,538	11.3	"
1880	122,481	12.3	"
1890	295,570	26.8	"
1900	569,768	49.0	Over 25; male only
1910	854,539	63.2	"
1920	3,250,247	97.6	Over 25; all adults
1930	3,884,489	98.1	"
1940	4,721,113	98.5	"
1948	5,433,663	96.6 *	Over 23; all adults
1963	6,748,611	98.6	"

* Decline mainly attributable to disenfranchisement of convicted National Socialists.
Source: Central Bureau of Statistics, *Statistiek der Verkiezingen* (1963), p. 8.

Appendix Table 6.2. Dutch Cabinets and Party Composition of Lower House of Parliament, 1888–1965 [1]

——— = Party members in government
≡≡≡ = Conditional support without direct representation in Cabinet

| | | | | | Nonreligious parties | | | | Religious parties | | | | | |
| | | | | | | Liberals | | | | | | | | |
Years	Cabinet	Duration in months	Election in year	Total seats, lower house	Socialists	Radicals	Center	Conservative	Catholics	Chr. Historicals	Anti-Revolutionaries	Others	Potentially definite government supporters [2]	Parties not in government [2]
1888–1891	Mackay	40	1888	100	1		46		25		27	1	52	48
1891–1894	Van Tienhoven	32½	1891	100		1	53		25		21	—	54	46
													Government ended by dividing all parties over franchise	
1894–1897	Röell	38½	1894	100		3	57		25		15	—		
													Conservative-Liberal government with no clear opposition	
1897–1901	Pierson	48	1897	100	2	4	35	13	22	6	17	1	52	48
1901–1905	Kuyper	48½	1901	100	6	9	18	8	25	9	23	2	57	53
1905–1908	De Meester	30	1905	100	6	11	25	9	25	8	15	1	36	64
													Liberal minority government defeated in December 1907 followed by minority government of religious parties (48 seats) which obtained majority at next election	

Cabinet	Years	Duration in months	Election year	Total seats, lower house	Communists	Socialists	Radicals	Center	Conservative	Catholics	Chr. Historicals	Anti-Revolutionaries	Others	Potentially definite government supporters [2]	Parties not in government [2]
Heemskerk	1908–1913	66⅔	1905	100		6	11	25	9	25	8	15	1	48	52
			1909	100		7	9	20	4	25	10	25	–	60	40
Cort van der Linden	1913–1918	60	1913	100		15	7	22	10	25	10	11	–	39(54)	46
														Liberal minority gov ernment which be came War Cabinet with support of all democratic parties	
Ruys De Beeren brouck	1918–1922	48	1918	100	2	22	5	6	9	30	7	13	6	50	50
Ruys De Beeren brouck	1922–1925	34½ (13 + 21½)	1922	100	2	20	5	Fusion of Liberals 10		32	11	16	4	59	41
														(Intermediate Cabinet crisis, when Socialists, Radicals, and minority of Catholics rejected Navy bill)	
Colijn	1925–1926	7	1925	100	1	24	7	9		30	11	13	5	54	46
De Geer	1926–1929	41	1925	100	1	24	7	9		30	11	13	5	46	
														Intermezzo Cabinet of "nonpoliticians" from all parties, except Socialists and Com munists; both govern ment and opposition uncertain	

Nonreligious parties · Religious parties

Years	Cabinet	Duration in months	Election year	Total seats, lower house	Nonreligious parties				Religious parties				Potentially definite government supporters [2]	Parties not in government [2]
					Communists	Socialists	Radicals	Liberals	Catholics	Chr. Historicals	Anti-Revolutionaries	Others		
1929–1933	Ruys De Beerenbrouck	45⅚	1929	100	2	24	7	8	30	11	12	6	53	47
1933–1937	Colijn	49 (26 + 23)	1933	100	4	22	6	7	28	10	14	9	65 (Intermediate Cabinet crisis caused by Catholic opposition)	35
1937–1939	Colijn	25	1937	100	3	23	6	4	31	8	17	8	56	4
1939	Colijn	½	1937	100	3	23	6	4	31	8	17	8	Cabinet of "strong" men of orthodox Protestant and Liberal background dismissed by combined vote of Catholics, Socialists, and Radicals	
1939–1940	De Geer	13	1937	100	3	23	6	4	31	8	17	8	68	28
													Became War Coalition under dissident Anti-Revolutionary Gerbrandy, 1940–1945	

| | | | | | | Nonreligious parties | | | Religious parties | | | | | |
Years	Cabinet	Duration in months	Election year	Total seats, lower house	Communists	Socialists	Liberals	Catholics	Chr. Historicals	Anti-Revolutionaries	Others	Potentially definite government supporters[2]	Parties not in government[2]
1940–1946	WAR CABINETS IN EXILE AND "NATIONAL" GOVERNMENT 1945–1946 (PROGRESSIVE-ORIENTED)					1940–1945 NO PARLIAMENT							
						1945–1946 EMERGENCY PARLIAMENT							
1946–1948	Beel	25	1946	100	10	29	6	32	8	13	2	61	39
1948–1952	Drees (31 + 18)	49	1948	100	8	27	8 / --	32	9	13	3	68 (76)	34
							(Intermediate Cabinet crisis caused by Liberal vote against Liberal Minister of Foreign Affairs)						
1952–1956	Drees (32½+17)	49	1952	100	6	30	9	30	9	12	4	81	19
							(Intermediate Cabinet crisis caused by disagreement about housing policy)						
1956–1958	Drees	26	1956	100	4	34	9	33	8	10	2	85	15
			1956	150	7	50	13	49	13	15	3	127	23
							(Socialist ministers resigned in December 1958 when majority in Parliament rejected tax bill)						

Years	Cabinet	Duration in months	Election year	Total seats, lower house	Nonreligious parties				Religious parties				Potentially definite government supporters[2]	Parties not in government[2]
					Communists	Pacifist Socialists	Socialists	Liberals	Catholics	Chr. Historicals	Anti-Revolutionaries	Others		
1958–1959	Beel	5	1956	150	7		50	13	49	13	15	3	77(90)	60
													Rump Cabinet presiding over tactical dissolution of Parliament	
1959–1963	De Quay	50 (19 + 31)	1959	150	3	2	48	19	49	12	14	3	94	56
													(Intermediate Cabinet crisis in December 1960, through dissension about housing policy)	
1963–1965	Marijnen	20	1963	150	4	4	43	16	50	13	13	7	92	58
1965–	Cals		1963	150	4	4	43	16	50	13	13	7	106	44

1. Before 1888 party affiliation and party composition of cabinets were too undefined to permit tabular representation.
2. The detached relations of government and Parliament which prevail in the Netherlands causes both parliamentary support and parliamentary opposition to be somewhat fluid. Governments with a fairly narrow official basis have in practice enjoyed considerable support from parties not represented in the government, while nominal government supporters have often opposed particular cabinets on particular issues.

Source: D. Hans, *Parade der Politieke Partijen* (Putten, n.d.), pp. 102, 103; Central Bureau of Statistics, *Statistiek der Verkiezingen, 1963*; *Parlement en Kiezer*, Yearbook, 1963–1964, List of cabinets and ministers since 1848.

Appendix Table 6.3. Percentages of Total Number of Valid Ballots Obtained by Parties in Elections for Lower House of Dutch Parliament Since Introduction of Proportional Representation and Universal Suffrage, 1918–1963

	1918	1922	1925	1929	1933	1937	1946	1948	1952	1956	1959	1963
1. Protestant parties												
Anti-Revolutionary Party	13.4	13.7	12.2	11.6	13.4	16.4	12.9	13.2	11.3	9.9	9.4	8.7
Christian Historical Union	6.5	10.9	9.9	10.5	9.1	7.8	7.9	9.2	8.9	8.4	8.1	8.6
Staatkundig-Gereformeerde Partij	0.4	0.9	2.0	2.3	2.5	1.9	2.1	2.4	2.4	2.3	2.2	2.3
2. Catholic Party	30.0	29.9	28.6	29.6	27.9	28.8	30.8	31.0	28.7	31.7	31.6	31.9
3. Liberals												
Liberals	10.0	9.3	8.7	7.4	6.9	4.0	6.4	8.0	8.8	8.8	12.2	10.3
Radicals	5.3	4.6	6.1	6.2	5.1	5.9	—	—	—	—	—	—
4. Socialists												
SDAP	22.0	19.4	22.9	23.8	21.5	22.0	—	—	—	—	—	—
Labor Party	—	—	—	—	—	—	28.3	25.6	29.0	32.7	30.3	28.0
Pacifist Socialists	—	—	—	—	—	—	—	—	—	—	1.8	3.0
5. Communists	2.3	1.8	1.2	2.0	3.2	3.3	10.6	7.7	6.2	4.8	2.4	2.8
6. Other parties with seats	8.3	2.4	3.5	3.2	6.4	6.3	—	1.3	2.7	—	—	2.9
7. Other parties without seats	2.2	7.1	4.9	2.9	4.0	3.9	1.1	1.6	2.0	1.4	2.0	1.5

Source: Central Bureau of Statistics, *Statistiek der Verkiezingen*, 1963, p. 13; and calculations by R. P. van den Helm.

Appendix Table 6.4. The Relation Between Religious and Nonreligious Parties in the Netherlands (combined percentages of all valid ballots, including votes for dissident parties)

	1918	1922	1925	1929	1933	1937	1946	1948	1952	1956	1959	1963
All Protestants [1]	21.9	27.7	26.0	25.9	27.1	29.0	23.5	24.8	23.3	21.2	20.4	20.4
All Catholics	30.0	30.9	29.8	30.4	29.5	29.4	30.8	32.3	31.4	31.7	31.6	31.9
Total: Religious Parties	51.9	58.6	55.8	56.3	56.6	58.4	54.3	57.1	54.7	52.9	52.0	52.3
All Liberals [2]	15.3	14.5	14.8	13.6	12.0	9.9	6.4	8.0	8.8	8.8	12.2	11.0
All Socialists and Communists [3]	25.9	21.6	25.3	26.8	26.7	26.1	38.9	33.4	35.5	37.5	35.1	33.8
Total: Liberals, Socialists, and Communists	41.2	36.1	40.1	40.4	38.7	36.0	45.3	41.4	44.3	46.3	47.3	44.8
Others [4]	6.9	5.3	4.1	3.3	4.7	5.6	0.4	1.5	1.0	0.9	0.7	2.9

1. Includes also Christian-Democratic Union, which fused with Socialists in 1945.
2. Includes also Vrijzinnig-Democratische Bond (Radical Party), which fused with Socialists in 1945.
3. Includes SDAP/Labor Party, Revolutionary Socialists, Pacifist Socialists, Communists.
4. Mainly interest parties and rightist groups, including National Socialists, Fascists, and Boerenpartij (Peasant Party).
Source: Calculated by R. P. van den Helm from data of Central Bureau of Statistics.

Appendix Table 6.5. Religious Divisions in the Netherlands, 1849–1960

	Roman Catholic	Dutch Reformed (Neder-lands) Hervormd)	Orthodox-Reformed (Gerefor-meerden)	Other Protes-tants	Jewish	Others	No church
1849	38.1	54.6	1.3	3.3	1.9	0.8	0.01
1859	37.1	54.9	2.0	3.1	1.9	0.8	0.1
1869	36.5	54.7	3.0	2.9	1.9	0.8	0.1
1879	35.9	54.5	3.5	3.0	2.0	0.8	0.3
1889	35.4	48.6	8.2	2.9	2.1	1.2	1.5
1899	35.1	48.4	8.1	2.9	2.0	1.1	2.3
1909	35.0	44.2	9.4	3.0	1.8	1.7	5.0
1920	35.6	41.2	9.1	2.7	1.7	2.0	7.8
1930	36.4	34.3	8.7	2.2	1.4	2.4	14.4
1947	38.5	31.0	8.6	1.8	0.1	2.8	17.0
1960	40.4	28.3	9.3	1.5	0.1	2.0	18.4

Source: Central Bureau of Statistics, *Jaarcijfers.*

*Appendix Table 6.6. Percentage of Children Attending Government and Private Schools in the Netherlands, 1860–1960 **

	Attending government schools	Attending private schools			
1860	78	22			
1870	76	24			
1880	75	25			
1890	70	30			
1900	69	31			
1910	62	38			
1920	55	45			
		Protestant	Catholic	Other	All
1930	38	25	36	2	62
1940	30	26	42	2	70
1950	27	27	44	2	73
1960	27	27	44	2	73

* In the analysis of this table it should be remembered that Catholics and orthodox Protestants have tended to have larger families over most of this period. According to J. P. Kruyt, *Verzuiling* (Zaandijk, 1959), p. 25, roughly 35% of *parents* send their children to Catholic schools, 28% to Protestant schools, and 37% to nonreligious schools (calculation for 1957).

Source: 1860–1890: Calculated from *Verslag van de Staat der Hoge, Middelbare en Lagere Scholen over 1890–1891,* Bijlage II. 1900 to date: Central Bureau of Statistics, *Zestig Jaren Statistiek in Tijdreeksen, 1959,* p. 31.

Chapter 7. Germany

Appendix 7.1

The following remarks contain some comments on a Hamburg public opinion poll[1] which, diffuse and ambiguous as it may be, throws some light on popular attitudes toward the German political system. To what extent is the German population at large conscious of the turn its political establishment has taken and how is it reacting to it? In November 1960, at the time when the SPD shift was already in full swing, a poll in Hamburg, Germany's biggest and one of its most cosmopolitan cities, asked what it would mean if the opposition were to take over the government: would it make a significant difference? Fifty-seven per cent failed to see that such a change would constitute a major event. A total of 5 per cent of the entire sample visualized the SPD's taking over the federal government in a positive light. They emphasized that such a change would not impinge on the democratic foundation of the system. All others evaluated the "no-change" situation in a more skeptical light: 17 per cent replying that the new *equipe* would anyhow have to go on as before; 13 per cent laying stress on the ideological similarities of the two major parties; and 10 per cent stressing the foreign policy commitments already incurred. Thus a great part of the German population seems to be increasingly aware of the limited significance of a change in the parties holding the reins of government. When a similar question was put in 1952, the number of those doubting the importance of a change was only 36 per cent.[2] This insight into the strictly limited meaning of governmental change was most conspicuous among those less than 30 years old: 63 per cent.

In the light of this skeptical attitude toward the meaning of political change, the continued high electoral participation (186.9 per cent throughout the country in 1965) remains puzzling. The rise in the invalid vote, at

1. Wolfgang Hartenstein and Günther Schubert, *Mitlaufen oder Mitbestimmen* (Frankfurt, Europaische Verlangstalt, 1961), p. 103.
2. *Jahrbuch der Öffentlichen Meinung, 1947–1955* (1956), p. 262. For the Hamburg figures see Hartenstein and Schubert, pp. 49–52.

its apex at 4 per cent in 1961 (2.4 per cent in 1965), possibly expresses a small nucleus of discontent with the political system, but it means little if held against such participation figures.[3]

A small indication of an interesting motivation for electoral participation is furnished by the reaction to the Hamburg poll question asking whether someone politically totally uninterested should vote. Among the 52 per cent who felt that such a person should nevertheless vote, a good 39 per cent felt that voting is a duty (p. 37); they thus look at voting as one of the many interconnected types of activity which modern society imposes on its citizens before releasing them to their private pursuits.[4]

That the act of voting may not itself connote meaningful participation in public life is clear from another group of answers. Asked how they would react if a law were to be passed unfavorable to their class of people, only 20 per cent replied in terms of some collective measure they would want to take. That unionists would figure prominently in this group (with 36 per cent) was to be expected. But voting for either of the two big parties has apparently no relation to one's preparedness to secure one's rights by some form of collective action (22 per cent for the SPD, 21 per cent for the CDU); 12 per cent would take individual steps, most of them (9 per cent) by contacting the competent authorities. Interestingly, only 2 per cent thought of voting as a form of response to legislation threatening their interests. This shows to what extent parties remain abstract entities to the citizens, scarcely related to their own life situations; 22 per cent would just gripe, having the feeling of powerlessness in the face of official action, and 33 per cent would not go beyond passive resignation (pp. 43–48).

However, this remoteness from the political process—the feeling of an outside event taking place way beyond their own life sphere and, while impinging on them, scarcely accessible to influence by them—does not result in any hostile attitude toward official institutions and belief systems. Quite the contrary, with one characteristic exception, official values are upheld with a good deal of intransigence against potential deviants. Even in Protestant Hamburg only 50 per cent of the people would allow an adversary of established religion to make a public speech and only 23 per cent would allow him to teach in an institution of secondary education (p. 60). Significantly, political deviationists would do much worse. Only 29 per cent would allow a public speech by someone attacking one of the

3. On the political significance of the invalid vote see R. Stiefbold, "The Significance of Void Ballots in West German Elections," *American Political Science Review,* 59 (1965), p. 391.
4. See also Sidney Verba, "Germany: The Remaking of Political Culture," in Lucian Pye and Sidney Verba, eds., *Political Culture and Political Development* (Princeton, Princeton University Press, 1965), which evaluates related German material.

official dogmas of the Federal Republic by accepting the Oder-Neisse line; only 18 per cent would allow such a dangerous character to teach in a high school. Professional people (55 per cent), skilled workers (46 per cent), and those with college education (60 per cent) would be more liberal in this respect. Among white-collar workers and public servants only 40 per cent, and among unskilled workers only 33 per cent (pp. 59–63), would be that liberal.

In one field both urban background and the experience of the '30s and '40s have produced a clear choice for tolerance and constitutionalism. A neighbor suspected of communism would be denounced to the authorities by only one out of three of those questioned, and by only one out of four among younger groups and skilled working-class families.

While the picture is far from uniform, some points seem to be beyond dispute. Integration of the population into the political system is not very far advanced, and there is some indication, as suggested by the answers to the question on the significance of political change, that the petering out of general political debate seems to have contributed to the characteristic distinction between the "we" and "they," the people and the rulers. Non-integration does not necessarily mean cleavage, especially under the

Appendix Table 7.2. Voting in Bundestag Elections, 1949–1961

	1949	1953	1957	1961	1965
Electorate and participation					
Registered voters (in millions)	31.2	33.2	35.4	37.4	38.5
Percentage turnout	78.5	86	87.8	87.5	86.8
Invalid (list) votes as percentage of votes cast	3.1	3.3	3.8	4	2.4
Valid (list) votes cast (in millions)	23.7	27.6	29.9	31.5	32.6
Party strength as percentage of valid votes cast					
CDU/CSU	31	45.2	50.2	45.3	47.6
SPD	29.2	28.8	31.8	36.3	39.3
FDP	11.9	9.5	7.7	12.7	9.5
DP	4	3.2	3.4	.1	—
BHE	—	5.9	4.6	—	—
BP	4.2	1.7	.9	—	—
Z	3.1	.8		—	—
KPD	5.7	2.2	—	—	—
DRP	1.8	1.1	1	.8	—
WAV	2.9	—	—	—	—
Others	6.2	1.6	.4	4.8	3.6

Abbreviations:
  CDU/CSU—Christian Democratic Union and Christian Social Union
  SPD—Social Democratic Party   FDP—Free Democratic Party
  DP—German Party   BHE—Refugee Party   BP—Bavarian Party
  Z—Center Party   KPD—German Communist Party
  DRP—German Rightist Party   WAV—Economic Reconstruction League

favorable economic circumstances of today. Official values, especially in the field of national interest, are upheld. They give way clearly only where the official value system suffers from internal contradiction between substantive and procedural goals—between the danger of communism and the need for constitutional safeguards—and where the substantive threat seems less real than past popular experience and the ensuing desire to safeguard one's privacy against all intrusion. More recent polls centering on the *Spiegel* affair would confirm the intensive concern for individual rights and procedural guarantees.

Appendix Table 7.3. Composition of the Federal Government at the Time of the Federal Chancellor's Election, 1949–1963

Date of vote	Composition of coalition	Strength of government coalition by individual factions	Total coalition strength	Strength of SPD faction and other opposition	Total number of Bundestag members entitled to vote *
Sept. 15, 1949	CDU/CSU	139	208	131	402
	FDP	52		plus 63 of	
	DP	17		small parties mostly in opposition	
Oct. 9, 1953	CDU/CSU	243	335	151	487
	FDP	48			
	DP	15			
	GB/BHE	27			
Oct. 22, 1957	CDU/CSU	270	287	169	497
	DP	17		plus 41 FDP temporarily not in the government	
Nov. 7, 1961	CDU/CSU	242	309	190	499
	FDP	67			
Oct. 16, 1963	CDU/CSU	242	309	190	499
	FDP	67			
Oct. 20, 1965	CDU/CSU	245	294	202	497
	FDP	49			

* Berlin members (19 since 1952) delegated by the Berlin City Assembly do not appear in these figures.

Source: The material for the tabulation has been furnished by members of the Institute for Political Science (Chair II) of the Institute for Technology at Darmstadt, Germany.

Explanations of Appendix Tables 7.2 and 7.3

Appendix Table 7.2 tells the story of the increasing concentration of votes on the three parties represented exclusively in the Bundestag since 1961.

Appendix Table 7.3 explains the story of government and opposition in terms of their respective strengths at the most important time of parliamentary history, the moment of the election of the new Chancellor. It shows that, with the exception of the first Bundestag and the third Bundestag, opposition and SPD were synonymous. Thanks to the workings of economic deprivation, a still fairly liberal election law, and old habits, the first Bundestag counted eight parties with 10 members and more. In 1953 there was a short-lived emergence of the Refugee Party, prohibited from running by fiat of the occupation authorities in 1949. But with this exception incipient prosperity helped along by a stricter election law eliminated the radical Right and Left and started the process of party concentration. By 1957 only four parties were left, with the fourth existing merely by sufferance of what was then the majority party. In the same year the FDP temporarily joined the ranks of the opposition. In the three-party system operating since 1961, the so-called opposition is restricted to the solitary ranks of the SPD.

Appendix Table 7.4. Analysis of Party Preferences (1963) in Answer to the Question: Which of Today's Parties Do You Like Best?
(in percentages)

	CDU/CSU	SPD	FDP	Others	No clear-cut answer
Total	33	34	8	2	23
Men	28	38	9	2	23
Women	38	30	6	2	24
Age groups:					
16–21	31	29	8	2	30
21–25	39	27	5	2	27
25–30	29	42	8	1	20
30–50	33	37	6	2	22
50–65	31	32	8	3	26
Older than 65	41	31	9	1	18
Monthly family income after deductions					
Below DM 400	38	26	6	3	27
400–600	31	39	7	2	21
600–800	31	39	6	1	23
800–1200	35	32	9	2	22
More than 1200	41	22	14	2	21
Professional categories					
Workers and agricultural laborers	26	43	4	2	25
White-collar	38	29	8	0	25
Officials	36	35	8	1	20
Self-employed and professions	37	21	16	3	23
Farmers	46	10	15	1	28
Retired	38	34	6	2	20

	CDU/CSU	SPD	FDP	Others	No clear-cut answer
Educational level					
Grade school (8 years)	32	36	6	2	24
Junior high (10 years)	40	27	13	0	20
Senior high, college, graduate school	32	22	18	4	24
Denominational structure					
Protestants	25	37	10	2	26
Catholics	49	27	3	1	20
Others: unaffiliated or no data given	19	41	10	5	25

Source: Appendix to *Emnid informationen*, No. 33, of August 12, 1963.

Appendix Table 7.5. Professional Affiliation or Background of Members of the Fourth Bundestag (as percentage of total membership)

	CDU/CSU	SPD	Total
Independent entrepreneurs	5.9	1	5.2
Business executives	6.4	5.9	6.5
Managers of Business associations	4.4	1.5	3.8
Retailers, innkeepers, etc.	4.4	1.5	3.1
Artisans and employees of artisan organizations	3.6	2	2.9
Farmers and employees of farm organizations	18.3	1.5	11.5
Employees and workers	4.8	7.4	5.6
Party functionaries	2.4	12.3	6.5
Functionaries of labor organizations	7.2	15.8	9.6
Lawyers and accountants	8	5.4	7.6
Academic professions, clergy, physicians, and architects	5.9	7.9	6
Publishers and journalists	3.6	11.8	6.9
Employees of public enterprises and officials	22.7	23.1	22.3
Housewives	2.4	2.9	2.5

Source: Deutsche Industrieinstitut Publication, No. 7 (July 3, 1962), p. 14.

Explanations of Appendix Tables 7.4 and 7.5

Appendix Table 7.4 has little meaning in terms of predicting voters' future decisions as such a large part of the sample (23 per cent) remains undecided. But it is of value for the correlation between party preferences and a variety of social characteristics of the electorate. In spite of a number of crosscurrents the tabulation confirms the continued existence of a working-class subculture with some, however attenuated, form of SPD loyalty (43 per cent). It is most marked among male non-Catholic workers in the 25- to 50-year age group, among people who never went beyond grade school and whose family income stays within the 400 to 800 DM limit. The lower-level SPD interest among the lowest income group (26 per cent) runs parallel to a high degree of political apathy or indecisiveness (27 per cent). It belongs to the same syndrome as lower SPD interest among women (30 per cent as against 38 per cent for the CDU) and among Catholics (27 per cent against 49 per cent CDU).

Other inquiries would show that the white-collar workers not only have a higher income than workers, but that even in the same income categories there is a marked difference in consumer goods preference (see Richard F. Hamilton, "Affluence and the Worker: The West German Case," in *American Journal of Sociology,* 71 (1965), 144–52, and Hans Paul Bahrdt in *Gibt es noch ein Proletariat?* Marianne Feuersenger, ed., Frankfurt, 1962 pp. 15–33). Both income differentials and different consumer habits are reflected in the appreciable difference in party preference (29 per cent SPD as against 38 per cent CDU). SPD and CDU are running neck-and-neck among officials (35 per cent SPD as against 36 per cent CDU); this reflects not only the fact that railroad men and postal clerks, for example, count as officials but also the fact that a sizable number of city and state administrations are SPD-governed. However, it should be noted that SPD strength remains appreciable throughout with both white-collar workers and retired people (38 per cent) suggesting a continued basis for the party's present attempt to cast a wide net for a multiplicity of social groups. Only among farmers has it scarcely any clientele (10 per cent). The same tabulation would show the precariousness of the social basis of the third party: with 14–18 per cent, the FDP has some position only among higher income groups, self-employed, professionals, farmers, and persons educated beyond grade school—mainly Protestant.

Appendix Table 7.5 shows that the professional background of members of the Bundestag is to some extent in keeping with party attractiveness to various social groups. The small percentage of agricultural representatives in the SPD faction corresponds to the generally poor response the SPD has among farmers (1.5 per cent as against 18.3 per cent for the CDU). Conversely, labor organization functionaries appear in more than double strength among the SPD as compared with the CDU 15.8 per cent as against 7.2 per cent. The fact that the SPD is to some extent still a membership party whereas CDU recruiting is handled by tributary and ancillary organizations is reflected in the drastic difference in the number of full-time party functionaries in the Bundestag: 12.3 per cent for the SPD as against 2.4 per cent for the CDU. Many of the 11.8 per cent publishers and journalists among the SPD ranks, too, are likely to be connected with party or related enterprises. However, the most important professional category in the Bundestag—evenly distributed among all parties—are employees of public enterprises and civil servants: 22.3 per cent. It is this element—emphasizing continuity, shared interests, proper procedure as well as administrative experience needed for the planning and running of extensive public services in the huge agglomerations of population—which is most characteristic of the German parliamentary scene.

Chapter 8. Austria

Appendix Table 8.1. Voting Percentages for Parliamentary Elections When Social Democrats Were in Opposition

	1920	1923	1927	1930
Government				
Christian Socials	42	45	—	36
Pan-Germans	17	13	—	—
Heimwehr (fascist)	—	—	—	6
Schober bloc	—	—	—	—[b]
Total	59	58	49 [a]	42 [b]
No. of seats	*113*	*92*	*85*	*80*
Opposition				
Social Democrats	36	39.5	42	41
Agrarian League	—	2.5	6	—
Others	5	—	3	3
Schober bloc	—	—	—	—[b]
Total	41	42	51	44 [b]
No. of seats	*70*	*73*	*83*	*82*

a. There was a common list for government parties.

b. The total vote for Schober-bloc candidates (Pan-Germans and Agrarian League) was 12 per cent. Nine of the elected members sat with the government, 10 with the opposition.

Appendix Table 8.2. Voting Percentages for Parliamentary Elections Under Coalition Regimes

	1919	1945	1949	1953	1956	1959	1962
People's Party (CS in 1919)	36	50	44	41	46	44	45.5
No. of seats	*69*	*85*	*77*	*74*	*82*	*79*	*81*
Socialists (SD in 1919)	41	45	39	42	43	45	44
No. of seats	*72*	*76*	*67*	*73*	*74*	*78*	*76*
Communists	—	5	—	—	—	—	—
No. of seats		*4*					
Coalition	77	100	83	83	89	89	89.5
No. of seats	*141*	*165*	*144*	*147*	*156*	*157*	*157*
Freedom Party (Pan-Germans, 1919, Independents, 1949, 1953)	18	—	12	11	7	8	7
No. of seats	*26*		*16*	*14*	*6*	*8*	*8*
Communists	—	—	5	5.5	4	3	3
No. of seats			*5*	*4*	*3*		
European Federalists	—	—	—	—	—	—	.5
Others	5	—	—	.5	—	—	—
No. of seats	*3*						
Opposition	23	—	17	17	11	11	10.5
No. of seats	*29*		*21*	*18*	*9*	*8*	*8*

Appendix Table 8.3. Party Strength in Chamber Elections
(percentage of vote)

Chamber of Labor (total)	1949	1954	1959
SPÖ	64	69	68
ÖAAB (ÖVP)	14	16	19
Communists	10	10	6
Freedom Party	12	2	4
Nonparty	—	3	3
Chamber of Labor (manual workers only)			
SPÖ	66	73	74
ÖAAB (ÖVP)	11	11	14
Communists	11	11	7
Freedom Party	12	2	3
Nonparty	—	3	2
Chamber of Commerce (contested elections only)	1950	1955	1960 *
ÖWB (ÖVP)	77	79	79
FWV (SPÖ)	16	16	8
Others	7	5	13
Chamber of Agriculture (aggregate of provincial elections)	1949–51	1954–58	1959–63
ÖBB (ÖVP)	82	85	83
ABB (SPÖ)	9	10	11
NB (Freedom Party)	8	4	5
Others	1	1	1

* Contested *and* uncontested election (FWV figures would be somewhat higher if total were for contested elections only).
Sources: H. P. Secher, "Representative Democracy or 'Chamber State,'" *Western Political Quarterly*, *13* (1960), 890–909; *Wiener Zeitung*, October 18, 1959; compilations in archive of ÖVP.

Appendix Table 8.4. Party Strength in Presidential
Elections
(percentage of vote)

	1951 1st ballot	1951 2nd ballot	1957 (and 1965)	1963
SPÖ	39	52	51	55.5
ÖVP	40	48	49	40.5
VdU	15.5	—	—	—
KPÖ	5	—	—	—
EFP	—	—	—	4
Others	.5	—	—	—

Chapter 10. Italy

Appendix Table 10.1 Elections—Chamber of Deputies
(percentage of total vote, with number of seats in parentheses)

	1946 Constit. Assembly	1948 1st Legislature	1953 2nd Legislature	1958 3rd Legislature	1963 4th Legislature
PCI	18.9 (104)		22.6 (143)	22.7 (140)	25.3 (166)
		31.0 (183)			
PSI	20.7 (115)		12.7 (75)	14.2 (84)	13.8 (87)
PSDI	—	7.1 (33)	4.5 (19)	4.5 (22)	6.1 (33)
PRI	4.4 (23)	2.5 (9)	1.6 (5)	1.4 (6)	1.4 (6)
DC	35.1 (207)	48.4 (304)	40.0 (262)	42.3 (273)	38.3 (260)
PLI	2.8 (16)	3.8 (19)	3.0 (13)	3.5 (17)	7.0 (39)
PDIUM (and other Monarchist parties)	—	2.8 (14)	6.9 (40)	PMP 2.6 (14) PNM 2.2 (11)	1.7 (8)
MSI	—	2.0 (6)	5.8 (29)	4.8 (24)	5.1 (27)
Other parties	18.1 (90)	2.4 (5)	2.9 (3)	1.8 (4)	1.3 (4)
Total	100.0 (555)	100.0 (573)	100.0 (589)	100.0 (595)	100.0 (630)

Source: Through 1958, "Analisi statistica dei risultat," Schepis, Tavola XII; for 1963 results, *Tempi moderni, 13* (April 1963), 75.

BIBLIOGRAPHY

Chapter 1. Great Britain

The development of the institution of organized parliamentary opposition is traced in Archibald S. Foord, *His Majesty's Opposition 1714–1830* (Oxford, Oxford University Press, 1964), but the period from the 1780s is inadequately covered. History is treated as background to present political institutions in John P. Mackintosh, *The British Cabinet* (London, Stevens, 1962). The most recent editions of Walter Bagehot, *The English Constitution* (Fontana Library ed. London, Collins, 1963), and A. V. Dicey, *Introduction to the Study of the Law of the Constitution* (10th ed. London, Macmillan, 1959), contain introductions by R.H.S. Crossman and E.C.S. Wade, respectively, referring to developments since the authors' times.

On the landed aristocracy and the "governing class" in the nineteenth century see F.M.L. Thompson, *English Landed Society in the Nineteenth Century* (London, Routledge, 1963), and G. Kitson Clark, *The Making of Victorian England* (London, Methuen, 1962). On the rise and decline of "movement politics" see Donald Read, *The English Provinces c. 1760–1960* (London, Arnold, 1964).

On the crises before the First World War see Roy Jenkins, *Mr. Balfour's Poodle* (London, Heinemann, 1954); Harold Nicolson, *King George the Fifth* (London, Constable, 1952); Robert Blake, *The Unknown Prime Minister* (London, Eyre and Spottiswoode, 1955); and A. P. Ryan, *Mutiny at the Curragh* (London, Macmillan, 1956). For the history of the Labor Party and Governments see Carl F. Brand, *The British Labour Party* (Stanford, Stanford University Press, 1964); G.D.H. Cole, *A History of the Labour Party from 1914* (London, Routledge, 1948); Margaret Cole, *The Story of Fabian Socialism* (London, Heinemann, 1961); Ralph Miliband, *Parliamentary Socialism* (London, Allen and Unwin, 1961); and R. Bassett, *Nineteen Thirty-One* (London, Macmillan, 1958).

On Parliament see Sir Ivor Jennings, *Parliament* (2nd ed. Cambridge, Cambridge University Press, 1961). On the electoral and party systems see D. E. Butler, *The Electoral System in Britain Since 1918* (2nd ed. Oxford, Oxford University Press, 1963); R. T. McKenzie, *British Political Parties* (2nd ed. London, Heinemann, 1964); and the Nuffield College studies of British general elections since 1945, especially the latest, D. E. Butler and Anthony King, *The British General Election of 1964* (London, Macmillan, 1965). On organized groups and pressure politics see S. E. Finer, *Anonymous Empire* (London, Pall Mall Press, 1958), and Allen Potter, *Organized Groups in British National Politics* (London, Faber, 1961).

On the social setting see Anthony Sampson, *Anatomy of Britain* (London, Hodder and Stoughton, 1962), and *Anatomy of Britain Today* (London, Hodder and Stoughton, 1965) and W. L. Guttsman, *The British Political Elite* (London, Macgibbon and Kee, 1963). On politics in the social setting see Jean Blondel, *Voters, Parties, and Leaders* (London, Penguin, 1963); Richard Rose, *Politics in England* (Boston, Little, Brown, 1964); and Samuel H. Beer, *Modern British Politics* (London, Faber, 1965). The contributors to *The Twentieth Century* (October 1957) special number on "Who Governs Britain?" answer or evade the question in a variety of ways.

Chapter 2. The American Oppositions

Probably no political system has ever had so much written about it as that of the United States. A reader who wishes to pursue the topics discussed in this chapter should consult the various works cited in the footnotes. There are also a number of short works that provide excellent overviews of certain aspects of American politics and good critical bibliographies:

Fred I. Greenstein, *The American Party System and the American People* (Englewood Cliffs, N.J., Prentice-Hall, 1963); Nelson W. Polsby, *Congress and the Presidency* (Englewood Cliffs, N.J., Prentice-Hall, 1964); Robert E. Lane and David O. Sears, *Public Opinion* (Englewood Cliffs, N.J., Prentice-Hall, 1964). David Truman's now classic *The Government Process* (New York, Knopf, 1953) is rich in bibliographical references. Two standard works cited in the footnotes that are of central importance to this chapter are Angus Campbell et al., *The American Voter* (New York, Wiley, 1960), and V. O. Key, *Public Opinion and American Democracy* (New York, Knopf, 1961). One should also consult Seymour M. Lipset, *Political Man* (Garden City, N.Y., Doubleday, 1960) and his *The First New Nation* (New York, Basic Books, 1963).

Chapter 3. Norway

GENERAL HISTORY: There is no dearth of narrative histories of Norway but very little serious work on developments after 1905. The standard history of the first three decades after 1814 is Sverre Steen's five-volume *Det frie Norge* (Oslo, Cappelen, 1951–62). In contrast to other general histories this is well annotated and documented. Useful summaries of further developments are found in W. Keilhau's three volumes (8–10) of the series *Det norske folks liv og historie gjennom tidene* (Oslo, Aschehoug, 1931–35), and his *Det norske folks historie i vår egen tid* (Oslo, Aschehoug, 1938). More recent summaries are found in M. Jensen, *Norges historie fra 1660 til våre dager* (Oslo, Gyldendal, 1949; pocket ed. Universitetsforlaget, 1964), and in the multivolume series edited by T. Dahl, *Vårt folks historie*, vols. 5–7 (Oslo, Aschehoug, 1963–64). A useful collection of essays on a variety of aspects of national development is *Dette er Norge*, vols. 1–3 (Oslo, Gyldendal, 1964).

Among English-language histories Karen Larson, *A History of Norway* (Princeton, Princeton University Press, 1948), is particularly useful for earlier periods but highly inadequate for an understanding of developments since 1905.

POLITICAL HISTORY: The standard work on the history of Parliament is *Det norske Storting gjennom 150 år* (Oslo, Gyldendal, 1964), vols. 1–4. The first volume, by Alf Kaartvedt, covers the *ancien régime* until 1869. The second volume, by Rolf Danielsen, covers the critical period from 1870 to 1908 and constitutes the first thorough analysis of the changes in procedures and alignments brought about through the great struggle over constitutional principles in the '70s and '80s. The volume by Tim Greve on the period since 1905 leaves much to be desired.

A leading interpreter of nineteenth-century political developments in Norway is Jens Arup Seip. His most important contributions are: *Det opinionsstyrte enevelde*

(Oslo, Universitetsforlaget, 1958), an illuminating analysis of the absolutist heritage and of the early conceptions of representation and popular sovereignty; "Det norske system," *Historisk tidsskrift 39* (1959), 1–58, an analysis of the influence of Saint-Simonian ideas on the policies of the leading officials; *Et regime foran undergangen* (Oslo, Tanum, 1945), a pathbreaking analysis of the strains within the official leadership in the decade before the breakdown of the *ancien régime; Fra embetsmannsstat til ettpartistat* (Oslo, Universitetsforlaget, 1963)—essays on the development of the Norwegian system from a regime of king's officials to the rule of one party.

A work of major importance for an understanding of developments in the '80s is Alf Kaartvedt, *Kampen om parlamentarisme 1880–84* (Oslo, Universitetsforlaget, 1956).

A Swedish work on the period 1905–35 is still a major source of information: Arne Björnberg, *Parlamentarismens utveckling i Norge sedan 1905* (Uppsala, Almqvist and Wiksell, 1939).

There are hardly any detailed analyses of the politics of the years between the two world wars. A thoroughgoing account of the controversies over foreign and military policy and their importance for the development of party alignments in the Storting is found in Nils Orvik, *Sikkerhetspolitikken 1920–1939* (Oslo, Tanum, 1960–61).

On World War II and its aftermath see especially M. Skodvin, *Striden om okkupasjonsstyret i Norge* (Oslo, Universitetsforlaget, 1956); T. Chr. Wyller, *Nyordning og motstand* (Oslo, Universitetsforlaget, 1958); and *Frigjøringspolitikk* (Oslo, Universitetsforlaget, 1963).

CONSTITUTIONAL COMMENTARIES: The basic work on the Constitution of 1814 is still T. H. Aschehoug, *Norges nuværende Statsforfatning*, vols. 1–3 (Christiania, Aschehoug, 1875–85). The standard textbook is F. Castberg, *Norges statsforfatning*, vols. 1–2 (3d ed. Oslo, Universitetsforlaget, 1964). A summary presentation is given in J. Andenæs, *Statsforfatningen i Norge* (Oslo, Tanum, 1945 and later eds.).

An important review of constitutional developments is given by T. Eckhoff in "Utviklingslinjer i norsk statsstyre og forfatningsrett," *Tidsskrift for Rettsvitenskap*, 77 (1964), 171–231.

A summary presentation in English of the Constitution and the principal organs of government can be found in J. A. Storing, *Norwegian Democracy* (Boston, Houghton Mifflin, 1963). This conventional text is unfortunately marred by a few inaccuracies and misinterpretations.

ELECTIONS AND PARTIES: A review of Norwegian research on elections and parties is given in S. Rokkan and H. Valen, "Parties, Elections and Political Behaviour in the Northern Countries," pp. 103–36 in O. Stammer, ed., *Politische Forschung* (Cologne, Westdeutscher Verlag, 1960).

Analyses of early electoral developments are presented in S. Rokkan and H. Valen, "The Mobilization of the Periphery," pp. 111–59 in S. Rokkan, ed., *Approaches to the Study of Political Participation* (Bergen, Christian Michelsen Institute, 1962), and in S. Rokkan, "Geography, Religion and Social Class," in S. M. Lipset and S. Rokkan, *Party Systems and Voter Alignments* (New York, Free Press, 1966).

An excellent review of early party developments is found in R. Danielsen's chapter on Norway in "Framveksten av de politiske partier i de nordiske land på 1800–tallet," pp. 131–50 of *Problemer i nordisk historieforskning* (Oslo, Universitetsforlaget, 1964). A useful contribution to the analysis of the growth of urban party organization has been published by Ulf Torgersen in the collective volume edited by E. Allardt and Y. Littunen, *Cleavages, Ideologies and Party Systems* (Helsinki, Westermarck Society, 1964).

The official party histories published since the 1930s (the latest ones are for the

Labor Party, 1887–1962, and for the Communist Party, 1923–40) contain very little serious analysis. On the development of the Labor Party there is useful information in H. Lange, *Fra sekt til parti* (Oslo, Universitetsforlaget, 1962); K. Langfeldt, *Moskvatesene i norsk politikk* (Oslo, Universitetsforlaget, 1961); and I. Roset, *Det norske Arbeiderparti og Hornsruds regjeringsdannelse i 1928* (Oslo, Universitetsforlaget, 1964).

The best introduction in English to the study of parties and electoral behavior in Norway is H. Valen and D. Katz, *Political Parties in Norway: A Community Study* (Oslo, Universitetsforlaget, 1964). For a broader treatment of regional variations, see the paper by S. Rokkan and H. Valen in E. Allardt and Y. Littunen, eds., *Cleavages, Ideologies and Party Systems*, and S. Rokkan, "Geography, Religion and Social Class."

The findings of the long-term program of electoral research at the Christian Michelsen Institute in Bergen and the Institute for Social Research in Oslo are being published in a series of reports in English and in Norwegian. Particularly detailed accounts of electoral arrangements, party organization, candidate recruitment, turnout, and the ecology of the vote will be given in forthcoming volumes by S. Rokkan, H. Valen, et al., in the series *Valg i Norge*.

MOVEMENTS AND ORGANIZATIONS: There is no general work on the growth of popular movements and interest organizations. A useful *aperçu* is given in Sverre Steen's collected essays, *Tusen års norsk historie* (Oslo, Cappelen, 1958), pp. 182–86. For a quick review of the growth of "organizational society," see T. Chr. Wyller, *Nyordning . . .*, Sect. 3.

The standard works on the unions are G. Ousland and A. Skar, *Fagbevegelsen i Norge*, vols. 1–3 (Oslo, Tiden, 1949), and W. Galenson, *Labor in Norway* (Cambridge, Mass., Harvard University Press, 1949). Cf. also the latter's chapter on Scandinavia in W. Galenson, ed., *Comparative Labor Movements* (New York, Prentice-Hall, 1952).

On white-collar unions, see specifically E. Fivelsdal, *Funksjonærenes syn på faglige og politiske spørsmål* (Oslo, Universitetsforlaget, 1964). On the employers' associations: E. Petersen, *Norsk Arbeidsgiverforening 1900–1950* (Oslo, Arbeidsgiverforening, 1950). On farmers' organizations: O. A. Johnsen, *Norges Bønder* (Kristiania, Aschehoug, 1919); G. Werner-Hansen, ed., *Norges Bondelag 1896–1956* (Oslo, Bøndernes Forlag, 1956); and J. Tveite, *Jord og gjerning* (Oslo Selskapet Norges Vel, 1959). On the Folk High School movement: Erica Simon, *Réveil national et culture populaire en Scandinavie* (Paris, Presses Universitaires, 1960). On consumer cooperatives: I. Debes, *Forbrukerkooperasjonens historie*, vols. 1–2 (Oslo, Norges Kooperative Landsfortund, 1956).

A Register of Norwegian associations and organizations has been prepared by J. Moren at the Christian Michelsen Institute and is scheduled for publication in 1966.

The growth of "corporatist" bodies of consultation and decision-making has been described by J. Moren in *Organisasjonene og forvaltningen* (Bergen, Norges Handelshøyskole, 1958).

THE MASS MEDIA: The political role of the press has been analyzed in S. Rokkan and P. Torsvik, "Der Wähler, der Leser und die Parteipresse," *Kölner Zeitschrift für Soziologie*, 12 (1960), and in S. Høyer, "Pressens økonomiske og politiske struktur," *Tidsskrift for samfunnsforskning*, 1964 (4), 221–42.

THE CENTRAL DECISION-MAKING ORGANS: The basic works on Parliament are T. Lindstøl, *Stortinget og Statsrådet 1814–1914*, vols. 1–4 (Kristiania, Steenske, 1914); V. Haffner and K. Bjørnstad, *Stortinget og Statsrådet 1915–45* (Stortinget, 1949); and the already cited 150-year history, *Det norske Storting gjennom 150 år*, vols. 1–4. On legislative procedure the indispensable manual is V. Haffner, *Om Stortingets lovbehandling og Stortingets voteringsordning* (new ed. Oslo, Universitetsforlaget, 1964).

On the Cabinet a straightforward reference work is J. Debes, *Det norske Statsråd 1814–1949* (Oslo, Cammermeyer, 1950). A useful description of its procedures is given in K. Bloch, *Kongens Råd* (Oslo, Universitetsforlaget, 1963).

A standard history of the central bureaucracy is H. K. Steffens, *Den norske Centraladministrations Historie 1814–1914* (Kristiania, Stenersen, 1914). A team of young historians and political scientists is currently preparing an analytical history of developments department by department from 1814 to 1964.

Knut D. Jacobsen's *Teknisk hjelp og politisk struktur* (Oslo, Universitetsforlaget, 1964) presents a major breakthrough in the study of processes of administrative change in Norway; it deals with the development of administrative machinery for agriculture from 1874 to 1899.

Useful compendia for students are Per Stavang, *Parlamentarisme og maktbalanse* (Oslo, Universitetsforlaget, 1964), and Ulf Torgersen, *Norske politiske institusjoner* (Oslo, Universitetsforlaget, 1964).

Chapter 4. Sweden

BIBLIOGRAPHY: E. Håstad, "Swedish Political Science," in *Contemporary Political Science* (Paris, UNESCO, 1950), pp. 150 ff.; Sarah Thorelli, "Political Science in Sweden," *American Political Science Review, 44* (1950), 977 ff.; L. Frykholm, "Swedish Legal Publications in English, French and German 1935–60," *Scandinavian Studies in Law, 5* (1961), 155 ff.

PERIODICALS: *Statsvetenskaplig Tidskrift* (Lund) from 1897; *Scandinavian Political Studies* (Helsinki) from 1965.

GENERAL WORKS: I. Andersson, *A History of Sweden* (2d ed. Stockholm, Natur och Kultur, 1956); E. Lundberg, *Business Cycles and Economic Policy* (London, Allen and Unwin, 1957).

CONSTITUTIONAL PROVISIONS, SWEDISH GOVERNMENT AND POLITICS: *The Constitution of Sweden*, Documents published by the Ministry for Foreign Affairs, 1953 (also in French); N. Andrén, *Modern Swedish Government* (Stockholm, Almqvist and Wiksell, 1961); B. Arneson, *The Democratic Monarchies of Scandinavia* (New York, Van Nostrand, 1939); E. Fahlbeck, N. Herlitz, and N. Stjernquist, "Die Entwicklung des öffentlichen Rechts Schwedens in den Jahren 1933 bis 1953," *Jahrbuch des öffentlichen Rechts*, N.F.(4)1955; R. Fusilier, *Les Monarchies parlementaires* (Paris, Éditions Ouvrières, 1960); W. Haller, *Der schwedische Justitieombudsman* (Zürich, Polygraphischer Verlag, 1964); N. Herlitz, *Sweden: a Modern Democracy on Ancient Foundations* (Minneapolis, University of Minnesota Press, 1939); E. Håstad, *The Parliament of Sweden* (London, Hansard Society, 1957); H. Tingsten, *The Debate on the Foreign Policy of Sweden 1918–1939* (London, Oxford University Press, 1949); D. A. Rustow, *The Politics of Compromise: A Study of Parties and Cabinet Government in Sweden* (Princeton, Princeton University Press, 1955); D. Verney, *Parliamentary Reform in Sweden* (Oxford, Clarendon Press, 1957).

R. Malmgren, *Sveriges grundlagar och tillhörande författningar med förklaringar* (9th ed. Stockholm, Norstedts, 1965); N. Herlitz, *Svenska statsrättens grunder* (2d ed. Stockholm, Norstedts, 1956); R. Malmgren, *Sveriges författning, en lärobok i svensk statsrätt*, vols. 1–2 (Malmö, 1941–52); Författningsutredningen, "Sveriges statsskick, 1. Lagförslag, 2. Motiv, förslag till regeringsform, 3. Motiv, förslag till riksdagsordning," *Statens offentliga utredningar*, 1963, Nos. 16–18 (Stockholm, Ministry of Justice,

1963); G. Heckscher, *Svensk statsförvaltning i arbete* (2d ed. Stockholm, Studieförbundet Näringsliv och Samhälle, 1958); N. Herlitz, *Grunddragen av det svenska statskickets historia* (6th ed. Stockholm, Norstedts, 1964); H. Meijer, *Kommittépolitik och kommittéarbete* (Lund, Gleerups, 1956) (with an English summary); O. Nyman, *Parlamentarismen i Sverige* (4th ed. Stockholm, Bokförlaget Medborgarskolan, 1963); *Sveriges Riksdag*, vols. 1–17 (Stockholm, 1931–38).

POLITICAL PARTIES AND ORGANIZATIONS: R. Fusilier, *Le Parti socialiste suédois* (Paris, Éditions Ouvrières, 1954); G. Heckscher, "Interest Groups in Sweden," in *Interest Groups on Four Continents*, ed. H. W. Ehrmann (Pittsburgh, University of Pittsburgh Press, 1958); T. L. Johnston, *Collective Bargaining in Sweden* (London, Allen and Unwin, 1962); F. Schmidt, *The Law of Labour Relations in Sweden* (Stockholm, Almquist and Wiksell, 1962).

G. Heckscher, *Staten och organisationerna* (2d ed. Stockholm, KF:s Bokförlag, 1951); H. Johansson, *Folkrörelserna och det demokratiska statsskicket* (Lund, Gleerups, 1952); O. Ruin, *Kooperativa Förbundet 1899–1929* (Stockholm, Rabén and Sjögren, 1960) (with an English summary); T. Vallinder, *I kamp för demokratin, rösträttsrörelsen i Sverige 1886–1900* (Stockholm, Natur och Kultur, 1962) (with an English summary); J. Westerståhl, *Svensk fackföreningsrörelse* (Stockholm, Tidens förlag, 1945).

IDEOLOGIES AND RELIGION: C. A. Hessler, *Statskyrkodebatten* (Stockholm, Almqvist and Wiksell, 1964) (with an English summary); H. Tingsten, *Den svenska socialdemokratiens idéutveckling*, vols. 1–2 (Stockholm, Tidens förlag, 1941).

ELECTIONS AND MASS MEDIA: Official Statistics of Sweden: *The Elections to the Riksdag During the Years 1961–1964* (Stockholm, Central Bureau of Statistics, 1965); A. Y. Pers, *The Swedish Press* (Stockholm Forum, 1963); H. Tingsten, *Political Behavior: Studies in Election Statistics* (London, King and Son, 1937); C.-G. Janson, *Majoritetsval* (Stockholm, 1958); C.-G. Janson, *Mandattilldelning och regional röstfördelning* (Stockholm, 1961) (with an English summary); L. Sköld, *Kandidatnominering vid andrakammarval* (Stockholm, 1958) (with an English summary); B. Särlvik, *Opinionsbildningen vid folkomröstningen 1957* (Stockholm, 1959); G. Wallin, *Valrörelser och valresultat, andrakammarvalen i Sverige 1866–1884* (Stockholm, 1961) (with an English summary); J. Westerståhl and C.-G. Janson, *Politisk press: Studier till belysning av dagspressens politiska roll i Sverige* (Gothenburg, Political Science Institute, University of Gothenburg, 1958) (with an English summary).

Chapter 5. Belgium

GENERAL HISTORY: J.-A. Goris, ed., *Belgium* (Berkeley, University of California Press, 1946); J. A. van Houtte et al., eds., *Algemene Geschiedenis der Nederlanden*, vols. 9–13 (Zeist and Antwerp, Standard Boekhandel, 1956–58); Henri Pirenne, *Histoire de Belgique*, vols. 5, 6, and 7 (2d ed. Brussels, Lamertin, 1921, 1926, and, for vol. 7, 1948); J. Deharveng et al., eds., *Histoire de la Belgique contemporaine* (3 vols. Brussels, Dewit, 1928–30).

POLITICAL HISTORY: Frans van Kalken, *La Belgique contemporaine* (2d ed. Paris, Colin, 1950); Carl-Henrik Höjer, *Le Régime parlementaire belge de 1918 à 1940* (Uppsala, Almqvist and Wiksell, 1946); E. R. Arango, *Leopold III and the Belgian Royal Question* (Baltimore, Johns Hopkins Press, 1963); Msgr. A. Simon, works cited in footnote

2, especially *Le Parti Catholique Belge, 1830–1945* (Brussels, Renaissance du Livre, 1958); Léon Delsinne, *Le Parti Ouvrier Belge des origines à 1894* (Brussels, Renaissance du Livre, 1955); K. van Isacker, *Werkelijk en Wettelijk land . . . 1863–1884* (Antwerp, Standaard Boekhandel, 1955); sections in various volumes of G. D. H. Cole, *History of Socialist Thought* (5 vols. in 7, London, Macmillan and St. Martin's Press, 1953–60), and of Carl Landauer, *European Socialism* (2 vols. Berkeley, University of California Press, 1959). See also the recent book by Jean Meynaud, Jean Ladrière, and François Perin, for the Centre de Recherches et d'Information Socio-Politiques, *La Décision politique en Belgique: Le pouvoir et les groupes* (Paris, Colin, 1965).

POLITICAL INSTITUTIONS AND ELECTIONS: André Mast, *Les Pays du Bénélux* (in series *Comment Ils Sont Gouvernés*) (Paris, Librairie Générale du Droit et de Jurisprudence, 1960); Raymond Fusilier, *Les Monarchies parlementaires* (Paris, Editions Ouvrières, 1960); John Gilissen, *Le Regime représentatif en Belgique depuis 1790* (Brussels, Renaissance du Livre, 1958); R. E. De Smet, R. Evalenko, and W. Fraeys, *Atlas des élections belges, 1919–1954* (Brussels, Institut de Sociologie, 1958); Institut Belge de Science Politique, a number of works, especially its *Aspects de la Société Belge* (Brussels, Librairie Encyclopédique, 1958), *Le Contrôle parlementaire de l'action gouvernmentale* (Brussels, Librairie Encyclopédique, 1957), *Le Problème des grandes agglomérations en Belgique* (Brussels, Librairie Encyclopédique, 1957); and articles on "La campagne électorale de mars 1961," in *Res Publica, 3,* no. 4 (1961); Felix Oppenheim, chapter on Belgium in Sigmund Neumann, ed., *Modern Political Parties* (Chicago, University of Chicago Press, 1956); Jan Dhondt, "De evolutie van de partijen tussen de twee wereldoorlogen," *Res Publica, 4,* no. 4 (1962), 370–80; and T. H. Reed, *Government and Politics of Belgium* (Yonkers, World Book Co., 1924).

SOCIAL MOVEMENTS: B. S. Chlepner, *Cent ans d'histoire sociale en Belgique* (Brussels, Institut de Sociologie Solvay, 1956); Léon Delsinne, *Le Mouvement syndical en Belgique* (Paris, Sirey, 1936); and R. Rezsohazy, *Origines et formation du catholicisme social en Belgique, 1842–1909* (Louvain, University of Louvain, 1958).

REGIONAL AND LINGUISTIC PROBLEMS: S. B. Clough, *A History of the Flemish National Movement* (New York, R. H. Smith, 1930); A. W. Willemsen, *Het Vlaams Nationalisme, 1914–1940* (Groningen, Wolters, 1958); *Revue Nouvelle,* special number August–September 1961; Telemachus, "De Spanning tussen de Taalgroepen: een sociologische benadering," *De Maand, 6* (1963), 332–44 (French version in *Revue Nouvelle,* Oct. 15, 1963, 303–14); and M. van Haegendoren, *De Vlaamse beweging: verweer en aanval!* (Hasselt, Vlaamse Pockets, 1964).

CURRENT ANALYSIS of parties, interest groups, social movements: periodic and other reports of the Centre de Recherche et d'Information Socio-politiques, 1959—.

BIBLIOGRAPHY: Most complete historical bibliography in the volumes of the *Algemene Geschiedenis* (see under General History); *Res Publica,* current bibliography in each issue and special bibliography on political parties, 1830–1962, in vol. 5, no. 4 (1963); and extensive annual bibliographies on Belgian history by Jan Dhondt and associates in *Revue du Nord* (Lille) and *Revue belge de philologie et d'histoire.*

Chapter 6. The Netherlands

GENERAL HISTORY: The most recent and complete general history, J. A. van Houtte et al., eds., *Algemene Geschiedenis der Nederlanden* (Utrecht, W. de Haan, 1949–55), is not available in English. But extensive data can be found in the writings of P. J. Blok, *History of the People of the Netherlands* (5 vols. New York, Putnam's, 1898–1912); *Britain and The Netherlands,* papers delivered at the Anglo-Dutch Historical Conferences (2 vols. London, Chatto and Windus, 1960, and Groningen, Wolters, 1964); Pieter Geyl, *The Revolt of The Netherlands, 1555–1609* (2d ed. London, Benn, 1958); *The Netherlands in the Seventeenth Century,* Parts I and II (London, Benn, 1961–64), and *History of the Low Countries—Episodes and Problems* (London, Macmillan, 1964); E. Kossmann, *In Praise of the Dutch Republic: Some Seventeenth-Century Attitudes* (London, 1963); G. J. Renier, *The Dutch Nation: An Historical Study* (London, Allen and Unwin, 1944); and I. Schöffer, *A Short History of The Netherlands* (Amsterdam, Allert de Lange, 1956).

In addition, a number of works on the Netherlands were published in English during or just after the Second World War: see A. J. Barnouw, *The Dutch—A Portrait Study of the People of Holland* (New York, Columbia University Press, 1940), and *The Making of Modern Holland* (New York, Norton, 1944); B. Landheer, ed., *The Netherlands* (Berkeley, University of California Press, 1943); J. Veraart, *Holland* (London, Macdonald, 1944); and especially B. H. M. Vlekke, *The Evolution of the Dutch Nation* (New York, Roy, 1945).

POLITICAL HISTORY: The most important study of institutions in the time of the Dutch Republic is S. J. Fockema Andreae, "De Nederlandse Staat onder de Republiek," *Verhandelingen der Koninklijke Nederlandse Akademie van Wetenschappen,* Nieuwe Reeks, 68 (Amsterdam, 1960). The development of the Dutch States-General is described by a number of authors in S. J. Fockema Andreae and H. Hardenberg, eds., *500 Jaren Staten-Generaal in de Nederlanden* (Assen, Van Gorcum, 1964). For the history of politics in Parliament see W. J. van Welderen Baron Rengers, *Schets eener Parlementaire Geschiedenis van Nederland, 1848–91,* new edition by C. W. de Vries and new volumes by De Vries, W. H. Vermeulen and L. G. Kortenhorst, *1891–1918* and *1945–46* (5 vols. The Hague, Nijhoff, 1948–56), and P. J. Oud, *Het Jongste Verleden* (6 vols. Assen, Van Gorcum, 1948–51), covering the period 1918–40. An excellent analysis from orthodox Protestant perspective is given by P. A. Diepenhorst, *Onze Strijd in de Staten-Generaal* (2 vols. Amsterdam, Dagbl. en Drukkerij De Standaard, 1927–29).

GENERAL PARTY HISTORIES: H. Daalder, "Nederland," in section on political systems in *Repertorium van de Sociale Wetenschappen,* vol. 1: *Politiek* (Amsterdam, Elsevier, 1958), pp. 213–38; D. Hans, *Parade der Politieke Partijen* (Putten, Terwee, nd. [1938?]); C. E. van Koetsveld, *Het Ontstaan, de Beginselen en de Geschiedenis van Onze Politieke Partijen* (Utrecht, Jac. C. van der Stal., 1904). On the orthodox Protestants, J. A. de Wilde and C. Smeenk, *Het Volk ten Baat, de Geschiedenis van de A. R.-Partij* (Groningen, Jan Haan, 1949); on the Catholics, N. de Rooy and L. J. Rogier, *In Vrijheid Herboren* (The Hague, Pax, 1953). There is little literature in English on Dutch socialism: G. D. H. Cole's treatment in *History of Socialist Thought* (London, Macmillan, 1953–60) is often erroneous.

For Dutch sources see the literature mentioned in the footnotes to Chapter 6 and the full bibliography in Fr. de Jong Edz, *Om de Plaats van de Arbeid* (Amsterdam, De Arbeiderspers, 1956).

POLITICAL INSTITUTIONS AND PARTY SYSTEM: In English: R. C. Bone, "The Dynamics of Dutch Politics," *Journal of Politics, 24* (1962), 23–49; H. Daalder, "Parties and Politics in The Netherlands," *Political Studies, 3* (1955), 1–16, and *The Relation Between Cabinet and Parliament in The Netherlands,* report to the International Political Science Association (Rome, 1958); B. W. Schaper, "Religious Groups and Political Parties in Contemporary Holland," in *Britain and The Netherlands, 1,* 204–20; Amry Vandenbosch and S. J. Eldersveld, *Government of The Netherlands* (Lexington, University of Kentucky Press, 1947). In French: Raymond Fusilier, *Les Monarchies parlementaires* (Paris, Éditions Ouvrières, 1960), Ch. VI; André Mast, *Les Pays du Benelux*, in series *Comment Ils Sont Gouvernés* (Paris, Librairie Générale du Droit et de Jurisprudence, 1960). In Dutch: see especially the thorough constitutional law treatises by R. Kranenburg, C. W. van der Pot, and P. J. Oud.

SOCIAL STRUCTURE AND VERZUILING: A. N. J. den Hollander et al., eds., *Drift en Koers: een halve eeuw sociale verandering in Nederland* (Assen, Van Gorcum, 1962); J. P. Kruijt, *Verzuiling* (Zaandijk, Heijnis, 1959); and special issues on *Verzuiling* of *Sociologische Gids*, vol. 3, no. 2 (1956), and *Socialisme en Democratie*, no. 1 (1956).

ELECTIONS AND POLITICAL BEHAVIOR: A full bibliography and data on elections and the electoral system are given in G. H. Scholten and G. Ringnalda, chapter on the Netherlands in S. Rokkan, ed., *An International Guide to Electoral Statistics* (forthcoming). In English, see Hans Daudt and Henk de Lange, *Youth and Politics in The Netherlands*, and L. van der Land et al., *Voting in The Netherlands: A Panel Study in an Amsterdam Suburb*, both reports to the International Political Science Association (Geneva, 1964); A. Hoogerwerf, *Protestantisme en Progressiviteit* (Meppel, Boom, 1964) (with English summary); and English summary to *De Nederlandse Kiezer* (The Hague, Staatsdruk-Kerij 1956). In French, see J. Barents and J. J. de Jong, *Partis politiques et classes sociales* (mimeo. Paris, Association Française de Science Politique, 1955). In German, see Georg Geismann, *Politische Struktur und Regierungssystem in den Niederlanden* (Frankfurt, Athenäum Verlag, 1964) (with many data, if a one-sided analysis).

BUREAUCRACY: A. van Braam, *Ambtenaren en Bureaucratie in Nederland* (Zeist, W. de Haan, 1957).

INTEREST GROUPS: A. D. Robinson, *Dutch Organized Agriculture in International Politics, 1945–1960* (The Hague, Nijhoff, 1961); John P. Windmuller, "Post-War Wage Determination in The Netherlands," *Annals of the American Academy of Political and Social Science, 310* (1957), 109–22 (with full bibliography).

For contemporary developments, see the English-language journal *Delta: A Review of Arts, Life and Thought and in The Netherlands*, 1958 to date.

Chapter 7. Germany

In addition to the books and articles listed in the notes, the following writings are germane to our subject.

ARTICLES: O. K. Flechtheim, "Zur Frage der Innerparteilichen Demokratie," *Neue Kritik*, No. 8 (1962); W. Hennis, "Parlamentarische Opposition und Industrigesellschaft," *Gesellschaft, Staat Erziehung*, No. 5 (1956); S. Landshut, "Form und Funktion der Parlamentarischen Opposition," *Wirtschaft und Kultursystem* (Rüstow Festgabe), ed. G. Eisermann (Zurich and Stuttgart, Eugen Rentsch Verlag, 1955); H. Kremer and L. Meunier, "Gemeinsamkeit ist eine Zier . . . ein politische Portrait Willy Brandts," *Der Monat*, 17, No. 197 (February 1965), pp. 5–15; E. Krippendorf, "Das Ende des Parteienstaats," *Der Monat*, No. 160 (1962), pp. 64–70; G. Loewenberg, "Parlamentarism in Western Germany: The Functioning of the Bundestag," *American Political Science Review*, 55 (1961), pp. 87–102; J. Seifert, "Innerparteiliche Opposition," *Frankfurter Hefte*, No. 11 (1960); D. Sternberger, "Über Parlamentarische Opposition," *Wirtschaft und Kultursystem* (Rüstow Festabe), ed. G. Eisermann (Zurich and Stuttgart, Eugen Rentsch Verlag, 1955).

BOOKS: Douglas A. Chalmers, *The Social Democratic Party of Germany* (New Haven, Yale University Press, 1964); K. W. Deutsch and L. J. Edinger, *Germany Rejoins the Powers* (Stanford, Stanford University Press, 1959); L. J. Edinger, *Kurt Schumacher: A Study in Personality and Political Behavior* (Stanford, Stanford University Press, 1965); Th. Eschenburg, *Institutionelle Sorgen in der Bundesrepublik Politische Aufsätze 1957–1961* (Stuttgart, Kurt E. Schwab Verlag, 1961); A. Faul, ed., *Wahlen and Wähler in West Deutschland* (Villingen, Ring Verlag, 1960); J. Habermas, *Struktur der Öffentlichen Meinung* (Neuwied, Luchterhand, 1962); U. Kitzinger, *German Electoral Politics* (Oxford, Oxford University Press, 1959); M. G. Lange, ed., *Parteien in der Bundesrepublik* (Stuttgart and Düsseldorf, Ring Verlag, 1955); U. Lohmar, *Innerparteiliche Demokratie* (Stuttgart, Ferdinand Enke Verlag, 1963); Theo Pirker, *Die SPD nach Hitler* (Munich, Rütten and Löning, 1965); C. Schmid, *Politik und Geist* (Stuttgart, Ernst Klett Verlag, 1961); R. Wildenmann, *Macht und Konsens als Problem der Innen- und Aussenpolitik* (Frankfurt–Bonn, Atheneum Verlag, 1963).

DOCUMENTS: *Verfehlt die Opposition Ihre Aufgabe?* (Does the opposition fail to do its job?). Debate between Rudolf Augstein, publisher of *Der Spiegel*, and Heinz Kühn, SPD Land chairman for Rheinland-Westphalia, at Freiburg University, January 19, 1965. Reprinted as an insert in *Der Spiegel*, February 20, 1965.

Chapter 8. *Austria*

The only English-language books on the Second Republic are Richard Hiscocks, *The Rebirth of Austria* (London and New York, Oxford University Press, 1953) and Gordon Shepherd, *The Austrian Odyssey* (London and New York, Macmillan, 1957). For the politics of the First Republic, see Mary MacDonald, *The Republic of Austria, 1918–1934* (London and New York, Oxford University Press, 1946), and Charles A. Gulick, *Austria from Habsburg to Hitler* (2 vols. Berkeley, University of California Press, 1948). Catholic politics in the First Republic is discussed in Alfred Diamant, *Austrian Catholics and the First Republic* (Princeton, Princeton University Press, 1960), and Socialism in the First and Second Republics in Kurt L. Shell, *The Transformation of Austrian Socialism* (New York, State University of New York, 1962).

The following are the most rewarding volumes in German: for the political history of the First Republic, and a discussion of the *Lager*, Henrich Benedikt, ed., *Geschichte der Republik Österreich* (Vienna, Verlag für Geschichte und Politik, 1954); for a Socialist account of the Second Republic, Adolf Schärf, *Österreichs Erneuerung* (Vienna, Wiener Volksbuchhandlung, 1955); for a Catholic account, mostly of the First Republic, Eduard Ludwig, *Österreichs Sendung im Donauraum* (Vienna, Österreichische Staatsdruckerei, 1954); for a critical account of the Coalition, Alexander Vodopivec, *Wer regiert in Österreich?* (2d. ed. Vienna, Verlag für Geschichte und Politik, 1962); and for a penetrating critique of Austria's political ethos, Günther Nenning, *Anschluss an die Zukunft* (Vienna, Europa-Verlag, 1963).

Austria's major political monthlies are *Die Zukunft* (SPÖ) and *Österreichische Monatshefte* (ÖVP). The cultural monthly *Forum* has significant articles on politics. All three are published in Vienna.

Chapter 9. France

Extended critical bibliographies can be found in F. Goguel and A. Grosser, *La Politique en France* (Paris, Colin, 1964) and in A. Grosser, *La Quatrième République et sa politique extérieure* (Paris, Colin, 1961).

The most detailed institutional study of present France is Pierre Avril, *Le Régime politique de la 5. République* (Paris, Librairie Gale. de Droit, 1964) (bibliography).

On the very important problem of legitimacy at different moments, see *L'Affaire Henri Martin*, Commentaire de J. P. Sartre (Paris, Gallimard, 1953); Michèle Cotta, *La Collaboration* (Paris, Colin, 1963); Jacques Duquesne, *L'Algérie et la guerre des mythes* (Paris, Desclée, 1958); Otto Kirchheimer, *Political Justice* (Princeton, Princeton University Press, 1961); *Le Procès de l'attentat du petit Clamart* (Paris, A. Michel, 1963); *Le Procès du Maréchal Pétain* (2 vols. Paris, A. Michel, 1949); Jacques Weygand, *Le Serment* (Paris, Flammarion, 1960) (novel).

On the attitudes of political and social organizations (with historical and sociological explanations), see Gérard Adam, *La CFTC 1940–1958: histoire politique et idéologique* (Paris, Colin, 1964); Axel von Campenhausen, *L'Église et l'état en France* (Paris, Éd. de l'Épi, 1964); Georges Dupeux, *La Société française 1789–1960* (Paris, Colin, 1964) (bibliography); Raoul Girardet, ed., *La Crise Militaire française* (Paris, Colin, 1964); Annie Kriegel, *Le Congrès de Tours* (Paris, Julliard, 1964), and *Aux Origines du communisme* (2 vols. Paris, Mouton, 1964); M. de La Fournière and F. Borella, *Le Syndicalisme étudiant* (Paris, Éd. du Seuil, 1957); Maurice Labi, *La Grande division des travailleurs: la première scission de la CGT* (Paris, Éd. Ouvrières, 1964); Jean Meynaud, *Nouvelles études sur les groupes de pression en France* (Paris, Colin, 1962); Jean Meynaud and A. Lancelot, *La Participation des français à la politique* (Paris, P.U.F., 1961); René Rémond, *La Droite en France* (Enlarged ed. Paris, Aubier, 1964); Jean-Daniel Reynaud, *Les Syndicats en France* (Paris, Colin, 1964); Gregor Siefert, *La Mission des prêtres-ouvriers* (Paris, Éd. de l'Épi, 1963); Georges Vedel, ed., *La Dépolitisation, mythe ou réalité* (Paris, Colin, 1962).

Chapter 10. Italy

The literature on Italian politics is voluminous. This bibliography can only suggest how the interested reader can begin to acquaint himself with available materials, especially those in English.

Numerous studies of the historical and economic background are available. Useful introductory bibliographies on Italian history can be found in general histories of Italy such as that of Denis Mack Smith, *Italy: A Modern History* (Ann Arbor, University of Michigan Press, 1959). For an introduction to the Italian economy see Shepard B. Clough, *The Economic History of Modern Italy* (New York, Columbia University Press, 1964). There is no good general book on the socio-cultural context of Italian politics; an excellent beginning in a work directed to another problem is Joseph LaPalombara, *Interest Groups in Italian Politics* (Princeton, Princeton University Press, 1964), pp. 1–102. For an introduction to the sociological literature see Filippo

Barbano and Mario Viterbi, *Bibliografia della sociologia italiana (1948–1958)* (Turin, Edizioni Romella, 1959).

Although the number of empirical studies published is growing each year, works on Italian politics are largely legalistic, philosophical, historical, or polemical. Many significant works (few of them based on empirical research) have been cited in the notes to the chapter on Italy and will not be repeated here. Two general works in English are John Clarke Adams and Paolo Barile, *The Government of Republican Italy* (Boston, Houghton Mifflin, 1961), and Norman Kogan, *The Government of Italy* (New York, Crowell, 1962). An extremely useful volume for the student of Italian politics is the *Annuario politico italiano,* compiled by the Centro Italiano Richerche e Documentazione and published by *Comunità.* It contains a review of the past year's politics, biographical and statistical information, and an extensive bibliography of Italian books and articles of political relevance published during the previous year.

There is no general work on Italian parties either in English or Italian. An introduction is Carlo Morandi, *I partiti politici nella storia d'Italia* (Florence, Felice Le Monnier, 1963); the text ends with the advent of fascism, but the excellent bibliography contains references to publications issued through 1962. Some useful studies in English of the postwar PCI are the following: Aldo Garosci in Mario Einaudi, Jean-Marie Domenach, and Aldo Garosci, eds., *Communism in Western Europe* (Ithaca, N.Y., Cornell University Press, 1951); Norman Kogan, "National Communism vs. the National Way to Communism—An Italian Interpretation," *Western Political Quarterly,* 11 (1958), 660–72; Giorgio Galli, "Italy," in Walter Laqueur and Leopold Labedz, eds., *Polycentrism* (New York, Praeger, 1962), pp. 127–40; and Galli, "Italy: The Choice for the Left," in Leopold Labedz, ed., *Revisionism* (New York, Praeger, 1956), pp. 324–36.

The best introduction in English to the postwar Socialist Party is Raphael Zariski, "The Italian Socialist Party: A Case Study in Factional Conflict," *American Political Science Review,* 56 (1962), 372–90. On the Christian Democratic Party see Mario Einaudi and François Goguel, *Christian Democracy in Italy and France* (Notre Dame, University of Notre Dame Press, 1952). For an evaluation of neofascism see R. Taylor Cole, "Neofascism in Western Germany and Italy," *American Political Science Review, 49* (1955), 131–43.

On the Church in politics see A. C. Jemolo, *Church and State in Italy 1850–1950* (Oxford, Blackwell, 1960); Richard A. Webster, *The Cross and the Fasces* (Stanford, Stanford University Press, 1960); and Leicester C. Webb, *Church and State in Italy, 1947–1957* (Melbourne, Melbourne University Press, 1958).

The Italian Resistance is treated in Charles F. Delzell, *Mussolini's Enemies: The Italian Anti-Fascist Resistance* (Princeton, Princeton University Press, 1961). On the political situation at the end of the Second World War see Norman Kogan, *Italy and the Allies* (Cambridge, Harvard University Press, 1956).

CONTRIBUTORS

SAMUEL H. BARNES is associate professor of political science, University of Michigan. He has contributed articles to *The American Political Science Review, The Journal of Politics, The Review of Politics, Industrial and Labor Relations Review,* and *The Journal of Conflict Resolution.* He is completing a study of communications and participation in an Italian Socialist federation. In 1962–63 he held a Fulbright lectureship at the University of Florence, Italy.

HANS DAALDER, professor at the University of Leiden, the Netherlands, is a former Rockefeller Fellow in Political Science (1960–61) at Harvard and Berkeley. Dr. Daalder has published (in English) *Cabinet Reform in Britain, 1914–1963,* and various articles on Dutch politics, the military in the emerging countries, and Marxist theories of imperialism.

ROBERT A. DAHL is Sterling Professor of Political Science, Yale University. His publications include *A Preface to Democratic Theory; Who Governs? Democracy and Power in an American City; Modern Political Analysis;* and (with C. E. Lindblom) *Politics, Economics, and Welfare.*

FREDERICK C. ENGELMANN, professor of political science and chairman of the department, University of Alberta at Calgary, Canada, has written articles on political parties, Canadian politics, and Austrian politics.

ALFRED GROSSER is director of studies and research at the Fondation Nationale des Sciences Politiques, professor at the Institut d'Études Politiques, University of Paris, visiting professor at the Bologna Center, S.A.I.S., The Johns Hopkins University, and, in 1965, Kratter Visiting Professor of Modern European History, Stanford University. His most recent books are *La Quatrième Republique et sa politique extérieure; The Federal Republic of Germany; La Politique en France* (with François Goguel); and *La Politique Extérieure de la Vᵉ République.*

OTTO KIRCHHEIMER, Dr. jur., professor of government, Columbia University, died in November 1965. His recent publications included *Political Justice* and *Politik und Verfassung;* he was a co-author of "The Speigel Case," in *Politics in Europe* (Carter-Westin, eds.)

VAL R. LORWIN, professor of history, University of Oregon, is the author of *The French Labor Movement* and has written a number of articles on American, international, and comparative labor history and French and Belgian politics.

ALLEN M. POTTER is professor of government, University of Essex, England. His publications include *American Government and Politics* and *Organized Groups in British National Politics.*

STEIN ROKKAN is director of research for comparative politics, Christian Michelsen Institute, Bergen, Norway. He has been a visiting professor at Yale and the University of Manchester. He was co-editor and co-author of the UNESCO publication *Democracy in a World of Tensions* and has contributed a number of reports on electoral research: *Approaches to the Study of Political Participation; Regional Contrasts in Norwegian Politics* (with H. Valen), *Party Systems and Voter Alignments* (edited with S. M. Lipset), *International Guide to Electoral Statistics* (edited with J. Meyriat). He is currently a member of the Executive Committee of the International Political Science Association.

NILS STJERNQUIST is professor of political science, Lund University, Sweden. His published works deal mainly with Swedish and Danish government and politics.

INDEX

453

A
PASSAGE
NORTH

A
PASSAGE
NORTH

A NOVEL

ANUK
ARUDPRAGASAM

LONDON / NEW YORK

Published in the United States by Hogarth,
an imprint of the Random House Publishing Group,
a division of Penguin Random House LLC, New York.

HOGARTH is a trademark of the Random House Group Limited,
and the H colophon is a trademark of Penguin Random House LLC.

LIBRARY OF CONGRESS CATALOGING-IN-PUBLICATION DATA
Names: Arudpragasam, Anuk, author.
Title: A passage north : a novel / Anuk Arudpragasam.
Description: London ; New York : Hogarth, an imprint of Random House, [2021]
Identifiers: LCCN 2020044443 (print) | LCCN 2020044444 (ebook) |
ISBN 9780593230701 (hardcover) | ISBN 9780593230718 (ebook)
Classification: LCC PR9440.9.A78 P37 2021 (print) |
LCC PR9440.9.A78 (ebook) | DDC 823/.92—dc23
LC record available at https://lccn.loc.gov/2020044443
LC ebook record available at https://lccn.loc.gov/2020044444

Printed in Canada on acid-free paper

randomhousebooks.com

10 9 8 7 6 5 4 3 2 1

Book design by Jo Anne Metsch

A
PASSAGE
NORTH

MESSAGE

1

THE PRESENT, WE assume, is eternally before us, one of
the few things in life from which we cannot be parted. It over-
whelms us in the painful first moments of entry into the world,
when it is still too new to be managed or negotiated, remains
by our side during childhood and adolescence, in those years
before the weight of memory and expectation, and so it is sad
and a little unsettling to see that we become, as we grow older,
much less capable of touching, grazing, or even glimpsing it,
that the closest we seem to get to the present are those brief
moments we stop to consider the spaces our bodies are occupying, the intimate warmth of the sheets in which we wake, the
scratched surface of the window on a train taking us somewhere else, as if the only way we can hold time still is by trying
physically to prevent the objects around us from moving. The
present, we realize, eludes us more and more as the years go by,
showing itself for fleeting moments before losing us in the

world's incessant movement, fleeing the second we look away and leaving scarcely a trace of its passing, or this at least is how it usually seems in retrospect, when in the next brief moment of consciousness, the next occasion we are able to hold things still, we realize how much time has passed since we were last aware of ourselves, when we realize how many days, weeks, and months have slipped by without our consent. Events take place, moods ebb and flow, people and situations come and go, but looking back during these rare junctures in which we are, for whatever reason, lifted up from the circular daydream of everyday life, we are slightly surprised to find ourselves in the places we are, as though we were absent while everything was happening, as though we were somewhere else during the time that is usually referred to as our life. Waking up each morning we follow by circuitous routes the thread of habit, out of our homes, into the world, and back to our beds at night, move unseeingly through familiar paths, one day giving way to another and one week to the next, so that when in the midst of this daydream something happens and the thread is finally cut, when, in a moment of strong desire or unexpected loss, the rhythms of life are interrupted, we look around and are quietly surprised to see that the world is vaster than we thought, as if we'd been tricked or cheated out of all that time, time that in retrospect appears to have contained nothing of substance, no change and no duration, time that has come and gone but left us somehow untouched.

Standing there before the window of his room, looking out through the dust-coated pane of glass at the empty lot next door, at the ground overrun by grasses and weeds, the empty bottles of arrack scattered near the gate, it was this strange sense of being cast outside time that held Krishan still as he tried to make sense of the call he'd just received, the call that had put an end to all his plans for the evening, the call informing him that Rani, his grandmother's former caretaker, had died. He'd come home not long before from the office of the NGO at which he worked, had taken off his shoes and come upstairs to find, as usual, his grandmother standing outside his room, waiting impatiently to share all the thoughts she'd saved up over the course of the day. His grandmother knew he left work between five and half past five on most days, that if he came straight home, depending on whether he took a three-wheeler, bus, or walked, he could be expected at home between a quarter past five and a quarter past six. His timely arrival was an axiom in the organization of her day, and she held him to it with such severity that she would, if there was ever any deviation from the norm, be appeased only by a detailed explanation, that an urgent meeting or deadline had kept him at work longer than usual, that the roads had been blocked because of some rally or procession, when she'd become convinced, in other words, that the deviation was exceptional and that the laws she'd laid down in her room for the operation of the world outside were still in motion. He'd listened as she talked about the clothes she needed to wash, about her conjectures on what his mother was making for dinner, about her plans to shampoo her hair the next morning, and when at last there was a pause in her speech he'd begun to shuffle away, saying he was going out with friends later and wanted to rest a while in his room. She would be hurt by his unexpected desertion, he knew, but he'd been waiting all afternoon for some time alone, had been waiting for peace and quiet so he could think about the email

he'd received earlier in the day, the first communication he'd
received from Anjum in so long, the first attempt she'd made
since the end of their relationship to find out what he was
doing and what his life now was like. He'd closed the browser
as soon as he finished reading the message, had suppressed his
desire to pore over and scrutinize every word, knowing he'd be
unable to finish his work if he let himself reflect on the email,
that it was best to wait till he was home and could think about
everything undisturbed. He'd talked with his grandmother a
little more—it was her habit to ask more questions when she
knew he wanted to leave, as a way of postponing or prolonging his departure—then watched as she turned reluctantly into
her room and closed the door behind her. He'd remained in the
vestibule a moment longer, had then gone to his room, closed
the door, and turned the key twice in the lock, as if double-
bolting the door would guarantee him the solitude he sought.
He'd turned on the fan, peeled off his clothes, then changed
into a fresh T-shirt and pair of shorts, and it was just as he'd
lain down on his bed and stretched out his limbs, just as
he'd prepared himself to consider the email and the images it
brought to the surface of his mind, that the phone in the hall
began to ring, its insistent, high-pitched tone invading his room
through the door. He'd sat up on the bed and waited a few seconds in the hope it would stop, but the ringing had continued
without pause and slightly annoyed, deciding to deal with the
call as quickly as possible, brusquely if necessary, he'd gotten
up and made his way to the hall.

The caller had introduced herself, somewhat hesitantly, as
Rani's eldest daughter, an introduction whose meaning it had
taken him a few seconds to register, not only because he'd been

distracted by the email but also because it had been some time since the thought of his grandmother's caretaker Rani had crossed his mind. The last time he'd seen her had been seven or eight months before, when she had left to go on what was supposed to have been just a four- or five-day trip to her village in the north. She had gone to make arrangements for the five-year death anniversary of her youngest son, who'd been killed by shelling on the penultimate day of the war, then to attend the small remembrance that would be held the day after by survivors at the site of the final battle, which was only a few hours by bus from where she lived. She'd called a week later to say she would need a little more time, that there were some urgent matters she needed to attend to before returning—they'd spent more money than planned on the anniversary, apparently, and she needed to go to her son-in-law's village to discuss finances with her daughter and son-in-law in person, which wouldn't take more than a day or two. It was two weeks before they heard back from her again, when she called to say she'd gotten sick, it had been raining and she'd caught some kind of flu, she'd told them, would need just a few more days to recover before making the long journey back. It had been hard to imagine Rani seriously affected by flu, for despite the fact that she was in her late fifties, her large frame and substantial build gave the impression of someone exceptionally robust, not the kind of person it was easy to imagine laid low by a common virus. Krishan could still remember how on New Year's Day the year before, when they'd been boiling milk rice in the garden early in the morning, one of the three bricks that propped up the fully laden steel pot had given way, causing the pot to tip, how Rani had without any hesitation bent down and held the burn-

ing pot steady with her bare hands, waiting, without any sign
of urgency, for him to reposition the brick so she could set the
pot back down. If she hadn't yet returned it couldn't have been
that she was too weak or too sick for the ride back home, he
and his mother had felt, the delay had its source, more likely, in
the strain of the anniversary and the remembrance on her already fragile mental state. Not wanting to put unnecessary
pressure on her they'd told her not to worry, to take her time,
to come back only when she was feeling better. Appamma's
condition had improved dramatically since she'd come to stay
with them and she no longer needed to be watched every hour
of the day and night, the two of them would be able to manage
without help for a few more days. Another three weeks passed
without any news, and after calling several times and getting no
response, Krishan and his mother had been forced to conclude
that they were wrong, that Rani simply didn't want to come
back. It was surprising that she hadn't bothered to call and tell
them, since she was usually meticulous about matters of that
kind, but most likely she'd just gotten so sick of spending all her
time alone with Appamma that it didn't even occur to her that
she should let them know. Confined to a small room in a house
on the other side of the country, forced to tolerate the endless
drone of Appamma's voice every day and night, unable to go
outside the house for significant periods of time, since she
didn't know anyone and couldn't speak Sinhalese, it made
sense, they'd agreed between themselves, if Rani had decided
after almost two years in Colombo that it was time finally to
leave.

Krishan had told Rani's daughter that his mother wasn't at
home, that it would be a couple of hours before she would re-

turn, had asked whether there was any message he could pass on, and after pausing for a moment she'd told him, without any particular emotion in her voice, that Rani, her mother, had died. He hadn't responded at first, the words he'd heard strangely devoid of meaning in his head, then after a few seconds had managed to ask how, what had happened, when. It had happened the previous night, she told him, after dinner, her mother had gone to get water from the well and had fallen in, nobody knew exactly how. They'd begun looking for her about twenty minutes after she'd disappeared, had searched all over for three quarters of an hour till her eldest child, Rani's granddaughter, had gone right up to the well, leaned over the wall to look inside, and begun to scream. She'd fallen headfirst and broken her neck, either by striking the wall on the way down or the floor of the well, which contained no more than a foot or two of water. Krishan asked how she'd fallen, whether it had been an accident, not knowing whether this was a foolish or insensitive question, and Rani's daughter replied that of course it was an accident, it was dark and there was no light, her mother must have tripped on the elevated concrete platform that surrounded the well, or perhaps she'd fainted while drawing water and fallen, she'd been complaining about headache and dizziness earlier in the day. She said all this in a somewhat mechanical tone, as if nothing about what had happened was shocking or surprising to her, and had then fallen silent, as if there was nothing more to say on the matter. Krishan wanted to know more, and wanting perhaps to ward off more questions Rani's daughter added that the funeral, if he and his mother could make it, would be on Sunday afternoon. Krishan said he would let his mother know and that they would cer-

tainly come if they could, a statement that immediately felt absurd, not only because he was unsure whether the suggestion
that they attend was something Rani's daughter actually desired or merely a formality, but also because he realized as he
gave his answer that he still didn't quite believe what he had
been told. He felt an urge to ask more questions, to ask who
else had been present the night before, whether there'd been
any other signs earlier in the day, had Rani said or done anything odd or unusual, had she been having headaches or dizziness regularly, had she finished dinner, what had they been
eating, to ask for any detail really, however trivial, for there is
always a need at such times to seek out more information, not
because the information itself is important but because without it the event cannot be believed, as though you needed to
hear all the circumstantial details that connected the unlikely
death to the so-called real world before you could accept that its
occurrence was not in opposition to the laws of nature. It was
the fact, above all, that sudden or violent deaths could occur
not merely in a war zone or during race riots but during the
slow, unremarkable course of everyday life that made them so
disturbing and so difficult to accept, as though the possibility of
death was contained in even the most routine of actions, in
even the ordinary, unnoticed moments of life. Suddenly the
small details that are glossed over in your usual accounting of
life took on an almost cosmic significance, as though your fate
could be determined by whether or not you remembered to
draw water before it became dark, by whether you hurried to
catch the bus or decided to take your time, by whether or not
you said yes or no to any of the countless trivial decisions that
come only in retrospect, once the event has occurred and noth-

ing can be changed, to take on greater significance. Krishan couldn't think of anything to ask without seeming insensitive or overly inquisitive, and wanting to extend the conversation however he could he'd asked how far their village was from Kilinochchi town, what the best way was to get there. His mother would know, Rani's daughter said, once they got to town they would have to take two buses, after which they would have to walk or take a three-wheeler to the village. There was another pause, and unable to think of anything else to ask, seeing that Rani's daughter was unwilling to say or add anything more, Krishan was forced to say goodbye.

He'd remained standing there in the hall for some time, long after he heard the click on the other end of the line, and it was only when the phone began to make a continuous and disconcertingly shrill beep that he put it back down on the hook and drifted back to his room. He locked the door, walked slowly back to his bed, and sat down where he'd been sitting earlier. He picked up his cellphone, thinking to tell his mother the news, then remembered she was teaching and wouldn't be able to answer till classes were over at seven-thirty. Putting the phone aside he looked around the room restlessly, at the miscellanea of things on the dressing table opposite, at his work clothes inside-out on the floor in front of him, the books and clothes and DVDs strewn on his brother's unused bed. He picked up his trousers and turned them the right way around, folded them and placed them neatly on the bed. He did the same for his shirt, then looking around the room once more, got up and went to the window. Leaning upon the sill with both hands, forehead pressed lightly against the grille, he gazed out at the balcony of the house on the other side of the empty lot, at the clothes strung out on the line and the small TV satellite on the darkened terra-cotta roof. He tried to think about the phone call and what he had learned, of Rani's death and how it had occurred, but the news still felt unreal to him, like something he couldn't yet appreciate or understand. He felt not so much sadness as a kind of embarrassment for the way the news had caught him, in the midst of his self-involved thoughts about Anjum's email and his impatience in dealing with his grandmother, as if by jarring him out of his ordinary consciousness the call had compelled him to think, paradoxically, not about Rani but himself, to look at himself from the outside and to see from a distance the life in which he'd been immersed. He thought of the way he'd responded to the arrival of the email that afternoon, the way he'd leaned up close to his laptop and stared at the screen without moving, the quiet surprise he'd felt as he read the message and the quiet anticipation that had followed, an anticipation he'd done his best to stifle, knowing it couldn't be justified by the content of the message itself. The email had been fairly short, consisting of three or four carefully rendered sentences, deliberate and yet quietly lyrical, sentences that were intended to divulge no more and no less than Anjum wanted. They told very little of her life and asked very little of his too, this of course being Anjum's way, her way not just of writing but of being also, though perhaps, he thought to himself, she'd written so little only because she hadn't wanted to impose on him without permission, because she'd wanted to offer him the possibility of communication without obliging a substantial response. She'd been in Bombay for a couple of weeks, she'd written, where she'd taken a short break from the work she was doing in Jharkhand, the first time she'd returned to that city after the two of them had gone there four years before. She'd gone for a walk along the coast and had been reminded of the walk they'd taken there on the last day of their trip, had wondered how he was doing, whether his time since returning to Sri Lanka had given him everything he sought. She thought of him from time to time and hoped he was doing well, that he'd managed to find in his new home, with the passage of time, a solution to all his yearning, concluding the body of the email by attaching to that very specific word, yearning, the almost paradoxical idea of a solution, then signing off with only her first initial.

The message revealed nothing of the nature of Anjum's occasional thoughts of him, Krishan had noted almost immediately, and made no mention either of how Anjum's own life in the previous years had been, whether the home she'd set up in rural Jharkhand with her activist friends had given her what she wanted, whether she was fulfilled or disenchanted, satisfied or disappointed with what life had brought. It was unclear whether her decision to write now was related to some process of taking stock, of reflecting on other paths she might have taken or might still take, or whether on the other hand it was a matter only of disinterested curiosity, of the ordinary, passing interest that people often had in the lives of their former lovers. She'd written, too, as though their parting of ways had been mutual, as though each of them had been moved in their own directions by their own separate desires and histories, attributing a kind of agency to him that, he knew, he hadn't actually possessed in the relationship. Anjum had decided to leave Delhi long before she met him, had been planning for some time to make a base in Jharkhand with her friends and other activists she knew, with her comrades as she often put it without irony. The limited nature of their time together in Delhi had been decided therefore from the very beginning, and already from the beginning their future separation was something he'd known he'd have to plan for and expect. He himself had loosely considered the possibility of leaving Delhi before meeting Anjum, of abandoning the life he'd built there over several years and the PhD program he'd recently begun, of returning to Sri Lanka to contribute somehow to the efforts to rebuild and recover after the war. He'd become obsessed, in the years since the end of the fighting, with the massacres that had taken place in the northeast, become more and more possessed by guilt for having been spared, coming to long for the kind of life he might lead if he left the inert spaces of academia he'd become sequestered in and went to live and work in a place that actually meant something to him. This abstract longing to be in his imagined homeland had receded to the periphery of his mind soon after meeting Anjum, for whom, he realized very quickly, he was willing to abandon all his other hopes and plans, so unparalleled was their time together, so unlike anything that had come before or since. He'd hoped as they became closer that Anjum would consider rethinking her own plans, that she would consider including him in her new life or at least giving him access to her once she moved away, but she seldom took up any of the allusions he made to the possibility of a shared future together, implying with a combination of silences and stray remarks that the project she was beginning signified a complete break from her life in Delhi, a break that would be compromised if she remained with him after she moved.

It was their relationship, ironically, that had given content to his abstract earlier notion of return, not so much through conversations they had, since Anjum seemed reluctant to discuss her work in much detail with him, as through the example she herself embodied of what a life organized around a social or political vision could be. She didn't look down on his academic pursuits exactly, but he could tell she gave them little importance, and the longer he spent in her presence the more respectable his earlier ideas of abandoning academia seemed, the more earnestly he began to wonder whether a life governed by some ideal of collective action was possible for him as well. Anjum's unwavering dedication to the women's and labor movements she worked for in Delhi had already been making him feel, almost as a kind of self-defense, that he too needed to devote himself to a cause larger and more encompassing than himself, and knowing that he'd be unable to remain in Delhi once she left, driven by a need to prove both to himself and to her that he had a cause of his own, an independent destiny that would lead him somewhere with or without her, he'd actively begun redirecting his thoughts of the future toward the idea of a life in the northeast of Sri Lanka. It was a naïve idea in a way, since he had no notion what social work in the former war zone would entail, had none of the specific skills or experiences that would help him in this kind of vocation, but unable to bear the thought of waiting impassively as Anjum's impending departure drew nearer he'd begun to cultivate once more his sense of having a destiny in that place he'd never actually lived, fantasizing about what it would be like to walk over the same land his forebears had, to help create out of near annihilation the possibility of

some new and compelling future, as though living a life simplified in the way that only war can simplify he too would be able
to find something worth surrendering to.

It was strange to think how much had changed between
then and now, Krishan thought as he stood there in front of the
window, not in any sudden or decisive way but simply with the
decision to move back and the slow accumulation of time, how
what had once seemed like a distant, inaccessible, almost mysti-
cal place was now such an integral part of him. The predominant associations he'd had of the northeast for most of his life
had been formed during short trips to Trincomalee and Vavuniya when he was a child and a longer trip to Jaffna during
the cease-fire, when he was seventeen or eighteen, from the
painfully nostalgic accounts he'd always heard from older relatives living abroad about how idyllic their childhoods in the village had been. For most of his life he'd visualized, when he
thought of the northeast, wide landscapes of salt flats and palmyra trees, the copper-colored dirt roads of the Vanni and the
tracts of hard, dry earth that made up most of the peninsula,
the piercing, lilting rhythms of devotional music rising up from
temples during festival season, the sound of people speaking
their untainted Tamil loudly and musically, without restraint.
These images had filled him with a sense of freedom, with the
possibility of living a life radically different from his own, but
they'd been suffused at the same time with a dreamlike quality
that made it hard to think about them in any concrete way, just
as the news that arrived each day in the newspapers about shell-
ings and skirmishes, about advances, retreats, and cease-fires,
had always been of importance and concern but rarely disrupted the flow of events in his own life in the south of the

country, part of the white noise of life that he'd learned since childhood to take for granted.

It was only much later that events in the northeast began to penetrate more deeply into the pattern of his everyday life, toward the end of the war in 2008 and 2009 when it was beginning to seem, for the first time, that the Tigers might be defeated, and with them the idea of a Tamil-speaking state in the northeast. He'd been in the final year of his undergraduate course in Delhi at the time, in the midst of applying for graduate programs in political science, and he could remember spending days trying without success to work in the blissfully ignorant silence of his college library, anxiously refreshing the news websites he kept permanently open on his computer at the time. There were rumors of vast numbers of civilians being killed by the army, and he'd known very well that the government's account of a humanitarian rescue mission in the northeast was a falsification, that nothing he read in the newspapers could be trusted. He'd spent hours poring through the internet in English and Tamil, going page by page through blogs, forums, and news sites that shared images and videos taken during the last months of fighting, most of these sites set up by diasporic Tamils who posted material that survivors had taken on cellphones and cameras and managed somehow to send abroad. The internet, he realized, was rife with the civilian photographic archives of recent wars around the world, each one a seemingly endless maze of nameless violence, and in the months following the war's end he'd spent much of his time exploring these archives at leisure, gazing blankly at images of bloated bodies and severed limbs, of molested corpses, burning tents, and screaming children, many of which remained imprinted in his mind with disturbing clarity. It was impossible to forget these images once they'd been glimpsed, not just because of the violence they showed but also because of their strikingly amateur quality, for unlike the highly aestheticized, almost tasteful shots of war one often came across in books and magazines, the images he found online were of jarringly poor composition. The images were grainy and blurred, carelessly framed and focused—a ruptured tube of toothpaste on the ground beside a corpse, a stunned old woman swatting flies from her wounded leg—as though taken on the run or as though the individuals taking them didn't want to look at what they were capturing. They were images, he couldn't help feeling, that he wasn't supposed to see, depicting people in positions they would sooner die than be discovered in, the fear in their eyes due less to the terror of the situation than the terror of being captured in states of such intimate agony, their gazes filling him with shame even as he was unable to turn away.

For a long time the horror these images elicited remained buried inside him, a morbid reality that he was constantly feeding and yet unable to express, as though unable to fully believe or understand what they depicted. It was only when the Channel Four documentary came out in 2011, accusing the government of war crimes and genocide, when later that year the UN published its report giving an estimate of how many civilians had died, that he was finally able to speak about what had happened, to accept that the images he'd become obsessed with were not some strange, perverted creation of his subconscious life, that they represented things that had really happened in the country he was from. Even now he felt ashamed thinking about his initial reluctance to acknowledge the magnitude of what

had happened at the end of the war, as though he'd been hesitant to believe the evidence on his computer screen because his
own poor, violated, stateless people were the ones alleging it, as
though he'd been unable to take the suffering of his own people seriously till it was validated by the authority of a panel of
foreign experts, legitimized by a documentary narrated by a
clean-shaven white man standing in front of a camera in suit
and tie. Like most Tamils his age living outside the war zone,
whether Colombo or Chennai or Paris or Toronto, he'd
watched the documentary and read the report several times,
had continued trying to find out everything he could afterward,
reading every article and essay that came out in both English
and Tamil, watching all the interviews he could find with survivors on YouTube. His initial disbelief gave way first to shock,
then to anger, and then to shame at his own easy existence, this
shame giving rise, over the months that followed, to an un-
canny sense of unreality, as though the world he was inhabiting
in Delhi was somehow illusory, his courses at university and
future academic plans, the protests and demonstrations he
went to almost as a pastime, the various friends, lovers, and
crushes who made up his social life. Nothing around him
seemed to register the extent of what had happened—even on
the final day of the war life in college went on more or less as
usual, everyone immersed in studying for their end-of-term
exams—and this incongruity between his environment and
what was going on inside him—his growing sense that the
world as he understood it had come to an end—led him to feel
that the spaces he inhabited lacked some vital dimension of reality, that his life in Delhi was a kind of dream or hallucination.
It was probably some dissonance of this kind, it occurred to

him now, that had led so many Tamils living in foreign countries to such acts of desperation, that led that boy whose name
he could no longer remember to travel from London to Geneva so he could set himself on fire in front of the UN building
in February 2009, that led tens of thousands of protesters, most
of them refugees, to spontaneously gather three months later
on one of Toronto's major highways and bring the entire city's
traffic to a standstill—as if these exiled Tamils were willing to
go to any length to force the alien environments in which they
now lived, so far from the northeast of Sri Lanka, to come at
least briefly to a stop, to reflect or register in some way the cessation of life that they knew was occurring in their place of
birth.

Perhaps because he'd grasped the enormity of what had
happened only after everything was already over, when there
was no longer anything that could be done, perhaps because
he'd had no Tamil friends in Delhi with whom he could talk or
process his feelings, his own response to the end of the war had
taken a more inward direction. Thinking of that period now he
was slightly taken aback by the quiet intensity of his reaction,
by the unhealthy fervor with which he immersed himself in all
the images and videos he found, the diligence with which he
tried to reconstruct that situation from which he'd been spared.
He'd begun making mental timelines of the displacement of
civilians from their villages across the northeast, of the locations of the various hospitals that had come under attack by the
government, of the sites of the no-fire zones at which the worst
massacres had occurred, studying all the maps of the war zone
he could find and learning everything he could about these different places. He did his best to obtain every little piece of infor-

mation he could, noting the different kinds of shell the army had used and the different kinds of sounds they made as they fell, the weather conditions and soil composition at all the different sites of killing, guessing or inventing all the details he couldn't verify, re-creating those sites of violence in his mind so meticulously that his intention could only have been to personally inhabit them somehow. There was an element of self-hatred in these labors, he knew, a desire to punish himself for what he'd escaped by exposing himself to it as violently as he could, but it struck him now that perhaps there was also something religious in his devotion to understanding the circumstances under which so many people had been erased from the world, as though he was trying to construct, through this act of imagination, a kind of private shrine to the memory of all those anonymous lives.

Looking out through the window at the empty, endless sky, still golden yellow but streaked now by long, ribbonlike clouds of rose, Krishan thought of a poem he'd read many years before in the *Periya Purānam*, parts of which they'd had to study in some detail for literature at school. He'd had little interest in old Tamil literature at the time, had spent most classes gazing out through the window at the cricket ground next door, but the story of Poosal had, for some reason, always stayed with him. Poosal, according to the poem, was an impoverished man from a far-flung village who was possessed of unusually intense religiosity. From a young age his thoughts and feelings had always been lovingly directed toward Siva, and his entire adult life had been spent nurturing this instinctive love and trying to make it stronger. For a long time he'd been seeking a way by which he could honor his lord, the poem explained, and deciding after much reflection that the most fitting tribute would be to build a temple for Siva to live in, Poosal had energetically begun searching for all the necessary land and materials. For several months he looked into every possibility, going to every town and village in the area and meeting every important personage he knew, but gradually, after many failed attempts, it began to dawn on him that he'd never be able to obtain the resources needed to build his temple, that he was simply too poor to serve his lord the way he wished. Devastated, he sank into a state of deep despair, a condition of hopelessness he remained submerged in for some time, apparently, till reflecting on his situation one day it occurred to him that he could, instead of building a physical temple for Siva, simply build a temple for him in his mind. Stunned by the obviousness of this idea, Poosal had set to work at once. He found first a perfect plot of land in his mind, then began acquiring in his imagination all the materials that would be needed for his labor, from the smallest, most finely made tools to the heaviest slabs of stone. He solicited, mentally, all the best carpenters, masons, craftsmen, and artists, and then on an auspicious date, lovingly and attentively, laid the imaginary foundation stone deep in the center of the plot of land, following all of the stipulations set down in the relevant texts. With great care and studious rigor he began to work on the structure of the temple, refusing to sleep even at night, first completing the foundation, then adding layer upon layer to the edifice, so that over a period of several days the temple took form in his mind, from the halls and columns to the molding above the portals and the plinths. When all the towers and subsidiary shrines were completed, when the tank was dug and filled and the outer walls at last raised, he put the finial into place, saw to all the necessary details, then finally, exhausted but satisfied by his labor, chose an auspicious time for the consecration of the temple to Siva.

According to the text the king of the realm had, at the same time, been putting the final touches to a temple that he himself had been building in honor of Siva, and had happened to choose for the consecration of his temple the very same auspicious day and time that Poosal had. The royal temple was of unprecedented scale, built over many years and at vast expenditure, but the night before Siva's image was to be installed there, according to the poem, Siva appeared in the king's dreams to inform him that he wouldn't be able to attend the ceremony, that it would have to be postponed, since he'd decided instead to attend the consecration of a grand temple constructed in his honor by a man called Poosal, a loving devotee of his from the faraway village of Ninravur. Waking up the next morning, the king was stunned that a common man had built a temple that Siva preferred to the one he himself had built. He set off with his retinue for Ninravur, and when after many days of traveling they at last approached the lush groves of the village, the king ordered the locals to take him so he could see what Poosal had built. They knew who Poosal was, he was told in response, but he was a poor man, and he hadn't built any temple. The king was nonplussed on hearing this but ordered to be taken to Poosal regardless, and dismounting from his horse out of respect for the devotee he went to his modest dwelling place by foot, where he found an emaciated man sitting cross-legged on the ground, eyes closed and blissfully unaware of anything around him. The king called out to the man and asked him where his temple was, the one that everyone in the world was praising—

he'd come to see it because Lord Siva himself had said he was
going to be installed there that day. Bewildered by the regal
voice, Poosal opened his eyes with surprise and looked up at
the man speaking to him, whom he recognized at once to be
the king. He recounted humbly how he'd lacked the means to
build a physical temple for Siva, how he'd painstakingly thought
a temple into existence in his mind instead, and amazed by the
devotion of this man who'd lacked any resources and nevertheless managed to honor his lord, the king had fallen to the
ground in praise of Poosal, his fragrant garlands mingling with
the earth.

Krishan would not have been able to say, as he stood there in
his room, to what extent this poem he'd read so long ago had
influenced his reaction to the events of the war, but it occurred
to him now that the structure Poosal had constructed so meticulously in his mind was not so different, in a way, from the
one he himself had constructed in the months and years after
the war's end. He too had more or less abandoned the world
around him to cultivate a kind of alternative space in his mind,
and even if the time he'd spent dwelling in this site had been
painful rather than joyful, driven as much by shame as by love,
he too had in some way hoped that the object of his thoughts,
the suffering of his partly real, partly virtual community, might
receive through his labor a recognition it hadn't received in the
real world. Thinking of his first months working in the northeast after his return to the island, Krishan could still remember
the distinct sense he'd had of physically entering a place he'd
imagined into existence, the feeling he was moving not so
much across solid earth as across some region in the outskirts
of his mind. He'd begun working for a small, local, under-

funded NGO in Jaffna, earning little more than he needed to survive, and traveling on broken roads between bombed-out villages that glimmered with the corrugated steel and aluminum of makeshift homes, past the resentful glances of men who could no longer protect, the tired eyes of women who now bore all responsibility for the continuation of life, it was as though the scenes of prior violence he'd re-created in his mind were superimposed over everything he saw. The last shells had long since fallen, the last bodies been long since cleared, but the mood and texture of this violence suffused the places he went to such an extent that even his way of walking changed while he was in the northeast, his gait acquiring the same quiet reverence of someone moving in a cemetery or cremation ground. There were glimpses occasionally of a simplicity and beauty hearkening back to another kind of life—the joyful laughter of two girls sharing a bicycle on their way to school in the morning, the careless splashing of an old man filling up buckets of water at a well in the gathering dusk—and seeing the violence of the final years of war everywhere around him but also, at such moments, visions of possible futures, he'd given himself up to the work before him with vigorous, single-minded discipline.

He'd become, during his time in the northeast, less abstract and more grounded, more connected to the land and people that till then he'd seen mainly on screens, gradually internalizing the cyclical rhythms of rural life, where time never seemed to be heading anywhere but was always circling, returning, and repeating, bringing the self back to itself. He'd envisioned participating in some kind of dramatic change, in some kind of sudden rising or flourishing after all the pain and grief, but as

the months turned into a year and as one year turned into two
he began to realize that these visions would never be achieved,
that some forms of violence could penetrate so deeply into the
psyche that there was simply no question of fully recovering.
Recovery was something that would take decades, which even
then would be partial and ambiguous, and if he wanted to help
in a meaningful way it would have to be in a way that was sustainable for him in the long term, without having to abandon
all his needs for its sake. As his initial urgency and unity of purpose wore away, he began spending more of his weekends in
Colombo, making the seven-hour journey back home two,
sometimes even three times a month. The city had transformed
dramatically in the years since the end of the war, its widened
roads brightly lit by shop signs and electronic billboards, its skyline populated by sleek hotels and luxury apartment buildings,
its new cafés, bars, and restaurants teeming with people he
didn't know and couldn't place. Krishan registered these
changes with resentment, as if the city's sudden modernity was
in direct relation to the evisceration of the northeast, but he
couldn't help being drawn to the easy distractions this urban
life seemed to offer, and when a position opened up at one of
the large foreign NGOs in Colombo—highly bureaucratic,
well-compensated, and concerned mainly with applications
and reports—he'd decided it was time to return, not for very
long, he told himself, just until he'd saved up some money and
had a better sense of what his next steps were. He'd settled back
into life at home with his mother and grandmother after the
better part of a decade away, old habits and routines returning
but mingled with the freedoms of adulthood, his free time
spent meeting old friends and new acquaintances, seeing the

occasional or potential lover, reading and watching films at home. These small but varied pleasures had distracted him for a while, but there was a difference between pleasure that soothed and lulled one to sleep and pleasure that drew the self more widely and vividly into the world, and thinking of his return to Colombo now it seemed to him, as he stood there in front of the window, that something vital had been lost over the course of the previous year, the sense, so strong for most of his twenties, that his life could be part of some larger thing, part of some movement or vision to which he could give himself up.

Krishan turned from the window and looked around at the room in front of him, the room he'd grown up in with his younger brother and which, in the last few years, since his brother moved abroad, he'd had mostly to himself. The room was still suspended in the warm glow of early evening, but the shaft of light that fell from the window had moved along the floor, indicating that he'd been standing there for a considerable amount of time. He remembered the call from Rani's daughter and realized that he'd been thinking only about himself since returning to his room, that he'd failed to bring himself any closer to the fact of Rani's death, as though he was trying, somehow, to evade the significance of what he'd learned. He went to the dressing table, picked up his phone, and after hesitating a moment, dialed his mother's number. There was still time before her class ended but he hoped she would pick up, that in communicating the news to her he himself might better understand its meaning. The phone rang for a while before playing the network's automated message, informing him that the number he was calling was not available, and putting the phone down Krishan thought of his grandmother, who was probably sitting in her room with nothing to do. He hadn't yet told her about the call, and he could perhaps go to her room now and let her know. The news would sadden her, no doubt, but his grandmother wasn't the kind of person who was easily affected by the deaths of other people, in a way would even be grateful to learn what happened to Rani, obtaining from it the urgency and excitement that even a painful happening can generate in the life of someone without much to do. Relieved there was someone he could talk to, the one person ironically who always wanted to talk to him, he went to the door, turned the key in the lock, and took the four short steps across the vestibule that separated their rooms. It was only when he put his hand on the doorknob that he began to have doubts, realized that informing his grandmother right away might not actually be the wisest way to proceed. It was Appamma after all who would be most affected by Rani's death, Appamma who'd shared a room with Rani for more than a year and a half, and perhaps the best course of action was to keep the news from reaching her altogether, to let her go about her life with no notion that Rani had died alone in a well the night before. He remained in front of his grandmother's door, wanting to go in and talk but unsure whether it was a good idea, till feeling at last an urge to glance into her room, as if by getting a glimpse of her he would know what to do, he let go of the doorknob and knelt down in front of the door, closing his left eye and squinting in through the keyhole with his right.

2

APPAMMA'S DOOR WAS in line with the chair by the window, and peering into her room Krishan could make out her figure from behind, her body slumped forward on the chair, her arms placed along the armrests, and her legs stretched out on the stool in front of her, in accordance with her belief that keeping them horizontal was beneficial for her circulation. Her head was tilted to the side and hanging forward slightly, as if she were staring down at her lap, and from time to time it jerked up like something had startled her before sinking back down. His grandmother, Krishan realized as he stared through the keyhole, had accidentally fallen asleep. It was not an occurrence that was rare, given her difficulty sleeping during the nights, when she sometimes got up to go to the bathroom four or five times before dawn, but it wasn't something he could have counted on or expected either, especially not in the evenings when she was generally most on her guard. It happened

usually only in the early afternoons, when she was lying in bed
with the afternoon movie playing on the TV, very occasionally
in the late mornings too, when she was sitting in her chair waiting for lunch to be brought up to her room. His grandmother
didn't like being caught sleeping in the daytime, he knew, especially if it was obvious that she hadn't fallen asleep intentionally. Accidentally falling asleep indicated that she wasn't in
complete control of her body, that sometimes her body acted
of its own accord, independently of her own wishes, which
wasn't something she could let other people think. If she ever
woke up after a nap and discovered that someone had come
into her room she would strenuously deny that she'd been
sleeping, even if she hadn't been asked or challenged, would
claim to have been resting with her eyes closed, enjoying the
breeze, even if just a moment before her mouth had been hanging wide open and her snoring audible through the door. Seeing no reason to hurt her pride Krishan always avoided going
near his grandmother at such times, had learned, over the years,
if for some reason he did need to wake her up, to make a loud
noise from afar before entering her room, to bang a door or
pretend to sneeze so she would have time to compose herself
before he was in front of her. He took these measures in part so
she wouldn't feel anxious or embarrassed, so she wouldn't feel
the need to persuade him she'd been awake and not asleep, but
even more than this because it bothered him that his grandmother was willing to tell such obvious lies to convince him she
was in good health. Almost everyone told falsehoods, it was
true, in order to maintain in their minds a certain image of
themselves, but whereas everyone else told these lies skillfully,
without exposing the insecurities at their source, his grand-

mother's lies revealed that she was capable now of only the most transparent attempts at maintaining her preferred self-image, betraying herself far more in uttering them than if she'd simply kept silent.

Krishan moved back a little from the keyhole. He didn't want to wake his grandmother up, and was sure now that he shouldn't inform her about Rani's death, that for the time being at least it was best to let her continue existing in her state of ignorance. He didn't want to return to the stillness of his room either, and feeling an urge suddenly to put as much distance as possible between himself and the house, it occurred to him that he could leave to go for a walk, that being out in the open for a while, smoking a cigarette in his usual spot, he would be able to collect his thoughts. He went to his room, changed quickly into a pair of trousers, and put his pack of cigarettes and lighter into his pocket, left his phone on the desk and went downstairs. Stepping out of the house he saw with a little relief that it was still relatively bright outside, the sky still a pale, weightless blue, and closing the gate behind him he made his way up the lane with quick, determined strides. He passed the neighboring houses, the construction site where the workers were finishing up for the day, the sound of trickling water audible from their makeshift shower on the ground floor, turned left at the end of the lane and headed in the direction of Marine Drive. An un-broken stream of cars and vans was rushing past in both direc-tions, the vastness of the sea glimmering beyond them, and crossing the road as soon as a break emerged in the traffic he began to head south, keeping to the pavement between the road and railway tracks except for occasional stretches where the pavement seemed to disappear. Taking his lighter out and sparking it with his thumb he looked around distractedly as he walked, at a parked three-wheeler with an icon of the Buddha attached to its rear window, concentric circles of colored LED lights creating the illusion of a halo revolving around his head, at an elderly Muslim woman doing her best to keep up with a young girl and boy, her grandchildren most likely, who were tugging at her hands. Cars, vans, and three-wheelers continued to rush past in both directions, as though keen to avoid the twilight, and the people passing him seemed fully absorbed in their various destinations too, tired commuters hurrying to the station to catch the next train home, aging men and women taking their evening exercise in T-shirts and tracksuits, swinging their arms with exaggerated motion as they power walked toward some imaginary goal. It took a while to fall into a rhythm after the quiet of his room, to assimilate the sound and movement of the city into a workable state of equilibrium, but putting more distance from their house he began to feel calmer, to relax into a more even pace as he made his way along his habitual route.

His walks had become an unexpected routine in the previous few months, one of the few effective strategies he'd found for escaping the restlessness that had begun taking hold when he returned in the evenings from work. In his first months of being in Colombo he'd still been engrossed by all the possibilities of life in the city, by the prospect of going out in the evenings, drinking and smoking weed, being obnoxious or lighthearted with friends, meeting attractive people with whom he could flirt. These activities had given movement and structure to his time, a sense of something to look forward to, the possibility of an encounter that could change the course of his life, but perhaps because he'd met so few people in Colombo who really moved him, whether intellectually or politically or romantically, perhaps because he was less easily sustained by the things that had attracted and stimulated him when he was younger, the desires that led him to move back and the short-lived satisfactions they offered soon came to feel misleading, like distractions or diversions from a more basic absence. Solitude in the past had always been a pleasurable way to pass time, a kind of consolation for the demands and disappointments of the world, a tender solicitousness he could obtain simply by withdrawing into himself, but a quiet restlessness began to surface whenever he found himself alone at home in the evenings, as he moved here and there in his room, wasted time on the internet, tried to read books he'd been meaning to read. He tried to cope in whatever way he could, even if it meant going to his grandmother's room and listening to her discuss how mosquitoes were managing to enter the room despite her precautions, but the unease continued to lurk just below the surface, growing continuously over the course of the afternoons and evenings and reaching a peak during the last, dying moments of the day, when the sun was setting and the golden yellow light giving way, suddenly and dramatically, first to pink, then to violet, and finally to the lighter and darker blues of night. There was something about twilight that heightened his anxiety, which brought it to the surface of his consciousness and made it palpable, as though with the gradual disappearance of the horizon the last hopes and promises of the day too were disappearing from view, another day coming and going with nothing to show for itself.

He would set off well before the sky began darkening, moving with an intentionally slow, steady pace meant to calm him down, taking long, meandering routes through different parts of the city at first, out of a desire to familiarize himself with its significantly altered topography. No matter how many different paths he took he continued feeling out of place amid all the new signs and façades, markers of a new trajectory of development that he could find no way of relating to, and gradually he began circumscribing his walks to the residential areas closer to home, to the numerous small, scraggy lanes and byways of Wellawatta and Dehiwala, areas he'd rarely explored when he was younger on account of the war, the army checkpoints put up every hundred meters and the omnipresent risk of being interrogated and detained. He passed the small, old houses, most of them with people living in them, some of them converted into small offices and showrooms, passed the newer apartment buildings occupied mostly by Tamil and Muslim families, and thinking as he walked of the weight of life that all these structures contained he would begin to feel less burdened, as if with every step he took from his own house he was leaving behind some heavy and unnecessary part of himself. He was still full witness to the dramatic changes occurring in the sky above, but something about being outside and in the direct presence of these changes made them easier to bear, as if being out in the open, unbound by four walls, a floor, and a ceiling, whatever was weighing him down in his chest was free to spread out and dissipate. Listening to the sounds of the waves breaking gently against the rocks, the birds flapping their wings against the push of the warm breeze, he gradually became less restive, the present ceasing to be a void and becoming instead, for a short period of time, a place he could inhabit comfortably and securely. There were few moods that could persist after all when one was in full view of earth and sky, and even the more deep-seated moods one carried through the course of the day—those moods that maintained themselves in the chest against all the conflicting feelings that came one's way while out in the world—even these moods thinned slowly into nothingness when confronted by the immensity of the horizon, so that one could feel, at such moments, if not satisfaction or contentment then the peace at least of a brief inner extinction. When he returned to the enclosed spaces of his house and room after these walks he was usually too tired to feel the unease that had led him to leave, and getting on his bed, salty from perspiration and the breeze of the sea, a pleasant ache in his calves and thighs, he would lie there in the cocoon of his exhaustion, getting up only when it was time at half past eight to go downstairs and bring dinner up to his grandmother, when it was already dark and the most difficult part of the day, the transition from evening to night, was over and done with.

It was during these walks that he'd once more begun smoking, at first if only because smoking a cigarette at the halfway point allowed him to justify his otherwise purposeless walks, to feel he wasn't just walking because he had nothing to do or nowhere to be. He'd smoked casually since going to India for college, where most of his friends smoked too, but it had only become a serious habit later, when he started spending time with Anjum, who smoked frequently and with an elegance he found himself wanting to emulate. He'd given the habit up on moving to the northeast, mostly because of how harshly smoking was viewed in the environments in which he worked, though perhaps, it occurred to him now, his disavowal also had to do with Anjum, with the more general attempt he'd made to distance himself from her after they parted ways, to eliminate not only the various traces of their relationship that remained on his phone and computer but also the various gestures and phrases he'd picked up during their time together, most of which continued displaying themselves in his body despite his efforts to discard them. He hadn't felt the need to resume smoking upon returning to Colombo, not wanting to deal with hiding the habit from his mother while living at home, had limited his consumption initially to cigarettes he scrounged when drinking or joints he smoked with his friends. The occasion for his return to the habit had come only a couple of months earlier, when stopping at a small snack shop to buy a Milo during one of his walks, he'd observed the man in front of him asking for three single Gold Leafs, paying for them and collecting them from the counter with a self-satisfaction that made him wonder what was stopping him from doing the same. He'd asked for a Gold Leaf and a box of matches when it was his turn, had walked for a while with the cigarette tucked carefully in his shirt pocket, bringing it up to his face every so often to savor the smell of the tobacco. Crouching at the corner of a small, deserted lane, he'd struck a match and put the flame delicately to the tip, taking pleasure in each of the various motions, in ashing the cigarette with a sharp tap of his index finger, in bringing it leisurely back to his lips, listening to the burning of paper as he sucked in slowly and watching the smoke waft up in the air as he exhaled. He smoked a cigarette at the halfway point of each of his next few walks, soon began buying not one but two, one for smoking immediately and the other for before he went to sleep, transporting the extra cigarette with care in his shirt pocket, taking pains to ensure it remained crisp and unbent, going out to the balcony later in the night when no one else was awake to smoke in silence under the stars. The number of cigarettes he smoked proliferated in the weeks that followed, so that soon he started buying packs instead of singles and replaced his matchbox with a lighter. Smoking became a way to help time pass, an activity he could look forward to in the intervening periods, something that made the present more bearable even when he wasn't smoking because it meant the present was leading to something good. Unlike the prospect of going out in the nights, which engendered hopes and expectations that were ultimately illusory, the pleasure of smoking a cigarette was a real one, a pleasure, however modest, that was itself and nothing else, that contained no false promises, and that he knew he could rely on as long as his supply of cigarettes remained steady. He didn't stop going out in the nights or trying to meet new people, but smoking allowed him to accept that there was nothing more than what was visible before him, opening the present up, making it more expansive but also more inhabitable, so that even when he returned home with none of his hopes for the night fulfilled he was consoled by the certainty of one last cigarette before bed.

Looking up Krishan saw that he was coming to one of his preferred spots for smoking, chosen because he could sit there by the water without being visible to pedestrians on the road. Veering right from the pavement he made his way up the grassy mound to the railway tracks, paused to make sure there was no train coming, since there was a news story almost every month about a pedestrian or cyclist being knocked down somewhere or other by a train, then crossed to the other side. He walked

down to the slender outcropping of rocks that formed the
boundary between land and sea, where making his way to a
section that was relatively free of rubbish, he took out his pack
of cigarettes and lighter and lowered himself down. There was
a young couple sitting a good distance to his right, their bodies
not touching but their heads leaning together as though sharing a secret, while far off to the left a few men in tattered clothes
were fishing on the rocks closest to the water, appearing and
disappearing among the thick clouds of spray. Krishan turned
and looked out at the silver-gray sea that stretched out calmly
in front of him, at the golden-gray sky, backlit by the sun, suspended like a canopy over the horizon. Drawing a cigarette
from the pack he rotated it slowly between his fingers, as if
surprised by its insubstantiality, then turning away from the
water and hunching to guard against the breeze, he lit the cigarette and took in a long first drag. He tried to direct his thoughts
toward Rani, toward the unexpected and slightly absurd nature
of the way she'd died, the strikingly mechanical tone of her
daughter as she'd relayed the events over the phone, but found
himself dwelling, for some reason, not so much on Rani or her
daughter as on the scene he'd glimpsed through the keyhole of
his grandmother's door, the sight of his grandmother so un-
knowingly, helplessly asleep. Why the sight of her sleeping
bothered him so much was hard to say, especially when there
was something far more urgent and important to think about,
but gazing out at the water that extended from the rocks at his
feet, his eyes drifting across its shifting gray surfaces, all he
could think about was the vulnerability that had emanated
from her sleeping body, a vulnerability that should have been
obvious but had caught him by surprise, as if the real condition

of his grandmother had been invisible to him all this time, as if
he himself had been complicit in keeping it hidden.

His grandmother's withdrawal from the world had begun,
of course, long before he was born, but the event that first made
him conscious of its inevitable trajectory, Krishan could remember, the event that first made it clear to him that she would
not remain in his life forever, had occurred when he was twelve
or thirteen, when his grandmother must already have been seventy or seventy-one years old. She'd been working in the garden that afternoon, according to what she told them afterward,
plucking out weeds from a spot in the corner where she planned
to plant a few bitter-gourd seeds she'd obtained. It hadn't been
strenuous work but she'd found herself, as she came up the
stairs afterward, panting in a heavy, alarmingly hurried way,
and despite going straight to her room and sitting down on her
chair to rest the panting had become more pronounced, followed shortly afterward by a kind of shivering that radiated out
from deep inside her chest. They'd taken her at once to the
hospital, where a battery of tests run in quick succession indicated that one of the arteries near her heart was clogged. She
hadn't exactly had a heart attack or a stroke, the doctors said,
but she was in fact in danger of both, and it was advised that
something called a bypass surgery be performed, an operation
in which the length of a vein that ran from her right ankle
to her right calf would be extracted and used to replace the
problematic artery near her heart. Of the days that followed,
Krishan could remember only his surprise at how easily his
grandmother seemed to submit to everything that took place,
how willingly she seemed to give her body up to the authority
of the doctors and nurses around her. When she returned

home after the two weeks of monitoring that followed the surgery, seemingly healthy and flattered, clearly, by all the attention being lavished upon her, she'd given no sign of seeing the
events of the previous month as anything but a brief, almost
refreshing interruption of her daily existence. With a satisfaction she hardly concealed she furnished all the relatives who
visited her in the following days with a detailed account of
everything that had happened, from the initial panting and
shivering, which she always clarified was not a heart attack or a
stroke, to her final discharge from the hospital three weeks
later, dwelling at length on the quality of the various meals
she'd been served before ending her account by lifting her sari
to display the operation scar on her right leg, as if to provide
evidence that all she'd described really had occurred, that nothing had been fabricated merely for the sake of her audience's
entertainment.

It had been his habit, at the time, to go to her room in the
nights to talk to her before she went to bed, and he could remember how, in the weeks and months after the operation, as
the nervousness and excitement of the event were finally absorbed back into the mundane exigencies of daily life, Appamma's conversation during these nighttime visits came more and
more to center on the subject of her health. Her health was
something his grandmother had always talked about to some
degree, but it became now the topic toward which every conversation with her invariably converged. He would go to her
room just as she was turning off the lights, around nine o'clock
when the last TV show she followed for the day had finished,
and lying on the bed next to her in the darkness he would listen
as she discussed how many times she'd walked up and down

the hall that day for exercise, how she still cooked and cleaned and was therefore fitter than other people her age, how any medical professional who met her for the first time was always astonished when she revealed how old she was, since she looked much younger, they never failed to tell her, than any other person in their late sixties they knew. He would speak from time to time during these conversations, either to show his grandmother he was listening or when it was obvious she wanted him to confirm or verify something she said, but mostly he remained silent, detecting in the way she spoke something that made him hesitant to change the subject or interrupt her, a kind of confessional quality in her voice and the room, as though what she was sharing with him were not something she would share with anybody else, a kind of fear or anxiety that she was reluctant to communicate directly but which, as they lay next to each other in the darkness, their faces invisible to each other, he could sense in her body beside him. Only rarely did this fear or anxiety enter the actual words she spoke, usually only after she'd been talking for some time, when she'd established to her satisfaction that she was still as healthy as before despite having needed the surgery, which, in her view, was nothing but a precautionary measure. She would mention at these times, lowering her voice as though making a parenthetical remark or an unimportant aside, that so long as she could take care of herself she would be fine, that the only thing she didn't want was to become incapacitated, to be unable to walk or dress or bathe herself, to be confined to her bed, a nuisance and a disturbance to others. Not knowing what to say at first Krishan responded to these admissions with silence, but as he grew accustomed to them he learned to tell his grandmother

that she was wrong, that she wouldn't be a nuisance or a disturbance to look after, that he at least would take care of her happily, without any sense of obligation. It was a response she
appreciated but usually chose to ignore, preferring to focus instead on the possibility that she would never be immobile or
confined to bed, that she would always be able to take care of
herself and would never have to worry, therefore, about being
a burden.

The years that followed had brought with them various
signs of deterioration, the first appearance of the swelling that
eventually beset both her legs, the discoloration of the small
patch of skin just above her collarbone, the jarring whiteness of
which none of the ointments she applied could efface. Most of
these developments Appamma dismissed as either temporary
or irrelevant, and it was not till five or six years later, when relatives were visiting from Toronto and they'd decided, on the last
day of the visit, to go to a nearby Indian restaurant for dinner,
that she was once more forced to confront the fears and anxieties that had surfaced in the months following the operation.
There'd always been a kind of buried tension in Appamma's
face when she was compelled to leave the house and traverse
the unfamiliar terrain of public spaces, an anxious strain in her
features as she navigated the slender line between shame and
danger, shame, on the one hand, of the ungainliness of her
body and uncertainty of her feet, of the fact she was slowing
down everyone else in the party and becoming an object of
pity, danger, on the other hand, of trying too hard to keep up,
of making a misstep and falling, which would of course have
only made her even more an object of pity. Krishan always tried
to slow down in such situations, letting the rest of the party go

on ahead while he walked in step with his grandmother, pretending they had the same natural pace so she would feel less pressure to keep up with everyone else, sometimes also offering her his own arm for support, though this was a gesture she usually rejected, thrusting his hand aside as if it were an insult. These offers to help were, in fact, mostly unnecessary, but it was at just such a moment, approaching a part of the restaurant where the floor was very slightly raised, wanting to show their relatives she was capable of walking without help, that rejecting his hand with a flourish Appamma had tripped and fallen facedown, striking the floor in a strangely soundless fashion, as if the impact had been absorbed wholly into the soft mass of her large body. In the sudden rush to help often witnessed at such times—the immediate scrambling of the rest of the party, the quick, purposeful strides of waiters moving toward the scene of the accident, the scraping of chairs as diners stood up and tried to express concern on their faces—in the sudden rush Appamma struggled to assert herself, to smile dismissively despite being visibly shaken, to get up on unsteady legs and continue moving toward their table. Someone immediately brought over a chair and she was made to sit down right there in the middle of the restaurant, given a thorough examination while all the waiters and diners looked on uncomfortably, unsure whether or not to retain their postures of concern. She'd managed somehow to avoid the hard edges of the tables and chairs on her way down, but despite her protests and to her great embarrassment—it had been just a little fall, she argued almost indignantly, the kind that happened to everyone from time to time—it was decided that they should ask for takeaway and have their dinner at home.

It was partly at the instigation of the relatives who'd witnessed the fall that Krishan's mother had bought the walking
stick, a somewhat costly purchase that Appamma reacted to
with an irritation bordering on hostility. She refused to use the
walking stick despite all her daughter-in-law's attempts to persuade her, and because she'd become noticeably more cautious
after the accident, moving more circumspectly around the
house, clutching the furniture and walls for support, her
daughter-in-law's insistence eventually fell away. The walking
stick assumed a more or less permanent position in the corner
of her room next to the TV, like a souvenir from a trip or a me-
mento of a special event, and the question of her mobility was
forgotten until a weekend three years later, when standing in
front of the gas cooker in the kitchen, frying the sardines Krishan ate for lunch—the only real cooking she was allowed to do
by that point, and which she insisted on doing so he would feel
indebted to her in some way—Appamma had once more collapsed to the ground. Once more she somehow managed to
avoid striking her head on the way down, and when she was
rushed to the hospital immediately afterward it was discovered
that her heart had stopped beating for a few seconds while she
was cooking, as a result of which she'd lost consciousness and
fallen. The natural signaling system that was responsible for the
regular beating of the heart sometimes weakened with age, the
doctors explained, more to Krishan and his mother than to Appamma, who looked on powerlessly from her wheelchair as
they discussed her condition among themselves. If, for whatever reason, a signal didn't go through properly, the heart could
skip a beat, which could sometimes lead to dizziness or faint-
ing. The only way to prevent a more serious accident happen-

ing in the future was to install a small battery-operated device called a pacemaker inside her chest, which, by producing its own electrical signaling, would keep the heart beating steadily even if its natural signaling system failed momentarily or broke down.

Appamma had feared she'd be forced to use the walking stick upon returning home, and buoyed by this unexpected diagnosis, which indicated that she wasn't to blame for the fall and that it wouldn't happen again if a pacemaker were installed, she energetically assented to being operated upon a second time. Sensing that her daughter-in-law would probably try to make her use the walking stick regardless, she began rehearsing arguments she could use to defend herself, that the unusual curvature of the walking stick's handle made it difficult to hold, that the walking stick actually increased the likelihood she would fall, that it was in fact safer for her to walk holding the walls and furniture for support. She returned from the hospital ready to negate her daughter-in-law's efforts, feeling as strong and vital as ever, as if with the aid of the battery-operated device installed in her heart she was now invincible. Entering her room she found, waiting for her next to the bed, not the walking stick that had been bought three years before but a new apparatus, a walker consisting of four hollow, rubber-tipped aluminum legs, joined at the top by a U-shaped frame with foam grips on each of the three sides. Caught off guard by this new device, Appamma's feeble attempts to object were easily countered by Krishan's mother, who was prepared this time to put up a fight. She'd already been lucky twice, his mother argued, and if she fell again, for whatever reason, she could be bedridden for the rest of her life—if that happened it was she, her daughter-in-law, no one else, who would have to bear the burden of looking after her. Appamma immediately fell silent, pierced by the thought of being reduced to an obligation. When her daughter-in-law left the room she simply sat there staring at the walker, as if at an unwanted guest she could not send away, and for the next three days she hardly spoke or left her room. Krishan's mother wondered whether she'd been too harsh, whether she should relax her demand or find some other way to appease her mother-in-law, but then after lunch on the fourth day Appamma emerged from her room clutching the walker tightly with both hands, her eyebrows pinched in concentration as she inched her way matter-of-factly into the hall. She didn't say a word as she sat down in her usual place on the armchair in front of the TV, as if there were no significance in the fact she'd come out of her room with the walker, as if there'd been no adjustment or concession to reality in her decision to use the new apparatus. Sensing her reluctance to acknowledge the change Krishan and his mother exchanged sidelong glances but pretended not to notice, and from then on, as if she'd gone through a kind of metamorphosis over the three days cocooned in her room, Appamma used the walker whenever she needed to go anywhere. She would push the walker forward a short distance, lean her weight on it, then take a step forward before repeating this sequence of movements, which soon became so second nature that it was hard to imagine her moving differently. When relatives came to visit she would demonstrate its different features, how the height could be adjusted by means of the metal knobs on the legs, how the frame that connected the front legs to the back legs could, by swiveling, allow for a greater range of movement when she turned, as though she'd come to see the walker not as a mark of weakness or vulnerability but of strength and capability, as something that postponed and even halted her withdrawal and therefore something she could accept as part of herself.

The walker didn't help her negotiate the staircase, of course, and over the course of the subsequent years Appamma was forced to limit the frequency of her visits downstairs. She would decide to make the journey a full day in advance, and approaching the stairs with intense focus when the moment arrived she would clutch the banister face-on and move not forward but sideways, parallel to the banister, first bringing her lead foot down to the stair below and then, looking down to check that the foot was firmly planted, bringing her back foot down beside it. Krishan or his mother would stand on the step directly below watching every movement, ready to catch her in case she stumbled, and when after several tense, painstaking minutes Appamma made it all the way down she would take a moment to catch her breath, exalting in a combination of triumph and relief. Clutching the walker, which was always brought down beforehand, she would head immediately in the direction of the kitchen, where moving along the counters with renewed vigor she would throw open all the drawers and cabinets, peer inside the various compartments of the fridge, try to take stock of all the kitchen's contents so she could form some notion of what had changed and what had stayed the same, like an emigrant who returns from exile to visit her native land and is consumed with understanding how things stand. The loss of this knowledge would have been too great to bear, and when the trips downstairs finally came to an end Appamma compensated for her loss of physical access to the

kitchen by means of more oblique strategies, the most important of which was to ask, pointedly and unceasingly, as many
questions as possible about what was happening downstairs.
Appamma had always asked about matters she couldn't verify
directly—why had Krishan been late from work, who'd rung
the doorbell, how come her younger brother in London hadn't
called in so long—but she began making these inquiries with
much greater frequency and insistence than before, piecing together theories about the external world on the basis of the information she gathered like an injured general who cannot
participate in the battle and is forced, as a result, to rely on secondhand reports and satellite images of the fighting. Having
little else to do on weekday afternoons and weekends, when
there was nothing to watch on TV, she devoted herself to the
formulation and development of these theories, coming up
with more and more questions to ask as they grew in complexity, since there came, with the increase in theoretical complexity, a need for further, more specific information by which they
could be confirmed, disproved, or elaborated. Krishan and his
mother found themselves, soon, in thrall to endless questions
about a world that neither of them had any interest discussing. They would tiptoe past Appamma's room, hoping she
wouldn't hear them and call out to them, would cut short their
conversations with her as if they had somewhere else to be,
Krishan's mother especially, who was burdened enough having
to do all the shopping, cooking, and housework without being
forced to justify every banal detail to her mother-in-law. Even as
she became aware of their attempts to avoid her Appamma
pursued her quest for information relentlessly, asking them
both the same questions so as to cross-check their answers for

consistency, furrowing her eyebrows and pursing her lips till she had every detail down correctly, as though the continued movement of the world upon its axis hung upon whether the small chili plant in the garden was bearing fruit or whether left-overs remained from the previous day's fish curry, as though something catastrophic could happen to the transition of day to night and night to day if she failed to properly oversee these matters from afar.

Krishan had always thought of death as something that happened suddenly or violently, an event that took place at a specific time and then was over, but thinking now of his grandmother as he sat there on the rocks, it struck him that death could also be a long, drawn-out process, a process that took up a significant portion of the life of the dying person. It was an obvious fact, in retrospect, but perhaps because of how his father had died, in the Central Bank bombing of 1996, perhaps because of the frequency of sudden and violent death in the country in which he was born, he'd never really stopped to consider the fact that people could also die slowly, that dying could be a process one had to negotiate over the course of many years. Ever since he was old enough to follow the news he'd been hearing of people dying in abrupt and unpredictable ways—in road accidents and race riots, by snakebite, tidal wave, and shards of shrapnel—and it had never really occurred to him that for most people in most places, even Sri Lanka, death was a process that began decades before the heart stopped beating, one with its own logic and trajectory. It was a process that began almost imperceptibly, with the minor changes in appearance that one was inclined at first to regard as merely superficial, the loosening of the skin, the thinning of the hair, and the deepening of the lines of the face, which only afterward began expressing itself in deeper, more unsettling ways, in the stiffening of joints and flattening of reflexes, in the subtle but suggestive deteriorations of motor activity that led sooner or later to constant second-guessing, making it impossible to see what was happening as merely skin deep. Changes occurring deep inside the body began making themselves felt, changes in energy, menstruation, metabolism, and libido that appeared with the force of inevitability, and tests taken, if one had the privilege of taking tests, showed that cholesterol or sugar or blood pressure had increased and that the body's internal indicators would need to be more carefully monitored, unless they didn't, in which case the relief that accompanied this news forced one to prepare for the occurrence of such developments anyway. In either case one began to treat oneself differently, in either case one became wary of overexerting oneself, of not eating in the right ways, not sleeping enough, or not doing enough exercise, in either case one began acting with increasing restraint and participating in life more selectively, a decrease in participation that was not so much a personal decision as the defining feature of aging: of the slow, meticulous process by which the same body that once moved so freely and easily between environments begins, gradually, to withdraw from what is called the world. The bones became brittle, the muscles slackened, and soon one could no longer walk at the pace of others; one's aptitude and reliability decreased, one was less able to do one's work, whether one's work was inside the house or outside. Vision worsened and so did hearing, things had to be repeated because they went unheard or were forgotten, and soon one ceased working altogether, venturing out into the so-called real world even less. Soon one became even less aware of what was happening to other people in other places, frequenting only a few specific locations, the hospital for checkups and the houses of a few relatives, so that soon, scarcely able to move, one was confined not just to one's house or flat but one's room. Interaction with the outside world slowed to a stop, leaving one with no idea what to do or how to pass the time, with nothing to think about but oneself and one's drastically reduced future, so that when at last it was time for one's natural death, which was in fact far less natural than a sudden or violent death, being mediated at every juncture by doctors, nurses, tests, and medications, when at last it was time to leave behind what remained of the body, one's first, most intimate environment, the small section of world over which one earlier possessed full mastery, it was something that one was if not exactly prepared for then not at least surprised by, since it was only, after all, the last stage in a withdrawal that was already long under way.

Krishan's notion of the elderly had always been of people who accepted this condition—some of them only begrudgingly, doing what they could to make the process easier, irritable about their situation but on the whole resigned to its inevitability, others almost gracefully, capable even of laughing at their age-related limitations. Appamma, on the other hand, was simply incapable of accepting her withdrawal from the world, and though there was something childish in this, as if she alone were unable to handle this process that so much of humanity had to experience, it struck Krishan now that maybe there was also something admirable about his grandmother's response to her situation, something deserving of more than just pity or condescension. In a way it was hard not to admire the resoluteness with which she'd fought against what was happening to her, her unwillingness to compromise on what she took herself to be entitled to, even if this unwillingness lacked the grace or the practicality of her peers, even if part of her resistance involved lying to herself and others, even if it was doomed, in the end, to failure. Her participation in the world had never been great—she'd never finished her schooling, had been married at a young age, had never had control or influence over anything but domestic matters—but she'd fought to preserve this participation as single-mindedly as she could, ceding the territory she saw as hers only after defending each inch of it to the utmost of her ability. He remembered how, on one of her final trips to the garden, exhausted from the journey downstairs and her visit to the kitchen, Appamma had walked haltingly over the grass to a pot she'd planted some seeds in a few days earlier, wanting to see whether there was any sign of life emerging from the soil. Two tender little shoots were visible, each of them a bright fragile green, but most of the surface was covered with weeds that seemed well entrenched in the soil, for despite tugging at them several times they didn't budge. He had been on the verge of going and offering to help when he saw Appamma's jaw suddenly clenching, her eyes flashing with anger, when he saw her bending down to almost a right angle, taking hold of the weeds one by one, tugging at them with such force and such vigor, her whole body somehow electrified, that they came out together with several clumps of soil. She flung the weeds into the corner of the garden, patted down the disturbed top layer of the soil, and inspected the two delicate green shoots that, miraculously, had remained unharmed in the center of the pot. She regarded them for a while, caressing the shoots with a delicacy totally at odds with her previous action, had then turned toward him and smiled, a luster in her eyes that remained for some time and returned, or so he imagined, whenever he came back to her with a positive account of how her plants were faring. What his grandmother found so captivating in such matters Krishan couldn't say, but it was mostly to tend to such things that she fought to remain in the small, self-contained spaces that had become for her the world, and he couldn't help feeling there was something worthy of admiration in this fierce and humble loyalty to life, in the way she preserved and nourished this life however she could, with all the resources at her disposal, even as her body was being inexorably broken down, even as the people around her ceased needing or depending on her, even as Rani, her last link to the wider world, was now gone.

3

FLICKING HIS CIGARETTE into the water at the base of the rocks, Krishan stood up slowly and stretched out his arms and legs. He'd planned to be gone just a short amount of time, since he didn't have his phone and knew that his mother might return his call, but wanting to remain outside a little longer he crossed the tracks, made his way down to the pavement, and resumed his earlier path, watching as the vehicles to his left accelerated and decelerated in spurts, as the walkers and joggers on the pavement pursued their destinations intently in both directions. The section of Marine Drive along which he was walking had changed little since the end of the war, still comprised of the same modest houses and flats, the only additions a few small cafés and restaurants that had sprung up here and there, mostly to cater to the influx of Tamils who'd begun visiting from abroad and wanted to stay near relatives. Among the various signboards Krishan saw the red cross of the small pharmacy he'd frequented in the past to buy medications for Rani, an establishment he hadn't entered in several months now and which, he realized, he'd hardly even noticed on his recent walks. He remembered the slight awkwardness with which he would slip Rani's prescription across the counter, the quiet, composed manner with which the thin, dignified pharmacist would read the long list and begin retrieving the items from the shelves. The pharmacy always had all the items on the prescription— the antidepressants, the antianxiety medication, the sleeping pills, blood pressure tablets, and liver medication—and usually they stocked multiple brands of both the antidepressants and the antianxiety medication, suggesting a much wider demand for these medicines than he would otherwise have suspected. He'd often wondered after his visits how many other people in the area took medications for psychological issues or mental illness, whether there was anyone else nearby who came to the pharmacy in need of a similarly diverse assortment of drugs, and he wondered now whether there was anyone else who'd moved to the area from the northeast after experiencing a catastrophe like Rani's. He continued making his way down Marine Drive, his movement stiff and somewhat forced, and it was only when looking up after a while, seeing that he was nearing the mouth of the Kirulapone Canal, that he felt his body beginning to loosen. The canal was the union of several smaller canals that moved silently through the inland parts of the city, the culmination of a centuries-old drainage system that collected the city's rainwater, channeled it toward the coast, and cast it out to sea. Its dark green water was calm and leisurely, its motion invisible except around the tips of the ferns that dropped down from the stone walls, pricking its otherwise smooth surface, and making his way along the walkway Krishan felt his quick steps giving way to a longer, more composed stride. Listening to its gentle gurgle during the lulls in traffic, he imagined the quietly profound meeting of waters that was taking place beneath the pavement, the slow, placid water of the city giving itself up to the deep, heavy, undulating water of the sea, and it occurred to him that it was perhaps this sense of an invisible but constant renewal taking place below that was the source of the reassurance he so often felt while crossing the canal, the intimation that subterranean processes might be occurring deep inside him too, even when, on the surface of his life, everything remained exactly the same.

Resuming his way along the unpaved path on the other side, Krishan's thoughts returned not to Rani, exactly, but to the trip to London his grandmother had made two years before, the ill-advised journey from which she'd returned in a state of almost total collapse, the ill-fated journey that had been responsible, eventually, for Rani's entry into their lives. The trip had not actually been his grandmother's first time abroad, for unlike his mother and him, who'd only been to the UK once in their lives, on an extended trip several years before that took them first to London and then to Toronto, Appamma had actually visited London four or five times over the previous twenty years, each time as the guest of her youngest brother. Her brother, who was actually her half brother and eighteen years her junior, had been raised by Appamma for several years in Jaffna, and despite their different personalities and trajectories the two siblings had remained close, speaking on the phone at least once a month ever since they'd moved to different places. Her brother had joined one of the smaller separatist organizations operating in

Jaffna in his twenties and had been forced to leave the country in 1986, traveling first to India and then to Europe before ending up finally with asylum in the UK. He'd already been well into his thirties when he arrived in London, had never finished his schooling and spoke hardly any English, but was handsome and charismatic and had ended up managing a supermarket not far from where he lived. Unable to return to Sri Lanka on account of his former activities, having no wife or children that he needed to provide for, he would buy return tickets for his eldest sister every few years, so she could come and stay with him in London for five or six weeks. Appamma had always looked forward to these visits, in part because of the prestige of flying, the sense of power they gave her, in part because of the reassurance they provided that she wasn't completely dependent on her daughter-in-law, that there was someone else in the world who wanted to see her and spend time with her. Her brother had none of the scruples her daughter-in-law had, was more than happy to let her wander into the small back garden of his house or spend afternoons in the kitchen preparing lunch, dinner, and various greasy desserts, and the prospect of being in a foreign environment—even if she seldom left the house—was a perennial source of invigoration for her. The idea of traveling abroad broke the monotony of life confined to her room by giving her something to look forward to, an event in the future around which to organize the otherwise shapeless passage of the months, a longer-term correlate of what her TV programs did for each day and what her Sunday baths did for each week, coming, over the years, to be indispensable to her manipulation of time.

Her brother would buy her tickets six months ahead of her

departure in order to get the best price possible, and from the
moment Appamma was informed of their purchase, the abstract notion of going abroad becoming tied to a concrete date,
she would begin anticipating the journey ahead with a kind of
slow, sweeping pleasure. Her preparations began a full two
months in advance of her departure, with the chili powder she
always took for her brother and other relatives, a process she
would spread out over a couple of weeks, first leaving the curry
leaves and chili out to dry in the sun, then having them ground
together with coriander, turmeric, fennel, and cumin, sealing
the resulting powder in airtight plastic bags so it was ready to
be packed for international travel. The chili powder done, she
would begin taking out the various items of clothing she'd kept
stored in her armoire since her previous trip, mostly some nice
saris and a few sweaters and socks she had no use for in Colombo, washing and folding them then laying them neatly
aside. She would start pressing her daughter-in-law to begin the
visa process, to buy the supply of heart and pressure medications she would need during her time abroad, would begin
looking through her drawers for the various miscellaneous
items, safety pins, rubber bands, pens, and batteries, that would
come in handy during her stay. Finally, three weeks before the
trip, she would order Krishan or his brother to bring out the
two battered suitcases that were stored under their beds, leaving them open in a corner of her room, partitioning them into
different compartments, and carefully filling them with the
things she'd gotten ready. She would finish all her packing at
least a week in advance of her departure, would spend the remaining days visualizing her daily routine in London to make
sure there was nothing she was forgetting, making small addi-

tions and modifications to her bags, taking pleasure in their order and fullness, in the fact that she was prepared for any outcome or eventuality, so that when the day of her flight finally came all that was left was for her body and her suitcases to be flown to London, her mind having settled serenely in the spare room of her brother's house long in advance.

When her brother had called three years before to suggest she make her next visit the following June, proposing they use the occasion to celebrate her eighty-fifth birthday in style, inviting not just their relatives in London but those who could come from Europe as well, Appamma had, needless to say, been flattered by the suggestion. Despite her attempts at nonchalance she was visibly gratified by the notion of going to London to celebrate her health and longevity, by the thought of having all eyes on her, the old but still vigorous matriarch of the family, the fulcrum around which the members of their dispersed family were brought together. Krishan and his mother had been a little more hesitant, for though Appamma's trip four years before had been without any issue, her health had been declining steadily in the time since. Her body had become frailer, especially her legs, as a result of which she'd abandoned her trips downstairs, and her bladder had become less reliable, so that sometimes she went to the bathroom once every two or three hours, which in turn affected her ability to sleep. Her hearing too had gotten weaker, though she refused to use the hearing aids she'd been prescribed, making conversations more difficult to sustain and even her regular TV shows harder to follow. Increasingly forlorn as a result of her deepening isolation, the idea of a birthday party in London struck Appamma as precisely the intervention needed, energizing her so dramatically that neither Krishan nor his mother had the heart to air their reservations. In the weeks that followed she began exercising more, practiced moving without her walker over short distances; she became vigilant about what she ate and obsessed about her appearance, applying a cream with clinical regularity to the rash that had begun spreading across the back of her neck. Her initial excitement about going abroad, it soon became evident, was turning into anxiety about how she would perform on the trip and above all at the party, about whether she would be able to impress their relatives with her mental and physical vitality, and it was this anxiety perhaps that was responsible, as her departure drew nearer, for the unforeseen further decline in her condition, her loss of weight, her forgetfulness and repetitiveness in conversation, the increasing time she spent in bed.

By the time the trip was two months away both Krishan and his mother had begun to doubt it was safe for her to go at all, and his mother decided at last to broach the subject with her, suggesting that maybe the flight should be postponed or that maybe it was better for her not to go. Appamma shrugged the suggestion off lightly at first, but when it became apparent that her daughter-in-law was serious she responded with uncharacteristic rage. She would be able to handle the long flight perfectly well, she stammered in fury, there would be attendants to wheel her through the airport, and during the journey all she had to do was stay seated. It would be a complete waste of her brother's money to change plans now that tickets had already been bought, and if her daughter-in-law was tempted it could only have been out of jealousy that she herself didn't have the chance to travel abroad. Krishan's mother replied that she didn't care about going abroad, that it was only concern for her mother-in-law that was prompting her to intervene—how could Appamma hope to fly halfway across the world, she asked, when she couldn't even make it down the stairs? Appamma had turned away angrily, and after the exchange they were both cautiously taciturn, each acting as though it were obvious the other would soon concede. The issue came to a head six weeks before the flight, when Appamma asked Krishan's mother why she hadn't begun the visa application, whose outcome couldn't be taken for granted and which in the past she would have initiated much earlier. His mother ignored the question, and Appamma responded not with argument or accusation but a profound silence, refusing to eat or to speak a word, rising from the chair in her room only to go to the bathroom or when it was time to sleep. Krishan's mother pretended to ignore what she saw, hoping her mother-in-law would soon give in, but Appamma held firm in her fast and vow of silence till two days later, fearful she would collapse, his mother was forced to concede, informing Appamma through Krishan that she would apply for the visa, that she didn't want to cause anyone such misery and that if going to London was so important then she might as well go. Appamma's condition improved in response to the victory, and by the time the visa arrived Krishan and his mother both felt less nervous about the trip. Watching through the glass divider a few weeks later as an attendant whisked her through check-in they felt confident that nothing disastrous would happen, that the flight would go smoothly and that she would be handed over without issue to her brother on the other side, so that waving goodbye as she was wheeled off toward immigration neither of them could suppress their anticipation for the six weeks they would be able to spend by themselves.

They received a call from Appamma's brother in London the next day, informing them she'd arrived safely. She was tired from the flight and hadn't wanted to eat, her brother had said cheerfully, but she was jet-lagged and would be better after she slept. He called again the next day, some alarm in his voice, to say that Appamma still wasn't eating. She had trouble moving, wasn't really talking, and didn't seem herself somehow, though what was different he couldn't really say. He called each of the following days, repeating each time that he wasn't sure what to do and that he was worried she would get worse, and then on the eighth day called to say he thought it best to send her back as soon as she was well. Appamma was eating now and had gotten a little better, he told them, she still wasn't quite herself mentally, but would very likely keep improving in the coming days. She would soon be fit enough to travel, he felt, and though it would be expensive to change her ticket it was probably a good idea for her to return sooner rather than later, just in case her condition deteriorated again. They'd have a small gathering for her the following Saturday instead of a birthday party, would take her the day after to the airport so she could board a direct flight to Colombo. It wouldn't quite be the party they'd planned, since their relatives from Europe wouldn't have arrived, but there was, in his opinion, no other sensible option given the circumstances. Krishan's mother hadn't objected, knowing it would be hard for Appamma's brother to look after her in London if she did become unwell. A week later she and Krishan left once more for the airport, sitting beside each other in nervous silence the whole journey and arriving an hour in advance of the flight. They sat down in the cavernous hall for arrivals, their gazes shifting between the notifications board that hung from the ceiling and the automatic doors through which newly arrived passengers emerged, most of them tourists from Europe, Russia, and North America, large, oblivious-looking people who'd begun flocking to the country ever since the end of the war. Appamma's brother had already called twice to ask whether Appamma had arrived, his impatience betraying real concern about how she would fare on the flight back, and they sat there in a state of tension till finally the arrival of the flight was announced. They kept their eyes pinned to the automatic doors, scanning each new wave of passengers several times over, trying to determine whether they matched the demographics they expected of a direct flight from London, or whether they were likely to have come from elsewhere. Half an hour passed without any sign of Appamma, and unable to remain sitting Krishan's mother got up and elbowed her way to the crowd standing up front. Leaning on the railing between tour operators holding up their signs she rotated her phone anxiously in her hands, her eyes darting to the sides of the hall as though there might be an entrance she was unaware of. Another half an hour passed and then another, they began to feel sure something had happened, that they needed to find an official to speak to, and just as they were about to abandon their positions they saw the door slide open and a wheelchair being pushed slowly into the hall.

It took a moment to register that the person being wheeled out was the same person they'd said goodbye to eleven days earlier, for Appamma had lost so much weight that her sari gathered in folds around her body. Her blouse was falling loosely over her right shoulder, her bra strap visible over her skin; her cheeks were slightly hollowed and there was a glazed, uncomprehending quality in her eyes as she looked in disorientation at the wide, high-walled hall. Krishan and his mother signaled to the man pushing the wheelchair and quickly ran toward her, but seeing them Appamma only clutched her handbag and gave them a look devoid of recognition, the black of her pupils completely dissolved in the indistinct brown-gray of her irises. They repeated her name several times, heedless of the obstruction they were creating and all the people watching, and though something seemed to resolve in Appamma's eyes each time her name was pronounced they dissolved back quickly into indistinctness, glistening like drops of oil behind the soft, drooping folds of skin that enclosed them. It was only when Krishan's mother took her hands and introduced herself, slowly and loudly, as if to a child, that a partial clarity emerged in Appamma's face, her features drawing together in recognition, and watching her during this brief moment of awareness, which couldn't have lasted more than a couple of seconds, Krishan felt sure he could see a glimmer of embarrassment or shame in his grandmother's eyes, as if she'd understood, in that brief moment, everything that had happened, the fact that all her hopes and plans for the trip had gone astray, that she'd come away having won not admiration from their relatives but pity. She mumbled something about her brother, her birthday party, and how time either had or hadn't come around, repeated the latter several times before lapsing, once more, into a state of confusion. It was a condition she remained submerged in during the long days and weeks that followed, days and weeks in which she was unable to string words into coherent sentences, unable to feed or wash herself, urinating and sometimes even defecating on her bed, and thinking of that moment at the airport now as he continued making his way down Marine Drive, Krishan couldn't help feeling that his grandmother had chosen to abandon her lucidity on purpose upon recognizing them that day, that she'd sensed in that moment that remaining conscious would mean accepting the powerlessness of her situation and decided, in some interior part of herself, that it was preferable from then on to be absent.

The number of pedestrians on the pavement had begun to diminish, the vehicles on the road moving faster now on the emptier roads, and looking up at the deepening blue of the sky Krishan realized that it was getting late, that he'd come a significant way from the house. In the distance ahead, on the other side of the road, was the little Pillayar temple that was the last of the landmarks he used to measure his progress on Marine Drive, and deciding that he would continue walking just a little longer, smoke one last cigarette before turning back, he glanced quickly in both directions and crossed to the other side of the road. The temple was more of a shrine than a temple, consisting of no more than a single, tiny room, but like the canal closer to their house Krishan was always reassured by its presence on his walks. Approaching it now he paused and looked in through the iron grille, at the Pillayar's childlike smile flickering behind his trunk in the light of the small lamp, nodding at him in a kind of acknowledgment before he turned and continued walking. The temple had no official name, but growing up Krishan had always heard it referred to as the Visa Pillayar temple, since it was to petition for the granting of a visa that most people went to pray there, a petition that, in many cases, the Pillayar was said to have answered favorably. Flicking through Google Maps shortly after his return to Colombo he'd noticed the temple had been labeled Visa Pillayar by Google too, that thanks, no doubt, to the efforts of a grateful Tamil abroad whose visa had been granted, its colloquial name was now legitimized with a semiofficial status. No one he asked seemed to know much about how the temple had become associated with visas and emigration, and his main source of information about the place came from a long, nostalgic account of its history that he'd discovered in an anonymous comment on some diaspora blog. It was a comment that had clearly been authored by someone who'd lived many years in the area and then moved abroad, perhaps the very same person who'd campaigned to have the temple named on Google Maps, there were so many diasporic Tamils who haunted the internet in such ways, he knew, people who'd left or fled the country and now lived in bitter cold on the other side of the world, people who spent their free time trying to convince themselves that their pasts on this island really had taken place, their memories more than fantasies or hallucinations, representing people and places that really had taken up space on the earth.

According to the comment what was now the site of the temple had originally been an ordinary middle-class residence, a small, single-story house that had been vacated by its owners in the early nineties, when the government was reclaiming land close to the sea in order to construct the road that would become Marine Drive. Among the rubble of the half-demolished house that was visible to passersby afterward was an abandoned stone sculpture of Pillayar, sitting there with his usual placid expression despite being plastered in dirt and exposed to the elements, too heavy, the anonymous poster hypothesized, for his owners to have taken to their new residence. Flowers would occasionally be seen strewn in front of the Pillayar, sometimes even an offering of fruit, and at some point someone had washed off the dirt encrusting his face and trunk, cleared a path through the rubble so he could be accessed easily from the street. This had been in the mid-nineties, when thousands of Tamils displaced from the northeast had come to Colombo hoping to find a way to leave the country from there, to make it somehow to Canada or the UK or Europe or any other place that could be identified with the possibility of future prosperity. Most of these people stayed in Wellawatta, where they had the relative security of being in a Tamil area even in the country's far south, and it was some individual or group of individuals from among these displaced people, according to the anonymous commenter, who'd first built a small shed for the Pillayar, so he didn't have to sit under the open sky. A small brass lamp had been placed in front of him soon afterward, not long after a till box for donations as well, thus setting up the makeshift shrine that, over the course of a few years, thanks to donations received from local residents, soon became housed by a permanent concrete structure, a structure that deserved to be called a temple, the commenter stressed, despite being maintained not by male Brahmin priests but by older women of presumably different castes.

The darkness around him was becoming heavier as Krishan left the temple behind and entered the final, deserted stretch of Marine Drive, where there were hardly any shops or streetlights, silence except for the occasional passing car and the gentle breaking of water against the rocks. There was a bus parked with its lights off by the side of the road, and making his way around it he saw that he'd come to the unmarked stop for overnight buses that made direct journeys between Colombo and Jaffna, the same spot he'd been picked up and deposited on so many of his visits home while working in the northeast. There was nobody there now, it was still a little too early for departures, but he continued walking till he'd gone a good distance past the bus stop just in case, stopping finally at a narrow, unlit lane that went up to Galle Road, one of the last such lanes before Marine Drive came to an end. Standing with his back to the wall of an empty lot he looked past the road and tracks at the water stretching out darkly from the shore, the shimmering lights of cargo ships visible now in the distance, charting their heavy, patient paths between port and sea. He remained there unmoving for a while before he drew out a cigarette, turning away to light it then looking back at the water as he took a first drag, remembering for some reason the time when Rani, who didn't of course smoke cigarettes, had told him she chewed betel leaf. It was a confession he'd found hard to believe at the time, partly because it was a habit he associated with laboring men, partly because he'd never seen Rani chewing betel at home. He'd never seen Rani getting up and going to the toilet or garden to spit out the viscous, blood-red cud, and she'd hardly ever left the house by herself either, certainly not enough to maintain an addiction or even a mild habit. She only chewed betel when she was back home in the village, she'd told him with a smile, obviously proud of her self-control, it wasn't something she'd let herself do in another person's house. It wasn't something she'd always done either, she told him, she'd started only recently, about a year or so after the end of the war.

She liked chewing betel, found that it soothed her, though she was careful not to do it too much, since she didn't want to become too dependent on it. He hadn't asked her more at the time, perhaps because it would have felt too intrusive, perhaps because he simply hadn't thought to, but thinking of her confession now Krishan wished he had, for there was always something more to how people began such habits, not just with betel or cigarettes but with other, more addictive substances too. Whether an addiction came about quickly, before one knew what was happening, or whether it happened more gradually, with the tacit consent of the individual involved, there was always a story that divulged something about the specific or general sense of absence that allowed the dependency to develop. Addictions were, so often, at the beginning at least, a way of tolerating or managing yearnings that were too intense or too painful, a way of catching hold of desire that floated too freely, without an object to which it could be fastened, functioning for so many people as a means by which desire could be taken hold of and brought back down to the earth, relocated in easily acquired and reassuringly concrete objects like cigarettes, betel leaves, and bottles of liquor. Rani's habit of chewing betel had been a response no doubt to everything she'd seen and lost during the war, but what specific role it had played in her last years, what specific consolations it had given her, he had no idea, and having failed to ask or find out when she was still alive it would remain unknown to him, he realized, like so many other things about her life.

Rani was so different from them, her history and experiences so far from anything they were familiar with, that thinking of her now Krishan found it hard to believe they'd shared a living space, that their lives had intersected in any substantial way at all. The first time he encountered her, he remembered, had been more than two and a half years before, on an after-noon when he'd been taking a tour around the psychiatry ward of the General Hospital in Vavuniya, where he'd gone to speak with the doctor in charge about a program for trauma victims being run by his organization in Jaffna. He'd been walking with the doctor just outside the ward, no longer talking about the program specifically but about how things worked at the ward more generally, when glancing through the tall iron gratings that looked into the ward he had noticed, sitting up on one of the beds, quietly reading a book of some kind, a woman in a neat purple frock. The woman was heavyset, her skin black-ened around the eyes, and lowering her book as they passed she'd looked up and smiled gently. Struck by the disjunction between her calm, reflective demeanor and the slightly un-hinged appearance of the other occupants of the ward, most of whom seemed to be in varying states of psychosis, he'd asked the doctor once they were past earshot who she was and what she was doing there. The woman, the doctor told him, had had three children, two boys and a girl, and had lost both sons dur-ing the war. The elder one had been killed while fighting for the Tigers in 2007, and the younger one, only twelve at the time, had been hit by shrapnel on the penultimate day of fighting in 2009. The woman was suffering from post-traumatic stress dis-order with severe depression, and came to stay at the ward for a few days every month, officially to get medication and to re-ceive electroshock therapy, but also just to be able to leave home for a while, where she was plagued by endless thoughts of her sons. She was better now than when she'd first begun receiving treatment, the doctor told him, but it had been three years since then, and there was no hope of her condition improving while she remained at home. At home she was forced to spend too many long stretches of time by herself, trapped in her own mind, and there were too many associations with her two sons for her to be able to move on, not that moving on would ever be fully possible for cases such as hers.

It wasn't long after this encounter that Appamma had made the trip to London, and though Krishan's mother was able to take care of her by herself for a while, it soon became clear that someone else would be needed to look after Appamma when school started and his mother's teaching duties resumed. A professional nurse or caretaker turned out to be too expensive, and his mother spent several weeks asking almost everyone she met whether they knew someone who might be willing to stay and look after Appamma for a salary of some sort. Failing to find anyone as the start of the term drew closer, exhausted and having no idea what to do, she'd remembered the story Krishan had told her about the depressed woman who needed to leave home in order to get better, had asked him to get in touch with the doctor to see if the woman might be interested in taking the job. The suggestion had seemed out of the question to Krishan, not only because Rani hardly seemed capable of looking after herself, let alone another human. She'd lived through the last two years of the war, losing both her sons and seeing unimaginable violence all around her, and even if she said yes he would feel uncomfortable about her living with them in their two-story house in Colombo, would feel guilty living opposite someone who'd suffered so much and now had nothing, not even her mental health. Her status in the house and the work

she did would be ambiguous too, since she wasn't a professional nurse, and there was no guarantee she would be treated
respectfully by Appamma either, who was sometimes extremely irritable in her state of infirmity. His increasingly exhausted mother refused to let go of the idea, pointing out that
if what the doctor said was true then maybe it would be good
for Rani, that in any case the choice was hers to make, that it
wasn't for him to decide whether or not she should take the opportunity. Krishan finally gave in, confident the idea would be
rejected as absurd, and apologizing on behalf of his mother he
put forward the suggestion to the doctor, who, to his surprise,
immediately agreed. It would be good for Rani to leave the
north for a time, the doctor said, and perhaps looking after
someone else would help get her mind away from her own
troubles—he would ask her if she was interested and would let
them know. Two days later he called to say that Rani was indeed interested, that she would come the following week.

When he went to pick her up at the Pettah bus station late
at night the following Sunday, Krishan had found Rani standing
near the station entrance, hair disheveled, sari full of wrinkles,
the duffel bag containing all her things thrown over one of her
hefty shoulders. She was looking at the city around her uncertainly, at the density of bright lights, private vehicles, and tall,
multistoried buildings, at the paved streets and the people
around her speaking a language she couldn't understand. It
must have been unsettling, Krishan realized as he descended
from his three-wheeler, to be seeing Colombo for the first time,
to come here after having lived all her life in a small village on
the far side of the country, under Tiger control for more than
fifteen years. It must have been unsettling to have looked out

the window of her bus at the miles of continually built-up area that led, through the densely populated outskirts and suburbs, into the central parts of the city, to see up close the money and power of the state against which so many people she knew had given up their lives trying to fight. When she saw him coming toward him Rani had smiled as though he were an old acquaintance and begun walking in his direction. She didn't say much on the ride home, despite his attempts at making conversation, not so much out of shyness, it seemed, as from simply having nothing to say. There was something confident about her manner, even in the uncertainty of the new environment, and unpacking her things as soon as they arrived at the house she made herself at home with relative ease. She did everything that was needed of her, with more attention to detail than Krishan or his mother had been able to give, not hesitating even when she needed to help Appamma in the toilet or the shower. The first week passed without any of the discomfort Krishan had feared, and soon he felt he'd been wrong to be skeptical about Rani coming to stay with them, that maybe it had been a good idea after all. There were occasional tensions with Appamma, of course, who especially early on, when the childishness brought on by her condition was still strong, disliked not being the main subject of attention, but Rani didn't seem to take issue with any of her occasional rude or insensitive remarks, either because she knew Appamma was not in her right mind or because she simply didn't care. She smiled in his presence and engaged in conversation with all three of them, though she rarely initiated a conversation herself, and except for her appearance, her darkened eyes and often uncombed, unruly hair, the only sign she gave of being less than well was the way her gaze sometimes seemed to slip away from what was in front of her, as if there were other things on her mind than the work that occupied her hands. Krishan wondered what she was thinking at such times, whether she was remembering her sons or what had happened during the last months of the war, but he'd never dared broaching the subject explicitly, and in the first few weeks the closest they got to acknowledging her life in the northeast were moments in which she discussed the family she still had left, when she had reason to mention her alcoholic son-in-law, or the stepdaughter she'd helped raise, or her two young granddaughters, who, it was clear, she cherished more than anyone else alive.

It was strange to reflect on the fact that Rani was dead, this person who'd lived in their home for over a year and a half, this person to whom each of them had, in their own particular ways, become so attached. It was strange too to think that after having survived so many shells and so much shrapnel during the end of the war she'd died the previous day in such an arbitrary, almost careless way, her neck broken at the bottom of a well. Her nephew too had died in an accident after the war, he had learned from Rani during conversation one day—he'd been nineteen or twenty, his motorcycle had collided with a lorry, and he'd died on the spot, his body thrown up in the air by the force of the impact. That incident too had felt strangely arbitrary when he heard about it, strangely careless given all that the boy had seen and survived during the last two years of the war. Krishan had dismissed it simply as coincidence at the time, as yet one more of the cruel flukes of the world they lived in, but the thought occurred to him now that perhaps the boy's death hadn't been purely accidental, that perhaps Rani's death hadn't been accidental either. There'd been so many stories of accidents in the northeast in the years since the end of the war, drownings, fires, mine explosions, and road accidents above all, so many brief second- or third-page news items that noted how some or another unknown person from the former war zone had died in some or another bizarre or unexpected way. Accidents happened everywhere, of course, but these accidents had to have been more than just bad luck, for how could such hardy people, people who'd gone through so much and still come out alive, allow themselves to die so easily now and with such docility? It was as though there was some other, more obscure logic at work than mere chance, as though death was in some way following these people who'd managed to survive, as though they were in some way marked, the various statistically high probabilities on which ordinary life was based beginning, for them, to alter, to change more and more in favor of their unforeseen demise—as though they themselves walked with open arms in the direction of these seemingly accidental deaths, as though they themselves welcomed them or even willed them to take place.

Standing there with his back to the wall, his gaze following the lights of a ship lost in the black water, Krishan thought again of Rani's daughter's voice on the phone, her affectless tone and her eagerness to be done with the call. It made sense, of course, since she'd probably had to repeat the same story countless times, since she probably had a lot of work to take care of before the funeral, but all the same he had the feeling she was trying to hide something. He would have to leave early on Sunday morning for the funeral, he realized, and he would have to go alone, the journey there and back was too demand-

ing for his mother, who would anyway need to stay home to
look after Appamma. It would be his first time returning to the
northeast since he'd moved to Colombo, his first time in almost
a year, and he'd be going not just anywhere he knew but to Kilinochchi, ground zero of the war. He would have to go to the
town, which the army made a show of keeping oppressively
clean and well organized, would have to travel through miles of
impoverished countryside to find Rani's village, which he
would be seeing for the first time. It was the place she'd grown
up and spent all her life in, which she'd been displaced from
with her family during the fighting and returned to afterward
without her sons, and the thought of being there made him
suddenly uncomfortable now. He wanted to go, wanted to pay
his respects to Rani, to acknowledge her in some way and to
have that acknowledgment be seen by her family, but he would
feel guilty in front of her family members, none of whom he'd
ever met before. He would feel guilty seeing the well in which
she'd died and guilty for the fact he'd done nothing to prevent
her death, which even if accidental he felt certain now had been
foreseeable and even predictable somehow. Krishan remembered the way Rani would hug him when he visited Colombo
on his breaks from work, the way she would press his face
tightly against her ample cheeks, as if welcoming back a son
she hadn't seen in years, and standing there looking at the darkness of the sea he felt his eyes beginning to water, the significance of the phone call at last beginning to sink in. He heard,
approaching from outside his field of vision, the faint clanging
of heavy iron, and looking to the right saw the hazy yellow
headlights of the commuter train in the distance, their circles
becoming sharper and brighter as the train advanced along the

faint arc of the coast. Its movement became louder and more convulsive as it drew nearer, the pounding of its wheels on the tracks almost deafening by the time the front carriage hurtled by and cut off his view, each subsequent carriage superimposing itself so rapidly over the preceding one that the train appeared stationary while it moved. He watched as the open-door carriages passed motionlessly one by one, their fluorescent light falling on the multitude of bodies sitting and standing and leaning out, fixing their postures briefly against the night, the scene unchanging for what felt like an impossible amount of time till finally the train vanished and the jolting faded and only he remained, gazing at the water from the deserted road.

JOURNEY

4

HIS BODY HEAVY from having woken up so early, Krishan was sitting on his haunches, leaning back against one of the tall iron posts that rose from the platform, watching the people around him with the dense, trancelike clarity that often takes hold when one is up before the day, when everything outside is still shrouded in the pitch-black darkness that directly precedes dawn. The train, which was scheduled for a quarter past five, had not yet arrived, and the platform had filled up with people, with middle-aged men, older couples, and families sitting or standing in the cool darkness of the morning, gazing out in silence at the trains arriving and departing on the other tracks. He was watching a family of five who had stopped not far from where he was sitting, standing in a circle near the edge of the platform around three large pieces of luggage. The mother and father were looking around the station with quiet but focused curiosity, as if they might be called upon to draw the scene from memory later on, the three teenage children, two girls and a boy, leaning on the bags with seeming indifference, lost in the dim blue glow of their phones. The parents looked like they might still live in the country, but it was obvious from the appearance of the children that the family was visiting from abroad, their foreignness, like that of many diasporic children, immediately recognizable by the clothes they wore, their tight, branded shirts and tank tops, their loose tracksuits and formfitting jeans. On another day Krishan might have tried to speculate about the family's origins and the circumstances under which they'd left, studying how the parents were dressed, whether the children spoke Tamil or the language of their adopted home, how nervous or at ease they seemed to be returning to their place of origin. Today, though, he simply gazed at them without curiosity, not in the mood to analyze or conjecture, content to give sensation precedence over thought as he sat there waiting for the train.

He'd been in a strange mood over the last day and a half, distracted and somewhat removed from himself, unable to shed any tears since his walk on Friday evening, unable for any sustained period of time to think about Rani, who'd once more begun to seem distant and elusive in his mind. He had told his mother the news on returning home from his walk and they'd decided it was best not to inform Appamma till the next morning, so she wouldn't have to spend the night reflecting on the death by herself, and retreating to his room he'd spent the rest of the evening trying to read, his thoughts drifting now and then to the email he'd received from Anjum, the question of how to respond. When they told Appamma after breakfast the next morning she hadn't been as shocked or upset as they'd

feared, responding with surprise as she asked for all the details
and then falling silent as the information sank in. She was sad
but her sadness was muted, calmer and more thoughtful than
they'd expected the night before. Shrugging her shoulders, her
eyes watering slightly and a kind of wistful smile on her face,
she told them that Rani had suffered a lot, poor woman, that
maybe it was for the best she was gone. She'd been silent for a
while and then asked his mother to take out twenty thousand
rupees from her bank account, to be given to Rani's daughter
to help with expenses for the funeral. It was money Krishan
didn't know his grandmother had, money she'd apparently
saved up over the years from her monthly pension payments,
modest sums she received because her husband had been a
teacher in their village in Jaffna. He'd been surprised to learn
Appamma had a bank account, that she was actively keeping
track of the money she received, had been even more surprised
at the generosity of the gesture given the childish self-absorption
he'd come to associate with her old age. He'd known his grandmother was close to Rani, that the two of them had spent
nearly every day together for almost two years, but the majority of their relationship had taken place while he was elsewhere,
it made him realize, while he was busy with other things, and
listening to his grandmother reminisce about Rani at various
points over the previous day he could tell, despite her measured
response, that the two of them had been intimate in ways he
had no inkling of.

The platform began to resound beneath his feet, lightly at
first and then more heavily, and looking to the right Krishan
saw that their train was approaching the platform slowly from
the distance. The exterior was a dull red that had been stained

over the years by rust, smoke, and grease, not one of the sleek new models bought recently with loans from China but one of the older, heavier, boxier trains purchased decades before from India. Everyone who'd been sitting and standing as if half-asleep immediately clutched their bags and began hurrying in search of their carriages, roused by the thick smell of diesel, but Krishan remained where he was, watching as the family from abroad began making its way through the crowd, the three children listlessly following their parents toward the front of the train. He waited till they disappeared into the crowd, then standing up heavily and throwing his backpack over his shoulder, proceeded to the second-class carriage where his own seat had been booked. He climbed the vertical steps up to the carriage, and squinting in the harsh fluorescent light of the compartment made his way to his seat, which, he discovered to his satisfaction, was by the window. The boy in his early twenties sitting next to him smiled and stood up to let him into his seat, probably Sinhalese from the look of him, which meant, Krishan noted happily, that he would probably be getting off somewhere in the south, that there was a chance the seat beside his would be empty for the remaining portion of the journey. Resting his bag on his lap he sat down and looked out at the now much emptier platform, listened to the calls of the men who went up and down the platform selling tea, coffee, and peanuts to passengers through the windows. He wondered whether he should try to sleep, since he'd only gotten three or four hours that night, but decided he would try to stay up despite his fatigue, to preserve for as long as possible the calm focus that had held his mind since waking. He took out of his bag the book he'd brought, a book about Indian militarism and the occupation of Kashmir that he'd wanted to read for some time but had been struggling to make progress with in the previous few weeks. He flicked through the pages thoughtlessly, more to hear the sound of the flicking than to find the place he had stopped, till a heavy clanging sounded from deep inside the train and caused the carriage to shake—the familiar yet always surprising sound that signified the train's imminent departure and came, he liked to assume, from the massive pressure of the brakes being released. The train jerked forward a little bit, hesitated for a few seconds, then began to stagger forward. The fluorescent lights in the carriage went off, shrouding everything in the blue darkness of dawn, and grateful that reading was no longer a possibility Krishan put the book down and leaned back as the train made its way out of the station. The thin floor reverberated beneath his feet and the glass windows trembled against their frames, the clanging of the wheels against the tracks growing heavier and more rhythmic as the train picked up speed. It was his first time traveling all the way north by train, and looking out at the abandoned carriages and cluttered workshops just outside the station, at the shanty settlements strung out along both sides of the tracks, strangely desolate in the small, bright circles of light cast by occasional lamps, he began to feel, despite his fatigue and the somber purpose of his journey, a mood of anticipation rising gently inside him, the same sense of possibility he'd always felt when embarking on long train journeys, the sense that he was leaving behind everything that limited and constrained him, moving toward some vast and unspecifiable future.

It had been some years since he'd felt this mood of optimism while traveling, for though Krishan had traveled fre-

quently between north and south during his time in the
northeast, he'd always traveled by bus on these journeys. The
train hadn't been functional till the previous year, the northern
section of the line having been completely destroyed during the
war, and bus in any case was the more utilitarian option, faster,
cheaper, and more easily arranged at the last minute than train.
There was something much more stressful about traveling by
bus, Krishan felt, for traveling out of Colombo by road you
were constantly blocked or impeded by traffic, especially in
buses because of their unwieldy size and the narrowness of the
roads. Bus drivers were so often in a state of physical tension,
their hands tightly clutching the steering wheel and the gear-
stick, their feet constantly pushing down on the pedals, suddenly accelerating and breaking in the pointless attempt to
overtake slower vehicles, attempts borne out of a deep anxiety
to finish their routes as soon as possible despite the fact that it
was impossible, no matter how quickly they went, to speed up
even the longest journey by a meaningful amount of time. The
constant frustration of the drivers, which invariably communicated itself to the passengers too, seemed only to make them
tenser, to spur them on more recklessly, pushing them to overtake on bends and when vehicles were approaching on the opposite lane, a frustration that was no doubt one of the major
causes of the road accidents that took place around the country
each day. They spent the majority of their lives in such a state,
Krishan knew, and imagining these drivers as they lay awake in
their beds at night, their bodies still caught up in the tension
and strain of the day's driving, he wondered sometimes what
their dreams were like when they were finally able to fall asleep,
whether they saw visions of broad, empty, smoothly tarred

roads unlike the ones they came across in real life, roads that stretched out into the horizon and down which they could accelerate into infinity, endlessly and without obstacle, as long as they pleased.

Traveling by train was different, for even if there were occasional delays and breakdowns there was never any traffic on train rides, no effort or strain required as you were borne smoothly and inexorably toward your goal. Looking out at the silhouettes of the city passing by in the darkness, Krishan thought of all the hours he'd spent on trains during his time in India, when he was on holiday from university and had the chance to leave Delhi, to see other parts of that vast, seemingly endless country. He'd spent most of those journeys sitting or lying on his seat or berth, reading, listening to music, or simply looking out at the small, unpeopled rural stations, the hot wind rushing into the carriage through the open doors and windows, allowing him to breathe in the air of the places they passed and absorb their smells, as if he were in some kind of communion with these small towns and villages as they flitted by. The constant movement of wind through the carriage would feel like a calling to him from outside, and leaving his seat he would go down every so often to the linking section between carriages, where standing in a corner he would look to make sure nobody was watching, light himself a cigarette, and pull open one of the heavy train doors, one hand tightly clasping the grip on the door frame so he didn't fall into the passing landscape, the other holding the cigarette in front of his body so that no one passing behind would see that he was smoking. The warm, fragrant air of the countryside buffeting his face, he would look out at the wide expanses of farmland, brush, and forest, at the plains that went by for sometimes hours at a stretch without stopping, and he felt, at such moments, something close to a sense of liberation, if not quite liberation then the sense at least of being on the verge of liberation. It was as if, at such times, he was permanently suspended in the blissful but always vanishing space between desire and satisfaction, in that region of the self where one is no longer anguished by the absence of something one feels to be necessary for one's salvation, but not yet saddened by the disappointment that attainment of desire always seemed to bring, for strong desire, desire that radiates outward through all the regions of the body, always seemed to involve the hope or belief that attainment of the object of desire, whether a person, place, or situation, will change everything completely, will end all absence and yearning, all effort and struggle, that it will stem, somehow, the slow, sad passage of time. We experience, while still young, our most thoroughly felt desires as a kind of horizon, see life as divided into what lies on this side of that horizon and what lies on the other, as if we only had to reach that horizon and fall into it in order for everything to change, in order to once and for all transcend the world as we have known it, though in the end this transcendence never actually comes, of course, a fact one began to appreciate only as one got older, when one realized there was always more life on the other side of desire's completion, that there was always waking up, working, eating, and sleeping, the slow passing of time that never ends, when one realized that one can never truly touch the horizon because life always goes on, because each moment bleeds into the next and whatever one considered the horizon of one's life turns out always to be yet another piece of earth.

His thoughts had often returned to *The Cloud Messenger* during those long journeys, the famous Sanskrit poem of yearning that he'd read in translation early on during his time in India, before he'd begun to understand how intimately the Sanskrit language was tied to the mythology of Hindu nationalism, before he'd begun to understand the everyday racism of North Indians toward people of darker skin like himself, a racism that hadn't affected him greatly but had, nevertheless, played its own small part in his desire to leave. The language and imagery of the poem had moved him so much all those years ago, and looking out now as the darkness of early morning gently let up, he found himself thinking, once more, about the painful longing so elegantly expressed in its verses. The unnamed main character of the poem was a yaksha, a kind of divine or semidivine spirit who served the god of wealth, and the poem began with an account of how, as punishment for neglecting his duties, the yaksha had been exiled by the god of wealth from Alaka, his beautiful native city in the foothills of the Himalayas. He'd been compelled to wander far south to the plains of central India, thousands of miles away from the cool climes of his birthplace, a parched, arid wilderness that to the author and his audience of elites must have signified the outer limits of civilization, an area of total darkness. The yaksha had already been wandering alone in this wasteland for many months at the start of the poem, unable to stop thinking about the city he'd been exiled from and above all the wife he loved so much, losing so much weight from the sadness of separation, according to the poem's narrator, that even the bracelets on his thinning arms had slipped off. It was late July or August, the time of year when the annual monsoon rains finally began to reach the plains of

central India on their northward journey from the southern
coast, and climbing up to the top of a mountain in his dazed,
hopeless state the yaksha had noticed a single dense, dark cloud
heading in his direction from the south, descending so low it
almost touched the peak of the mountain before pausing there
as if for rest. Gazing at this cloud the yaksha was lost for a long
time in thought, hardly able to hold back his tears, until realizing at length that the cloud was a forerunner of the imminent
monsoon, that it would, in all likelihood, continue traveling
north till it reached the Himalayas, it occurred to him that he
could ask the cloud to carry a message for him to his wife. Although most rational beings know, the narrator remarks in the
fifth stanza, that a cloud was nothing but a conglomeration of
vapor, light, water, and wind, an object incapable of being ra-
tionally addressed, individuals consumed by love were unable
to distinguish between the sentient and the insentient, as
though to the individual overcome by passion the whole world
was populated by beings whose sole purpose was either to support or thwart their love. So taken up was the desperate yaksha
by the possibility of communication with his wife, the narrator
goes on, that looking up he began to address the cloud out
loud, praising its beauty and auspiciousness before asking it
whether it would be willing to bear a message from him to his
wife on its way north.

All this took place within the first six stanzas, and the large
substance of the poem that followed, one hundred and fifteen
stanzas in all, consisted of the detailed set of directions that the
yaksha gives to the cloud in order to find his city and wife, directions, the yaksha assures the cloud, that will lead it through
all the grandest, most opulent cities of the subcontinent, allow-

ing it to stop, on the way, at wide-flowing rivers and dense jungles so it could gather itself and rest, absorbing water into its body and rejuvenating itself so it could maintain its bodily integrity as it continued the long journey north. It should begin, the yaksha tells the cloud, by heading north from their present location and then a little west toward the Vindhya mountain range, whose flanks are covered with wild mango trees and kutaja flowers, where welcomed by the cries of watery-eyed peacocks it would be able to drink to its heart's content at the source of the Narmada River. Though it might want to dwell there in the mountains for some time, the yaksha goes on, it should try not to tarry too much and should continue quickly on its journey, which would as it knew take several weeks to complete. Heading north from the Vindhyas the cloud would reach the country of Dasharna, its garden hedges white with the buds of ketaki flowers and its trees busy with the nest-building of crows, flocks of flamingos dwelling on the forests of rose apple at its outskirts. At its capital, Vidisha, the cloud would be able to drink from the waters of Vetravati, the yaksha says, after which it should continue north, going a little out of its way in order to see the famous city of Ujjain with its terraced mansions, where the morning breezes carried the drunken warble of cranes and were fragrant with the scent of blooming lotuses, a city so beautiful it looked like a fragment of heaven on earth. The cloud should visit the famous shrine to Siva in Ujjain and then spend the night there, asking its wife, lightning, to descend in silence every now and then to give light to the women who were making their way secretly to their lovers. From Ujjain the cloud should head farther north, past the Gambhir River in Rajasthan toward Devagiri, where it could worship at the temple to Siva's son Skanda. It should then proceed toward the Chambal River, where again it could rest and take up water, and from there it should travel northeast past Kurukshetra, the battleground of the famous ancient war depicted in the *Mahābhārata*. The cloud should afterward make its way east toward the city of Kanakhala, the yaksha says, where it could drink from the great Ganges, continuing its journey north till it reached the source of the Yamuna River, a mountain white with snow where the rocks were fragrant with the musk of deer and bamboo swayed softly in the wind. On the last leg of its journey it would have to travel north around the flanks of the Himalayas till it reached Mount Kailasa, home of Siva, the snow on its slopes white as freshly cut ivory, and once there it should head toward the waters of Lake Manasa, full of golden lotuses, where the gossamer on the wish-fulfilling trees by its banks was fanned continually by the misty breeze.

It was from the banks of Lake Manasa, the yaksha says, that the cloud would finally be able to see his much-longed-for city Alaka, which it would recognize at once by the enormous mansions with bejeweled floors and the soaring palaces with turrets that kissed the sky. The city itself was located in the lap of the mountain and contained enormous parks and gardens where the flowers of winter, spring, summer, and autumn were all in simultaneous bloom, a detail that had struck Krishan when he first came across the poem, as though the narrator was suggesting that all seasons were collapsed there into a single season, that time itself stood still or that all times were contained in a single time—as though, the narrator was suggesting, in ordinary life we are pulled in different directions by our contradictory desires, so that what we imagine as heaven is a place where these conflicting longings are somehow reconciled, in which the separate and seemingly incompatible times of their fulfillment are brought together, uniting our otherwise divided souls. The citizens of Alaka, according to the description the yaksha gives to the cloud, consist of male and female yakshas obsessed with love and sex, the male yakshas constantly drinking aphrodisiacs, carrying flowers in their hair that looked like the reflections of stars, while up in their private chambers the female yakshas, torn between embarrassment and desire in the company of their lovers, threw fistfuls of powder at the tall-flamed lamps while their lovers untied their robes. His own home, the yaksha tells the cloud, was to the north of the god of wealth's own house, recognizable by its arched gate and the young mandara tree beside it. There was a tank with emerald-paved steps, its waters crisscrossed by golden lotuses, and to the side of the tank was a rockery with a girdle of golden plantains where his wife often spent time, in the center of which was a golden perch where a peacock came to roost at day's end. By these signs the cloud would recognize his home, and if it went down discreetly to the house and cast a glance inside, it would finally be able to see his wife. The intense longing of separation would be weighing her down, her once beautiful appearance having changed like a lotus laid waste by frost. Her face will have become swollen from crying, her lower lip discolored from the heat of many sighs, and when the cloud saw her she would probably be painting pictures of him, the yaksha went on, or speaking to the caged mynah about him, or perhaps trying to play a song on her lute to remind herself of him, wetting its strings with her tears. She might be marking out the days and weeks left for his exile to end, or perhaps lying there on her bed fantasizing about the two of them in the throes of passion, for these, he explains, were the many ways that lovers whiled away their time when separated. The cloud should wait until nighttime before alerting his wife to his presence, since it was at night that loneliness would most affect her, when she would be most in need of his words. It should go down to the window of his wife's chambers, and if she was sleeping the cloud should let her sleep on for the first watch of night, just in case she was dreaming of him. When the first watch was over, he goes on, it should wake her up by sending in a cool breeze through the window, and it is only at this point in the poem, after addressing the cloud for an entire eighty-nine stanzas, that the yaksha finally shares the message he wants to send.

The cloud should begin by announcing to his wife that it has been sent by her husband, he says, which will guarantee that she listens attentively, since to a person separated from their lover, news of the lover was almost the same as being physically united again. The cloud should inform her that her husband is alive and well, that he is wondering how she is doing, and that he cannot stop thinking of her. He sees her image everywhere around him—her arms in the slender vines, her flirtatious eyebrows in the ripples of a stream—and he wonders constantly how to make the rest of his allotted term of exile pass more quickly. He asks her not to become disheartened or grow suspicious of him, promises that he will be back as soon as possible, and with this the yaksha ends his brief message, a message that, after his richly described account of the path the cloud should take on its journey, after his meticulous instructions for how to find Alaka and how, having arrived there, to recognize his home and his wife, strikes the reader as remarkably superficial. It is as though, after giving what amounts to an extended literary map of half the subcontinent, a vast poetic travelogue of all its great cities and natural wonders, the yaksha realizes he doesn't actually have much to say to his wife, that words will never bridge the distance between him and her, the geographical but also the temporal and psychic distance, the distance between all that has happened and all that has changed in the time since their separation. Having delivered his message the yaksha looks up at the cloud, which has not, of course, said a single thing during his entire monologue, then expresses his hope that the cloud will carry his message without delay, adding that in no way does he consider its silence a refusal. His request is unusual, he acknowledges, but the cloud should take pity on him, and he will pray, in the meantime, that the cloud never be parted in a similar manner from its wife lightning. It is with this last statement that the yaksha ends his speech and the poem too comes to an end, though Krishan could never think about the poem's last lines without dwelling also on the image suggested so obliquely by its ending, the image of the yaksha looking up from that lonely mountaintop as the monsoon wind blows in from the south, the image of that desperate, homesick, divine or semidivine being watching helplessly as the cloud is ushered north, its edges slowly dissolving as it is pushed farther and farther into the distance, its bodily integrity imperceptibly dwindling and with it the message entrusted with so much longing, till finally, like the dissipation of desire into yearning, it evaporates soundlessly into the nothingness of the horizon.

Recalling this image of the separated lover as day opened out over the scenes passing by outside, the small, cheaply constructed houses and huts rushing by, the vegetation between

them becoming increasingly unruly, Krishan thought once
more of the trip to Bombay he'd made by train with Anjum
almost four years before, during his last year in Delhi, that short
but somehow timeless trip that had been the prolonged climax
of the overwhelming months they'd spent together but also, in
retrospect, despite having stayed together for some time afterward, the point he first began to sense that their relationship
might not last forever. He could still see Anjum sitting opposite him on their berth that day, cross-legged in her beige shal-
war kameez, her head propped up on her hands, the mahogany
of her eyes brighter and more vivid than usual in the light that
seeped in through the window, could still see the way she would
glance at him and then look away as she talked about her time
in Jharkhand, about the small village where she and the few
activists she worked with had been running a workshop on
labor rights for women working in the mines. They hadn't seen
each other in three weeks when they'd met that morning outside the station, had hardly spoken or texted either, Anjum not
being the kind of person who liked calling or texting unless it
was necessary. After just a quick, lighthearted embrace they'd
made their way to the platform without further physical demonstration of their feelings, each of them conscious of the other's physical presence but neither making any attempt to touch
or hold the other after that brief contact, as if in tacit agreement that they had to maintain strict distance from each other
in that intensely public place. They'd booked an upper and
lower side berth, so they wouldn't have to share the uncomfortable intimacy of a four-person compartment with strangers
who'd spend the entire trip trying to figure out whether they
were married, but the positioning of the side berths, which ran

along the side of the train, still subject them to the gaze of others, put them directly on view to the people in the compartments opposite and to anyone walking through the carriage. He'd tried to listen as Anjum described the village, which was strikingly verdant despite the aridity he generally associated with Jharkhand, as she described the struggles of the women living there and how the right-wing Hindu politicians in the area, suspicious of what was going on, had ordered their people to keep tabs on the workshop. He'd wondered almost every day, while she was away, how she was spending her time there, what she was thinking and feeling and saying and doing in that small village in that state he'd never been to, but sitting opposite Anjum on the berth, finally in her presence after three weeks of separation, he found himself paying more attention to the small movements she made with her body than to what she actually said, to the way she kept running her hands through her short hair, or rotating the ring she wore on the middle finger of her left hand, or pulling up her sleeves, which, for some reason, kept falling back down onto her forearms. It was unsettling to sit so stiffly and so far apart from this person with whom he'd spent so much time in various states of union, this person he was unable or reluctant to disentangle himself from in private, even to go to the bathroom or pick up his phone, and it was because perhaps of this physical distance that they also avoided sustained eye contact with each other as they talked, because their inability to touch seemed to give the small space between their bodies a palpable erotic charge, so that despite and also because of this distance it felt like they were touching each other when they were in fact only looking at each other, as if with their eyes they were reaching out and caressing each other in front of everyone else there, so that even their eye contact became overly intimate and uncomfortable, not just because it alerted their neighbors to the nature of their relationship but also because it exposed the superficiality of all their attempts at verbal communication, made obvious all the ways it fell short of what they really wanted from each other as they sat there opposite each other on that train hurtling heavily through the plains.

Conversation did become a little easier as the journey went on, as the gazes of the other people on the train fell away and they adjusted to their new situation, reconciled themselves to being next to each other without losing themselves in each other, they had done it before, after all, whenever they chose to meet in some public place rather than in one of their flats, a postponement that often brought its own particular kind of pleasure. They talked about various things as the train made its way south and west, what exactly he could no longer say, but after a while conversation seemed to dwindle, as if they were running out of things to relate to each other, which worried him a little, though it also made sense, Krishan told himself, for they would be on the train for almost twenty-one hours, it would be impossible to talk the whole time, a realization that in a way signaled the true beginning of their three-week-long trip together, the moment when silence as a way of being together took precedence over speech. They ate the greasy samosas they'd gotten at the station for lunch, passed most of the warm, lazy afternoon reading or gazing out at the passing landscapes, listening to the rhythmic clanging of the wheels against the tracks, occasionally breaking their silence to share something from what they were reading or to mention a thought or story that found its way to their minds. Krishan did his best to read the book he'd bought but found it more and more difficult to concentrate as the afternoon wore on, reading and rereading the same few lines as his thoughts drifted again and again to Anjum, to whether she still felt the same way about him as he did about her, the same way she had seemed to feel before their three-week separation. He couldn't help feeling there was some subtle but noticeable change in her attitude toward him, even if it was true she'd been glad to see him at the station, even if it was true she'd wanted to talk to him about her time in Jharkhand, to share with him at least a significant part of everything that had happened. Looking up at her without trying to hide it—she was so absorbed in what she was reading that she didn't even notice him looking—he couldn't help suspecting that her feelings had changed, that she no longer felt the same overwhelming urge to put aside everything else so they could give themselves up to each other, for why, if she did, were they still sitting so far from each other, why were they making no attempt, at least covertly, to touch each other, to let their toes at least graze?

It couldn't have been fear of disapproving looks from the other people on the train, Krishan knew, for Anjum wasn't the kind of person to care about such things, was always ready to confront people who voiced their disapproval about how she dressed or spoke or conducted herself. It could only have been that her feelings had changed somehow, maybe she had met someone during her time in Jharkhand, another activist like her perhaps, a woman or a man whose life was more similar to hers than his and who she could identify with more than she could with him. Maybe she'd never even felt the same way about him as he did about her, maybe he'd been mistaken thinking his feelings reciprocated to begin with, in the four months they'd known each other she'd been reluctant to give their relationship any kind of name, after all, would dismiss any attempt he made to share his feelings with her explicitly, closing her eyes, shaking her head, and smiling in a slightly ironic, playful manner, as if to say he should know better, that there was no need to make such statements, that such statements were always false or cheapening or manipulative. It was a view he agreed with on principle, knowing enough by then to be suspicious of the ready-made expressions and conventional sentiments with which new lovers usually tried to allay their fears, expressions and sentiments which, he knew, if they weren't deployed with utmost caution, always had the consequence of domesticating love, of containing and constraining its vastness. Anjum's insistence on avoiding such statements had bothered him though from the very beginning, perhaps because of the single-mindedness with which he could sense that she pursued her convictions, and thinking about their namelessness he began to feel even more anxious as he watched her sitting in front of him, totally absorbed in her reading. In the absence of concrete words and gestures, which had a solidity you could cling to in a way you could not cling to unexpressed feelings, he found himself doubting all his convictions about the time they'd spent together, as if his memory of that time might be wrong or inaccurate, as if that time might not even have taken place at all, as if it might have been nothing more than a dream, the person sitting opposite him a total stranger. Sitting there pretending to be as engrossed in his book as she was in hers he began poring over the past several months, trying to find in that slow cascade

of images and sounds some moment that would give irrefut-
able proof against his doubts, that would allow him to dismiss
the distance he felt from Anjum as merely an illusion, no more
than the ordinary, temporary impasse that lovers often felt on
reuniting after a separation.

The first time he'd encountered Anjum had been at a panel
he'd gone to in Delhi with his roommate Rajiv five or six
months before, the subject of which was the relationship between the modern Indian state and queerness, the ways in
which Indian nationalists, mimicking the white rulers of India
before them, had sought to eliminate or to conceal queerness
in the subcontinent. The event had been delayed slightly due to
technical issues, and the two of them had been standing in the
small garden outside, smoking in silence, when they noticed
Anjum walking in through the gate, tall and long-limbed, her
skin darkly lustrous, hair cut short, wearing jeans with a large
shirt that hung loosely from her shoulders. She'd come with
two other people, a girl and a boy, the girl good looking but in
a more conventional way, the boy quite average. The three of
them had gone inside, then learning the panel hadn't started
had come out to the garden to smoke. Krishan tried to find
something to say to Rajiv, to give the impression of being absorbed in conversation, but neither he nor even Rajiv, who was
only attracted to men, had been able to stop themselves from
looking at Anjum through the corner of their eyes, at the elegance with which she brought her cigarette to her mouth and
then drew it away, at her sharp, judgmental features and boyish
grace, the strange quality of not belonging to the world that
seemed to emanate from the way she held herself and the way
she moved. When the panel began she sat down with her

friends on the floor in front of the stage, hidden from where he and Rajiv sat toward the back of the hall. Despite being unable to see her Krishan couldn't help wondering what her response was whenever one of the participants said something of interest, whether she was smiling or nodding or impassive, whether she was furrowing her eyebrows in agreement or indignation, as if his own responses to the discussion onstage would be ill-judged or in poor taste if they didn't cohere with hers.

When the panel finished everyone began making their way haphazardly outside, and spotting Anjum in the crowd Krishan tried discreetly to lead Rajiv closer to where she and her friends were standing. Leaning back against the wall in a performance of casualness he did his best once more to seem engaged in conversation, privately devoting his mental resources to discerning the nature of the relationship between Anjum and her attractive female friend, who, he felt sure, must also have been her lover. He lit one cigarette after another, trying not to seem distracted as he spoke to Rajiv's various friends, glancing back whenever he had the chance at Anjum and the people she was talking to, all of whom seemed far more intriguing and far more attractive than the people he was with. He wasn't close enough to hear anything she said but could tell that she was aware of the attention she commanded as she stood there, a cigarette in her right hand, her left hand sometimes on her hip and sometimes gesticulating as she talked, her upper body leaning forward as she spoke and moving back slightly when she laughed, her manner full of ease, as though she was at a friend's home and not in a public or semipublic place. When, midway through his third or fourth cigarette, she and her two friends left with two other boys, it was as if something had been extracted painfully but soundlessly from deep inside him. Everything remained exactly the same as before and yet her silent departure left the scene in the garden feeling empty and arbitrary, the crowd around him suddenly devoid of interest. It wasn't so much that he'd failed to introduce himself to Anjum or to insinuate himself into one of her conversations, such strategies didn't suit him, he knew from experience, he was still too shy and too awkward at the time to go up to people he didn't know in such contexts. What he'd wanted was simply to continue being in her presence, to continue occupying the same space that she was occupying, as if simply by being in her proximity something might happen that might somehow be of significance, in the same way perhaps that in the East Asian tradition of Pure Land Buddhism, which he'd been reading about at the time, devotees who felt Buddhahood to be too great a challenge for them as individuals could attempt, instead of striving to achieve nirvana, simply to be physically near the Buddha, to obtain a place in the strange force field like sphere that surrounded him no matter where he went, a space that assumed the aspect of heaven and that was, according to the tradition, the next best thing to enlightenment that a human being could strive for.

He'd been unable, in the weeks that followed, to forget Anjum, the stern beauty of her face and her distinctly southern darkness, the way she'd walked in so silently and unexpectedly through the gates of the building and into his mind. Images of her would rise to the surface of his consciousness unannounced at various moments of the day and he would think of the way she'd seemed to move through space that evening, her strange ease and ethereality, as though she subsisted not in the ordinary atmosphere but in some other medium, as though the path she carved through each day was light and effortless, free of resistance, her movement through the world like the long, fluid, unbroken descent that a diver makes through the air before cutting soundlessly into the water, disappearing beneath its surface. He'd come across such people before, of course, not frequently but from time to time, girls but also boys, people who were sometimes strikingly attractive in appearance but who always aroused in him much more than merely an urge to thrust forward or upward with his hips. He'd had glimpses of such people on the metro, in supermarkets, or simply walking down the street, people who seemed to materialize into the midst of everyday life, their faces sharp and angular, their bodies slender, their penetrating gazes directed high above the throng of other humans, as if nobody they saw could possibly interest them, as if everything they needed was already contained in the place they were headed, people who possessed that same quality of seeming to belong to a different, more timeless world that Anjum had, a quality he thought of, for lack of a better word, as beauty. Such people had always drawn his attention, made him stop what he was doing and turn around, made him wish he could follow them to wherever they were going, but watching them disappear into the crowd, a painful twinge in his chest, they would sooner or later leave his thoughts. Why he was unable to stop thinking about Anjum on this occasion, by contrast, it was difficult to say. Rajiv had mentioned that he'd seen her before at other queer events, that he'd been introduced to her briefly once before but had been too intimidated to talk to her, and perhaps she'd stayed in his mind because he sensed they were vaguely part of the same larger circles, that there was a chance he might come across her again in the future. He felt, upon learning her name from Rajiv, that he'd obtained a real, concrete connection to her, a thread that would lead him to her eventually, and the first thing he did was try to find her on Facebook, going through all the listed Anjums as well as the friend lists of dozens of Rajiv's friends, not knowing at the time that Anjum didn't use social media at all. He daydreamed of running into her at random places, on his way to or from campus or while out with his friends, imagining these encounters would lead to a life completely different from the life he lived, to a life that lay, in some way, outside time. He believed in the possibility of these encounters so intensely that he actually felt cheated when he failed to encounter her at a bar or party or a political event or panel, deciding with a little bitterness, once he was sure of her absence, that the place had nothing to offer him. It was funny how similar desire was to loss in this way, how desire too, like bereavement, could cut through the fabric of ordinary life, causing the routines and rhythms that had governed your existence so totally as to seem unquestionable to quietly lose the hard glint of necessity, leaving you almost in a state of disbelief, unable to participate in the world. You could follow the thread of habit day in and day out, lost in studies and in work, among friends and colleagues and family, clasping this thread tightly with both hands so as not to lose your way, and then all of a sudden one morning or afternoon or evening, sipping on a cup of tea at work or going to a friend's house on the weekend, you could come across a person or place or even an image of a person or place that suggested other possibilities, that brought to mind a completely different life, a life you might have lived or might still live, so that suddenly the life you'd been living for the last so many months or years, a life that till that very moment seemed fulfilling, satisfactory, or tolerable at least, became, with the soundless flicking of a switch, empty and hollow, lacking any connection to the person you felt you were or wanted to be.

It was hard to understand now how he'd been so drawn to Anjum when he'd known nothing about her at all at the time, not that she was from Bangalore, not her financial situation or her political views, not that she didn't like having her picture taken, that she slept without a pillow, or that she showered with cold water in the mornings, not even whether she was attracted to men. He'd become obsessed after that initial encounter with not so much a person as the image of a person, an image lacking a caption containing even the most basic details, had begun to long and pine for someone he knew nothing about but who, nevertheless, he imagined could somehow save him. In a sense his response to Anjum was no different from that of so many people, men especially but women too, who seeing someone whose external appearance could sustain all their fantasies, proceeded to project everything they desired onto this person, acting surprised when they realized, weeks or months or years later, that the actual person was different from the image they'd formed, that the actual person had a history and an identity of their own that would not remain silent, responding to this discovery with indignation, as if they'd been lied to or misled, sometimes using persuasion, manipulation or force to compel the unsuspecting person to conform to that initial mental image. And yet his obsession with Anjum could not have been simply an idealization, Krishan knew, for how else could it have turned out, if the image in his mind had been nothing but the blind projection of his own desires, that the more he got to know Anjum the more his desire for her seemed to intensify, how could it have turned out that everything he learned about her subsequently served to expand and elaborate the image in his mind rather than contradict it, filling it out, giving it dimensions and solidity, adding to his desire rather than undercutting it? There must have been more to it than mere projection or mere idealization, even if he'd known nothing concrete about Anjum after that first encounter, for a lot could be said after all on the basis of a single image, a lot could be learned about a person even on first glance, from the composition of the face, which was shaped not just by bone structure but also by the muscles around the cheeks, eyes, and jaw, each of them sculpted in different ways and to different degrees by the ways they were used, each mood and expression requiring a different combination of flexion and relaxation in the different parts of the face, so that one could learn, if one was perceptive enough, to tell whether a person spent most of their time in a state of attentiveness or indifference, melancholy or exuberance, skepticism or hopelessness or earnestness. One could tell by observing the movement of their eyes whether a person spent most of their time feeling shame or self-assuredness or desire or yearning or self-containment, one could tell from the readiness of the smile how vulnerable a person was and from the furrows above the brows how much they were plagued by anger or anxiety, could tell by the posture and the gait and the movement of the hands how lively they were, how open to the influence of others and how ready to influence others, so that perhaps his longing for this person he did not know was due not so much to projection or idealization as to the sometimes almost prophetic nature of

a glance, which under the right light and the right circumstances could reveal so many of the possibilities and tendencies
of a person's character, which was also why, perhaps, when
everything finally ended between them, this too, in retrospect,
had seemed like something he'd known about right from the
very start, something he'd already glimpsed in that first, silent,
one-sided encounter but chosen, subsequently, to ignore.

5

TWO MONTHS AFTER that first encounter, when he learned about a screening organized by a group that Rajiv knew, Krishan had waited all week with anticipation, knowing there was a chance he might encounter Anjum there. Queer events occurred in Delhi with greater frequency than they did in other big Indian cities, but they were still relatively rare, lacking places to host them and money to fund them, as a result of which when they did occur they functioned as a kind of meeting point, a gathering place where people could show their faces and reassure each other that they continued to exist. The event was at a small office space in South Delhi used by a wedding photography business during working hours, and entering the space Krishan had looked around for Anjum almost immediately, despite having told himself he wouldn't. He loitered near the entrance chatting with people he knew, his eyes returning to the door whenever someone walked in, and when the event began with still no sign of her he went reluctantly to find a place to sit with Rajiv, chastising himself for his foolishness as he tried to prepare himself for the screening. The film was an independent documentary about the long marginalized community of transwomen in Hyderabad, hijras, as they were usually referred to in India. It depicted the community's preparations for one of their year's most important festivals, touching also on the relationship between the hijra community and the small but relatively new and more mobile community of queer activists in the city. Krishan found himself being drawn slowly into the film, into the perhaps misleading intimacy with which it showed lives he would otherwise have no access to, and it was only toward the end of the film, after the thought of her had long disappeared from his mind, that he noticed Anjum sitting on the floor close to the front of the room, not far from the door, the light from the screen playing on the slant of her attentive face. Despite doing his best to continue paying attention he found himself unable to concentrate on the film, his heart beginning to beat faster, a tension beginning to spread through his arms and legs. Something inside his chest or stomach seemed to lunge each time he noticed her shift her weight from left to right or cross and uncross her legs, each time she smiled or shook her head in response to something in the film, and feeling that he wouldn't be able to wait another two months to see her again he began to wonder whether he should find a way to talk to her afterward or whether, rather, it was better to wait, there was something inappropriate, he knew, in him showing overt interest in a woman in such a situation, one of the few spaces in Delhi explicitly intended to support less normalized modes of desire.

It turned out, to Krishan's scarcely containable joy, that Rajiv knew some of the people that Anjum had come with, and chatting outside in a group of nine or ten afterward it was suggested, to his even greater joy, that they go to someone's flat nearby to hang out and smoke weed. Trying not to show too much excitement, though in the privacy of his mind he was unable to believe how effortlessly their paths were converging, Krishan nodded his assent to the plan, too hopeful and nervous to really talk to anyone as they walked toward the flat, which was only fifteen or twenty minutes away by foot. He did his best, over the course of the evening, to avoid looking at Anjum more than was appropriate, not wanting to impose himself on her, on the one hand, but also not wanting to alert anybody in the room to his interest in her. He was unable to shake the sense, whenever he was looking elsewhere, that she was looking at him, but each time he glanced up her gaze was in fact directed elsewhere, usually toward whoever was speaking, her long, thick eyebrows furrowed in a kind of skeptical curiosity, her eyes darting tirelessly from one person to another as the conversation shifted from political matters to personal updates to lighthearted teasing to gossip, breaking up from time to time into smaller conversations before coalescing back into a larger one. There was something about Anjum's gaze that elevated its object above everything else in the environment, he felt, so that whatever her eyes were resting on seemed more important than anything else in the room, whichever person she was listening or speaking to more interesting or attractive than anyone else, as if her gaze bestowed not merely significance upon what it was directed toward but existence itself, as if while she was present nothing existed except what she was looking at.

She would smile generously and sometimes laugh in response to what the others were saying, occasionally making her own comments or jokes or qualifications or rejoinders, all of which she expressed with a kind of irony, a skepticism not so much about the particular subject matter of her speech, he felt, as about whether speech in general was worth the effort of speaking. He used every occasion she spoke to study her, grateful to have an excuse to look at her without seeming conspicuous, and he tried too to participate in the conversation, not just so she might pay attention to him but also so he didn't seem out of place in that room full of mostly unknown people. As the evening wore on, as the group slowly grew smaller and those remaining grew progressively more stoned, their eyes did begin to meet more frequently, he sensed, perhaps because he was glancing at her a little more boldly as he grew more intoxicated, perhaps because sooner or later a person always came to know when they were the object of another person's gaze, the eyes had a strange power of attracting the attention of whoever they were looking at, after all, whether the person looking was immediately in front of you or on the other side of a large room, as if simply to look at another human, to recognize them, was also to ask or demand silently to be acknowledged back. On the first occasions they both looked away somewhat quickly—not too quickly, since looking away too quickly gives the impression of having something to hide or some ulterior motive—but after a while Anjum began holding her gaze for longer periods of time, in what felt like an intentional way, as though challenging him to make clear the intent of his own. There was something excruciating about the way her dark brown eyes bore into his at these points, something impenetrable about her own face that made these moments of recognition doubly difficult to withstand, even though they could have lasted at most a second or two, and looking away from her each time he would scold himself immediately for his cowardice, increasingly hopeful, at the same time, that these extended moments of contact were not just accidental, that some kind of silent communication was unfolding between them, that it wasn't just his desire leading their eyes to meet but hers too.

The two boys who Anjum seemed to know best in the group left after a couple of hours, and not long afterward Rajiv made an excuse and took his leave too, leaving only him, Anjum, and the two girls who shared the flat, one of whom immediately began rolling another joint. Anjum didn't seem to know either of them particularly well, which gave Krishan the hope that maybe she was staying behind because of him, and when the joint was finished and Anjum indicated that she needed to leave, that it was getting late, he took the initiative and asked whether she too was planning to take the metro. She was, it turned out, she was heading in the same direction that he was, both of them living in the north of the city, and it was decided that they would make their way to the station together. Taking leave of their hosts, they went downstairs, she first and he following, opened the gate and headed in the direction of the main road. It was only a week after Diwali, as most North Indians referred to the festival, and the air was thick and smoggy, still heavy with fumes from the firecrackers and fireworks of the week before. The only light came from the mute sodium glow of occasional streetlamps, which served more to underscore the lack of visibility than to improve it, and there was a postapocalyptic quality in everything they passed, in the empty roads, devoid of life, the closed shops and lightless buildings, everything around them coated in dust, even the leaves of the plants and trees, as if the city had been abandoned for years. Making their way through this desolation they found themselves talking about the differences between north and south, a subject Krishan had wanted to bring up since learning earlier in the night that Anjum was from Bangalore, sensing it would be a way of bringing them closer together, of giving the two of them some kind of shared racial or mythical origin that would put them in league against the city around them. She'd left Bangalore when she was nineteen to come to university in Delhi, Anjum told him, hadn't lived there or anywhere else in the south since then. For several years she'd hardly visited either, though she'd gone back twice in the year before last, a situation that had to do, as Krishan learned later, with the end of the three-year relationship with her ex-girlfriend, a relationship she'd told her parents about and that had compelled her to break ties with them for some time. The physical distance between them seemed to lessen as they walked, their arms brushing lightly against each other as they negotiated their way through the unlit, uneven roads and pavements, physical contact that momentarily obliterated Krishan's consciousness and which he had to try hard not to be overwhelmed by. Reaching the station they descended the long, steep staircase into the gleaming interior, where slowing down for a moment in uncertainty, stunned by the fluorescent brightness after walking so long in near darkness, they made their way through the long corridor that led to the main lobby, their movements suddenly stiff, almost embarrassed, keeping more distance between their bodies as they walked, their footsteps resounding behind them in the silence. They kept their gazes fixed ahead or on the floor in front of them, as though they couldn't look at each other, as though the brightness of the station exposed a vulnerability that they'd managed till then to keep hidden from their faces, for it was only in the darkness, after all, that you could look at a person you desired without fear of exposing yourself, which was why parties and liaisons and intimacies and sexual transactions were almost always reserved for the night, the lights kept to a minimum or even turned off completely, so you could see well enough for eye contact to be made but not for your need to be revealed. It was only in the darkness that you could approach another person and let your desire be known without allowing the sense of insufficiency or abjection that is so often part of desire to become visible, those desperate, vulnerable parts of the self you always had to skirt or sidestep during flirtation and which, when flirtation failed, when the veneer of coolness or nonchalance suddenly fell away, were painfully betrayed on your face. Krishan tried to find something to say to ward off this possibility, making a silly comment about how clean and well-lit all the metro stations in Delhi were compared to the deserted city above, a comment Anjum responded to almost immediately, to his gratefulness, saying that in a way she found them both similar, especially at night when the metro stations were largely empty, the large echoing halls and long underground corridors a strange futuristic mirror of the city above.

Entering the lobby the two of them went through security, he through the men's queue and she through the women's, putting their bags through the machines, walking through the purely ornamental metal detectors, letting themselves be frisked carelessly by the listless soldiers on duty. They went

down the staircase to the mostly empty platform, the flow of
their conversation back to normal, the moment of danger successfully averted, and no sooner had they stopped near the middle of the platform than they saw the lights of a train within the
tunnel to the left, its twin circles becoming larger and more
distinct as it entered the station almost silently, slowing to a
soundlessly smooth stop in perfect alignment with the mark-
ings on the floor. They entered the carriage, surprisingly
crowded given the emptiness of the station, and carving a space
to stand just in front of the doors, fell silent as the train began
to move. Several of the men in their section of the carriage
were looking at them, Krishan could tell, a few of them studying him out of a kind of secondary interest, but most of them
looking at Anjum, who was, he noted with discomfort, the only
woman in the carriage. They looked at her not with that gaze
with which men so often looked at women in Delhi, eyes reaching out like hands about to take hold of inert everyday objects,
a glass of water or a remote control, but with a slightly more
subdued, slightly more respectful gaze, a respect they gave only
begrudgingly, Krishan knew, because of his presence beside
her. Anjum had told him at length much later about what it was
like for women to move through public spaces in Delhi, about
how the gaze of men in Delhi seemed to lack a kind of shame,
there was no other explanation, she felt, for the persistence
with which men of all classes would try, simply by staring, to
pull the inner life out from inside the woman who was their
object of interest. You could feel the gaze of men in cities like
Chennai and Trivandrum and Bangalore too, she had told him,
but men's gazes in most other parts of the country, in most
parts of the south, for example, felt somehow less relentless,

less direct, and less violent, more likely to falter when they were responded to or challenged, as if the gazer, upon being gazed back at, could feel he was doing something wrong and withdrew. In Delhi and many of the Hindi-speaking states more generally male stares were different, were intensely unselfconscious and intensely unrelenting, so that even when you weren't being harassed in more explicit verbal or physical ways you still had to use all of your psychological resources to resist these gazes over the course of each day, to prevent these men from trying to enter your soul through your eyes, like strangers who enter the privacy of your house without permission and without even bothering to take off their shoes. You had to employ these psychological resources so constantly over the course of the day, losing even the freedom to think autonomously in your own mind, that by the time you returned home you were always utterly exhausted. The cumulative effect of years of being subject to these gazes was that women who lived in the capital had learned to curb the movement of their own eyes to remarkable degrees, restricting their gazes in public spaces to areas where their eyes couldn't be intercepted, toward their feet or their laps or into the screen of their phones, though she herself made a conscious effort not to constrain her vision, Anjum added, to let her eyes move as freely as she wanted, which was also why she made a point of never using the women-only carriages at the front of the train, no matter how crowded the other carriages were.

He'd thought many times since that conversation about what Anjum had said and the words and images she'd used, not just because it was one of the first examples he'd had of her striking eloquence, the sharpness and intelligence of which he hadn't encountered anywhere in his university, despite having just begun coursework for his PhD. What she'd said had helped him understand not just the entitlement with which men in Delhi used their eyes on women but also the amorphous tension that lay over interactions between men in Delhi too, the vague and omnipresent air of threat that sometimes seemed to hover like an electric charge over the entire city, a charge you felt that at any given time and in any given place might coalesce and then explode without warning into a sudden eruption of physical violence. He remembered sitting opposite a man on the metro one night, relatively light-skinned, strong jawed, a roughness about his face emphasized by the small scar above his right eye that cut into his brow. He was in his mid- to late twenties probably, wore the uniform of mutely colored shirt, sleeveless sweater, trousers, and sandals so common among men in the city, and was sitting beside two friends who seemed a little more well off than him, one of whom had his arm slung around his shoulder, though the man who'd caught Krishan's eye wasn't really paying attention to either of them, was simply staring at the floor in front of him, listening to music with earphones on. Sensing perhaps that he was being watched the man had looked up at Krishan, his face devoid of expression, causing Krishan to look away immediately with embarrassment, as if he'd been caught doing something wrong. After a while, when he felt sure the man had forgotten about him, Krishan looked at him again, why exactly he wasn't sure, there was something intriguing about his presence, about his rough handsomeness and the way he seemed totally absorbed in his thoughts. Again the man looked up, holding his gaze this time, causing Krishan, after one or two seconds in which neither of them gave any

indication what they were thinking, to look away. Staring down
at the floor he could feel the man continuing to look at him, his
gaze like a physical weight forcing his eyes down, and he felt
suddenly not curiosity or embarrassment but fear mixed with
shame, fear for what the man might to do to him, shame for
having looked away and for continuing to avert his gaze from
this stranger who was, he felt, now intentionally staring him
down. There was always something so unbearable when two
strangers looked at each other for an extended amount of time
without obvious reason or purpose, a kind of tension that built
up from each person's sense that the other person could see
inside them, into everything you wanted to keep hidden and
out of sight, a tension that soon became so uncomfortable you
felt compelled to smile or frown or speak, to do anything, whatever it was, to distract the other person from what they might
see through your eyes. Looking at a person in such a way was
an act of great intimacy, which was also why it could give rise
so easily to violence between men who didn't know each other,
each man interpreting the other as attempting to penetrate
him, to make him vulnerable and to possess whatever these
vulnerabilities offered. It was for this reason too that there was,
so often before these sudden eruptions of violence, a kind of
staring contest that took place between the men involved, as if
each was trying to challenge the other to enter him with his
eyes while also trying to enter the other with his own, a contest
that had become standard fare during televised boxing matches,
when the two boxers stared at each other during weigh-ins or
right before the fight began, a staring contest that starts out as
a performance but soon becomes very real, a contest that was
actually less about peering into another than showing one's

willingness to be peered into, about showing that there was nothing one was ashamed of or afraid of exposing, nothing one would not put on the line.

Krishan chastised himself for looking away, which was beginning to feel like an unacceptable act of cowardice, for though he was looking down he could feel the man continuing to stare at him, almost gloating. He kept his eyes averted for the next couple of stops, trying to work up the courage to look up at the man, not out of curiosity now but out of self-respect, despite his fear, as if to prove to himself that he had nothing to be ashamed of, that he too could own himself in the way that was required to withstand another person's gaze. He looked up finally, and the man, who had returned to looking at the floor, looked back up almost immediately with the same expressionless gaze as before, though now there was something menacing about his look, which had become almost a leer. Krishan forced himself to keep looking but the longer the two of them stared at each other the more nervous he grew, the man seemed tough, he was with his friends, they could beat him up easily if they wanted, nor would he be able to defend himself in an argument, his Hindi was too poor to come to his aid in such situations and would give him away as an outsider, which would of course only embolden them. Unable to bear the weight of the man's eyes but not wanting to concede and look away, he had tried finally simply to smile, to give, at the last minute, a nonviolent direction or interpretation to their staring, a smile that the man responded to by leaning forward and continuing to stare at him for a few seconds longer before suddenly, to Krishan's surprise, himself breaking out into a smile, a wide, friendly smile devoid of aggression, after which he called the attention of his friends, stood up, and pushed his way through the crowd—they had just arrived at a station—out through the doors of the train. It was a response that had left him confused at the time but also greatly relieved, acutely aware, as he breathed out heavily and rested back against his seat, of the power that human eyes had, their power not just to beckon other people silently from the distance but their power also to inquire, assert presence, and threaten, to enter another person with or without their will, the way they were used, by so many men, almost as a sexual organ, a tool of penetration and reception. There was an intense vulnerability that the gaze of another could make you feel, for the eyes were, as was so often said, a window into the soul, though what a gaze meant, he had realized that day, whether it meant intimacy or violence, was also dependent on the features of the face that surrounded the eyes, on the meaning given to the gaze by the lips and cheeks and eyebrows, so that when two people looked at each other it was a moment both of total knowledge and of total indeterminacy, a way of acknowledging another person that was open to the most radical of interpretations, so that when the meeting of eyes was unaccompanied by a determinate expression on the face or a determinate purpose or context it was one of the few moments in ordinary life when it seemed, somehow, that the rules that governed normal interaction between humans were suspended, as though for a moment at least, within the slender line that existed between their gazes, anything at all was possible between strangers.

Krishan was pretending to look at the little electronic signboard above the door that indicated the stops on the train's route, and realizing after a moment that Anjum was looking straight at him he lowered his head and tried to return her gaze. She was standing with her back to the doors, one hand holding the grip that hung from the ceiling and the other folded behind her back, her body loose and relaxed as she swayed gently with the movement of the train. Her expression was difficult to read, the dark brown of her irises thinned to a rim around her dilated pupils, and she was gazing at him as though totally oblivious to the fact that the two of them, especially she, were the center of attention in the carriage. He waited for her to speak but she remained silent—anything they said would be immediately audible to the people around them, even if they kept their voices low—and realizing that she'd been looking at him for some time, that this looking was, moreover, intentional, Krishan felt even more uncomfortable in the crowded, brightly lit carriage, not just because he once more felt exposed but also because Anjum's gaze was intended now, he couldn't help feeling, as a provocation to the men staring at her, as a kind of demonstration that she refused to curb the movement of her eyes and the desire it contained, a demonstration not just for the sake of the men staring at her but also, he felt, for him, as if she could tell he felt threatened by these gazes and wanted him to know that she, unlike him, was not. Not wanting to show his discomfort he forced himself to respond to her gaze, doing his best to avoid her eyes and look instead at the other parts of her face, at her dark, curved forehead, fully visible because of her short hair, the light furrows between her eyebrows, which contributed to the sternness of her gaze, the stud on her left nostril, and her lips, though each of her features always led him back to her eyes, large and dark and insistent, or perhaps it was her eyes themselves, staring earnestly at his, which constantly drew his gaze back to hers. They were almost the same height, he only an inch or two taller, and standing opposite her he noticed how perfectly aligned their bodies were, that if he moved just a short distance forward his chest would be pressed against her chest, his waist against her waist, his groin against hers. He'd been aware since the beginning of Anjum's physical presence, both her stature and also the way she had of moving, but standing in front of her now—he was careful to keep his eyes on her face, not to look down at the rest of her—he felt newly alert to her body, as if realizing for the first time that it existed in the same space and time as his body, a body that could come into contact with his, that could rock and press and shift and push with and against his own. He still didn't know whether she was attracted to men, everything he'd interpreted till then as possible interest could just as well be disinterested friendliness, and even if she was attracted to men in general it didn't, of course, imply that she was attracted to him. Her gaze, though, was gradually becoming gentler, more open and more suggestive, no longer seeming to challenge or interrogate him so much as to be making a kind of invitation, and the longer he looked at her the more everything else seemed to fade away, the gazes of the men around them diminishing in force, becoming almost mute, the sounds around them too becoming fainter, the announcer's voice as they approached various stations, the whoosh of the doors sliding apart, the shuffling of feet as people entered and left the train, as if only the two of them existed on the train as it wound its way through the subterranean city, everything else reduced to a faint echo from a distant world. He felt their bodies moving closer together, their foreheads almost but not quite touching, as if they were about to share a secret with each other though neither of them said a thing, no longer because they feared being heard by the people around them, none of whom existed anymore, but because it seemed there was no more need now to speak, because conversation was no longer required to distract from or conceal what each was feeling, because it was somehow becoming clear, standing opposite each other in the heavy, rhythmic clarity of their intoxication, that they were interested in one and the same thing.

Krishan didn't know how long they stood there looking at each other, stoned but with total lucidity, their bodies rocking gently with the movement of the train but never touching, but at some point Anjum leaned toward him so that her mouth was near his ear and asked whether he had to sleep early that night, whether he wanted to smoke a little more before he went his own way, a question that even if Krishan wasn't exactly expecting didn't exactly surprise him, and to which he'd responded with a silent nod of his head. Getting off at her station, which was only two stops past his, they took a three-wheeler in silence to her flat, their knees pressing against each other over the course of the bumpy ten-minute journey, she looking out on her side at the pavement cascading under the wheels of the three-wheeler, he looking out on his side at the passing streets, desolate as a moonscape, their hands covertly making their way toward each other so that they could clasp each other while continuing to look out their respective sides. When they arrived Anjum whispered that they needed to be quiet, and leading him up several flights of stairs, unlocking her door, she took his hand and guided him through the darkness of the flat. He waited by the door as she went in and turned on a light, a small bedside lamp on the floor that lit up the room with a soft yellow glow. The room was small and bare, empty of furniture except for a wooden desk in the corner and a thin mattress on the floor along the wall. The walls were lined with folded clothes piled on sheets of old newspaper and several stacks of books in English and Kannada, the English ones mainly political or historical, as he came to learn later, the Kannada ones mainly poetry. Anjum put her things in a corner and sat down cross-legged on the mattress, her back against the wall. Krishan sat down next to her, not against the wall but facing her at an angle, watched as she took from beside the mattress an engraved metal box, a small clay lamp containing the butts of several old cigarettes, and a slender volume of Kannada poetry. She took out from the box a small, marble-sized ball of hash, which, she told him as if by way of explanation, she'd been gifted by a friend, hash being too expensive for her to buy herself, then heating the hash up gently under the flame of a lighter, she began to break the softened ball up with her fingernails into tiny crumbs that she deposited onto the cover of the book. Not quite able to believe that he was alone with this person he'd spent the previous two months fantasizing about constantly, Krishan watched as she mixed the little shreds of hash with tobacco from a cigarette and then rolled the joint with elegant, practiced fingers. She put the book away, dusted off the mattress, and lit up the joint, and he asked as she took her first drag whether she read a lot in Kannada, to which she responded that it was mainly poetry she read in Kannada, most of it from a slightly older generation of female poets in Karnataka. She didn't really enjoy poetry in English or Hindi, the other two languages she spoke, the emotional valences of the words and images not resonating as much with her as they did in her mother tongue. She wrote in Kannada too, in her journal or notebook—she preferred not calling it a diary—but that had been a relatively recent development, something she'd begun doing only in the last two or three years. When she lived in Bangalore she'd preferred writing in English, probably because in Bangalore, where she spoke mainly Kannada, English had been a way for her to remove herself from her environment, to feel, when she was alone with herself, that she was far from everything around her. It was for this same reason probably that she'd started writing in Kannada again now, because in Delhi of course she communicated primarily in Hindi and English, so that now writing in Kannada rather than English had become her primary mode of being elsewhere, not necessarily a way for her to be back in Bangalore or back in Karnataka, places she felt quite ambivalent about, but a way for her to feel elsewhere at least than Delhi.

Their fingertips came into quiet contact each time the joint passed between them, each of them taking long, indulgent drags before passing it on. It shortened quickly, faster than Krishan would have liked, and taking the last drag, stubbing the joint out firmly in the clay lamp, Anjum looked up at him silently, a shy but assured smile on her lips. There was nothing in their hands to distract them now, nothing to help them pretend they weren't sitting next to each other, alone and unhindered, free to do what they wanted. Both of them shifted slightly where they sat, and Anjum put her hand lightly on the inside of his knee, tracing it upward across his thigh. Krishan brought his face forward to kiss her but leaning to the side she skirted his mouth and kissed him not on the lips but on the side of his jaw, near his ear, then down toward his neck, only gradually making her way up toward his lips. In the soft, effortless sequence of movements that followed almost instinctively, as if the ground beneath them was giving way and holding each other they'd begun falling downward through space, their clothes came off and she sat astride him, her movement slow at first, then more voracious. He lay beneath her, contributing to this movement and supporting it with his hips, his hands moving from her thighs to her waist to her sternum just as hers moved from his chest to his shoulders to his neck, occasionally becoming conscious of what was happening, regarding the woman on top of him with quiet amazement before becoming submerged again in their deep motion, clutching her body more tightly in their increasing momentum as though to prove to himself that she really existed, that the image he'd carried of her in his mind was in fact more than an image, something solid, not fleeting, made of flesh and skin that he could hold and clasp, which gave off smells he could breathe in and sweat he could feel his hands slide over. Her breathing was becoming faster, her groin pressing harder and more intently against his, and sensing what was happening he did his best to hold himself in check, to focus his mind as he tried to accommodate her increasing urgency, though soon he felt himself being overwhelmed and joined her in reaching, unexpectedly, a breathless, briefly overlapping peak. When it was over Anjum leaned forward, still astride him, and buried her face between his neck and head, her chest pressing against his as she breathed heavily in and out. She stretched out her legs so she was lying flat on top of him, her feet upon his, each of them listening as the quick beating of their hearts against their chests became slower and more measured. They lay there in silence, each of them buried in the quiet exhaustion of their bodies, watching as their intoxication surfaced slowly from the ruins of their urgency, neither of them feeling any desire to speak, as though swathed in the warm afterglow of exertion and pleasure they were fully suspended in the present moment, without thought of past or future, a present that like a womb seemed sufficient to contain everything they needed so long as their bodies remained in contact.

They remained this way for fifteen minutes, half an hour, or maybe even an hour, it was difficult to say, it was as if time wasn't passing, or as if all time was contained in this one time, though at some point, shifting onto her side, Anjum placed her hand on his thigh and traced lightly up toward his groin in inquiry. Her hand dwelled there till she sensed a shifting, which soon turned into another series of movements, which led them again to a slow, vigorous immersion into each other, this time longer and more explicit, each of them plundering the other more boldly now, taking as much pleasure in taking as in being taken from. They shifted from one position to another, consuming each other in turns with their eyes and hands, each of them torn between the urge to physically possess the other body and the urge to be able to admire the other body at a remove, caught between the conflicting needs for proximity and distance so central to desire. When they slowed down once more they lay side by side on their backs in exhaustion, his right leg sprawled over her left leg, her left arm stretched out over his stomach, each of them staring at the ceiling in the warm glow of the lamp. They were silent for some time and then began to speak, Krishan could no longer remember about what, to speak with the strangely confessional intimacy that so often arises between new lovers as they lay beside each other after sex, an intimacy that sometimes feels artificial or performed but which, when two individuals have been longing for each other so much that their desire isn't exhausted in the act of union, can feel strangely profound, an intimacy in which each person feels that what they are sharing is something they've kept deep inside themselves all their lives and have only now, in the safe vulnerability of the moment, become capable of expressing. It was an intimacy Krishan had felt once or twice in the past with other people, but which was magnified now to a degree he'd never experienced, as though the words he spoke at that moment to Anjum and which she spoke to him would not, as most words did, fade gently into the world's endless stream of sounds and silences, as though their words were somehow really being heard or really being received, being given some kind of objective validation outside the boundaries of their individual selves, as though in speaking at that moment within the warm cocoon of their bodies they were writing their souls out into the sky or inscribing it into the earth, making themselves, by means of their words, permanent somehow or eternal.

They did not sleep that night, moving continuously in and out of these states of vigorous exertion, peaceful exhaustion, and quiet, confessional revelation, as though none of these states were distinct from each other, as though none of them had any beginning or end but were all simply different aspects of the same larger condition. At six or six-thirty in the morning, knowing he would have to go home before going to campus, Krishan got up to search for his clothes in the mess of things beside the mattress. He put them on with some awkwardness, knowing that Anjum, naked under the sheets, was watching him, then kneeling down on the mattress he kissed her on the cheek with a chasteness she did not seem to expect and took his leave. Outside the day was colder than he'd expected, perhaps because he hadn't been outside so early in the morning in a while. The morning light was pleasantly dusky through the thick fog and dust, and he felt as he walked a gentle invigoration from having not slept all night and not eaten. Despite the poor visibility the scenes around him possessed an unusual clarity, the edges of things sharp and their surfaces distinctly colored, the tea shops already open, fruit and vegetable sellers already pushing their carts, laborers going here and there, the roads packed with cars, vans, buses, and three-wheelers throwing up large quantities of noise and smoke into the air. Looking at all the people around him already beginning the day, already fully engrossed in obligations, in the routine of their daily lives, he felt as though he'd stepped from one realm of existence into another, each of which seemed to deny the possibility of the other. As though the appearance of the world of everyday life, which had seemed so far away just a few hours ago, called into question now the existence of the world he'd just left behind, a world so different in nature that he might actually have begun to doubt its existence had he not been carrying the smell of it still in his body, the scent of sweat and bodily fluids and the faint pungency of condoms, all of which enveloped him against the morning cold like a warm, invisible layer, a constant proof and reminder of the night before. The scent remained with him on the ride home and even after he had showered, changed his clothes, and gone to campus, leaving him only after he'd slept in his own bed that night and then bathed again the next morning, and perhaps it was its dissipation that was responsible for the quiet anxiety he felt in the following days, as if reimmersed into his ordinary life without any physical token of the ever more distant world he'd shared with Anjum, he could no longer be sure whether the profundity of the experience had been real or just imagined, whether Anjum had felt the same way or whether, blinded by his heavy intoxication, he had misread the situation, in which case, it occurred to him, it was possible she might not even want to see him again. They did in fact meet a few days later, this time at his flat rather than hers, and this second night too had gone the way of the first, the two of them again hardly sleeping, again moving in and out of those different modes of bliss, and again followed, not long afterward, by a kind of anxiety, less this time about whether he'd actually felt what he remembered feeling or even about whether Anjum had felt the same way, but about whether, rather, what they'd experienced together could possibly continue, whether it wouldn't somehow just vanish into thin air. Even if their two meetings had been as revelatory for her as they'd been for him, how could he be sure she would continue to find in their encounters that same quality and pitch, how could he be sure it would continue, not just for her but for him too, for how after all could such intense desire and attraction really last, how could a way of being so manifestly at odds with the so-called real world possibly be sustained?

In the three or four months that followed, time that felt, in his memory, strangely outside time, Krishan had oscillated continuously between these two conditions, between the thoughtless, rapturous, and seemingly endless present that he experienced in physical proximity to Anjum, and the restless, agitated uncertainty that he felt when they were apart. They met each other usually no more than once a week and sometimes even less frequently, depending on Anjum's schedule, for most of her free time was devoted to her political work, to organizing, going to protests, and running workshops, for which she often traveled out of Delhi on weekends too. When they did meet they would spend extended periods of time together, sometimes, if they met on the weekend, up to two days without break holed up in one of their rooms, smoking cigarettes and hash, having sex, talking and reading to each other, the sleepless nights followed by mornings and afternoons in which they drifted continuously between dreams and coitus. Even in the excursions they made out into the world to eat or to obtain fresh air they were unable to break away from the cocoon they formed together in bed, so that even sitting in tea stalls and smoking cigarettes, walking together directionlessly in parks, standing opposite each other on trains, they were as though wholly ensconced in each other, unable to break away from each other, as if the world consisted of only the two of them, as if everything outside them was some kind of trick or illusion or lesser reality, a feeling no doubt related to the strange quality that time seemed to acquire while they were together, for though this time could be measured objectively, could be counted, once it was over, in terms of hours and minutes, it seemed at the same time recalcitrant to the metrics of standard time, as though it had a duration that was fuller or vaster than the time that constituted the other parts of their lives, as though while they were with each other they were held together in a single, depthless moment that could be stretched out forever and that, while they were in it, went on endlessly, though eventually of course it always came to an end. The longer they spent together in this way, hardly eating and hardly sleeping, as if their time together were some kind of ascetic practice, the more dangerous being together somehow seemed, their personalities beginning to disintegrate, their private moods beginning to dissipate, as if in the time they spent together they were pushing farther and farther into some realm of existence or being that was connected to the so-called real world by only the slenderest of threads, so that the farther they went into this other realm the more possible it seemed that the thread might be cut, that they might find themselves suspended, suddenly, in some other place, unable to return to their familiar selves. It would seem more and more urgent for each of them to obtain brief moments alone so they could verify that they continued to exist as individuals, so they could attempt, in whatever small ways, to preserve at least scraps of their individuality, one of them going outside in order to buy cigarettes, taking what was obviously a longer amount of time than necessary, the other spending several minutes in the bathroom, answering the various messages that had accumulated on their phones under the pretext of having to use the toilet. Having reassured themselves of their separate existences they would lose themselves once more in the world they formed together, this dissipation or disintegration of the self holding such an ineluctable pull over them, despite the need they felt for self-preservation, that they couldn't stop themselves from spending more time together, though eventually of course it would be necessary to separate, eventually the pull of the outside world and their separate lives grew so strong that they could no longer continue ignoring it even as they tried, postponing their social or personal commitments and sometimes even canceling them, extending or prolonging the moment of departure in small ways, one last cigarette, one last cup of tea, or one last quick, urgent ripping apart of clothes, so that five minutes more became half an hour and half an hour more became three full hours.

When they did finally manage to part ways Krishan always felt a quiet relief, mingled with the sadness of having to confront the strange nonexistence of his person, a nonexistence he felt as a blissful, exhilarating condition in the presence of Anjum but that, as soon as he was on his own, he experienced only as an unsettling loss of self. Too exhausted to think or feel or do anything productive he would go home and lie down for a while, and when he finally recovered the strength he would go to the bathroom and shower, attempting, by washing his body, to recover something of his former self. He would try then to do something quiet, to sweep his room, the rhythmic, repetitive motion of which always comforted him, to read, which allowed him to feel he had an inner life of his own, to try in whatever way he could, in other words, to rebuild his depleted resources and reconstruct a self that was independent of Anjum. Sooner or later though he would feel the need to contact Anjum, to hear from her and to obtain from her some kind of external corroboration of the thoughts and feelings still lingering in him from their encounter, some kind of proof that these thoughts and feelings were justified, a consolation for the loneliness he began to feel as their separation became more concrete. Anjum rarely responded quickly to his texts once they'd separated, often taking hours to text back, sometimes more than a day. Her responses were sometimes sweet, sometimes more matter of fact, but they were never long and seldom conducive to further conversation, as though she wanted to maintain some distance from him once they were no longer in the same physical space. Maintaining such distance was healthy, Krishan knew, it was necessary for regeneration, which was necessary in turn not only for the endless task of daily living but also, more importantly, in order to be able to see each other again. He did his best not to seem desperate or needy, not to create the impression that he wanted her more than she wanted him, never sending more than one text message at a time, never sending a second message till he received a response to the first, always waiting at least an hour before replying to the messages he finally received, even if he wanted to respond immediately. He did his best to appear unbothered by Anjum's silences, but obtaining little reassurance from her that she was thinking about him as much as he was thinking about her, that she wanted to see him as soon as he wanted to see her, he would begin in the days following their meetings to feel anxious, to wonder whether he might have said or done the wrong thing, whether she was beginning to get bored of him, whether the profundity of their time together was being lost to repetition and routine. Such anxiety was, of course, experienced to some degree by every person newly in love, by every person who finds in another a bliss or rapture that they were unaware till then was possible and that they became terrified, having experienced, of losing. It was an anxiety that usually diminished as time passed, as interaction became a little more habitual and as each person became to the other someone whose continued presence could be taken for granted, and Krishan's anxiety too began to diminish a little with the passing of time, as he became more confident that the quality of transcendence in their encounters was not going to subside just because they were becoming more familiar with each other. He could tell how much Anjum liked him, not just his body but his sensibility and the things he said, could tell how interested she was in him from all the questions she asked about his youth in Sri Lanka, which seemed to her like a distant, mythical place. He could tell from how she sometimes held him while they slept that she was opening herself up to him, allowing herself to become more attached to him, but even as she seemed to become more vulnerable, even as he sensed, in the way she sometimes looked at him or sometimes touched him, that she too was perhaps developing the tenderness that marked the transition between falling in love and actually loving someone, Krishan couldn't suppress the sense that in some private way she was resistant to becoming too close to him, that despite being willing to abandon herself fully when they were actually beside each other, she was wary of spending too much time with him or of incorporating him into the rest of her life—as though she felt that what they experienced together could not go on forever, that it would inevitably cease to be gratifying or fulfilling if it did, as though the yearning for other worlds he sensed so vividly in her could be permanently satisfied only by something else.

He'd wondered initially whether this resistance might have to do with wanting to be with other people, for Anjum would often express her attraction toward people they knew or saw in passing, both boys and girls, making these remarks almost conversationally, as if she couldn't possibly imagine him being affected by what she said. She sometimes mentioned lovers she'd had in the past and during her previous relationship, which had been open for two years, and it occurred to him that maybe she wanted to sleep with other people—maybe women in particular, who could give her something he could not—that possibly in fact she already had other lovers, which was maybe why they

saw each other no more than once a week. Or perhaps she was
in some way embarrassed by him, embarrassed to be seen in a
conventional relationship with a male, and maybe this was why
she seemed so reluctant to meet him at social events and in the
company of friends. He didn't raise the issue with her explicitly,
partly out of shyness and partly out of fear of what he would
learn, and it was only two or three months into their relationship that he began to sense that Anjum's distance came not so
much from desire for others or embarrassment at their relationship as from the fact, simply, that she didn't seek transcendence in sexual or romantic relationships at all. She liked
intimacy, of course, had a strong, sometimes overwhelming
need for sex, and was clearly capable of losing herself in the
rapturous world they experienced when they were alone, but
for some reason it was as though she didn't fully trust this world
of theirs, as if she didn't believe it could do justice to what she
ultimately yearned for. This yearning, Krishan began to understand as they spent more time together, as he learned more
about her life outside their meetings, was a yearning she saw
only her political work as capable of fulfilling, not exactly the
utopian vision that animated this work, since she was too cynical to imagine that a perfect world could ever be brought about,
but the life she hoped to create with the community of people
with whom she did this work, with her comrades, as she liked
to call them. Listening to the way she talked about the various
cases of gender and caste violence she saw at her job, the way
she talked about the protests she went to and the police violence she'd witnessed, the fervor with which she discussed
plans and visions for future work, always collaborative, always
with comrades, it dawned on him that Anjum was willing to

give up everything for these plans and visions, that if the circumstances were right she would drop everything for their sake and disappear, and though he sometimes hoped, in moments when he felt close to her, that he too might be able to share in this life she sought, that she might at some point be willing to invite him into it, he couldn't help suspecting, at other, weaker moments, that she viewed the time they spent together as only a distraction, that no matter how much she liked or even loved him their relationship was something she allowed herself only as a break from what really mattered to her, that she was, like the female Tiger cadres he'd read about and listened to in so many articles and interviews, one of those people for whom love, no matter how otherworldly it seemed, was always bound to the so-called real world, a world whose basic structure she could never accept, that she was, in other words, one of those people whose being was so taken up with yearning for another world that no single person, no love or no romantic relationship, could ever fill the absence in her soul.

6

IT WAS THIS thought Krishan kept returning to as he sat opposite Anjum that evening on the train to Bombay, he pretending to read while all the time stealing glances at her, hoping she would glance up from her book and give him a sign, that she would reach out with her hand to touch him or raise her head up to look at him at least. He was able, usually, to suppress such anxieties when next to Anjum, not wanting to let them affect their time together, but having not seen her in three weeks and having hardly heard from her at all, unable now, even in her presence, to obtain the instant reassurance that her touch always gave, Krishan couldn't help worrying that something had changed during her time in Jharkhand, that the urgency for union he'd always sensed when they met in person was no longer present, as if the distance she so often tried to maintain when they were physically apart had crystallized now into something more definite. Dinner was beginning to be served

in their carriage, the staff moving quickly from berth to berth
with trays marked vegetarian and nonvegetarian, and becoming aware of the commotion around them Anjum had closed
her book finally and looked up. She asked him how his novel
was going, and looking down at the book still open in his hands
he replied that it was going okay, that he'd read a little too much
for the day and wasn't really in the mood to keep reading. She
too was a little distracted, she told him, a little too upset to
read. He looked at her inquiringly, surprised at this admission,
and after hesitating for a moment she told him she'd been fighting with her mother, that no matter how much she tried to put
the matter aside it had kept returning to her thoughts. Krishan
waited for her to continue, but she seemed unsure about
whether to share more, and it was only when he prodded her a
little, asking what had happened, what was the reason for the
fight, that Anjum sighed and began to explain. It had started
with an accusatory comment her mother had made on the
phone three weeks ago, chastising her for having not returned
to Bangalore in so long. She'd gone twice the year before but
hadn't been back in the previous year, and her mother had been
pestering her continuously about her next visit. She'd told her
mother it wasn't her fault, that her work had been overwhelming and that she simply hadn't had time to visit, but her mother,
who'd been irritable from the start of their conversation, had
insinuated that there must have been some other reason. What
did she mean, she'd asked, what other reason, and her mother,
without skipping a beat, had told her that her ex-girlfriend
must have been the reason, that either she'd gotten back with
her ex or that she was wasting her life away in some other infantile way. Anjum had been silent at first, not having expected this

accusation, then remembering all the things her mother had said in the past concerning Divya she'd suddenly become furious, had shouted and hung up the phone. On both occasions her mother had tried calling since then, ostensibly to patch things up, the subject had come up again, neither of them backing down, and on both occasions the line had been cut amid shouting and recriminations.

Krishan had heard a little about how Anjum had fallen out with her parents over Divya, but it was something she'd never seemed to want to dwell on at length, despite his attempts at inquiry whenever the subject came up, and he was a little taken aback now by how patiently she began to relate the story behind the recent fight, a story that was, she made a point of telling him, nothing particularly surprising or remarkable. She'd been together with Divya for almost two years at the time, she told him, had been living together in the same flat with her for several months, and because she'd felt certain the relationship was going to last she'd decided that she should finally let her parents know. It was a matter she'd known they wouldn't respond to well, especially not her mother, but her parents were relatively permissive and understanding so far as parents went, had always supported or at least sympathized with whatever she and her sister wanted. She'd assumed that eventually they would come to accept the relationship, even if they had to go through a long period of adjustment before that could happen, even if they never made any effort to meet Divya or bring her into their lives, which wasn't, in any case, something she particularly cared for. She'd fully expected the fury of her mother's initial response, had fully expected the long campaign of manipulation that came afterward, the tears her mother frequently

shed in an attempt to make her feel guilty, her claims that Anjum's father was becoming ill in response to what she'd told
them. She'd expected the vicious remarks, calculated to induce
shame, had expected the quietly poisonous words that sank in
and took root long after they'd been spoken and heard, but
what she hadn't quite expected, what she hadn't quite prepared
herself for, was that she herself would be so affected by everything her mother said. She'd been close to her mother during
childhood, almost inseparable, but their relationship had become troubled when she was a teenager, and she'd made a concerted effort when she left to Delhi for university to distance
herself from her parents and her home. Her mother would still
make disparaging comments every so often about the way she
dressed or the way she looked, would chastise her if she didn't
want to spend time with relatives when she returned home, but
by the time she'd graduated and begun to work her mother had
become less controlling, sensing perhaps that she had less
power over her daughter now that she was making her own
way in the world.

She'd assumed, when she told her parents about Divya, that
no matter what her mother said she would be able to stay patient and composed, remain unaffected by the attempts her
mother made to bring the relationship to an end, but the truth,
she'd realized, stunningly obvious in retrospect, was that her
mother was still after all those years capable of piercing her, of
making her doubt not only her convictions but her sense of
self. She'd borne her violent words as long as she could, hoping
they would eventually come to an end, but the fighting had
continued for months, leading to deeper and deeper resentment, till finally, no longer able to hear her mother's voice with-

out feeling her chest constrict in anger, she'd been forced to break off ties. They didn't talk for a year and a half, not till several months after the relationship with Divya ended, and even then she didn't tell them about the breakup immediately, not wanting to give her mother the satisfaction of knowing it was over. When she finally learned what happened her mother took care not to seem overjoyed, persuading her to come home for a week, making her special curries and desserts almost every meal, never once making reference to the relationship. She'd known that nothing had really been resolved, that her mother would continue pretending she was straight, but she'd accepted the conciliatory gestures nevertheless, the reassurance and security of being in touch with her parents convincing her to let the matter go. As time passed and things became more normal she gradually forgot what happened, which felt increasingly in the past and increasingly insignificant, especially since things with Divya had ended for other reasons. It was only now that she was realizing how resentful she must have remained, for how else, when her mother brought Divya up on the phone, could all that rage have resurfaced, so suddenly and forcefully that it surprised even her? In a way her mother's intuition had been right—the fact she hadn't returned home in so long testified, no matter how she tried to rationalize it, to a smoldering anger about all the things her mother had said, an anger she'd suppressed for a long time and which, when her mother provoked her that day on the phone, had finally exploded into the open.

Anjum fell silent as their trays were brought to them, each of them moving to the edge of the berth and resting the trays on their laps. They opened the little plastic containers to examine what was inside, nothing but a few small, slightly soggy chapattis and a yellow-colored fish curry, and leaning forward to avoid spilling they began to eat. When the two uniformed men had served the opposite berths and moved beyond ear-shot, Krishan turned again toward Anjum and spoke in a low voice. Was she sure that her mother's pressure hadn't been partly responsible for her decision to break up with Divya, that her mother's role in the breakup wasn't the source of her unex-pected anger? Anjum thought for a moment, looking at him as she finished swallowing what was in her mouth, then shook her head. No, she said. If anything her mother's response had made her even more determined to be with Divya, if anything it had made her stay with Divya even longer than she would have oth-erwise. She wouldn't have let her mother or any of her family members affect her choices, she'd been with other women too since Divya, and wouldn't hesitate to be with a woman again in the future, if that was what she wanted. She paused for a sec-ond, then smiling at him as if making a joke added that if she was spending time with him now, it was because she liked him, not because he helped her satisfy some subconscious desire to please her mother. Krishan listened as she began to speak about her previous relationship openly and at length for the first time, as she described Divya's possessiveness and the various other problems that had led to the end of their time together. Her voice was less grave now, more earnest, as if in talking about her mother and Divya she was getting something off her chest, and Krishan felt the anxiety he'd felt all afternoon melting away. He understood now why Anjum had been so out of touch these last three weeks, why she'd seemed distant for most of the day, and he could sense, in the way she was talking about Divya, that she was trying in part to reassure him, to convey that she hadn't ignored him on purpose and that there was nothing he needed to worry about. She was focusing on him fully, her eyes fully on his, and he couldn't help feeling grateful that she was telling him all these private, intimate details, she who was usually so reserved about what she shared, as if this person who'd maintained till then such a smooth façade of invulnerability was willing at last to open herself up to him. Sure that nothing had changed between them, that they had, in fact, somehow grown closer over the past three weeks, Krishan felt silly for all the anxiety he'd been feeling, anxiety that now felt misplaced and childish. He should have guessed that something else was happening, they were after all going on this trip to Bombay together, were going to spend three weeks with each other in a kind of semi-domesticity, something they'd never done before and that Anjum wouldn't have suggested if she wasn't in some way serious about him. She could have told him of course that she was fighting with her mother, in which case he would have tried to comfort her instead of getting worked up on his own, but that was just how Anjum was, she was secretive with her thoughts and liked to deal with things on her own, a quality that made her confidences all the more precious when she shared them. They stayed up talking as the passengers in the carriage around them began going to bed, turning off their compartment lights and drawing the curtains over their berths, their conversation moving from Anjum's mother and Divya to parent-child relationships, to the question of financial independence and other more far afield topics, Krishan becoming more and more cheerful as they talked, as if only now were things between them becoming normal again, making jokes, reaching out and touching Anjum on the knee or forearm, causing her to laugh and touch him back. When, around nine or nine-thirty, the main lights in the carriage were turned off and Anjum yawned, told him she was sleepy, he couldn't help feeling slightly let down, not because he'd thought any other end to the night was possible but because he'd only just begun feeling connected to her, and wanted to remain in that feeling. He watched as she stood up and pulled down her bag from the upper berth, began to spread out the sheets and cover, then getting up with some reluctance he began clearing the lower berth, dusting off the crumbs from their meal and spreading out his own sheets. When Anjum was done setting up her bed she came up from behind and touched his left elbow, squeezing it lightly as she leaned in close and whispered good night. Climbing nimbly up the small iron ladder, she made some last adjustments to her berth, then drew her curtain and disappeared from view.

Krishan finished making his bed and sat down at the edge of his berth, looked to his left and right and wondered what to do. There were no signs of life or movement in the carriage, the curtains had been drawn across all the berths but his, the bright fluorescent ceiling lights turned off and replaced by two small bulbs in the corners of the carriage that gave the darkness a dull amber hue. There was a reading light that he could turn on in the upper corner of his berth, he knew, but he didn't really feel like reading, especially not after having read or tried to read for so many hours that afternoon. The sudden and intense fluctuations in his mood that day had left him exhausted, in a quiet, ruminative mood, and what he wanted above all was to be with himself for a while. Deciding to lie down and watch what could

be made of the passing night, he took off his sandals, brought
his legs up onto the bed, and drew the curtain so he was enclosed in the darkness of the berth's womb-like space. Through
the scratched horizontal pane of the window the countryside
outside was flitting by quickly, shrouded ghostlike in the blue-
black dark. He brought his face to the glass and tried to discern
what kind of landscape they were passing, but couldn't make
out anything except for very occasional lights in the distance
and trees here and there, as though everything passing by was
anonymous, only the continuous pounding of the train's wheels
below to mark their progress against the immensity of the
night. Raising his hand, Krishan caressed the soft leather underside of Anjum's berth. He could sense her presence above him,
in her own separate enclosure, and the thought of being so
close to her and yet so sealed off magnified his feeling of being
alone, not in a way that caused anxiety or distress but in a peaceful, almost pleasant way. It had been a while since he'd last felt
this kind of solitude, this sense of calm self-containment or self-
sufficiency so different from the loneliness that had been taking
hold of him in the past few months. Unlike that loneliness, which
was full of a desperate, almost helpless desire to be in Anjum's
presence, a constant anxiety about whether Anjum really wanted
to be with him, what he felt now oddly was a sense of needing
nothing outside himself, not even Anjum, a sense of being able to
relinquish the world and everything it offered, to accept instead
the person he was, incomplete though he was and so full of
voids.

He'd never thought of himself as being needy—even now,
in his state of calm, he found the word difficult to use—but the
truth was that he'd become, in the last few months, so depen-

dent on the signs of interest and affection that Anjum gave him, his moods so responsive to everything she said or failed to say, did or failed to do, that sometimes he seemed pathetic even to himself. He'd found himself becoming envious and even possessive on occasion, resentful of the fact that the time he spent with Anjum was determined solely by reference to her availability, and even if Anjum's own nature was partly responsible for these feelings—it was no coincidence, he felt, that Divya too had been possessive while she was with Anjum—he still couldn't help detesting himself for the pettiness of the thoughts he sometimes had. When his desperation was at its peak he often felt his only recourse was to pull back completely, to attempt to psychologically extricate himself from Anjum altogether, partly out of frustration or indignation or even perhaps a desire to wound, but above all to save himself from the pain of feeling desire too strongly. He would listen, at such moments, to a recording of the *Sivapurānam* he'd bought a few years before, not long after having heard it for the first time at a funeral in Colombo for some distant relative. A singer had been hired for the funeral, and listening to the man as he stood singing beside the corpse for the small audience, he'd been moved, despite having hardly known the deceased, to the point of shedding tears, entranced by the singer's rich, unornamented voice, by the slowly building, incantatory rhythm of the song, written in a Tamil from several hundred years before that he could hardly understand but which, he knew, was about the pain of being embodied, of having to live many different lives, as a blade of grass, a worm, and a human, of having to endure countless existences dominated by earthly desires while all the time yearning to give up earthly life, to be shorn of attachment and the weight of the body and joined to the feet of Siva. Listening to the song or singing the lyrics to himself in those moments of desperation he was able to more easily bear the uncertainty of being with Anjum, would feel consoled by these visions of total removal from the world, by the possibility of cutting off all ties with Anjum and leaving her completely, a severance that was at that point only a fantasy but nevertheless one that comforted him. There was probably something unhealthy, he suspected, about this need to either identify completely with Anjum or completely withdraw from her, about his difficulty finding a reasonable middle ground, and he wondered in less impassioned moments whether it was possible to relate to her differently, to accommodate himself better to this person who clearly wanted to be with him but seemingly only in a temporary or provisional way. He wondered whether he could simply be grateful for her presence when it was available and content by himself when it was not, whether he could take pleasure in her company when he could but remain unworried and unconcerned at other times, to avoid in this way the debilitating anxiety he so often felt when she was out of touch or vague about plans or withdrawn. He would think, listening to the *Sivapurānam*, of the sea in Sri Lanka as it was during the calmer months, specifically of the sea in Trincomalee as he'd seen it once on a warm, late June evening, the water a calm, waveless sheet of glimmering, glistening blue that stretched out silently toward the sky. He would think of how the water unfurled itself so softly across the gentle slope of the beach, how it swept over the smooth, polished sand with such tenderness and how reaching its full extension, just as it was losing all its momentum, it would pause as if taking a breath in a last brief embrace of the earth, clasping the land for as long as it could before being drawn back with a sigh into the sea. He would think of the sea, rolling and unrolling itself softly and placidly across the edges of the earth in this way, coming into contact with the shore so lovingly and gratefully and then, when it was time, withdrawing so gracefully, and he would wonder whether it was possible for him too to be in Anjum's presence and then return to himself with such grace and equanimity, to attach himself to the thing he loved and then detach himself without each time ripping apart his soul, though the truth, he knew, was that such a stance was only possible at certain moments, at least for him, moments in which he was, for whatever reason, briefly in possession of himself, for it was difficult to be philosophical in the midst of desire, it was difficult to be as removed from the world as religious devotees claimed to be when you were caught up in the bliss of union or in the desperation of being parted.

How long he sat there looking out the window it was hard to say, immersed in the darkness of the world passing by and simultaneously lost inside himself, but at some point, maybe half an hour, maybe an hour after she'd said good night and withdrawn for the night, Krishan heard the creaking of Anjum's berth directly above him, the sound of Anjum moving on her bed. He assumed at first that she was simply shifting or rolling around, since Anjum moved constantly from one side to the other as she slept, but a few seconds later he noticed the flapping of the curtain on the far side of his berth, the momentary entry of the carriage's amber light into the enclosure. A hand parted the curtain and he saw Anjum's face looking in, her eyes squinting as she tried to locate him in the darkness of the berth. She was trying to determine whether or not he was

awake, he realized, and quickly drew in his legs to let her know
he was up. Parting the curtain more widely, letting more light
in, Anjum glanced around to make sure no one was looking,
then entered the berth and drew the curtain so the enclosure
was once more shrouded in darkness. She moved toward him
on her hands and knees, her movement confident despite the
berth's narrowness, and he slid down so that he was lying on his
back and she was able to move closer. Their bodies weren't
touching but her head was directly over his, their eyes trying to
distinguish each other in the shadows, neither of them moving,
neither of them, he could feel, breathing. They didn't need to
speak, he could sense why she'd come and now that she was
there felt no surprise at all, as if he had in fact been waiting for
her to come all the while. He could smell the light perspiration
on her skin, which he had not been this close to in three weeks,
and despite feeling an urge to wrap his arms around her and
bring their bodies together he remained unmoving, arms by his
side, partly to preserve the self-possession he had just been feeling, the sense of not being in need of her or anybody else, but
partly also to prolong his anticipation of the contact he felt certain was going to come, the loss of self he knew he was going
to give into and that he wanted more than anything else despite, just moments before, having felt so self-possessed. He
traced Anjum's thigh lightly with his right hand, wanting to
draw her body closer to him but still wary of more solid contact, and Anjum lowered her head down and brushed her lips
against his. Her mouth hovered above his for a moment, the
warmth of her breath on his skin, then moving to his neck she
began not to kiss him exactly but to caress him with her closed
lips, making her way up from his neck to the side of his face,

across his forehead and then down to his mouth, where again she did not kiss him so much as touch her lips to his, the rest of their bodies taut as this brief contact was made. A shaft of silvery blue light entered the berth through the window and then disappeared, and raising her head up to look outside Anjum became still. They were passing a station probably or perhaps some small town, nothing to worry about it seemed, and as another shaft of light passed into the enclosure, filling the berth with a soft, electric glow, she turned back and their eyes found each other wordlessly, she looking down at him and he up at her. Their faces were illuminated only for a moment but it seemed much longer to Krishan, as if in that brief silver light he could see every detail of Anjum's face simultaneously and with great clarity, the stud on her nose, the lashes over her dark brown eyes, the soft fuzz of her earlobes, like a dark room lit up by lightning so that everything is taken in as an instantaneous whole, each detail of her face imprinting itself so vividly in his mind that when the light fell away and they were engulfed again in darkness he continued to see her just as she was in that brief moment, their eyes locked, their bodies tense, still keeping their distance in case the train came to a stop and people began to enter or leave. The carriage continued rocking from side to side, the berth and the windows vibrating from the hammering of the iron wheels below, and breathing out softly Anjum lowered herself down again so their bodies were in full contact, each of them drawing deeper and more immersed in the other, each of them losing awareness of everything that existed outside the movement of their limbs and the smell of their skin and their hushed groans and murmurs as they were borne aloft together through the anonymous night.

They remained there for some time, each of them breathing slowly in and out, saying nothing for a while, receding back into their own separate worlds as they emerged slowly from their cocoon. Krishan asked whether she wanted to smoke a cigarette, a habit of theirs after having sex, and Anjum whispered back that yes, a cigarette would be nice. She went out first, and waiting a couple of minutes he began making his way down the darkened carriage himself, taking care to move quietly despite there being little chance that anyone was up. Opening the carriage door and going out into the small space between carriages he was met with a rush of cool air on his face, and squinting in the fluorescent light he found Anjum standing on the left, looking out through the open door at the passing scenes. He put his hand gently on her shoulder, and turning around immediately she unlatched the heavy iron door from the wall, closed it to stem the flow of wind. She reached into her pocket and took out her pack of cigarettes, offering him one and then taking one herself, lighting both cigarettes in the stillness of the enclosed space. Opening the door again and latching it to the wall, she resumed her earlier position as the wind rushed once more into the carriage, leaning against the doorframe in silence and looking out. He looked over her shoulder at the wide expanse of land they were passing, the silhouettes of occasional trees and scattered brush, everything engulfed in the seemingly endless night. It was cumbersome to smoke with Anjum immediately in front of him, and wanting to be by himself for a moment, to make sense of everything that had just happened, Krishan squeezed her lightly on the back of the neck and went to the closed door opposite. Pulling down on the handle, opening the door, and latching it to the wall so that he too could lean

out into the landscape, he took a drag of his cigarette and
watched as the foreground rushed past while the lightless horizon in the distance remained still, the wind buffeting his face,
the thin steel floor trembling beneath his feet. They could have
been anywhere in the immense stretch of land between Delhi
and Bombay, could have been anywhere in that endless country
that he'd always associated with both the beginning and end of
human time, and staring out at the silvery outlines of trees and
electricity pylons that punctuated the land's flatness he suddenly felt drawn again to Anjum, an urge to wrap his arms
around her and tell her how much he loved her, how much he
wanted her, to confess how sad he'd been while she was away.
He finished his cigarette and flicked it out, watched as its fire
glinted for a second before disintegrating into the receding
darkness, then turned around toward Anjum, who sensing his
gaze perhaps threw out her own cigarette and turned toward
him. She stood there unmoving in the doorframe opposite his,
her body leaning to the right, one hand still gripping the bar
along the wall, the large shirt she'd changed into billowing in
the wind. In the white light that fell from the ceiling her face
was starkly visible, her eyes squinting slightly, her thick eyebrows furrowed, a tired, peaceful smile softening her sternly
beautiful face. Behind her vast tracts of unlit land passed by
each second, miles and miles of unknown places containing
people living unknown lives appearing and vanishing every moment, but continuing to look at her, not taking his eyes off her
as she gazed back at him, it felt like the two of them were lost
in that distant night that the train was hurtling through, as if
those vast distances were contained right there in the space between them, as if what was distant and what was proximate

had collapsed somehow into a single space. He was unsure
what was going to happen between the two of them, could tell
in the clarity of the hour and the mild intoxication of the tobacco that nothing was certain, that as long as he continued to
be with Anjum he would continue experiencing those rapid,
unsettling transitions between rapture and disquiet. Watching
her as she watched him, the landscape rushing by behind her
but aware only of the blinking of her eyes and the beating of
his heart, Krishan was grateful that they were part of the same
place and the same time, that for now at least they were together in the same moment, a moment that contained not only
what was proximate and what was distant but also what was
past and what was future, a moment without length or breadth
or height but which somehow contained everything of significance, as if everything else the world consisted of was a kind of
cosmic scenery, an illusion that, now that it was being exposed,
could quietly fall away. What for lack of a better word was
sometimes called love, he had realized that night, was not so
much a relation between two people in and of themselves as a
relation between two people and the world they were witness
to, a world whose surfaces and exteriors gradually began to dissipate as the two individuals sank deeper and deeper into what
was called their love. Falling in love, or what deserved to be
called falling love, he had realized that night, was not so much
an emotional or psychological condition as an epistemological
condition, a condition in which two people held hands and
watched in silent amazement as the world around them was
slowly unveiled, as the falsities of ordinary life began to thin
and dissolve before their eyes, the furrowed eyebrows and
clenched jaws, the bright colors and loud noises, the surface

excitements and disturbances all dropping away so that what remained—time stripped bare—was the only way the world could truly be apprehended, so that even if this condition did not last, even if it was lost, as eventually it is always lost, to habit or circumstance or simply the slow, sad passage of the years, the knowledge that it has imparted remains, the knowledge that the world we ordinarily partake in is somehow not quite real, that time does not need to pass the way we usually experience it passing, that somehow it is possible to live and breathe and move in a single moment, that a single moment could be not a bead on an abacus of finite length but an ocean that can be entered into, whose distant shores can never be reached.

It had been almost four years since that trip, since that moment standing opposite each other on the overnight train to Bombay, and sitting now on this other train, traversing the length of his country of birth, Krishan thought once more about how much time had passed, about how much had happened and how much had changed. He'd thought several times, since reading Anjum's email on Friday afternoon, about what kind of message he might send in response, how much or how little he should share with her of the life he was now living, how earnest or aloof he should try to seem. He'd imagined telling her about what he'd been doing since his return to Sri Lanka, about his two years in the northeast, the initial fervor and subsequent disillusionment, about his recent time in Colombo, the books he'd been reading and his walks in the evenings. He'd wondered what her response would be as she read what he wrote, had imagined her impressed as she learned about everything he'd seen and done, as she saw how much more he understood now about himself and the world. She

would respond not immediately but after an interval of perhaps a week or two, her response would lead to the growth of
a slow, thoughtful, and somewhat confessional correspondence, and finally the two of them would meet at some halfway point, he fantasized, where she would be quietly taken
aback to see him in person after four years, surprised by the
way his body had grown into itself, his shoulders a little broader,
his arms and legs stronger, his cheeks more hollowed out, by
the confidence with which he now spoke and carried himself.
The idea of writing such a letter had given him some hope on
Friday afternoon, as if an unexpected possibility was opening
itself up to him, the possibility of reconnecting with a past he'd
left behind and perhaps even of reunion with Anjum, but thinking again about writing to her he began to second-guess these
thoughts, to feel they were somewhat naïve. There was a tendency, he knew, when thinking about people from the past, to
believe that they'd remained the same while you yourself had
evolved, as if other people and places ceased moving once you'd
left them behind, as if their time remained still while only yours
continued to advance. The tendency in general was misleading,
people and their situations were always changing, but with
Anjum especially it was wishful thinking, Krishan knew, for
Anjum especially was too quick and too active to remain the
same, always inclined toward what was unknown, ready to absorb and assimilate it if she found it worth her while. She would
probably not be too surprised or impressed by how he'd
changed, for she too had no doubt experienced much over the
last four years, she too had no doubt grown and developed, not
just in opinions and outlook but probably in habits and mannerisms too. It occurred to him that he didn't even know whether

she still tilted her head back in the same way when she laughed, whether she still had that habit of rotating the silver ring on her middle finger when she was thinking about something, whether she still even wore that ring at all. It was not where she was living and what she was doing that he wanted to know but these small details, these small, almost imperceptible changes in habit and manner that could signify, sometimes, a total alteration in a person's stance toward the world. He wanted to know whether she too had felt the weight of things increasing upon her in the last few years, whether she too had become just a little more fatigued with the passing of time, but it was precisely these answers that couldn't be communicated via email, precisely these answers that couldn't be given or asked for in words sent through the void. Even if he managed to compose an email he would, like the yaksha in Kalidasa's poem, be unable to share what he really wanted to share, for how would it be possible to convey all that had happened to him in the intervening years, to convey all the events and all the experiences, one change building upon another, accumulation upon accumulation, how would it ever be possible to really begin or end? What was the point of trying to account for all the time that had passed like a river between them, gone and impossible to retrieve, what was the point when all that writing could accomplish was to remind them how much they'd once shared, when the only way to respect what had existed between them was to remain apart, to acknowledge that no words could bridge the vast distance between them?

The train was slowing down, the boy on the seat beside him and others in the carriage beginning to stir, and looking outside Krishan saw that they'd arrived in Anuradhapura, the ancient

Buddhist center of learning and the last major Sinhala town before the north. Almost half the passengers in the carriage got off as the train came to a stop, almost all of them Sinhalese from what Krishan could tell, so that with the exception of a few neatly dressed, clean-shaven men with buzz cuts—soldiers who were returning to their various bases after having spent their leave in the south—it was mainly Muslim and Tamil passengers left now in the carriage. The station master sounded his whistle after a while, the train hesitated, then resumed moving with a jolt, and leaning his head against the window Krishan adjusted his gaze to the scene that opened up as the train left the station and town. The landscape had become flatter and drier, still a lot of vegetation and still occasional paddy fields but no longer the lush, overabundant growth of the south, no longer the same thick density of ferns and flowering plants, the dense clusters of bright green paddy shooting out of silvery water. The profuse foliage had been replaced by fields of tall grass interspersed with quiet stands of trees, and the villages they were passing too seemed emptier and sleepier, small single-story houses and huts deserted except for the occasional old man or woman sitting on a plastic chair, watching with boredom as trains passed by on the tracks. Krishan remembered that his mother had asked him to call when he reached Anuradhapura, and though he didn't really feel like talking, he pulled his phone out of his pocket and dialed her number. His mother picked up after a while, her voice lower and more somber than usual, and he told her they'd just passed Anuradhapura, that they'd probably get to Kilinochchi in the next two hours. He asked whether she'd heard anything from Rani's daughter, which she had not, then asked how Appamma was doing. She was not doing so well, his mother told him after a pause, she'd gone to her room in the morning and found her sitting with her face buried in her hands, the TV turned off even though one of her favorite programs was on. Her eyes were wet, she'd obviously been crying, and his mother had been at a loss for how to comfort her, since it was so rare to see Appamma cry. Krishan asked whether Appamma had been sobbing or just tearing up, to which his mother responded that she didn't know but that it seemed like she'd been crying a good deal. She hadn't wanted breakfast in the morning, she added, and had neglected to take her weekly head bath too. Krishan tried to inquire further but his mother became irritated with his questions, dismissing Appamma's state as a natural response to what had happened, a response that would eventually pass. They talked a little longer, his mother repeating the directions for how to get to Rani's village, asking whether the money he was taking with him was safe, then bringing the call to an end.

Putting his phone down on the empty seat beside him, Krishan turned listlessly and looked out again through the window, unsure what to think as he replayed in his mind what his mother had said. He was bothered by the image of Appamma crying in her room, since it was true as his mother said that his grandmother seldom cried, but even more unsettling was the fact that she'd neglected to take her Sunday head bath. Her head baths were one of the primary rituals by which his grandmother gave movement to her time, an activity that taxed her body but that she continued performing with meticulous regularity, so that if she hadn't wet her hair and shampooed it that morning it could only have been, he knew, because she'd been thoroughly shaken by Rani's death. He'd assumed from her initial response that the news would leave her saddened but mostly untouched, that it would leave her unaffected the way many of the seemingly important deaths in her life had, the death of her sister several years prior, for example, which she'd been upset by for a few days and then seemed to forget about completely, or even the death of her husband decades before, at whose funeral, according to his mother, she hadn't even cried. It was obvious now that Rani's death had the potential to affect his grandmother more gravely than these other deaths, that the psychological impact of the loss might be severe enough to have a physical effect on her too. It had been due largely to Rani that Appamma had been brought back from the brink, after all, due to Rani's nursing and attention during those first few weeks but also, even more significantly, to the constant human presence that Rani had provided in the subsequent months. She'd played a vital role in Appamma's overall recovery, putting an end to the isolation she experienced spending hours on end alone in her room, coming over time to represent the wider world from which she'd been sundered. Appamma had taken personal affront to her unannounced departure, to the fact that Rani had ended their relationship without even informing her, and it had required significant work on her part to forgive the betrayal, to come up with an acceptable narrative for why Rani had cut off ties so abruptly. Whatever the plausibility of Appamma's narrative, which appealed of course to Rani's instability and not to any dissatisfaction with her situation in Colombo, it was possible now, Krishan knew, that the connection to the outside world that Rani had symbolized could be severed by the news of her death. There was a real chance now that Appamma could return to her earlier state of isolation, to a life lacking in meaningful stimulus, her mood and energy once more beginning to deteriorate, her mental sharpness and along with it her physical vitality, her mind and body spiraling in tandem once more toward oblivion.

It was striking now to think about how close his grandmother had become to Rani during their time together, about how much his grandmother had come, in spite of all her initial suspicions and resentments, to trust Rani and depend on her, to become, even, a kind of friend. He'd been nervous at the beginning about how Appamma would receive her, about whether she would treat Rani as a nurse or whether she would treat her as a servant who was at her beck and call, whether she would give her the respect and understanding due to someone who'd lost so much. The first weeks of Rani's stay in Colombo had actually gone smoothly, Appamma still possessing only the most basic modes of awareness, scarcely even conscious of Rani's presence in her room, taking her for granted the same way a newborn child takes for granted the fact it will be fed and washed and cleaned. It was only in the weeks that followed that his initial fears had begun to materialize, Appamma becoming more cognizant of her surroundings, surfacing from her unconsciousness to find that her existence was now bound to that of a stranger. She saw Rani as an alien presence in the household, an imposter who symbolized her new helplessness and was constantly taking her family's attention away from her, attention, she felt, that belonged by rights only to her. With the gradual recovery of her speech and memory Appamma became, paradoxically, more infantile than before, incapable of recognizing anything but her own desires and far more irritable when those desires went unmet. Krishan remembered how, on a weekend afternoon relatively early on, not more than two months into Rani's arrival, he'd gone to his grandmother's room and found Rani stretched out on the floor on her thatched mat, her hands covering her face as if for protection from the light. It always made him uncomfortable to see Rani sleeping on the floor, as if this habit were a subtle critique of his way of life, but she'd insisted on it despite him setting up his brother's bed in Appamma's room, not being used to sleeping on a mattress, as she told him, preferring instead the cool hardness of the floor. She had turned slowly toward him as he entered the room, as though she hadn't been sleeping but lying there lost in thought, her eyes red and her hair in greater disarray than usual. He'd asked whether everything was okay, and she'd told him she was fine, that she hadn't slept at all the night before, that was all. She hardly slept on most nights, she said, she was unwell, and her illness made it difficult to sleep. Krishan had known what Rani meant by the word unwell, but it was the first time the question of her mental state had come up explicitly, she having brought it up herself, and wanting to let her say more if she wanted he'd asked her what she meant. She'd show him, she replied, and standing up a little unsteadily she went to the corner of her room where her bag was kept, rummaged through it till she found a cardboard folder. This is the reason I'm unwell, she'd told him, taking out two medium-size photographs from the folder and holding them out for him to see, the first of a boy about fifteen or sixteen, wearing a black suit two sizes too big for him, taken in a studio with a sky blue backdrop, the second of a boy about ten or eleven, wearing trousers and a shirt, taken in the same studio with the same blue background. The first was her eldest son, she explained, the one who'd died fighting, and the second was her youngest, the one who'd died in shelling on the seventeenth of May, the penultimate day of the war.

Taking the photos uncertainly in his hands Krishan looked at the two boys, both of whom held their arms awkwardly by their sides, neither of them, it seemed, having posed for a formal photograph before. He was wondering whether to ask Rani what their names were or whether to wait till she told him of her own volition when he noticed, through the corner of his eyes, that Appamma was beginning to shuffle around on the bed with irritation, as if to attract his attention. She didn't like him having long conversations with Rani, he knew, since in her mind she was the one who was ill and needed to be looked after, whereas Rani was perfectly well and was there only to look after her. Not wanting to encourage her indignation he kept his gaze fixed on Rani, who was beginning to describe the circumstances of her youngest son's death. It had been early morning when it happened, she was saying, and they'd been trying to cross the front lines from what remained of Tiger territory, which had been shelled every day and night for the previous several months. They had been unsure whether or not to cross for some time, afraid of being killed in the cross fire and about what the soldiers would do to them if they went over to the government side, but they'd decided finally that it was safer to try crossing over than to remain behind under constant shelling. Appamma, whose shuffling on the bed was becoming more conspicuous, interjected suddenly that the afternoon's film had been no good, that when there was no good film playing she preferred the TV to be off. This was irrelevant, of course, the TV in any case being off, and trying to show Rani that he was paying attention Krishan asked who she'd been with at the time. She'd been with her husband, her youngest son, her daughter, and her sister's family, Rani replied, all of whom she'd been together with throughout the various displacements. They'd been walking for about half an hour through the shelled debris of the camp, trying to find the best place to cross, when they heard a high-pitched whistling in the sky, a sound that indicated a standard-issue shell, she explained, for every kind of airborne weapon had its own sound, the cluster bombs, the rockets, and even the drones. They began to run, not knowing whether they were moving toward the shell or away, and after a few seconds it had fallen, not close but not far away either. Looking around in the rising dust and smoke she saw that her youngest son had fallen down and was unable to get up, and running toward the body she realized that he'd been struck by a piece of shrapnel in the stomach and died instantaneously, without so much as a sound.

Rani, whose eyes had been welling up, wiped away a tear, and as Krishan was wondering what he could say to console her he heard his grandmother calling his name from the bed. He tried to ignore her, but she repeated his name with irritation until he was forced to turn around. She was pointing to the dressing table beside the TV, at several tins of canned tuna that her brother had put in her bags before she returned from London. She'd forgotten about them till finding them that morning, she said loudly, that was how much her brother loved her, he was always thinking of her, even while she was sick he'd thought to buy canned tuna for her, knowing they were her favorite food. She wasn't planning on opening any yet, since there was plenty of fish available these days, she would save them for later, she'd decided, when the price of fish was higher. Krishan nodded quickly and turned back to Rani with a look of apology, terrified she would be hurt or offended by the interruption, but Rani continued as though Appamma hadn't spoken at all. They'd had no choice but to keep running, she went on, they'd had no choice but to keep running since the shells were continuing to fall. She wasn't able to bury her son's body, her daughter had been with her, and she couldn't put her at risk by staying there any longer—what happened subsequently to her son's body she'd never managed to find out. Appamma, who'd taken Krishan's curt response to her statement as a snub, raised her voice and shouted across the room that some of the tins were not ordinary tuna but were in fact flavored, some lemon, some pepper, and some tomato, but Rani, too caught up in what she was saying to take heed, simply raised her voice and continued, describing how they'd escaped finally and made it to the other side of the front lines, how they were frisked by the Sri Lankan army, extensively interrogated, and then interned in camps for more than a year and a half. Krishan kept his gaze fixed on Rani as she told him how they'd lost almost all their belongings in the last few months of fighting, how the only tokens of her sons she'd managed to hold on to were the two photographs he was holding in his hands. He didn't look away till she finished her account, transfixed, despite his fear of another interruption, by the strange tension and immediacy in her eyes, which were directed not into the distance as they often were, not far away the way the people's eyes usually were when describing an event from a different time and place, but vividly alert and present, as if the world she was describing was somehow in front of her as she spoke, as if she'd never left that other world behind.

Such incidents occurred a few times in the first two or three months of Rani's arrival, but Rani would always ignore them or respond to them quickly and sharply, rarely seeming to take them to heart. They became less common as time passed, partly because Krishan's mother made a point of scolding her mother-in-law whenever she overheard a rude remark or demand, but mainly because the childishness induced in Appamma as a result of her trip gradually began to subside on its own. As time passed and her condition improved, Appamma became more capable of seeing things from the perspective of others and more aware of how much she owed to Rani, in whom she had, she discovered, a person she could count on for all her personal and social needs, a companion who wouldn't desert her even when everyone else had said good night. It was to Rani that she directed her questions about what was happening downstairs, what they were going to have for dinner, how much the onions, coconuts, or brinjal cost, how the various plants in the garden were doing, questions that previously she would have had to ask Krishan or his mother and to which Rani, unlike the two of them, was compelled to give some response. Rani's eyes and ears and hands and feet became, over the course of her recovery, her proxy sensory and motor organs, and not only did Appamma's ability to understand and participate in the affairs of the household begin to improve but so too did her consciousness of the world beyond the house. Through Rani her conception of the world began to expand to include the north and east, parts of the country she'd grown up and spent her married life but hadn't seen in decades. She learned from Rani about the war and about Kilinochchi and Jaffna, about how things had worked in the areas under Tiger control and how they worked now under government control, and it was because of Rani too that Appamma began reading the newspapers, paying more attention to the evening news, forming political opinions and keeping abreast of political developments, things Krishan had never noticed her caring about till then. All this knowledge, this sense of being once more part of the world, together with the presence of a full-time interlocutor and companion, someone with whom she could watch TV, express her opinions, quarrel, and make jokes, had the effect of energizing Appamma, improving her moods, so that not only did she recover her condition prior to the trip to London but soon surpassed it too. She became healthier and more mobile, more youthful and more vital than she'd seemed in several years, making it obvious that her deterioration in the years leading up to the trip had its source not so much in the physical process of aging as in the withdrawal that came about as a result, the loneliness and isolation of having nothing to do and nobody to engage with, a withdrawal that led to the atrophy of the body far more quickly, it seemed, than any merely physical process.

Krishan remembered how another day later on, when all Appamma's faculties had been fully restored, he'd gone into their room in the morning and found the two of them talking, both of them in a seemingly good mood, Rani explaining to Appamma some development in the TV show they'd just finished watching. He'd said hello to Rani and asked his grandmother how she'd slept the previous night, to which she'd

responded by slapping her hand dramatically against her forehead in a kind of mock frustration, a sly smile on her lips as she
told him she'd spent the entire night looking after Rani, as if
she were Rani's caretaker and not the other way around. He'd
glanced nervously at Rani, unsure how she would respond to
this statement, but she too was smiling, partly out of embarrassment and partly because of the liveliness of Appamma's account. She'd woken up the previous night, Appamma explained,
to the sound of sudden screaming and shouting, had been worried there was a thief in the house or that some other terrible
thing had happened. She'd sat up in a state of disorientation,
not knowing what the source of the commotion was, then
turning around had realized that Rani was the one yelling, that
she was having one of her nightmares again. She'd gone over
and begun shaking Rani by the shoulders, trying to wake her
up, but even after she woke it had taken several minutes to calm
her down. They'd tried going back to sleep but the entire night
Rani had tossed and turned, mumbling loudly to herself, and
two more times she'd woken up screaming and shouting. It was
fine for Rani, Appamma went on, still pretending to be upset,
the smile on her lips widening into a grin, for Rani always made
up for her lost sleep in the afternoons. What about her though,
she who could never sleep in the afternoons, what was she supposed to do? The three of them had laughed at Appamma's
humorous narration but Krishan had been left somewhat unsettled, for the nightmares Rani had, he knew, were nightmares
about the last months of the war, most often about the death of
her younger son, sometimes about other things she'd seen or
heard. For him these were subjects that had to be discussed
with utmost gravity, subjects that had to be approached with

the solemnity reserved for funerals, and he found the lightness with which Appamma treated them disturbing. He'd still been living and working in the northeast at the time, but despite coming across countless people who'd suffered just like Rani during the war, he hadn't become close enough to anyone to witness their traumas firsthand. It was only on moving back to Colombo and living opposite his grandmother and Rani, observing the dynamic that had formed between the two women, that he began to wonder whether it was his own stance that had been misplaced. The trauma Rani had suffered during the war was, for better or worse, part of her ordinary life, something she couldn't help thinking about or reacting to, whether she was waking up, eating, performing her duties, or sleeping, and it had been foolish of him to think it belonged to some separate sphere. Trauma for Rani was something that had to coexist with all the various exigencies of daily existence, and precisely for this reason she couldn't afford to treat it with the same weight or seriousness that he did. In treating Rani as someone she could tease, argue with, and exchange stories with, as someone with whom she had to compete for the attention of her grandson and for power within the household, Appamma was in a way treating Rani as an equal, as someone who was going through something that was normal and not unusual, someone who didn't have to be stopped and pitied or treated with excessive caution. Even if she sometimes hurt Rani with her cavalier stance, Appamma's way of dealing with her had probably made Rani more comfortable on the whole, and perhaps it was this nonchalance that had allowed a camaraderie and even a kind of friendship to form between the two women, between that rapidly aging woman who was fighting to remain in the world and that invisibly wounded stranger who didn't seem to care about whether she stayed or left, a bond that despite all his guilt and despite all his efforts he himself, he felt now, had been unable to forge over the course of Rani's time with them.

7

IT WAS STRANGE to think of the two years Rani and Appamma had spent together in the latter's small room, the unlikely confluence of paths that had brought them together, one of them ostensibly the caretaker and the other ostensibly the charge, even though each was unwell in their own way, even though a remedy was being sought in the arrangement for both of them. Krishan had worried initially that Rani's trauma might actually be worsened by moving from her village to the south of the country, where she had neither friends nor relatives and could speak hardly a word of the majority language, but both he and his mother had sensed an improvement in her condition soon after her arrival, and even the doctor had said as much when she returned to Vavuniya for a checkup after two months in Colombo. Being in a different environment had helped her get some distance from her traumas, and having a job to do, however undemanding it was, gave her purpose and direction, prevented her from spending her days lying about as she had while living with her daughter. The fact she was earning more than her daughter and son-in-law too had an important effect, gave her new standing in her family, since far from being a burden she'd now become an essential source of financial support, lending money sometimes to her daughter, sometimes to other relatives who needed help too. She bought presents for her two granddaughters whenever she went back to her village to visit, dresses, hair clips, chocolates, whatever she could afford that took her fancy, and whenever she spoke on the phone with her daughter the two of them would grab the phone from their mother, demand to know when their grandmother would next be visiting. Talking about her granddaughters, Krishan noticed, one of whom was five and the other seven, both apparently very talkative, very intelligent, and very stubborn, was one of the few things that caused Rani's face to visibly brighten. The fact she took up so much space in their minds was obviously a source of much joy to her, and it had occurred to him more than once that Rani was trying in some way to substitute her two lost sons with her two granddaughters, though perhaps the pleasure she took in her granddaughters was just the ordinary joy that anyone who'd come in contact with so much death took in the vitality of the young. The nightmares continued, of course, as did the bad days, days when Rani hardly spoke a word, burdened by a weight none of them could see, but for the most part this aspect of her condition seemed controlled, held within manageable bounds that allowed her to live with relative normalcy. It was only well into her stay in Colombo, after a year had passed and she'd become fully integrated into the household, inseparable from its routines and rhythms, that Rani's trauma once more seemed to surpass these bounds, making its presence felt again in her mood and energy. The relapse had to do no doubt with the deaths of her husband and nephew within a span of a few weeks, her husband of cancer and her nephew in a motorcycle accident, but outwardly at least Rani didn't seem greatly shaken by either death, not even that of her husband, who she hardly ever talked about and who, as Krishan learned later, she'd married at the insistence of her parents despite being twenty years his junior. He couldn't help feeling that the deaths were only catalysts, that the resurgence of Rani's illness had more to do with the depth and the pull of her original trauma than anything else, a trauma she could never fully escape, which the novelty of her new life in Colombo had temporarily concealed and which, as she became more used to her new situation, had begun once more to exert its hold on her. Whatever its source, Rani began to talk less, to sleep less in the nights and more in the afternoons, to take less care of her physical appearance. She began complaining about feeling unwell, about dizziness and a constant, dull pain in the back of her head, physical symptoms, Krishan came to suspect, that signified psychological distress more than any specific bodily malady. She spoke to the doctor a few times on the phone, and began at his suggestion going up to Vavuniya more frequently for sessions of electroshock therapy, traveling north by bus every month and a half to spend a few nights in the ward.

Krishan had known for a long time that Rani received electroshock therapy, ever since that afternoon in the ward when he first encountered her and first learned who she was, but the idea of Rani sleeping next to psychotic patients during the nights and receiving current to the head during the days continued to bother him, as if her need to continue receiving the treatment was a mark of their own shortcomings, a sign that they'd somehow failed her. Electroshock therapy was a form of treatment that was no longer in use, he'd believed for most of his adult life, an obsolete mode of therapy from the long-gone era of asylums for the insane. His vague sense of it had been shaped by harrowing scenes in old American movies he'd watched about the mentally ill, scenes in which the patient was strapped into a chair or bed with a bit in their mouth and electrodes attached to their temples, in which a switch was casually flicked and heavy current passed through the patient's body like thunder and lightning, causing the eyes to widen, the jaws to clench, and the body to jerk, the veins on the neck and forehead to vividly distend. It was the most effective treatment for the severest, most recalcitrant forms of depression, the doctor had told him when Krishan first inquired about it, Rani was already taking several medications, medications for depression, anxiety, and sleeplessness, as well as for her liver, which was adversely affected by the other medications. None of them were having any significant effect except the electroshock therapy, the doctor explained, which wasn't painful, lasted only a few minutes, and was administered only after the patient had taken a general anesthetic, ensuring that no pain could be felt while the current was being passed. Krishan continued to be suspicious of the treatment despite this justification, and when the topic came up with Rani of its own accord one day he'd asked her what the treatment was really like, whether there really was no pain or discomfort. Rani had looked at him, almost surprised by the question, then shook her head. She never felt anything while it was actually happening, she told him, since she was never actually conscious during the treatment, and she didn't feel bad afterward either, mainly just a little groggy from the anesthetic. Krishan noticed that she did in fact seem better whenever she returned, more active, more talkative, and in a general way more present, though sooner or later she always seemed to return to her previous condition, taciturn, distracted, and lethargic, as if this condition possessed some magnetic hold over her that the electricity could only temporarily dispel. Each time she went back to the ward the doctor would deem it necessary to give her a slightly more intense course of treatment, so that whereas at first she received only one or two doses administered over two or three days, toward the end of her time in Colombo it had become three, four, or even five doses over six, eight, or ten days. In the months before she finally left Colombo she became increasingly forgetful as a result of the therapy, sometimes losing the thread of conversation, sometimes getting confused about whether or not she'd taken her medications, sometimes going down to the kitchen to get something and then forgetting why she'd gone. The treatment she received on her last visit to the ward was so severe that for several weeks afterward her hands and feet were shaking, leaving her unable to bring up Appamma's afternoon cup of tea without spilling. He'd called the doctor to ask what to do, concerned about the side effects but also wondering whether the treatment as a whole was making any difference, whether it was really worthwhile given all the side effects. It had been almost six years since the end of the war and the death of her sons, she'd been doing shock therapy for almost four, and she'd still shown no sign of permanent improvement—was it really sustainable, he'd asked, for Rani to continue receiving current to the head like this indefinitely? The doctor had told him that nothing could be done—he'd increased her medications but they were having no impact, and the side effects of the shock therapy would only be temporary, whereas if she didn't continue receiving treatment her condition would almost certainly deteriorate rapidly. It wasn't so much a question of helping Rani get better, which was increasingly unlikely as the years went by, as simply of helping her cope with ordinary life as best as possible. She herself had been asking for higher doses of therapy, was finding ordinary consciousness increasingly intolerable, and it was his opinion, given the situation, that nothing else could be done.

It was shortly after this conversation with the doctor that Rani had had the accident in the kitchen, Krishan remembered, an accident he'd forgotten about completely till then and which seemed now, in light of the news of Rani's death, to have carried with it a warning or omen that they hadn't perceived at the time. His mother had started asking Rani to come downstairs to cook with her in the evenings, partly because she needed help but also because she felt it would be good for Rani to move her body, to be involved in some physical activity and have a break from Appamma's endless chatter. Rani initially seemed to enjoy these hours in the kitchen with his mother, happy to have the opportunity to talk to an adult without Appamma's constant interjections, but her thoughts also often drifted while she was in the kitchen, leading her on two occasions to accidentally cut her hands while using the coconut grater. One evening Rani had been cutting vegetables while Krishan's mother was turned the other way, busy making batter for the thosa, the regular beat of Rani's knife against the cutting board audible behind her. At some point the sound of the slicing behind her came to a stop, and turning around his mother had found Rani standing totally still, her left hand held up in front of her face, bright red blood dripping profusely from her hand onto the bright orange carrots she'd been slicing. Rani was silent, looking at her hand as though at a curiosity, and Krishan's mother had screamed hysterically, asking what had happened, what had happened, rushing over to look and discovering that a chunk of flesh from the top of Rani's middle finger, about an inch long, was dangling from the rest of the finger. She'd cut it accidentally while slicing the carrots, Rani told her calmly, it was probably best to just cut the whole thing off now, and screaming again Krishan's mother had stopped Rani from picking up the knife, shouting that she was mad and calling for Krishan to come down. The two of them had taken her to the hospital immediately to get the severed piece of finger reattached, and all through the process Rani had been remarkably silent, as if she felt no pain or urgency, only an abstract embarrassment for having made herself the cause of so much concern. They had accepted Rani's explanation that it had just been an accident, like the two accidents with the coconut grater earlier, a result of her distracted state of mind, her inability to fully focus on what was in front of her. The event had soon been forgotten, but reflecting on it as he sat on the train now, it occurred to Krishan that perhaps it hadn't been accidental, that perhaps the incidents with the coconut grater earlier hadn't been accidental either, that perhaps on all of these occasions Rani had actively been trying to harm herself, that perhaps she'd

been asking for higher doses of electric shock for the same reason too, out of a desire to extinguish her consciousness and all
the heaviness it involved. He thought again about what he'd
learned from Rani's daughter on Friday evening, about the way
Rani had been found at the bottom of the well, and the thought
came back to him that her fall had somehow been willed or intended. He'd tried to put the possibility out of his mind for the
last two days, hoping it would fade away if he didn't think about
it, but he was realizing now that suicide was a real possibility,
that he wouldn't be able to rule it out till he went to the funeral
and saw Rani's daughter face-to-face, till he actually spoke to
her in person and searched her eyes for some indication of what
had really transpired.

Krishan looked out to see if he could get a sense of how
close they were to Vavuniya, whether they'd made it out of
Anuradhapura district yet, but nothing in the monotonous vegetation that lined the tracks or the brief glimpses of landscape
beyond gave any indication where they were. There was no
sudden change in ecosystem between south and north, he
knew, both sides of the border region looked more or less the
same, mainly scrubland with occasional stands of trees but
sometimes denser, more crowded sections of jungle too. He'd
never actually traveled anywhere in the North Central Province, always having associated that part of the country with ancient Buddhist temples and ruins, places he not only had no
interest in but generally went out of his way to avoid. Growing
up he'd associated Buddhism mainly with the Sri Lankan government and army, with the statues they constructed all over
the country to remind Muslims, Tamils, and other minorities
of their place, and it was only during his time in India, ironi-

cally, as he finally began learning more about its history, that he'd begun considering it a religion or philosophy in its own right. It was during his time in Delhi that he'd learned that Buddhism was viewed as a religion of emancipation among the oppressed castes of India, that at one time there'd been Tamil Buddhists in the south of India and even in northeast Sri Lanka, that what most Sri Lankans called Buddhism was in fact just one particular version of Buddhism. He himself had just as much entitlement to the Buddha as most of the Sri Lankans who called themselves Buddhists, he came to realize, and coming across a translation of *The Life of the Buddha* by chance in a bookshop in Delhi one day, flicking through it and deciding it was finally time to try to understand Buddhism with a more open mind, he'd bought the book on a whim and begun to read it on the way home. The poem, which was written by the north Indian poet Ashvaghosha in the first century, under circumstances that couldn't have been more different from the Sri Lanka in which he lived, had begun with a moving and detailed account of the birth of the Buddha that was familiar but slightly different from the versions he'd heard growing up. The young prince Siddhartha, according to the poem, had appeared in his mother's womb without any act of conception, and was delivered apparently without passing through her birth canal, his skin gleaming like the sun, his large, dark, unblinking eyes capturing the gazes of those around him like the moon. Shortly after his birth his father was visited by a highly revered seer who'd examined the newly born child, declaring that he would become either a conqueror of vast worlds or a conqueror of the soul. Conquering the soul meant taking the path of renunciation, meant leaving behind family, society, and the world at large, and the king was greatly disturbed by this news, not ever wanting to be parted from his son. Knowing that any exposure to pain or suffering could lead the young prince down the path of renunciation, he decided to raise Siddhartha in such a way that he experienced only the pleasures of the world, none of its bitterness, hoping in this way to ensure that he became a conqueror of worlds rather than a conqueror of the soul. As the young prince came of age, according to the text, he became a youth of startling beauty and intelligence, and the king assigned him chambers in the very top floors of the palace, where he spent the days and nights with male friends and female consorts. He was married at a relatively young age to a princess named Yashodhara, a woman of exceeding beauty and noble bearing, and not long afterward she bore him a son, which meant, his father thought happily, that the prince would be too bound to earthly life to ever renounce. Siddhartha continued to spend most of his time in his private chambers even after his son's birth, taking his pleasure with the women his father had sent to entertain him. Listening to the soft sounds of the women's golden tambourines, watching as their lithe bodies moved to the music, laughing and drinking with them in the evenings and sleeping with them in the nights, for many years he saw hardly any reason to descend from the cloud-topped chambers in which he lived.

It was only in his twenty-ninth year, according to the poem, hearing about the lush parks and groves in which his female consorts passed their time in the city, that Siddhartha began to wonder about what existed outside the confines of his chambers and the palace. Increasingly bored by his life of endless sensual and material pleasure, this curiosity slowly turned into yearning, and one day the prince asked his father for permission to venture beyond the palace grounds, something he'd never done before. The king was troubled by the request, but decided eventually to let his son be escorted around the city, though only on a predetermined route that would be shorn of anything that might upset the prince. He had the areas around the route beautified with flowers and banners, had all the poor, disabled, and sick removed from sight, and finally, at an appointed time, sent Siddhartha on his way with a trusted charioteer. Multitudes of people, women especially, who'd never seen a man so attractive, gathered around the road to try to catch sight of the young prince, and seeing the order and splendor of the city and the droves of respectful citizens, all dressed in clean, dignified clothes, the prince rejoiced, according to the text, as though he'd been born for a second time. Everything went according to plan till he caught sight, near the edge of the crowd, of a white-haired woman with a wrinkled face, her body slumped and her back unnaturally bent, holding a walking stick for support as she tried to catch a glimpse of him from the distance. Never having seen a person in such a condition before, he asked the charioteer what had happened to the woman and was told the woman had reached old age, a state in which beauty and strength were destroyed, in which memory dissipated and the sense organs deteriorated. Perturbed, the prince asked the charioteer whether such a thing could happen to anyone, or whether it was the fate of that particular woman alone. When the charioteer said it would happen to everyone who lived long enough, that it would without doubt happen to him one day too, the prince became dejected, and soon asked for the chariot to be turned around toward the palace, where he retreated to his chambers to be alone. Unable to find peace there, he decided after a few days to go on another trip around the city, hoping it would help him come to some clarity. On this second journey too however he saw a sight that upset him, a middle-aged man with a severely distended abdomen, his shoulders drooping, his limbs thin and pale, grunting in pain as he moved with the help of someone beside him. Siddhartha asked the charioteer what had happened to the man, and the charioteer explained that the man was afflicted by sickness. The prince asked whether sickness affected that man alone or whether it was something that could happen to all people, and the charioteer replied that sickness had many forms and that anybody could get sick, that there was no way to guarantee against it. Once more Siddhartha fell silent. Asking to be taken back to the palace, he stayed alone in his chambers for several days in a state of despondency. The king grew furious that his orders hadn't been followed to the letter, and hoping that a positive experience might change the prince's mind, he commanded that a different route be found, that it be decorated so as to be even more beautiful than the first, and that any person whose sight might in any way be upsetting to the prince be removed from the area. He pleaded with his son to go on one more excursion, to which the prince agreed, but on this occasion too he saw something he wasn't meant to see, he saw, on an adjacent street, beyond the crowds that had gathered to see him, a motionless body being carried by a number of people in mourning. He asked the charioteer why the person was being carried in this way, to which the charioteer replied, reluctantly, that the person had died. The prince didn't know what death was, and on being told that it was a state without consciousness, a state in which a human was no different from a log or a stone, unable to see or hear or talk or feel, the prince suddenly became inconsolable. The cheering, smiling, laughing people who'd gathered by the road began to take on a sinister aspect, and looking around at them he began to feel they must either be insane or completely deluded, for how, otherwise, could they go about their lives unaffected by the fact that they would get old, that they would get sick, and that eventually they would die? Returning to the palace Siddhartha continued to reflect on what he'd seen, unable to take pleasure in anything he'd previously enjoyed, neither wife, son, consorts, nor friends, unable to see the life he'd been leading as anything but a farce. It was his inability to move on from these facts, according to the poem, that had eventually led the twenty-nine-year-old prince to leave the palace in secret one night, embarking on that long and famous journey that led, finally, after six years of homelessness, penance, self-mortification, and meditation, to liberation from the cycle of birth and death, from the misery and bitterness of the so-called real world.

Krishan had been greatly moved by the story of Siddhartha's disillusionment, which despite having heard so many times growing up he was only then fully considering, and dwelling on it now as he was borne toward Rani's funeral it occurred to him how similar, in a way, Siddhartha's disillusionment was to Rani's, how similar what he'd gone through must have been to the experiences of most people who'd lived through the end of the war. Just as Rani's life and the assumptions on which it was founded had been exploded over the course of the few short months that left both her sons dead, so too had Siddhartha's life and his assumptions that sickness, old age, and death years of rigid austerities and unfathomable deprivations, the violence he inflicted on himself in search of a life free from what he'd seen on his excursions, what else could have explained any of it except a pathological response to a profoundly shocking event, a condition that had been treated, in Rani's less fortunate case, by regimens of electroshock therapy that left her hands and feet in a state of constant spasm?

The train was slowing down, the clanging of the wheels on the tracks becoming more dispersed, and noticing the small huts and houses that lined the tracks, the weathered posters for various Tamil political candidates pasted on their corrugated steel walls, Krishan realized that they'd arrived at last in the Northern Province. The train made its way a short distance through the town and then into the station, grinding slowly to a stop as it passed the board labeled VAVUNIYA at the head of he platform. A few of the passengers still remaining in the carriage stood up—a young Tamil couple with a child, a middle-ged Muslim man, and two soldiers—and collecting their things ney made their way out onto the platform, which was empty xcept for the stationmaster, a soldier, and three armed police-en. Looking out through the opposite window at the other atform, where a small group of people were waiting for the in headed south, Krishan noticed a large, freshly pasted bill-ard on the far end, its left half depicting a rough sea under k clouds that seemed on the verge of erupting. Tossing and ning in the midst of the waves, seemingly on the point of ng engulfed, was a small, rickety fishing boat, and in thick Tamil letters, emblazoned across the center of the image, e the words THERE'S NO WAY: YOU WILL NEVER BE ABLE SET FOOT IN AUSTRALIA. The right half of the billboard

did not exist, that the body and the world could go on liv
harmony forever. Just as the end of the war had left Ra
trievably traumatized, so that again and again images c
her of her two dead sons, the younger one especially, i
backs when she was awake and in nightmares when s
asleep, leaving her unable to return to ordinary life aft
so too had Siddhartha been traumatized by what he'd
his three excursions, sights so fundamentally at o
everything he'd come to believe over the course of h
he simply could not go on as before. His youth, if /
sha's account was anything to go by, had been ver
from the childhoods of ordinary people, since m
were, from their earliest days, continually exposed
sickness, and death. Ordinary humans were, from
ginning, slowly and gently exposed to these facts o
never subsequently strayed too far from their min
learned to take pleasure in the world despite the co
transitory quality of its pleasures, to value small
pinesses in spite of the fact that they would no
Siddhartha by contrast had been systematically
ally blinded to the existence of sickness, old age,
never even considered the possibility that the
dulged in might one day dissipate or disappear
was leading might one day end. His sudden an
to these facts over the course of a few short
have resulted in shock so great as to be traun
medical sense of the word, for what else co
his desire to so abruptly leave behind his
friends, and lovers, to so mercilessly reject e
stituted the world he knew? What else coul

consisted of a black background with dense white text that Krishan couldn't decipher at first, though as the train jerked back into motion and his carriage moved past the billboard he was able to make out a few of the lines, which stated that traffickers were trying to profit by cheating people who wanted to move to Australia, that Australia was no longer accepting people who tried to come to the country by boat, that boats attempting to reach the country would be steered back into deep waters by the Australian navy. He'd heard similar advertisements on Tamil radio stations and TV channels, usually aired in prime-time spots in the late evening and night, but this was the first billboard he'd seen and it was no accident, he knew, that it had been put up at Vavuniya, the first station in the Tamil part of the country. The Australian government had put tens of millions of dollars into such advertisements, not just in Sri Lanka but in other countries with large displaced populations like Iraq, Afghanistan, and Bangladesh, hoping to stem the tide of people from these countries who tried to make the long and arduous journey by boat. It was difficult to say whether the advertisements actually worked, for most of the people who made the journey chose to make it despite the exorbitant sums they had to pay the middlemen, knowing very well the danger of crossing thousands of miles of deep sea in dilapidated fishing boats, tightly packed for weeks with other asylum seekers in nearly uninhabitable conditions. Such people made the journey knowing their chances of reaching Australia were slim, that even if they did survive the boat trip they were likely to be kept in illegal offshore detention centers for years. The majority of them were people who'd lost everything during the war, people who, even if they hadn't been detained, bereaved, tortured, or raped, had seen untold amounts of violence, for whom life in their homeland had become more or less unbearable. It was true probably that severe trauma could never be escaped, that you carried it with you wherever you went, but trauma Krishan knew was also indelibly linked to the physical environments in which it was experienced, to specific sounds, images, languages, and times of day, as a result of which it was often impossible for people to continue living in the places they'd seen violence occur. It was often hard, he'd read somewhere, to convince a person who'd had a serious car accident to get back into a car, many such people preferring to take other modes of transport whenever they could from then on, and if this was the case with car accidents then how much harder must it have been to convince people to remain in places they'd been bombarded by shelling, places they'd come face-to-face with punctured bodies and severed limbs? Even if they were the only places they'd ever known, places their forebears had lived and that they them-selves had never imagined leaving, how was it possible to con-vince such people not to risk their lives going elsewhere, not to attempt migrating to countries that seemed, in their minds, far removed from these sites of trauma, even if they knew they were likely to die in the process and even if they knew, in their heart of hearts, that most people in places like Australia and America and Europe would never let them live in their coun-tries with full dignity?

It always made Krishan a little uncomfortable that he'd cho-sen to return while so many Tamils were willing to risk every-thing to leave, a choice that had only been possible, he knew, because of the fortune and privilege of his circumstances, the safe distance of his own life from the violence and poverty of the northeast. It was true that his father had been a casualty of one of the Tiger bombings in Colombo, that he had in this sense been deeply affected by the war, but the fact was that he'd grown up in comfort, in a house of his own far away from the actual fighting, that he'd never had to experience violence directly, neither gunshots, shelling, nor displacement, nothing more than casual racism here and there, threatening interrogations by police and soldiers on the street. The idea of doing social work in the northeast would have never even occurred to him, probably, had he not been so insulated from the traumas of the war, and in a way his departure after two years had only underscored how different his life was from those who'd spent their lives in the northeast, those for whom coming and going wasn't simply a matter of choice. Krishan looked at the scenes passing outside as they left the town, the outlines of the trees in the distance distorted by the intensity of the heat, and feeling a little restless he took out his phone and looked at the time. They were less than an hour from Kilinochchi and he wasn't sure what to do with himself, whether to try reading or listening to music, neither of which he felt like doing. He didn't want to remain seated, had been sitting for several hours and felt an urge to stand up, then realized that he hadn't yet smoked that day, that it would be nice to leave the carriage and have a cigarette now that he was finally in the north. He reached down and took out his lighter and pack from his bag, glanced around quickly to make sure no one happened to be walking through the carriage, then stood up and began making his way along the aisle, holding the seat backs for support till he passed out into the small corridor between the carriages. He waited a few seconds to make sure he was alone, then lighting a cigarette discreetly against the wall he pulled open the train door, latched it to the wall, and leaned outside, his face immediately assailed by a blast of hot, dry wind, his eyes by the penetrating, preternatural brightness of the day.

Just a stone's throw from the train he could see the A9 running in parallel with the tracks, veering sometimes closer and sometimes farther away, the air above its smooth black surface trembling from the heat of the tarmac. The highway was hardly a highway, consisting of only a single lane for each direction of traffic, but because it was the main road linking north and south it had assumed a kind of epic proportion in the minds of everyone who'd lived through the war. The southern section had been controlled by the government for most of the fighting, the northern section by the Tigers, each side manning their portion of the border with heavy fortifications and multiple checkpoints, so that for the better part of twenty-five years it had, like the train line, been completely inoperative. It had been reopened finally in 2009, just a few months after the defeat of the Tigers, the military quickly filling up the craters, demining the adjacent land, and repaving the road so it was ready for civilian use, though for a long time soldiers continued checking every single vehicle that crossed the border, going methodically through every single compartment and every single piece of luggage if the passengers were Tamil. The train line had taken much longer to be put back into operation, not only because all the stations on the northern section of the line had been bombed out, but also because every inch of track and every nut and bolt had been stripped away by the Tigers, who'd made use of the iron for weapons, bunkers, and anything else they required in their typically meticulous way. It had taken several years for the government to relay the track, and when the line was officially reopened the previous year it had been celebrated with great fanfare, the government using the occasion to symbolize how the entire island was now back under its control, a marker of their achievement as liberators of the country. That had been in 2014, toward the end of his time in the northeast, when he'd become so used to traveling by bus that he didn't even think to use the train, and looking at the highway from his slightly different vantage point now, Krishan found himself thinking of all the journeys he'd made between Colombo and Jaffna since returning to the island, the intense longing he'd felt, during those first months especially, as he gazed out from his bus window at these same unending landscapes of brush and palmyra, landscapes so flat and dry and unforgiveable that it seemed sometimes almost miraculous that so many generations had worked life and sustenance out of the earth.

It was hard to say what it was about the northeast that had drawn him there after so many years abroad, what it was that had taken root so deeply inside him that he abandoned the life he'd built for himself in Delhi in search of another one here. It was true that guilt had played some part, guilt for the relative ease of his life growing up, guilt for the fact that he'd spent so much of his twenties lost in academic texts, but there was also something in the sparse, desolate beauty of the region that had brought him here, he thought as he gazed out the train, something much stronger and more substantial than guilt. He'd spent so many hours looking at images of the northeastern countryside during his time in Delhi, not during his initial obsession with the war's final massacres but afterward, sensing in those images of sprawling fields and thick jungle something ancient and almost mythical, something that made him dream of a possible fulfillment without knowing how or from what source. Compelled by some need to dwell more on the origins of the war, to understand the nature of the longings that had led to such a devastating conclusion, he'd begun reading about the earlier, more idealistic days of the separatist movement, and it was the story of Kuttimani more than anything else, he remembered now, that had captivated him at the time, that had crystallized the longing to live in the northeast that was just beginning to take hold of him. He'd known about Kuttimani since childhood, about his role in the early days of the separatist struggle, his trial, incarceration, and subsequent murder, but it was only during his time in Delhi that he'd actively tried to find out more about the life of that early insurgent, about the circumstances in which he'd grown up, the moods with which he'd lived. He'd been unable to find even the most basic biographical information, not even his date or place of birth, and the only material of value he'd found were a few scanned newspaper photographs, most of them taken during his trial or just afterward. He could still see two of those images vividly in his mind, both of them black-and-white, grainy and out of focus, the first showing Kuttimani in the courtroom, probably immediately after the verdict had been pronounced, clean-shaven, smartly dressed in a white shirt and sarong, handcuffed arms raised above his head in a sign of victory despite the fact that he was surrounded by policemen and had just been sentenced to death. The second showed him leaving the courtroom after the trial, his handcuffed arms held out in front of him, the side of his handsome mouth curled into a smirk as he looked straight into the camera with his squinting, sun-shaded eyes, his taller, thinner, mustachioed comrade Thangathurai standing beside him, also looking at the camera, though with an expression that was noticeably less triumphant. In both images Kuttimani was fresh-faced and seemingly well in possession of himself, exuding a sense of calm, easy assurance, a bearing that had probably been achieved only with great effort, Krishan knew, for the newspaper article that contained the pictures also gave a long list of the tortures to which Kuttimani, Thangathurai, and Jegan, the third accomplice in the robbery, had been subject by police, a list that included, among other things, being stripped and beaten by batons and rifle butts, being forced to inhale the fumes of burning chili, having metal rods inserted into their anuses, and steel wire inserted into the urethral opening of their genitalia. It could only have been after much inner struggle that Kuttimani found the composure required to present himself in court the way he did, Krishan knew, to make the arguments and the famous last statement that were published the next day on the front pages of all the major newspapers, sending ripples from the south of the country all the way north.

The crime for which Kuttimani had been arrested, the robbery of eight million rupees from a People's Bank in Jaffna in March 1981, had not, in fact, been his first. In 1969, when he was probably in his early twenties, he'd formed, together with Thangathurai, an informal separatist organization that later became the Tamil Eelam Liberation Organization or TELO, an armed separatist group that funded most of its activity through the smuggling of contraband and the robbery of state or state-affiliated institutions. He'd been arrested by Indian police in 1973 while seeking a safe haven in Tamil Nadu, and after being deported at the request of Sri Lankan authorities had been imprisoned in his home country without trial till 1977, when he was finally released due to foreign pressure. He rejoined the insurgency, organized increasingly more daring attacks and robberies that culminated in the 1981 People's Bank robbery in Jaffna, leading to a vigorous manhunt by government authorities. He was arrested off the coast of Jaffna by the Sri Lankan navy only two weeks later, on a small motorboat trying to make his way with Thangathurai and Jegan to Tamil Nadu, where he'd been hoping to hide once more till the search for him died down. The trial, which took place at the Colombo High Court over a year later, was packed with journalists and members of the interested public, and was followed throughout the country with intense scrutiny. Kuttimani was charged with murder—there had, apparently, been people killed in the course of the robbery—and wanting no doubt to make an example of him to other separatists, the court had sentenced him to death. The judge asked whether he had any final words or requests that he wanted the court to hear before it was adjourned, and in response to this suggestion, according to the article, Kuttimani had proclaimed to the court that he was guilty of no crime whatsoever. He was an innocent person, taken into custody by the police and forced to sign a confession after months of unbearable torture. The court's verdict, he went on, which nobody in the country would find surprising, would only add new urgency to the separatist movement growing in the northeast, would only give new and more compelling reason for the establishment of the new state of Tamil Eelam. More and more Tamil youth would be arrested on false charges, and as this went on the movement for Tamil liberation taking hold in the northeast would only further be strengthened. He ended his speech by asking that he be hanged not in Colombo, where the trial was taking place, but in his ancestral village in Jaffna, that his vital organs be given to Tamils who needed them, and that his eyes in particular be donated to a young Tamil boy or girl who could not see, so that even if he himself never had the opportunity to see Tamil Eelam, as he put it, his eyes at least would one day have the chance.

Reading of Kuttimani's capture on one of the small boats that militant groups had used throughout the war to smuggle arms, money, and people between the northeast coast of Sri Lanka and the southern coast of India, Krishan had remembered another image he'd found on the internet, an undated color photograph taken somewhere on the northeast coast much later, probably at some point in the nineties. In the foreground of the image were two Tiger cadres standing at the edge of the beach, both barefoot, wearing shorts that left much of their thighs exposed, the shorter, thinner man on the left wearing a baggy button-up shirt, the taller, stockier man on the right wearing a camouflage T-shirt. Both of them were holding AK-47s, the man on the right with a magazine of bullets slung across his left shoulder, and both were looking out intently at the still, golden sea that stretched out from their feet. About thirty or forty feet from the shore a small motorboat sat quietly on the still water, inside it the small, blurred outlines of three or four seated men, while wading through the knee-high water, just disembarked from the boat, four more figures were making their way toward the shore. They were, most likely, returning from Tamil Nadu, where they'd gone either for some kind of military training, or to procure arms that they could smuggle back to the island. The two armed men standing barefoot on the edge of the shore had probably been stationed there to await their arrival, though they didn't seem to have much interest in the boat or in the men making their way back from it, such arrivals and departures probably being extremely routine. They seemed, instead, to be gazing to the northwest, across the enormity of the motionless sea, toward that line in the distance where the edge of the silently bright water became indistinguishable from the bright, cloudless horizon, a point so distant from their small section of beach that it could only have been on or near the Indian coast. It was while looking out at that same convergence of sea and horizon, Krishan couldn't help imagining, that Kuttimani had been arrested on his way to Tamil Nadu, and perhaps it was even because he'd been distracted by the sight of that distant meeting point that he'd let himself get caught. There was something so freeing or fulfilling about looking out across such distances, after all, such a feeling of freedom even in the act of stepping out under open sky, where one's eyes were no longer hemmed in by walls and roofs and could range, without constraint, over earth and sea. It was precisely for this reason, Krishan couldn't help feeling, that Kuttimani had asked for his eyes be given to a sightless child, so that they too might look into the horizon, so that they too might look across the distance at the land that belonged to them and the possibilities it contained. The freedom that Kuttimani desired, the freedom that perhaps all liberation movements sought, was not just the freedom that came when one could move freely over the land on which one's forbears lived, not just the freedom that came from being able to choose and be responsible for one's own life, but the freedom that came when one had access to a horizon, when one felt that the possible worlds that glimmered at its edges were within one's reach. It was only when looking at a horizon that one's eyes could move past all the obstacles that limited one's vision to the present situation, that one's eyes could range without limit to other times and other places, and perhaps this was all that freedom was, nothing more than the ability of the ciliary muscles in each eye—the finely calibrated muscles that contracted when focusing on objects close by and relaxed when focusing on objects far away—nothing more than the ability of these muscles to loosen and relax at will, allowing the things that existed in the distance, far beyond the place one actually was, to seem somehow within reach.

Kuttimani was moved, on being sentenced to death, to Welikada, the maximum-security prison built by the British in Colombo in 1841 and still, seventy years after their departure, the largest prison in the country. Krishan had never been inside Welikada, but he'd passed its imposing façade on Baseline Road plenty of times, the dominating white wall emblazoned with the crest of the Department of Prisons at the top, below it a long, beaten copper mural depicting the different stages of the rehabilitation of criminals. The mural began on the left with images of men committing crimes like murder and theft, followed to the right by downcast, penitent figures standing trial in orderly courtrooms, then by inmates engaging in manual labor of various sorts, laying bricks, painting, and shoveling, ending, finally, with scenes of joyful, sober individuals walking out of the prison under the watchful but caring eye of the guards. The mural, together with the large text printed below stating that PRISONERS ARE HUMANS, gave the impression that Welikada was a humane and progressive environment, an impression that Krishan always suspected to be false and that was discredited beyond doubt as he learned more about the massacre of Tamil prisoners there in July 1983. These massacres, which according to the government were simply the result of Sinhala prisoners getting out of hand, had taken place during the larger anti-Tamil pogrom that occurred in Colombo that month with the collusion of the government, leading to the destruction of eight thousand Tamil homes, five thousand Tamil shops, and the death, on some estimates, of up to three thousand Tamil people. The prison killings took place on two separate days in the midst of this pogrom, on the twenty-fifth of July and then again on the twenty-seventh, and were, according to the book Krishan read in the hope of learning more about Kuttimani's death, far from accidental or unplanned. Fifty-three Tamil inmates, all of them political prisoners, were killed, and the government story that the killings were the result of Sinhalese prisoners getting out of hand was, according to the authors of the book, patently false. No prison guard was killed or hurt during the violence, which almost certainly would have been the case if they had made any attempt to stop the Sinhala prisoners. Armed military personnel stationed within the prison grounds took no action to stop the killings either, apparently on orders from above, and after the attacks these same personnel refused to allow the still breathing Tamil prisoners to be taken to the hospital, which led eventually to them dying of their wounds. The conflicting evidence given by prison guards and officials made it clear, the authors of the book argued, that the killings were politically motivated at the highest levels.

Kuttimani had been housed, apparently, in a prison building

named the Chapel by the British because it was shaped like a cross, with four rectangular divisions on each floor and a central lobby on the ground floor. The seventy-four Tamil political prisoners held there had been jailed in three divisions of the ground floor, while the fourth division on the ground floor as well as all the upper floors housed Sinhala prisoners convicted of murder, rape, and other violent crimes. Kuttimani was held in an eight-by-eight cell together with his associates Thangathurai and Jegan, according to the book, and it was in this cell presumably that he spent the large part of his sixteen months in prison. Reading this detail Krishan couldn't help wondering how Kuttimani passed his time there with his two comrades, during all those long days and nights before their unscheduled killing. Probably they'd talked about news relating to the war, which must have come to them in bits and pieces through prison guards, and probably they'd discussed and debated the separatist movement and the political situation, not only among one another but also, during mealtimes and the recreation period, with the other Tamil prisoners, most of whom also belonged to separatist armed groups or political parties. The TELO were explicitly anti-ideological, in the sense that they had no specific ideas or proposals for what kind of country the people of the north and east would live in when the freedom struggle was finally won. Their first and only demand was for a Tamil homeland—all other matters would be considered after their homeland was won, they argued, since doing so beforehand would only be a distraction. Other groups, such as EROS or the PLOTE, were more strongly ideological, most of them socialist or Marxist, with strong anti-imperialist stances and distinct social and political visions of what the Tamil homeland would look like. These more abstract, intellectual articulations of the future were eventually destroyed by the Tamil Tigers when they annihilated or violently assimilated all of the other armed groups in the years that followed, less because of ideological differences—the Tigers too, like the TELO, believed that ideology was mostly a distraction—than simply to consolidate their position as the most powerful separatist group in the north. The prisoners couldn't have discussed politics all day, of course, especially since their news of what was happening in the world outside must have been limited, and Krishan wondered how Kuttimani must have spent the rest of his time in prison, whether he read, or wrote, or exercised, whether there was a window in his cell from which the sky could be seen. He liked to imagine Kuttimani looking out through a window, liked to imagine that he spent time looking into the distance even if there was no actual window, even if the cell contained no light, for even when you were fast asleep it was possible, Krishan knew, to dream of wide landscapes and endless roads that led all the way to the horizon, so that waking up it was as though you'd spent the last several hours in the outside world and not in a cramped cell with your eyes tightly shut.

What actually happened on the day Kuttimani was killed was unclear, but according to the book the attack of the twenty-fifth started around two in the afternoon, when some four hundred Sinhalese prisoners escaped their cells, no doubt with the help of some of the prison guards. Gathering in the lobby of the ground level they obtained the keys to all the Tamil cells, then attempted to enter the three sections of the ground level that housed the Tamil prisoners. Feeling a loyalty to the Tamil prisoners inside the section he guarded, one Sinhalese prison guard apparently told the mob they would have to kill him to enter, in response to which the mob left that noble guard unharmed and entered the other two Tamil sections, where the guards in charge gave them free entry. It took the disorganized mob some time before they were able to work out which keys opened which cells, and this allowed the Tamil prisoners to organize some resistance to the attackers. The Sinhala prisoners vastly outnumbered them, though, and were armed with weapons that, according to the text, could only have been procured for them by the guards. Entering the cells one by one they cut down and battered the occupants, leaving most of them dead and the rest seriously wounded. The mob was no doubt aware who Kuttimani was—accounts of what he'd said during his trial the year before must have spread through the prison—for when they entered the cell he shared with Thangathurai and Jegan, the attackers made sure not to kill him immediately. It was reported that after knocking the three occupants to the ground several of the attackers had held Kuttimani fast on his knees, while another used an implement of some kind, most likely a knife but perhaps also a key, to gouge out, one after the other, both of Kuttimani's eyes. The process must have taken some time, Krishan knew, each eye must have been scored out slowly and clumsily, losing its delicate integrity in the process rather than being scooped out whole, and when the eyes were removed they had probably been crushed in the carver's hands or trampled under his feet, for it was difficult to imagine the prisoners leaving them as they were.

Leaning out of the train door as the hot, dry wind buffeted his face and the train wheels pounded heavily over the tracks below, Krishan felt he could see, with stark clarity, the figure of

Kuttimani kneeling down in his grimy prison cell, two dark wounds in his head where previously his eyes had been. It was strange how sometimes scenes one has never witnessed could appear before the mind's eye more profoundly than memories from actual life, but looking out over the flat, arid landscape rushing before him, its far edges flickering in the distance like a mirage, the same landscape Kuttimani had no doubt imagined so many times from his cell, Krishan had the strange sensation that what he was seeing now was not exactly his own vision but the superimposition of Kuttimani's upon his own, the superimposition not just of Kuttimani's vision but the vision of all those many people from the northeast whose experiences and longings had been archived or imagined in his mind. He had the strange sensation that the images he was seeing were a product not just of the light entering his eyes from outside but of all the various images he'd come to associate with the northeast over the course of his life, the firsthand images from his childhood visits and his two years living there as an adult, the secondhand images from all the photographs he'd seen in books, newspapers, and websites, the images he'd constructed in his mind out of all the things he'd read and heard, idyllic images of rural life and horrific images of war, images depicting a life he might have lived had history been just a little different, the faint traces of these countless images all projected now over what his eyes actually saw as the train raced north. He could see the leafless thickets of brush rushing past in the foreground before him, the white-hot horizon melting into the cloudless sky in the background, could feel the thin steel floor vibrating beneath his feet and his shirt billowing in the wind, but standing there leaning out through the door of the train, knowing that soon he would be arriving in Kilinochchi and that soon he would be in Rani's village, attending the funeral of a person he still could not quite accept was dead, he couldn't help thinking, as the train hurtled closer toward his destination, that he'd traversed not any physical distance that day but rather some vast psychic distance inside him, that he'd been advancing not from the island's south to its north but from the south of his mind to its own distant northern reaches.

BURNING

8

IT WAS A little past four in the afternoon, the light softer now and more diffuse, the intensity of the day's heat beginning to wane, and standing by himself in a corner of the garden Krishan was observing the people gathered in Rani's house for the funeral, somewhat unnerved, after his long and meditative journey, by how quickly he'd found himself in this place so different from his point of origin, this setting that, despite conforming to all his abstract expectations, had nevertheless managed to catch him off guard. The sense of calm, peaceful self-containment he'd felt on the train had remained with him on the two quiet buses from Kilinochchi, and it had persisted too on his long walk from the bus stop, as he made his way slowly along the network of paths that ran through the noticeably deserted village. The properties on either side of the lanes were marked off by low fences of dried palm fronds thatched together with wire and rope, most of them fronted by small, well-cultivated gardens, each with its own little vegetable plot and an assortment of trees—drumstick, banana, coconut, curry leaf, as well as others he couldn't identify. The houses themselves were simple and unadorned, the larger concrete ones containing a kitchen and one or two rooms, the smaller ones consisting of mud walls and thatched roofs and no more than a single all-purpose hall. He'd taken his time noting and regarding everything he passed, as if he'd come for no other reason than to discover what effect the surroundings had on the trajectory of his thoughts, and it was only as he turned into the lane where Rani's house was located, as he heard the low, irregular beat of funeral drums rising up from the end of the lane, that he began to realize his journey was over, that he'd finally arrived at his destination. He wondered suddenly how he should comport himself, what he should say to Rani's daughter when they met, how he could give her his grandmother's money without drawing attention to himself, questions he'd had the whole day to consider but had avoided thinking about till then. Approaching the house he saw first the band of drummers standing just behind the palm-leaf fence, four men aloof from everyone else in the garden, looking at one another intently as they rapped the small, flat, beautifully constructed drums that hung from their necks—members, he knew, of one of the most marginalized castes in the northeast. In the garden behind them a large crowd had already assembled, two or three hundred people at least, almost all of them people from the village it seemed, which explained perhaps why the village had felt so quiet on his walk. Some of the attendees looked desolate or forlorn, some merely bored, but most of them were talking in low voices, as if using the gathering as an opportunity to dis-

cuss whatever matters were on their minds, the women wearing black, gray, or white saris, some of them in pale, unobtrusive
colors, the men wearing mainly shirts and formal white sa-
rongs. The band began to drum louder and at a faster tempo as
he made his way toward the gate, giving, Krishan realized with
discomfort, what was in effect a kind of announcement of his
arrival. Walking through the garden he did his best to ignore
the curious faces of the people as they turned and looked at
him, all of them aware no doubt that he was not from the village, most of them probably able to tell from the way he was
dressed, from his trousers and dark blue collarless shirt, that he
wasn't from any of the neighboring villages either. The house
was on the larger side of the houses he'd passed on his brief
walk through the village, with white concrete walls, an untiled
asbestos roof, and smooth red cement floors, and climbing up
the two short steps to the veranda, where the crowd was more
concentrated and nobody seemed to notice him, he took off his
sandals, left them by the collection of footwear near the entrance, and went up to the threshold of the front door.

In the center of the room, elevated on a kind of low table or
cot, was an open wooden casket overlaid with plastic lamina-
tion on its surfaces, and standing around the casket were a
number of people, mainly women, some of them looking into
the casket and whimpering or crying, a few quietly reciting
hymns from small booklets they held in their hands, verses
most likely from the *Sivapurānam*. Seated a little away on the
floor in front of one of the walls was a priest, an array of fruit,
coconuts, lamps, and other items spread out on banana leaves
in front of him, and sitting cross-legged opposite him was a
broad, muscular man of about thirty, wearing a white sarong

and a white thread tied diagonally across his otherwise naked torso. The man was conducting the rites for the deceased, which meant, Krishan guessed, that he was Rani's son-in-law, the husband of Rani's daughter, the responsibility of performing the rites generally falling on a son-in-law if the deceased didn't have any sons. Krishan scanned the room for Rani's daughter, and his gaze soon came to rest on a woman whom several other people in the room were watching too, a woman in her mid- to late twenties standing by the head of the casket, her arms supported by a couple of older women as if they were worried she might faint. She had Rani's dark complexion but didn't quite resemble her on first glance, her build much less substantial, her face rounder and softer. She wasn't crying so much as out of breath, it seemed, her eyes not quite focused, as if she wasn't able to see clearly, and it was only when he noticed the two young girls holding on to her dress and looking somewhat lost, the only children present in the room, that Krishan realized the two girls must be Rani's granddaughters, that the woman they were holding must be Rani's daughter. Not knowing how to approach her Krishan remained at the threshold, wondering what to say, studying Rani's daughter till the older woman beside her noticed him standing there and gestured him toward them. He went up and introduced himself, looking first at the older woman and then at Rani's daughter, trying to diminish his stature and summon a look of grief on his face. This was the moment he'd feared most since learning about the death two days before, the moment Rani's relatives finally came face-to-face with him, looks of silent accusation on their faces, but registering who he was Rani's daughter only smiled sadly and welcomed him, her voice soft and plaintive, very different from how it had been on the phone. So you managed to make it, she said looking straight at him, you managed to find the house. I'm glad you were able to come. Turning to the two women she was standing next to she explained who he was, that it was at his house that her mother had been staying in Colombo, that it was his grandmother her mother had been looking after. Krishan looked at the women with an uncertain smile, searching their faces for any sign of resentment, for any sign that they, if not Rani's daughter, might hold him responsible for what had happened, but they too simply looked at him knowingly and warmly, as if to them he was merely one more mourner at the funeral, not the object of any ill will.

The older woman motioned him toward the casket, which he'd carefully avoided looking at till then, and drawing closer to it, slightly hesitant about looking directly at Rani, the first things Krishan noticed were the two oversize garlands draped over her chest, the way the plain white sari she was wearing blended in with the white satin interior of the casket. Her strangely pale, almost white hands were patiently folded over her waist, and her equally pale, unadorned feet were tied together by a thread that linked her two big toes. Taking in these details Krishan allowed himself to get a little closer, glancing at last toward the head of the casket at Rani's face, at the hair combed neatly back, at the eyes closed, the lips slightly pursed, the skin just as strangely pale as her hands and feet, coated, he realized, with several layers of talcum powder. Her face was expressionless, or rather wearing an expression that didn't seem exactly coherent, certainly not consonant with the mournful faces around her, and standing there with his hands by his sides Krishan was not sure what exactly he should be feeling or what exactly he should do. He was somehow moved, but he didn't feel any sadness or tears rising to his eyes, only a softer, tenderer version of the alienation he'd felt upon hearing the news two days before. Even if he no longer had difficulty remembering who Rani was and what she was like, even if he could remember all her mannerisms, her gruff but warm way of speaking, the sadness and longing she always carried with her, he struggled to connect the image of Rani in his mind with the body now lying in front of him, which seemed, with its ghostlike face, hands, and feet, with the unfamiliar white sari and strangely formal posture, to belong to someone he didn't know. He heard at that moment, coming from behind him, the sound of a woman wailing, and turning around saw that an older couple had entered the room. The woman held Rani's daughter's hands in her own for a moment, then pulled her hands away and began striking them against her temples, crying out that she could not believe Rani was gone, that first it had been her sons, then her husband, and now Rani herself. She repeated these statements rhythmically and without break, becoming even more strident as she left Rani's daughter and approached the casket, causing some of the women who were already standing beside it to begin crying louder themselves.

Krishan watched the scene for a while, surprised by the pitch of the woman's emotion, especially since Rani's daughter herself was so subdued, and decided that the woman must have been a close relative or perhaps an intimate friend. Turning to look at Rani's daughter, seeing that for a moment nobody was paying attention to her, he took from his shirt pocket the envelope his grandmother had given him and went up to her, leaning forward as he told her, almost in a whisper, that his

grandmother had asked him to give it to her in order to help
with the funeral expenses. Rani's daughter looked a little surprised, even though his mother had told her about the money
the day before, then nodded her head in acknowledgment as
she took the envelope. Looking away she hesitated for a second, then turning back and meeting his eyes she spoke to him
again. My mother felt very close to your grandmother. She enjoyed staying in Colombo a lot, and would always talk about
your family when she came back for visits. I don't know why
she ever decided to leave, I kept telling her that she should go
back, that that was what the doctor had said was best, but she
was so stubborn about remaining here. She didn't want to stay
in Colombo anymore, and she didn't want to go back to the
hospital for treatment either. She said that the only thing she
wanted was to stay at home with her granddaughters, that she
didn't want to miss them growing up. My mother loved my two
girls so much, even more than she loved her youngest son, I'm
glad she was able to spend some time with them at least before
she left us behind. Rani's daughter paused upon saying this, reflecting on what she'd said in the distinctive manner the bereaved sometimes have when talking to other people, appearing
on the surface to be engaging in conversation when all the
while speaking only to themselves. Krishan nodded and tried to
smile, glanced at the girls who were now standing next to the
priest and their father, observing the men with a mixture of
interest and confusion. He was unsure what to say and waited
to see whether Rani's daughter would say more, but smiling
with an air of finality she turned and went into the adjacent
room to put the envelope away. He waited there a little longer,
hoping they might continue speaking when she returned, but

by the time she did another family had entered the room and begun giving their condolences. Seeing no point to remaining inside, Krishan looked once more at the casket, touched his hands to its base, then slipped out to the garden and looked for an uncrowded place to stand, somewhere he could watch the proceedings unobserved and reflect on what he'd seen and heard.

He'd believed till then that he would be able to learn what happened to Rani by attending the funeral, that merely by studying her daughter's face he would be able to ascertain the nature of Rani's death, but seeing her daughter in person at last it was evident to him that his expectations had been misplaced, and not only because the constant stream of people coming in to give their condolences made conversation impossible. He'd expected, for some reason, to be able to obtain some kind of decisive affirmation or refutation of his suspicions, but the moment he heard Rani's daughter talking he realized that no unambiguous verdict was possible, that even if he waited till the funeral was over to talk to her the subject of suicide would never come up explicitly, that he would be left in the end with only his own interpretations of whatever she told him. He'd been relieved by the warmth and openness with which she'd received him, so different from the distant, mechanical tone of her voice on the phone, and he'd been relieved too by what she'd said about Rani's feelings toward Appamma, which meant his fears that Rani resented their life together in Colombo were unfounded, that she hadn't left because she disliked staying with them but for other, more significant reasons. She had said she wanted to spend time with her granddaughters, and this was no doubt true, but he got the sense from Rani's daughter's account that Rani had left more because she wanted to escape her mind and her mental condition than anything else, that she'd left in the same way that so many of those who are chronically depressed move from one place to another or back and forth between different places, hoping that a change of environment will make things better, though at the end of the day they were compelled to take their minds with them wherever they went, like movable, invisible prisons in which they were trapped. He'd been struck, too, by the palpable tone of regret in Rani's daughter's voice, as if her mother's decision to leave Colombo and stop therapy had led to the worsening of her condition and perhaps ultimately to her demise, as if her mother's depression and her death were connected in some significant way. This more than anything else made him wonder whether his suspicions about suicide might be right, but there was a good chance he was reading too much into the way Rani's daughter had spoken, he told himself, for there was often a certain kind of regret in the way the bereaved talked about how the people they'd lost had died, as if they believed that the death would not have come about if some small detail had been different, as if they believed that not only the more specific death but also the more general phenomenon of dying itself could have been avoided. There was an openness or vulnerability in Rani's daughter's bearing that felt incompatible with the possibility that Rani had committed suicide, for if she really did believe or suspect that her mother had killed herself she would have been a lot more guarded, he felt, would have spoken less freely about her mother, not only out of shame but out of fear that someone might guess what happened. Even if there had been concrete signs that Rani had killed herself it was clear her daughter was oblivious to them, that either she hadn't noticed the signs or, more likely, if there were such signs, that she'd intentionally averted her eyes from them. There was no sense, after all, in pursuing the possibility that her mother had committed suicide unless the facts were undeniable, and since there was no concrete evidence that this was the case, it was probably just easier to assume it had been an accident and leave the matter at that. In a way Krishan was grateful to be able to stop there, to learn that he would not be able to find out anything more, that he could let the issue go with the relative likelihood that Rani hadn't ended her own life. Even on the off chance that it had been suicide, he told himself, it was clear from what Rani's daughter had said that his family couldn't have been responsible, that they'd done their best to help her and that what she'd done to herself, if indeed she'd done anything, was the result of far more subterranean forces inside her, forces that had their genesis outside their lives.

Looking up from the patch of ground he was staring at Krishan saw that the crowd in the garden was getting larger, the buzz of low voices around him louder now and more sustained. New arrivals were continually trickling in, acknowledging the various people they saw as they walked toward the house, everyone knowing everyone, it seemed, which was in a sense what defined village life, the total absence of anonymity, nobody a stranger to anyone, even if not everyone was friends. Entering the house the new arrivals all went straight to Rani's daughter to give her their condolences, the women crying loudly and dramatically as they took her hands and then breaking out into loud waves of lamentation as they approached the casket, beating their chests, raising their hands up to the sky, speaking to Rani's dead body as if she were still alive. Coming back out to the veranda, wiping their tears away with their hands or their sleeves, a few of these women seemed to undergo a remarkable transformation, as if having left the presence of the body and the bereaved they were immediately able to regain the composure they'd lost while inside. Krishan had often heard his mother, who'd grown up in Jaffna and had always resented village life, disparaging the lamentations she claimed could be heard at every village funeral, not the lamentation of the bereaved, whose grief was of course usually sincere, but the lamentation of everybody else, the people who were much less affected by the death and who sometimes didn't even really know the deceased, people who, according to his mother, would come to the funeral whistling a tune or telling jokes, who would break out into histrionics in front of the body and then afterward, when no one was watching, go on with their lives as though nothing had happened. It was all just acting, his mother had said contemptuously of such women, a performance they put on to show everyone else how close they'd been to the deceased. It wasn't just the people who came to the funeral either, she went on, at some funerals the family of the deceased themselves hired people for the purpose of lamenting, just like they hired drummers and a priest, in order to show everyone how important their relative had been, how loved they were and how missed they would be. It had been hard for Krishan to actually understand what his mother meant at the time, never having been to a village funeral at that point, and because his mother was generally suspicious of emotion, preferring to cry in private if she had to cry at all, he'd dismissed what she said as simply another example of her general cyni-

cism regarding the expression of emotion. Listening now to the
crying and wailing of the new arrivals though, not all of whom
could have been close relatives or friends, observing how coming back out to the veranda they returned so quickly to a state
of equilibrium, he couldn't help wondering whether perhaps
his mother had been right, especially since the only woman
who didn't seem to be shedding any tears was Rani's daughter
herself, the one person who should have been more affected
than anybody else. Despite being in a state of visible distress
and vulnerability Rani's daughter was not, Krishan could tell,
completely beside herself like many of the other women were
or were pretending to be, perhaps because she was too exhausted to really feel grief, because she was still processing
everything that had happened, perhaps because there was no
natural correspondence between the moments conventionally
prescribed for grief and what the bereaved actually feels.

The man directing the funeral, a middle-aged man with a
slight limp who was casually dressed in trousers and shirt, came
out to the veranda and began calling out to everyone assembled
in the garden, shouting that everybody who wanted to put rice
into the deceased's mouth should come forward. Several people on the veranda and a few in the garden stood up and went
into the house, filling up the already crowded front room, and
Krishan too took a few steps forward, not to go inside but to get
a better view of what was happening. He watched as one by
one the close relatives and friends of the family went up to the
casket, took a small handful of dry rice, and let the grains fall
gently from their palms over Rani's mouth, an act whose meaning or significance he had never been quite able to understand.
All he could think about as he watched was the irony of Rani

being accorded the full set of funeral rituals, she who'd mentioned on more than one occasion during her time in Colombo how much she wished, instead of having to leave her youngest son by the side of the road for the flies, she'd been able to give him a proper funeral. She'd been unable to do not just the funeral, Krishan knew, but also any of the other ceremonies, certainly not the kaadaatru, which was supposed to come the day after the cremation, when the ashes were picked up from the cremation ground and taken home. Interned inside army camps, she probably hadn't been able to do the function that was supposed to take place on the fifth or seventh day after the cremation, the ettuchelavu, as it was called, when all the deceased's favorite foods were offered up symbolically to a garlanded photograph, and not having any of her son's ashes she wouldn't have been able to conduct the anthiyetti either, the ceremony in which the ashes were scattered into a river or a tank or the ocean, probably the most significant of all the post-cremation rituals. The only ceremony she'd been able to perform was the annual death anniversary, the thuvasam, for which neither the body nor the ashes were necessary, only a photograph, a garland, and a priest. Rani had done the thuvasam for both her sons every year since leaving the camps, and in the previous two years she'd used the money she earned looking after Appamma to organize them with great lavishness, inviting everybody in the village and leaving Colombo more than a week in advance to undertake preparations. They'd been watching the news one evening in Appamma's room, Krishan remembered, listening to a report about a monthslong protest in a small village organized by the aged mothers of disappeared Tamil men, the women demanding that the government investigate the tens of thousands of Tamil people who'd vanished without a trace during the war and immediately afterward. They wanted some kind of verdict on their disappeared sons, husbands, and brothers so they could finally have a measure of peace, one of the women was telling the reporter, so that they could conclusively learn what had happened to the people they loved. Rani had turned to him after the segment was over and told him, shaking her head, that she was grateful for having seen her dead sons' bodies, for having managed to hold the younger one in her arms for a few seconds, that she didn't know what she would have done had either of them suddenly gone missing one day, had she been forced to live in uncertainty about whether they were alive or dead. When you didn't see and hold the body of a dead child you couldn't understand that they were gone, she told him, and unlike her the relatives of people who'd gone missing were forced as a result to live their lives in a kind of suspended state, unable to accept that their sons or husbands or brothers were dead, knowing there was a chance they might be alive in some unnamed cell somewhere, though at the same time they were hesitant to give this possibility too much credence, afraid to believe in it given how many unmarked graves they knew were scattered around the north and east.

Krishan had always assumed that Hindus cremated the bodies of the dead and scattered their ashes as a kind of acknowledgment of the body's impermanence, of its vulnerability and transience, and so it was strange for him now, watching as one by one people dropped grains of rice over Rani's mouth, to think that nevertheless the physical body played such a central role in Hindu funerals, that it was given such prominence in all

the mourning rituals. It was acknowledged not just at the funeral, where the body was dressed up, caressed, and talked to
by the people who came to mourn, but also in the cremation
and the rituals that followed, first in the ash that was collected
in the urn after the body had been burned, the urn becoming a
kind of materially reduced body that was treated, even after the
cremation, with all the reverence due to the original body. Even
when the ash was dispersed over water thirty-one days later,
when this materially reduced body that had been held on to for
a month was given up, even then a kind of symbolic body was
retained in the physical object of the photograph, which was
garlanded and placed on a wall of the house, taken down every
year during the death anniversary and prayed to and offered
food, as if the image itself were capable of consumption and
digestion, the photograph becoming, in other words, not so
much a representation as a physical manifestation of the dead.
The process of letting go of a person was always done in gradual stages, from what he'd seen, from the actual body to a reduced body to a symbolic body that was always kept in the
house, an acknowledgment both of the difficulty of giving up
the body and also of the fact that the bodies of the ones we love
can never be fully renounced. And perhaps this was why the
symbolic acts of feeding were so important in the mourning
rituals, it occurred to him, in the pouring of rice over the mouth
of the deceased and in the offering of food to the photograph
of the deceased, for it wasn't surprising that in a culture in
which food and the activity of eating were so important, in a
culture in which feeding was one of the primary acts of care,
in which to ask whether somebody had eaten was to ask whether
they were well, in which the question of whom you can eat

with and whose food you can eat was a way of enforcing the boundaries between castes, that in such a culture the acts of serving and eating were also the physical processes that the bereaved found most difficult to part with, so that even after the body had stopped consuming and digesting food the bereaved continued to find solace in the act of feeding the deceased.

Standing there in the garden looking into the house Krishan thought of the cemeteries for fallen cadres that the Tigers had built all over the northeast, cemeteries that no longer existed and that harkened back in his mind to a time, only a few years before, when the northeast had been an entirely different place. The Tigers, though they consisted mostly of men and women who prayed in private to Hindu gods, had always buried their dead instead of cremating them, a practice inspired, Krishan had learned somewhere, by the significant population of Christian Tamils in the northeast. Cadres who died on campaigns that were successful in capturing new land were buried in new cemeteries constructed on the land they'd fallen fighting for, while the other dead were buried, symbolically if their bodies could not be recovered, in one of the several massive cemeteries already established across the north and the east. Krishan had never been to any of these cemeteries but he'd seen photographs and videos of them—vast, open spaces filled with endless rows of large horizontal stone tombs, identical except for the small engravings at their base indicating who rested there. The cemeteries, which were swept every day and kept open through the night for anyone to come and mourn their dead, were festooned on special occasions with the small red-and-yellow flags of the Tigers strung out high above the rows of tombs, and during Maaveerar Naal, the annual day for the remembrance of the war dead, masses upon masses of people would gather at these sites from all over Tiger-held territory to listen to speeches and cry over the sons, daughters, brothers, and sisters they'd lost, taking sorrowful pride in their sacrifices as they listened to Tiger songs of fearlessness and devotion blaring from loudspeakers, scenes of immeasurable pain and sadness that Krishan had never once seen in person but which were, somehow, etched into the back of his eyes. All those cemeteries, containing hundreds and thousands of dead fighters, had been razed to the ground by the army after the end of the war, their huge Chinese-made bulldozers mowing down graves indiscriminately, hardly a trace of them left anywhere in the northeast now, hardly a trace of any of those male and female cadres who'd died fighting in anonymity for a future that never materialized, not even of Rani's eldest son, who, Krishan realized now for the first time, must also have been buried in one of those cemeteries, must also have had his remains destroyed and removed from their place of rest.

It was not just the cemeteries that had been destroyed, naturally, for all the former Tiger offices, bases, and weapons depots had been destroyed too, all their signs, posters, and statues, after which the army had begun the labor of clearing rubble from bombed sites, of extracting the land mines buried all over the northeast, of relaying shelled-out roads and train tracks. Soon the only external signs that there'd once been a separatist movement and a war were the tents in which people still lived and the scars still inscribed on their bodies, the hairless skin on what remained of people's amputated arms and legs. The purpose of all the government's demolition and renovation in the northeast had, of course, been to erase any memory that might spur the Tamil population back toward militarism, and in this it had been more or less successful, for one hardly heard ordinary people talking about the Tigers in the northeast now, one hardly heard anyone giving them more than a passing thought. It was strange to consider, since for decades the Tigers had been the central fact of life in the northeast, but it also made sense to a degree, for memory requires cues from the environment to operate, can function only by means of associations between things in the present and things in the past, which meant that remembering became far harder when all the cues that an environment contained were systematically removed. Without the physical objects that allowed it to operate organically, memory had to be cultivated consciously and deliberately, and how could the average person in the northeast afford to actively cultivate their memory of a world now gone when there were so many more urgent concerns, how to make ends meet, how to rebuild their homes, how to educate their children, concerns that filled up all their mental space? The truth was that eventually most people would have ceased remembering the past anyway, even if all remaining traces of the Tigers had been left untouched, for the truth was that all monuments lose their meaning and significance with the passing of time, disappearing, like the statues and memorials in Colombo dedicated to the so-called independence struggle against the British, into the vast unseen and unconsidered background of everyday life. Deliberately or not the past was always being forgotten, in all places and among all peoples, a phenomenon that had less to do with the forces that seek to erase or rewrite history than simply the nature of time, with the precedence the present always seems to have over what has come before, the precedence not of the present moment, which we never seem to have access to, but of the present situation, which is always demanding our attention, always so forceful and vivid and overwhelming that as soon as one of its elements disappears we forget it ever existed. A shirt we wore every week for several years can be thrown away and then forgotten forever the week after, a table on which we ate two meals a day for a decade can be replaced and the strangeness of the new arrangement gone within a month, and even when something vital disappears, something our lives have centered on for years, even then we move on very quickly, very quickly adjusting to the new circumstances, so that within a few months or years the new way starts to seem like the way things have always been.

Forgetting was, of course, something we ourselves chose to do on purpose sometimes, as when after the end of a painful relationship we delete all traces of it that existed in our phones, attempting to excise it from our lives, and in this sense forgetting was not so different from remembering, an important and necessary part of life, just as central as remembering when it came to establishing an identity and orienting ourselves toward the future. And yet there was a crucial distinction, Krishan knew, between the forgetting that takes place as a result of our consent, which is a forgetting we need in order to reconcile our pasts and presents, and the forgetting that is imposed on us against our own will, which is so often a way of forcing us to accept a present in which we do not want to partake. Whenever forgetting was imposed in this way it would always give rise to people who insisted stubbornly on remembering, people who resisted not only the specific erasures of the past by those in power but also the more general erosion that would anyway have been brought on by time, people who remained committed to commemorating the world taken away from them no matter what happened, sharing stories and images and songs and videos that they kept safe inside their heads and their hard drives, trying to ensure that even if all the objective evidence was taken away, even if there was no means in public spaces for the communication of such histories, that their pasts would continue to exist somewhere, somehow. Even if sharing what happened during the war was painful, even if it was easier for most people to pass over these wounds in silence, suppressing their memories of the world they'd helped construct and the violence that had destroyed it, even so people would remain who insisted on remembering, some of them activists, artists, and archivists who'd consciously chosen to do so but most of them ordinary people who had no other choice, people like Rani who, in the most basic sense, simply couldn't accept a world without what they'd lost, people who'd lost their ability to participate in the present and were thus compelled to live out the rest of their lives in their memories and imaginations, to build in their minds, like the temple constructed by Poosal, the monuments and memorials they could not build in the world outside. Perhaps this, it occurred to Krishan as he stood there in the garden of the funeral house, was why Rani had seemed to spend so much of her time in Colombo lost in thought, not because she was sad or depressed but because she was busy constructing in her mind a place where she could be reunited with the sons she'd lost, a place she could occupy as an alternative to the world that bombarded her senses with its emptiness every single day and night.

The sound of the lamentations was more or less continuous

now, rising out of the front room in waves and mingling with the drumming from the gate, the tempo and volume of which in turn had been increasing, the quicker, louder beat that announced new arrivals becoming almost indistinguishable from the beat that was rapped out in the interim. Looking up Krishan saw the funeral director come out to the veranda again, this time to say that it was the last chance to see the body, that they were about to close the casket, upon hearing which the people who'd been waiting in readiness in the veranda and the garden gave a collective stir, those in the garden moving toward the veranda, those on the veranda forming a line near the door so they could enter the house. Krishan made his way toward the house, which was more or less packed with people now, joining the haphazard line that went in through the front door. Those already inside were thronging around the body, jostling to get closer in the same way devotees jostled in temples to catch sight of the deity when the curtains were drawn, the men touching the casket with their hands, some of them crying and talking to the body but most of them stone-faced, the women stroking Rani's face and shoulders and arms, raising their hands to the sky and beating their chests as they wailed out loud. The lamentation was reaching a peak, all the women crying in unison, their voices rising and falling so loudly and rhythmically that at moments it seemed even to eclipse the drums, whose sole function now was to provide accompaniment to their voices, to give the music of collective lamentation a beat on which it could fall back. Overwhelmed by the scene around him, so different from the staid funerals he'd witnessed in Colombo, Krishan caught sight of Rani's daughter as he edged deeper into the sea of mourners. She was standing behind the head of the casket and no longer fully in control of herself, her feet not quite steady, supported by the two women who were standing beside her earlier, sobbing loudly as she touched her mother's face. This was the last time she would see her mother, only men being allowed to accompany the body to the cremation ground, and goaded perhaps by this knowledge, by the intensity of the drums and the wailing of all the women, she too had begun to speak to the body, to cry and lament with the other women, though what she was saying was lost among all the other voices rising and falling in the room. Krishan still couldn't tell how genuine most of the lamentation was but it occurred to him, as he was pushed toward the center of the room, his feet trampling and trampled by the feet of the others crowded around him, the heat of their bodies and their breathing pressing in against him, that perhaps he was wrong to think of lamentation in terms of sincerity or insincerity, that perhaps the crying and wailing and sobbing all around him was intended not as an expression of emotion but as a kind of service offered to the bereaved, a performance in some sense but a performance that, together with the drums and the rituals, was meant only to help the bereaved with their own lamentation, to ease out, like the calm rhythmic words and firm kneading hands of a midwife during a difficult birth, the tears that the bereaved so often found impossible to bring out by themselves. It was difficult after all to understand what a death meant, even for those who will be affected most vitally by the loss, it was difficult to really accept a death, to really let go of oneself and in doing so begin letting go of the other, and perhaps the custom of lamentation was meant above all to help the bereaved in this process, the friends and relatives and community of the bereaved trying to help the bereaved cry by crying themselves, even if they did not feel the same pain. Nearing the casket Krishan was seeing Rani's body for the second time now, her powdered face, the grains of rice that had fallen from her mouth onto the white satin of the casket, her pale hands clasped together over her waist. He was unable to cry, unable to produce anything more than the welling in his eyes, but caught up in the density of people around him, in their pushing and pulling and jostling, in the wailing and lamenting and the sound of the drums, he now felt totally immersed in what was happening, a participant in this process, whatever it was, rather than a spectator, capable of feeling fully the force of what was happening, as if something inside him too was being channeled by everything around him, being called to the surface of his mind. He brought his hands together and touched Rani's shoulder lightly, brought his hands to his eyes and blessed himself with her, touched her neck and forehead and blessed himself again, and understanding now that it was really Rani lying in front of him he stood there in front of the casket looking at her till the pushing of people behind him compelled him to move, to shuffle around the casket and make his way back out to the garden.

Outside there was an air of anticipation, the drums beating with a feverish intensity, the four drummers still standing in the same place behind the fence, immersed in the rhythm of their drumming. More and more of the people who'd gone inside the house returned outside, the funeral director calling more impatiently now for people to leave the front room as he tried to clear a space around the casket. Krishan watched as the two women supporting Rani's daughter, who was still standing by the head of the casket, drew her back a little, as the director and his assistant carefully lifted the lid of the casket and then low-ered it over the body. The two of them came out, went to the side of the house, where a bier consisting of two wooden poles was leaning against the wall, the two main poles held crosswise by several sticks that were bound by rope and covered by a patchwork of dried palm fronds. The two of them carried the bier around the side of the house and placed it on the ground a few feet in front of the veranda steps, the director trying to shout above the wails and the drums for everyone to give them space. He signaled to his assistant, who went back inside and, together with four or five other men, heaved the casket up. The director leading the way, clearing the path in front of them, they brought the casket out through the door to the veranda, moving slowly and vigilantly, doing their best to keep the casket stable, Rani's daughter coming out behind them together with all the women who'd been inside from the beginning, all of them beating their hands against their chests, their wailing loud and unabating. The men moved with the casket down the ve-randa steps and into the garden, shouting at one another over all the noise to coordinate their movements, then cautiously, almost delicately, they lowered the casket down onto the bier. Everybody in the garden crowded around this central point de-spite the repeated cautionings of the director, watching as the men began to secure the casket to the bier with rope. The drummers had already made their way out through the garden gate, Krishan saw, were beating their drums out on the lane, and Rani's daughter's husband, who was carrying a large and seemingly heavy clay pot on his right shoulder, followed them out without expression. The funeral director shouted for the people around the bier to give them space, and the casket now loaded firmly onto the bier, the men gave a count of three and heaved the bier up onto their shoulders in a single motion, two men in front, two behind, and two on each of the sides. The lamentation reached a crescendo, a chorus of mainly female voices rising up into the air, and shepherded through the garden by the director, the bier was carried in stops and starts toward the gate, the crowd following them as they went. Struggling a little at the narrow gate the men carried the bier out into the lane, the women in the crowd following them only up to the fence, raising their arms to the sky and continuing to wail, the men following the body out through the gate, forming a cortege that Krishan too joined as the body began to move away from the house. Turning back Krishan saw Rani's daughter standing in front of the fence, no longer crying or wailing, entirely silent, chest heaving, struggling for breath it seemed as she watched them, her figure becoming smaller and more spectral as they moved farther and farther from the house, till they turned a corner and she was lost to sight. The procession continued at a slow but even pace, led in the front by Rani's son-in-law, who carried the clay pot on his shoulder in silence, followed by the bier and the rest of the all-male procession, some of whose members dropped out as they passed their homes, the rest continuing to walk soundlessly behind the body. They made their way slowly through the village, not toward the main road where he'd gotten off the bus but farther and farther away from all links to the outside world, through narrow, winding, unpaved lanes that opened out, eventually, into a sprawling landscape of grass and brush. They scarcely seemed to advance as they walked through this vastness, making no discernible progress against the palmyra trees that stood solemnly in the distance, their tall figures turning into silhouettes as the sun began tracing the visible portion of its descent, as the afternoon moved toward its climax and the golden-yellow light began enfolding the land around them, as Rani began making her last, silent journey into the distance beyond.

9

THEIR PROGRESS REMAINED slow, subject to the burden of the body, the wide and gently rolling landscape ahead becoming gradually more verdant, swathed by grasses, plants, and shrubs that burst forth in undisciplined abandon, by clusters of trees weighed down by the density of their branches and leaves. Except for a cyclist who passed by in the opposite direction, easing to a stop as he neared the procession and then pulling over beside the path, there was little sign of human life as they made their way, little movement around them except for the small, weightless white butterflies that flitted in and out of the vegetation as though in slow motion. Krishan had traveled for seven hours from Colombo by train, for three hours from Kilinochchi town to the village on two separate buses, had felt upon arriving at Rani's house that he'd traveled as far interior as possible within the northeast, but having made his way now to the far side of the village and out into this unexpected space, walking along this unpaved path miles from any main road, he couldn't help feeling he was entering a sphere of vast remoteness, a place undiscoverable on any map and untouched by any written history, a place that felt, all the same, somehow familiar, as though he'd walked through it in a dream or a previous life. He was still at the back of the procession, the men in front of him, maybe twenty or thirty in all, moving silently and patiently, their gazes directed at the ground in front of them or at the path ahead, the drummers rapping their drums quietly behind the body, their accompaniment serving only to amplify the silence surrounding them. Inside the small, contained space of Rani's house and the neatly fenced-off boundaries of the garden he had been overwhelmed by all the emotion, by the clamor of the lamentation and the drumming, the sight of the body and the people thronging all around it, but moving out in the open now, the late afternoon sky stretching out before them, these feelings seemed small and almost petty, as though forced into a wider relief, into a contrast with the world's expansiveness that dissolved them into nothingness, so that deprived of the shared emotion that had united him with everyone else during the funeral he was returning now to his own thoughts once more, remembering once more his own identity.

In the distance ahead the land seemed to gradually flatten, the area to the left of the path becoming a vast glimmering surface that reflected the pale gold of the sky. The butterflies became scarcer, the quicker, more mercurial movement of dragonflies taking their place, and as they drew closer the glimmering surface resolved into what was actually an immense lake, its near banks covered with ferns and tall grass, its distant banks too far to make out, merging silently with what looked like hills or cloud on the horizon. It was hard to say whether the lake had formed naturally or whether it was one of the man-made tanks constructed centuries ago by old kings and chief-tains, tanks that had been around so long that they were now an intrinsic part of the ecology, but studying it as he continued walking, the water calm and waveless, lapping softly and peace-fully upon its banks, the feeling grew in Krishan that he'd been to this place before, that he'd walked across this same path and sat there by the banks of this same lake. There couldn't have been many bodies of water this size in the northeast, he knew, and taking out his phone he tried to see if he could find the place on Google Maps, which was unhelpful since there was, he saw, no signal on his phone. He wondered whether it was pos-sible he'd passed it on one of the visits he'd made to the district back when he was based in Jaffna, but he knew for certain that he'd never been to Rani's village before, and couldn't remem-ber having spent much time in the general vicinity before ei-ther. He could ask one of the men in the procession for the name of the lake, but none of them seemed to be paying it any attention and it would have been out of place to ask in any case, he felt, especially when everyone seemed so lost in their own thoughts. His gaze continued to return to the lake obsessively, as if at a face he'd come across somewhere but for some reason could not place, and it was only when he noticed a few reeds projecting out of the shallows that something clicked in his mind and everything seemed to resolve, when he realized with slight disbelief that the lake was familiar to him not because he'd been there before but because he'd seen it before on the internet, in a scene from a documentary he'd watched several years before in Delhi. It was a documentary he'd rewatched

two or three times and which he'd been fixated on for several
months afterward, which he'd stumbled across on YouTube not
long after his obsession with Kuttimani, in that period when his
attention had shifted from the traumas at the end of the war to
the longings at its beginning. The film, whose name he could
no longer remember, was not much more than an hour long,
and though it had been made by a filmmaker from Denmark or
Norway or one of those other northern European countries
that were hard to distinguish, it had been devoid of the false
benevolence common to so many British and European documents of violence and suffering in former colonies, devoid of
the knowingness or righteousness so easily conjured up in such
materials. The film's narrative centered around the life of a
twenty-four-year-old woman named Dharshika, who he could
still vividly recall, a woman who was, at the time of filming, an
active member of the Black Tigers. The Black Tigers were the
elite, much feared division of the Tigers that specialized in carefully planned and meticulously executed suicide missions—
from assassinations of political figures to bombings in public
spaces to small but devastating attacks on Sri Lankan army and
navy bases—and it had been clear, watching Dharshika talk and
move over the course of the documentary, that there was indeed something elite about her too. It was if she had in some
way been divinely ordained for her role, not just because of the
severe beauty of her appearance, her sharp, almost haughty
features and darkly lustrous skin, but also because of the penetrating steeliness of her gaze and the certainty of her posture,
the conviction with which she spoke about the brutality of the
Sri Lankan government and her readiness to fight and die to
protect her people. There'd been thousands of women like her

but it was hard not to wonder, listening to her as she spoke, how such a person was possible and how she'd come to be, what experiences and what inner affinities had led her down this path so different from those taken by other men and women her age, a path that was headed so clearly toward death and the total extinction of consciousness it brought but that she followed, nevertheless, with such ease and confidence, as though she couldn't wait to reach its end.

According to her mother, whose estranged relationship with her daughter formed, Krishan recalled, one of the central subjects of the documentary, Dharshika had only been two years old when war broke out in Jaffna. Their family had lived in the midst of the fighting from its very earliest days, the most banal activities of their ordinary lives filled with great risk, sudden mêlées between the army and the Tigers often forcing them to stop what they were doing and run to take shelter. Even when there was no fighting there was the constant presence of soldiers who patrolled the villages, who would use security checkpoints as an excuse to harass and inappropriately touch girls and young women, as a result of which the movement of females outside their homes had to be severely restricted. As a young girl Dharshika had been extremely close to the aged priest of the nearby church, her mother told the camera, always sitting next to him during mass and prayers, assisting him in whatever ways he needed. It had been her daughter's goal from a young age to join the order as a nun, she added plaintively, so she could spend the rest of her life devoted to Mother Mary. Standing in front of the bombed-out ruins of this church in the next scene, asked by the filmmakers about this lost period of her childhood, Dharshika spoke at length about how the violence she'd seen had changed the course of her plans, recalling in particular an incident in which the army had shelled the church while civilians were sheltering there during the fighting, leaving behind a slew of bodies on the floor next to the fallen cross. On the verge of breaking down as she talked about these childhood memories, she managed to hold herself together for the length of the segment, wiping away a tear with the palm of her hand as if swatting away a fly before going on to criticize the Christian notion of turning the other cheek, asking how a God who cared about justice could let such things happen in his own house. These objections had led Dharshika to turn her devotion away from God and toward the movement and its Supreme Leader, but they hadn't, interestingly, been enough to turn her away from Mother Mary, and she still returned to the church grounds whenever she could, she told the camera matter-of-factly, where she would sit in front of the lone statue of the Mother that still remained and speak her heart out for hours at a time.

All of these experiences had no doubt played a role in her decision to join the Tigers, but it was above all the death of her father, her mother made clear, that led Dharshika to run away from home when she was still a young girl. Her father had been a peon at the post office in Jaffna town, and he'd been killed along with twenty-four other people by an aerial bomb that the army had dropped one morning in the center of town, opposite the main bus depot. Some children were able to bear the pain and grief that came as a result of such events, Dharshika's mother explained, while others lacked the capacity to return to ordinary life afterward. Her daughter belonged to the second category, and on an afternoon not long after the one-year anniversary of her father's death, at the age of about twelve or thirteen, she'd secretly left home. In what capacity she initially joined the Tigers was unclear from the documentary—she might simply have been a resident in one of the many orphanages they ran, or worked as a volunteer in one of their many nonmilitary organizations, or she might have joined as a recruit straightaway and been sent away to some secret location for basic training. What is clear is that at some point in her later teenage years she ended up joining one of the Tiger's all-women combat units, that she was selected eventually for one of the few highly coveted positions available in the Black Tigers. Speaking with a mixture of grief and pride at their family home, Dharshika's mother explained with a tinge of embarrassment that she'd had very little contact with her daughter since she left at that young age, that she saw Dharshika only once in a while, when her duties permitted it, and even then only for very short periods of time. She'd heard that her daughter had done well in the Tigers, that her courage and talent had earned her the respect of the other cadres and her superiors in the organization, but she herself had no idea whether her daughter was the same person she used to be, how her character had changed and to what degree, had no idea even whether she continued to pray. Dharshika herself, interviewed presumably somewhere close to her base, spoke of her mother without sentimentality, as though she were talking about a distant relative who'd died years before, and listening to her Krishan had wondered whether some kind of rift had developed between Dharshika and her mother in the year following

her father's death, whether the daughter had formed some kind
of resentment against the mother who'd been forced to raise
her and her siblings alone after their father's death.

This refusal to show any sentimentality, it became clear, was
part of a more general toughness that Dharshika seemed keen
to present in front of the camera, a toughness that was mir-
rored to some degree by her best friend Puhal, the other main
subject of the documentary, but underscored at the same time
by their differences. Puhal was twenty-four and in the same unit
as Dharshika, the same height but of slenderer build, and somewhat softer in her way of speaking and moving. She too seemed
keen to emphasize her toughness, but she generally took more
time responding to the questions she was asked and was often
hesitant in the answers she gave, her conviction undercut by a
willingness to reflect on her vulnerability in ways that Dharshika seemed unable or unwilling. The two of them had spent
every day together for seven years, and their comfort and intimacy with each other was clear from the brief glimpses the
documentary gave of their shared daily lives. In one scene the
two women, both advanced belts in karate, sparred against
each other in the early morning, ending their session with a set
of three-finger push-ups that they performed in parallel and at
the exact same speed, while in another Puhal stood behind
Dharshika and combed out the latter's beautifully rough, unruly hair, straightening it out and plaiting it into two neat braids
with an almost maternal tenderness and familiarity. In the interviews they did together they seemed to enjoy playing off
each other, Dharshika's bravado against Puhal's thoughtful-
ness, as in a scene in which Dharshika joked about the US government gifting them an American tank that had been sold to

the Sri Lankan army and then captured by the Tigers in battle, in response to which Puhal chided her as though she were a child, scolded her for making light of the losses that had been suffered in the course of winning the tank. In one of the scenes Krishan had been most struck by, the two women took turns discussing the modus operandi of the Black Tigers, whose missions, Puhal explained, involved taking out a major target with the use of very small, highly trained groups of cadres instead of relying on large numbers as the regular Tiger units did. They would be given their target months in advance of the mission, and for months their training would revolve around the specificities of that mission—its particular location, the season and time of day, and the nature of its target, military, political, or civilian. They were sent in with Claymore mines strapped around their chests, which they used either to destroy their targets along with themselves or, if they'd destroyed their targets by other means, to blow themselves up at the end of the mission so as not to be captured, which would of course have meant being subject to torture by government forces. Each member of the unit was always extremely eager to be selected for the next mission, Dharshika told the interviewer, each one of them begging and pleading to be selected, for which reason a kind of lottery system was used to choose teams, so that nobody could complain about being unfairly overlooked. No Black Tiger had ever returned alive from a mission, successful or not, and none of them went in with any expectation that they would return from their missions alive. You tended to stop caring about death after joining the Black Tigers, Puhal explained, learned gradually to take the inevitability of your own death for granted. This was the case for all Tigers, of course, but what distinguished Black Tiger cadres from ordinary cadres was that whereas ordinary Tigers could die at any moment, depending on the vicissitudes of battle, Black Tigers knew months before they died the exact location, moment, and method by which they would die, a death for which they trained for months once their mission was assigned and which they planned and visualized endlessly in the lead-up to that final moment. Krishan had been struck by the tone with which Puhal made this remark, as though she felt it was one of the virtues of being a Black Tiger that your death was totally in your own hands. There was an element of bravado perhaps in this remark, but it was clear that Puhal truly did find some solace in the thought that death could be planned and controlled—that this phenomenon that had been so omnipresent throughout their lives, that could strike at any time and was therefore a constant source of uncertainty and anxiety, could be something you chose rather than something imposed from the outside. There was something in the way both women spoke about their training and their future mission that made him feel that they not only had no fear of dying but were in fact looking forward to it, that they were in a sense even impatient for it, as though they felt they would, upon dying, be reborn into the nation for which they'd just died, as though they saw the nation for which they were fighting as a kind of heaven, as though death, for them, was not the end of real life but its beginning.

The scene that took place at the lake they were now passing, which had remained fixed in Krishan's memory as the climax of the documentary, began with Dharshika and Puhal sitting together on its banks in full military fatigues, looking out over the water and trying to make out whether it was mountains or cloud that lay on the lake's far side. The interviewer had just asked them, presumably, whether they thought much about the battles they'd fought in, for nodding her head at the camera Dharshika said with a smile that scenes of battle played in her mind every time she closed her eyes. She often dreamed of being in battle too, she went on, snapping off a leaf from one of the plants in front of her and beginning to shred it into little pieces, would often have dreams of seeing the enemy approach and trying to shoot but having her gun get stuck, or of shooting enemy soldiers but having no effect on their progress, the soldiers continuing to march zombielike toward her despite all the rounds she emptied on them. These were just dreams, of course, she added after a brief pause, drawing out a tiny glass vial that hung like a pendant from a string around her neck, in reality they knew they would never be captured, on account of the cyanide they carried with them wherever they went. No matter what happened they could always bite down on the capsule and end their lives if they were about to be captured, though if by chance they bit into the vial while they were asleep and dreaming, she said, glancing at Puhal and laughing, then that would be that, they would simply never wake up. Puhal then described how the capsule had to be used in the middle of battle or a mission, explaining that you had to bite into the vial with your teeth so the cracked glass would cut into your tongue, causing the cyanide to enter your bloodstream and kill you immediately. Even if you'd been wounded and were too weak to properly bite down, all you had to do was smash the vial and let a few drops of the cyanide drip onto your wounds, and this would be sufficient to obtain the desired effect. They talked as if the cyanide capsules were heirlooms that had been passed down generation after generation with these exact instructions, long-cherished reminders of their forbears and identities, and listening to the reverence with which they spoke on the subject Krishan had had the sense that they were, already in that moment of filming, talking to the camera as though from some other realm.

The two women were then asked what friendship meant to them, for Puhal turned her head away from the camera and looked shyly at Dharshika, a slightly embarrassed smile on her face, causing Dharshika in turn to laugh. It was clear from their smiles that the two friends hadn't discussed their relationship with each other explicitly before, perhaps because it was more natural for such matters to be negotiated through gestures rather than words, perhaps because the impending approach of their deaths in the form of an as yet unknown mission made discussions of their relationship seem futile. Friendship for them, the two cadres told the camera, their expressions quickly turning serious, meant sharing in each other's emotional lives. It meant sharing in each other's happinesses and sadnesses, and it meant helping and supporting each other in whatever practical ways they could, though they were of course prepared to separate, they hastened to add, if one of them had to be transferred to another location. The discussion then turned from friendship to the subject of betrayal, the gravest offense a cadre could commit, one that the Tigers punished with execution, Krishan knew, even when there was little certainty about the allegation. The two women tried to justify the harshness of the punishment, explaining that the Tigers were fighting for the good of the people, that if a single traitor could, by sharing military information, put the entire cause in jeopardy, then it was better the traitor be shot than the movement and the people be endangered. Looking at the interviewer Dharshika then added, apropos of nothing it seemed, that if someone were to tell her that Puhal had betrayed the cause, if the accusation were to be firmly proven, that she herself wouldn't hesitate to shoot her best friend. A look of uncertainty passed shadowlike across her face as she said this, as though she herself was surprised by what had just come out of her mouth, and falling silent she looked away from the camera, as if she'd spoken too quickly and needed more time to consider the hypothetical situation on which she'd just pronounced. She looked down at the reeds in front of her, then turned back toward the camera a second later and nodded her head gravely, as if to confirm that her initial instinct had indeed been correct, that she would indeed kill Puhal if she betrayed the cause. Puhal, who'd been looking out over the water all that while, turned and regarded Dharshika, who raised her head and looked into the distance to avoid her gaze. There was a period of long silence, in which only the gentle sound of the water lapping against the banks and the faint buzzing of dragonflies in the background could be heard, Dharshika continuing to pluck bits of leaf from the plants in front of her, examining them distractedly in her hand, shredding them, and letting them fall. Puhal then began to speak, breaking the silence with her own take on what Dharshika had said. Everything they did eventually made its way to the Leader, she said—if they did something good the Leader would hear about it, if they did something bad the Leader would hear about it, and if they committed an act of betrayal the Leader would hear about that too. If the Leader verified that Dharshika had indeed committed an act of betrayal, then most likely he would have somebody else execute her, but if for whatever reason it was she who had to do the job, then she too would shoot Dharshika, just as she was ordered. Puhal gave a small but triumphant smile as she said this, as though proud to show that she too was willing to kill her best friend for the sake of the cause, then rubbing the tip of her nose she immediately furrowed her eyebrows and looked away, an expression of irritation on her face, though it was hard to say whether her anger was directed at the interviewer recording the scene, at Dharshika for first so brazenly claiming that she would not hesitate to kill her, or at herself for responding in kind. The two women fell silent again, Puhal looking out over the water, Dharshika dissecting another leaf in her hands, and the film then cut to a wide landscape shot of the Vanni, of two large, seemingly unused buildings in the distance, surrounded on all sides by dense vegetation, the two women standing side by side in a corner of the screen, guns strapped tightly across their shoulders.

Krishan had been struck by that scene the first time he saw it, by the way it so vividly captured Dharshika and Puhal's relationship and situation, something simultaneously so moving, challenging, and disconcerting about how these two women had abandoned everything to join the Tigers, their homes and villages, families and friends, about how they'd formed, in exile from their previous lives, such an intimate bond, and how, despite waking together almost every day for seven years, they were ready to give each other up for the cause they'd joined, even to kill each other if the need arose. The two of them were no longer alive, Krishan knew, they'd died most likely within a few years of filming those scenes, probably in one of the increasingly desperate suicide missions the Tigers had ordered toward the end of the war or while defending the rapidly shrinking land still under Tiger control. It was strange to think that he might now be walking past the very same lake that these two women had once looked across, walking on the very same earth that they might have trod upon all those years before, and it was strange to think how different he himself was now from the person he'd been when he'd come across those scenes for the first time, to think how far he'd felt from the northeast during his time living and studying in Delhi, as if it was a place from which he'd been exiled and as if, with the end of the war and the destruction of the world that had existed there, it was a place for which his yearning could never be fulfilled. He'd been seeing Anjum for about two months at the time, and he could still remember now the urgency with which he'd wanted to share the film with her afterward, his eagerness to show her some glimpse of that destroyed world he felt to be a part of himself, his certainty that she would be impressed to learn that this was the lineage from which he came, even if he didn't fully agree with everything that all the other members of this lineage had done. He'd told her about the film the next time they met and they'd agreed to watch it together, but this had turned out to be more difficult to accomplish than expected, for Anjum was rarely in Delhi during the weekends and rarely able to meet more than once a week even when she was in town. They were spending entire days together when they did see each other by that point, and there was of course always time available in the literal sense of the word, but all they could seem to do when they were in proximity to each other was gaze at and be gazed at by each other, consume and be consumed by each other, so that even when he remembered the film he hesi-

tated to bring it up, worrying that watching a film was too
mundane an activity to do together, that sitting together but
not paying attention to each other would fail to do justice to
what they felt for each other.

It was for this reason probably that when he and Anjum did
finally watch the documentary, the first and only film they
watched together, it was toward the end of their time in Bombay, toward the end of that trip that was the first occasion in
four or five months that they spent continuous time with each
other, in which the urgency for transcendence that they'd previously felt gave way to the possibility of other, more gentle ways
of being together. They were staying in the room of a friend of
Anjum's who was out of town, and after the initial awkwardness and uncertainty of the train journey they'd spent the first
couple of days much as they would have in Delhi, smoking,
talking, and sleeping together, occasionally going outside but
even then not very far, the only difference being that this time
there was a totally different city in the background, a city by the
sea of immense wealth and poverty, a city that seemed, even
more than Delhi, like a veil or a mirage or an illusion that surrounded them. It became clear soon enough that they could
not spend the entire trip this way, that being together for an
extended period of time meant they would need to pay attention to all the various human and animal needs they more or
less ignored in Delhi. They needed, first of all, to eat, and since
they couldn't afford to always eat out they'd had to plan their
meals, to buy meat and vegetables and cook together. Their
sleeping patterns too became more regular, no longer a capitu-
lation to fatigue as it had been earlier, for if they didn't sleep in
the night they wouldn't be able to see the city during the day,

which was ostensibly part of why they'd come to Bombay to begin with. Anjum had a few friends in the city with whom she was supposed to spend time, people she'd gotten to know over the years through her activist work, and so they appeared together in social contexts for the first time as well. He'd been surprised by how charismatic Anjum could be in the presence of others, how friendly and lighthearted, qualities he'd intuited during their initial, public encounter, but which he'd somehow forgotten about in the time since. She continually asked her friends questions about their thoughts and opinions, their habits and routines, thoughtful, thorough, and disarming questions that came from a generous curiosity about other lives but were also, he sensed, part of a strategy that allowed her to avoid sharing too much of herself. He noticed that she was careful not to say or do anything that would allow anyone to perceive them as a couple, and though these moments troubled him he forgot about them with relative ease, reassured by how close they were otherwise becoming on the trip, by how much more open and accessible Anjum seemed to him now. He'd become familiar with so many of her invisible patterns and rhythms, with all those tendencies of being that were revealed only when one spent extended time with another person—the variation of mood in accordance with time of day, energy, digestion, and environment—and he'd begun, for the first time, to glimpse what a more substantial relationship between them might look like, what it would be like to actually share a life with Anjum. A calm and tender domesticity began to emerge as they cooked and ate together, went on long walks together and met other people together, the rapture and otherworldliness of their time in Delhi transformed, during their three weeks together, into a gentle and patient coexistence with their surroundings, washed by waves of desire that never ceased flowing, but that no longer made it impossible to participate in the outside world. He had known from previous relationships how quickly desire began to dissipate when two people became used to each other, how quickly the hope of transcendence with which infatuation begins was replaced by mere comfort and security, the safety of habit and routine, but he realized during their short time in Bombay that domesticity didn't have to signify the domestication of desire, that it could mean not its dullening and deadening but its deepening and widening, habit becoming something that fortified and buttressed desire without at the same time stifling it, like a glass case that protects the delicate flame of a candle while being open enough to let in the oxygen needed to keep the flame burning.

It was as they were rolling a joint on the afternoon of their penultimate day in Bombay, their last full day in the city, that the idea of watching the documentary came up again and they decided to finally watch it together. Drawing the curtains, placing the laptop on the bed between them, they lit the joint and let the video play, watched the scenes unfolding on the screen before them in a deepening trance. They sat there watching in silence till the very end, listening to the music that played as the credits rolled, and when the video at last came to an end Anjum closed the laptop gently and they both remained unmoving for a while, reluctant to speak or look at each other in the same way that when a film ended at the cinema and the lights came on, there was a moment in which you were reluctant to make eye contact with the person beside you, as if to do so would be to acknowledge the transience of the world in which you'd just been immersed. He asked whether she'd liked the film and she nodded that she had, that she too had been moved by it and could see what had attracted him so much to it, after which they said little else about the film, deciding in a kind of tacit agreement to remain in their thoughts a little more, to let the impression it had made linger inside them a bit longer. Outside the sky was already turning into the lavender gold of early evening, it was getting late, they realized, and they would have to leave the flat soon. They'd planned to spend their last night walking the length of Marine Drive, the long C-shaped road that ran along the sharply curved southwestern coast of the island city, a road that shared the same name as the road in Colombo near which Krishan had grown up, but that was so much more immense that no comparison was possible. They got ready and took the local train down as far south as possible, crushed into each other by the constant press of people in the carriage, then took a three-wheeler from the station down to the southernmost tip of Marine Drive. The sun had just gone down but the concrete was still exhaling heat as they began to make their way up the length of the broad pavement, cars rushing by on the road to their right, tall apartment buildings reaching up into the monumental sky behind them, the water breaking gently against the man-made rocks to their left, the boundlessness of the ocean stretching out into the distance beyond. They talked about various things, what things exactly he could no longer remember now, their gazes directed above the countless people they passed, commuters, students, walkers, joggers, and couples, and it was only when they'd covered about half the length of the promenade that the documentary came up again in conversation, when deciding to sit down and

smoke on the concrete ledge that gave onto the sea they began
to talk about the dynamic between the two cadres, the nature
of the friendship that clearly meant so much to each of them
but that both had taken such pains to disavow.

She couldn't stop thinking, Anjum told him as they looked
out at the darkening sky, about the scene by the lake, the scene
in which Dharshika and Puhal had claimed to be willing to kill
each other for the sake of the movement. Dharshika would not
have made such a cruel statement unless she'd actively wanted
to wound Puhal in some way, she felt, unless she'd held some
secret resentment against her friend that she wished to punish
her for. It was the kind of deep, unspoken resentment that was
only possible between people who loved each other intensely
and yet sensed the possibility of being hurt by each other, between people who needed each other and were yet unable to
fully acknowledge this need to each other for fear of becoming
vulnerable. It was a form of cruelty common in families and
close friendships, where people are so dependent on each other
but also so hemmed in and restricted by each other, and it was
a form of cruelty that was an intrinsic part of the dynamic between lovers too. Watching the two cadres interact she'd wondered whether there might not be something deeper hidden
behind their friendship, between the brasher, more assertive
Dharshika and the somewhat more approachable Puhal, there
was something almost erotic, she couldn't help feeling, in the
alternating boldness and shyness with which their eyes continually met, their gazes continually moving toward each other and
then away. Anjum said all this more or less at once, as a clear,
fully formed thought that she articulated, as was her wont,
only after having dwelt on it by herself, and surprised by the

suggestion, which he would never have otherwise considered, Krishan asked her whether she thought the two cadres had been lovers, adding that he thought it unlikely given how rigidly disciplinarian life for Tiger cadres was supposed to be. Anjum shrugged in a slightly indifferent way, as though the veracity of her interpretation was not really what mattered, then turned and looked out at the sea, rotating the ring on her middle finger absentmindedly. The documentary had reminded her, she went on after a moment, about a collection of old Buddhist poems she'd recently read, a collection of poems written between the third and sixth centuries B.C. by Buddhist nuns from all over the subcontinent, collected, translated into Pali, and passed down in the tradition as a single work. The poems were written across the social spectrum, by oppressed-caste women and upper-caste women, by serving women and prominent ladies, all of them evincing the same veneration for the Buddha and for the liberation that came with following his doctrine of radical detachment. Several of the poems depicted the situations that led to the conversion of their authors in surprising detail, many of them single women who'd joined monastic life as a way of escaping the compulsion to marry men they had no interest in, many of them married women who'd sought escape from the drudgeries of domestic labor and the unwanted sexual demands of their husbands, from what would now be called marital rape. Some had wanted freedom from the sexual violence casually inflicted on them by upper-caste men, while some had wanted freedom from the violent heat of their own high libidos and uncontrollable sexual urges, a coolness they found in Buddhism. Many of the women, Anjum added, had also joined the order as a way of coping with grief, with the untimely death of a son or daughter or brother or sister, the Buddha's teachings on death providing the only consolation that really made sense of all their suffering. All of these elder nuns had, in other words, two thousand five hundred years before, left their homes and relatives in order to find, through the monastic order, liberation from the societies in which they'd been born, and she couldn't help thinking about the parallels with Dharshika and Puhal, with all the other women who'd left their families to join the Tigers. Like the Buddhist nuns, they too had given up attachment to their bodies in response to the traumas they'd experienced, and like the nuns they too had joined a movement for liberation, a movement founded and led, like Buddhism, by a man, a movement that to their minds promised not only the possibility of freedom from the Sri Lankan state but also real and immediate freedom from their own society's expectations and oppressions.

There was some truth to the comparison Anjum was making, Krishan knew, for he'd watched interviews where female cadres talked about how joining the Tigers had helped them escape from certain of the patriarchal tendencies of Tamil society, had read in various places about the fact that many of them had experienced one form of violence or another at the hands of men in occupying forces, that even the Black Tiger cadre who'd assassinated the Indian prime minister in 1994 had been raped as a young girl by Indian soldiers stationed in Jaffna. There was something in the authority with which Anjum spoke though that seemed to suggest more, as though she perceived herself to be more closely connected to Puhal and Dharshika than he was, as though, Krishan couldn't help feeling, she was trying in some way to appropriate what he'd wanted to share with her of himself. The sentiment bothered him but it wasn't without basis either, he knew, not merely because of the possibility that Dharshika and Puhal might, like her, have sought something beyond heterosexuality, but more importantly because they, like her and unlike him, had the conviction to follow a path that involved abandoning the ordinary world, the strength to cut off ties with family and society in order to devote themselves fully and absolutely to a cause. Krishan thought of how Anjum had avoided touching him in the presence of her friends, how she'd introduced him as a friend from Delhi, things she hadn't seemed to do with any explicit intent or purpose but that had served, nevertheless, to remind him in those moments that he could not take their relationship for granted, that soon she would be moving away and that their time together would soon be coming to an end. He'd known these things already, of course, they had after all been the source of all the anxiety he'd experienced since meeting Anjum, but in a way he'd been evading these facts over the previous three weeks, he realized, in a way he'd allowed the comfort and familiarity that had developed between them to shield himself from their implications. It was this subject that Anjum was trying to broach now by likening herself to Dharshika and Puhal, Krishan realized, as he looked at the thoughtful, almost brooding expression on her face, not explicitly, since that was not Anjum's way, but lightly and gracefully, hoping he would be perceptive enough to understand what she was doing without the heaviness of having to tell him directly. It was their last evening in Bombay and she was trying, gently, to remind him that she was different from him, that her own path in the world had already been staked out and that he would need to find his own, and it was at this moment, turning and looking out over the darkly shifting sea, that he finally felt the inevitability of their parting of ways coming home to him, a kind of sudden, silent shift taking place in the geology of his mind, a fact he responded to not with anxiety now or desperation, as he had in the past, but with the silent conviction that he too had a path ahead of him, that he too had a history and a destiny of his own. It had been at that moment, sitting beside Anjum with the ocean before them and the city of Bombay to their backs, having spent all his adulthood, almost seven years at that point, living in India, that the thought first came to him of returning to the country of his birth, of leaving behind his graduate studies and his plans of being an academic, of devoting himself to working in the northeast, a thought that had no doubt been preparing itself in his mind for some time, encouraged by his obsession with the war but also by his time with Anjum, the model she'd provided for a life governed by the vision of another world. He felt a kind of sadness come over him, not so much the sadness of separation from Anjum as the sadness of being separated from a life he'd become familiar with and comfortable in, but stronger than this sadness was the sense of possibility he suddenly felt rising through his body, the sense of possibility that came with extinction of the self and submission to higher powers, from the prospect of leaving behind all the difficulties of loving someone who couldn't be with him and devoting himself instead to the project of a new world, a world that would give him the same sense of liberation he felt with Anjum but without the sadness and the desperation, a world that would take him away from this person he loved but would also, somehow, bring them closer.

The two of them finished their cigarettes quietly, each of them lost in their own thoughts, then resumed walking down Marine Drive, slowly and in silence. Even though nothing exactly had happened, even though their conversation about the film had been abstract and unrelated to their relationship, it was as if each of them sensed that some turning point had been reached. It was as if the logic that had begun to unfold five months ago, when their eyes first made contact, was coming finally to its end, and it was in response to this feeling, perhaps, that they held hands for the first time as they walked, clasping each other not firmly or with fullness of contact, not giving each other promises they could not keep, but loosely and tenderly, only their little fingers intertwined. It was dark now, the pavement lit by the sodium glow of the tall streetlamps on the road to their right, and stretching out to their left the water glimmered in the warm night, the city's reflected intensities fluctuating on its surface. To their right, curving outward with the coastline into the distance ahead, high-rises rose up to form the skyline, the first of endless lines of buildings that comprised the island of Bombay, buildings that contained within their small compartments tens of millions suffering and striving people from all across the country, a condensation of human life so dense and so rich that it was impossible to believe such a place existed till one saw it with one's own eyes. It was as though, as they walked together holding hands that night, they were being presented with a crystallization of two contradictory possibilities of liberation that existence on earth offered, the possibility, on the one hand, that one felt whenever one came across an immense number of people living in a single place, the possibility of finding among all those millions a per-

son or people with whom one could be happy, and the possibility, on the other, that was felt whenever one looked into the
endless, lightless reaches of the night sea, the possibility of liberation that was associated with oblivion, with the cutting of
ties and voyaging out into the unknown. Krishan held Anjum's
hand a little more tightly, and looking at her as she looked back
at him, her tall, graceful form silhouetted by the silver-yellow
halo of the city behind her, she appeared to him just as she'd
appeared the first day they met, just as she'd appeared that
night on the train with the countryside rushing past behind her,
with that combination of sadness, longing, and conviction that
he would, he'd felt with certainty that moment, never forget.
He continued gazing at her, at the severity of her profile and
the vulnerability of her gaze, and it was as though he could feel
the sight of her penetrating his eyes in real time, burning itself
delicately into the film of his retinas, forming an image that
would remain imprinted in the back of his eyes like a shadow or
like tracing paper over everything he saw subsequently. And
maybe it was for this reason, it had occurred to him at that moment, that eyesight weakened with the passing of the years, not
because of old age or disease, not because of the deterioration
of the cornea or the lenses or the finely tuned muscles that controlled them but because, rather, of the accumulation of a few
such images over the course of one's brief sojourn on earth,
images of great beauty that pierced the eyes and superimposed
themselves over everything one saw afterward, making it harder
over time to see and pay attention to the outside world, though
perhaps, it occurred to him now, four years later in the country
of his birth, walking at the back of the procession bearing
Rani's body for cremation, Rani who'd seen so much that she

had never been able to forget, perhaps he'd been naïve back then, perhaps it was not just images of beauty that clouded one's vision over time but images of violence too, those moments of violence that for some people were just as much a part of life as the moments of beauty, both kinds of image appearing when we least expected it and both continuing to haunt us thereafter, both of which marked and branded us, limiting how far we were subsequently able to see.

10

THEY HAD LEFT the lake behind some time ago, the vegetation along the road less exuberant as they moved farther from the water, merging into the dustier, browner landscapes of tangled brush and gnarled trees that had dominated the scenery from station to village. They'd been walking for maybe half an hour and he could feel the moisture trickling down his back and sides, his body beginning to feel heavier and more cumbersome despite having no part to play in shouldering the bier. Krishan knew that cremation grounds were generally located some distance outside villages, a fact that had to do with the supposed impurity of funeral rites and of those compelled to base their livelihoods upon them, but he wondered now whether the distance between village and cremation ground might also be related to the process of grieving, whether it might also be meant to give the relatives who carried the pot and bore the body a more vivid sense of the materiality of what was being lost. He continued moving at the same slow, even pace, trying to calculate how far they had come from the village, to keep track of the path they were taking so he could make his way back alone if needed, and it was some time before he made out, coming up on the right, a large plot of land bounded by crumbling gray cinder-block walls, the sprawling land inside visible through a collapsed section of wall, overrun by brush and weeds. The four drummers, still playing lightly at the head of the procession, entered the plot of land on reaching the gate, followed by the casket-bearers, and Krishan realized that it was this walled-off plot of land, hardly distinguishable from the landscape surrounding it, that functioned as the village's cremation ground. He'd never been to a cremation ground in the northeast before, only in Colombo, where in addition to a kind of pavilion for cremations there were usually also large sections containing Muslim and Christian tombstones, physical graves that gave those sites the atmosphere of being populated. The ground they were entering now felt strangely empty in comparison, devoid of anything human, only the section near the center of the ground cleared of vegetation, the only permanent structure there a small cement platform that was level with the ground. Four thick iron bars were anchored into the rectangular platform at its corners, and it was within the confines of these iron bars that the pyre had been prepared, a number of dry, unevenly hewn pieces of wood stacked between them to a height of two or three feet. A small distance away several items had been laid out on the ground in readiness for the cremation, another small pile of wood, a dried palmyra leaf, a sack of hay, and a bottle of kerosene along with a few smaller items. The funeral director helped guide the cas-

ket to the center of the ground so the men carrying it could
lower it onto the pyre, several other members of the procession
joining as they let the front of the casket down and then slid the
rest forward till its weight was entirely supported by the pyre.
The drummers drew off to a side to continue drumming lightly,
as unconcerned with the proceedings as they'd been at the funeral house, and the rest of the men in the procession gathered
on one side, the closer relatives nearer to the pyre and the others farther back. Krishan watched as the director unfastened
the lid of the casket and Rani's body was revealed once more to
the light of day, her face still ghostly pale, her eyes still closed,
her body still laden with garlands of flowers. With the help of
his assistant he began taking the garlands off Rani's body, the
still fresh flowers probably an impediment to the burning, lifting them up one by one with both hands and putting them
carefully down on the ground a short distance away. Taking a
large, curved, sicklelike knife the director severed the thread
tying Rani's big toes together, separated her feet from each
other, then unfolded her hands and separated those too, this
too presumably to aid the burning. From the small pile on the
ground he began to carry pieces of wood one by one to the
casket, placing them gently, almost reverentially, upon Rani's
body, the assistant helping him till her body was mostly concealed, so that looking at the casket it was hard to say whether
the purpose of the additional wood was to help with the body's
burning or to shield spectators from the sight of it disintegrating under the flames, from the disturbing scene of human
turning into mineral right before their eyes.

The director called to Rani's son-in-law, who was standing a
few feet away from the pyre observing the proceedings, the

clay pot still on his left shoulder, and he made his way dutifully toward the head of the casket. The director gave him the torch he'd been carrying, a short stick of sandalwood that had already burned halfway down, and taking it in his right hand Rani's son-in-law held it behind his back with the smoldering end pointing away from his body. The director took the curved knife in his hand and stood just behind the son-in-law, who, like a man about to be shaved at a barbershop, remained where he was with almost nervous stillness. Gripping the knife not by the handle but by the blade itself, the director marked a spot near the base of the clay pot and struck at it sharply with the point of the knife, making a small, precise crack in the pot out of which water began to trickle. The drummers immediately began playing louder and more intensely, and in accordance with the director's instructions Rani's son-in-law began walking counterclockwise around the casket, solemnly and cautiously, the pot on his left shoulder and the torch in his right hand. The director followed close behind him, using his right hand to guide the trickling water away from the casket, slapping it as it fell in a gesture whose significance Krishan didn't quite understand. He stopped Rani's son-in-law at the head of the casket after one circumambulation, and taking the knife in his hand tapped sharply a second time at the back of the pot, this time a little farther down, creating a second hole so that the stream of water became a little broader, wetting the path that Rani's son-in-law now took for a second time around the body. Krishan had registered the son-in-law's physical presence in passing at the funeral house, but he was struck by his handsomeness as he moved now in the softness of the evening light, by his dark, muscular upper body, bare except for the white thread strung across his torso, the broadness of his chest and shoulders. The entirety of his back, he noticed, was marked by scars, making his stoic, graceful bearing even more impressive as he moved, and studying them as the pot was struck a third time and he began his third revolution, Krishan wondered whether perhaps they'd been inflicted by the army after the end of the war, which would have made sense, he knew, since Rani's son-in-law would have been in his early twenties at the time, and regardless of their affiliation with the Tigers most men that age would have been treated with suspicion. When he finished the third round the director stopped him at the head of the casket, turning him around so he was facing away from the body, then instructed him to throw down the pot and light the pyre without turning to look. Rani's son-in-law hesitated for a moment, as though he'd developed an attachment to the pot he'd carried with him all the way from the funeral house, then threw it down in front of him and watched as it shattered with a heavy thunk upon contact with the ground, the exploded water spilling onto the dry earth before him. Still looking away from the body, he reached toward the casket uncertainly with the smoldering torch, groping till he made contact and then letting the torch fall into the pyre. The pyre remained unlit, which was of course the standard course of things, the lighting of the pyre by the male relative usually nothing more than a symbolic act, and ushering Rani's son-in-law quickly to the other side of the casket, the director cut the thread around his torso and deposited it in the casket by Rani's feet. He opened a small packet of camphor tablets, deposited a few of the tablets on the ground by the foot of the pyre, then handed Rani's son-in-law a matchbox. Crouching down in front of the camphor tablets Rani's son-in-law lit a match and set the camphor alight, then getting on his stomach and stretching out his body on the dusty earth in front of the flame, prostrated himself before Rani one last time. He stood up slowly, still taking care not to turn his face toward the body, then turned around and began walking away from the pyre, back toward the entrance of the cremation ground. There was shuffling among the men behind him, and turning Krishan saw that several of them too had begun heading for the entrance. It was some kind of defilement to watch the body burning, he knew, but he didn't want to abandon Rani before the pyre began to burn, it didn't make sense having come all the way, and looking around, seeing that a few of the men were still standing there with hands behind their backs, no intention of leaving till the actual lighting took place, he turned his gaze back to the scene before him.

The director was taking out bales of hay from the sack beside the pyre, inserting them one by one into the gaps and crevices between the wood piled above and below the body, rendering Rani completely invisible. He began tearing out the white satin lining on the inside of the coffin lid, revealing the bare wood beneath, then picking up the dried palmyra leaf and taking the long stem in both hands, thrust the fan of the leaf inside till it was lodged inside the stack of wood. He lit a match and brought it to the part of the leaf that was now inside the pyre, lighting the fan at a few different points and then blowing in order to encourage the fledgling flames. Krishan had heard the news of Rani's death two days prior, had seen and touched her lifeless body just two hours before, but it was only now, watching the director trying to light the pyre, that he truly began to register that Rani would soon be gone, that she was, in fact, already gone. It was only now that he was realizing what it meant for her body to burn, what it meant for a fire to build in the hay and the wood, for it to spread to the casket and to the surface of Rani's body before entering, finally, inside her. Her hair would be the first to burn, he knew, the wild and unruly hair of her head that had been combed and domesticated after her death, followed by her eyelashes, her armpit hair, and the hair on her arms and legs, then by the softer, tenderer parts of her exterior, her lips, her eyes, and her skin, which would probably melt before they burned. The director had managed to consolidate a small fire beneath the casket, the fan of the leaf and the bales of hay burning in unison, the individual stalks blackening and curling as fire ran through them, and though the flames hadn't yet spread to the wood, let alone begun touching the casket, Krishan could sense within his own body what he knew would soon be occurring to Rani's. He thought about the burning of her eyes, so fragile and delicately constituted, thought about the melting of the eyelids, the dissolution of the iris and the lens into the simmering water of the tear glands, thought about the retina curling up and with it all the images that had been imprinted there over the course of Rani's lifetime, images of beauty and violence that had been superimposed over everything she saw. The fire was spreading slowly and evenly below the casket, crackling as it burnt up the hay and the shavings on the surface of the wood, spitting out embers as it ate its way through the fan of the palmyra leaf, and Krishan thought of how, if there still remained in Rani's body any trace of memory or consciousness, this too would soon be extinguished. He wondered whether this was what Rani had, during all her time in Colombo, secretly desired, the complete dissolution of all her thoughts and feelings, the extinction of consciousness that she could never hope to achieve through sleep the way most people did, that she hadn't been able to achieve through the mind-numbing quantity of sleeping pills she took or any of her other medications either. It was an extinction she'd tried and failed to obtain through shock therapy, through the general anesthetic she took and the electricity that was passed through her brain immediately afterward, an extinction she'd tried and failed to obtain through her various attempts at self-harm as well, hoping perhaps that severe physical pain, which had the effect of reducing all consciousness to the site of injury or laceration, of reducing the world to a point on the body's surface, leaving nothing else available for thought or consideration, would allow her to forget her other, deeper and less tangible pain.

It no longer mattered whether Rani's death had been planned or accidental, Krishan understood now, there didn't need to be a sharp line between these two kinds of death, a meticulous plan wasn't necessary for a death to have been intended. All it took sometimes was a vague desire for self-destruction in order for a person to become just a little more careless when crossing the road or leaning out of the train, to become just a little less vigilant when lighting a firecracker or fixing a hole in the roof, all it took sometimes was a silent half-wish for oblivion in order for the line between accidental death and planned death to be blurred, for death to become something the deceased would, eventually, be pushed toward. The idea of Rani being driven toward such a death seemed more and more plausible to him now, even if he had no evidence except the regret in her daughter's voice when she'd spoken of

wishing that Rani had never left Colombo, even if her daughter
herself seemed untouched by the possibility that her mother
had wanted to die. Rani had lived for six years since the loss of
her two sons, had been unable to recover despite her best efforts and the best efforts of everyone who knew her, and it
made sense, after all that effort and all that time, if death, the
total and irrevocable cessation of consciousness, had seemed to
her in some instinctual, primordial way like the only way to
achieve the extinction she sought. Thinking about the possibility no longer made him feel guilty, his brief interaction with her
daughter at the funeral house having made it clear that Rani's
death was not something he or his mother or grandmother
could have prevented, not something they had caused or been
responsible for. Rani's fate had been sealed long before their
paths came together, on that day before the end of the war
when a shard of shrapnel had sliced through her younger son,
as though a fragment from that same shell had pierced her too
that day, entering her not through her skin but her eyes, a small
but insidious fragment that had entered her pupils like a needle
and gradually made its way deeper inside her body over the
years, eventually becoming the cause of her death too. What he
felt was not so much guilt as a kind of amazement that he'd
shared a home with such a person to begin with, that their lives,
so different in quality and tenor, had somehow run in parallel,
that Rani had been part of their lives for so long without him
being able to foresee what was now so obvious, the inevitable
endpoint of the trajectory along which she'd been silently advancing, though perhaps such trajectories only became visible
when everything was over and it was already too late, perhaps
they only began to seem inevitable or necessary in retrospect,

once they'd already been incorporated into a new, more sober conception of reality.

Watching as the wood beneath the casket began to catch fire, the fire beginning to spread from the center of the pyre as the long stem of the palmyra leaf slowly burned through, Krishan remembered a conversation he'd had with Rani on New Year's Day, back when he was still living and working in the northeast. He'd returned to Colombo for the occasion and had planned to go out, less because he cared about New Year than from a desire to get intoxicated with friends after the sobriety of the previous months in Jaffna, drawn by the appeal of being out among people his own age in a state of heightened receptivity, the slim but enticing possibility of meeting someone new he always felt in such situations. The plan was to have dinner and drinks with a few friends before going out later to a house party they'd been invited to, and he'd gone that evening to his grandmother's room to say good night a little earlier than usual. Appamma and Rani had just finished eating and were watching the news with absorption, listening as the presenter discussed the various preparations for the night that had been undertaken throughout Colombo, while in the background of the studio, behind the presenter, flakes of digital snow were soundlessly falling, an embellishment that felt especially absurd given the drought that had been afflicting the country that year. The screen cut to clips of the president and prime minister wishing all Sri Lankans the best for the new year, snippets of their speeches dubbed into Tamil by the station, then to scenes of fireworks and celebrations from Sydney, Tokyo, and Beijing, where the New Year had already begun. Appamma had asked him what his plans for the night were, what time he was planning to come back, and he told her for what must have been the third or fourth time that day that he wasn't sure, that it would probably be late depending on what his friends wanted to do. He'd asked Rani whether people celebrated New Year's in the north, more for the sake of making conversation than to really find out, knowing that for most people in the north the New Year began not in January but the middle of April, in accordance with the Tamil calendar. Rani responded that people acknowledged the day, since it was a government holiday, but that nobody she knew really celebrated it, not at least in the way it seemed to be celebrated in Colombo. It occurred to Krishan as she said this that Rani might like to go and see the fireworks at Galle Face that night, that she might enjoy experiencing this aspect of Colombo that she wouldn't otherwise have the chance to see. Rani didn't generally like leaving the house, he knew, but Galle Face for some reason was always heavily frequented by Muslim and Tamil families and she would feel safe there, especially if he was with her too. He knew it would complicate his plans for the night, but not bothering to think the matter through he asked whether she wanted to join him, saying he could come back home shortly before midnight to pick her up and then bring her back once everything was over. She would get to see all the fireworks, he went on, there would be a big display, she probably hadn't seen anything like it before, and it was only on saying this that he realized that being in Galle Face could actually be triggering for her, that the sound of laughing, shouting Sinhalese voices and the sudden, chaotic explosions of firecrackers going off around them might remind her of the end of the war. Rani smiled to show she appreciated the offer but said that she couldn't, that she and Appamma were planning to watch a film that night. He looked at Appamma with surprise as if to ask whether this was true, to which Appamma had nodded her head and told him that yes, they'd made their own plans, that he wasn't the only one with something to do. They were airing a special film for New Year's, Rani explained, a new Vijay film that would play at midnight, the kind of film you would otherwise have to go to the cinema to see. Krishan shook his head in mock disapproval, as though he was jealous of being left out of their plans, then smiling stood up and kissed each of them good night, relieved that his offer had been turned down but warmed, at the same time, by the fact that Rani and Appamma had made their own plans for the New Year.

He'd gone out to dinner with his friends as planned, had drunk and smoked weed at one of their homes before heading out to the party, the kind of party he would be unlikely to meet anyone interesting or thoughtful, he'd known beforehand, but which he was nevertheless keen to attend, too drawn by the possibility of flirtation or intimacy to be put off by its more obnoxious elements. He could no longer remember any of the specific details of the night, the flat had been loud, smoky, and crowded, populated mainly by English-speaking people in their twenties and thirties, liberal people who said liberal things but became uncomfortable whenever identity or tradition was foregrounded too strongly. Everyone was drinking, smoking, and talking, and as midnight approached the party migrated to the roof to watch the fireworks, remaining there for a while after the fireworks had peaked and then making their way back down, everyone looser and more familiar with each other for having shared the intimate moment of transition. The music became louder, the movement and interaction more lively,

more people beginning to dance as their drunkenness deepened, a few people arriving after having spent midnight at other
parties, the ashtrays slowly filling up and the empty bottles and
cups accumulating. When, around four-thirty in the morning,
the energy of the party began dwindling and people began fil-
tering out, first the couples and then everyone else in little
groups, Krishan did his best not to give way to the sense of
disappointment he always felt at the end of such events, when
it began to dawn on him that the promises with which the night
had started were failing to come to fruition. He and the two
friends of his who were still at the party were heavily intoxicated, had been smoking joint after joint through the night, and
not yet wanting to return home but knowing they'd be over-
staying their welcome if they remained much longer, had decided to smoke one last joint and go to Galle Face, where they
could talk for as long as they liked and where there might still
be people. They managed to find a three-wheeler after wandering the roads for a while, and were relieved when they arrived
to see that the place was still lively, the long, wide lawn far less
crowded than earlier in the night no doubt but still full of activity, mainly groups of boys and young men dancing obliviously
to the clashing music that sounded from different speakers,
though there were also, surprisingly, a large number of families, mothers and fathers, babies, children, and grandparents sitting peacefully on mats they'd brought from home, some of
them talking as they sipped on cups of tea or coffee, others
stretched out and fast asleep. The grass was full of the debris of
the night, spilled food, ice cream wrappers, empty plastic bottles, and the burnt remnants of firecrackers, but managing after
a while to find a section that was relatively untouched, the three

of them sat down in a small circle and made themselves comfortable. They lit cigarettes and talked under the wide, starless sky, the salt breeze of the sea cool on their tired skin as the darkness gradually let up, the crowd becoming sparser as the sun came up quietly behind them. Increasingly weighed down by their intoxication and from having spent the entire night talking, their conversation soon petered out, each of them losing themselves in their own heavy, swaying thoughts as they looked out over the calm January sea that was making itself visible beneath the pale dawn light.

He had known it was time to make his way home, his throat was parched from smoking one cigarette after another, there was nothing he could possibly obtain by staying up longer, but feeling a kind of restlessness at the thought of leaving, a reluctance to admit that the night was coming to an end, he'd persuaded his friends to stay just a little longer, citing the length of their friendship and the fact that he would soon be returning to the northeast. It was normal of course to be reluctant to go home when you were inebriated and unfulfilled, not just on New Year's but whenever you were out and about, but thinking of that night at Galle Face now Krishan wondered why it had always been so difficult for him to end such nights unless he was absolutely exhausted, till going home was no longer a choice but a necessity. It didn't simply happen when he was out with other people, he knew, he found it hard to go to bed at a reasonable hour even when sober in his room, some part of him always resistant to going to sleep, as though going to bed was a kind of concession or surrender, as though by staying up something might happen that would justify having lived through the day. In Delhi, where for the most part he'd had no fixed schedule, he'd frequently found himself trapped in cycles of going to bed later and later every night, waking up later and later every morning, cycles he would attempt to correct by forcing himself at last to wake up early one morning, hoping he would fall asleep early the next evening out of sheer fatigue, cycles that repeated themselves no matter how hard he tried to maintain a consistent schedule. The pattern had been broken to some degree during his time in the northeast, where work was often so physically exhausting that he came home looking forward to sleep, but it had resurfaced once more upon moving back to Colombo, where despite having to get up early for work he went to bed late almost every night, losing sleep almost every day of the week and then compensating for the loss over the weekend. He often wondered about people who managed to keep regular hours of sleep with little effort or discipline, people who went to bed at the same time each night as though naturally in sync with the revolutions of earth, sun, and moon, as though the movement of their bodies was in some kind of inner harmony or alignment with those of the solar system. It was as though the desire that drew one out into the world each morning in the hope of some small fulfillment or some profound discovery was counterbalanced, for each person, by the disappointment and struggle that moving through the world entailed, as though by the end of each day most people's longing was equaled or exceeded by the fatigue the world produced, so that at a certain moment each evening they became content to stop searching and return to the comfort of their homes, to yield finally to sleep and the concession to reality it involved. It was as though for most of his life he'd been driven by a longing that was somehow stronger or more insistent than that of most people he knew, by a desire that had to meet more resistance than average before it could be vanquished, as though his body was adapted not to a twenty-four-hour day but a twenty-five- or twenty-six-hour day, so that what he and others like him needed, he couldn't help feeling, was nothing so much as a world of vaster circumference, a world whose movement through space could do justice to the longing he felt inside him.

By the time he'd said goodbye to his friends it had been seven or seven-thirty in the morning, the new year already well under way, and entering the house quietly he'd gone straight to his room, not wanting to alert his mother to his presence in such an unkempt state. He'd peeled off his clothes, full of the stale, damp odor of cigarette smoke, then stepped directly under the shower, letting the cool water wash over his hair and body. Turning off the tap he'd heard the sound of Appamma's door opening and closing outside, of Rani announcing to his grandmother that she'd brought up their tea, and knowing that if he went to bed he wouldn't wake till afternoon, that it would be nice to wish the two of them while it was still early morning, he dried himself off, put on a pair of fresh clothes, and went to their room. The two of them were sipping their tea in silence, Rani on her chair, Appamma at the edge of the bed, and kissing each of them on both cheeks he wished them a Happy New Year. Appamma was under the impression he'd just woken up, that he'd come home early the previous night, and after explaining that he'd just returned and hadn't yet gone to bed he asked how the film had been, whether they'd stayed up to watch the whole thing. Rani had looked at Appamma with a teasing smile, then told him that his grandmother had fallen asleep five minutes after the film started. Appamma immediately interjected, a mixture of embarrassment and indignation on her face, insisting that she'd been tired all of the previous day, that she'd hardly slept the previous night, that she didn't like watching all these new Indian films and that seeing the introductory part was enough for her to know that she was better off going to bed. He asked Rani if she too had gone to bed without watching the film, knowing she might have felt let down by Appamma's withdrawal from their plan, but Rani shook her head with a smile, told him she'd switched off the lights and stayed up to watch the film anyway, the volume turned off so not to wake his grandmother. With the volume turned down or with the volume turned all the way off, he'd asked, taking her last statement to be an exaggeration, to which Rani confirmed that she had indeed watched the entire thing without sound, shrugging as though there was nothing surprising in this. He asked how she'd managed to watch without being able to understand the dialogue, not quite believing she'd spent two and a half hours in front of a soundless screen, and she replied that it hadn't been too difficult to follow, that you could tell the emotions of the characters simply by looking at the expressions on their faces.

Krishan had talked to Rani and Appamma a few minutes more, had gone to wish his mother for the new year, then returned to his room, where despite the tiredness in his eyes and the lightness in the back of his head he was unable to fall asleep at once. Lying on his back with his eyes closed he thought about what Rani had said, the image fixed in his mind of her staying up by herself in that silent room, surrounded by darkness except for the images moving on the screen and the flickering light it cast on the walls. There'd been a similar occasion a few months earlier, when entering Appamma's room he'd found Rani sitting by herself in front of the TV, the sound blaring this time as some unrealistically dramatic scene, a kidnapping or assault, unfolded before her on the screen. He'd watched beside her for a while and then asked what had happened, what was the cause of the scene's exaggerated violence, in response to which Rani had looked at him with slight confusion for a moment before telling him, embarrassment on her face, that she wasn't exactly sure, giving him some vague explanation of the scene that didn't quite make sense. She'd been sitting there staring at the TV, he'd realized, without actually paying attention to what was happening, had been watching the screen as if it were showing her a sequence of images and sounds without meaning or connection to each other. Every time he saw Rani watching TV since then he'd wondered whether she was actually paying attention, and the fact she'd been able to watch an entire film without sound the previous night confirmed these suspicions to him now, for there was no way she could have followed the film without knowing what the actors were saying, especially since she wouldn't have been able to hear the music, which such films relied upon so heavily to set up the emotional valence of a scene, to tell the audience whether they should be sad or hopeful or anxious or fearful. She couldn't have had any sense of the plot, any sense of why something was happening and what consequences it would have for the characters, and if Rani really was content to watch a film this way then it must have meant that its logic and meaning were in some way irrelevant to her, that she was watching it without wanting or being able to inhabit it the way a spectator normally did. The sense of hearing was vital to the sense of participating in a situation, after all, and to watch a film without listening to it was to experience it at a remove, to observe the moving colors and shapes the way you might observe the patterns of passing clouds or the ripples on the surface of a lake. We can direct our gazes toward what lies in the distance whenever we want, toward things that have nothing to do with us and lack the power to affect us, but usually we can hear only what is in our vicinity and has the potential to affect us, so that sound, unlike sight, was associated with the physical presence of a thing and the possibility of interaction with it. It was for this reason perhaps that ghosts and spirits and phantoms were so often depicted as silent presences in films and books, as beings we can glimpse but cannot hear, that can watch but cannot speak, as though to signify that while these beings are in some way present to us they cannot participate in our world, no longer have the power to act and affect us, just as we ourselves are present in some way to them but cannot engage in the world to which they have been cast. What it was like to live in this way, to see but never hear, to be seen but never heard, Krishan did not know, but standing there as the fire grew beneath the casket he couldn't help feeling that this was what Rani's life had been like since the end of the war, physically located in a world that was shorn of the people she loved and unable therefore to participate in it, her mode of existence more akin to that of ghosts than humans, even if she'd existed in a body that possessed weight and could move physically through space, even if she'd remained capable of love and pain, laughter and generosity, even if the life inside her had been undeniable to anyone who saw her.

Krishan watched, mesmerized, as the fire engulfed more and more of the pyre, the wood inside crackling and bursting in response to the heat, the flames beginning to lick the bottom of the casket, the smoke beginning to rise up in thick, dark clouds. The director was still adding occasional handfuls of hay to different parts of the pyre, using his knife to prod and nudge the wood inside, but he too was more of a spectator now than a participant, watching the fire as it began to burn of its own volition, as though conscious of its own existence and the need to keep itself alive. The man standing beside him turned and began walking back toward the entrance, and looking around Krishan saw that nobody else from the procession remained now but him, that except for the funeral director and his assistant he was the only person left standing before the pyre. He too would have to leave soon, he knew, the intensity of the light in the sky was waning, it must have been five o'clock or later, and he didn't want to make his way back to the village in the dark. He remained standing there transfixed as the fire spread to the foot of the casket, as the wooden panels that formed its sides began to smolder and smoke, as the wood above Rani's feet began to catch flame. Picking up the end of the still burning stem of the palmyra leaf, the director drew the stem out from below the casket and inserted it into the wood above the body. He picked up the bottle of kerosene and sprinkled the oil over the wood, as though impatient for the casket to begin burning, took whatever hay was left in the sack and inserted it wherever he could. Rani was being exposed to the flames directly for the first time, Krishan could tell, and though her body hadn't started burning yet, though in any case it was concealed from sight, he felt he could hear the fire nearing her, hissing and sputtering as it spread. Listening to these sounds he suddenly felt anxious—it bothered him that Rani remained silent as the flames surrounded her body, that he himself stood there doing nothing, even though there was nothing he could do—and making eye contact briefly with the director, he took a first step back. He wondered whether to make some gesture of obeisance to Rani, but not wanting to seem foolish he turned and began to walk, moving slowly and deliberately back across the ground. He began feeling calmer as the sound of the burning receded into the distance, as though what was happening behind him, no longer audible, was happening in another sphere or medium, and it was only when he reached the entrance, drawn by some lingering curiosity, that he turned to look back once more.

The pyre, much smaller in the distance, was burning densely and brightly in the center of the ground, deep amber-orange in the early twilight, its smoke wafting up and dissipating into the air. Beyond the walls of the ground the pale blue horizon had taken on a gray hue, its vastness interrupted here and there by the palmyra trees dotting the landscape, and looking into this vastness Krishan felt, coming over him, the strange sense that there was nowhere left for him to go. His gaze moving between the soundlessly burning pyre and the landscape of brush and bramble that spread out on all sides he wondered what had brought him to this place so far removed from the world he knew, what forces had led him to leave the life he'd created for himself in India, to come to this place he'd never actually lived, this place that had hardly figured in his life growing up. He wondered what movements of fate had led to his seemingly accidental encounter with Rani in the hospital ward, to her arrival in their home just a few months later, to her unexpected death two days before and his attendance now at her cremation, unable to shake off the sense that his presence in this scene of desolation had been decided somewhere long before, that something inside him had been driving him toward it long before the end of the war, something more than just guilt, something like freedom, even if he could not say what exactly freedom was. The specific path a life took was often decided in ways that were easy to discern, it was true, in the situation into which one was born, one's race and gender and caste, in all the desires, aspirations, and narratives that one came thereafter to identify with, but people also carried deeper, more clandestine trajectories inside their bodies, their origins often unknown or accidental, their modes of operation invisible to the eye, trajectories which were sometimes strong enough to push people in certain directions despite everything that took place on the surface of their lives. It was such a trajectory, set in motion by the things they'd seen, that had led so many young men and women to join the separatist movements decades ago, it was such a trajectory that had led Rani and so many people like her to their accidental or intentional deaths in the years after the war, and it was such a trajectory, Krishan now felt, that had led him too, in his own quiet and unremarkable way, to this cremation ground at the end of the world. His own path through life had been decided when he was much younger, not long after the death of his father perhaps, though what came to mind now was not so much his father's death as a period several years later, his final months of school and the long, aimless months he'd spent waiting for exam results, those endless days and weeks filled with yearning for a life he couldn't articulate and didn't know where to find. The cease-fire had been breaking down at the time and the war in the northeast was beginning to resume in full force, as a result of which his mother rarely let him or his brother leave the house by themselves, overly anxious that they would be stopped and interrogated, taken away by soldiers or policemen, overly fearful she might lose a son after having already lost her husband. He'd begun feeling trapped having to spend all that empty time within the walls of their small home, and although he hadn't understood it at the time it had probably been this sense of entrapment, this loss of freedom, that led him to pass so much time on their roof in those months, climbing up on the balcony railing and then onto the gentle slope, lying there for hours at a stretch in the nights while his brother, mother, and grandmother slept, listening to music while gazing up at the ocean of blue suspended above, at the silvery translucence of the clouds that he'd always felt were carrying messages to him from afar, thinking as he lay there, in that naïve and moving way of adolescents, how large and unknown the world was, how much it seemed to contain.

It had been in those months of waiting probably that he'd first become aware of the absence inside him, the longing for a life that existed beyond the boundaries of the Colombo and Sri Lanka he knew, an absence that he hadn't felt as an absence so much as a kind of willingness to be drawn elsewhere, an absence that had made him, paradoxically, more present to the world around him, more delicately aware of its surfaces and textures and moods. He'd not had any sense, back then, of what it was that life could offer, hadn't yet known what it would be like to live in another place, to live by himself and be responsible for his own decisions, to kiss, have sex, or be in love, to make a home for himself somewhere or to move from place to place. He hadn't yet experienced the objects of any of his desires, whether people or places or situations, his desires at the time no more than images in his mind, abstract objects possessing meanings he couldn't glean, things to which he attached significance without knowing why. What he'd felt at the time was not so much desire as a kind of yearning, for though both desire and yearning were states of incompleteness, states involving a strong, sometimes overwhelming need for something outside one's life, what was called desire always had a concrete object, a notion of what was necessary to eliminate the absence one felt inside, whereas to have what was often called yearning was to feel this absence and yet not know what one sought. To desire, in a sense, was to know or think one knew what one wanted, to know or think one knew the paths by which it might be reached, even if those paths turned out to be too difficult to follow, even if the things they led to, the things one desired, turned out not to provide the liberation one thought. To yearn on the other hand was to be lost, to lack bearings in the world because one did not know what one was seeking or where it could be found, so that unable to distract oneself, by frenetic activity or single-minded pursuit, from the painful sense of lack, one's only consolation was to look out across vast distances, as if surely somewhere in the expansiveness of the horizon, across space and sea and sky, some possibility was contained that could make life self-sufficient and devoid of need, some possibility that could bring an end to time. That such a possibility didn't exist he was now old enough to know, but it was a yearning of this kind that had led him here, he felt as he gazed at the pyre burning soundlessly at the center of the ground, that had led him along all the many paths he'd taken and brought him here at last to Rani's burning body—Rani, whose

vividly painful longing contained both the particularity of desire and the directionlessness of yearning, the knowledge of
what exactly she needed and the knowledge that it could no
longer be found—as though to tell him that any attempt to cure
or solve absence would lead, sooner or later, only to death and
the extinction of thought.

The evening was gathering over the landscape, and standing
there at the entrance to the cremation ground Krishan gazed
for a last time at the brilliant red glow of the pyre, all of it alight
now, the wood and the casket and most likely the body inside
too, all of it burning brightly in the lifeless gray light of the
evening. It would take several more hours for the burning to
be complete, he knew, the human body contained a lot of material, not just flesh and bones and organs but feelings and visions, memories and expectations, prophecies and dreams, all
of which would take time to burn, to be reduced to the sooth-
ing uniformity of ash. It was these ashes that Rani's son-in-law
would pick up the next day, which would be kept for a month in
their home and then dispersed afterward over a body of water,
perhaps over the sea on the northern or eastern coast, perhaps
over the lake they'd passed on the way to the ground, in either
case dissipating, eventually, into the long wide arc of the world.
Eventually nothing would remain of Rani's body, eventually
nothing would remain of what she'd thought or felt or seen or
heard, though watching as the flames flickered in the distance,
shooting out embers into the void, Krishan no longer felt any
particular sadness at the thought of Rani's body being reduced,
perhaps because he could no longer hear the actual sound of
the burning, perhaps because he understood now that Rani had
already left the world. He watched as the scarlet glow of the

fire grew brighter in the darkening evening, as the air around it warped with strange clarity in the intensity of the heat, watched as the substantiality of a human life was transmuted, like a mirage or hallucination or vision, into thick clouds of smoke billowing up into the sky, thinning as they rose and then disappearing into the evening, a message from this world to another that would never be received.

ACKNOWLEDGMENTS

THIS NOVEL WAS a more collaborative effort than my first novel, and would not have found its present form if not for the generosity of many people: my editors P.E. at Hogarth and L.B. at Granta; J.B., R.R., and the rest of the team at Hogarth; my agent A.S. at ICM; my sister and first reader A.A.; my long-time mentor P.K.; and my dear friends A.G., A.T., B.M., C.E., G.K., H.B., J.R., L.S., M.L., O.N., S.K., T.M., T.T., and V.S. My thanks also to *The Paris Review* for excerpting part of the novel in their fall 2019 issue.

The text incorporates a number of works of translation and documentary: the version of Poosal's story from the *Periya Purānam* in the first chapter is based on a translation from the Tamil in David Shulman's *Imagining the Real;* the version of *The Cloud Messenger* told in the fourth chapter is based on James Mallinson's translation from the Sanskrit; the version of the *Life of the Buddha* told in the seventh chapter is based on a translation from the Sanskrit by Patrick Olivelle; the story of Kutti-mani's death told in the seventh chapter is based on Rajan Hoole's account in *The Arrogance of Power: Myths, Decadence, and Murder*; the documentary described in chapter nine is Beate Arnestad and Morten Daae's *My Daughter the Terrorist*; the account in chapter nine of Buddhist women's poetry is based on a translation from the Pali by Charles Hallisey.

This book is for my mother and father.

ABOUT THE AUTHOR

ANUK ARUDPRAGASAM was born in Colombo, Sri Lanka. He studied philosophy in the United States, receiving a doctorate at Columbia University. His first novel, *The Story of a Brief Marriage*, was translated into seven languages, won the DSC Prize for South Asian Literature, and was shortlisted for the Dylan Thomas Prize. He currently divides his time between India and Sri Lanka.

anukarud.com

ABOUT THE TYPE

This book was set in Dante, a typeface designed by Giovanni Mardersteig (1892–1977). Conceived as a private type for the Officina Bodoni in Verona, Italy, Dante was originally cut only for hand composition by Charles Malin, the famous Parisian punch cutter, between 1946 and 1952. Its first use was in an edition of Boccaccio's *Trattatello in laude di Dante* that appeared in 1954. The Monotype Corporation's version of Dante followed in 1957. Though modeled on the Aldine type used for Pietro Cardinal Bembo's treatise *De Aetna* in 1495, Dante is a thoroughly modern interpretation of that venerable face.